D1433344

By the same author
In the Twilight of Socialism
The Smaller Dragon: A Political History of Vietnam
Vietnam: A Dragon Embattled

Vietnam: A Political History

Drawing by Tran Tan Thanh (after an illustration by L. Ruffier
in *La Dépêche Coloniale*, Paris, 1909)

VIETNAM:
A POLITICAL
HISTORY

JOSEPH BUTTINGER

ANDRE DEUTSCH

ANDRE DEUTSCH

FIRST PUBLISHED 1969 BY
ANDRE DEUTSCH LIMITED
105 GREAT RUSSELL STREET
LONDON WCI
COPYRIGHT © 1968 BY JOSEPH BUTTINGER
ALL RIGHTS RESERVED
PRINTED IN THE UNITED STATES OF AMERICA

SBN 233 96107 0

Preface

Vietnam: A Political History is based almost entirely on my earlier books on Vietnam—*The Smaller Dragon* (1958) and the two-volume *Vietnam: A Dragon Embattled* (1967). The only completely fresh material in the present work is its final chapter on the Americanization of the war now being waged. This concluding portion brings the account up to the present—that is, to the beginning of June, 1968, when the last lines of the Postscript were written. For the rest, this volume is an abridgment of the earlier books, that is to say of their main text, not of the wealth of material contained in the thousands of notes. This omission, inevitable though it may be, is regrettable, since the notes won the approbation even of persons otherwise critical of my work. Yet the absence of such vast detail also has its advantages. Being unencumbered by information of interest primarily to the specialist, and concentrating on the main events in the history of Vietnam, the book, it is hoped, may thereby gain in appeal for the general reader.

Abridgments and condensations of published works pose very special problems. Those acquainted with the two works that form the basis of this condensation may not always agree with the method used. I confess that I myself did not know how to solve the problems involved. I am therefore doubly indebted to Cecile Akin, who tackled the thankless job of condensation, and to Jean Steinberg, who prepared and edited the final version. If I say that I cannot see how this could have been done any differently or any better, I am passing judgment on their work, not on my own.

I am aware that my treatment of the period covered by the last chapter differs from my approach to the history of ancient, colonial, and postcolonial Vietnam up to the fall of Ngo Dinh Diem. It is my intention to return to the subject of Vietnam once the events of the present have become past history. This can be done only when the termination of the present tragic phase of Vietnamese history ushers in a new chapter in the evolution of the Vietnamese people.

—JOSEPH BUTTINGER

Pennington, N.J.
June, 1968

Table of Contents

vii

Part Three: VIETNAM AT WAR

LIST OF MAPS

Part One

The Smaller Dragon

I

Introducing Vietnam

1

Aʟᴛʜᴏᴜɢʜ ɪᴛ ɪs one of the smaller countries of Asia, Vietnam has, for more than 2,000 years, played a prominent role in the history of the Far East, a role quite out of proportion to its size and economic resources. The explanation of Vietnam's historical importance can be found, at least in part, in its geographical position. Vietnam lies at the southern border of China, within the region for which the term Southeast Asia has come into general usage since World War II. Southeast Asia comprises the peninsula jutting out between India and China and the vast archipelago south and east of it that includes Indonesia and the Philippines. Vietnam lies on the mainland part of Southeast Asia—the so-called Indochinese Peninsula. Three of the six countries on that peninsula—Burma in the west and northwest, Thailand in the center, and Vietnam in the east—occupy more than 80 per cent of its surface.

3

The Indochinese Peninsula has been known by a variety of names. In German it is called Hinterindien; the French have long called it l'Inde extérieure (this, however, refers only the "Indianized" western part). Although some of these names are no longer in use, much confusion still exists about the name of the peninsula, partly because during the Indochina War the term "Indochina" became synonymous with French Indochina, the former French-controlled association of Cambodia, Laos, and Vietnam. Present-day Vietnam thus is a part of Indochina—the eastern portion of the Indochinese Peninsula.

Perhaps confusion might best be avoided by calling the entire peninsula Indochina, as accurate and useful a designation as can be found, given the geographic, ethnological, and historical factors. The peoples inhabiting the peninsula, which lies between India and China, as close to one as to the other—although the territory is in fact an extension of the Chinese land mass—are neither Indian nor Chinese. The mountain ranges of southern and southwestern China extend down into Indochina along the entire northern boundary. The narrow river valleys have since time immemorial been the migration routes of the peoples who, coming down from southern China and Tibet, have populated Southeast Asia.

China's proximity has, historically speaking, been largely neutralized by India's ready access to the Indochinese western coast, and by the land connection in the northwest. The sea, unlike the massifs on the mainland, does not separate the countries of Asia; rather, it serves to connect them with one another and the rest of the world. Consequently Indochina has been influenced equally by her two big neighbors. Indian trade and religion have contributed to the development of Indochinese civilization as much as Chinese philosophy and conquests. Although India and China dominated Indochina's religions, philosophies, art, and political organization for two millenniums, the cultures of Indochina never were mere copies of either one or the other. They evolved along individual lines, taking from one as well as the other.

French Indochina therefore was never anything but the smaller and only partly Indianized eastern portion of Indochina, a product of Western imperialism, and unrelated to the geographic, racial, and cultural factors that have molded the Indochinese world.

2

Western intervention in Indochina has given rise to another semantic problem, this one in connection with Vietnam. Before 1946, it would have been difficult to find reference works carrying entries under "Vietnam." One would have had to look under French Indochina—an area comprising Tongking, Annam, Cochinchina, as well as Cambodia and Laos.

The land which in the wake of French political and military intervention became known as Annam (Tongking and Cochinchina were regarded as somehow connected with Annam) was in fact a highly centralized state officially renamed Vietnam back in 1802. Under the inverted form Nam Viet, the name had already been used to designate the regions inhabited by the ancestors of the Vietnamese people in the third century B.C. The term "Viet" has, in one form or another, been part of the name of the country ever since Vietnam regained independence in the year 939, after more than a thousand years of Chinese domination. Vietnamese patriots have pointed out that their people and their country were known by their present name while France was still the country of the Gauls.

Vietnam lost its name, its unity, and its independence in a series of colonial wars waged by France between 1858 and 1883. Vietnamese national leaders never accepted the names imposed on their divided country by the French, but only when the country regained its independence did it also win back its name.

Vietnam is considerably smaller than either Thailand or Burma, but with 36 million inhabitants it is the most populous of the Indochinese states, and though the population density given in terms of total area is by no means great, the unequal population distribution within the country presents a major problem: almost 80 per cent of the population inhabit 20 per cent of the land. On the one hand, there are vast, only sparsely populated stretches, and on the other, there are rural areas in the North with a population density of more than 1,000 persons per square mile.

Some of the reasons for this uneven pattern are historical and economic, but the determining factor is the country's topography:

the vast stretches of mountains, jungle, and forests with their sparse expanses of cultivable land, and the plains and fertile river deltas which form less than one-fifth of the country. The difference between the plains and mountain regions is underlined by the racial and cultural differences of their populations. The mountain population is composed almost exclusively of the various ethnic minorities, while the Vietnamese people, the great majority, crowd the valleys and deltas. The mountain peoples represent a bewildering racial and linguistic mixture. Their exact number has not yet been established, nor have they been completely classified. The Vietnamese majority, on the other hand, possess a remarkable cultural unity, speak the same language everywhere, and resemble one another physically as much as the members of any other highly unified nation.

3

The minority peoples of Vietnam offer a panoramic view of the country's prehistory and history.

Indochina is the home of about a million so-called Moi, an aboriginal, not highly civilized people, most of whom live in the highlands of central and southern Vietnam. Moi, a derogatory term meaning "savage" in Vietnamese, has now been largely discarded in favor of "montagnard," and with emphasis on tribal names such as Rhadé, Sadang, Jarai, Stieng, and others. The racial diversity of these montagnards—their color varies from very light to the darkest black—tends to support the view that the peninsula's original Austro-Negroid population, the first wave of immigrants into Indochina, was not completely displaced but partly absorbed by peoples of Indonesian stock, who, though themselves migrants from southwest China and Tibet, were old settlers in Indochina at the time of the first Mongolian migrations.

The Thai tribes of North Vietnam are descendants of a group of Mongolian migrants, presumably the third great human wave to reach Indochina from China. This last migration, which probably began less than three thousand years ago, has never come to a complete stop.

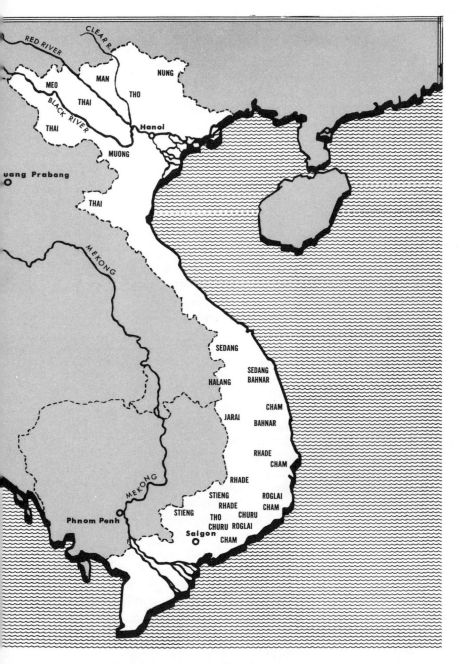

DISTRIBUTION OF POPULATION
Geographical distribution of ethnic minorities in Vietnam

According to Chinese sources, the Thai were already on the move in the sixth century B.C. They advanced toward Indochina along the rivers and through the valleys slowly and as a rule peacefully. There were only two massive, violent outbursts against Vietnam and northern Burma, one in the ninth century and another around the end of the thirteenth, when the Thai, harassed by the Mongol masters of China under Kublai Khan, pushed into the center of the peninsula and there began to develop one of the major Indochinese states.

The arrival of Thai peoples in Vietnam probably dates back to the emergence of the Vietnamese themselves, and their influx continued even after the mainstream began to move down the middle of Indochina toward the Gulf of Siam. At least one Thai tribe, the Nungs, settled in Vietnam as late as the sixteenth century. Today the Thai are the most important minority group of Vietnam. They are racially quite heterogeneous, and they also differ from other Thai peoples in other parts of Indochina. The designation Thai is in fact hardly anything more than a linguistic classification.

In customs and degree of civilization, the Thai resemble their neighbors the Muongs, who inhabit the lower mountain regions around the Red River Valley. The Muongs, who number about 250,000, are probably the product of a series of racial mixtures in which the Mongol element predominates. In this respect they resemble the Vietnamese. They are, in fact, the only ethnic minority whose dialect is closely related to the Vietnamese language. The Muongs also share many of the primitive religious practices of the Vietnamese, and their social structure has been described as a replica of Vietnamese society before the conquest of Vietnam by the Chinese.[1]

If, as seems likely, the Muongs represent a racial and cultural transition from some extinct Austro-Indonesian tribe to the ancestors of the Vietnamese, then the first appearance of the Vietnamese people can be determined with a fair degree of accuracy. Non-Chinese Mongolian immigrants into the Red River Valley mixed with and gradually absorbed the Austro-Indonesian stock, thus producing a number of new racial mixtures. Some of these new peoples disappeared; others, like the Muongs, just managed to survive after being pushed out of the valley. The ancestors of the Vietnamese seemingly were the only ones who were able to survive in the country of their origin and eventually to develop as a separate and homogeneous nation. It is now believed that they were the product of a racial union of the original Indonesian inhabitants of the Red River Valley with a Thai people and a branch of the so-called Viets, another non-Chinese people from the regions south of the lower Yangtze. The Viets probably moved into southeast China and toward the Indochinese Peninsula between 500 and 300 B.C.

4

Another minority people of southern Vietnam are the Chams. A study of the montagnards in the south and the Thai and Muongs in the north helps to throw light on the great migrations into Indochina, the racial structure of the peoples of that region, and the origin of the Vietnamese people. A study of the Chams will help to clarify some of the early history of Indochina, and of Vietnam in particular.

Estimates of the number of Chams in Vietnam range from twenty thousand to forty thousand.[2] They live in miserable villages, and in their dialects, matriarchal structure, and customs, they resemble the most primitive of the montagnard tribes. They, too, belong to the Indonesian peoples who at one time dominated the peninsula. But although the Chams are now a primitive people, they, unlike the montagnards, are remnants of a highly civilized nation conquered and almost extinguished in centuries of wars with the Cambodians and Vietnamese.

The kingdom of Champa probably came into existence at the end of the second century of our era. It appears to have originated in the province of Quang Nam, just below Hue, but soon extended over 200 miles south to the Bay of Cam Ranh and west beyond the Annamese mountain chain into the Mekong Valley of present-day Cambodia and southern Laos. The first mention of Cham activity is contained in a memorandum of 280 A.D. written by the governor of a southern Chinese province to the Chinese emperor. It speaks of attacks by the Chams on Chinese-held territory and complains that the Chams were supported by raiders from a kingdom called Funan, located south and west of Champa. The kingdom of Funan, which may be described as a precursor of the kingdom of Cambodia, was one of a number of early Indochinese states fated to disappear. The first Chinese account of Funan dates from the middle of the third century, by which time Funan had already become a highly developed state, with walled cities, great palaces, libraries and archives, as well as a mighty fleet, and an early system of taxation.

In the south, Funan extended over the whole Mekong Delta, but this does not necessarily establish any historical connection between Funan and Vietnam. The conquest of the delta by the Vietnamese did not begin until the end of the seventeenth century, and Funan had already disappeared by the end of the sixth. What is significant for an understanding of Vietnam, however, is that the recorded facts about the people and history of Funan apply largely also to Champa and the Chams, whose role in Vietnamese history is second only to that of the Chinese.

Lively commerce with India probably resulted in the adoption of Indian customs, religious practices, and Indian art and culture by an upper stratum of the peoples of that region long before the kingdoms of Funan and Champa appeared. The first organized states that arose in Indochina at the beginning of our era were indeed essentially a product of Indian cultural penetration. But the Indian priests, scribes, and officials whom the first Chinese emissaries to Funan claimed to have found there were soon to become Indochinese, and neither they nor their culture ever became the instruments of Indian political domination. Cultural development in the territories north of Champa, inhabited largely by the ancestors of the Vietnamese, was the by-product of Chinese military expansion and political rule. Seven hundred years were to pass between the arrival of the first Chinese in the kingdom of Funan and Chinese recognition of the independent kingdom of Vietnam in 981. The very next year, the first major Vietnamese expedition against Champa was under way. It was the beginning of a process of territorial expansion that lasted more than eight hundred years and scattered the Vietnamese people from the Red River Valley along the east coast of Indochina all the way down to the Gulf of Siam.

When Vietnam gained her independence, Champa was still a strong, aggressive power. Five hundred years later, in 1471, the Chams suffered a cruel defeat at the hands of Vietnam, and soon afterward Champa came to an end. Vietnam, continuing her expansionist policy, attacked the kingdom of Cambodia, which had arisen as the successor of Funan in the latter half of the sixth century and had reached its height at the end of the twelfth. Cambodia, threatened also from the north by the advancing Thai, was unable to halt Vietnam's infiltration of her rich but sparsely populated provinces in the south. The descendants of the Cambodians who remained in the Mekong Delta region after the Vietnamese expansion now constitute one of the minority peoples of South Vietnam. Their exact number is a point of major controversy between Cambodia and Vietnam. The Vietnamese, although they consider this minority as being largely assimilated, admit to a number of about 400,000.

5

The unity and continuity of Vietnamese history from its pre-Chinese past to the present day stand out amid the shifting mosaic of races and cultures on the Indochinese Peninsula. The development of the "Moi" was arrested at the dawn of history, and that of the Muongs soon thereafter. The Chams, who came on the scene of history later than the Vietnamese and were never subjugated by China, have all but disappeared. Nothing is left of the great kingdom of Funan, and Cambodia, the once powerful successor of Funan and center of Indochinese culture long before Vietnam consolidated her independence, was in decline when European intervention changed the course of Indochinese history. The Vietnamese alone have remained, and have become the strongest of all Indochinese nations.

The reasons for the survival and strength of the Vietnamese people lie at least partly in the vitality that the peoples whom they vanquished, displaced, or absorbed seemed to lack. The decline of the Chams and of the Cambodians and the rise of the Vietnamese may be seen as a clash between the civilizations of

India and China, in which the Sinized Vietnamese checked the spread of Indian cultural penetration of the peninsula. But before the Vietnamese people could set forth on their own, they had to throw off the yoke of China and develop the will and determination to prevent its reimposition. This in turn resulted in one of those curious paradoxes in which the poorly charted history of Vietnam seemingly abounds: the subjugation and education of the early Vietnamese by the Chinese turned out to be the main reasons for China's failure to establish herself permanently on the Indochinese Peninsula. All Chinese attempts at reconquering Vietnam were defeated by the skill and tenacity of the Vietnamese resistance.

Thus the main features in the development of the Vietnamese people from their pre-Chinese origins to the present time can be summarized as follows: Mongolian racial components and a willingness to absorb the higher culture of the Chinese gave the inhabitants of the Red River Valley an early advantage over their migratory neighbors in the surrounding mountain regions and their piratical Indonesian cousins farther south. Despite the threat by the peoples who kept coming through the mountains in the north and northwest, the Vietnamese stayed in the valleys and deltas that were their homes. They broke the power of the Indianized kingdoms to the south and carried elements of Chinese civilization as far as the Gulf of Siam. In the course of this process they asserted their right to a separate national existence against the Chinese, the Mongols under Kublai Khan, and the later European invaders. And in all likelihood they have remained the strongest barrier against a Chinese advance into Southeast Asia to this very day.

6

Though historians may disagree over the reasons for Vietnamese territorial expansion and the methods employed by the Vietnamese, there can be little difference of opinion about the kind of country this development eventually produced.

The Vietnamese started to spill over the confines of the Red

River Valley and a few smaller deltas farther south soon after having won their independence. Theirs was a slow advance that lasted more than eight hundred years, carried out primarily by the sort of peasant soldiering for which the Vietnamese seemed to have developed a special aptitude. The Vietnamese peasant turned soldier whenever an enemy approached and reverted to settler once a war ended.

Vietnamese expansion could proceed in only one direction. Population pressure and Chinese military power in the north were far too strong, and the country not nearly attractive enough to tempt the Vietnamese into trying to expand into southern China. Their eastern border was the sea, and to the west they saw nothing but infertile mountains populated by primitive peoples. The rice land they sought was to be found only to the south of the Red River Valley along the coast, in the territories belonging to the still partly nomadic and predominantly seagoing Chams. And so the Vietnamese began their southward march, looking for new plains beyond every layer of mountains, pushing along the narrowing flatlands between the mountains and the sea, settling in valley after valley, until they finally reached the open spaces of the Mekong River Delta, even deeper and wider than the Red River Delta 800 miles to the north, their starting point.

This was the famous March to the South of the Vietnamese people. Thus their country grew and acquired its present-day shape. Vietnam's expansion came to an end only some two hundred years ago, when Cambodia ceded to her the provinces of Sadec and Chaudoc.

7

One result of the above-described process is the peculiar shape of the country. It is about 1,000 miles long; in the north, between the coast near Haiphong and the mountain crossings into the Chinese province of Yunnan, it reaches a depth of more than 250 miles, but between the nineteenth and the sixteenth parallels, its average width is no more than 50 miles. The southern half down to the Gulf of Siam is a little wider, ranging from about 90 miles to a maximum of 120. However, the mountains—and only the Mekong Delta region has no mountains—reduce the habitable area of Vietnam to a slender coastal strip of plains and small deltas even narrower in some areas than the plains in the provinces north of the sixteenth parallel. The two large deltas, in the north and the south, and the expanse of narrow coastal lands have been represented pictorially as two baskets of rice suspended from the two ends of the bamboo pole used by the Vietnamese peasant to carry his load.

The preservation of Vietnamese racial and cultural unity in this long and narrow country with its enormous difficulties of internal communication emphasizes the qualities that evidently helped the people survive. Geographic, economic, and specific historical circumstances—e.g., the Chinese empire with its pioneering civilization—all contributed to the shaping of the Vietnamese people. In this mechanism of complex historical causality the early development of a solid social organization no doubt is a major contributing factor. The basis of this social organization is economic, but it could not have developed and become stable were it not for the impact of Chinese technology and Chinese civil and moral law.

Rice cultivation involves a definite cycle of economic activity. Much work must be performed at a given time, requiring more labor than may be available. Once the work is done, the labor force becomes largely idle. Therefore, the support of large numbers of underemployed is an economic necessity. The size and cohesion of the Vietnamese family—the basic working unit of the country—are rooted in this fact.

Though nature has supplied Vietnam with an abundance of water, she has done so in a most erratic fashion. Hence, the rice needed to feed the population of the Red River Valley could not be grown without irrigation and flood control. No individual Vietnamese family by itself, however large and industrious, could have coped with these tasks. Economic survival required cooperation on a village, provincial, and country-wide basis. The need for a system of dams, canals, and other hydraulic installations thus led to the early formation of social structures that have retained their stability in the midst of developments that tended to destroy both their substance and form.

The customs and religious ideas of the people reflected the peculiarly Vietnamese conditions for economic survival, as did the civic code and philosophy of state. The administrative hierarchy won early religious sanction, and the respect for the bureaucracy, a Chinese import, developed long before the powers of heaven were enlisted in the glorification of the Vietnamese kings. Yet at the same time no culture ever developed stronger family bonds nor a greater degree of solidarity among the people of the same village.

All these factors combined to make the Vietnamese a profoundly social, strikingly nonindividualistic race. Not that Vietnamese society lacked in opportunities for individual courage or for achievement by the gifted and strong. Nor did it lack the talented and brave men and women to use the opportunities offered. But a Vietnamese of the year 1000 or 1500 would never have dreamed of leaving his family or native village to go out by himself in search of land. The March to the South was a series of displacements, both voluntary and forced, of groups of individuals and families, groups large enough to found communities similar to the ones they had left behind. The need for protection by the state, under whose auspices territorial expansion usually took place, did not allow for political independence of newly won territories. The gradual nature of the process which made possible the full administrative integration of every new province into the Vietnamese state was equally favorable to the preservation of the unity of the new settlers. Their higher technics, their language, their deeply rooted customs and beliefs, and above all their functionaries, shielded them against absorption by the peoples they met on their way. Thus every new settlement in every new delta and valley in the long stretch of narrow coastal lands became a link between north and south. The unity of Vietnam is, in the words of Paul Mus, like the unity of a chain.[3]

In addition to being among the world's great rice growers, the Vietnamese are renowned for their skillful handling of river and ocean vessels. The Englishmen who came to Vietnam in the seventeenth and eighteenth centuries considered the Vietnamese the best sailors in the Far East. This should not be too surprising in view of Vietnam's physical characteristics—the long coastline and the many rivers connecting the populated regions with the sea. The vast majority of the people, moreover, live within 50 miles' distance from the sea. Thus salt and fish, vital parts of the Vietnamese diet, are easy to come by, and the proximity of the ocean to all important centers of population compensates for the difficulty of overland transportation and communication. The sea also has helped to promote Vietnamese unity. When, at the end of the eighteenth century, political unity was restored in the country after many years of partition and civil war, maritime transportation played a major part.

The sea not only unites the various parts of the country with each other, it is also the major link between Vietnam and the rest of the world. In a more tranquil past, Vietnam was called the "balcony of the Pacific." Yet because of its long coastline, combined with the fact that it lies along the sea route connecting India with China and China with the main Indonesian islands, Vietnam has always been highly vulnerable to attack from the sea. Its excellent harbors and bays seem to invite aggression despite the generally forbidding nature of the coast. The Chinese tried to subdue the Chams in maritime expeditions as early as the fifth century. Naval attacks by the Malays and Javanese were frequent during the eighth century, and again in the thirteenth, when China was in Mongol hands. And France first came to Vietnam in the middle of the nineteenth century because the Vietnamese coast offered convenient anchorage for French ships supporting England during the wars with China. The narrowness of the country and its extensive coastline made invasion by sea an ever-present danger.

8

Among the other natural phenomena that influence the conditions of life of the people on the eastern coast of Indochina, the climate is by far the most important. It determines the seasonal shift from great economic activity to underemployment, the cycle of work and inactivity, the people's state of health, the type of houses they build for themselves, the clothing they wear, and the food they eat. The abundant vegetation and the paucity of animal life, the types of natural catastrophe that tend to befall the country, even the periods of active hostilities in times of war are solely or largely determined by the climate.

Vietnam lies within the tropical zone. Its farthest northern point is on the latitude somewhere between Miami and Havana; the Point of Camau at the southernmost tip is almost as close to the equator as the tip of India. From north to south it is a tropical country subject to monsoons, the seasonal winds of the Indian Ocean and Southeast Asia which determine the length and character of the country's two seasons—dry and wet. Between April and October, when the wind comes from the southwest, depressing rains saturate the country day after day. Between October and April, the monsoon gives way to dry and cooler winds from the Asian mainland, and in these months little rain falls on most of Vietnam.

The regularity of this alternation, however, is somewhat modified by a number of geographic factors in the north, center, and south that affect the length and amount of local precipitation as well as the time of the rainy season, which begins in the center when it ends in the south. The amount of rainfall can vary considerably from one region to another. Thus the Cape of Padaron has an annual precipitation average of less than 3 feet, and the Atonat mountain region southwest of Hue a high of almost 10 feet. Moreover, the averages in the same region vary considerably from one year to the next. This variation has been one of the main causes of human misery in the valleys and deltas of Vietnam. One would be hard put to say whether the people in the Red River Valley have been victimized more by invading armies, by the swollen waters of the Red River in the many years of excessive rainfall, or by the equally calamitous droughts. In fact, only the people in the Mekong River Delta are less subject to the vagaries of nature, the dangerous high and low waters, one spelling flood, the other drought, with famine the inevitable consequence of either.

This cycle has raged most violently in the Red River Valley, the cradle of the Vietnamese people and to this day the most populated part of Vietnam. The Red River, after receiving the waters of the Black and Clear Rivers about 30 miles above Hanoi, carries an average of 141,000 cubic feet of water per second through the 100 miles of the delta from Viet Tri to the coast. In a dry year, the volume may fall below 24,600 cubic feet. When that happens, its waters can no longer reach the scorched rice fields, thirstier even than the feverish, malaria-ridden peasant himself. But the peasant knows that the rains that can bring deliverance are fraught with new dangers, not only to his crop but to himself. With the excessive rainfalls, the water level of the Red River rises to dangerous heights, occasionally up to forty times its normal volume.

How, in view of these extremes, was it possible for the Vietnamese to settle the Red River Valley? Only a gigantic effort on the part of the people could make the area habitable and productive. The force of the river had to be utilized. The waters rolling across the delta had to be contained and channeled into the river bed, and some of the excess waters stored for use in time of drought. This was accomplished through a system of dams, dykes, and canals controlling the rivers and regulating the water flow. The Red River now passes through the delta between two gigantic dykes that irrigate the fields, suspended, as it were, above an apprehensive population.

Some of the hydraulic installations in the Red River Valley must have been started long before the formation of an independent Vietnamese state, perhaps even before the arrival of the Chinese.[4] Today the dykes extend over an area of 1,600 miles. Along the tops of these dykes some of the oldest roads in the land run between villages and provinces. Built by the labor of the Vietnamese peasants, these dykes rise above the flatlands of the delta, monuments to man's industry and ingenuity, true ramparts of civilization.

II

One Thousand Years of
Chinese Rule

1

THE STORY OF THE first Vietnamese state and dynasty—which constitutes the legendary period of Vietnamese history—is based entirely on a collection of myths characteristic of a hunting, fishing, and partly agricultural people with totemistic and animistic beliefs.

According to legend, Vietnam began as a kingdom called Van Lang (or Van Tang, "Country of Tattooed Men"), ruled by a dynasty called Hong Bang for more than 2,600 years—from 2879 to 258 B.C., when the last of its kings was overthrown.[1] Van Lang was conquered by the king of Thuc, an aggressor from the north who allegedly united his own country with Van Lang and became the founder of the second Vietnamese kingdom, Au Lac. This semilegendary state lasted for only fifty years. Its disappearance in 207 B.C. (it was overrun by armies coming down from southeastern China) marks the beginning of authenticated Vietnamese history.

The attempt to invest Vietnam with a history as old as China's does not stand up to investigation. Though a kingdom of Van Lang seems in fact to have existed, its size and precise location are not ascertainable. None of the Vietnamese or Chinese sources describing the region that might have been Van Lang predates the fourth century, and its descriptions of the people do not fit the third or second millennium B.C. Rather, it seems in line with the centuries just before the incorporation of these territories into the Chinese empire—the third and second centuries B.C. Thus if Van Lang did indeed exist, and if it was the earliest Vietnamese kingdom, it could certainly not have come into being before 1000 B.C., and probably not even until 500 B.C.

The king of Thuc who allegedly conquered Van Lang and founded the short-lived kingdom of Au Lac has caused more problems for the students of Vietnamese history than all the legendary kings of the Hong Bang dynasty put together. Though he is generally believed to have existed, his kingdom cannot be pinpointed. Some believe it to have been a large country in the vicinity of the present-day Chinese province of Szechwan, others think it was a small state in the vicinity of Van Lang. But since Au Lac is known to have been liquidated by the Chinese in 316 B.C., it could hardly have conquered Van Lang fifty-eight years later. Furthermore, Van Lang cannot be found. This lends weight to the theories of those who maintain that Thuc was the name not of a kingdom but of a Van Lang clan, one powerful enough to have overthrown the last ruler of the old dynasty, allegedly a wastrel and drunkard who, unable to arouse himself from his stupor to defend his invaded capital, threw himself into a well on hearing the shouts of the victorious army of Thuc.

2

The myths about the appearance and downfall of the kingdoms of Van Lang and Au Lac are symbolic tales of the encounter of different races, of the struggles that accompanied their attempts to live together, of the bloody battles when these attempts failed, and of the painful fusion of originally dissimilar people.

Asia has always had a greater migratory population than any other part of the world, and these migratory peoples turned Indochina into a meeting ground of many different races. New streams of peoples were forever moving from the north, clashing as they progressed with those already settled in the valleys and the deltas in the south. In the first millennium B.C., these conflicts developed into lasting antagonisms between the peoples of the mountains and those of the plains and of the areas bordering the sea. These antagonisms form the basic theme of the myths surrounding the origin of Van Lang and Au Lac, a theme that recurs in the folklore of all the peoples of Southeast Asia, who share "a mythology imbued with a cosmological dualism of mountain versus sea, winged beings versus water beings, men of the mountains versus men of the coast."[2]

The end of Au Lac as a separate kingdom in 207 B.C., although an established historical fact, is also the subject of a myth which sees the Vietnamese people under the protection of a supernatural sea creature—Kim Quy, the Golden Turtle. It seems that a claw attached to the king's bow made him invincible, but after being robbed of the magic charm, the king was defeated and driven back to the coast. Before his pursuers caught up with him, he chopped off his daughter's head (she had been involved in the theft of the magic claw) and departed from this world by following the Golden Turtle into the sea.

This legend grew out of the subjugation of Au Lac by a Chinese general, Trieu Da, the governor of a large province in southeast China inhabited mostly by Viets. Exploiting the crisis that led to the fall of the first Chinese dynasty, the Ch'in, Trieu Da killed all Chinese loyal to their emperor, expanded the territories under his control to the north and south, and proclaimed himself the ruler of an independent new state, Nam Viet. The capital of the new kingdom was located near the site of present-day Canton; the territories of Au Lac formed the southern provinces of Nam Viet. Au Lac ceased to exist when Nam Viet came into being.

Vietnamese historians of old, wishing to assert the identity of their people, saw the kingdom of Nam Viet as an early realization of the separate statehood of their people. But this is nothing more than patriotic self-deception, of which the Vietnamese are as capable as any other nation. For if the kingdoms of Van Lang and Au Lac had been genuinely Vietnamese, as these historians assert, then the appearance of Nam Viet did not realize but rather wiped out whatever separate statehood the Vietnamese had achieved by the end of the third century B.C.

Nam Viet, neither Chinese nor Vietnamese, held out against imperial China for almost one hundred years. It succumbed to the armies of the powerful new dynasty of the earlier Han in 111 B.C., the year that ushered in the more than one thousand years of Chinese rule over the Vietnamese.

3

The kingdom of Nam Viet founded by Trieu Da was inhabited predominantly by Viets. No one seems to know how closely or remotely these people were related to the Chinese. They are known to have inhabited large portions of southern China in the third century B.C., and are believed to have come from the lower Yangtze Valley, where a Viet kingdom was destroyed by the Chinese in 333 B.C. Until fairly recently it was thought that the Viet Lac, the only Viet tribe to have preserved their ethnic identity under Chinese rule,[3] were the ancestors of the Vietnamese. This theory has now been discarded. The Viets probably were among, but not the only, ancestors of the Vietnamese. As Mongolians they were related to the Thai and the Chinese. The Viets were not part of the Austro-Indonesian racial group, whereas the Vietnamese represent a racial mixture of Austro-Indonesian and Mongolian elements. The theory of the mixed ancestry of the Vietnamese is also supported by a wealth of ethnological findings. The Vietnamese language is a blend of Mon-Khmer (monotonic Indonesian) and Thai (variotonic Mongolian) elements. The totemistic beliefs of the early Vietnamese, their custom of tattoo-

NAM VIET

The approximate borders of Nam Viet before its conquest by the
Han empire in 111 B.C., the date when the territories inhabited by
the Vietnamese became a Chinese province

ing their bodies and of chewing betel nuts, are common to all Southeast Asian peoples of Austro-Melano-Indonesian strain. The earliest social organization of the Vietnamese, on the other hand, as well as many of their religious customs, derive from their Mongolian ancestors. Some Thai in the mountains between the Red River and Laos have preserved a social organization that is amazingly similar to the type of feudal society found in Chinese accounts of the early Vietnamese.

Historical research has not yet been able to fix a precise date for the first appearance of the Vietnamese, but the area of their evolution can be defined with a fair measure of accuracy. It is believed that some Austro-Indonesian tribes went north into the present-day Chinese provinces of Kwangsi and Kwantung, where they mixed with Mongoloid ancestors of the Viets. Subsequently the earliest Thai or some other wave of the Mongolian migration into Indochina may have descended to the coast of Vietnam, where they mixed with the Indonesians in the deltas. The Red River Valley is believed to have been the center of this entire process.

The inhabitants of the Red River Valley before the last century B.C. probably led a primitive agricultural existence, supplementing their cereal diet by hunting and fishing. The ocean tides affected the water levels far into the flat delta and irrigated the rice fields. The tool these early people used was a hoe made of polished stone. (Ploughs and water buffalos were first introduced by the Chinese.) However, bronze was already known to the early Vietnamese and was used for the points of their poisoned arrows. The New Stone Age was just beginning to give way to the Bronze Age when Chinese expansion catapulted the Vietnamese people onto a higher level of civilization.

The advantages of a sedentary existence in a fertile delta must have become evident to the rice-growing Vietnamese soon after they began to develop some irrigation techniques—that is, before their contact with the Chinese. And once a substantial number had settled in clusters, the need for a stable relation of the people to the cultivable land became imperative. Whose land was it? How much of it could one family work without interfering with the life of others? Was it "owned" in perpetuity or only temporarily? Who would protect the weaker against the stronger, or a settlement against strangers trying to oust the settlers from their land? The earliest social organization of the Vietnamese people grew out of the attempt to find answers to these questions.

The solutions found resulted in a strictly feudal society, remnants of which still exist among the Muongs. In such a society, vassalage prevails—i.e., the dependence of a lower group on the next higher one, reaching from the broad base through various stages to the head of the feudal order, the king. The dependence of the lower on the higher orders is rooted in the power of the upper ranks to apportion land. Although among the early Vietnamese all land theoretically belonged to the people, it was held in trust by the king. The king in turn divided the country among his brothers and sons and among others whom he elevated to the upper nobility, and these feudal lords became heads of provinces. They in turn subdivided their domains among the lower nobility, the chiefs of villages or groups of villages. Their charges and privileges, like those of the higher nobility, were hereditary. They were civil, military, and religious authority rolled into one. They administered justice, led wars, presided over local festivities and religious ceremonies, and were in effective control of all the land. Originally their privileges and powers probably derived from military leadership in defensive wars against nomadic mountain peoples.

Although control of the land and the exercise of power were highly decentralized in this hierarchical setup, the common people shared in neither. The Van Lang and Au Lac eras may have brought the people a degree of security and protection, of order and justice, but their lives remained hard, and the better future they were promised by their seers is still an unfulfilled hope today, after two thousand years of suffering.

During its first thousand years, Vietnam was a Chinese province known in Chinese annals as Chiao Chi. The entry of the Chinese into the burning capital of Nam Viet in the year 111 B.C. marks the beginning of the recorded, verifiable history of Vietnam.

In that period, the Chinese not only wrote and dominated Vietnamese history, they also contributed to the making of the Vietnamese people. Vietnamese history must therefore be looked at against the background of Chinese history and civilization.

4

The China of which Vietnam became a part was a new empire. The extension of Chinese rule to non-Chinese peoples began only under Han Wu Ti, the most famous of the Han emperors, whose reign began in the year 140 B.C. China proper—i.e., the single, unified state comprising all the regions inhabited by the Chinese people—was less than a century old when Han Wu Ti embarked on his expansionist policies. But new though China was when the Chinese came to the Red River Valley, its civilization dated back at least fifteen hundred and possibly more than two thousand years. The cradle of this ancient civilization lay in the north of China along the Yellow River. There fertile land invited man to settle and rewarded his labors. The Yellow River, China's great provider and perennial curse, also created the great, fertile plain of northeast China. From this region, Chinese civilization spread north and east over the great plain, south and southwest into the mountains of Szechwan and down the Han River toward the Yangtze Valley, and finally west and northwest up the Wei River Valley into the upper regions of the yellow earth.

These vague territorial boundaries obtained throughout the first millennium of Chinese history, during the era of the Chou dynasty, from 1200 to 221 B.C., and the semihistorical phase of the Shang, perhaps going back as far as 1500 B.C. This period ended around the third century B.C., when the greater, mightier China began to emerge under the Ch'in.

This old Kingdom of the Middle, which began when some of its hunting, fishing, migratory peoples became agricultural settlers, gave birth not only to the archetypal peasant, but also to the warrior, vagabond, social philosopher, and pirate. But above all, it gave birth to the mandarin, the prototype of the bureaucrat, durable as the Chinese empire itself, and combining within himself something of the peasant, vagabond, pirate, warrior, and philosopher.

In 221 B.C., the first Ch'in emperor began to reorganize the whole of China. The old feudalism was attacked at its roots. The powers and functions of the lords were divided among provincial military and civil administrators appointed by the emperor. The

Ch'in imposed many major and lasting reforms, such as a single script, a unitary system of measurements and weights, and a road net connecting all parts of the country with the capital. The many walls around the former kingdoms were torn down, and one Great Wall built as a barrier against the Huns and other nomadic invaders. Regionalism was fought ruthlessly by mass deportations and mass transfers of populations. In fact, the Ch'in reign was a perfect example of totalitarian rule. Twenty-one hundred years before the leaders of Communist China were born, the people of China were already organized into small units and ordered to spy on each other.

These and other drastic methods of political rule could not fail to arouse dissatisfaction, and opposition to them was given expression by the Confucian scholars. The emperor barred these "utopian dreamers" from disseminating their ideas, had many of them executed or exiled, and ordered all but purely technical books burned. This *Realpolitik*, however, was successful only so long as the first Ch'in emperor was alive. After his death in 210 B.C., the edifice he had erected collapsed.

In 202 B.C., an able general who appropriately enough had begun his career as a pirate chief appeared on the scene. He reunited China and founded the Han dynasty. The Han continued and completed the work begun by the Ch'in. The new dynasty won the support of the scholars, and their teachings furnished the ideological foundation for the now unified, centrally administered state. With this active participation of the scholars, the mandarins established themselves as the class which more than any other helped to perpetuate the social and political structure created by the Han. When the reign of Han Wu Ti came to an end, in 87 B.C., the Chinese empire stretched "across Central Asia to Western Turkestan, across the Korean Peninsula to the heights of Seoul, and across Indochina to the approaches of Hue."[4]

5

The first annexation of Vietnam by the Chinese was a bloodless affair of little immediate effect. In 207 B.C., the founder of Nam

Viet had divided Vietnam into two provinces headed by viceroys but under the control of the old local lords. After the fall of Nam Viet, in 111 B.C., the two viceroys submitted to the victorious Chinese general and pledged allegiance to the Chinese empire. By confirming both these men in their functions, the Chinese rulers made themselves the overlords of the Vietnamese lands. Soon thereafter they divided the country into a number of military districts under Chinese prefectures and Chinese governors but did not interfere with local political institutions. The feudal chiefs who, with only one exception, had offered no resistance to the Chinese, continued in their positions, but they ruled with a somewhat heavier hand, for now they had to extract from the people the tribute demanded by the Chinese. This regime lasted more than a century, during which time Vietnam was nothing more than a leniently governed Chinese protectorate.

Local interference which ultimately led to direct Chinese rule only began after the onset of our era. In their relations with the Chinese in the Nam Viet era, the Vietnamese had already been subjected to Chinese cultural and technical influences. As their contact with Chinese civilization became more direct it also became more active. The plough was introduced, draft animals, new tools, and new materials were imported, and Chinese customs and learning were spread by the growing number of officials, soldiers, colonists, and refugees from China. Many of these new arrivals were former officials and scholars, the intellectuals of old China, who were among the first to flee when economic conditions undermined the existing order, bringing chaos, revolution, and foreign invasions.

The Chinese governor of the Vietnamese provinces between the years 1 and 25 A.D. welcomed these refugees as political allies against the successor to the Han dynasty, whom he and other provincial commanders refused to recognize, and as instruments of the Sinization of the Vietnamese. He opened schools to teach the language, writing, and ideas of the Chinese, and he introduced his country's more advanced techniques and civilized customs. The proselytizing effort of China, which made so many regions of the Asian mainland completely and permanently Chinese, met with a curious fate in the southern provinces of former Nam Viet. The people of the Red River Valley were quite willing and certainly gifted enough to learn what the Chinese had to teach them; but the more they absorbed of the skills, customs, and ideas of the Chinese, the smaller grew the likelihood of their ever becoming part of the Chinese people. In fact, it was during the centuries of intensive efforts to turn them into Chinese that the Vietnamese came into their own as a separate people, with political and cultural aspirations of their own.

It is not difficult to see why the Chinese were so successful in transplanting their culture to the Red River Valley. No other plain or valley south of the Yangtze is so rich in alluvial soil and lends itself so well to Chinese agricultural methods. The superior Chinese methods of irrigation and soil treatment, the manufacture of tools, weapons, and pottery, had developed in response to the same needs as those of the inhabitants of the Red River Valley, and under almost identical economic conditions. Moreover, as agricultural peoples whose crops and lives were forever threatened by invading nomads and the unpredictable furies of rivers, the Chinese and early Vietnamese were bound to develop similar attitudes. This made it easy for the Chinese to transplant their customs and ideas to the Red River Valley.

Yet despite all these factors, and a thousand years of military, administrative, and propagandistic efforts notwithstanding, the Chinese failed completely in their attempt to assimilate the Vietnamese. One probable reason for the failure was the long prehistory of the Vietnamese. The roots of their culture probably reached deeply into their pre-Chinese past. Another reason is purely geographic. Being situated on the periphery of the Chinese empire, Vietnam has always been able to expel the Chinese when their military power declined in times of dynastic decadence or internal discord. But mere hope for success could never have aroused the Vietnamese to fight Chinese domination had it not been for other, more compelling motives. It is the story of Chinese rule which contains the final explanation for the ethnic durability of the Vietnamese: When the Vietnamese, after many unsuccessful attempts, finally broke away from China, they had forever passed the stage when a people can become anything other than its own riper self.

6

One of the earliest undertakings of the Chinese in Vietnam was the construction of roads, waterways, and harbors to facilitate communication with China and to ensure administrative and military control of Vietnam. The indigenous feudal regime was ill equipped to carry out these technical innovations, or to promote Chinese learning and customs. The Chinese governors adapted the old order to the needs of a state in the process of modernization by creating their own administrations and filling new posts with Chinese personnel.

The benefits the Vietnamese people derived from these reforms did, however, carry a price tag. The Chinese rulers needed Vietnamese labor, tributes, and recruits for their armies. The cost of progress was high and discontent spread. But though the peasants may have been the hardest hit, active political opposition and conscious rejection of Chinese rule developed first in the ranks of the feudal lords. The hereditary local chiefs feared that the new Chinese policy of reform would seriously endanger their positions. They saw their power and prestige being whittled away. Feudal resentment turned into opposition; opposition brought repression; open rebellion was the only road open to the lords. When threatened with extinction, the hereditary rulers of the Vietnamese decided to fight.

The first Vietnamese uprising against China occurred in 39 A.D. A new Chinese governor, who added brutality to the repressive measures of his predecessors, created the atmosphere as well as the occasion that unleashed the revolt. The insurrection was started by a noblewoman whose husband had been killed by the Chinese as a warning to the restive lords. Led by the Lady Trung Trac and her equally fearless sister, the lords and their vassals attacked and defeated the Chinese forces guarding the governor's residence, stormed Chinese fortifications, and proclaimed the Trung sisters queens. Their kingdom, founded in 40 A.D., lasted little more than two years. Defeated by a Chinese army, the Trung sisters committed suicide by drowning.

Vietnamese historians have always treated the Trung sisters and their ill-conceived, ill-fated rebellion very kindly. When Vietnam became independent, they were proclaimed national heroines. The circumstances of foreign rule were bound to distort the true nature of this first Vietnamese "national revolution." But at that time there was no Vietnamese "nation," and even the evolution of the Vietnamese as a separate people was far from complete. The revolt of the Trung sisters was primarily an attempt of the indigenous chiefs to preserve their privileges and powers, and the battle was fought by and for the feudal minority whom Chinese interference threatened with extinction.

The defeat of the old feudal class marked the beginning of Vietnam's long Sino-Vietnamese period. Now the traditional local rulers no longer obstructed Sinization. Most of them had been killed in battle, and many of the survivors fled south. Those who stayed were demoted and hundreds of families were deported to China. Only the lower ranks were allowed to stay in their jobs, working increasingly under Chinese officials and an autocratic central government usually headed by the commanders of the Chinese troops stationed throughout the country. Vietnam, in brief, became a colony governed by Chinese proconsuls. With only brief interruptions, this new order was to last nine hundred years.

Both the organizational frame and spiritual foundations of Vietnamese society were altered by the waves of technical, social, political, and religious innovations that came down from China. The process, to be sure, was a tangle of accident, blind force, and conscious direction, but the result stands out clearly: a Vietnamese nation with its own, unique characteristics.

After crushing the ephemeral kingdom of the Trung sisters, the Chinese set up a completely new administration. They replaced the old feudal chiefs with more modern, more competent, and more reliable local and provincial administrators who were not independent rulers but rather servants of a centralized state. In order to keep the growing number of Chinese employees in Vietnam they were given land. However, they were not the only ones thus employed or rewarded. In line with their policy of Sinization, and in need of officials familiar with the people and local customs, the Chinese retained the subdued remnants of the old aristocracy.

Soon they also began to employ those Vietnamese whom they had educated and trained. However, they were cautious in using them, appointing them only to minor posts, as if preparing the Vietnamese for the distant future, when the same policy would be pursued by the French.

Before long, these high and low officials, provincial and local commanders, and scholars serving the state constituted a privileged new upper class. Three characteristics of this Chinese-created new class were to determine the curious political role it was destined to play during the many centuries of Chinese domination. It was semifeudal (its members acquired more and more land and succeeded in making their privileges quasi-hereditary); it was semi-mandarinal (the positions of the officials depended on their education); and it was largely foreign, for although the number of Vietnamese in this group continued to grow, the class as a whole remained predominantly Chinese. Its culture was Chinese, and it kept on being replenished with Chinese appointees, many of them refugee intellectuals.

7

The fall of the Han dynasty in 220 A.D., like all major convulsions in Chinese history, had repercussions in the extreme south of the empire which opened a new line of development in the political history of Vietnam. As a direct consequence of the empire's declining military power, a "barbarian" state by the name of Lam Ap had arisen on Sino-Vietnamese territory north of Hue. Founded in 197 A.D., Lam Ap became the nucleus of Indianized Champa, Vietnam's dangerous contender for supremacy along the east coast of Indochina.

More important yet for the future of Vietnam were the developments in the provinces while the Han dynasty was in its decline and after its defeat. Under the governorship of Che Sie, who ruled in the Red River Valley from 187 to 226, the Vietnamese territories became virtually independent of China. Although Che Sie payed China the tributes he owed and pursued a policy of Sinization, he ruled like a sovereign king over an independent state.

When China toward the end of Han rule was split into three contending kingdoms, Che Sie established a formal subordinate relationship with the heads of the Wu, who ruled southern China from Nanking. Upon Che Sie's death, his son decided to succeed him before the court of Wu had a chance to act. On receiving news that Nanking would not confirm his governorship, he prepared to defend with arms his father's provincial autonomy. He was defeated and killed by the Wu forces.

Because they were proponents of autonomy, Che Sie and his son, although Chinese, may be called the forerunners of the great Ly Bon, the first true champion of Vietnamese independence. The rebellion he led in 542 broke Chinese domination five hundred years after the Trung sisters; his reign as emperor lasted just about as long as theirs. But Ly Bon not only was a leading member of the Chinese-created, essentially Sino-Vietnamese ruling class; he himself was a descendant of a Chinese refugee. What, then, made him a Vietnamese? What turned him into a rebel and the leader of a foredoomed undertaking?

If in the five centuries between the Trung sisters and Ly Bon the Vietnamese of the new upper class were becoming more and more Chinese by virtue of their education and culture, its Chinese members evolved in the opposite direction: they were becoming more and more Vietnamese. The class as a whole developed common interests rooted in local positions, and these interests differed from and became increasingly opposed to those of the Chinese imperial rulers. Why, they asked themselves, should they pay tribute to China, why should their laborers become Chinese soldiers and their profits from international trade be transformed into Chinese revenues? The many new and unique features developed by Chinese culture on Vietnamese soil undoubtedly made for a prenationalist mood among the Sino-Vietnamese upper class, but the motive force behind their fight for autonomy or independence was a desire to preserve their wealth, uncurtailed by the needs and demands of the empire.

The new upper class in fact had staged its first insurrection in 248 A.D., three hundred years before Ly Bon, shortly after the defeat of Che Sie's son and the reimposition of strict Chinese control. The revolt failed, but it gave Vietnamese history yet another heroine, the twenty-three-year-old Trieu Au, who fought the enemy at the head of a thousand-man army. Defeated by the Chinese, she too committed suicide.

The size of Trieu Au's army bears out that the early Vietnamese uprisings against Chinese rule were primarily upper-class revolutions in which the mass of the people played little part. That is one of the reasons for their failure. When success came in the tenth century, it was due not only to China's internal problems but also to the fact that the struggle for independence no longer rested on a narrow social base. Gradually it took on the character of a national revolution.

8

What happened to the Vietnamese peasant in the course of the thousand years of Chinese rule? How were he and his village affected by the spread of Chinese civilization?

Chinese technical progress revolutionized the economic basis of Vietnamese life. With the expansion of rice lands, the wealth of the country increased more rapidly than that of any other Chinese territory south of the lower Yangtze.

This prosperity, however, was accompanied by a social, political, and cultural transformation as costly and detrimental to the peasant as progress can possibly be. The country grew rich while the peasant remained poor. The needs of the ruling minority and the demands of the state took more from him than technical innovation gave him. This is a crucial factor for the understanding of Vietnamese ethnological survival under Chinese rule.

Vietnamese history stresses the role armed rebellions against Chinese rule played in the emergence of a national community strong enough to resist absorption. The dozen or so anti-Chinese uprisings between the years 39 and 939 must indeed have contributed greatly to the growth of national feeling. The peasant, in particular, must have longed for an end to oppressive conditions. His interests conflicted more sharply with Chinese rule than those of the rebellious upper classes. He wanted to rid himself of a foreign rule under which he suffered greatly, profited little, and could expect nothing. If for centuries he did not engage in active resistance, it was mainly because he lacked the self-awareness as well as the possibility for organized action of the ruling class. But when the time of decision came, it became apparent that the passive resistance of the peasant had contributed more to the survival of the Vietnamese people and to national consolidation than all the upper-class revolts. After a thousand years, the villages of the Red River Valley and along the coast were still inhabited by a people essentially untouched by Chinese efforts to change and absorb them. The peasant clung to his pre-Chinese customs and religious practices, as in some respects he does to this day. This resistance to change should not be confused with a lack of receptivity toward new ideas. The Vietnamese villagers, inquisitive and eager for knowledge, accepted a great deal that was new, but they transformed or adapted it to their own preferences and needs.

Yet another and more fundamental factor affected the developmeant of the Vietnamese nation. Once the Chinese had introduced their agricultural improvements, the villages neither needed nor were intrinsically capable of radical change. As in China itself, all innovations on the village level were limited by the nature of an essentially static economy. Neither the Chinese overlords nor the local Sino-Vietnamese elite wished to interfere with the basic productive force of the country, its only permanent and reliable source of wealth.

Seen thus, the motives and causes that form the complex pattern of the birth of this nation reveal some clearly perceptible, unbroken lines. But such are the ways of history that for centuries the two principal currents of national independence ran counter to each other: The interests and aspirations that sparked the revolt of the upper class against the Chinese at the same time estranged them from the mass of people, the peasants who had resisted Sinization. The hostility of the peasants, on the other hand, was directed primarily against the local upper class, which, though Chinese-trained, was nevertheless the pioneer of national independence.

Not until the ninth century did these conflicting trends begin to converge. The village emerged as the source from which the national spirit drew its strength, but it was in the ranks of the upper class that this spirit had come to life. The upper class now made the peasants aware of the connection between the national interest and their needs and harnessed their forces for action against the Chinese. The upper-class rebels ceased to see the peasant merely as an object of exploitation and began to look at him as an indispensable ally in their fight for independence. They mobilized the peasants by appealing to their common interests, and they stressed those factors which separated both of them from the Chinese. They began to speak the language of the villagers and to honor the peasant's pre-Chinese customs. In preaching the national gospel, they transformed themselves into something more genuinely Vietnamese than they had ever been before.

The evolution of the Vietnamese people toward national separateness thus reached its final phase. The basic features that would distinguish the Vietnamese as a separate member of the family of man were fully developed by the time the thousand years of Chinese rule came to an end. Not only had the Vietnamese people preserved their pre-Chinese culture, but by modifying and even "Indianizing" the Chinese elements they had added to their own, they created something new. One day the world would recognize the Vietnamese as the truest son of Indochina, enduring, indomitable, and dauntless, perhaps because he drew his strength from more than one source.

III

Nine Hundred Years of
Independence and Growth

1

VIETNAM BECAME AN independent state in the tenth century. The Vietnamese in 939 defeated the Chinese armies and drove them out of the country in a bloody encounter, one in a long series between Chinese imperial forces and Vietnamese rebels in the Red River Valley. The smaller dragon had at last become strong enough to refuse obeisance to the bigger.

Although by no means internally secure and out of danger, Vietnam, separate and independent, had become a historic fact by 940, and such it was to remain except for one brief interruption, for well over nine hundred years—until 1883, when France won her twenty-five-year struggle for domination. The one interruption of Vietnam's nine hundred years of independence was a brief period of Chinese rule from 1407 to 1427. But this interlude ended in an overwhelming resurgence of Vietnamese national vigor.

The Chinese interregnum divides the nine centuries of Vietnamese independence into two almost equal periods. The changes in the country during these periods make such a division not only convenient but also meaningful. Between 940 and 1400, Vietnam developed a stable and efficient political regime. The state was built around a hereditary monarchy and the country united under a central government. Although Vietnam underwent phases of disgraceful dynastic corruption and political debility, it always remained strong enough to repel all invasions from the north and to hold its own against aggression by its neighbors to the south, Champa and Cambodia. Yet in all this time, despite its unity, highly developed political structure, and military strength, Vietnam did not expand. Its territory comprised the Red River Valley, the mountainous back country, and a narrow coastal strip extending to the south like a spear into Champa. When the Chinese reconquered Vietnam in 1407, 90 per cent of the territory that makes up present-day South Vietnam was not yet part of the country.

Vietnam's physical expansion was, however, not the only new feature of Vietnamese history after the Chinese interregnum. In the sixteenth century Vietnam suffered its first political division, which lasted more than fifty years. And in 1620, only thirty years after its reunification, the country was again split in two. This second division lasted more than a century and a half, and more than one-third of that period was taken up with fruitless attempts to reunite the country through war. A nationwide revolution that began its irresistible course soon after 1770 briefly succeeded in uniting the two parts of the country. But this unification did not become permanent until 1802, after a long civil war won by the South with foreign technical and military help.

2

The initial years of Vietnamese independence were filled with crises. Native governmental institutions evolved only slowly and painfully. In its first seventy years of independent statehood, Vietnam went through three dynasties—the Ngo, the Dinh, and the Earlier Le. This time of stress contrasts strikingly with the subsequent four hundred years, after political consolidation had been achieved. Between 1010 and 1400, Vietnam had only two ruling houses, the Ly and the Tran, each lasting approximately two hundred years.

The greatest of all Vietnamese dynasties, the Later Le, was born in 1427, the product of a ten-year war of liberation. The Le dynasty remained in possession of the throne for more than three hundred and fifty years, surviving both partitions of Vietnam. During the first partition, brought on by the rise of a usurper, the legitimate dynasty headed the smaller part of the country, but during the second, its emperors were recognized as the nominal heads of the country by the actual rulers of both parts—the Trinh in the North and the Nguyen in the South—as well as by the subjects of divided Vietnam. The Le dynasty remained nominally in power until the thirty-year civil war that preceded the country's reunification in 1802, when a member of the Nguyen family—one Nguyen Anh—founded the last dynasty of Vietnam.

The Nguyen emperors led Vietnam into hopeless isolation from the West—one reason that their efforts to resist French conquest during the second half of the nineteenth century were ineffective. The dynasty expired with the dismissal of Bao Dai in October, 1955.

3

The feudal chiefs of the tenth century who helped ·throw off the Chinese yoke did so, it would seem, only to gain a freer hand over their own subjects. Once the central authority of the state was removed, the existing social structure of independent Vietnam proved very much to the liking of the semifeudal and semimandarinal local bosses. Their main objection to the Chinese had been the taxes they had to hand over to the central administration and interference in local rule. These same factors aroused them also against their own rulers after the expulsion of the Chinese. Hence the Ngo and Dinh rulers did what their Chinese predecessors had done: They fought their feudal antagonists. If at times they fought them with less success than the Chinese, they also fought them with more justification, for the anarchic situation these chieftains helped to create was fraught with grave dangers to the new country.

When the country eventually became stabilized under later dynasties, its social and political structure had been preserved, but even under the strongest kings Vietnam's unity and order rested upon a compromise between the need for a centralized authority as represented by the monarchy and the interests of the local chiefs and provincial nobility.

Great strides toward a stable central administration were made by Le Hoan, the founder of the Earlier Le dynasty, who ruled for twenty-five of his dynasty's twenty-nine-year life span, from 980 to 1005. After holding off a Chinese invasion attempt in 981, he concluded a peace with the Sung emperor that brought formal Chinese recognition of Vietnamese independence. Subsequently, Le Hoan waged a successful campaign against Champa.[1] By putting his sons at the head of important provinces, he hoped to strengthen the monarchy without destroying the governmental structure inherited from the Chinese. But royal power and central administrations did not become secure until the reign of the Ly dynasty, which lasted from 1009 until 1225.

With the reign of the Ly, the Vietnamese monarchy at last entered a stage when its energies were no longer being dissipated in the struggle for mere survival. They could devote themselves to the construction of dykes, the building of canals and other irrigation projects, and in expanding available rice lands through deforestation and the requisitioning of fallow land. If the young nation was to survive, the existing land had to be made productive; new land had to be added to feed a growing population and meet the demands of a "progressive" state.

The social and political implications inherent in these tasks were numerous and tremendous. One was a loss of feudal autonomy on the provincial level and the ensuing consolidation of central state authority. Perhaps the people and rulers had drawn a lesson from the tenth century, when the hated rule of the Chinese was followed by political and economic chaos, the result of feudal dissension. But whatever the reason, the country had the good fortune—so rare in the history of Vietnam—to be given a number of rulers who possessed both the vision and energy to face up to the required economic tasks. Much was accomplished during the eleventh and twelfth centuries. The Ly moved the seat of government from a higher region of the Red River Valley back to Hanoi, the economic center of the country. Better inspection and quicker repairs of dykes were promoted through the establishment of ten-family peasant cooperatives, and even military service was adapted to the needs of agriculture by allowing soldiers to return for work in their villages six months in every year. In 1224, Thai Ton, the founder of the Tran dynasty, ordered the dykes of the Red River to be extended all the way to the coast.

As promoters of agriculture the early Tran rulers were surpassed only by the fifteenth-century Le monarchs, in particular Le Thanh Tong, who conquered most of Champa and ruled Vietnam from 1459 to 1497. The Le created a permanent staff of dyke inspectors, provided for the indemnification of landowners whose land was claimed for dykes, confiscated all idle land, and gave it to anyone willing to work it. In times of peace the army was used to increase the rice-land surface by clearing jungles, draining swamps, and building dykes, roads, and canals. Soldiers were even sent south into territory wrested from Champa to defend and colonize the fertile regions of central Vietnam.

In addition to promoting agriculture, the monarchs of the Ly and Tran dynasties were anxious to discover new sources of dynastic power. They sought to organize a strong, unified, centrally administered state on the model of China. Thus in 1089, the Ly established a fixed hierarchy of state officials with nine degrees of civil and military mandarins. A civil-service training institute and an imperial academy had already been set up in 1076. Both these schools were open to children of officials and to young princes and nobles. Examinations for public office were compulsory, and literary competitions to determine the grade of officials were introduced. Textbooks were published, classical writings imported from China, and the elite of the Buddhist clergy appointed to the highest positions in education, administration, and diplomacy. In 1225, the Tran founded an officers' training school. But universal military service dated back to the Ly, who created an army that was no longer the semiautonomous instrument of princes and local nobility. The armies of the Ly, the Tran, and the Later Le were raised by the monarchy and led by officers appointed and paid by the monarch, as were all economic, religious, educational, and administrative officials. In short, the state was no longer held together by military force alone, but rather by the much more stable institution of a specialized, well-trained bureaucracy. The great Le monarchs of the fifteenth century completed the work of their predecessors. Vietnam became the most advanced and the strongest of all Indochinese states.

4

The economic and administrative measures of these dynasties no doubt were more effective in preventing political strife than brute force would have been, yet the country continued to be plagued by feudal dissension and civil war. The reason for this was a basic social conflict: In order to survive, Vietnam had to have a progressive, centralized state, but its essentially agrarian economy did not allow for a nonfeudal ruling class. No matter how often the monarchy expropriated rebellious lords and smashed the power of ambitious local administrators, Vietnam's agrarian economy continuously re-created the social basis of a local type of feudalism. At times the landowners, who constituted a large part of the ruling class, modified dynastic policy to their own advantage, and at other times a king might decide that the only way the country and peasants could be saved from economic ruin was by curtailing the rights, possessions, and powers of the landowning class. The very frequency of such intervention, however, proved its ineffectiveness. A weak ruler or dynasty inevitably brought on a breakdown in public order and civil war, usually the result of a rebellion by members of the ruling class. When this happened, local chieftains or high officials would raise armies to fight powerful rivals or to overthrow a monarch and proclaim themselves the heads of new dynasties, or the ruling dynasty would fight and defeat the rebels. But whoever won would replant the seed of Vietnam's special brand of feudalism by rewarding his loyal followers with land or the control over land and those who worked it.

CAMBODIAN EMPIRE

Approximate borders of Vietnam, Champa, and of the Cambodian empire at the height of its power, during the twelfth century A.D.

5

In 1276, Kublai Khan, grandson of Genghis, master of an empire greater than any the world had ever known, ousted the Sung emperor of China and resumed the imperial policy of Han Wu Ti. Like others before and after him, Kublai Khan recognized the strategic importance of the east coast of Indochina in his expansionist schemes. He occupied Champa and invaded Cambodia in 1282. But in order to maintain and extend his foothold in Indochina, he had to eliminate the main obstacle to control of the peninsula—the strong and independent state in the Red River Valley. Five hundred thousand Mongol troops, so the annals say, invaded the Red River Valley in 1284, the darkest year in the history of Vietnam. The small country was not unprepared. It had built up an army of two hundred thousand which fought with great skill and valor. And because the whole people threw itself body and soul into the fight against the foreign invader, the Mongol armies were defeated. They were beaten again in 1287, when they returned three hundred thousand strong.

Without waiting to recover from the ravages of the Mongol invasion, Vietnam resumed its war against Champa, turning it into a feudatory state in 1312. But in 1326, Champa freed itself, and by 1371 it had become strong enough to invade the Red River Valley and pillage Hanoi. By that time, the Tran dynasty had lost its vigor and force. Vietnam was weakened by Thai minority insurrections, by defeats imposed by a small kingdom in the west (the future Laos), and by renewed Cham attacks that ended in the loss of provinces previously wrested from Champa.

Military campaigns and royal incompetence finally led to an economic crisis such as Vietnam had never before known and which hastened the end of the Tran dynasty. Amid this turmoil, an even greater catastrophe than the Mongol invasions befell Vietnam. In 1406, a vast Chinese army descended on Vietnam, sent by China's new rulers, the Ming. One year later, Vietnam was once more under Chinese rule.

The rule of the Ming was probably worse than anything Vietnam had ever experienced. The country was bled white. Battalions of forced laborers were sent into mines, forests, and to the bottom of the sea to extract Vietnam's natural wealth for China. But the main booty were the high taxes levied against all products and economic activities.

The economic exploitation was accompanied by radical measures designed to denationalize the people. Chinese became the language of instruction in the schools. All local cults were suppressed, and only Chinese rites and religious ceremonies were tolerated. Whatever national literature had been produced was confiscated and shipped to China. The women were made to dress in the Chinese mode and men forced to let their hair grow long. To help control a people that was not known for its obedience to the Chinese, the Ming governors also issued identity cards to the Vietnamese. In these years of Ming rule, the Vietnamese people learned to live with burning hatred in their hearts and to conceal their anguish until the time was ripe for revenge.

6

Vietnam's most powerful movement of national resistance started in the province of Thanh Hoa, south of the Red River Valley, in the year 1418, under the leadership of an aristocratic landowner, Le Loi, the first ruler of the Later Le dynasty, which was to last 360 years. Stirred by the misery of the people and outraged by the degrading spectacle of collaboration with the enemy by members of his own class, Le Loi proclaimed himself "Prince of Pacification" and embarked upon the stupendous task of expelling the Chinese. Le Loi, the courageous leader of a war that lasted more than ten years, can indeed be called the architect of national unity and a pioneer in the art of guerrilla warfare.

The Chinese had lost most of the country by 1427, but they hung on to the fortress of Hanoi for almost a year. But after Le Loi had defeated two armies sent to relieve the beleaguered forces in Hanoi, the Chinese capitulated and evacuated the country early in 1428.

Le Loi adopted the name of Le Thai To and ascended the throne shortly after the Chinese left the country. One of his first acts was an attempt to solve the problem of the landless, whose number had increased under Chinese rule and the years of war. Le Thai To ordered the redistribution of land among the entire population. Everyone, from the highest mandarin down to the poorest peasant—men, women, and children—was entitled to a share, but not an equal one. The members of the new royal family had to be taken care of first. Then the deserving military leaders and faithful allies of Le Loi had to be rewarded and elevated to the ranks of princes, lords, and high officialdom. Only those large landowners who had collaborated with the Chinese were expropriated. Other land for distribution came from the holdings of landlords who had died during the war, from devasted areas, and from villages whose population had been decimated during the war. But despite Le Thai To's agricultural reform, welcome though it was, too many peasants remained as miserable as before. There simply was not enough land to go around.

The problem of the landless peasants abated somewhat under later fifteenth-century rulers. Le Thanh Tong, whose thirty-six-year reign ended in 1497, made existing community lands inalienable and untransferable in order to protect them against further depletion by the landowners. But as the population increased, the land available for periodic redistribution grew scarcer, even under strong monarchs able to enforce any measures they thought necessary.

The conquest of Champa, virtually completed by Le Thanh Tong in 1471, brought a welcome interruption. Thousands of men were absorbed by the army and quite a number of them settled in military colonies and on state-owned landholdings. Even before Champa was defeated, mandarins and nobles sent "vagabonds" and landless peasants south, where land allegedly was just waiting to be taken. Under the aegis of the monarchy, new Vietnamese villages of small landholders with enough communal land for everybody sprang up all the way down the coast of central and southern Vietnam. The number of private holdings, however, grew equally fast. In fact, under Le Thanh Tong, deserving officials were given land that did not revert to the state after their death. Vietnam became stronger and wealthier, but its social structure remained unchanged.

The social conflicts and political struggles under the Le dynasty remained essentially the same as under the Ly and Tran, except that everything ran in higher gear. The monarchy climbed to greater heights but it also plunged to lower depths. Periods of remarkable achievement alternated with periods of bottomless decline. Some of the Le monarchs were the best and strongest rulers Vietnam had known, others the most depraved and most incompetent. In keeping with the spirit of national rejuvenation generated during the war against the Chinese, Le Thai To imposed a strict puritanical regime to speed up the process of reconstruction. He instituted a penal code that made laziness and gambling major offenses, and he forced Buddhist monks and Taoist priests to leave their monasteries. But only ten years later, at a time when a peasant caught gambling still had his hand cut off, his successor died from the effects of overindulgence.

7

The next two centuries and a half of Le dynastic rule were marked by political ineptitude and moral debasement, feudal impertinence and usurpation of royal powers, occasional vain efforts to secure economic stability by aiding the peasants, and bloody civil strife. The periods of general prosperity and domestic peace were brief and rare.

Why could these two hundred and fifty years of peaceful relations with the outside world not have been a time of domestic peace and prosperity as well? Why were Vietnam's valleys and coastal areas, its deltas and mountains, drenched with the blood of its people? Vietnam, instead of enjoying peace and well-being, became the scene of palace intrigues and assassinations, local and national uprisings, minority rebellions and peasant revolts, until finally, an explosion of feudal rapacity culminated in the ultimate political madness: the division of the country into two discordant halves.

The feudal cancer in the body politic had been allowed to grow until it threatened the survival of Vietnam as a homogeneous nation. The country was torn in half twice, once in the first half of the sixteenth century and again almost one hundred years later, and each of these divisions was followed by more than fifty years of civil war between the North and the South.

Those who believe that history repeats itself may find confirmation in the first division of Vietnam. But this division also attests to a far greater historical truth, namely, that although events do repeat themselves, they do not within the context of a different time have the same meaning, nor do they produce the same results.

Between 1504 and 1527, Vietnam had no less than eight rulers, six of whom were assassinated either by relatives or would-be usurpers, one of whom, Mac Dang Dung, succeeded. A former governor of Hanoi, Mac ascended the throne in 1527, and before another ten years had passed another Chinese army was massing at the border. But Mac did not send his troops out to fight this new threat. Instead, he welcomed the invading generals with presents and even offered China a part of Vietnam in exchange for a promise not to fight him. Thereupon the Chinese withdrew their troops and Peking recognized the newly founded dynasty.

The Le, however, did not cooperate with the Chinese. They decided to support Nguyen Kim, another ambitious Vietnamese, who planned to overthrow Mac and install himself in his place. In 1540, Nguyen Kim, head of a government-in-exile nominally headed by a descendant of the Le, prepared to wrest Vietnam from the Mac with the help of the Laotian king. Five years later Vietnam was divided in two. Nguyen Kim had won control of the southern half up to Thanh Hoa, at the edge of the Red River Delta. But when Nguyen Kim was assassinated in 1545, the Mac were still in firm control of the North. In fact, it took almost sixty years of warfare before the Mac were driven out of Hanoi and the Le put back into power at the head of a reunited Vietnam.

In 1592, reunification was only a brief interlude in a long history of division and armed conflict between North and South. After the defeat of the Mac, power in Hanoi rested in the hands of the Trinh family, whose chiefs had led the forces of the Le after Nguyen Kim's death. When the Mac were defeated and the Le reinstalled, the Trinh formalized their position as the real rulers of Vietnam by making themselves hereditary princes in charge of the government, although leaving the Le on the throne.

During the Trinh-led struggle against the Mac, Nguyen Hoang, a surviving son of Kim, had been appointed governor of the country's troublesome and underdeveloped southern regions. Under his administration the territory prospered and became virtually independent of the rest of the war-torn country. By the time the war ended, the Nguyen family controlled all of Vietnam south 'of the seventeenth parallel.

When death ended Nguyen Hoang's long and successful rule in 1613, he transferred his powers to his oldest son. From that time on, the Nguyen family ruled the South as autocratically as the Trinh governed in the North. Although both the Trinh and the Nguyen paid lip service to the legitimacy of the Le monarchs, Vietnam was again divided into two separately governed halves.

In 1620, the Trinh unsuccessfully attempted to oust the Nguyen, whereupon the latter discontinued the payment of all revenues to the government in Hanoi. Subsequently, in 1627, the Trinh launched a major land and sea offensive against the South. This too failed, but the South remained on the defensive. Although the North was far more powerful, the South, by exploiting the narrowness of its coastal plain, was able to repel the far stronger armies of the North. The Nguyen built two enormous walls, and in seven major campaigns, the Trinh never once succeeded in breaching these walls. It took the North fifty years to realize that military conquest might not be the way toward reunification.

In 1673, the Trinh ceased their attacks, and the war between North and South came to an end. The fifty-year struggle between the rival houses was followed by a hundred-year truce. When this truce was broken in 1774—again by the North—an entirely different movement of national reunification, directed against both the Nguyen and the Trinh, was already under way.

8

The one hundred and fifty years of separation under the Trinh and Nguyen constitute an inexhaustible source of controversy and speculation. Why, if the population of the North was three times that of the South, did the Trinh fail to vanquish the Nguyen?

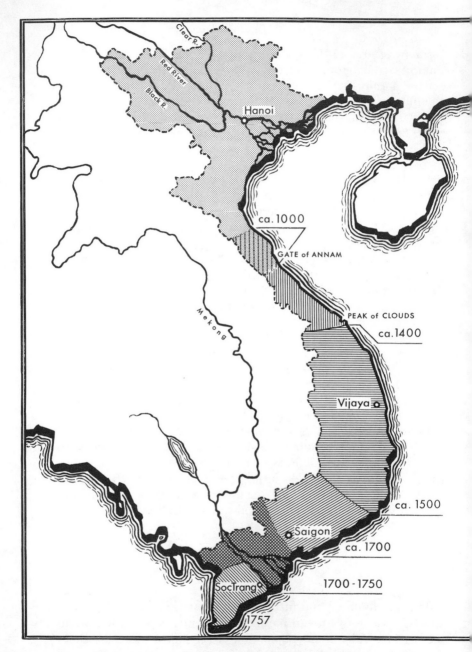

Clear R.
Red River
Black R.
Hanoi
Mekong
ca. 1000
GATE of ANNAM
PEAK of CLOUDS
ca. 1400
Vijaya
ca. 1500
Saigon
ca. 1700
1700-1750
SocTrang
1757

"MARCH TO THE SOUTH"

Through the "March to the South," the Vietnamese eliminated Champa and advanced to the Gulf of Siam at the expense of Cambodia

How was it possible for the South not only to survive cut off from the North, but even to pursue a policy of territorial expansion? And what forces were responsible for the survival of one Vietnamese culture and national sentiment in the long years of division and conflict between North and South?

The Trinh were not only stronger than the Nguyen; they also enjoyed the support of the Dutch, who were trying to gain a foothold in Vietnam. This brought them into conflict with the Portuguese, who consequently sided with the Nguyen. Portuguese military assistance in the form of weapons and technical advice helped the Nguyen to counterbalance the numerical superiority of the Trinh. This, together with the South's geographic advantages, no doubt helped to defeat the Trinh attempt at unification by force. But these factors were not decisive, and they certainly do not explain how a separate Vietnamese state could survive, expand, and remain wholly Vietnamese despite being cut off from the Red River Valley, the source of Vietnam's vitality.

The Vietnamese had worked and fought their way south for centuries, but the new territories they occupied at the end of the sixteenth century—600 miles of coastland and valleys housing less than one fifth of the population of the North, and possessing an even smaller portion of the country's wealth—could never have become anything but an awkward appendage to the North had it not been for one region that the Vietnamese now began to penetrate: Cambodia's enormous Mekong River Delta.

The discovery and settlement of the Mekong Delta represents a turning point in the history of Vietnam. The obstacles confronting the Vietnamese pioneers who came to this new land were enormous, but so were the opportunities. Not only the poor and desperate came, but also the bold and the strong.

This southward expansion constitutes the positive side in the long history of Vietnamese national disunion. The weaker Nguyen were able to resist the powerful Trinh because their country was developing. They could satisfy the need for new land. There were fewer aspirants for high position and more opportunities for those seeking administrative posts, for in 1632, the Nguyen introduced the Chinese system of recruitment for government service by competitive examination. A steady stream of immigrants and refugees from the North poured in. Some came because they were tired of war; others were looking for land; and still others came in search of greater personal security. Neither the methods nor principles of government in the South were any different from the North, but there was more room and there were greater opportunities for work and privacy.

However great the merits of the Nguyen in settling and organizing the South, the story of their successful expansion has its negative aspects as well.

Vietnamese dynastic power for centuries had been anchored in the Red River Valley. Outside that region, wherever local economies could flourish independently, provincial autonomy had always been strong. The farther south one went, the larger became the regions able to function autonomously. Hanoi had long ceased to be the center of the country, and with its expansion, provincial separatism grew stronger.

The great landowners and local mandarins had always fought national institutions not subject to local jurisdiction. And their position was further threatened by economic undertakings not rooted in the villages under their control. Activities such as small manufacturing and trade originating or developing beyond the spheres of their local domains met with the hostility of landowners and mandarins. For they knew that any such development, in addition to creating a rich merchant class and urban centers of political power, would only strengthen the central authority of the state. They knew that their privileges and powers were more secure if the existing order remained unchanged.

For these reasons, Vietnam's economy was not permitted to rise above the village level despite the country's fantastic growth. Vietnam possessed the most advanced native administration in all of Southeast Asia,[2] but its peculiar feudal social structure prevented further economic and social growth. The mandarins continued to oppose economic progress even after it had become obvious that the only alternative was stagnation and military impotence in the struggle against the West.

This, however, explains only what the country's ruling classes wanted, not how they were able to block economic development. They were able to do so because their prosperity as well as the minimum conditions for the peasant masses were compatible with a static, village-based economy. They did not have to develop a national market in order to safeguard the traditional way of life. Consequently there was no need for such innovations as, for example, a countrywide transportation system. In short, no economic necessity was at work to break the country's semifeudal, bureaucratic, ideological chains. The entrenched forces of separatism were even able to destroy the unity of the state without substantially altering the conditions of life of the people and without dealing a death blow to Vietnam.

9

The powerful Vietnamese lords and the local mandarins accomplished what no foreign power had been able to do: split the country and interrupt the development of a unified national community for almost two hundred years. However, Vietnam's national unity survived, because of the forces rooted in the Vietnamese village, in the peasant's way of life, north and south. The forces of the village, as inexhaustible as the fertility of the Vietnamese soil, bound together what the lords, the mandarins, and the country's rulers were tearing apart.

The Vietnamese peasants have to their credit the two most outstanding achievements in the history of Vietnam: territorial expansion and the preservation of national unity. How did the country reward the labor and dedication of its peasantry? "I am always bathed in sweat," goes an old Vietnamese song, "and all that is left of my torn garment is its collar."

Buttressed by an economic structure that neither territorial expansion nor dynastic rule was able to alter, the feudal and bureaucratic powers sowed misery and social discord. The central authorities in both parts of the country needed the support of its local forces and therefore they gave the lords and mandarins a free hand in the exploitation of the peasants. As the number of landless, semislaves, and vagabonds increased, so did the financial problems of the state. Both the Nguyen and the Trinh had trouble in holding their respective domains together. Provincial dissidence and local revolts increased again during the eighteenth century, but with one significant difference: more and more, the forces of peasant rebellion were stronger than those of upper-class political ambition.

But even though despair drove him to rebellion, the peasant was never able to develop political aims of his own. If he raised any demand at all, it was for the return of the land that he had owned or rightfully used. He was leaderless. And though his rebellions led nowhere, hardly a year went by in either the South or the North without at least one peasant insurrection. Vietnam was the home of people who, in the words of a French historian, "had nothing and were ready for everything."[3]

But the day was approaching when this cycle of hopelessness would be interrupted. By the middle of the eighteenth century, on the eve of the American and French revolutions, new social forces, albeit feeble, were beginning to appear on the Vietnamese scene. One local rebellion, at first not very different from all the others before, spread until it took on the dimensions of a national uprising. Starting in the South in 1772, it was led by three brothers, named after their native village, Tay Son.

Both French and dynastic Vietnamese historians have tried to cast the Tay Son brothers in the part of bandit leaders. But more important than the personal motives of these three men were the social forces that brought their movement national success. Not only did the Tay Son brothers enlist the support of the masses of landless, miserable peasants, they also gained the financial support of the small, emerging merchant class.

The Tay Son rebellion brought to an end the rule of the Nguyen in the South. They fell in 1777. But the Trinh, who had tried to exploit the problems of the Nguyen and invaded the South in 1774, were also marked for doom. No sooner were the Tay Son in control of the South than they decided to march into the Red River Valley. In 1786, Hanoi fell to the South; Vietnam at last was reunited. A year later, the Tay Son also got rid of the moribund Le monarchy.

The rule of the Tay Son was brief—the last of their rulers was overthrown in 1802—but the unity of the country survived.

IV

Missionaries, Merchants, and Conquerors

1

IN THE SIXTEENTH CENTURY, Portuguese explorers and conquerors, prodded by merchants and missionaries, became the pioneers of Western imperialism in the Far East.

The Portuguese arrived in Vietnam in 1535. However, long before Columbus' accidental discovery of America, the Portuguese had sailed down the west coast of Africa in the hope of reaching the Indies by sea and of breaking the trade monopoly of the Venetians and Arabs, the intermediaries in the trade between the Far East and the West.

When Vasco da Gama succeeded in reaching India in 1498 after sailing around the Cape of Good Hope, he opened up a direct route to the Asian world for the West. The Portuguese immediately began to settle portions of the Indian coast and to fight the Arabs for control of the neighboring waters. They succeeded in cutting the old trade route from the East (via Alexandria to Venice) by blocking access to the Red Sea. Five years after da Gama first landed in India, European merchants could buy pepper in Lisbon at a fraction of its cost in Venice. Lisbon became the main European outlet for Oriental products.

From India, the Portuguese under the leadership of Admiral Albuquerque penetrated farther east. In 1510, Goa became the first Portuguese stronghold in Asia and the capital of all its Indian possessions. Malacca, the center of a budding Mohammedan empire on the west coast of Malaya, was conquered and turned into a Portuguese stronghold in 1511. This gave Albuquerque control of the routes leading into the Gulf of Siam, the South China Sea, and the waters of the vast Indonesian Archipelago. Thereupon the Portuguese pushed on toward Siam and China and down into the Java Sea. They swarmed over Asia, convinced that the worlds they had discovered were there for only one purpose: to make Portugal strong and rich.

From the very outset, the Portuguese had been reaching out toward the spice treasures of the distant Ceram and Molucca Islands. The Javanese shippers of these spices to Malacca were attacked as fiercely as was Arab navigation between Malacca and the Red Sea. The Portuguese also fought the Spanish, who had begun to intrude into the Moluccas after Magellan's first voyage. Portugal's methods were such that "even their own historians were ashamed of their crimes in the Moluccas."[1] According to St. Francis Xavier, who came to Amboina in 1546, Portuguese learning was restricted to the conjugations of the verb *"rapar,"* in which they showed "an amazing capacity for inventing new tenses and participles."[2] Such talents naturally limited the effectiveness of the missionaries eager to stem the conversion of Indonesia to the Moslem faith. But the unhappy union of Christian zeal and naked greed was to become the model for the colonial behavior of a number of other nations as well.

Their efforts on behalf of the spice islands did not prevent the Portuguese from sailing all over East Asia, from Malaya to Japan. In one tremendous push they opened the doors of most Eastern capitals for contact with the West. The first European to come to Ayuthia, the capital of Siam, was a Portuguese, and the first Westerner to see the spectacular ruins of Angkor also most likely was Portuguese. Soon after Malacca fell into their hands, the Portuguese secured trading concessions in both Thailand and Burma. They landed on the Chinese coast near Canton in 1513 and reached Japan in 1542. However, a regular trading base between these more remote countries and the West was not established until 1557, when the first Portuguese settled in Macao.

2

Albuquerque's lieutenants had long been attracted by the inlets and harbors of the east coast of Indochina. One of his captains, Antonio da Faria, who entered the Bay of Tourane in 1535, had no trouble finding and taking what he was looking for—a suitable site, less than 15 miles south of Tourane. He decided on Faifo as another possible center of Portuguese trade and shipping. Although he did not succeed in making Faifo into a stronghold similar to Goa or Malacca, by 1540 it had become the main port of entry for foreign goods into "Cochinchina," the name given by the Portuguese to Vietnam.

During the sixteenth century, the Portuguese effectively controlled all Western trade with Vietnam. From their strongholds, they dominated Asian waters and held off all competitors. This was the time of Portuguese maritime greatness.

The first signs of Portugal's decline began to appear toward the end of the sixteenth century. Holland and England, at war with Portugal and Spain, were barred from access to the Lisbon market. Angry and envious, the Dutch and English began to treat Portugal as Portugal had treated the Arabs and Venetians, and they began to sail the seas in search of new trade routes and new worlds. Moreover, the Dutch were eager to best Philip II of Spain, who had ascended the Portuguese throne in 1580.

Although the cutting down of Portuguese power in Asia was the common aim of the English and Dutch, their European alliance against Portugal and Spain never developed into joint action in the Far East. As it turned out, England's rise to colonial supremacy was still a century away. The seventeeenth century in Asia was the century of the Dutch. They were wealthier than the English and more experienced navigators and traders. They became the heirs of the Portuguese chiefly by concentrating their efforts on Southeast Asia.

The English founded their East India Company in 1600, two years before the Dutch, but for ten years they made no headway in India itself. Only after defeating a Portuguese fleet in Indian waters in 1612 were they able to acquire their first trading concession on Indian soil. By that time, however, their trading stations in Southeast Asia were already under heavy attack by the aggressive Dutch.

When the Dutch founded their East India Company, they amalgamated a number of existing companies that had been operating for years on a small scale. The capitalization of the Dutch company was almost ten times that of the English. By 1605, the Dutch had visited every major port in Southeast Asia and set up their trading posts throughout the archipelago, from Malaya to New Guinea.

From the outset, the Dutch made things difficult for the English wherever they could. They tried to prevent them from entering any place they considered theirs by virtue of having gotten there first. Political considerations connected with their position in Europe forced the Dutch to tolerate the English in Asia, but they did all in their power to prevent them from gaining a foothold in Eastern trade. By 1615, the Dutch traders had become convinced that they could no longer tolerate the English. Their profits were declining, they said, because they had not pursued a sufficiently aggressive policy toward the English. And they contended that the Dutch company was bound to fail unless it secured a trade monopoly in Asia.

The Dutch succeeded in replacing the Portuguese as the dominant colonial power in Asia. By 1668, the Portuguese were definitely defeated. They were able to hang on to Goa and Diu in India and to Macao, but they lost their possessions between India and China and their control of Far Eastern navigation. The Dutch had the Cape of Good Hope, and they controlled the coasts of Malabar and Coromandel as well as Ceylon. They also had won Malacca from Portugal in 1641. Dutch power in the archipelago was supreme. They had wiped out every single independent state in the spice islands of eastern Indonesia. They were also the only ones permitted to trade with Japan after Japan expelled all Westerners in 1641.

3

The Dutch made their appearance in Vietnam exactly one hundred years after the Portuguese. They established their first trading post in 1636 in the southern half of the country. When the government at Hanoi a year later permitted them to set up a post in Pho Hien, the Dutch immediately switched the bulk of their trading activities to the North, the richer half of the country.

The Trinh, eager for support against the Nguyen, allowed the Dutch to establish themselves in the capital, who in turn supported the Trinh so strongly that they incurred the enmity of the Nguyen. Portuguese intrigues helped to nourish this hostility, and in 1654 the Dutch were forced to leave the South.

In keeping with the pattern of Western penetration in the East, the English were the next to appear at the gates of Vietnam. But their days of glory in Asia had not yet come. They had failed in India and Indonesia, and they were not too successful in Vietnam. An early English attempt to enter Faifo met with disaster. Later efforts to gain a foothold in either the South or the North were blocked by the Portuguese and the Dutch. Not until 1672 were the English able to open an office in Pho Hien, which they later moved to Hanoi, hoping that the trade thus gained would justify their efforts.

In the meantime another power, France, had made its appearance. The French had founded their East India Company in 1664, more than sixty years after the English and the Dutch. In 1676, they acquired the site of Pondicherry, on the east coast of India. They also managed to set up a post at Bantam, on the western tip of Java. Although a French ship had sailed up the Red River in 1669, the first regular French trading office in Vietnam was not opened until 1680 in Pho Hien, the starting point of both the English and Dutch. Portuguese merchants had already been in Vietnam for well over a hundred years when the French came to Pho Hien, ignoring the warnings of their already established Western competitors. Trade with Vietnam, they were told, was bad and getting worse. The French came to Vietnam at the risk of having their ships sunk by Dutch saboteurs, their representatives murdered by Portuguese conspirators, and their reputations slandered by the English. But they were ready to fight back.

However, when the French arrived on the scene, trade with Vietnam was in fact becoming unprofitable. Soon some pessimists were heard to complain that they had boarded a sinking ship. When the Dutch in the wake of their conquests on Java drove the French and English out of Bantam, the isolated French trading position in Vietnam was doomed. The only comfort the French could derive was that their more powerful rivals suffered a similar fate. The English closed their Hanoi post in 1697; the Dutch, in 1700. Only the Portuguese were able to continue their traffic between Macao and Vietnam, though on a reduced scale.

When the English East India Company tried to re-enter Vietnam in 1822, after a century of troubles on the Indian subcontinent, it warned its agents against a repetition of the errors committed by Europeans, which they held responsible for the failure of previous Vietnamese ventures.[3] The counsel was no doubt wise, but the diagnosis only partially correct. If after 1672, the year the English started to trade with Vietnam, business began to decline, it was due largely to the fact that the long war between North and South had come to an end that year. Vietnam no longer needed military equipment from the West. Vietnamese domestic peace did more to ruin Dutch and Portuguese trade with Vietnam than European abuses or English and French competition. And peace in Vietnam was followed by a series of long European wars which had a detrimental effect on intercontinental traffic and trade.

However, other and more fundamental reasons were responsible for the West's failure to turn trade with Vietnam into as profitable an undertaking as with other parts of Asia. In Vietnam, the West could not engage in the same piracy and plunder as elsewhere, for both the South and the North had strong governments, effective armies, and even naval forces with which to defend themselves.

Vietnam's educated upper class was experienced in war and in administration and determined to remain in control of the country's wealth. As long as the blood and the sweat of the peasants were at their disposal, the rulers of Vietnam were able to handle all outside threats.

If they wished to add Vietnam to their profit-making Asian ventures, the seafaring nations of Europe had to forgo their usual methods of brute force. For the time being, trade was the key to whatever treasures the country held. The English and French efforts were probably made at considerable cost to themselves. They were slow to realize that the trade was disappointing. Vietnam, though potentially rich, was not yet ready for large-scale trade. Only the government and a handful of wealthy people were able to purchase European goods. In short, Vietnam was not yet ripe for exploitation.

4

Mercantile penetration had failed and conquest by force seemed patently ill-advised. The year 1700 might therefore have marked the end of contacts with Europe and of Western influence in Vietnam were it not for an entirely different kind of Western activity in Asia: the missionary work of the Catholic Church. After the last European traders left Vietnam in 1700, Holland and England were definitely out of the picture. Portugal and France, however, retained representation, for most of the missionaries in Vietnam were either Portuguese or French.

The beginnings of Catholic proselytization in Asia are inextricably linked with the history of Portuguese trade and expansion. When Pope Alexander VI, in 1493, for the purpose of spiritual and territorial conquest divided the world between Portugal and Spain, the Portuguese managed to seize Asia as their spiritual domain. Missionaries to Asia had to leave from Lisbon and be "cleared" by the Portuguese in Goa. They worked under Portuguese supervision, political as well as ecclesiastic. The Portuguese guarded their exclusive right to oversee the transformation of the heathen Asians into Christians so jealously that it outlived their trading monopoly for more than half a century.

The history of Catholic missionary work in Asia is one of hopeful beginnings and astonishing recoveries from near fatal blows, but compared with the results in Central and South America it must be regarded as a failure. This is true also of Vietnam, although there the Catholic Church was more successful than in any other part of Asia except the Philippines.

Very little is known about the beginnings of missionary work in Vietnam. According to Vietnamese annals, one Ignatio came to Vietnam and preached in the province of Nam Dinh in 1533. A little more is known about a Spanish Dominican by name of Diego Adverte, who arrived in Vietnam in 1596. For a while he was allowed to preach, but the appearance of Spanish warships soon after his arrival aroused suspicion, and the authorities literally chased him on board one of those unwelcome ships.

Organized religious propaganda began twenty years later, after Portuguese merchants in Faifo invited a group of Jesuits from Macao. Two missionaries—one an Italian, the other a Portuguese—left the Jesuit academy at Macao for work in Vietnam, arriving in Tourane in January, 1615. Among the many who hurried to join the mission they founded at Faifo was Cristoforo Borri, the first European to write about Vietnam and the Vietnamese people and to praise their "natural kindness and hospitality" to the skies. Borri thought the Vietnamese superior to the Chinese both in intelligence and courage, and to all other Asian peoples in friendliness, good manners, and their thirst for knowledge.[4]

Soon afterward, a gifted, strong, dedicated Frenchman, Monsignor Alexander of Rhodes, a native of Avignon, came to Vietnam. Within six months he had mastered the language and begun to preach in Vietnamese.[5] He wrote the first catechism in the Vietnamese language and published a Vietnamese-Latin-Portuguese dictionary. Moreover, these were the first works to be printed in Quoc Ngu, the name by which the transliteration of Vietnamese sounds into Latin script is known.

In 1627, Rhodes was sent to Hanoi. He was well received by the court and gained the affection of the people. Rhodes then was thirty-seven years old. He lived for another thirty years, and remained active throughout.

Rhodes' life mirrored the turbulent history of the Vietnamese missions. He was expelled from the North in 1630, and at about that time the South also began to be apprehensive about the effects of this new religion. Throughout the duration of the civil war, both the North and the South were lenient in the enforcement of their anti-Catholic measures, lest the foreign ships bearing their precious cargoes of war materials failed to return—a frankly voiced Jesuit threat. Rhodes was permitted to return to Vietnam, but in 1645 both the Nguyen and the Trinh barred him from the country.

Exasperated by the lack of vigor of his Portuguese superiors, Rhodes in 1649 went to Rome to agitate for support of the struggling Vietnamese missions free from Portuguese control. He submitted a training program for indigenous priests. The Vatican bureaucracy, fearing a conflict with Portugal, did not act, whereupon Rhodes turned to France for support, a power whose passion for influence in Asia he was aware of and was determined to exploit. The Vietnamese, he wrote, were wealthy because their soil was fertile. They had gold mines and great quantities of pepper, and they were so rich in silk that they used it for fishing lines and cords.

Rhodes succeeded in enlisting French priests for work in Vietnam and in gaining the support of the French Church. In addition, the aristocracy and circles interested for a share in Asian trade contributed money for his projected training of an indigenous clergy. In the midst of his efforts, however, Rome sent Rhodes to a mission in Persia, where he died four years later, far away from the people whom he had hoped to bring into the arms of the Church. But he died knowing that Rome had at last recognized the merits of his project. His plan for Vietnam received official sanction in 1658, despite Portuguese opposition to two Frenchmen who were appointed to head the Vietnamese mission.

5

The evangelization of Indochina was to become the prerogative of a special French-directed organization, the Society of Foreign Missions, which was founded in Paris in 1664. It owed its existence to the same impulses, even the same people, who that very year had founded the official French East India Company—merchants and missionaries from Paris and Rouen.

This union of religious and mercantile interests, a memorable chapter in the history of Western colonialism, was forged around 1650. The French had opened a house in Hanoi ostensibly to organize Franco-Vietnamese trade, but its residents were in fact missionaries disguised as French merchants. Some trade was conducted, but it served mainly as a cover for clandestine proselytizing.

The meeting of two different lines of action originally quite unrelated to each other created a curious state of affairs. Both churchmen and traders realized that in the struggle for a share of Asia their intimate cooperation was a condition for success. A maritime trading company provided for the free transportation, provisioning, and establishment of missionaries and their helpers in exchange for clearly specified trade services by the missionaries. François Pallu, one of the two apostolic vicars to Vietnam, was even more blunt than the merchants who provided for his voyage to the East. In a report submitted in 1667, he assured the directors of the French company that they would have as many promoters of trade as there will be bishops, priests, and believers.

Immediately after his appointment as head of the Tongking mission in 1658, Pallu stated that although the voyages were undertaken for the glory of God, their practical aspects ought not to be neglected. Once the French started to compete with the Portuguese, English, and Dutch, no Frenchman proved more knowledgeable about the prospects of Western trade than the Apostolic Vicar François Pallu.

Pallu and his colleague, Monsignor Lambert de la Motte, tried to resume the work that Rhodes and his colleagues had been forced to abandon, and the obstacles the two Vietnamese governments erected only served to strengthen the churchmen's alliance with business. Because missionaries were barred from entering the country, Pallu and de la Motte smuggled them in disguised as merchants and used them to promote trade. But when trade with the West declined, the fate of the missions depended on the degree of acceptance of their religious activities by the Vietnamese.

6

Monsignor Rhodes' impressive statistics and claims notwithstanding, the educated, wealthy elite was not readily converted. The early converts came from among the poor and downtrodden.

The conflict between the Vietnamese governments and the Catholic missions was not so much religious as political. The Vietnamese, convinced that most of the Westerners pursuing spiritual goals were allied with the agents of worldly conquest, treated the missionaries as members of a fifth column and the Catholic communities as part of a political movement in the service of foreign powers. These Vietnamese fears and suspicions were strengthened by a combination of religious, political, and military moves through which France tried to conquer the kingdom of Siam in 1685. Pallu in particular was a political schemer who went far beyond his instructions. He might be called the inventor of the colonial practice of shaping policy in Paris by the method of the *fait accompli.*

Another factor in Vietnamese opposition to the activities of the Church were the conflicting Christian and Confucianist views on the relation of the individual to the state, and the fact that some Christian doctrines which sought to govern individual behavior beyond the private sphere would, it was feared, destroy the moral foundations of a Confucianist society. From the mandarins' point of view, the missionaries' influence on individual conduct was bound to affect the principles of Confucianist society. The Church's attack on polygamy was of little consequence per se, but actions according to one's private conscience in violation of the principles on which society rested were immoral. Moreover, the Confucianist mandarins maintained, the conscience of a Vietnamese Christian was shaped by the doctrines of an institution taking its orders from abroad. Therefore, they maintained, being a Christian was not only immoral but also subversive.

For these reasons the Vietnamese governments did not permit the Catholic Church to function freely, frequently jailed its native leaders, and deported its missionaries. In the course of their two hundred years of illegality, missionaries and native Catholics paid for their beliefs with their lives. But in spite of occasional violent outbursts instigated from above, the Catholic communities of Vietnam were never in danger of extinction. As a matter of fact, two hundred years after the expulsion of Rhodes, they had become important and influential enough to provide France with a pretext for military intervention.

7

As the eighteenth century unfolded, it became apparent that Western penetration of Vietnam was suffering reverses. The volume of trade between Vietnam and the West diminished. What foreign trade there was was carried on largely by a Chinese colony at Faifo.

In the eyes of some forward-looking Western colonialists, this state of affairs was regrettable more from a Vietnamese than a European point of view. They believed that if Vietnam remained closed to European trade and shipping, the country inevitably would one day have to be opened by force. The only question was which of two contending powers, England or France, would undertake such military intervention.

It was this Anglo-French rivalry, however, and England's determination to destroy the positions of the Portuguese and Dutch in India, that gave Vietnam its long respite from European interference. England's attention was turned on India, which forced France to concentrate her efforts on the defense of her Indian position.

It was only after England's decisive victory over her European rivals in India, and the conclusion of the Treaty of Paris, by which France ceded most of her Indian possessions, that French traders and missionaries began again to advocate the conquest of Cochinchina, as compensation for the Indian holdings and also to prevent the English from getting there first. Their campaign led nowhere. Conditions in Vietnam after the Tay Son rebellion in 1772 seemed to invite European interference, but the financial difficulties of France, the Seven Years' War, and the American Revolution helped to save Vietnam at that critical juncture. Later,

the French Revolution and the Napoleonic wars absorbed both
the military and political energies of the Western nations.

However, it was in this period that another French churchman,
Pigneau de Béhaine, Bishop of Adran, almost succeeded in securing Vietnam for France's future colonial empire, sixty years before
her costly Indochinese venture.

French policy toward Indochina during the eighteenth century,
although essentially negative, nonetheless constitutes an important chapter in the history of French colonialism. It was in the
eighteenth century that some of the basic features of French
colonialism in Indochina emerged more clearly than at any time
in the future. Thus it was made obvious that the conquest of
Vietnam was not an undertaking demanded by the French people, or even by the government. French intervention grew out of
the initiative of private persons and the unauthorized actions of
military men and colonial officials in India and the Mascarene
Islands who combined service to their country with the promotion
of their private interests. The story of French intervention in
Indochina thus is largely the story of the efforts of individuals
to engage the power, wealth, and prestige of their country to
promote their private schemes. The missionaries sided with the
vocal advocates of intervention, though until the Bishop of Adran
joined the forceful advocates of the cause, their voices seemed
timid besides those of the traders, officers, and officials.

One of the most outstanding of these advocates of force was
Joseph François Dupleix, France's first great colonial statesman-
soldier. From his position in India he tried repeatedly to open the
ports of Vietnam to French commercial vessels and to trick the
Vietnamese rulers into letting him establish a military base along
the eastern coast of Indochina.

The Vietnamese rulers, although alert to the dangers of Western infiltration, were generally ready to talk and trade. In spite
of this readiness, the efforts of Dupleix and the others came to
naught mainly because they lacked official French support.

Premature and ineffective though it was, the early colonial
propaganda was nevertheless marked by a concreteness and candor
not found in any later French statements about Indochina.
Words like "civilization," "cultural mission," "French honor,"
even "religion," were not then part of the colonial vocabulary.

One agent of the French East India Company wrote in 1755 that the acquisition of the island of Condore not only would give France a flourishing Asian trade, but would put her in a position to destroy English and Dutch trade. And one enthusiastic churchman, the Abbé de Saint-Phalle, exclaimed: "They have gold in their mines and rivers, even in the excrement of their ducks; there is hardly a country in Asia where labor is cheaper than in Cochinchina."[6]

But the French Government and the East India Company frankly told the churchmen, traders, and officials that it could not raise the funds for ships and soldiers, that France could not risk widening its conflict with England and Holland, and that the defense of its holdings in India were more important than dissipating its strength in a distant, comparatively unknown land.

The work of Pierre Poivre, a pioneer of French Indochina, vividly demonstrates the futility of the efforts to overcome the then existing French resistance to action. Poivre began his career in 1720 as a missionary, but while in Asia he switched to his father's business, the silk trade. After two years in Canton, he returned to France, where he tried to promote trade with Vietnam. He then went to Cochinchina on behalf of the East India Company, bringing with him goods and rich presents for the Nguyen king. But while he had no trouble getting rid of his presents, he found it more difficult to dispose of his goods, and though he could see that the poverty of the people was one reason for his commercial failure, he put the blame on the dishonesty of the mandarins. He thereupon decided that his country should come to the rescue of its trade. He failed.

Poivre and his compatriots in Vietnam were completely blind to the effects of two hundred years of European actions in Asia. All Europeans were regarded as thieves who would stop at nothing, including murder, to gain their objectives. To cheat them was not considered dishonorable. The behavior of the mandarins, many of whom were probably as dishonest as Poivre claimed, was a response not only to the white man's past actions, but also to what they believed his future intentions to be. The mandarins proved to be correct.

In 1758, one Count d'Estaing, a French naval captain, conceived an elaborate plan for invading Hue and robbing the imperial palace of all its treasures. D'Estaing's project received the official approval of Governor Lally-Tollandal of French India. The expedition got under way in October, 1759, but the Count's uncontrollable desire to follow his piratical bent by attacking English trading posts on the west coast of Sumatra ruined his scheme. He lost many of his men in battle and through disease and missed the monsoon that was to carry his ships to Hue.

Nine years later, in 1768, the Count, now "matured and hardened,"[7] proposed that three thousand soldiers under the leadership of Picrrc Poivre land in Tourane, fortify the port, and make it the base of a vast commercial and political operation. But if France had had the money for such an expedition, she would have sent the men to protect her possessions in India, whose fate overshadowed all of France's colonial aspirations and stopped her from acting in any other Asian area.

8

This was the moment when Pigneau de Béhaine appeared on the Vietnamese scene. He was not quite twenty-five years old when the Society of Foreign Missions sent him to the Far East. He arrived at the province of Hatien in southwestern Vietnam in March, 1767. There for two and a half years Pigneau headed a seminary, until its destruction in the wake of a Siamese invasion. After two months in a Hatien jail, Pigneau fled Vietnam together with some of his pupils. They reached Malacca on a Chinese junk.

In 1770, the seminary was reopened in French India and its twenty-nine-year-old head appointed Bishop of Adran. In 1775, Pigneau was back in Hatien. A twenty-year-old ban against the Christian religion had been lifted by the last of the Nguyen kings shortly before the Tay Son rebellion put an end to the Nguyens. The king's sixteen-year-old nephew, Nguyen Anh, escaped the royal massacre, and the Bishop of Adran saved the young man's life by hiding him from his pursuers and helping him to an island in the Gulf of Siam—an act of Christian charity and at the same time a well-thought-out political step.

Pigneau—churchman, educator, and scholar—discovered his

true vocation—politics—after his encounter with Nguyen Anh. From the first day he met the young Nguyen Anh, Pigneau turned into a passionate politician. The Bishop of Adran was destined to become one of the greatest statesmen and military leaders in the history of Vietnam.

Pigncau probably did not give any thought to what extent he was interfering with the destiny of Vietnam when he rescued a young prince in 1777. Twenty-five years later, Nguyen Anh had conquered the whole of Vietnam, exterminated all members of the Tay Son family, and founded the last dynasty of his reunited country.

In order to secure their possessions against the Trinh in the North, the Tay Son, after subduing the South, moved the bulk of their armies to central Vietnam. No sooner had they done so when the sixteen-year-old Nguyen Anh reappeared in the country, rallied the followers of the old regime, hired Cambodian mercenaries and Chinese pirates, and in a series of lightning campaigns conquered several provinces and the city of Saigon, from where he ruled as the "King of Cochinchina" for four years. In 1782, the Tay Son attacked him by sea and shattered his army and his young administration. Another attempt by Anh, for which the King of Siam had provided an army of twenty thousand, also ended in disaster. The end of 1784 found Anh a refugee in Siam, pondering the problem of whether to reverse the tide with European military help. Pigneau, who had rejoined the young Nguyen Anh in Saigon in 1778, had been advising him to seek such help, and to seek it from France. Nguyen Anh in fact had been considering asking the English, the Dutch, and the Portuguese for assistance. He had even tried to enter into negotiations with Spain. But the French were the only ones with a permanent advocate on the spot, and moreover one whom the young man liked and admired. In November, 1784, Nguyen Anh asked Pigneau to negotiate the price for which France would be willing to support his aspirations to the Vietnamese throne.

When the Bishop arrived in Pondicherry in February, 1785, he came there as the authorized ambassador of the "King of Cochinchina" to negotiate the terms for France's military assistance. The French authorities in Pondicherry, however, were impressed neither by Pigneau's credentials nor by his audacious plans.

For fifteen months Pigneau fought to overcome the resistance of the French officials in India. In despair, he entered into talks with the Portuguese. But while the Portuguese were considering the matter, Pigneau reconsidered his step and decided to submit his project directly to Paris. He left Pondicherry for France in June, 1786, taking with him Nguyen Anh's five-year-old son.

9

The month of June, 1786, was a crucial one in the history of Vietnam for another reason as well. The Trinh rulers, who had taken advantage of the Tay Son uprising to invade the South in 1774, were driven out of Hue and their armies chased back to the Red River Valley. In a brilliant, brief campaign, the youngest of the Tay Son brothers marched from Hue to Hanoi, thus simultaneously bringing to an end Trinh rule and the division of Vietnam. The Tay Son were in unchallenged control from the Gulf of Siam to the borders of Yunnan and Kwangsi.

Pigneau's arrival in France six months later spelled the beginning of another battle for Vietnam, this one waged in Paris in the salons of the aristocracy, in the ministries, and in the royal palace. In this fight, which lasted from February to November, 1787, Pigneau proved himself an inspired public-relations man. The boy prince he had brought with him charmed the ladies, and he himself impressed the military and the custodians of the public purse. By November he had vanquished all opposition and apparently achieved his objective. His persuasiveness induced a reluctant government and king to sign an agreement they were unable to keep. He arrived at Pondicherry in May, 1788, as Royal Commissioner of France for Cochinchina with a treaty of alliance between the King of France and the "King of Cochinchina." However, four days after the signing of his precious treaty, the agreement was virtually annulled by the instructions the French Minister of Foreign Affairs sent to Governor Conway in Pondicherry. Conway, who was to provide the ships and troops for Pigneau's expedition, was known as an opponent of further French expansion in Asia. He was secretly told by Paris that it was up to him to decide whether Pigneau's expedition against Cochinchina should begin immediately, at a later date, or not at all. Conway reached no decision whatever, but permitted the difficulties of the project to delay all action indefinitely.

Unaware of his government's duplicity, Pigneau fought a furious personal battle against Conway, who apparently was a lover of intrigue as well as a tower of weakness. Although the Royal Council decided in October, 1788, to approve Conway's refusal to act, Paris did not inform Pigneau that the "expedition could not take place"[8] until April, 1789.

This was the moment for the Bishop of Adran to show the full power of his determination. "I shall make the revolution in Cochinchina alone," he is reported to have said.[9] Rejecting an offer by the English to do for him what his own country had refused, Pigneau raised money from French merchants in the Mascarene Islands and India, bought two ships, weapons, and ammunition, hired volunteers and deserters from the French Navy, and left Pondicherry at the head of his private expedition on June 19, 1789—four weeks before the storming of the Bastille set off the French Revolution.

Pigneau sailed directly to Vietnam because his royal protégé was back in Saigon. Nguyen Anh had returned to Hatien in 1787, where he soon afterward relighted the fires of war that were to burn in Vietnam for another fifteen years. When Pigneau joined him at the end of July, 1789, Saigon and the southern provinces of Cochinchina had been in Anh's hands for almost a year.

While Pigneau was fighting his political battles in Pondicherry and Paris, the Tay Son movement was beginning to lose ground. It had not fulfilled the hopes of the people, the earlier spirit of reform was dying; the social impulses that were the secret of its initial success had wrought no change in the country's social structure. The Tay Son had been able to arouse the people against a foreign invader, but the people had no stake in a war against Nguyen Anh. The peasants wanted peace, and they began to side with Nguyen Anh when he showed signs of being able to defeat his opponents.

For Pigneau's men, the war was a slow and disappointing business. Most of them were young adventurers who had joined Pigneau in the hopes of quick wealth. Only a handful stuck it out. Pigneau himself was ready to drop the venture. Nguyen Anh refused to take any unnecessary risks. Because he was in no hurry, his French advisers thought him timid, unenergetic, and perhaps incapable of victory. It took more than a dozen campaigns before Nguyen Anh succeeded in landing his troops near Hue. But in 1802, Hue fell, and once Hue had fallen Hanoi also fell, and with this the Tay Son lost the war. Nguyen Anh proclaimed himself Emperor of Vietnam, taking the name of Gia Long.

Pigneau's real aim in Vietnam had been the advancement of his religion. He had planned and fought not to give France an Asian empire but to give Vietnam a Catholic ruler in the person of his beloved pupil, the young Prince Canh, son of Nguyen Anh. But even if Pigneau had succeeded in converting the boy, he would have failed in his goal: the young prince died twenty years before his father. When Pigneau died, in 1799, Cochinchina probably had fewer than 30,000 Christians.

10

Vietnam turned against the West in Gia Long's lifetime, who, although he respected and honored his French helpers, did not trust any European power. His alleged friendship for France, a major tenet of French colonial propaganda, was never put to the test. During the Napoleonic wars and the early years of the Restoration, France made no serious political or mercantile efforts to exploit Gia Long's reputed good will. The last of Pigneau's aides left the court of Hue a few years after Gia Long's death, and Vietnamese-French relations were again restricted to contacts between the people and the missionaries.

The hostility of Gia Long's successors toward the West was the result largely of the new tide of European aggression sweeping over India into Malaya and Burma and up along the Chinese coast. Gia Long himself foresaw this and appointed as his successor a man hostile to the West. Five years after his death, the missionaries were again treated as agents of a subversive movement. An imperial edict of 1825 charged the "perverse religion of the European" with "corrupting the hearts of men."[10] Between

1833 and 1838, seven missionaries were sentenced to death and executed. The lifework of Pigneau was being undone.

In the meantime, the forces of Western imperialist aggression were steadily growing stronger. The threat to Vietnam's independence became apparent under Gia Long's immediate successor, Minh Mang, who ruled from 1820 to 1841, and it increased during the brief rule of Thieu Tri, one of Minh Mang's forty-nine sons. The final clash came under Tu Duc, the last emperor of an independent Vietnam.

Tu Duc ruled over his unfortunate country from 1847 to 1883. The first year of his rule also was the year of the first French attack on Tourane. When Tu Duc died, the northern and central parts of his country were about to become the two French protectorates of Tongking and Annam. The South, which the French had already wrested from Vietnam, had become the French colony of Cochinchina.

Vietnam's nine hundred years of independence had come to an end.

V

The Conquest of
French Indochina

1

FRANCE HAD REAPPEARED on the Far Eastern scene in 1817; exactly forty years later, in July, 1857, the French Government decided to organize a military expedition against Vietnam. In these forty years, French policy toward Vietnam went through three distinct phases. In the first of these, which lasted from 1817 to 1831, France tried through diplomatic efforts to obtain trading privileges and to persuade Vietnam to forge closer political bonds with Paris. Both these efforts were unsuccessful, and after a series of setbacks the French abandoned their attempts to gain a foothold in Vietnam by diplomatic and peaceful means.

In the second phase, which lasted about ten years, France showed little interest in Vietnam and in fact pursued no policy whatever. Aside from the missionaries, no Frenchmen had any contacts, either official or private, with any Vietnamese. Yet these years turned out to be more crucial for the future of Franco-Vietnamese relations than any since Alexander of Rhodes first set foot in Vietnam, for it was during these fateful years that the anti-Catholic policy of Minh Mang turned the missionaries into exponents of French military intervention.

If the missionaries and their supporters at home abstained from pushing for immediate military action it was because they were not yet ready. The last phase, one of open and mounting hostility toward Vietnam, may be said to date back to 1838, when a young naval officer by the name of Fourichon revived the idea of a military attack on Tourane. Two years later, another naval officer made a similar proposal and even persuaded some French cabinet members to submit it to the government. But the Minister of Foreign Affairs, François Guizot, was more concerned with restoring France's position in Europe than in Asian expansion, and he furthermore feared that such action might impair his friendly relations with England. But despite Guizot's caution, France only three years later found herself deeply involved in Asia, and exactly in the kind of trouble that Guizot had feared.

2

When the English broke into China during the Opium War and took Hong Kong in 1841, a new era of Western expansion in Asia was about to begin. The major Western powers fell on China like vultures. Since the European nations were establishing themselves in Asia, Guizot now argued, France no longer could stay out, and so, in 1841, he sent a mission to the Far East to explore the chances of trade with China. Two years later, his government decided that a naval detachment be stationed in the seas of China and Japan to protect French political and commercial interests.[1] Sizable naval forces under the command of Admiral Cécille and Captain Charner were dispatched to Asian waters.

The French fleet, arriving in Macao in August, 1844, brought with it a diplomatic mission with orders to secure for France the same trading privileges that England had won through the Opium War. The French accomplished this objective in December, 1844, but Guizot's orders went beyond that. He instructed Cécille and de Lagrène, the political head of the mission to China, to acquire positions that would give France the advantages England enjoyed in Singapore and Hong Kong, and Portugal and Spain in Macao and Manila. But he also warned his envoys to abstain from any action along the Vietnamese coast. Fearing the English, he said that Vietnam was unhealthy and that mainland positions there would be too difficult to defend.[2] Guizot's warnings were heeded, and Vietnam was once more reprieved. France gained temporary possession of Basilan, an island between Borneo and the Philippines which Cécille thought might become a strong point equal to Hong Kong. Spain, however, claimed that Basilan was a Philippine dependency and Spanish protests forced Paris to relinquish the island.

After this incident, Guizot was in no mood to listen to any more proposals by the frustrated naval officers in the East smarting under the Basilan fiasco. Admiral Cécille, who had had his sights fixed on the Indochinese coast and his heart set on a Vietnamese harbor ever since his arrival in the East, proposed that France gain a foothold in Vietnam by supporting the claims of Le descendants to the Vietnamese throne. According to Cécille's information, the Le pretender had numerous supporters in the North who were ready to rise. And once the Le dynasty was reinstalled, so Cécille's missionary friends assured him, France would be given a naval base and the missionaries would be free to proselytize.

In the meantime, the trouble Guizot most feared had come: a clash with England over the French acquisition of Tahiti. After weeks of trepidation, with England threatening war, Guizot was able to hold on to Tahiti by compensating England financially. But he now became more determined than ever to avoid all conflict with his European allies, and therefore he firmly rejected Cécille's plan.

3

Guizot's unyielding attitude infuriated the naval people in the Far East. What was the point of their presence, they asked, if they were not allowed to do for France what the Portuguese,

Spanish, and English navies were doing for their countries? The trade they were supposed to protect and defend was practically nonexistent, and their voyages cost the state as much as would campaigns to expand France's colonial possessions.

These views were enthusiastically endorsed by two groups: the missionaries and their political supporters at home. The missionaries, almost the only Frenchmen with whom the naval officers came into contact in the Far East, not only "constituted the only tangible aspect of national interest with which naval officers could concern themselves,"[3] but they were also the only ones who knew something about the East, including Asian languages, which made them almost indispensable in any negotiations. The feelings of the missionaries about official French policy were well expressed by the Jesuit Father Douai, who compared French action in the Far East with "little dogs that bark from a distance but never bite."[4] The French missionaries who came to Asia after 1820 were generally politically aggressive and confident that their countrymen at home admired and supported their efforts. And indeed, Minh Mang's persecution of the missionaries aroused French Catholic opinion more than any other event outside of France. After 1840, Catholic propaganda openly demanded French intervention on behalf of the missionaries. The anticlerical Guizot refused. But by 1843, public pressure had become too great. Guizot authorized the naval officers "to afford protection to French missionaries threatened with personal violence, if that could be done without involving the French flag in any altercation."[5]

In May, 1845, Admiral Cécille learned that a French missionary, one Monsignor Lefèbvre, had been sentenced to death in Vietnam, though not executed. Thereupon Cécille dispatched the commander of the "Alcmène," Captain Fornier-Duplan, to Tourane. Fornier-Duplan not only was handed Lefèbvre, unharmed, but also presents for himself and his crew. Thieu Tri obviously did not wish to persecute the missionaries, but only get rid of them and the French warships as quickly as possible. However, the naval officers and some of the missionaries were interested in peace only on their own, unacceptable terms. Whatever prospects for an agreement with Thieu Tri existed after Monsignor Lefèbvre's release were ruined completely and forever by the action of French warships in the harbor of Tourane in April, 1847.

Again it was Monsignor Lefèbvre who set off the chain of events that led to this first act of French aggression against Vietnam. In May, 1846, he tried to re-enter Vietnam, but he was intercepted and once more sentenced to death. Admiral Cécille eagerly seized upon this as a pretext for dispatching two warships to Tourane and to demand freedom to practice the Catholic religion and the release of Monsignor Lefèbvre. The two commanders of the expedition, Captain Lapierre and Captain Rigault de Genouilly, reached Tourane in the early spring of 1847. Neither knew that Monsignor Lefèbvre had been released by the Vietnamese and shipped to Singapore four weeks before their arrival. In an attempt to force the mandarins to accept Cécille's letter to the emperor, Lapierre had the Vietnamese ships in the harbor stripped of their sails. After waiting for two weeks for a reply, the French captains grew impatient. On April 15, they thought that four Vietnamese ships were approaching them in the harbor. Lapierre, feeling threatened, decided to shoot. Within seventy minutes, French guns had taken a hundred times more lives than all the Vietnamese governments in two centuries of missionary persecution. Without bothering further about Lefèbvre's fate, Lapierre and Genouilly steamed out of Tourane, leaving the other missionaries at the mercy of the enraged Vietnamese. Before they had a chance to repeat their Tourane performance, Lapierre and Genouilly ran aground in shallow waters near the Korean coast. They escaped punishment for losing their ships and for their unauthorized action in Tourane only because influential missionary leaders defended them in the highest Paris circles. The most exalted of these spokesmen was one Monsignor Forcade, who claimed that even the Pope himself would approve rigorous measures against the "Annamite king."[6] He was joined by Admiral Cécille, who, after returning from the East in 1847, demanded that France henceforth talk to Vietnam "only with guns" and see to it that Thieu Tri have a "good successor."[7]

4

The aggressive stance of the missionaries and naval officers reversed a Vietnamese drift toward moderation that had begun under Thieu Tri, and it destroyed any chance of reconciliation between the Catholic Church and the Nguyen regime. Tu Duc, who succeeded Thieu Tri in 1848, saw no alternative to fighting the missionaries and the Vietnamese Catholics. He and his mandarins knew that the missionaries were clamoring for more French warships in Vietnamese harbors, that they supplied the French with military and political intelligence, and that their leaders in France were agitating for military intervention. They also knew that Vietnamese Catholics had been implicated in the South's uprising against Minh Mang and in the North had conspired with the Le pretender, whom Cécille had wanted to put on Thieu Tri's throne. And before long, Tu Duc himself had to deal with a Christian-supported rebellion in the North which aimed at putting one of his own brothers on the throne.

Tu Duc, reputedly a mild man, decided to frighten the missionaries out of Vietnam and to force the Vietnamese Catholics into submission. After putting down the rebellion in the North, he had a French missionary executed; a year later, a second one was executed. He issued two edicts against the native Catholics which, had they been enforced, would have destroyed the Catholic community.

About forty French missionaries were in Vietnam during this time, and they were not idle. Life after the Tourane attack was becoming increasingly more difficult for them. For a long time thereafter, no French vessel came to Vietnam, and the missionaries grew bitter against their own country. However, changes were taking place in France: the anticlerical regime of Louis-Philippe and Guizot was replaced by the pro-Catholic Second Empire of Louis-Napoleon. As a consequence, Paris after 1852 was ready to listen to both the complaints and proposals of the missionaries.

After 1851, the complaints became louder and the calls for action more urgent. Monsignor Retord, an "unpolitical" churchman who in 1848 had asked for nothing more than diplomatic intervention, now asked that negotiations be backed up by military might. He said that he would agree to a treaty with Vietnam only if France were given a part of Vietnam. In 1852, eight missionary bishops appealed directly to Louis-Napoleon to send naval forces to Asia to dispel the false idea that France was too weak to come to the aid of her persecuted missionaries. Peaceful, conciliatory tactics, they said, had ceased to be effective.

5

In that same year of 1852, the missionaries scored a major success by converting the key French diplomat in the Far East, Count Bourboulon, to their interventionist position. Bourboulon was the first to use the phrases that were to become so popular among the French during the next thirty years of conquest and "pacification." Vigorous action would be "in the interest of all humanity"; all "civilized nations" would applaud France for punishing these "wretched and insolent barbarians."[8] France had to insist on religious tolerance for Christians, or at least on "complete security for French and Spanish missionaries," and on the cession of the port of Tourane, as reparation for the blood of missionaries shed over the years. Should Vietnam refuse to accept these "reasonable conditions," then the French Navy should take Tourane and the surrounding territory. In this manner, "relations of friendship and commerce" between France and Vietnam could be established "on a new liberal and equitable basis."[9]

Bourboulon had two main counselors and informants: the procurator of the Society of Foreign Missions in Hong Kong, Father Libois, and a Lazarist missionary from southern China by the name of Huc. Neither man had ever seen Vietnam, but the energetic Monsignor Retord supplied them so well with reports and ideas that they felt no compunction about expressing a wide variety of opinions, including military judgments about the harbor defenses of Tourane.

Bourboulon's suggestions were well received in Paris. Louis-Napoleon was only too willing to strengthen his power and prestige by force. However, in 1852, he was preoccupied with the consolidation of his dictatorial regime, and in 1853, with preparations for the Crimean War.

Throughout this period, the struggle between Tu Duc and the missionaries went on unabated. The missionaries, showing remarkable fortitude, kept silent about their own plight, stressing instead the numerous advantages France would gain by establishing herself in Vietnam. The prospect of an uprising in favor of the Le was seen as a "useful diversion" in the case of French intervention, and possession of Tourane had become a condition of "profitable commerce" and a device to gain access to the "unexploited riches of Cochinchina and Tonkin."[10]

Finally, in September, 1856, France again launched an attack at Tourane, but politically and militarily it was poorly coordinated. The first ship to arrive in the harbor brought a letter from M. de Montigny, the newly appointed envoy to the court at Hue. He himself had been delayed in Cambodia. The mandarins refused again to accept and forward this letter to Hue. The captain of the ship, afraid of a Vietnamese attack, shelled the harbor defenses and landed a troop detachment. A second French vessel arrived in October, but the ship bringing Montigny did not get to Tourane until January, 1857. By that time the "Catinat," the ship that had shelled the harbor, had already left for China, in compliance with previous orders.

Montigny's request for direct contact with the court of Hue was rejected. If he wanted war, he was told, let him fight. Lacking both the means and the authority to use force, Montigny had no choice but to discontinue his futile efforts. After threatening punitive action by France if religious persecution did not stop, Montigny left Tourane on February 7, 1857.

6

The missionaries' reaction to the failure of the Montigny mission was put forth drastically by Monsignor Retord. "Our brave compatriots," he wrote, "have left us helpless in the clutches of the tiger after having stirred him up against us. . . . They came without a summons from us and they left after compromising us. They began with an act of provocation and ended up with an act of cowardice."[11]

But even though the missionaries were losing patience with their government, they continued to fight for intervention with undiminished fervor. Count Bourboulon, prodded by Retord, informed Paris on October 12, 1857, that Spain stood ready to support an expedition against Vietnam with an army of Catholic Filipinos.

The missionary efforts of more than thirty years reached their climax in 1857. Two of the most forceful advocates of intervention, Father Huc and Monsignor Pellerin, went to Paris to plead their cause. Huc was received by Napoleon in January and assured the Emperor that the occupation of Cochinchina was a simple matter that would bring highly gratifying results. He prophesied that the Vietnamese people would greet the French as "liberators and benefactors," and it would not take long "to make them all Catholics and devoted to France."[12] Monsignor Pellerin was more circumspect. He delivered impassioned sermons in the churches of Paris about the struggle of the Vietnamese Christians and the duty of France to come to their aid. Napoleon received him in July, and again in December, after Pellerin's return from Rome, where he had sought the Pope's blessing for French action against Vietnam.

7

When Monsignor Pellerin returned from his first audience with Napoleon, he was pleased—and somewhat astonished—to find that the Emperor had "granted him more than he had asked for."[13] He could not have known that Napoleon had by then already made up his mind to intervene.

How did the decision to invade Vietnam come about? Was it the result of missionary propaganda and Catholic political pressure? Only a few months earlier, prospects for the success of the missionaries' cause seemed rather poor. As late as March, Count Walewski, Napoleon's Foreign Minister, told the Emperor that he saw neither reason nor necessity for so hazardous an undertaking.[14] Yet only four months later, Walewski had changed his mind. Between March and July, he had received very intensive political training. A Commission on Cochinchina had persuaded the leaders of France that drastic revision of France's Far Eastern policies was long overdue and that France had to enter the race for Asian possessions or else be reduced to a second-rank power.

On November 25, 1857, the French fleet in the Far East was instructed to take Tourane. The orders given the commander were unequivocal: He was to establish himself solidly through military force, without any further efforts to negotiate with the Vietnamese.

The execution of these orders was delayed by the Anglo-French action against China and by the allied negotiations for the treaties of Tientsin, which lasted until the end of June, 1858. Admiral Rigault de Genouilly, the commander of the French forces, set out for Tourane in August with fourteen vessels and twenty-five hundred men. At his side was Monsignor Pellerin, who had managed to become the Admiral's political and military adviser.

The expedition reached the Bay of Tourane on August 31. The harbor defenses were attacked on September 1, and the town occupied the next day. Resistance was weak. However, there were no signs of popular rejoicing, nor of the Christian uprising predicted by missionary propaganda. The Vietnamese people simply vanished, and the French found themselves without the indigenous labor force with whose help they had hoped to turn Tourane into an impregnable base. Moreover, heat and disease immobilized their own troops. Four weeks later the rains ruined their plans to reach Hue by land, and they lacked the shallow-draft river boats needed to sail up the Perfumed River.

"The Government has been deceived about the nature of this enterprise," Admiral Genouilly informed Paris.[15] He angrily blamed Monsignor Pellerin for having misinformed the planners of the expedition. The Bishop in turn accused Genouilly of a lack of vigor in the execution of his task. Pellerin demanded that the North be attacked. There were more Christians in Tongking, he said, than in any other part of Vietnam, and they would rise against Tu Duc's mandarins if the French entered the Red River Delta. The Admiral replied that he could not subordinate strategic considerations to more or less problematical religious interests. Instead, he decided to try to take Saigon.

Genouilly's decision to advance on Saigon was based on two considerations: He wanted to capture the rice stores of the South, and he believed that Saigon was destined to become an important commercial center once the port was opened to Europeans. Leaving only a small garrison at Tourane, Genouilly sailed south on February 2, 1859. By February 17, Saigon was in French hands. Again the local Christian population failed to rally around the French, and Genouilly became persuaded that local support would not be forthcoming in the future either.

The end of the rainy season and news of Vietnamese attacks on his men in Tourane forced Genouilly to return to his embattled garrison. Tourane turned out to be as miserable a place for the French in the spring and summer as it had been in the fall and winter. For every man killed in action, twenty died of tropical diseases; in June, more than two hundred men died in a cholera epidemic; in July, typhoid fever broke out; from May to December, an average of a hundred men died of disease each month. And all this time, Vietnamese resistance grew stronger. Genouilly came to realize that he would not be able to force the Vietnamese Emperor to his knees with the forces at his disposal. His hopes for reinforcements vanished completely when he learned of Napoleon's declaration of war on Austria in May, 1859. Embittered and discouraged, Genouilly asked to be relieved of his command. He left for Paris on October 31.

Genouilly's successor, Admiral Page, arrived in Tourane on October 19, 1859. Page's efforts to obtain through negotiations what force had failed to produce remained as unsuccessful as Genouilly's military efforts. It soon became clear that Tourane could not be held. On March 22, the last French soldier left the city.

8

Throughout 1860, France made no progress in Vietnam. The isolated French garrison at Saigon was able to hold out, and it even managed to keep the port open for European shipping, but its position became more precarious with each passing month.

After the Tourane fiasco, the struggle for Vietnam shifted back to Paris. Disappointed by Genouilly's expedition, Napoleon again became uncertain as to the policy he should pursue. But although missionary propaganda had become more restrained, the chorus demanding a new military effort grew bigger and louder. While France was failing in Cochinchina, these voices insisted, the English were gaining the upper hand in Burma and China, and if France were to withdraw from Saigon, the English would move into Victnam.

The party favoring renewed military action in Vietnam continued to make new converts. A new crop of angry generals, worried politicians, and frustrated naval officers protested a Far Eastern policy that seemingly turned France into a "satellite" of England. Backing them up were a growing number of merchants and manufacturers interested in overseas markets and a new breed of nationalist intellectuals who became the spokesmen for a new kind of "mission." It was the task of France, they asserted, to civilize the backward peoples of the world, to educate and guide the destinies of the black and yellow races.

These rationalizations had a profound effect on French thinking and attitudes, and they were instrumental in once more swaying Napoleon and in forcing every French government, whether reluctant or even antagonistic, to pursue an interventionist course in Indochina until Vietnam was conquered.

The party of aggressive imperialism gained a decisive victory when one of its most vocal spokesmen, François de Chasseloup-Laubat, was appointed to the post of Maritime Minister. Under his leadership, France once more embarked on an operation against Vietnam. In October, 1860, Admiral Charner, the commander of the French forces in the Far East, was ordered to go to Saigon and take up where Genouilly had been forced to leave off in the spring of 1859.

Charner began to make his way up the Donnai River on February 7, 1861, to relieve the Saigon garrison with seventy ships and thirty-five hundred men, and he was also given reinforcements from China. Vietnamese armed resistance was soon broken in a series of bloody battles, and by the end of June, the French had taken the main points of three provinces between Saigon and the Cambodian border. On July 1, 1861, Charner announced to the world that Saigon had become French.

The French thought that the Emperor of Vietnam, in order to restore peace in his mutilated country, would gladly accept their terms for a treaty. Tu Duc, however, was not yet ready to relinquish three of his richest provinces against a mere promise that France would discontinue her unilateral acts of war. He knew that disease was again decimating the French forces and that Paris was growing restive over the cost of the Vietnamese operation. Moreover, there was also hope that the refusal of the mandarins to collaborate with the French would add to Charner's administrative problems. If only the Emperor held out a little longer, the mandarins favoring resistance argued, the French, discouraged, might decide to return home.

When Charner was replaced by Admiral Bonard in November, these hopes were drowned in fresh rivers of Vietnamese blood. Bonard by violence and slaughter suppressed all resistance in the province of Bien Hoa and extended French control of the Mekong Delta to the west. He penetrated into the province of Vinh Long beyond Mytho, but by April, 1862, the French had once more spent their offensive power, and their undermanned, widely separated positions again became targets of Vietnamese guerrilla attacks. In these circumstances, Bonard was as eager as his predecessor to obtain through negotiations what military action could not win.

To the surprise of all concerned, the Vietnamese court sent emissaries with peace proposals to Saigon before Bonard presented Tu Duc with the full list of French demands. On June 6, 1862, a treaty was signed in Saigon giving France possession of the three provinces adjacent to Saigon and of the island of Poulo Condore, opening three Vietnam ports for trade with the West, granting missionaries freedom of action, and French warships free passage up the Mekong to the Cambodian border, barring Vietnam from ceding any part of her territory to other powers without the consent of France, and indemnifying France for the losses she suffered in her attack on Vietnam to the tune of 4 million piasters.

9

What prompted Tu Duc to petition Bonard for peace and pay such an exorbitant price? One reason undoubtedly was the loss of rice he suffered when Saigon fell into French hands, which considerably diminished his ability to raise and support a big enough army to fight the invaders. Another reason for his acceptance of the French terms was that he wished to gain time. He hoped that climate and disease would weaken the French, that the growing resistance of the people would break their spirit, and that the whole enterprise would turn out to be much more costly than Paris had anticipated. Once this happened, then those French circles opposed to the "Cochinchina adventure" would be able to persuade Napoleon to drop the project.

This line of reasoning was certainly not unrealistic, but it would have made a great deal more sense if Tu Duc had been able to mobilize his country's resources rather than sue for peace. However, the country's resources were undeveloped, and much of its wealth had been dissipated through mismanagement and corruption. Absolute power had made the mandarins arrogant and inefficient. Their laziness and dishonesty had built walls of hatred and indifference between the monarchy and the peasants, the country's true source of strength. After decades of isolation and estrangement from its own people, the Nguyen dynasty lacked both the authority and ability for the successful organization of the country's defense.

Tu Duc and his mandarins feared the Vietnamese people as much as they feared the power of France. The French success had brought on a crisis that threatened to bring down the regime even if the invasion were to end in failure. While Tu Duc was still fighting the French in the South, his own subjects were sapping his power with a rebellion in the North. Instead of rallying behind their emperor against the foreign enemy, the peasants chose to strike a blow at their enemies at home. Spurred on by missionaries who promised French support, a pretender of the old Le dynasty emerged in the spring of 1862 to challenge Tu Duc's authority over the Red River Valley. Tu Duc knew that the misery of the people made this movement more dangerous than any previous rebellion. In justification of their brutal repressive measures, he and his mandarins accused the rebels of being in league with the French.

But Tu Duc himself was in a far better position to help the French than were the desperate peasants in the Red River Valley.

His decision to use his military might against the rebels in the North accounted for his sudden willingness to talk peace with the French. He signed a treaty because he needed every one of his soldiers to re-establish his authority in the North. In order to re-conquer the provinces he had lost to the rebels in the North, he decided to relinquish the provinces he had lost to the French in Cochinchina. He made peace with his foreign enemies because he had to wage war against his subjects.

On the French side, political expediency led to a betrayal of similar magnitude. The missionaries demanded that France intervene on behalf of the Tongking rebels. If Tu Duc were to lose the North to a pro-Christian government, they argued, the Nguyen monarchy would soon collapse in the rest of the country as well. But Bonard put the interests of France above those of the Church. So long as Hue had refused to accept his conditions, he had threatened to support the Tongking rebellion, but once Tu Duc agreed to let France have Saigon and the three provinces, Bonard gave him a free hand against the Catholics in the North. In his refusal to support the Tongking rebels whom the missionaries had stirred up, Bonard was not out of step with Paris. For the French, "the missionary cause had long ceased to be a decisive consideration in determining governmental policy."[16] True, the treaty of June, 1862, promised the Vietnamese Catholics religious freedom, but it also allowed Tu Duc to slaughter them by the thousands after he had put down the insurrection. But the missionaries, though disillusioned about French motives and actions, never admitted publicly what had become obvious to them: that they had, in the words of a French historian, served merely as "the pretext for our intervention" and that they had supplied a "precious opportunity for establishing ourselves in the Far East."[17]

10

The struggle for Cochinchina did not, however, come to an end with the ratification of the treaty by Hue in April, 1863. The South had to be secured, and that task was shouldered by Admiral de la Grandière, who succeeded Bonard in May, 1863. It took another four years of military and diplomatic efforts against Vietnamese resistance, and in this period the proponents of French imperialism had to wage a determined campaign against their enemies and disgruntled sympathizers at home. De la Grandière eventually overcame the difficulties he faced, though he received little support from France in these crucial years.

The political troubles of the imperialist faction in France posed a greater danger to French control of Cochinchina than did Vietnamese resistance, and for two main reasons. For one thing, from 1863 to 1867, Napoleon showed little interest in Vietnam. His ill-fated attempt to put a Catholic emperor on the Mexican throne absorbed both his attention and his funds for overseas ventures. At this critical stage, Tu Duc made a move that proved most embarrassing to the proponents of further expansion in Indochina: He offered to cooperate with the French if Paris agreed to revise its demands.

Despite his victory over the rebels, Tu Duc's authority at home had been rudely shaken. The morale of Vietnam's ill-equipped army declined from year to year; the treasury of the empire was depleted by war and civil war and the loss of the rice from the South. The monarchy, in a disgraceful and desperate effort to replenish its empty coffers, lifted its ban on the sale of opium and, in an even more demoralizing move, permitted the sale of public offices. Anyone with enough money, qualified or not, could now become a mandarin.

By the spring of 1863, Tu Duc realized that he could check his enemies at home only if the threats from the outside ceased. Aware of Napoleon's difficulties, he decided to explore the chances for a permanent peace with France. The man he sent to Paris, the same one who had negotiated the Saigon Treaty, Phan Thanh Gian, was probably Vietnam's most capable high-ranking mandarin. What Tu Duc wanted was the return of the three provinces he had ceded to France, and he was willing to pay a high price. In return for reinstatement in his lost provinces, he agreed to a French protectorate over the whole of Cochinchina, to relinquish the cities of Saigon and Cholon as well as Cape St. Jacques, to pay a yearly tribute to France, and to open his country to French trade.

Tu Duc was far from happy with the success of his mission, but he had to have peace and a free hand against his domestic enemies if his dynasty was to survive. But Tu Duc and Napoleon no longer fully determined the policies of their respective countries. In the eyes of the advocates of French territorial expansion, the new agreement with Tu Duc was an unnecessary and dangerous retreat. The architects of the conquest of Indochina had become too strong to accept a partial withdrawal from Vietnam without a fight. The most active and articulate spokesmen held strategic positions and were able to force Napoleon's not so firm hand. They controlled the Navy both at home and in the East, and the naval captains and admirals had been the pioneers of French imperialism in the Far East. These men regarded the part of Vietnam already in their hands as only a bridgehead in a much bigger campaign, one that was to give France a vast and flourishing empire. From Chasseloup-Laubat down to the twenty-five-year-old Francis Garnier, an ensign who had fought under Charner and had become Inspector of Indigenous Affairs in Saigon, the Navy solidly opposed the main provisions of the new agreement.

The Navy's campaign for the retention of the occupied territories had the support of a number of other forces. The missionaries were outraged by the idea of a compromise before their freedom to proselytize had become firmly established. Their position was vigorously defended by the Catholic press. Moreover, a new group joined the Navy and the missionaries in their demands: the men of money and the practitioners of power whose appetites had been whetted by the brief taste of unrestricted authority over the "natives." The proponents of French expansionism knew what they wanted, which was more than could be said of their fumbling emperor. Napoleon capitulated. The agreement signed by his envoy was shelved, and Tu Duc was warned not to go back on the conditions of the Saigon Treaty.

11

Encouraged by this victory, the French imperialist faction decided to push forward. The new Governor of Cochinchina, Admiral de la Grandière, knew how to circumvent his government's inability to make up its mind. He took whatever steps he deemed necessary to expand French rule without waiting for orders or permission. Paris generally condemned these unauthorized actions, but it rarely renounced the gains they produced.

In one of his first actions, de la Grandière bullied the King of Cambodia into accepting a French protectorate over his country. De la Grandière claimed that the Saigon Treaty had made France heir to Vietnam's powers over Cambodia. By so doing he risked repudiation by Napoleon, who feared an armed conflict with Siam. The King of Siam had effectively controlled Cambodian policy for some time. The danger of a conflict with Siam was not removed until July, 1867, when Paris at last obtained Siam's consent to the establishment of a protectorate over Cambodia. The price for this consent was high, but it was not borne by France. The new protectors forced Cambodia to cede two of her provinces, Battambang and Angkor, to Siam.

That same summer, France dealt Tu Duc's crumbling regime a heavy blow: de la Grandière occupied all of Cochinchina south and west of the three provinces already in French hands. This new invasion had been secretly prepared in Saigon over many months, though at least one member of Napoleon's cabinet, Admiral Genouilly, knew and approved of the plan. De la Grandière attacked on June 17, 1867. A week later he was able to report to Paris that all of southern Cochinchina was in French hands. Vietnamese resistance, led by Phan Thanh Gian, viceroy of the three non-French colonies, was weak. De la Grandière accused the old, peace-loving mandarin of sheltering anti-French rebels and supporting their guerrilla activities, and used this charge as a pretext for the annexation of all Vietnamese lands betewen the Mekong and the Gulf of Siam. Phan Thanh Gian surrendered. Realizing that his policy of appeasement had failed, he committed suicide after making his sons promise never to collaborate with the French.

12

These actions completed the conquest of the Mekong Delta and made secure the French protectorate over Cambodia. The annexation of the Vietnamese south had taken the French a little more than eight years—from February, 1859, when they launched their first attack on Saigon, to June, 1867, the month they occupied the three provinces west of the Mekong. This ended the first phase of the conquest of French Indochina. As if to recuperate from overindulgence, France abstained from further aggression for several years. Between 1867 and 1872, the French made much progress in subduing resistance, organizing an administration, and preparing the colony for large-scale economic exploitation.

Before the aggression was resumed in 1873, a change of regime and of political temper had taken place in France which was not at all to the liking of the spokesmen of imperialism. Napoleon had foolishly maneuvered his country into a war with Prussia in 1870. As a result he lost his throne, and France lost Alsace-Lorraine. Napoleon's fall led to an uprising in Paris, and the victory of the Paris Commune brought on a bloody civil war. France recovered quickly, but for the next ten years political dissension and military weakness hampered support for imperialist ventures in the East. Nationalist sentiment in France was strong, but the public cry was for the return of Alsace-Lorraine rather than for military efforts to gain colonies.

The French in Indochina had only one alternative to inaction: to proceed on their own; to act without and if necessary against orders from Paris; to present Paris with *faits accomplis* which might force it to act.

Three men dominated the scene when aggression against Vietnam was resumed. The first was Admiral Dupré, Governor of Cochinchina since 1871 and a champion of expansion in the Far East. The second was Jean Dupuis, a French trader, imperialist, and explorer living in Hankow, where he had made a great deal of money selling arms to the Chinese. The third was young Francis Garnier, probably the most intelligent, eloquent, and passionate champion of French imperialism.

Dupuis and Garnier first met in June, 1868, in Hankow. Encouraged by a report that the Red River was navigable by large vessels, Dupuis, who had an arms contract with the governor of Yunnan, set out on a perilous journey to deliver his cargo of guns, rifles, and ammunitions without prior consent by Vietnam to sailing his ship up the Red River. With skill, daring, and bribes, Dupuis overcame all obstacles. He left in March, 1873, and returned to Hanoi with a cargo of tin in May. However, he was barred from taking a cargo of salt on a second journey to Yunnan. Not only was the export of salt forbidden by Vietnamese law, but the Vietnamese authorities were making a belated attempt to enforce their rule of keeping foreign shipping off the Red River. Dupuis' next move came as a surprise to all but those who had recognized him as a French *agent provocateur*. With the help of a heavily armed company of 150 Asians and 25 Europeans, he occupied a section of Hanoi in December, 1872, hoisted the French flag, and appealed to Saigon for help.

In Saigon, Admiral Dupré had been waiting for this appeal ever since Dupuis had arrived in Hanoi. Although motivated by other, less personal reasons, Admiral Dupré was as eager to go into Tongking as the impetuous Dupuis. "To establish ourselves in the rough country bordering on China," Dupré wrote in the spring of 1873, "is a question of life and death for the future of our rule in the Far East."[18] The Admiral was not the only one to hold this view. When Dupuis passed through Saigon in 1872, on his way back from France to China, General d'Arbaud, the acting governor in Dupré's absence, assured him that the French in Saigon would not abandon him if his attempt to sail up the Red River brought him into conflict with the Vietnamese authorities.

Admiral Dupré, on hearing of Dupuis' brazen defiance of the Vietnamese order to leave Hanoi, cabled Paris on July 28, 1873, that Tongking had been opened up by Dupuis and that if France did not act promptly, China or a European power would rob her of this unique trade route. "Need no help," he said. "Can act with means at my disposal. Success assured."[19] Paris replied with a warning not to create international complications through any action in Tongking.[20] But this warning did not reach Dupré until September, after he had taken measures to exploit the Hanoi incident for his own ends.

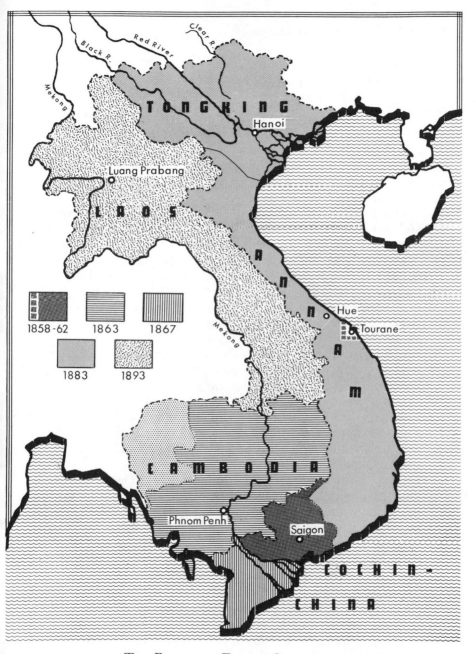

THE PHASES OF FRENCH CONQUEST

1858–1893—the five phases in the conquest of Indochina by the French

This map is reproduced by permission, from André Masson, *l'Histoire du Vietnam* (3d ed.; Paris: Presses Universitaires de France, 1967), a volume in the series *Que sais-je?*

13

Dupré had received assurances from Dupuis that disaffected local elements in Tongking were ready to support armed intervention by France. Dupré, convinced that the time for entering Tongking was ripe, made his first important decision in preparation for his coup. He sent for Francis Garnier, his choice for leader of his planned expedition.

Francis Garnier, the young officer, administrator, explorer, and writer, had returned to Paris to prepare the report of a Mekong expedition. In 1872, when this work was completed, Garnier resigned from the Navy and returned to China, apparently in the capacity of explorer and businessman. In July, 1873, on arriving in Shanghai after a three-month trip through the interior of China, he found Dupré's letter urging him to come to Saigon. He arrived in Saigon as a private citizen in August, 1873. By the end of October, when he reached Hanoi, the thirty-four-year-old Garnier was the most important French colonial leader in Asia. Admiral Dupré had granted him full military and political powers, and Garnier was determined to use them as he saw fit.

Garnier had Tu Duc's hesitant blessing for his move into Hanoi. Dupré, on Garnier's advice, had extracted the Emperor's approval by holding out the promise to oust Dupuis. But once in Hanoi, Garnier joined forces with Dupuis.

Once Garnier had convinced himself of Tu Duc's local weakness, he dropped any plan of negotiating the right to sail the Red River with Tu Duc's mandarins. Instead, he decided to settle the whole Tongking question by force. His calculated arrogance and brutality created such hostility and tension among the mandarins in Hanoi that the idea of reaching an understanding through negotiation became patently absurd.

Having thus laid the groundwork, Garnier arrogated to himself the role of Vietnamese lawmaker. On November 15, he issued a proclamation informing friend and foe alike that the Red River would henceforth be open to international trade. He also ordered the suspension of all customs tariffs and their replacement by rates more to the liking of Dupuis and other interested parties. On November 20, Garnier shelled and stormed the Hanoi citadel. After establishing himself in Hanoi as the self-designated "Great French Mandarin," Garnier attacked all important towns and fortifications between the sea and Hanoi. After three weeks of terror and the capture of Nam Dinh, lower Tongking was under French military control, and the nucleus of a French administration was established in all major cities. At this point, Garnier's meteoric career came to an abrupt end. On December 21, 1873, he was killed outside Hanoi.

The death of Francis Garnier came at a moment when the circles opposing Dupré's Tongking adventure were ready to throw their full weight against his course. The administration of Cochinchina was costly enough, and Paris was in no mood to weaken its rule in the south by spreading out over other parts of Vietnam. On January 7, 1874, Paris informed Dupré in no uncertain terms that a prolonged occupation of Hanoi or of any other part of Tongking was out of the question.[21]

The Tongking adventure of 1873 thus ended badly for the three men who had conceived and started it. Garnier lost his life, Dupré lost his position, and Dupuis lost his ships. But France, although she failed to get Tongking, could hardly be called a loser. By skillful maneuvering, the moderate faction of French colonialism won Vietnamese recognition of all French conquests in the south in a treaty signed at Hue on March 15, 1874.

As in the case of the Saigon Treaty of 1862, the main victims in this struggle between the dying mandarinal regime and the foreign aggressor were the Vietnamese people, particularly the Vietnamese Catholics, in whose interest the French campaign allegedly had been undertaken. According to some sources, twenty thousand Catholics in the north were killed for "cooperation with the French," and seventy thousand were made homeless.

14

Less than ten years after Dupré's ill-fated Tongking expedition, Vietnam's north became a French protectorate. Once again, a governor of Cochinchina, Le Myre de Vilers, sent an officer and a small force to Hanoi. But Captain Henri Rivière and his 233-man force were given more precise and more cautious instructions than Garnier. And unlike Dupré, de Vilers enjoyed the support of his government. No pretext was needed for this second attack on Tongking.

Captain Rivière reached Hanoi on April 3, 1882. He stormed the citadel and within a year succeeded in extending French control to lower Tongking. And like Garnier, Rivière too was killed near Hanoi. He died on May 19, 1883.

Rivière's death strengthened the forces in Paris determined to settle the "Tongking affair" by military means. But intervention had already been decided on by the Chamber of Deputies on May 15. Four days before Rivière's death, the Chamber voted the credits for the imposition of a French protectorate over Tongking.

The reason that the Tongking affair of 1883 took a different turn than the 1873 venture was written all over the face of France. During the 1870's, industry had expanded enormously; the demand for overseas markets and outlets grew louder with every year. For the first time since she first went into Vietnam, France almost unanimously stood behind the imperialist aggressors in the East.

In August, 1883, a strong expeditionary force penetrated into the Red River Valley and began the twelve years of slaughter known as the "pacification" of Tongking. At the same time, a French fleet shelled Hue, to teach Tu Duc a lesson. But Tu Duc was no longer there. He had died in July. The French gave no quarter and the mandarins capitulated. On August 25, 1883, they signed the Treaty of Protectorate which put an end to the independence of Vietnam.

At the time this treaty was signed, no one could have foreseen how long French rule would last nor where it would lead. But one thing was certain: neither the people nor the mandarins welcomed their new master or accepted his presence. In announcing the death of Tu Duc, the imperial court expressed Vietnam's will to regain independence. Tu Duc, the proclamation said, "was killed by sorrow over seeing foreigners invade and devastate his empire, and he died cursing the invader. Keep him in your hearts and avenge his memory."[22]

Part Two

From Colonialism to the Vietminh

VI

The Making of
French Indochina

1

THE COLONIAL HISTORY of France, more than that of any other Western country, abounds in periods of crisis resulting from neglect of necessary reforms. In the 1890's, a farsighted, concerned minority pleaded vainly for a re-examination of their country's Indochinese policies. This clamorous public debate was brought to a sudden climax by the death of Paul-Armand Rousseau, Governor of French Indochina, who died at his post in Hanoi on December 10, 1896.

Who, in 1896, believed that the emancipation of French Indochina held the key to the solution of the perpetual crisis—administrative, military, and financial—that forced France, ever since Vietnam was fully conquered in 1883, to pay so heavy a price for it in blood, money, and political dissension? The isolated voices demanding that France withdraw from the most un-

profitable regions—Tongking, the turbulent north of Vietnam—
were not considered as true expressions of existing sentiment but
only as an indication of the degree of national discontent over
the country's insolvent policy. The only realistic alternatives to
inaction and continuous deterioration were the sort of drastic
steps advocated by the proponents of administrative, fiscal, and
economic reform.

Among those urging such reform was Rousseau, whose untimely
death threatened to reopen the "question of Tongking," which
Paris thought had been settled. Rousseau had arrived in Saigon
on February 17, 1895. After struggling vainly all through that
year, he returned to Paris, determined to resign unless his demands for a settlement of the accumulated debts in the Tongking
treasury, a loan for public works, and more far-reaching administrative powers were granted.

Having won most of what he had fought for, Rousseau returned
to his post, leaving behind the feeling of confidence that a firm
advocacy of practical solutions never fails to arouse. Rousseau's
death was deeply felt and mourned. There is no way of knowing
what might have happened in Indochina, and above all in Vietnam, if fate had permitted Rousseau to serve out his full term.
Perhaps he would have been defeated by the forces resistant to any
change, as some of his predecessors had been. But it soon became
evident that his death opened the door for a period of reform
and transformation unique in the history of French Indochina.

When word of Rousseau's death reached Paris, the cabinet in
which Paul Doumer had served as Minister of Finance and in
which he had led a year-long fight for a tax reform had been
out of office seven months. This fight had not won him many
friends; the number of those who would have liked to see him
out of the way was considerable. Moreover, he was known to
have an extraordinary interest in Indochinese affairs. Thus it came
about that Paul Doumer on December 27, 1896, was appointed
Governor General of French Indochina.

If any one man can be credited with creating what after the
turn of the century became France's richest colony, that man
was Paul Doumer. It is no exaggeration to say that Doumer was

responsible for radically altering the course of Indochinese history for the next half century.

The man who brought about this change had no experience in colonial administration when offered the Indochinese post. He had never been to Indochina. His involvement with Indochinese affairs hardly went back beyond the year 1895, when he delivered an official report on the precarious financial situation of Tongking. Although Doumer soon acquired considerable knowledge of colonial affairs, it was confined largely to financial matters. Yet once he was appointed, the government and above all the pro-colonial French press believed at last to have found the man who could clear up the administrative chaos and promote economic development to justify the sacrifice in lives and money that France had made.

2

Almost four decades had passed since France first attacked Vietnam, and nearly fifteen years since the conquest of Indochina had been officially completed. Yet Indochina knew neither peace nor administrative order, neither cooperation between rulers and subjects, nor did it possess a government strong and unified enough to chart and pursue a promising course. Worst of all, the prospects for the early utilization of the country's economic resources were nil.

The center part of Indochina—Vietnam—proved the most troublesome for the French, but at the same time it held out promise for great gains. Vietnam had been divided by the French into three separately administered "states"—Cochinchina, Annam, and Tongking.

In Cochinchina, circumstances had forced the French to set up their own rule. Vietnamese noncooperation, the direct result of the methods the French applied in establishing themselves, led to a war that lasted almost two years, which was followed by years of brutal repression, a response to the guerrilla resistance that began after the defeat of the Vietnamese armies. The first governor of Cochinchina, Admiral Bonard, had intended to set up a protectorate type of regime in which the Vietnamese, subject to French control, would continue to function in the administration. He was eager not only to come to terms with the emperor of Vietnam, but also to gain the cooperation of the mandarins who, in the emperor's name, had been in charge of all civil, military, and judicial affairs, from the royal court down to the village level, ever since Vietnam regained its independence from China. Although Bonard succeeded with the emperor, he could not persuade the emperor's aides to work under the French. The mandarins knew well that they were beaten militarily, but politically they would not submit. They simply disappeared, taking with them or destroying indispensable records, and proclaiming, with the emperor's secret approval, that collaboration with the French was a betrayal of the national cause. On the lowest administrative level, therefore, a few "Christians or crooks,"[1] were the only ones whom the French managed to enlist.

The mandarins were replaced by French "inspectors of native affairs," young officers who, although ignorant of the country's administrative, fiscal, and judicial problems, were nonetheless given greater power than the mandarins had ever possessed. Cochinchina, instead of becoming a protectorate of France, thus became a directly administered colony whose government, under Admiral Bonard and his successors in the 1860's and 70's, was a purely military regime. The colony was in effect run by the Navy, under whose auspices Cochinchina had become French, and its governors up to the year 1879 were admirals, appointed by the Ministry of the Navy and Colonies, the metropolitan arbiter of all Cochinchinese affairs.

Although mutilated by the amputation of Cochinchina, an independent Vietnam consisting of Tongking (the north) and Annam (the center) existed until 1883. By the time the French had succeeded in making themselves masters of the entire country, their administration of Cochinchina had been solidified and long taken for granted. Yet when the north and center fell into their hands, they did not openly annex these regions, but concluded separate treaties of protectorate for Tongking and Annam with the Vietnamese emperor. The imperial court and the majority of the mandarins saw cooperation as the only way of preserving their positions. They had failed to regain Cochinchina, where resistance had dwindled to isolated gestures and where some rich Vietnamese and others soon made rich by the French had accommodated themselves to foreign rule. Only a minority of the mandarins continued to favor sabotage and armed resistance, and their hostility only intensified the desire of the French to gain the support of the neutral, the undecided, and the opportunistic. Cooperation was practiced for the most part, though inconsistently and in bad faith all around, both in Tongking and Annam, for at least twelve years before Doumer's arrival on the scene.

By the time Tongking and Annam had become so-called protectorates, a wholly French-staffed administration, allied with French commercial interests in Saigon, had turned Cochinchina into a French private domain. It was the opposition of these circles, organized since 1880 in the Colonial Council of Cochinchina, that doomed all attempts of Paris to set up a central authority capable of pursuing the political and economic interests of France. In 1887, France, urged on by spokesmen of a nationally oriented colonial policy, created the Indochinese Union, appointed its first governor general, and authorized a modest general budget for Indochina over and above the local budgets of the then separate four states—Cochinchina, Annam, Tongking, and Cambodia. It took the French in Cochinchina less than a year to kill both the Indochinese Union and the general budget to which they were expected to contribute. This meant that the authority of the governor general remained confined to Tongking and Annam.

Paris' next attempt to establish a central administration for the whole of French Indochina was made in 1891. The powers of the governor general were increased and once more explicitly stated to cover the entire territory of the revived Indochinese Union. But when Jean-Marie de Lanessan, the newly appointed governor general, sought to exercise his legitimate powers, his duel with the enemies of a central administration ended with his recall in October, 1894.

The strong government Doumer wanted for all of French Indochina demanded, at least so he thought, measures in Tongking and Annam that conflicted sharply with his desire to be liked and supported by the Vietnamese. A man who was determined to curtail the autonomy of his French brothers for the sake of a national purpose could not be expected to leave the administrative autonomy of Tongking and Annam untouched because a part of it was still Vietnamese-controlled. Doumer's plans called for a strong central government under French control. He therefore decided that all remnants of Vietnamese political authority had to be wiped out.

The interests and aims of the French had emerged very clearly when they imposed two separate protectorates for Tongking and Annam. In both, the emperor was recognized as the nominal head of the country, and the French actually left him in charge of the administration of Annam, albeit under their control. France thereby severed Tongking from the rest of Vietnam, as it had Cochinchina before.

In Tongking, direct French rule under the official cloak of a protectorate was in part the automatic result of widespread military action against the never-ending armed resistance of the Vietnamese and organized groups of Chinese pirates. There, too, collaboration with the mandarins soon was possible only under conditions fixed by the French. By an ingenious act that violated the Protectorate Treaty, the French also cut all contacts between the remnants of the old Vietnamese administration and the imperial court in Annam, and in 1887, the emperor's theoretical prerogatives over Tongking were transferred to a French-picked and French-controlled Vietnamese viceroy in Hanoi.

When Doumer started to bring order into Indochina affairs, the process of separating the north from the center and of abolishing Vietnamese authority in Tongking was nearly completed. Only one more step was needed to make Tongking as directly French-ruled as Cochinchina had always been, and Doumer took this step a few months later. In July, 1897, he abolished the office of viceroy and decreed that the emperor of Vietnam henceforth be represented in Tongking by a French resident superior in Hanoi. The new "representative of the emperor" was to take orders from one man alone, that man, of course, being Doumer himself.

With Tongking firmly in his grip, Doumer turned his attention to Annam. A few rough measures, taken in the sure knowledge that French military strength was sufficient to break all possible resistance, enabled him to achieve his aim within little more than a year. In September, 1897, he dissolved the Co Mat, or Secret Council, a sort of ministerial cabinet through which the emperor had performed whatever functions French control had left him. Indelicately but quite on purpose, Doumer chose the occasion of the coming of age of the young Emperor Thanh Thai to emasculate the last resort of Vietnamese political sovereignty. The Co Mat was replaced by a ministerial council in which every Vietnamese member had a French counterpart. This council was not headed by the emperor but by the French resident superior for Annam. The final blow, which made French rule in Annam as direct as in Cochinchina, fell less than a year later, in August, 1898, when the French administration took over the collection of all taxes. The emperor was granted a handsome allowance and the mandarins became French employees.

Doumer had never been quite as upset by the existence of separate Vietnamese "states" as he had been by the absence of French-controlled governments in them. Vietnam could well remain divided as long as the power of France over the entire country was united and firm. But sound though most Frenchmen in Indochina may have thought this approach, it does not explain why so passionate an exponent of administrative centralization as Doumer tolerated this complicated state of affairs once it ceased to be of advantage to the French. The reason that Doumer did not set up a single administration for Tongking and Annam was the existence of Cochinchina and the special economic and political status it enjoyed. Cochinchina produced money; Tongking and Annam so far had produced only debts. And in Cochinchina, the measures necessary for the establishment of a single French government for Vietnam would have had to be imposed on well-entrenched, rich, influential Frenchmen deeply interested in maintaining a local autonomy that promised ever-greater benefits as time went by, rather than on powerless "natives." Doumer knew that a unified French administration for Vietnam would involve the entire country. It was a problem that could be attacked successfully only if and when he became strong enough to make the French in Cochinchina accept that which he had forced on the Vietnamese in Tongking and Annam.

3

What kind of men were Doumer's French opponents in Cochinchina, and how had they gained the power to run the colony as if it belonged not to France but to them, rather like a jointly owned corporation?

The first French civilians to come to Cochinchina were the usual profiteers accompanying the armies and troops on whom they batten. They were soon followed by merchants who supplied the rapidly growing ranks of administrators, soldiers, and colons as well as the wealthier natives; by farsighted traders engaged chiefly in the export of rice; by land speculators; by contractors, doctors, pharmacists, journalists, and bankers. For the colons there was money to be made, more often than not at the expense of the public treasury. For the administrators, many of whom were in Cochinchina not because of their qualifications but because of political patronage, the new colony was a haven of sinecures made doubly attractive by that personal power which the poor in talent are always the first to grasp and abuse.

The attraction Indochina held for Frenchmen seeking government employment or wealth or both became shockingly apparent to Doumer in the three weeks between his appointment and his departure from Paris. The number of those applying for jobs was three times that needed for the already overstaffed provincial administration. The many businessmen urging their various schemes on him were equally dismaying. The less competent the promoters, the more ambitious were their proposals for the quick exploitation of Indochina's economic resources. Doumer's talks with these prospective colons reinforced his belief that the men already operating in Indochina put their own interests above the needs of France, whose protection he saw as his real mission.

What Doumer failed to acknowledge was that the motives of his countrymen for going into Indochina had always been frankly economic. Given the structure of French society around 1900, this meant that colonies, no matter how fiercely their acquisition was proclaimed to be in the national interest, necessarily became arenas of economic activity for private enterprise.

This was especially true of Cochinchina, so far the only part of Vietnam where private capital could be gainfully employed, and also the only part rich enough to support a costly administration. Cochinchina had been torn from Vietnam because it was looked upon as a region of great economic opportunity. This belief persisted even after the French had given up hope for trade with China by way of the Mekong. The Mekong irrigated Vietnam's richest rice lands and millions of acres still waiting to be opened up for production that could make Vietnam one of the biggest rice exporters. Eagerly anticipating this promising future, colons and administrators held on to what they possessed, even against pressure from Paris, and no governor had posed a serious threat either to the absolute rule of the French administrators on the spot or to the opportunities this rule offered to businessmen.

When Doumer met his overseas compatriots, their freewheeling commercial activities and unrestrained rule had already lasted for more than thirty years. The notion that Cochinchina was theirs had long found also institutional expression of a kind that angered Doumer to the point of his pleading for the rights of the Vietnamese, who, as he put it, could neither vote nor any longer were citizens of their own country. The main object of Doumer's indignation was the Colonial Council, created with the best of intentions by the first civilian governor of Cochinchina, Le Myre de Vilers, in 1880. Doumer had nothing but scorn for the composition and the prerogatives of the Council. "I did not believe it possible," he wrote in his memoirs, "that as strange and absurd a concept of colonial government as that created in Cochinchina could exist." After pointing out that only French citizens enjoyed voting rights, he stated: "Of the scarcely 2,000 French citizens in Cochinchina, 1,500 lived off the state budget, and not a few of the remaining 500 were connected with the administration in other ways. Thus, of a population of 3 million, 2,000 had the right to vote, and of these three-quarters were government employees." Doumer ascribed the power of the Council partly to its having a deputy in Paris and partly to its control over the colony's resources. "One easily grasps the beauty of this system," he wrote. "A majority of officials living off the budget decides what shall be spent and what taxes shall be collected."[2]

It came as no surprise to Doumer that his projected administrative reforms were bitterly fought by the men who headed the Colonial Council, of whom the most determined was a former colon named Paul Blanchy, who had been the Council's president since 1882 and mayor of Saigon since 1895.

The inevitable collision between the new governor general and the Colonial Council came in November, 1897, three months after the remnants of Vietnamese local power in Tongking and Annam had been wiped out. It was a clash Doumer had tried to avoid since he knew that it would delay his reforms. In spite of his impatience, partly the result of his unmatched capacity for work, he approached the institution of his reforms slowly and with great circumspection. "First those measures had to be proposed that would meet the least resistance in Paris."[3] He started by building a strong cabinet of four departments to control what he was about to create. Then he asked Paris to reinstitute the position of resident superior for Tongking, and, intending to confront the local Colonial Council with a higher body composed of representatives of all five states, he also asked for a decree establishing a superior council of Indochina. This decree was issued in July, 1897. The new council, whose forerunner had been killed by indifference in Paris and hostility in Saigon, was headed by the governor general. Sitting on it were the chiefs of the Army and Navy; the residents superior of Tongking, Annam, Cambodia, and Laos (Laos had been added to French Indochina in 1893); the lieutenant governor of Cochinchina; the presidents of the chambers of agriculture and commerce, as well as two high mandarins—for purposes of decoration, as some Vietnamese said. To these would later be added the directors of the General Services for Indochina.

The General Services, devised partly as a stratagem to gain more ready acceptance of governmental institutions for the whole of Indochina, were nevertheless essential administrative tools to bring order and vitality to the diverse services of the states. But the General Services were no less important as the organizational backbone of a central administrative and political authority over and above the local state governments. This was precisely why they were opposed by Paul Blanchy and his adherents; their personal prosperity was best protected if no one interfered with their way of running their state.

Only two of the General Services had been set up—one for customs and indirect taxes, the other for agriculture and commerce —when the Colonial Council was aroused by Doumer's request for a budget for all of Indochina to defray the costs of the central administration he was creating and to finance his ambitious public-works projects. In a meeting held in November, 1897, the Colonial Council condemned the idea of a general budget, refused to vote even modest funds for a study of railway construction in Indochina, denounced all measures so far taken to organize an all-Indochinese administration, and decided to appeal to Paris for support.

Doumer, who knew that his entire mission would be a failure if his request for a general budget were rejected, therefore submitted it to Paris immediately upon the Council's declaration of war. Paris' decision was long in coming—six months—but when Paris finally did speak in 'July, 1898, Doumer hailed the decree authorizing the general budget as "consecrating . . . the birth of Indochina."[1]

Within a few weeks after this crucial decision, Paris issued the other decrees he deemed necessary for his plans and which he had prepared and proposed while the battle between Paris and Saigon over the general budget was still raging. Before the end of his second year, Doumer had created and staffed the General Services of Post and Telegraph and of Public Works, as well as the so-called Directorate of Civil Affairs, a sort of ministry of the interior for Indochina. In September, 1898, the Superior Council for Indochina, now enlarged by the directors of the General Services, held a meeting in Hanoi. Instead of having to scheme how to build the government Indochina needed, Doumer was at last able to discuss the construction of railroads he envisioned for Indochina.

Cochinchinese regionalism, although not dead, was at least temporarily checked. Its main spokesman, Paul Blanchy, might in time very well have undone some of the reforms that Doumer had forced upon him and his clique had he not made the mistake of seriously underestimating Doumer and of championing a cause difficult to defend outside his own circles. His greatest mistake, however, was to die a year before his tenacious opponent left the scene of their strife.

4

Like a captain at last in command of a vessel without fuel, Doumer now attacked the problem of financing the general budget. He knew that he would have to raise the necessary funds himself, and with this in mind he turned his attention again to his "native charges," falling back on the tested, age-old method of taxation.

Doumer was neither the first nor the only man to think it natural that the Vietnamese or Cambodians should be asked to supply the money for what the French wanted to create for themselves. However, his dedication and ruthlessness in fiscal matters was unique.

To create order out of fiscal chaos and to make all five states of Indochina financially independent of metropolitan France was for Doumer the supreme purpose of his mission, from which the benefits France hoped for would necessarily flow. Now that he had made himself the head of an authoritarian administration, this masterly inventor of governmental techniques and institutions attacked and reduced the existing maze of taxation methods, simultaneously opening up vast resources for his general budget by a drastic but simple approach: making the local budgets of the states dependent exclusively on direct and personal taxes; and obtaining the revenues for the general budget from custom tariffs as well as from the whole area of indirect taxation, considerably widened through the creation of state-controlled monopolies for the production and sale of opium, alcohol, and salt.

The future would show that some of these measures were to do great damage to the edifice for which they now laid the foundation, but in terms of immediate results his fiscal reforms were a brilliant success. After only one year in office, Doumer succeeded in balancing the Tongking budget, a feat made more remarkable by the fact that alone between 1887 and 1891, Paris had had to pour no less than 168 million francs into the Tongking treasury.

Now Doumer could even begin to pay off the deficits of previous years. At the end of the second year, the Tongking treasury had miraculously accumulated a reserve of 4 million piasters. Nor had Doumer during these two years withheld his attention from Annam. In this least prosperous "state" of Vietnam, he raised tax receipts from 83,000 to 2 million piasters. Although the losses of the states, particularly of Cochinchina, were considerable when Doumer deprived them of the revenue from customs and indirect taxes, by the year 1900 all five local budgets were more securely balanced than ever before. They remained balanced even after Doumer forced the states to make sizable contributions to his public-works program.

These public works were financed chiefly by the new general budget for Indochina, for which the barely established central administration was able to collect 20 million piasters in 1899, and almost 40 million only four years later. When Doumer began to contribute 14 million francs yearly to the colony's military budget, which in the past had been carried by Paris exclusively, his efforts were rewarded: France complied with his request for money to build railroads by subscribing to a 200-million-franc loan.

5

Having thus confirmed that to whom that hath shall more be given, Doumer threw himself headlong into the task of supplying what he called "the great economic equipment" needed to exploit the natural resources that the country presumably possessed. Knowing that the remainder of his five-year term would hardly suffice to complete his numerous projects, he decided to start as many as possible, concentrating on those whose completion required decades, for he intended to determine once and for all in what manner Indochina should develop her economic wealth.

In an explosion of activity such as the French in Indochina had not witnessed before and would not witness again, Doumer revealed a capacity for work which strongly contradicted those who claimed even in those days that the French as a nation were in a decline. He grimly endured the hardships of constant travel, the by-product of his resolve to see for himself how his orders were being carried out. In order to speed up Indochina's transformation into a rich and modern country, he did not hesitate to open the gates for the massive recruitment of French personnel to help him plan, execute, and supervise what he had decided to build.

A modern state, Doumer maintained, had to have transportation facilities. Without roads, and above all railroads, the economy cannot flourish. The wealthiest countries were those with the densest railroad network. If France wanted Indochina to become rich, it was imperative to begin the construction of several vital lines. As a result, the public-works program for which he had obtained his 200-million-franc loan actually encompassed only one item: railroads. Moreover, most of the money for public works from the general budget was earmarked for railroads, roads, and the many bridges to cross Indochina's hundreds of small and large rivers. Doumer assured those who were frightened by his confident spending that "the budget will harvest, multiplied, the millions that are now being sowed," and with doubtful economic logic he expounded the cheerful view that "railroads, by facilitating the transportation of wealth, become themselves productive of wealth,"[5] not foreseeing that there would be "little to transport" in Indochina.[6]

Doumer's final railroad program called for two major lines with a total of 1,300 miles, one running from Haiphong on the Gulf of Tongking to Hanoi, and from there through the Red River Valley to the Chinese border at Laokay (later extended up to Yunnan-Fou in China); the other, even more ambitious, the so-called Trans-Indochinese line, was to connect Hanoi with Saigon.

6

With only three years left to complete what he regarded as the major part of his mission, Doumer started the railroad construction not only in a hurry, but also tackled as much of it as available manpower and materials would permit. Haste, therefore, was one reason that Indochina's railroads were a public scandal while they were being built. Insufficient preparations were responsible for engineering mistakes, for costly delays in construction, for faulty materials furnished by dishonest suppliers, and for the incredibly poor housing, feeding, and medical care of the native workers. More than 25,000 of the 80,000 Vietnamese and Chinese employed in the construction of the less than 300 miles of the Yunnan-Fou line died.

The superhuman effort expended unfortunately did not prove to have been worthwhile. The railroads turned out to be an economic fiasco whose dimensions became apparent only after Doumer's departure. The lines were among the most expensive to operate in the world, for their freight services were among the smallest. They never paid for themselves. Instead of multiplying the millions Doumer had invested, they became a drain on the budget. By 1910, Paris had become so disenchanted that railroad construction almost came to a halt, and the Trans-Indochinese railroad was not completed until 1936.

The final verdict on the Indochinese railroads must state that they benefited neither France nor the Vietnamese people. They were of profit solely for the men who built them, the contractors and engineers, and for the banks that granted the loans for their construction.

Of greater immediate and lasting usefulness than either railroads, roads, or bridges were the harbors Doumer built or enlarged, and the work done in hydraulic agriculture, such as the dredging of marshlands and the building of dams and canals. In contrast to roads and railroads, these works can be criticized only for being too few. But Doumer's most lasting, cheapest, and only undisputed achievements lay in the field of science. It was he who founded the renowned Ecole Française d'Extrême Orient, "a great scientific institution for developing the knowledge of the old civilization of the East and for protecting historical monuments,"[7] and the services for geography, geology, meteorology, statistics, and a medical school. Whatever applause France won for her achievements in Indochina was largely due to the men who labored in these fields.

Unfortunately, the scientists were not the only Frenchmen for whom Doumer's reforms and achievements opened the door to Vietnam. The institutionalization of the white functionary on all levels of French colonial rule was yet another product of his governance, and this despite his early awareness of the evils of French "functionarism." Not only did he fail to curb this evil, but he imported more French personnel for his federal apparatus, and this growing need for more personnel prevented him from checking the abuses and wasteful practices of French officials.

Doumer's unshakable self-confidence and lack of self-criticism nurtured his mistaken belief that the modern infrastructure he had created would make Indochina rich even in the absence of a modern economy. He remained stubbornly ignorant of the social and political consequences his fiscal and economic policies were bound to produce. Doumer left Indochina in March, 1902, after the great celebration that accompanied the completion of the bridge in Hanoi to which he had given his name, completely satisfied with what he had wrought. He looked upon his work and found it good, and he said so in the four hundred pages of his memoirs, in which he lauded his own achievements with a gusto that no one else could possibly match.

VII

The Methods and Aims of
French Rule

1

THE MAN WHO succeeded Paul Doumer as governor general of
French Indochina in October, 1902, was Paul Beau. Like
Doumer, Beau, too, was in the prime of life, a man of exceptional
talents, and with no experience in colonial administration. He
assumed the post in October, 1902, eight months after it had been
vacated by Doumer, at a moment when the reforms of his predecessor were beginning to have their portentous political effects.

Like the proverbial swallow that does not make a summer but
whose augural flight warms the hearts of men, a lonely voice
arose in Vietnam, presaging events no less inevitable because they
were still far off. It was the voice of Phan Boi Chau, who had
won first place in the competition for scholars and mandarins
held every three years at Vinh, but had rejected a French offer
to enter the administration. His mission in life was not, he told

friends, to serve as a symbol of Vietnamese readiness to cooperate with the French. It was to fight foreign rule. Chau went "underground" to organize a movement of national resistance. The first in a group of new leaders who spoke and fought for the liberation of Vietnam, he was the author of a pamphlet written "with tears of blood," dealing with the suffering and humiliation of his people.

Other voices, although not in the same revolutionary spirit, proved equally disturbing to the new governor general. They were the voices of the pro-French mandarins who honestly expected benefits for their country from cooperation with France. Pointing to the general discontent in Vietnam, to an emperor without authority, to the lack of moral authority, to dismay over the mounting tax burden, they voiced fear for the future.

The manner in which Beau, out of fiscal considerations, dealt with the problem of native discontent was truly pathetic. It was also a classical example of the kind of colonial rhetoric the French find harder to part with than with their colonies. In a speech at Nam Dinh before an assembly of Vietnamese scholars, Beau summed up his program by declaring that France, "respectful of human rights, would not injure the soul of the people of which she had assumed the guardianship."[1]

Unfortunately, Beau and his program did not enjoy his predecessor's good luck. Five splendid harvests had contributed much to Doumer's fiscal success. Beau's first harvest suffered from a terrible drought, and this catastrophe was only one in a series of three. It was difficult enough to collect taxes from the peasants in years when the harvests were good. In years of bad harvests taxes could be collected only by increasing pressure. From 1902 to 1906, the federal budget showed substantial deficits which only in part were a consequence of the poor harvests. The more immediate cause was the increasing costliness of Doumer's public-works program, which the country's economy could not sustain. Beau was unable to change his predecessor's plans; he could not have stopped work on the railroads even if he had not believed in their eventual benefit. Except for some agricultural measures, his economic program was essentially Doumer's. Not being an economic innovator, nor being primarily concerned with fiscal

or administrative matters, Beau devoted himself to hitherto
neglected fields: education and medical services. His efforts,
modest though they were, were held to be dangerously radical by
the French and dangerously insufficient by such Vietnamese patriots as Phan Chau Trinh.

Beau's efforts at reform did not change the way in which the
French treated native servants and workers, nor in which the
police handled political prisoners. Phan Chau Trinh, a brilliant
scholar, who had resigned as Minister of Ceremonial at the imperial court to assume the role of spokesman for Vietnamese
national aspirations, protested the brutal treatment of the native
population. He asked for more education for his countrymen,
for a larger role in the country's government, for a drastic reduc-
tion in taxes, and above all for an economic policy as beneficial
to Vietnam as to France. Unless these concessions were granted,
he warned, hostility to French rule would continue to grow.

Beau could do little to accommodate Trinh's demands. Forced
to maintain Doumer's policies of high taxation and exasperating
monopolies, of unproductive public works and opposition to Vietnam's industrialization, he could only allow for reforms that
involved little or no costs and did not antagonize his compatriots
in Vietnam. Thus he did what he could to aid Vietnamese education, to open the lowest ranks of the administration to Vietnamese, to set up medical services, and to abolish certain forms
of corporal punishments. But he forfeited what little confidence
he had gained among the Vietnamese. When Emperor Thanh
Thai, moved by the awakening national spirit, made what the
French called "fantastic" political demands, they pronounced
him "insane," removed him from his throne in September, 1907,
and exiled him to Réunion, one of the French-owned islands in
the Indian Ocean.

Thanh Thai's removal alienated the still largely monarchist and
traditionalist mandarins of Annam and Tongking, and Beau's reluctant adherence to a policy that shuttled back and forth from
leniency to force alienated the rest of the country. French-Viet-
namese cooperation was Beau's true objective. The establishment
of order was the objective imposed on him by circumstances. His
sincere attempt at "moral conquest" had failed.

2

When the French took possession of Vietnam, its system of free universal and higher education was in shambles. It collapsed because the mandarins and scholars, opposed to serving under the French, vanished, and the subsequent policy of "assimilation" aimed at making the colonial peoples French did not facilitate a revival. The plan was to substitute a rigid French system of education for Vietnam's Chinese-oriented system, which in the course of time would help to assimilate Vietnam and turn it into a province of France.

This was the theory that had prompted Cochinchina's first civilian governor, Le Myre de Vilers (1879–82), an ardent apostle of assimilation, to open schools in every village and canton. But he failed to remember that schools cannot function without teachers. There were none, and as he was unable to make provisions for the training of new teachers, his schools opened only to close again. Consequently, after ten years of foreign rule, a formerly literate region with more than 1.5 million inhabitants had fewer than 5,000 primary-school pupils. Higher education had ceased altogether.

In Tongking and Annam, the policy of assimilation proved sufficiently effective to impair the traditional system of education while failing to provide the new schools to preach the gospel of French culture to the Vietnamese. Resident General Paul Bert (January–November, 1886), an anticlerical scientist who believed in education as a political weapon, died before he could realize his plan for a French academy in Tongking. The first of his two energetic successors, Jean-Marie-Antoine de Lanessan, was chiefly concerned with appeasing mandarins and suppressing the guerrillas, while Doumer's sole contribution to education was the establishment of three small professional schools.

Paul Beau revived Bert's plan and laid the groundwork for the University of Hanoi, hoping that this would make the Vietnamese both more useful and more grateful to France. The sworn enemies of native education warned him that an educated native no longer meant simply "one coolie less" but one rebel more. Foremost among Beau's measures were provisions for the training of teachers. Quite aware that his university in Hanoi was no substitute for a Western institution of higher learning, he initiated the practice of sending gifted students to France. The high schools he founded realized a project conceived twenty years earlier by Le Myre de Vilers. He also tried with some measure of success to bridge the gap between a traditional Vietnamese education, still strongly entrenched in Tongking and Annam, and Le Myre's unsuccessful approach in Cochinchina, which did not differentiate between schools in Paris and Saigon. His curriculum retained much of Vietnam's Chinese-oriented system while also including Western subjects. To emphasize the importance of these innovations, Beau appointed a director of public education.

The humane impulse of Beau's native policy might well in time have won the people over. But though all of Beau's steps were in the right direction, they were too timid, they were taken too late, and they were successfully sabotaged. But the main cause for the hardening in the attitude of the Vietnamese was an external event—the victory of Japan over Russia in 1905. It taught the educated, and even more the young who longed for an education, an unforgettable lesson—i.e., that the only way for the East to assert itself against the West was by acquiring the scientific, technological, and general knowledge of the West. These are the weapons we need to regain freedom, wrote Phan Boi Chau from his exile in Japan, where a prince of the royal family had joined him, and where an increasing number of revolutionary students were going in the quest for knowledge to help them rid Vietnam of foreign domination.

A period of intense educational activity accompanied this awakening of the national spirit under the banner of "modernization." Study groups formed, patriotic merchants supported the publication of small newspapers that proclaimed eventual freedom for a Westernized Vietnam, traveling lecturers assured their listeners that education was a means of liberation and that Vietnam would rise again if it followed the path chosen by Japan. Poor and rich alike contributed to the cost of this movement, which culminated in the creation of the Free School of Tongking in Hanoi in March, 1907, largely under the stimulus of Phan Chau Trinh's campaign for a modernization of Vietnamese thought. Here the new movement found its organizational center and spiritual home. The subjects taught included the natural sciences, political economy, and national culture. Instruction was in Vietnamese, Chinese, and French. Moreover, in order to reach the widest possible audience, the Free School produced and distributed inexpensive educational brochures and manuals.

The French regarded the efforts of the "natives" to educate themselves along lines chosen by themselves as a political act against the colonial regime. The school in Hanoi was held to be no less subversive than the "exodus to the East," as the illegal movement of the students to Japan was called. Hence, no matter by what reasoning the Vietnamese justified their demand for modern education, in the eyes of the French it necessarily acquired an aura of political agitation. Even reading Montesquieu and Rousseau, whose works the Vietnamese obtained in Chinese translations, was considered an act of rebellion, since these books, although not formally banned, were not made available to the Vietnamese.

As the work of the school proceeded, the boldness of its founders and leaders increased. Under the guise of education for the masses, patriotic chants were printed and distributed, while traveling lecturers extolled chemistry and engineering as highways to national freedom. In short, education, a weapon being forged by Vietnam's teachers and students, became a threat to the colonial regime.

After watching these activities for eight months with growing impatience, the French took sudden and drastic action. The Hanoi school was closed and its teachers arrested. But this action failed to satisfy those who held Beau's leniency responsible for the "native" threat to French rule. Events seemed to bear them out. When the peasants of Annam, shortly after Beau's departure from Indochina, demonstrated openly against high taxes and the thinly disguised forced labor, the blame was placed on the activities of the Vietnamese educators. Hundreds of nationalists were arrested and death sentences pronounced against the leading members of the movement to create a new national elite. One scholar, Tran Quy Cap, was executed before protests from France could save his life, as they saved that of Phan Chau Trinh. But the latter and hundreds more, mostly teachers, were sent to Poulo

Condore, an island 50 miles off the southern coast of Vietnam, which the French transformed into a concentration camp.

Beau's closing of the Free School of Tongking and his reluctant adoption of a policy of force set the fateful tone for French behavior in Indochina. After Beau left, in February, 1908, the various local heads of the administration, now free of his restraining influence, reversed his policy and adopted measures that for years to come ruled out a more receptive attitude of the Vietnamese intellectual elite toward the colonial regime.

3

Although the French were right in suspecting the scholars of having had a hand in organizing the peasant demonstrations of March and April, 1908, they overestimated the influence of the nationalist leaders. The true significance of the demonstrations lay in the willingness of the peasants to participate. Striking back at the scholars did not alter the fundamental causes of peasant discontent: the high direct taxes for the local budgets, and, even more, the heavy indirect taxes of Doumer's salt, alcohol, and opium monopolies for the general budget.

No other single fact illustrates the enormity of French colonial fiscal practices better than the salt tax. In 1897, 100 kilos of salt cost little more than one-half piaster; by 1907, taxes had increased the price fivefold. In the same period, personal income taxes and local taxes in Tongking doubled, but only for the Vietnamese. The French paid almost no taxes. The flagrant injustice of the colonial taxation system, which favored the rich at the expense of the poor, the Europeans at the expense of the native population, was one of the chief reasons for Vietnamese discontent. The universal head tax, for example, was a trifling matter for the wealthy, but a major financial problem for the many who had almost no income at all. The man who made 50 piasters a year paid exactly the same head tax as did the man who made 5,000. The Vietnamese in Tongking paid 5 million piasters in income taxes per year; the Europeans, who controlled almost all business and made all the money, paid a total of 9,000 piasters. The pattern was more or less the same in the other four states.

More than half the tax revenue of Indochina was collected by the General Service of Customs and *Régies*, which administered the opium, alcohol, and salt monopolies. By creating what Virginia Thompson called "the triple-headed monster of monopolies," Doumer wished to secure revenues for the general budget that would make the government of Indochina an active force. Some of his successors doubled, then tripled, and finally multiplied the prices of opium, alcohol, and salt four- to sixfold, often with tragic results.

The high price of alcohol, measures against illegal distillation, and efforts to force the people to consume a French-made product considerably stronger than their rice alcohol placed a burden on those whose religious beliefs, customs, or personal habits prevented them from giving up alcohol entirely. The alcohol monopoly meant that alcohol could be produced and sold legally only by authorized French distillers and dealers. Illegal production was severely penalized. When a decline in alcohol consumption threatened the colony's tax revenue and the profits of the monopolies, each province was assigned a quota of alcohol it had to purchase, and every community was made responsible for its actual sale. Failure to consume the fixed norm resulted in the punishment of the village notables.

The opium monopoly also involved the purchase and distribution of the drug by the state. Licensed dealers conducted the sale of the opium. But although it was heavily taxed and a major source of revenue, the opium monopoly did not arouse popular hatred; only about 85,000 out of some 20 million inhabitants used it, and of these, 60,000 were Chinese.

The climax of fiscal brutality and administrative incompetence was reached with the production and distribution monopoly of salt, which took effect for the whole of Indochina in 1903. Unlike the alcohol and opium monopolies, the salt monopoly touched on the life of every Vietnamese, for everyone lived on a diet of rice and fish, and salt, usually as an ingredient of *nuoc mam*, a highly seasoned fish sauce, formed an indispensable part of it. By setting an exorbitant price and tolerating irregular distribution, the salt monopoly did in fact more damage to the health of the Vietnamese people than the monopolies that forced them to consume alcohol and encouraged them to use opium. It also ruined the many small fishermen, who had traditionally cooperated with the small salt producers. They now had to buy salt from the state at prices most of them could not afford.

The abolition of the monopolies, contemplated from time to time by Paris, never came to pass, because the private interests that profited from them had become too strong. Not one of the governors general who took a stand against them served out his full five-year term.

4

More than seven months elapsed between Beau's departure and the arrival of his successor, Antoni Wladislas Klobukowski, toward the end of September, 1908. It had taken Paris four months to appoint the new governor general, and another three passed before he reached Vietnam.

This delay in naming the most important colonial administrator, far from being an isolated case of official ineptitude, reflected the inconsistent and unsystematic conduct of colonial policy in France. Beau himself did not come to Indochina until eight months after Doumer's departure. No less than twenty-one months passed between the recall of Klobukowski and the appointment of the next regular governor general, Albert Sarraut. During the almost two-year search for the right man, the colony was run by two interim governors—Piquet and Paul-Louis Luce—whose main concern was to be relieved of an unrewarding duty. When, in 1928, during another period of sharp political conflicts in Indochina, Governor General Alexandre Varenne was virtually driven from his post, France spent eight precious months looking for a successor, thus giving colons and local administrators hostile to Varenne the chance to sabotage, if not undo entirely, his social and political reforms. Too many governors general lasted in their posts for only brief periods. Again and again, interim governors headed the colony for months and sometimes for years; quite a few lasted longer than the regular appointees.

Only a few outstanding men—e.g., Doumer, Beau, Sarraut, and

Varenne, and to a lesser extent Klobukowski and the antiliberal Martial Henri Merlin—were able to influence colonial policy and make some impact on the life of the native populations. The constant fluctuations of Indochinese policy might well be explained by the frequent change of administrators. Between 1886 and 1926, counting regular and interim governors, the French administration in Indochina changed heads no less than fifty-two times.

Equally detrimental were the political conditions in France that nullified the progress made when the direction of colonial policy was concentrated in the Ministry of Colonies in 1894; its head as a rule was the first victim of any change of government. Between 1896 and 1930, colonial affairs on the cabinet level were therefore directed by no less than forty-six different men of whom only a few had the talent, the tact, and the time required to bring about even a slight change for the better in Indochina.

In the light of these conditions, the changes of governorship merely confirmed that appointments of governors general were usually made after too great a delay and that the ideas of a new man were likely to be diametrically opposed to those of his predecessors. In the case of Beau and Klobukowski, the change was one from a decidedly liberal course to a period of harsh repression.

The seven months between Beau's departure and the arrival of his successor seemed the most critical period to the French in Indochina since the end of guerrilla fighting ten years earlier. It was not only a time of the first popular rebellion against the hardships brought on by Doumer's reforms. Peasant discontent was expressed openly in Annam. Older forms of national resistance were resumed in Tongking, where several hundred Vietnamese soldiers in the colonial service had apparently plotted an insurrection and some French soldiers of the Hanoi garrison had been poisoned on June 27, 1908, in preparation for an attack on Hanoi. These totally unexpected events created panic among the French population, and panic gave rise to a desire for revenge, two emotions that would henceforth be prime components of the French attitude toward all Vietnamese national movements.

An incident in Hanoi showed how dangers that were still imaginary were stirring up the European population. On June 30,

1908, Frenchmen aroused by the colonial press, which accused the authorities of laxity in the prosecution of Vietnamese nationalists, marched on the building of the Government General, broke in, and dispersed only after the interim governor, Gabriel Constantin Alphonse Bonhoure, assured them that normal judicial procedures, considered too slow in this "crisis," would be suspended and the arrested agitators punished without delay.

Suspension of normal judicial procedures meant that "justice" was handed over to the Criminal Commission, an institution "which the hysteria of the Hanoi French had instituted [in 1896] as an extra-legal method of dealing with the rebels."[2] Reinstituted in 1906, it consisted of four French colonial officials. Of the hundreds of Vietnamese who appeared before the commission between July and November, eighteen were sentenced to death.

Despite the fantastic proportions the crisis took on in the Saigon and Hanoi press (published by fierce opponents of a liberal native policy), it involved nothing more for the French than an increase in the activities of the military, the courts, and the police. But clashes did occur between the Army and some die-hard guerrillas, chief among them the old "great pirate" De Tham, with whom the French, unable to defeat him, had concluded a treaty of "coexistence." This had left De Tham in control of a portion of northern Tongking, a region that at the time was of no use to the French. The rebellious mood of his people and some prodding by younger nationalist leaders induced De Tham to break the peace and resume his attacks on the French. When he began to move beyond the confines of his anomalous sovereignty, rumors sprang up in Hanoi that his bands were approaching the city and were eager to wipe out the French, whom the administration, according to the local papers, did nothing to protect. De Tham was and continued to be a minor nuisance for the French until 1913, but Hanoi was no more threatened by him than was faraway Saigon. Yet exaggerated reports about his activities kept cropping up in the colonial press for several years, alongside the many articles pointing out that a class of educated natives were a menace to French rule.

It was this sort of propaganda more than anything else that had led to Beau's recall and to the appointment of a man chosen for his reputed willingness to adopt a tough antinationalist course.

Klobukowski, a son-in-law of Paul Bert, was an old Indochina hand. In government service since 1873, he had been chief of cabinet to Governor Thomson of Cochinchina in 1880, director of Paul Bert's cabinet in 1886, as well as resident general of Tongking. When chosen to replace Beau, he was attached to the Ministry of Colonies in Paris. Klobukowski was indeed determined to wipe out the Tongking guerrillas, to suppress all nationalist propaganda, and to stop Beau's dangerous experiments with higher education and minor administrative jobs for Vietnamese. When he finally arrived in Vietnam, he was greeted as the savior of colonial society.

The die-hards of colonialism were not disappointed in him. Beau, too, had resorted to repressive measures, but what he had done gradually and with a heavy heart, Klobukowski did swiftly and without qualms. His belief in the necessity of repression strengthened his conviction that there was real virtue in the use of force. For the guerrilla remnants this meant physical extermination, for the youth thirsting for education it meant the end of the meager opportunities provided by Beau, and for the scholars critical of the colonial regime it meant more arrests, more years in prison, even execution—measures that accomplished their purpose, at least temporarily, by putting an end to all overt nationalist agitation.

One of Klobukowski's first acts was to close the University of Hanoi. Next came the Directorate of Public Education set up by Beau, as well as the several consultative assemblies he had created to gain the support of prominent Vietnamese for the colonial regime. Order was apparently re-established and the country quiet on the surface, but the dissatisfaction of the masses and the hostility of the elite grew faster than under Beau.

Had Klobukowski remained satisfied to use force for direct political ends he might have remained the darling of colonial society. However, like Doumer and Beau, he regarded himself above all as a servant of France. Private interests that tended to undermine the position of France in Indochina had to be fought as firmly as Vietnamese national aspirations. To the surprise of the French, he began to take steps against the more odious practices in the enforcement of the alcohol and salt monopolies, thus threatening the scandalous profits made by a number of big

French firms. He abolished communal responsibility for alcohol consumption and forbade domiciliary visits without search warrants. That was as far as he got before a campaign of slander against him was launched in the local and Paris press. The violence of his opponents, according to Virginia Thompson, "conclusively proved the importance of the interests he attacked and the quality of his personal courage."[3]

Good or bad times for the tycoons of colonial society depended to a large extent on the man at the head of the colonial administration. The good times were times of prosperity under a complacent governor general and a Paris cabinet not interested in colonial affairs. The bad times, both for the colons and the many superfluous, corrupt, or brutal officials, were those when Indochina had a governor general who favored reforms and a more efficient administration. That is why every strong-willed head, from de Lanessan to Klobukowski, was hated by colonial society, and that is why the powerful business interests succeeded in having Klobukowski recalled after a mere sixteen months in office.

5

One of the by-products of French rule in Indochina was the vast number of articles and books in which colons and administrators described or told visiting journalists and writers what life in the colonies was really like. Most of these published accounts dwell on the hardships and frustrations of life in Indochina. In spite of much boasting about the qualities needed for mere survival, and the lack of modesty in talking of their achievements, the authors of all these memoirs produced primarily a literature of complaint.

Reasons for complaints were never hard to find. But the loudest cries did not, as might be expected, come from small colons and pioneers in uncharted economic ventures but from the men of big business when their scandalous profits were revealed and attacked. The businessmen launched counterattacks, and like all complaints of the colons, these were always directed against the mother country.

The complainants charged France simultaneously with neglect of and interference in colonial affairs. The most frequently heard was that Paris failed to support projects designed to develop Indochina's economic resources. Those who considered themselves thus neglected were generally those who had not managed to accumulate the wealth which had brought them to Indochina. The others who did well, the successful planters and businessmen, the shareholders of the Bank of Indochina, and the clique of higher officials, complained above all about interference, for which they blamed metropolitan ignorance of Indochinese conditions. Convinced that they were the best judges of the colony's economic, administrative, and political needs, the only ones who knew how the natives really felt and how they should be treated, they were always ready to make French policy in Indochina. They changed their tune only when they too sustained losses; then they joined those who called on the taxpayers at home to rush to the aid of Indochina's brave pioneers.

For almost two years after Klobukowski's recall, while Paris cast about for a new governor general, native policy in Vietnam was determined by the colonials themselves. Yet during this same period unfavorable reports about conditions in Indochina, particularly about the brutal treatment and ruthless exploitation of the natives, poured into France and began to have an effect on public opinion.

Still more important were the sensational reports submitted by two deputies, A. Messimy and Maurice Violette, to the French legislature between 1909 to 1912. According to these reports, relations between the French and the Vietnamese were infinitely worse in 1910 and 1911 than they had been in 1908, before Klobukowski embarked on his brutal course. Social conditions in the colony and the failure of French policy to win Vietnamese cooperation were as forcefully condemned in these official reports as in the books by the many writers who had visited Indochina and had returned filled with indignation against the colonial regime.

One of the first well-informed critics of French policy and colonial society in Indochina, Colonel Fernand Bernard, as early as 1901 had attacked the notion then gaining credence that as a result of Doumer's work all was at last well "out there." Bernard, who had come to Indochina in 1900 and was stationed in Tong-king, found no agricultural prosperity in the colony, at least none created by the French, and he showed that commerce, after forty years of the French "presence," was still insignificant and industry nonexistent. His worst predictions were confirmed by Jean Ajal-bert in 1909. Ajalbert, a lawyer by profession and a poet, play-wright, and novelist by avocation, had been sent to Laos and Thailand in 1903 by the French Government. He remained over-seas for five years, traveling widely throughout French Indochina. As early as 1906, Ajalbert, a passionate observer more familiar with native misery than any other writer on Indochina, had drawn attention to the price the Vietnamese people were forced to pay for Doumer's economically questionable achievements. In 1909, the sizable body of critical French literature on Indochina received a sensational addition from Ajalbert, who in his latest book charged that nothing was being done to improve conditions, while the harsh measures designed to secure the monopolies' finan-cial success added to the misery of the people.

Although Ajalbert understood how an inhospitable climate, the pressure of a hostile environment, and the white man's assumption of racial superiority could corrupt normally decent men, he un-compromisingly attacked the brutality with which the average Frenchman treated the natives. He described the public works as "ill-disguised deportation,"[4] called the salt tax "a permanent crime of *lèse-humanité*," and commented that the enforced sale of alcohol was ruled not by the law of supply and demand but by "the arbitrariness of an administrator who bets his future on the rise of consumption in his regional territory."[5] In describing the events of 1908, he warned of the much greater troubles to come unless French native policy underwent a drastic change. He was also the first French writer to discuss the profound reper-cussions of the Japanese victory over Russia among the young and the educated Vietnamese.

For a brief period before World War I, France shook off its habitual indifference toward colonial affairs, when Messimy and Violette, undeterred by attacks from procolonial speakers and writers, resumed the offensive in their 1911 and 1912 reports on the colony's budget. The devastating evidence they submitted about the denial of justice suffered by the native populations at the hands of the colonial society drew the attention of the entire country. Public opinion became receptive to the demands for a colonial policy that would no longer sacrifice the interests of France to the greed of a small group of unenlightened individuals.

6

The year 1909 was a landmark in the evolution of French thinking about colonial affairs. A substantial volume of critical literature had accumulated since 1901, when Colonel Bernard launched his attack on French policy in Indochina. By 1909, this policy had become a highly controversial issue. The impassioned national debate that got under way has continued to this day.[6]

French thinking about colonial policy had traditionally been dominated by a concept known as assimilation, which for a long time served to bridge the gap between genuine humanitarian intentions and the actual practice of colonial rule. In so far as it was applied at all, it might be described as a generous form of cultural imperialism. It gave birth to the idea of a special French *mission civilatrice*, which, although sprinkled with a dash of national conceit, was originally free of the hypocritical overtones it acquired in the nineteenth century, when colonies were seized and ruled by naked force for the purpose of economic exploitation. Assimilation, at least in the mother country, remained the doctrine of people for whom the so-called white man's burden was more than an empty phrase. The members of the uncivilized races in the overseas possessions were to be turned into brothers—*français de couleur*.

To be sure, the original concept of assimilation as a fraternal union between mother country and overseas possessions was dead, but the wish to change every belief, habit, and institution of the colonial peoples that obstructed the aims of the colonizers was very much alive. Assimilation, no longer called a civilizing intervention which one day would make the natives the equals of their rulers, became a mere set of supposedly practical necessities, some, such as the teaching of the French language, quite innocuous, and others, such as the abolition of traditional native education and the replacement of native penal law by French jurisdiction, destructive. There was much talk about the spreading of French culture, but action was centered on "modernizing" the colony's administration, which in fact meant that every important native official was replaced by French personnel. The ultimate aim was to produce natives who no longer felt like natives; they were expected to become French, but only up to a point, which would be reached as soon as they liked being governed by the French and became immune to anticolonial propaganda.

This was, of course, an illusion, but it kept the idea of assimilation alive even at times when the only policy in most French colonies was the use of force. As late as 1890, assimilation was still advocated before a National Colonial Congress, at which an important member of the French senate demanded that "the efforts of colonization in all countries under French authority be directed in the sense of propagation among the natives of the national language, the mores, and the processes of work of the metropole."[7] At the turn of the century, many Frenchmen still regarded their country's far-flung overseas possessions as "distant suburbs of Paris."[8] But in 1905, when the French deputy for Martinique, Gerville-Réache, suggested that France and her colonies form a single nation,[9] such a proposal was regarded as anachronistic. The concept of assimilation was dead, even in its later, imperialistic form; it had been effectively demolished by new schools of political theorists and thoroughly discredited by all attempts at practical application.

Long before the events of 1908 in Vietnam led to a reappraisal of colonial practices, assimilation had been criticized and rejected by two groups of writers whose books became more and more influential with the passage of time. One group, comprising chiefly anthropologists and sociologists, proved rather conclusively that assimilation, whether desirable or not, was in fact impossible. The most outstanding among these writers were Gustave Le Bon and Leopold de Saussure. Le Bon, as early as 1889, had called assimilation a "dangerous chimera"; ten years later, de Saussure, a more profound and also more influential thinker, published his widely read major work, *La psychologie de la colonisation française dans ses rapports avec les sociétés indigènes.* Both Le Bon and de Saussure maintained that a colonial policy which ignored the values, deep roots, and vitality of primitive cultures was doomed to fail.

The second group, composed mainly of political scientists and men either personally involved in colonial politics or professional writers concerned with the subject, shared two basic convictions: that the aims pursued by modern industrial countries in their overseas possessions were primarily economic, and that a quick and radical transformation of native customs and institutions was not only unnecessary but actually an obstacle to the achievement of these aims. Most of these writers, convinced of the economic necessity of colonies, were imperialists in the tradition of such earlier proponents of French overseas expansion as Jules Ferry and Pierre Paul Leroy-Beaulieu.[10] The slogan "France will be colonial or she will not be," which dominated the proceedings of the Colonial Congress of 1904, was an echo of Leroy-Beaulieu's battle cry of 1882: "Colonization is for France a question of life and death,"[11] as well as earlier calls for the exploitation of overseas resources and the civilization of these regions through commerce.

These men, although not cynics, ridiculed the humanitarian ideals of the advocates of assimilation. But they also attacked the measures applied in the name of assimilation on purely pragmatic grounds. They extolled the Dutch and British colonial systems because their goals were political and commercial, devoid of unrealistic proselytizing notions. "The Englishman," according to one writer, "hasn't the false pretension to be loved; he wishes to be comfortable and 'make money.' His goal has been attained."[12] What counted, according to such antiassimilationist writers as Charles Régismanset, was the amount of trade, not the number of civilized souls.

But what was to take the place of the policy of assimilation? It was over this point that the critics divided into two camps. One said that colonial peoples, at least for a long time to come, should and could actually be ruled only by force. The other camp believed that the futile attempt to make the natives French, and the accompanying policy of force, should gradually give way to a policy of cooperation with the natives. What gave strength to the arguments of the champions of force was the evident contrast between humanitarian theories and barbarian practice. Jules Harmand, one of the foremost exponents of French economic imperialism, spoke with disdain of the "lies of civilization" so popular in France, calling them "miserable hypocrisies that fooled no one."[13] Régismanset wrote that colonies were the result of naked force,[14] and Harmand added that in the struggle for markets and raw materials, force alone prevailed.

The economically oriented opponents of assimilation came out for a policy that soon became notorious under the label of "association." Association became the slogan of all who believed that in the long run Franco-native cooperation was the most beneficial and safest avenue. But not even its most extreme advocates thought of association as cooperation among equals. Cooperation was to be achieved through concessions to the native populations that would make them ready to work with the foreign masters of their country. Assimilation was rejected not only as unrealistic, but also because respect for native cultures and institutions was seen as an important condition of cooperation between colonial governments and their subjects.

Some said that there was nothing very new about this policy. De Lanessan, in his *Principes de colonisation*, contended that association was nothing but another name for a sound native policy, which in Indochina could be pursued only under a protectorate type of regime. Like Paul Bert before him, de Lanessan was convinced that only an economic policy of help also to the natives could assure France of substantial and lasting benefits in Indochina. August Billiard and Joseph Chailley-Bert, Paul Bert's son-in-law, were the most consistent advocates of association. In lectures both within France and overseas, Chailley-Bert openly advocated the restoration of genuine protectorates for the Indochinese states.[15] According to Billiard, France had colonies because she needed privileged markets.[16] He maintained that native consumption of French goods, the sought-for objective, was contingent upon an improvement of the native economy, and that this in turn demanded a policy of cooperation between, as he stated with appalling candor, intelligent direction and available brute labor.

As the debate went on, those advocating the economic advantages of association received sudden and unexpectedly strong support from people whose chief concern was the military defense of Indochina. That this defense was a real problem became apparent in 1905, when Japan's military exploits were recognized as only the first steps in an expansionist policy aimed at the domination of the whole of East Asia. General Théophile Daniel Pennequin, the Commander in Chief of the Army in Indochina, shocked colonial society by calling for the creation of a native army. Fully aware that this required a drastic change in the treatment of the Vietnamese, he called for a policy of genuine association, a colony without conquerors and conquered, in which Vietnamese and Frenchmen were part of the same empire.[17] His views were shared by such outstanding figures in the history of French colonization as Joseph Gallieni and Louis Hubert Lyautey, who, although they had no particular love for the Vietnamese, had deplored the exploitation policies of colonial society twenty years before Pennequin. In 1905, Albert de Pouvourville, long regarded an authority on Asian and Indochinese affairs, in his incisive book on Indochina, *Les défenses de l'Indochine et la politique d'association*, argued that native cooperation in the defense of Indochina was possible only if natives turned from "passive instruments" into "intelligent and voluntary collaboraters."[18] Henri Lorin, Professor of Colonial Geography at the University of Bordeaux, wrote that the colonized peoples would fight for themselves and for France only if they regarded the French as protectors and allies.[19] And the deputy from Indochina, François Deloncle, declared after an official special study trip that the colony could be effectively defended only if France was able to gain native cooperation.[20]

At this juncture, the so-called practical men of politics joined in the debate. The first official sanction of the principle of association came in 1905, from the Minister of Colonies, Etienne Clementel.[21] The call for the new policy went out also from the Colonial Congresses of 1905, 1906, and 1907. The Congress of 1906 specifically advocated the broadest use of natives in a colonial army.

Association became, at least on paper, the official policy of France, by virtue of the resolution adopted by the Chamber of Deputies in April, 1909, which stated that "the policy of association is necessary for the well-being of the populations and for the security of our possessions in the Far East; that in order to make it a reality, it is recognized that a change is necessary in the fiscal, judicial, and economic regime; that it is suitable to prepare gradually and wisely an advisory participation by the natives in public affairs."[22]

The Chamber's vote in favor of association posed two problems to the government: one, it had to determine the nature and scope of the reforms under the new policy, and two, it had to find a method for implementing the new policy in a colonial society hostile to reform. What concrete economic measures would alleviate the plight of the natives and at the same time safeguard the profits of the planters, mine owners, merchants, bankers, concessionaires of the state monopolies, and others for whom the exploitation of native labor had become the prerequisite for the acquisition of wealth? What kind of concessions would reconcile the natives to a lasting colonial relationship? And what kind of reforms would solidify rather than weaken French power?

In its quest for a solution, the government resorted to the simple expedient of deciding nothing. While continuing to stress the urgency of bold action, it in fact did nothing more than assert that sooner or later something would have to be done. Finding the right man for changes so radical in concept yet nonexistent in fact was apparently no easy task. What was needed was nothing less than a political wizard. No wonder that he was not found for twenty months after the recall of Klobukowski, and not for more than two and a half years after the Chamber had decided on a new regime for Indochina.

The man charged with bringing about what some people regarded as a near revolution in French colonial policy was Albert Sarraut, a young Radical-Socialist deputy and later senator from l'Aude, and, like his illustrious predecessor Paul Doumer, a rising leader within his party and in French political life.[23] Demanding and immediately receiving the authority to decide policy for Indochina, Sarraut was given powers greater than those enjoyed by any of his predecessors. Consequently, orders issued by the new governor general were equivalent to government decrees. Sarraut was also the only man to serve twice as head of the administration of Indochina, first from November, 1911, to January, 1914, and the second time from January, 1917, to May, 1919. Three rather undistinguished men served in the intervening years,[24] when bad health forced Sarraut to return to France.

Had French official attitudes toward Indochina ever been the result of rationally developed and consciously reached decisions, the appointment of Sarraut might easily pass as the one stroke of genius of which Paris could boast in its relations with Vietnam. This rather ambitious, ostentatiously liberal, and astute politician proved eminently qualified for his delicate task.

He succeeded in appeasing a major portion of the Vietnamese national elite without introducing a single reform likely to weaken the institutions upon which French domination rested. The means by which he achieved his extraordinary success were rather ordinary. He never dodged the issues of political concessions and social reforms, which, after all, were the essence of the policy of association he was charged with carrying out. He was eloquent, and he seized on his eloquence as an indispensable tool. And because he never failed to forecast the better days in store for his beloved subjects, he succeeded, by thus setting in motion new waves of hope, in mastering one crisis after another. Even in his farewell speech he managed to arouse the exciting expectation that taxes would soon be drastically reduced if not altogether abolished, and he hinted at the possibility of a limited form of independence. "Time was to show that Sarraut permitted himself to be carried away by his own eloquence, and to promise more than he could fulfill."[25]

To see Sarraut only as a political liar, as Vietnamese nationalists are wont to, underestimates him and does him an injustice. He was a perfectly honorable man who tried to accomplish what only the astute knew to be an impossibility. The fact was that the economic needs and political aspirations of the Indochinese people were not reconcilable with the preservation of colonial rule.

Sarraut's reputation as an innovator was not based on anything he did, but rather on the denunciations of the colons, who called him a "native lover" whose reforms would lead to the loss of Indochina. But the truly powerful men of colonial business were shrewd enough to realize that Sarraut's actions did not conform to his oratory.

7

The Sarraut legend, widely accepted even by critics of French colonial policy,[26] rests on three postulates. One, he is said to have inaugurated a new era in French colonial policy; two, he is credited with far-reaching reforms favoring the natives; and three, he allegedly was exceedingly popular with the Vietnamese people.

However, there never was such a thing as a new era in colonial policy. As de Lanessan had said, association was only a new name for an old policy, one tried repeatedly before Sarraut appeared on the scene; and even if Sarraut could have claimed that he was the first to aim at Franco-native cooperation, this policy, even to the extent to which it was practiced under him, was later abandoned, just as it had been dropped in the past.

If Sarraut figures in colonial history as a reformer, this is so chiefly because he favored more education, better medical care, and the hiring of natives for lower administrative jobs. These ideas, especially the employment of natives, was a reversal of Klobukowski's course, but the actual measures taken proved Sarraut to be not a fearless innovator but a prudent follower of Beau, the real pioneer in these important fields.

Sarraut's contributions to native education were modest indeed. He increased the number of *lycées* (secondary schools) to six for the whole of Indochina, but only three were open to the children of the 25 million natives; the others were reserved for the children of the few thousand French. And frightened by the attacks of colons, he did not reopen the University of Hanoi, which Klobukowski had closed in 1908, until April, 1917. He did nothing to increase the number of its students or improve the quality of the teaching, except to promise that both would be done when more money for such purposes became available. Students seeking a better education in France had to repeat their *lycée* and university courses, so that even the most gifted rarely obtained their doctorate before the age of thirty. Thus higher education, remarkably democratic in precolonial Vietnam, became the privilege of a small new plutocracy, the sons of the wealthy being rewarded for their support of the colonial regime. Time rather than any special effort on the part of Sarraut brought some improvement in elementary education, but so slowly that in spite of a great number of private and missionary schools, only about 200,000 out of a potential 2 million students attended regular though poor, overcrowded, and understaffed schools.

Sarraut, the passionate organizer who tried to rival Doumer in remaking Indochina, did bring order into the existing chaos of laws, decrees, ordinances, and local conflicting regulations on education in the five states. But his Code d'Instruction Publique was a reform benefiting only the colonial government, as did many of his other administrative achievements. He was effective in unifying and classifying the accumulated mass of frequently contradictory laws and regulations, as for instance the native and French-imposed penal codes. And to the surprise of many, he even eliminated some of the excessive centralization inherited from Doumer. Sarraut also succeeded in purging the civil service of many superfluous French employees, and he fared well with such reforms as setting up libraries, improving scientific services, and preserving the monuments of native history and art, thus proving himself a diligent, culturally progressive, and capable administrator.

Greatly exaggerated by Sarraut himself and by the conventional French efforts to exalt their achievements in Indochina were Sarraut's contributions to native medical care. To be sure, in 1913, two years after he took office, the country had 175 medical establishments, an increase of more than 100 over 1903. But many of these had been added by Beau, and others by Klobukowski. Besides, these figures say nothing about the quality of the medical care of natives. The larger and better of the few genuine hospitals were reserved for the French. The "medical establishments" were merely small, understaffed, and poorly equipped clinics and dispensaries, manned chiefly by so-called hygiene officers trained to perform simple tasks like inoculations and first aid. Nor could 175 medical establishments in a country of 25 million be called an impressive achievement.

In his fiscal and economic policy, Sarraut showed little originality. He merely followed in Doumer's footsteps. Unlike Klobukowski, Sarraut never tried to interfere with the monopolies; on the contrary, in 1913, he extended their contracts for another ten years. He even promoted their interests by pushing the sale of alcohol and opium with administrative methods no Vietnamese nationalist has ever forgiven. He did not shrink from encouraging the establishment of opium houses and taverns in communities which he felt did not have enough.[27]

When Sarraut, in January, 1917, started his second term, the French, with their country still in the midst of World War I, had already shipped a 140,000-man contingent of Vietnamese workers and soldiers to France to help in the war. Sarraut knew, condoned, and employed the cruel recruiting methods introduced by his replacement, and only the most brazen propaganda has ever attempted to deny or excuse them. The reprehensible recruitment of these persons was nothing more nor less than forced labor. Although Sarraut never tired of assuring the Vietnamese that they would be rewarded for their help, he never pursued a policy of genuine cooperation with the natives.

8

Sarraut's native policy was a failure even in areas that were neither financial nor political. Soon after his arrival he issued an edict forbidding colonials to strike natives. The order was remarkable for three reasons: first, that it should have been necessary at all; second, because it showed that Beau's earlier efforts to outlaw brutal treatment of natives obviously had proved unavailing; and third, because it exemplified the "liberalism" of colonial policy, which instead of providing justice for the weak merely asked the powerful not to abuse their might. The order remained ineffective because it could be ignored with impunity.

A labor code, long a crying need because of conditions in the mines and on the rubber plantations, was issued by Sarraut in 1913. But it had become obsolete even before efforts were made in the early 1920's to strengthen its moderate directives, which generally were observed in the breach. Not until Governor General Varenne's efforts on behalf of protective labor regulations were some of Sarraut's ideas about helping the viciously exploited Vietnamese workers translated into more adequate laws.

Aware of the abuses of granting land concessions to French colons and collaborating Vietnamese notables, Sarraut ordered a thorough study of the regulations that governed and the practices that had developed in the administration of government-controlled land. But the report and recommendations submitted to him by the commission he himself had appointed were shelved for fear of antagonizing the interested parties. They were not acted upon until 1927.

Equally ineffective in promoting better relations with the natives were the various provincial chambers of representatives Sarraut set up in Tongking and Annam. They never had any but consultative functions. Powerless as institutions of government, they also had no moral authority as representatives of the people. Vietnamese nationalists regarded them as "reactionary delegations of natives under the influence of the French."[28] This was particularly true of the Supreme Council of Indochina, which Sarraut renamed "Government Council," and whose native members were increased from two to five—one for each of the five states. Sarraut's greater policy-making powers made this council even less meaningful under him than it had been under Doumer, its founder.

Obviously France had not embarked on a new course when she sent Sarraut to Indochina, and clearly Sarraut was no innovator. What remains to be shown is that the claim of his popularity with the natives was as spurious as all the other propaganda claims.

If the Vietnamese ever had felt affection for the "great magician of the word," as he was called by some, there is every evidence to prove that they were disillusioned long before the end of his first term. And if he was ever really loved by some for the hopes his words stirred up, he would still have been hated by most for one single act: the revival, after some nationalist manifestations, of the Criminal Commission, which Klobukowski, after the suppression of the outbreaks of 1908, had suspended, and which Sarraut himself had once called a disgrace.

The year 1913 threatened to become as much of a nightmare for the French in Vietnam as 1908 had been. Agents of the Association for the Restoration of Vietnam, founded abroad by Phan Boi Chau and Prince Cuong De, became active in many parts of the country. They operated from their new base in China, which they succeeded in building up after the start of the Chinese revolution, an event that strengthened the spirit of national resistance in Vietnam as much as had the rise of Japan after 1905. On March 24, 1913, bombs were discovered in the vicinity of several public buildings in Saigon. On the twenty-eighth of the same month, unarmed peasants marched on Cholon, at the gates of Saigon, apparently intent upon voicing their grievances. With the memory of the demonstrations of 1908 still very much alive, the French brutally dispersed the marchers, arrested hundreds of nationalists suspected of being the leaders of the emergent movement, and sentenced thirty-four of them to prison as "insurrectionists." On April 12, the nationalist "underground" murdered a high Vietnamese official in Thai Binh; on the twenty-sixth, a bomb was thrown in Hanoi, killing two French officers and causing such panic among the French and such violent demands for action against the nationalists that Sarraut decided to revive the Criminal Commission. Two hundred fifty-four persons were arrested, many at random; sixty-four were brought before the Commission, which, as always, sentenced dozens of Vietnamese to death, including the absent Phan Boi Chau and Prince Cuong De.

The dubious premise of Sarraut's pronative policy produced the preposterous conclusion that the Vietnamese loved and admired him. He was praised as immoderately by historians for his alleged moderation in suppressing seditious movements as he was condemned for it by colonial society. If any conclusion at all can be drawn from this, it is only that under a different governor the number of Vietnamese killed as rebels might well have been greater than it was under Sarraut.

When the great "magician of the word" became silent, a moderate Vietnamese nationalist said after Sarraut's departure, the illusions created by his speeches quickly faded away. The "substantial reforms" he had promised in his farewell speech were not even mentioned by his immediate successor, Maurice Monguillot, an interim governor from the ranks of the administration who lasted from May, 1919, to February, 1920. Sarraut himself must have been aware that his policy of association had wrought no real change in the conditions of native unfreedom, for a few years later, in reviewing his own work and pleading once more for a policy of cooperation, he commented: "Less generous perhaps than other nations in the verbal liberalism of the constitutions granted, we compensate for the parsimony of our colonial franchise by sincere feeling."[29] In plain language this meant that French sincerity of feeling for the Vietnamese was proved by the fact that the Vietnamese enjoyed fewer rights than the natives of other colonial countries.

9

It would be tedious and fruitless to describe in detail French policy in Indochina between 1920, when a liberal governor general was about to be installed, and 1940, when a conservative had to make room for a military head of Japanese-occupied French Indochina. Up to the time when a world-wide crisis began to unhinge French power in Asia, French policy remained what it had been all along.

The new liberal governor general was Maurice Long, a Republican-Socialist member of the Chamber of Deputies. The reforms introduced by him during his tenure (February, 1920–April, 1922) either were of no interest to the mass of the population or too modest to affect their economic and political well-being. He increased the number of native members on the Cochinchinese Colonial Council from six to ten, but his appointees were spokesmen for the native plutocracy and the Council's French membership simultaneously was raised from twelve to fourteen. The colony's postwar prosperity gave Long more funds for medical care and education, but most of these were absorbed by the French. Long carried through some of the administrative reforms initiated by Sarraut, but his measures in the direction of liberalism were slow and timid. His boldest reform was the admission of natives as assistants into all but the highest administrative positions. This infuriated the French and failed to satisfy the nationalists. The colonials did not want any native officials, and the native elite resented the second-class status and a salary range considerably lower than the French. Long died in Ceylon, in August, 1922, on his way back to Indochina.

Long was succeeded by Martial Henri Merlin, a professed

opponent of higher education for the natives. He suppressed the faculty of law at the University of Hanoi, cut the budget for the *lycées,* and refused to sign a decree that would have admitted *lycée* and university graduates to higher schools in France. When the general budget showed large deficits despite continuing business prosperity in the colony, Merlin, instead of reducing administrative costs, increased the land tax of the peasants. An attempt on his life at a banquet in Canton in June, 1924, failed; "severe police measures"[30] against the Vietnamese national elite was his answer to this ominous warning. Merlin, appointed in August, 1923, was recalled in April, 1925, partly because of his inability to balance the budget, but chiefly as a result of the election victory of the French Left in 1924.

Proof that not even the firmest exponent of association could alter the miserable condition of the natives was delivered by Merlin's liberal, devoted, and determined successor, Alexandre Varenne, the first and only Socialist to occupy a high colonial position. An intelligent, able, and courageous man, he held exemplary liberal views about the relationship of France to her Indochinese possessions. Varenne's two most important contributions were in the field of labor protection and agrarian credit. His labor code, issued in October, 1927, regulated the recruitment of workers, hours, prevention of accidents, care for the sick, housing conditions, wages, and inspection procedures. But the power of the inspectors was very limited and the code was sabotaged. Not until 1936, after the Popular Front came to power in France, did the code become moderately effective.

Even more lamentable than Varenne's failure to protect labor was the failure of his efforts to save a debt-ridden peasantry from the greed of the moneylenders. The Banks of Popular Agricultural Credit he established in 1927 failed to promote the laudable aim of their founder; they fell into the hands of the moneylenders. Only one of Varenne's measures was of real help to the small borrowers: the abolition of prison sentences for peasants unable to pay their debts. Varenne was the first to act on the land-concession report Sarraut had commissioned in 1913. Although he did little for education, he achieved recognition in France of diplomas from Hanoi University, and he raised teachers' salaries. He also liberalized somewhat the control over the native press, and, to the dismay of colonial society, granted amnesties to political prisoners. Another of his reforms was to do away with the requirement of French citizenship for government employment. But when he tried to introduce an income tax, the attacks on him became virulent. He was the first to be accused openly of aiding the Communists,[31] who at that time had hardly appeared on the horizon of Vietnamese history. Varenne, alarmed by the storm he had aroused, and no doubt eager to compromise so as to be able to complete some of his projects, retreated on many fronts, but colonial society never learned to compromise, and they neither forgot nor forgave. Appointed in November, 1925, he was recalled in January, 1928.

Seven months passed before Paris decided on Pierre Pasquier to succeed Varenne. Pasquier had already spent thirty years in Indochina and like de Lanessan, Doumer, and Sarraut had secured for himself a place in colonial history also as a writer.[32] He lasted longer than any other governor general, from August, 1928, to January, 1934, when he was killed in an airplane accident.

It was under Pasquier that the then eighteen-year-old French-educated Bao Dai, the son and heir of Emperor Khai Dinh, was installed on the throne. Pasquier permitted the eager new sovereign to dismiss his old counsellors and surround himself with spokesmen for Vietnamese nationalism. But in 1933, when one of these men, the young Ngo Dinh Diem, behaved as though reforms were meant to be carried out, he was given the choice between accepting the French version of the policy of cooperation or quitting. He quit. Bao Dai's new chief counsellor, the gifted journalist Pham Quynh, proved a more pliable exponent of Franco-Vietnamese cooperation.

Pasquier combined a talent for appeasing the natives with modest reforms and the willingness to use utmost harshness in a vain effort to wipe out national resistance. In a time of economic crisis he kept the budget balanced, finished Doumer's hydraulic program, built the important canal between Song Can and Song Thi Long, and abolished the alcohol monopoly. These are among his undoubted accomplishments. But it was he who, after the uprising of the native garrison of Yen Bay on February 10, 1930, convened the Criminal Commission for the longest of its many sessions. The Commission sentenced 83 nationalists to death, and

546 to imprisonment and forced labor. But that was not all. That same year, 699 persons were summarily executed, 50 in Yen Bay alone. By the end of 1932, the number of nationalists arrested and held in prison was estimated at more than 10,000.

As resistance continued, repression became more and more cruel, under Pasquier as well as under his successor, the completely brutalized René Robin (February, 1934–September, 1936). Robin, who like Pasquier had served the colony for thirty years, had been resident superior of Tongking before he became governor general. Robin ran into trouble not only with the Vietnamese. When his budget was threatened, he cut salaries, and he even succeeded in getting a very mild income tax accepted, at least in principle. And despite his advocacy of the severest repressive measures against rebellious Vietnamese, he strongly opposed individual brutality against natives. Thus, after two years in office, the Vietnamese hated him and the colonials thought him their enemy. His recall, however, was not brought about by colonial society but by the election victory of the Popular Front. The new government decided that a new course was essential and a new man needed.

Jules Brevié, sent to Indochina in January, 1937, by Léon Blum's government, was a liberal. He was also an honest man. But he lacked boldness, and the concessions made under his administration were too modest and they also came too late. The Vietnamese people had made their choice. Not even a policy of genuine cooperation could have deflected them from their chosen road: resistance to the French until total independence was theirs.

VIII

The Movements of
National Resistance

1

IN 1883, WHEN TONGKING and Annam fell to the French, the
mandarins of Vietnam did not yet recognize that their role as
mentors and masters of the Vietnamese people had come to an
end. On the one side they saw the threat of extinction; in the
other direction they saw the glimmer of the hope that they could
continue their former lives. It is in such twilight periods of history
that tragic heroes often appear.

One such hero of Vietnamese history was Emperor Ham Nghi,
a tragic figure, if for no other reason than that his tender age
made him an innocent participant in the dreadful events connected with his name. He was twelve years old when made emperor in July, 1884, by two scheming mandarins of the Council
of Regents: Ton That Thuyet and Nguyen Van Tuong. Employing methods worthy of Richard III, they had already crowned

and removed three emperors since Tu Duc's death the year before. In 1885, they placed Ham Nghi at the head of an insurrection that for months reduced French control of Annam to a few strongpoints and left in its wake a trail of blood and fire. Yet the uprising, though carefully prepared, was a failure. Three years later, in November, 1888, Ham Nghi, then seventeen years old, was captured.

The young ruler fell into French hands through treachery. He and an aid had been hiding in the house of a Muong chief, whom the French bought with a large sum of money and the promise of high position. But the traitor did not live to reap the fruits of his betrayal. Only three days after Ham Nghi's capture, he was slain by Phan Dinh Phung, a great scholar, patriot, rebel, and leader of a future uprising.

In their victorious campaign the French had captured part of the royal treasure—more than twenty-five hundred bars of gold and almost six thousand bars of silver—which were now employed to extinguish the rebellion they were to have fueled. Young Ham Nghi, who met all questions of his enemies with contemptuous silence, was deported to Algeria. Every one of his captured followers was executed.

The legend of Ham Nghi grew while he was still being hunted by the French. During that time, the uprising at times reached the proportions of a truly national war of liberation. And even after the retreat of Thuyet's forces into northern Annam and the hill country near the Laotian border, the movement remained remarkably well coordinated. No longer was the rebellion led only by court mandarins, but also by private scholars who had never held office, and it was largely due to the scholars' moral authority that the peasants responded to the mandarins' call to arms. And it was they who continued the struggle after more and more court mandarins made dishonest peace agreements with the colonial regime.

The moral and military caliber of some of these rebel chiefs impressed even the French. Nghe One, who headed the rebellion in the province of Nghe An, lector at the imperial court, was known to the French as one of his country's greatest scholars. A French officer called Le Truc, a rebel chief in the provinces of Quang Binh and Ha Tinh, a "convinced patriot," with "integrity," and a man "to be respected."[1] Another man who impressed the French was Hieu, "the great agitator of Quang Nam," who, "still young and of rare energy, gave to the insurrection in his province the breadth and prestige of a national movement."[2] Cai Mao and De Soan were renowned rebel chiefs in the province of Thanh Hoa who built a fortress in the rice fields and made it their "capital." Ba Dinh, as it was called, comprised five villages connected by underground passages. Only after three murderous assaults by the French did the fortress fall, but its defenders managed to escape.

After three years, however, the national energies mobilized by the court's call to arms in July, 1885, were almost spent. Illness and death in battle had decimated the ranks of the rebels. Another factor in the decline of the movement was the betrayal of their hide-outs by Vietnamese Catholics, who, after the terror they suffered at the hands of the insurgents in 1885, cooperated more and more with the French.[3]

But the end of 1888, when Ham Nghi was caught and the exhausted survivors of the uprising who fought in his name were slowly wiped out, was not the end of resistance to French rule in Annam. The murder of the man who had betrayed Ham Nghi was the signal for another attempt to regain independence. This time the movement was led chiefly by scholars who had refused to serve or broken with the mandarinal regime. At their head was Dr. Phan Dinh Phung, another tragic figure in the history of the struggle for national freedom. As a member of the Council of Regents, Phung had fought Ton That Thuyet. His enemies at court jailed him and condemned him to death, but then thought it wiser politically merely to banish him to his native village. Yet when the court that had decreed his death rose up against the French, Phung joined the rebellion and fought for his emperor until Ham Nghi's capture. Then, in four years of clandestine travel and secret agitation, he prepared another attempt to oust the French. His insurrection, limited to North Annam, broke out in December, 1893. Phung established his headquarters on the mountain Vu Quang, a strategic spot that dominated the French-held fortress of Ha Tinh and the narrow foot paths and poor roads connecting North Annam with Laos and Siam.

For many months the French, whose outposts were constantly

attacked by Phung's small army of 3,000, were clearly on the defensive, unable effectively to control most provinces of North Annam or to protect collaborating mandarins and Catholics. It took the French almost two years of pursuit and terror to break the resistance. This humble scholar continued to fight long after the proudest mandarins had made their peace with the French. But ten years of guerrilla warfare had undermined Phung's health and weakened his army. He was driven from Mount Vu Quang and chased from one hide-out to another, up along the Laotian border, where, toward the end of 1895, he died of dysentery at the age of forty-nine. His followers surrendered on a promise of pardon, but all except his wife and son were beheaded.[4] With these executions popular resistance in Annam under the leadership of the mandarins and scholars of the ancient regime came to an end.

2

The story of resistance to the French was not quite the same in Tongking, where uprisings broke out earlier and lasted several years longer than in Annam. But the rebel movement in the north differed from that in the south and center in organization and later also in its aims.

The French were able to gain a measure of support in Tongking because they rid the countryside of the pirates that had been plaguing it. These pirates, largely Chinese refugees who had fled into Vietnam after the abortive Tai Ping revolt of 1865, pillaged villages, engaged in illegal opium traffic, and even traded in slaves. There is no doubt that some of the piracy was conducted under the guise of political rebellion. But denouncing all armed resistance as piracy, as French propaganda did, and treating all political rebels as criminals, exceeded even the dishonesty customarily employed in justifying political repression. But apart from the French-fostered confusion of rebels and pirates, the Tongking movement differed from the uprisings in Annam in two other respects. No attempt was made to coordinate resistance under a central leadership, and no agreement on a common political purpose was arrived at. The rebels fought their own local wars, often not aware or caring what was happening nearby. The mountain country offered the rebels a major geographical advantage, and they successfully defended fortified regions for long stretches of time. During the fifteen years it took them to "conquer and pacify" the area, the French in desperation made deals with the rebel chiefs, granting them the right to levy taxes and keep armies in return for pledges to stop opposition to the regime. Many rebel chiefs thus became *de facto* collaborators—until the French were able to attack and destroy them. Such treaties of temporary "coexistence" were concluded in 1890 with Deo Van Tri, a feudal leader of the northern Thai people; in 1893 with Luong Tam Ky, a Chinese outlaw; and in 1894 with De Tham, the "Tiger of Yen Tre."

De Tham, whose real name was Hoang Hoa Tham, was a former pirate who became an outstanding nationalist leader after 1883. With his strong army he fortified the province of Yen Tre and invaded the provinces of Bac Giang, Thai Nguyen, and Hung Hoa. Despite his treaty with the French he did not become a collaborator. In 1896, the French led by Gallieni set out to destroy De Tham, with only partial success. In 1897, they offered him another treaty, which left him in control of twenty-two villages in Yen Tre, and he remained a thorn in the side of the French for the next ten years. His army was smashed and he himself driven into hiding under Klobukowski. The French did not get his head, for which they offered an attractive price, until 1913.

The story of De Tham clearly spells out the geographical reasons for the difference between the resistance movements in the mountains and the delta regions. But there were others. To begin with, the people in the delta were not victimized by pirates, and pirate activity never discredited the genuine movements of national resistance. Consequently the delta rebels enjoyed widespread support. Their leaders, being either respected nationalist scholars or patriots from the lower ranks of the mandarinate, possessed greater political consciousness.

The most popular of these leaders was a former military mandarin by name of Nguyen Thien Thuat, who led the insurrection in Haidung, a large province between Hanoi and the sea. At the other end of the delta, in the province of Sontay, the resistance was led by De Kieu and the even more renowned and heroic Doc

Ngu. Doc Ngu governed well, fought well, and was loved by his people. In July, 1891, his bold partisans appeared in the vicinity of Hanoi, causing consternation among the French and the recall of Governor General Piquet.[5]

The delta movement was subdued in 1892. Nguyen Thien Thuat fled to China, Doc Ngu died, De Kieu surrendered. Most of the other leaders either committed suicide, died in battle, or were executed.

Why did it take the French almost ten years to defeat the rebels in the delta and fifteen in the remoter regions of the north? Part of the answer was found in 1894 by a famous quartet of colonels— Servière, Vallière, Pennequin, and Gallieni—who combined military talent with political sense. They realized that killing large numbers of Vietnamese was not designed to overcome resistance. Introducing social, economic, and political measures, they sought to counteract popular support for the guerrillas.

3

The number of lives lost between 1858 and 1896, in the first phase of national resistance against French rule, makes this one of the saddest periods in Vietnamese history. If dying for one's country is indeed noble, then the truly tragic aspect of this phase was not the number of its victims but its futility. The sacrifices had been made in vain. Not only was nothing won but nothing was learned, either by the victors or the vanquished.

Time was to show that the French misjudged their victory and the effect of defeat on the Vietnamese as badly as they had misjudged the causes of the rebellion, its strength, and the determination of its leaders. Having labeled resistance villainy, the French now equated acceptance of their rule with cowardice and political immaturity. They mistook the shrewd caution of the vanquished for apathy, even for love of the new masters. True, intelligent French observers as early as 1900 warned of new and still more violent conflicts, but these warnings were ignored by the policymakers and ridiculed by colonial society.

When the year 1900 passed without a flicker of life from the old rebel movement, the French believed that resistance had become a thing of the past. Even De Tham's private preserve in Yen Tre was no longer considered a threat but merely a blot on the brilliant canvas of total victory. De Tham too belonged to the past.

In a sense, the French were right. The period of armed rebellion under mandarinal leadership was over. Resistance, when it was resumed, was led by new men, inspired by new ideas, impelled by new forces, organized along new lines. The year 1900, therefore, became a point of departure in the political history of Vietnam.

French failure to see that their victory was only temporary was matched by the rebel leaders' failure to realize that their defeat was final. Tied to the past, the mandarin-rebels who had fled to China simply could not understand the forces of the present that devitalized their obsolete ideas and shattered their political dreams. Their continual optimism was a measure of their inability to grasp the reasons for their downfall. Confucianist China had remained their main source of inspiration even while the old China was crumbling under the blows of the West and Japanese imperialism was making its first onslaught. Nor could greater insight be expected of those fainthearted or opportunistic mandarins who decided to make peace with the French.

According to a deep-rooted, irrational, but highly potent popular Vietnamese belief, a dynasty that failed to avoid a catastrophe of such magnitude as the loss of its country's independence had lost the "mandate of heaven," which meant that it no longer had the right to rule. If national resistance was ever to gain sufficient strength, the rising new leaders concluded, it had to aim beyond the mere restoration of a mandarinal and royal past. But the new leaders were also not a true political avant-garde. All they wanted was to replace a puppet emperor with a legitimate national ruler, one willing to augment Vietnam's traditional values with Western scientific and technological ideas.

Such a modification of the past might satisfy a country's elite but not its suffering masses. The peasants who supported the new leaders did so only because their suffering left them no other choice.

Defeat had been the lot of the old mandarins, and defeat would also be the lot of the new generation, because they too were fighting for the goals of the elite, whose interests had little in common with the needs and awakening aspirations of the Vietnamese people.

4

The man who for the next twenty-five years personified the political character of Vietnamese national resistance was Phan Boi Chau. Born in 1867, in the province of Nghe An, a cradle of rebels, Chau began the political career for which he had carefully prepared himself in 1900. Up to then, he had devoted most of his time preparing for the great literary competitions at Vinh. But his aims differed from those of the traditional scholars. Although he had become contemptuous of the mandarinal career, he aspired to a high academic degree, for he knew full well that it would lend him prestige and thus help his revolutionary work. He received his degree in 1900.

Chau was the first prominent Vietnamese nationalist who realized that Asia would continue to be a victim of Western exploitation unless the East added modern Western knowledge and political ideas to its ancient store of knowledge. Between 1900 and 1905, the national movement fell under his spell. Working both overtly and clandestinely, he wrote a defiant pamphlet, *Letters Written in Blood*, which was secretly printed and distributed in 1903, tried to form small, armed groups to fight the French, and traveled throughout the country rallying young and old to his cause. In 1905, Chau went to Japan, where he met and was deeply impressed by exiled Chinese intellectuals who were to play a significant part in the movement led by Sun Yat-sen. Even greater was the impression made on him by Japan's modern leaders. He was convinced that Japan was destined to play a decisive role in ousting the white man from Asia.

Decisive for Chau's next moves was his encounter with Tang Bat Ho, a fellow patriot who had been to Japan and returned to Vietnam with an exciting political message. A royalist rebel, Tang Bat Ho had been forced to flee the country. He first went to Siam, then to China, and then back to Tongking, where he fought with Luu Vinh Phuc, the general of the Black Flags, an organization of Chinese pirates fighting on the side of the Vietnamese against the French. When resistance ended, Tang Bat Ho went to sea, touching every Asian port and making frequent trips to Japan. After returning to Vietnam at the end of 1904, he learned from the patriot Nguyen Than that Phan Boi Chau had become the new leader of Vietnamese nationalism.

The meeting between Tang Bat Ho and Chau opened a new phase in Chau's political career. His views became fixed, centering on Japan, and his life became one of travel, exile, prison, and eventual disenchantment.

The new phase in Chau's life comprised his most active years. Prominent nationalists rallied around him. In a series of meetings held in the house of Dinh Trach, a rich, retired mandarin, it was decided to send Chau to Japan and to organize an underground service to take young and talented Vietnamese to Japan for study —the so-called exodus to the East. During the next three years, some two hundred university students went to study in Japan. Chau himself set out for Japan in spring, 1905, in the company of Tang Bat Ho. There he wrote his second book, the *History of the Downfall of Vietnam*. He also met Sun Yat-sen, but it seems that the two men failed to reach an understanding. Sun Yat-sen proposed that the Vietnamese revolutionaries join his party and work for the victory of the revolution in China, while Chau thought that the Chinese revolutionaries should help oust the French from Vietnam before attacking the Manchu regime.

Chau returned from Tokyo in August, 1905. Unfortunately, his visit to Japan had convinced him that Vietnam's modernization did not require a political revolution, and that a reformed monarchy could work the same miracles for Vietnam that the Meiji emperors had worked for Japan. Another even more fateful misconception Chau brought back in his intellectual luggage was the idea that Japan would support Vietnamese national aspirations.

Chau disclosed his plans for a new monarch to his friends in Tokyo, and they advised him to bring the candidate he had found —Prince Cuong De, a descendant of Emperor Gia Long. Cuong De obtained French permission to leave Hue, joined Chau and Phan Chau Trinh in Hong Kong, and with them arrived in Tokyo in April, 1906. It was during this stay in Tokyo that Chau founded his first political organization and wrote two further pamphlets. But Chau also met with his first real disappointment in 1906. Although he had succeeded in getting his friend Phan Chau Trinh to Tokyo, he failed to convert this great patriot into an admirer of Japan. Trinh foresaw that Japanese imperialism aimed at the domination of Asia, and he did not believe in a policy of getting rid of the tiger by letting the panther into the house. Upon his return to Vietnam, Trinh started his own nonviolent movement for a modern and independent Vietnam with a bold open letter to Governor General Beau, dated August, 1906, in which he deplored the abuses and extortions openly practiced by the mandarins under the French regime.

The year 1907 was to provide Chau with his second major disappointment. The Vietnamese students whom he had brought to Japan became the victims of a Franco Japanese understanding. Held to be undesirable, their association was dissolved in 1908 and their residence permits canceled. They went either to China or Siam. The most severe blow was the expulsion of Chau himself and of Prince Cuong De at the request of the French. The Prince went to Hong Kong, and Chau to Siam.

In 1908, Chau, together with Japanese, Chinese, Korean, Indian, and Philippine revolutionaries, founded an East-Asian League, in the hope that it would become a solid alliance of Asian countries against Western imperialism. But while he, for more than ten years, combined his advocacy of revolutionary action with the moderate aim of a reformed monarchy, Phan Chau Trinh started a reformist movement whose much more radical aim was a democratic republic. Although still dedicated to revolutionary action in 1912, a time when the Chinese Revolution had won its first victories, Chau had to give in to the now dominant republican trend in the national resistance movement.

When the Chinese Revolution temporarily triumphed in Canton in 1911, both Chau and Cuong De rushed back to China. In Canton, they regrouped and reoriented their movement. Under the influence of the Kuomintang, Chau now decided to drop the concept of a renovated monarchy. His new organization, the Viet Nam Quang Phuc Hoi (Association for the Restoration of Vietnam), proclaimed the establishment of a democratic republic as its ultimate aim. Chau even formed a government-in-exile, with Cuong De as president and himself as vice-president and minister of foreign affairs.

For almost two decades, Chau was the most determined and radical Vietnamese agitator and the most effective political educator, the man the French regarded as the most dangerous nationalist revolutionary—and rightly so. Between 1907 and the end of World War I, probably no single plan or act of resistance was drawn up or carried out without Chau's direct help or inspiration, whether it was the movement to modernize education, the peasant demonstrations in Annam or Cholon, the planting of bombs in Saigon and Hanoi, the assassination of collaborators, the attacks on recruiting agents, or the flight of Emperor Duy Tan in May, 1916, and his pathetic effort at an uprising. The French made short shrift of Duy Tan's rebellion, just as, in 1917, they put down the first uprising of a Vietnamese garrison, which succeeded for one day in hoisting the flag of Chau's organization.

Yet as great a political agitator as Chau was, as a political thinker he gradually began to fall behind the demands of the national movement. The modernization of Vietnam was not a program, nor was he the only one to demand it. What the movement now needed were leaders who could formulate concrete immediate and long-range political and economic demands to attract the masses, as Sun Yat-sen had done in defining his famous three points.[6] But Chau and Cuong De still counted on outside help rather than on decisive action by the Vietnamese people. Cuong De did in fact go to Berlin to seek help, but beyond some token financial assistance no real support was forthcoming.

When counterrevolutionary forces prevailed once more in Canton, Governor General Sarraut went there for the specific purpose of getting Chau jailed. It seems that Chau was arrested sometime late in 1913 by General Lung Chi-kuang, who began negotiating with the French for ransom. But the outbreak of the war saved Chau from extradition. When Sun Yat-sen triumphed again in southern China in 1917, Chau and his fellow refugees were saved.

After the war and the Russian Revolution, Chau began to study Marxism. In the early 1920's, the Soviet Union began to organize its anticolonial campaign in the East. A young Vietnamese by the

name of Ly Thuy (alias Nguyen Ai Quoc, alias Ho Chi Minh), a
secretary to a Russian delegation of political and military advisers
to the Chinese Revolution stationed in Canton, proposed to Chau
and other Vietnamese patriots that they participate in founding a
World Federation of Small and Weak Nations to guide the struggle of these nations against colonialism and imperialism. The Vietnamese agreed, and Chau went to Hangchow to invite Nguyen
Thuong Hien, the exiled leader of the old Free School of Tongking, and other Vietnamese nationalists in central and northern
China to Canton.

After months of fruitless discussions, an associate of Ly Thuy
made the bold proposal to supply the revolutionary movement in
Vietnam with funds. He suggested that Phan Boi Chau, the most
famous of all the nationalists and the one the French were most
eager to capture, be sacrificed to the national cause. Not only
would this bring in money, but it could stir up the Vietnamese
people and arouse world opinion. Chau would undoubtedly be
condemned to death, but the French, in order to win sympathy in
Vietnam, would probably pardon and release him. Ly Thuy
agreed. One morning in June, 1925, Chau received an invitation to
attend the founding meeting of the Vietnamese branch of the
World Federation of Small and Weak Nations. As he was about
to board a ship for Canton in Shanghai, a group of men jumped
him and whisked him off to the French concession in Shanghai.
He was shipped to Haiphong and thence to Hanoi. Ho Chi Minh's
intermediary allegedly received 150,000 piasters from the French.[7]
Some sources question this version of Chau's arrest.

Chau was brought before the Criminal Commission on November 23, 1925. His trial lasted from 8:25 A.M. to 8:00 P.M., and he
was sentenced to hard labor for life. Just as the Communists had
predicted when they offered their plan to sell him to the French,
he was pardoned only a few weeks later by Governor General
Varenne, to live out his life confined to his house in Hue, barred
from receiving visitors, until his death on October 29, 1940.

With his capture, conviction, and pardon, Phan Boi Chau's
political career came to an end. The old revolutionary represented
a phase in the movement of national resistance that belonged to
the past. The end of his career marks the failure of a revolutionary

movement based solely on the political aspirations of a national elite. Chau as an organizer not only ignored the question of how to reach the hungry and restless peasants directly and how to control their spontaneous actions and broaden them into a popular rebellion. In his writings, too, he addressed himself only to the educated and concerned himself chiefly with the grievances of the elite. He failed to analyze Vietnamese society, to discuss the conflicting interests of the educated and the illiterate masses, and to formulate concrete proposals.

When Chau started on his arduous road, Ho Chi Minh was ten years old and Ngo Dinh Diem had not yet been born; Bao Dai, whom Chau would live to see become emperor, was not to come into the world for another thirteen years. When Chau died, in 1940, Bao Dai had already decided that the emperor of a French-ruled Vietnam fared better as a playboy than as a political reformer, Ngo Dinh Diem, after one abortive attempt to work under the French, had chosen political retirement, and Ho Chi Minh had gone into exile in China.

Of the three men whose names would dominate the next phases of Vietnam's history, only Ho Chi Minh seemed to understand that active resistance without the support of the people could not rid the country of the French. In 1925, while still calling himself Ly Thuy, Ho founded the Viet Nam Thanh Nien Cach Menh Dong Chi Hoi (Revolutionary League of the Youth of Vietnam) in Canton. The Thanh Nien was to become the nucleus of the future Communist Party of Indochina. Its appearance opened the most fateful chapter in the history of modern Vietnam.

IX

The Roots of Nationalism
and Communism

1

LONG BEFORE THE sadness of an unfulfilled life took zest and contentment out of Phan Boi Chau's old age, new forces had arisen in the camp of nationalism, guided by ideas and inspired by aims of which Chau would have been incapable. These new forces, with their fresh concepts and sources of ideas, were primarily the product of a social transformation which, in the course of sixty years, had created new classes with new economic interests, a new outlook on life, and new political aspirations. By 1930, Vietnam, although still badly underdeveloped and once more economically stagnant, was no longer the country in which Chau had grown to manhood. The economy had ceased to be purely agricultural and medieval; Vietnam now possessed what industries the colonial regime permitted her to have.

The main features of Vietnam's economic transformation be-

tween 1860 and 1930 have been treated by a number of authors.[1]
First of all, the 1860's saw the beginning of an enormous increase
in rice land in Cochinchina and in the export of rice. Second, the
post–World War I period brought a rapid acceleration in coal and
other mineral production. Third, the development of rubber
plantations during the 1930's made rubber the second-largest Indochinese export item. And finally, there was a slow growth of small
industries for the local market.[2]

The social consequences of these economic changes destroyed
traditional Vietnamese society as effectively as the conquest of
Indochina had destroyed the political structure of mandarinal
Vietnam.

Historically the process was one both of social regression and
advance. Its regressive feature was the rise of a semifeudal class of
big landowners on the one hand, and of a large class of landless
tenants and agricultural laborers on the other. The progressive
feature was the development, on a minor scale, and consistent with
foreign rule, of an upper class of capitalists, largely foreign and outside of Vietnamese society; a small middle class based partly on
property and partly on new economic and social functions; a relatively large intelligentsia no longer confined to mandarins; and a
working class composed of miners and plantation workers, public-
works employees, and industrial laborers.

2

The first wave of social change, the result of the French land
policies in Cochinchina, saw the creation of two new classes:
large landowners and landless peasants. The native landowners
were a perplexing social phenomenon. Although doubtlessly an
upper class, they exercised no political power, and although rich,
they did not participate in the development of capitalism. Only a
small portion of the native rich were engaged in manufacture, commerce, and banking. Their real economic function lay in renting
land to tenants, lending money at usurious rates, and selling rice to
French exporters. The colonial regime had created them, and it
preserved the conditions under which they flourished.

In precolonial Vietnam, the land question had been determined by the shortage of cultivable land. Under the French, the essence of the land question changed from country-wide shortage to unequal distribution.

The French, after a superficial study of Vietnamese land laws, decided that private ownership of land did not exist, that all the land belonged to the emperor. The peasant, at least in theory, was only a tenant of the state. In practice, however, the peasant was the owner of the land the emperors had allotted to his ancestors in the course of opening up new lands and creating new villages.

The admirals ignored custom in favor of the theory that they, as heirs of imperial power in Cochinchina, had the right to dispose of all untenanted and uncultivated land. The lands belonging to peasants whom war and civil war had driven from various provinces were the first to be given to colons and to collaborating, rich Vietnamese. When the displaced peasants returned to their villages, they were appalled to learn that their fields now belonged to someone else. The new owners offered them work on the land, or the rental of small portions of land at exorbitant rates, as a rule no less than half the harvested crop. Thus was created the new class of the landless tenants, or *tadien*, as they were called in Vietnamese, a class that, like the big landlords, had not existed in precolonial Vietnam. The creation of landlord and tenant classes proceeded much more rapidly after vast territories in western Cochinchina were opened up by the French through the building of canals and the draining of marshes. The land was neither distributed nor sold to peasants, but simply given or sold at ridiculously low prices to colons and collaborators.

Between 1880 and 1930, the rice-land surface in Cochinchina more than quadrupled, but the average holding of a peasant was smaller in 1930 than before the coming of the French. And although considerably more rice was grown than ever before, the peasants' share continued to decline. The French wanted to produce as much rice as possible because export, chiefly to China and Japan, promised quick and large profits. Whereas in precolonial Vietnam the export of rice had been forbidden, and the surpluses from the south sent to the deficit regions in the center and the north or stored, they were now sold. In 1860, when the French took control of Saigon harbor, 57,000 tons were exported; in 1877, the figure stood at 320,000. In 1937, rice exports reached 1.548 million tons, and before World War II, Vietnam had become the third-largest exporter of rice in the world (after Burma and Thailand).

These rising exports, and the corresponding profits, would not have been possible if the land made cultivable by the French had been given to landless peasants. The peasants would have eaten their fill, leaving very little for export. That is why the creation of large estates became a matter of policy, and landlordism with all its disastrous social and political consequences was preserved to the last day of French rule. Landlordism, the heritage of colonialism, has remained a problem with which South Vietnam is wrestling even now. By 1938, 2.3 million of Cochinchina's 5.1 million hectares of arable land were under cultivation, and most of this cultivated area was held by 2.5 per cent of all landowners. The small rice peasants, 183,000 of them, constituted 70 per cent of all landholders, yet they owned only 15 per cent of the land. Still worse off were the 354,000 families of landless peasants, not to speak of the rural laborers. The vast majority of Vietnam's large landowners, 6,300 out of 6,800, were in Cochinchina.[3]

Though Tongking had far fewer large landholders, conditions for the peasants in the north and center were in some respects worse than in the south. The population of the Red River Delta was 6.5 million in 1937, as compared to 4 million in Cochinchina; but the north had only half as much rice land as the south—1.2 million hectares. The population in the north increased almost as fast as in the south, but there was hardly any increase in the production of rice. This was true also for Annam. However, rural misery was not due solely to overpopulation and undercultivation. The approximately 500 large landholders, French and Vietnamese, owned 20 per cent of all land. About 17,000 medium landowners held another 20 per cent. Together, these two groups, constituting at most 2 per cent of all Tongkingese landowners, held 40 per cent of the land. The remaining 98 per cent were the poor. The total land in the hands of these 98 per cent was equal to that owned by the rich 2 per cent. The small and poor landholders numbered almost 1 million. Since they shared only about 480,000 hectares, their average holdings were less than half a hectare per family.

Once established, the large estates developed an inexorable tendency to grow at the expense of the small holdings. The reason was the poor landholders' constant need for money, which could be met only by loans from the rich. The larger estates increased when the small owner, unable to pay the interest on his debt, forfeited his land.[4] The attempt to remedy the situation through the establishment of agrarian credit banks failed. The money advanced by the government went through the hands of the rich notables. By passing on the government credits at usurious rates, the rich became richer still. Pauperization was the lot of most peasants and of all tenants north and south. Because the efforts of the peasants went unrewarded, they nursed "dreams of more happiness, of more justice."[5] By 1930, a great many peasants were ready to listen to any party whose leaders were willing to make the plight of the poor their chief concern. This fact, unfortunately, was grasped only by the Communists. When they proclaimed that independence was meaningful only if it brought about social improvement, they had won the first round in the fight for leadership of the nationalist camp.

3

But the peasants were not the only victims. Misery and suffering were the lot of the workers as well, particularly those in rubber production. Next to the increase in rice land, the greatest change brought about by the French in southern Vietnam (and parts of Cambodia) was the phenomenal growth of rubber plantations.

The development of rubber in Indochina was the kind of success story usually associated with American enterprise. Although an experimental rubber cultivation station had been set up in 1898, it was not until 1907 that rubber production was begun in earnest in Cochinchina. But these undertakings were still very modest. The majority of plantations in Cochinchina, most of them in the vicinity of Saigon, were owned by small colonists. Because British production in Malaya outstripped rubber production in Vietnam, the French planters asked for, and received, bank credits underwritten by the government. During 1923 and 1924, Cochinchina's rubber plantations began to recuperate, and the accelerated rise in rubber prices in 1925 brought a substantial increase in production. Between 1925 and 1929, the flow of French capital into Indochina's rubber industry was considerable. According to some sources, capital investments reached an estimated 700 million francs;[6] other estimates speak of 4 billion francs.[7] This enormous outpouring was due in part to the decline of the franc and in part to the fabulous earnings reported by the rubber companies.

Because rubber production was the result of French initiative, French investments, and French know-how, it became a French preserve. Only a few small plantations were owned by Vietnamese nationals. Most of the rubber was produced by large capitalist enterprises. The numerous small plantations—about 800 in 1934—accounted for only one-third of the production. The remaining two-thirds were produced by nineteen companies, the largest of which accounted for nearly 45 per cent of all the rubber grown in Vietnam and Cambodia.[8] In 1939, the profits of the large rubber companies in Cochinchina amounted to 309 million francs, and the total salaries to barely 40 million.[9] In World War II, the industry became stagnant; it recovered briefly in 1946, only to become a casualty of the hostilities between the Vietminh and the French.

One of the problems the French faced in exploiting this great new potential was that of labor supply. About 20,000 "coolies," as the French called the workers, were needed. In view of the hundreds of thousands of unemployed, it is difficult to see why the French could not get the necessary workers. The truth of the matter was that the peasants would rather starve in their native villages than become slaves on rubber plantations. Since no willing workers were found, forced labor—*corvée*—though outlawed, flourished. Before long, even the remotest villagers knew that only with exceptional luck could one expect to survive years of labor servitude. Working for the French was a fate to be avoided at all costs. Plantation workers were recruited by brutalized Vietnamese special agents—*cai*—who used the vilest methods in rounding up needed workers. Working conditions on the plantations were unspeakable, disease was rampant, and the death rate was four times the normal rate.

During the 1930's, rubber prices soared to fantastic heights. The planters became the most prosperous Frenchmen in Indochina. It was at this time that the Communists enjoyed a revival. No matter how extreme their accusations against the colonial regime, they were effective because the people had experienced their truth on their own bodies.

With rubber being grown in ever greater quantities, the question was raised whether it would not be wise to permit a local rubber industry to develop. Vietnam could provide the raw materials and cheap labor, and France the necessary capital and technical knowledge. But despite these ideal conditions, no rubber industry was developed. Latex, instead of being processed on the spot, was shipped to France, to the benefit of Michelin and other large concerns, and the finished products, tires in particular, then shipped back to Vietnam.

This failure to develop a rubber industry in Vietnam was an incomprehensible violation of economic common sense.[10] Not only did this ignore the economic needs of the colony and the interests of France, but it seemed to violate the self-interest of people forever on the alert for profits. But it was precisely the fierce pursuit of their own interests that blinded the French in Vietnam to the opportunities that the establishment of industries promised to open up. The guiding principle of French economic policy in Indochina had always been to put immediate profits before long-term economic considerations. It was this principle which led to the concentration on agriculture and the extractive industries. After World War I, no one apparently was interested in opening rubber-processing factories, but the number of mining concessions granted by the administration rose from 1,825 in 1925 to 11,587 in 1929.[11] Just as in the early days everyone wanted to buy and sell rice, and later to raise and export rubber, so everybody now tried to get rich quickly by exploiting the country's mineral resources with cheap labor. The administration favored the exploitation of the country's natural wealth. In order to lure investors into rubber, and also into developing tea and coffee plantations, it abolished all restrictions on the size of land concessions on November 4, 1928. The early theorists of colonialism had preached that France had to have colonies to gain access to raw materials and to secure markets for her own products; the practice of businessmen and investors all along was to export rice, rubber, and minerals, and to refrain from manufacturing goods that could be imported from France.

Yet Vietnam was well suited for large-scale industrialization. It possessed a large, cheap, highly adaptable labor force, particularly in the overpopulated north, it was richly endowed with sources of energy—coal and hydroelectric power—enough food was grown to sustain a large industrial population, and rubber as well as other raw materials were or could be made available. Conditions were favorable for the establishment of a chemical industry, for the industrial utilization of the large forests, for the manufacture of paper, glass, and much-needed fertilizers, and for the cultivation of natural silk, jute, cotton, and ramie.

4

Industrialization would have taken care of Vietnam's economic needs and helped to eliminate the appalling poverty of its people. It could have been achieved without cost to the metropolitan treasury and with no harmful effects on the economy of France. On the contrary, it would have served the interests of a great many industries in France and of French industries in Vietnam itself. However, it was feared that industrialization would create, as apparently it did in India, a politically ambitious middle class with national aspirations incompatible with foreign rule. For this very reason, the makers of colonial policy were deeply disturbed by the vehemence with which all factions of the nationalist movement demanded the development of industries. Their aggressively voiced economic demands confirmed the opponents of industrialization in their fear that economic progress leading to economic independence would only serve to strengthen the already existing desire for political independence.

But the arguments on either side, whether political or economic, carried little weight in the circles where the real decisions were made—the solidly entrenched special-interest groups both in France and Indochina. These established groups influenced the policy of the colonial administration, and administrative decisions could either open or block the way for private investments. This was how non-French capital, both foreign and indigenous, was kept out of big commerce, banking, mining, and rubber production. Through administrative regimentation, such as land controls which reserved the vast domains of red earth for rubber production to French nationals, these fields became jealously guarded French preserves.

The economic development of Vietnam was left to private enterprise, but private enterprise was obviously not equal to the task, and, until 1920, not at all enterprising.

At first sight it would appear that the absence of industry grew out of the attitude of two groups of French interests. One was the position of French companies selling their goods to Vietnam whose influence had secured them a protected market in Vietnam. They opposed industrialization and successfully demanded high tariffs. The second group comprised people active in the economic life of the colony. They, too, were not eager to have their preserve invaded by new investors. Their wish to reserve to themselves all opportunities for profitable investments was quite normal, but their failure to exploit the existing potential is not so easily understandable. Keeping industrial investors out of Vietnam required control of the financial market. Capital for investments in Vietnam could indeed be furnished on a significant scale only by already established French financial groups, the handful of large investors who dominated the economic life of Vietnam and who made such fantastic profits that the idea of new investments must have seemed absurd to them.

Far from being an incentive, their profits killed the spirit of their failure to exploit the existing potential is not easily under- enterprise. These people were not interested in investments but in the immediate distribution of profits. Even existing production was not expanded. The cotton mill at Nam Dinh with its 5,000 workers is a good example. In the 1920's, its profits actually distributed amounted to 52 million francs per year. Gains were not reinvested and production was not increased in more than twenty years. This kind of prosperity rested on colonial conditions that a general development of industry would very likely have upset. Labor might have become less cheap, tax exemptions would no doubt have come to an end, and labor laws would have had to be enforced.

But the individual factory owners eager to protect their parasitical positions were not powerful enough to determine economic policy. The powers that decided the economic fate of Vietnam were concentrated in a few banks representing both French banking and industrial interests. It was they, the controllers of French industry interested in export, who guarded the Vietnamese market for French goods and whose banking policy was to invest in readily exportable products of French-owned extractive industries. These banks were involved in large-scale financial operations throughout Asia. Their stockholders wanted the profits of their investments to revert to France; they were not concerned with the economic needs of Vietnam.

By far the most important of these was the Bank of Indochina. Founded in 1875, with the support of a "consortium of banking houses, including the Banque de Paris et des Pays Bas," it was granted "the privilege of issuing currency for twenty-five years, was also a discount and commercial bank . . . and acted on behalf of the Government General in its dealings with the French treasury."[12] In 1924, it absorbed the Industrial Bank of China and the French Colonial Financial Society. "In 1931 its privilege of issuing bank notes in Indochina . . . was renewed. . . . The French Government availed itself of this opportunity to acquire a 20 per cent interest in the Bank, together with the right to nominate six of the twenty Directors."[13] Its influence over the economy of Vietnam can hardly be overstated. The big and profitable mining and rubber enterprises, public utilities, and monopolies it controlled read like a Who's Who of French colonial holdings in Indochina.

There can be no doubt that to the extent to which economic policy for Vietnam was consciously made, it was made by the heads of the Bank of Indochina. They were the real masters of Vietnam. Rarely did Indochina have an administration which was not subservient to them, and never one that succeeded in changing the conditions under which the Bank and its retinue of smaller profiteers flourished. Neither the French economy nor the French consumer ever benefited from France's possession of Indochina. Rice and rubber were no cheaper in France than in countries without colonies. The French budget never profited from the gains made in Vietnam and never was compensated for the monies spent in conquering, pacifying, and, later, defending Indochina. Indeed,

Indochina, a source of colossal profits for a small group of financially powerful Frenchmen, was for France as a whole an everlasting drain on its resources. The men responsible were unable, either then or later, to realize what dreadful political consequences their policy of denying Vietnam industries would one day produce for France as well as for French Indochina.

5

One social consequence of this denial of industries was the small number of factory workers. In analyzing the composition and social nature of the Vietnamese working class, it is not enough to know that all its members were former peasants; what is more important is that the majority sooner or later became peasants again. Most workers experience the conditions of a genuine proletarian existence only for short periods of their lives, but the number of Vietnamese exposed to this existence was many times as large as the officially tabulated total number of wage earners. It is safe to say that between 1910 and 1940, millions of peasants for shorter or longer periods enjoyed the dubious blessings of proletarian life under the colonial regime. Only a small fraction became permanent members of the working class, but the impact that the development of capitalism in Vietnam had upon the outlook of large segments of the population was nevertheless great. Miners, factory workers, and coolies on rubber plantations alike were brutally treated and poorly paid. They lacked medical care; they worked ten to twelve hours a day; they were humiliated, insulted, and maltreated.

The working class remained small, but the nature of colonial capitalism spread the negative effects of modern labor exploitation over a vast number of people. It thus prepared not only the people in factories, mines, and towns, but also those in the villages, for the days when revolutionary leaders would seek the support of the masses.

Another no less important social consequence of the denial of industry was the smallness and unusual composition of the middle class. Not only was it numerically small, it also was of little social importance. The controlling positions in the economy's capitalist sector were held by the French, and to a minor degree by the Chinese. The negligible economic weight of the middle class was the main reason for its political weakness. The French knew well that this weakness had undesirable political consequences. Indeed, the class that might have formed the backbone of a nationalist movement immune to Communism hardly existed in Vietnam.

The main features of the society that grew out of Vietnam's underdeveloped economy were the same as in other underdeveloped countries. Yet the social structure had some peculiarly Vietnamese features, among them the unusually large proportion of professionals and intellectuals in its middle class. The French policy of keeping the Vietnamese away from industry and trade made it difficult for a Vietnamese to succeed in business. After fifty years of French rule, the Vietnamese still lacked the experience to run a bank or a commercial enterprise. French colonial policy reinforced the inclination of Vietnamese youth to seek professional positions. With a different policy, the Vietnamese attitude toward business would have changed. The disproportionally large segment of native lawyers, doctors, dentists, and other professionals and the lower and middle rank civil servants formed that portion of the middle class which political analysts have called the intelligentsia of Vietnam.

Because the country's economic sector remained underdeveloped, many of those with higher degrees failed to find suitable jobs, or even any jobs at all. All of them deeply resented the way in which the majority of the colonials continued to treat them.

The size of the intelligentsia and its deep discontent proved of far-reaching consequence for the development of the nationalist movement during and after the 1920's. In the struggle for independence, the role of the intelligentsia soon became more decisive than that of the peasants and workers, and its mood more important for the political orientation of the nationalist movement than the misery of the masses.

6

Although all classes of Vietnamese society opposed foreign rule, not all participated in the struggle for independence. The largest group working for a *modus vivendi* with the French, despite deep political discontent, were the landowners. They were a wealthy class created by the French. Yet the richer they became the stronger grew their longing to participate in the running of their country, a desire which clashed with their wish to maintain the social position French rule had created for them. Hence, most were willing to share the country with the French and never reached the point of total rejection of foreign rule. Only when elements of the middle class and the intelligentsia ceased to believe in French promises and began to raise political demands of their own did a new climate in Cochinchinese politics come about. The French gladly gave the landlords a free hand to exploit peasants and tenants, but they refused these same men a voice in the government of their country.

The history of the Constitutionalist Party, which was permitted to exist until it expired of excessive moderation, shows that Franco-Vietnamese collaboration was a promise the French never intended to keep. The Constitutionalist Party of Cochinchina was founded in 1923 by the journalist Nguyen Phan Long, the lawyer Duong Van Giao, and the agricultural engineer and landowner Bui Quang Chieu.[14] Chieu had studied in France and worked for the administration. His newspaper, *La Tribune Indigène*, founded in 1917, supported Sarraut. Nguyen Phan Long's paper, the *Echo Annamite*, represented the views of the Vietnamese civil servants.

The Constitutionalist Party started out well. It demanded more liberal press laws, greater opportunities for Vietnamese nationals in government positions, equal treatment of French and Vietnamese officials, liberalization of the requirements for the practice of law, and other such moderate reforms. Its leaders also wanted to make the Colonial Council, on which the Vietnamese had a minority representation, into a real legislative body. They put up their own candidates, and in spite of the severely restricted electorate—high officials, French-appointed collaborators, and rich landlords were almost the only ones given the right to vote—all their candidates were elected.

The Constitutionalist Party seriously strove to make association a political reality. Its leaders opposed both social revolution and demands for independence. The French, under Governors General Long and Varenne, instituted a few minor reforms, but the basic features had remained unchanged. Chieu in 1926 went to France to promote Franco-Vietnamese collaboration, but although well received, he failed to gain any real support. The movement, which was unsuccessful and had lost its more determined leaders and adherents, tried to save itself by moderating its demands. During the uprisings of 1930 and 1931 in Tongking and Annam, its leaders sided with the French. This may have assured the continued existence of their party, though only as a political corpse.

An attempt by the brilliant journalist Pham Quynh and old nationalists like Huynh Thuc Khang and Le Van Huan to create a reformist movement in Annam and Tongking failed from the outset. Their demand for permission to form a Vietnamese People's Progressive Party was rejected in September, 1926. The authorities also prevented them from joining the Constitutionalist Party. In view of the failure of the moderate leaders, Vietnamese intellectuals began to realize that the regime would yield nothing without a fight.[15] The decline of the reformist movement thus stimulated the revival of revolutionary nationalism. French intransigence was mainly responsible for the success the revolutionary leaders achieved after 1925.

In 1924, less than a year after the founding of the Constitutionalist Party of Cochinchina, an illegal though not as yet revolutionary party was founded in Annam and extended quickly also into Tongking. During its brief existence—it lasted until 1930—this group changed its name several times, until, after its views had evolved toward revolutionary concepts, its name became the Tan Viet Cach Menh Dang (Revolutionary Association of Vietnam). Its chief leader was Le Van Huan, one of the men whom the colonial regime had prevented from forming a legal organization in Annam. The main weakness of this group, aside from its small membership, was its lack of a precise and comprehensive program. The party rejected the monarchy but had little to say about social reforms and political institutions for an independent, republican Vietnam. Its failure to develop a program of social reforms and political action underlined the overriding importance of national independence in the political thinking of all nationalist groups. The elaboration of specific programs was considered a waste of time.

This, and not lack of sympathy with the masses, was mainly why the intellectuals never had a valid program of social reform. The rights they demanded were of concern only to the educated and the middle class. Long before 1930, the illegal nationalist groups had become convinced that independence could be won only by overthrowing the French by force. But none except the Communists knew that this could be done only by rallying the entire Vietnamese people behind the independence movement.

The lack of an adequate program led to the rapid decline of the Revolutionary Association. Its weaknesses were successfully exploited by the Revolutionary League of the Youth of Vietnam (usually referred to as Thanh Nien), which had been founded in China in 1925, and which must be regarded as the first successful step of the Communists to organize in Vietnam. Within two to three years, the Thanh Nien had built up a solid underground organization with thousands of members.

The success of the Thanh Nien was largely due to its precise and comprehensive program. By instigating mass action, exploiting popular discontent, and organizing peasants and workers, it also helped to satisfy the desire of the youth for positive political action. As a result, many non-Communist local nationalist groups joined the Thanh Nien. But before the Thanh Nien succeeded in completely absorbing the Revolutionary Association, a crisis within the leadership led to a split into three rival groups and to a temporary slow-down of the forward march of Communism in Vietnam.

In Tongking, meantime, dissatisfaction with the Revolutionary Association and the desire of many non-Communist nationalists for more direct action had, in 1927, led to the creation of the Vietnamese Nationalist Party, or Viet Nam Quoc Dan Dang, usually referred to as the VNQDD. The intelligentsia formed the core of the VNQDD's membership. Its revolutionary program aimed at a native military coup to oust the French. The party therefore spent much of its efforts in organizing Vietnamese serving in the army and in the stockpiling of weapons. It grew rapidly and gained more sympathy and financial support than any of its predecessors. But its leaders, young and inexperienced, were no match for the French Sûreté. Its chief was a twenty-three-old teacher named Nguyen Thai Hoc, whose political passion and illusions interfered with the need for caution. The police soon closed the party's publishing house. After the assassination of Bazin, the head of the private organization in charge of recruiting plantation workers, the French took vigorous action against all known and suspected members of illegal organizations. Although the leaders of the VNQDD managed to survive, they lived under constant threat of arrest and execution. Convinced that their desperation was shared by the entire country, they ordered a general uprising in which all major garrisons with Vietnamese troops were to take part for the night of February 9–10, 1930. It proved a lamentable failure. The garrison of Yen Bay in Tongking succeeded in killing its French officers and in holding out for one day; an unsuccessful attack was staged against the barracks at Hung Hoa, and in Hanoi, a number of bombs were exploded. But that was all.

"Repression," one writer noted, "was swift and brutal."[16] The panic of the French turned into brutal retaliation. The soldiers who had taken part in the rebellion were summarily executed. Eighty leaders of the party were condemned to death and hundreds deported to serve out life sentences of hard labor. Nguyen Thai Hoc and twelve of his collaborators were beheaded on June 17, 1930. Supported by the Kuomintang, a small group of its leaders survived as refugees until the end of World War II made it possible for them at last to return to Vietnam.

With both the Revolutionary Association and the Nationalist Party destroyed, the wide field of conspiratorial and revolutionary activity of Vietnamese nationalism was left to the well-trained, politically able, young Communists whom the Party sent from its bases abroad to replace the men it too had lost during the dreadful year 1930. A unified Communist Party of Vietnam had come into existence at congresses of all Communist groups of Vietnam in January and October, 1930, under the leadership of Nguyen Ai Quoc, who later gained renown as Ho Chi Minh.[17] Free of virtually all competition, the Communist Party now set out to become the leader of all forces determined to put an end to the colonial regime.

7

In writing the history of modern Vietnam, the question inevitably arises why the Communist Party gained such an enormous influence among the intellectuals, workers, and peasants. The same question can also be formulated differently: Why did the non-Communist nationalists fail to rally enough popular support to prevent the Communists from securing the leadership of the anticolonial forces?

It is idle to say that the Communist Party had better leadership. Other great nationalists, neither less able nor less dedicated, never gained national fame. But even if one were to concede that the Communist leaders were superior, there still remains another question, in fact the only politically relevant one: Why did the Communist cause in Vietnam attract so many highly qualified men?

The reason for the strength of Communism lay in a complex of economic, social, and political circumstances peculiar to the country. Most important was the nature of the colonial capitalism. It was a primitive, exploitative system that brought all the evils of early and none of the blessings of later capitalism, and above all, it was a completely foreign, not a Vietnamese phenomenon. The fact that capitalism was alien lent the nationalist movement its peculiar political bent. The position of inseparably linking nationalism and anticapitalism could have been weakened only if the Vietnamese middle class had been allowed to participate in the development of capitalism and if the Vietnamese economy had been promoted to the point at which capitalism would produce tangible benefits for the people. Neither was done.

Colonial capitalism, the root cause of Communism in Vietnam, did not mean the same thing to the middle class and intellectuals as to the peasants and workers. The middle class and intellectuals never objected to industrialization per se. Their chief complaint was that there was not enough industrialization, and what there was served to strengthen the French. When it became clear to them that they could never fulfill their aspirations as long as the French remained masters of their country, the question of how independence could best be achieved became the ultimate determinant for their political orientation. The color of the political banner under which the struggle for independence was conducted was secondary. Those able to conduct the fight with the greatest prospect of success became its accepted leaders. These, as history was about to show, were the Communists.

The Communists were superior to all other nationalist groups in two ways: They were trained in underground revolutionary activity and they possessed a workable political strategy for mass action. At no time after 1925 did the Communists have fewer than a dozen of their most promising young leaders in Moscow for training; before 1930, at least 250 men were indoctrinated and prepared for clandestine operations in a school in China. As to political strategy, the Communists knew well what image to present: anticolonialism and nationalism. As far as Vietnam was concerned, Communism was at best treated as a distant goal. The immediate aim was national liberation. For the nationalist middle-class leaders, anticapitalism was an acceptable and even welcome ideology; the Communists knew that only by professing a greater degree of nationalism than any other group could they hope to gain the leadership of the entire independence movement.

But the policy of the Communists was no mere attempt to outbid their rivals in the recital of nationalist slogans. Every single issue, no matter how seemingly unimportant, was related to the fact of foreign rule. They spoke of the need for lowering taxes, of the distribution of estates among the landless, of higher wages and better medical care for plantation workers, and of the right to organize unions, for they knew that the peasants and workers had to be shown that those who wanted independence understood their problems and their grievances. The Communists saw independence as the result of a continuous struggle waged by the masses, and they knew that the masses could be brought into the struggle if independence was presented not as a distant goal but as a result of a continuous fight on concrete issues of immediate interest to them. It was the chief weakness of all non-Communist groups never to have understood this connection. The nationalists never gained and never even consistently sought support among workers and peasants.

The constant denial of political rights prevented not only the development of a democratic movement based on the middle class, but also the rise of a democratically oriented labor movement. Labor unions were outlawed. Nationalists realized that they had to organize illegally. This in itself was bound to prevent the development of democratic political concepts. A firmly democratic party could have developed only under conditions of legality, something the French stubbornly and blindly refused to see. Only force could prevail against the French, and the Communists were the most consistent exponents of force. Only revolution could oust the French, and only mass action could bring about a revolution. Confronted with the alternative of fighting or of accepting outrageous conditions, all nationalists, including non-Communists, decided to fight, despite the risk that Communist preponderance in the nationalist camp might turn victory into a bitter fruit.

The revolution for which the Communists prepared themselves was described by their congress of October, 1930, not as socialist, but as bourgeois and democratic, as agrarian and anti-imperialist. With a large, organized following at their command, the Communists were soon ready for a type of political warfare of which the other nationalist groups never even dreamed. They decided to organize the peasants for open mass rebellion. Their rather fantastic aim was to destroy the established provincial authorities in wide regions of Vietnam and to establish local "democratic" institutions. If they succeeded to some extent, this was due largely to a prolonged period of famine in 1930, particularly in northern and central Annam.

Open rebellion started in northern Annam soon after May 1, 1930, a day on which hundreds of Communist-led demonstrators were killed by the French. Six months later, the peasants of the provinces of Nghe An, Ha Tinh, and Quang Ngai destroyed the local machinery of government and set up their own revolutionary regimes. Local "soviets" replaced the French-controlled administration over a wide territory of Annam and managed to maintain themselves for many months, in some instances until the spring of 1931. Somewhat later, the movement also spread into the Cochinchinese provinces of Ben Tre, Tra Vinh, Vinh Long, Sadec, and Long Xuyen. But there it did not succeed in establishing a revolutionary regime, not even temporarily.

1930 has been called the year of the Red Terror. It was followed by a year of White Terror. Early in 1931, the French had at last assembled sufficient military strength in northern and central Annam to re-establish the prerevolutionary order. Not until the summer of 1931 did the French, employing terror, succeed in restoring what they called normal conditions. Nationalist sources have estimated the number of victims at 10,000 killed and 50,000 deported. There is no darker year in the history of French rule in Vietnam than 1931. People were killed not in the heat of battle —there were no battles—but rather they were chased, hunted down, and murdered by a soldiery drunk on blood.

In 1932, a year after peace had been thus won, the French still held more than 10,000 political prisoners in jails and in their infamous concentration camp on Poulo Condore. The revolutionary organizations were either completely destroyed or unable to resume overt activity. "As a force capable of acting against the public order," declared Governor General Pasquier on December 17, 1932, "Communism has disappeared."[18]

8

In France, the events of 1930 and 1931 evoked indignation, shock, and shame. And in Vietnam itself, some of the more liberal Frenchmen urged that steps be taken to change the ugly political atmosphere.

When Emperor Bao Dai returned to Vietnam from France on September 8, 1932, the moderate colonials thought that this might become the occasion for political reforms. Bao Dai, enthusiastic, intelligent, and well meaning, was then eighteen. The first order he issued expressed his determination to seek the support and cooperation of the people. The degree of influence he might be able to wield depended, of course, on the French. On May 3, 1933, he upset the traditional mandarinal system of rule, took the reins of government into his own hands, and made the moderate nationalist Pham Quynh his Chief of Cabinet. A thirty-two-year-old mandarin by the name of Ngo Dinh Diem, his Minister of the Interior, was made head of a Franco-Vietnamese commission of reforms which accomplished nothing. After a few months of futile effort and frustration, Diem resigned. Bao's reaction to failure was also resignation, but not of his position. To assuage his disappointment, he took up the pursuit of worldly pleasures, something which the moralistic Diem never forgave. Another chapter in the history of Franco-Vietnamese relations had come to a sad end.

The three years that followed this new breaking of the promise of Franco-Vietnamese collaboration brought two momentous developments: the revival, after almost five years of decline, of Indochina's economy, and the election victory of the Popular Front in France.

Even in the absence of fundamental political reforms, the increasing benefits derived from the economic revival had a soothing effect on the political mood of all the people, French as well as Vietnamese. Concessions to moderate nationalism, although largely limited to Cochinchina, strengthened the legalistic elements of the nationalist movement at the expense of the nationalist extremists who seemed unable to recover from their disastrous defeat in 1930.

In this new setting the Communists again played a major though different role. Their new legality was merely a surface manifestation of their clandestine activities. Moreover, the Communist Party for several years was overshadowed by a Trotskyist movement so strong as to make it for a short time the leading group in the entire Communist and nationalist camp.

The rise of the Trotskyist movement in Vietnam began in 1933, soon after its founding by Ta Thu Thau, a brilliant French-educated Vietnamese. Their claim of a 3,000 membership in Cochinchina is supported by their extraordinary success in the elections to the Cochinchinese Colonial Council in 1939, a success the more remarkable as they were split into two camps—the so-called Struggle Group (named after the paper *La Lutte*), and the October Group (so-called after their paper), led by Ho Huu Tuong, who had spent many years in French prisons only to become a political prisoner under the Diem regime. The Struggle Group received the majority of all votes cast, and all of its candidates—Ta Thu Thau, Tran Van Thach, and Phan Van Hum—were elected, defeating all candidates of the newly revived Constitutionalist Party, as well as two Stalinists and several independent nationalists. Between 1933 and 1939, the Trotskyists were also highly successful in the elections to the Saigon municipal council, either running their own candidates or joining forces with the then much weaker Stalinists, with whom they temporarily cooperated in a number of legal, nationalist, front organizations, one of them the so-called Indochinese Congress. Behind these fronts, both Stalinists and Trotskyists worked feverishly to outorganize each other illegally, as if in preparation for the inevitable break in their "united front," which came when the defense of France against Germany and even of French Indochina against Japan became the overriding political consideration of the Stalinists—i.e., up to August, 1939, the time of the Stalin-Hitler pact.

Long before then, the Communist Party of Vietnam had regained much of the strength it had possessed before 1931. One of their organizational precautions had been to save as many of their most valuable cadres as possible by smuggling them into China. Another was to cooperate with moderate and "bourgeois" nationalist organizations in order to win recruits and camouflage their activities. In Tongking, the Party was able to operate under the cover of the Indochinese Democratic Front, which was led by two as yet unknown Communists: Pham Van Dong, later Premier of the so-called Democratic Republic of Vietnam, and Vo Nguyen Giap, the future Vietminh general who defeated the French at Dien Bien Phu. Many Communists also found cover in the Indochinese sections of the French Socialist Party and the League of Human Rights.

But the legal honeymoon of the Vietnamese Marxist revolutionaries was as short-lived as was the French Popular Front government. Even before that government fell, while a Socialist still headed the Ministry of Colonies, Ta Thu Thau was imprisoned because of an article which the colonists considered seditious. And on September 26, 1939, following the Stalin-Hitler pact, France outlawed its Communist Party. Simultaneously, drastic action was taken in Vietnam against all persons known as or suspected of being Communists. About 200 Stalinists and Trotskyists were arrested and both parties were once more reduced to illegality.

But a new wave of militant nationalism, formed and exploited by the underground Communist movement, arose toward the end of 1940, when France proved unable to defend Indochina and the Japanese occupied parts of Vietnam. The Communists started another insurrection in the Plaine des Joncs, which gained fame ten years later as a Communist base. But suppression again was swift. More than 6,000 persons were arrested and the Communist Party virtually destroyed. Yet its indefatigable leaders in and out of prison continued to recruit new followers.

The great event that prepared the Vietnamese Communists for their final forward march to power was Hitler's invasion of Russia. Overnight they turned into a prowar, pro-Allied, and in a sense even pro-French force that would soon be formally invited to join in the struggle to oust the Japanese. No longer were nationalists expected to fight French rule and colonialism, but only the lackeys of Fascism who ruled Indochina as a virtual colony of Japan. When Japan attacked the United States, the Vietnamese Communists also became "pro-American." They assumed that the expected defeat of Germany and Japan and the hoped-for union between a revolutionary China and the Soviet Union would bring about the fall of the Vichy regime in Indochina and very likely a general movement to rid Asia of European domination.

Preparing for the moment when power would be within their grasp became the supreme task of the Communist leaders. In May, 1941, Nguyen Ai Quoc held a meeting of his party's Central Committee in a small village near the Chinese border. There it was decided to found a new, all-embracing nationalist organization, the Viet Nam Doc Lap Dong Minh Hoi, or League for the Independence of Vietnam, known thereafter as the Vietminh. This was the instrument with which Ho Chi Minh entered the next phase of the duel between Communism and nationalism for the domination of postcolonial Vietnam.

X

The French Lose Indochina

1

$\mathbf{F}$OR SIX YEARS, from the outbreak of World War II until September, 1945, the fate of Vietnam was determined by the measures through which Japan turned Indochina into a military base. Less than a year after the outbreak of the war, France, defeated and occupied, was completely cut off from Asia. Japan was soon able to press the conquest of Southeast Asia, which for almost half a century had been the scene of intermittent Japanese military action. An early indication of Japanese intentions was the Chinese-Japanese war of 1894–95 for the control of Korea. Russia's attempt to wrest control of Korea from Japan brought on the Russo-Japanese War of 1904–5, which Russia lost. By 1910, Japan felt strong enough to annex Korea outright.

During the next decade, Japan attempted new incursions, but the West's victory in World War I thwarted her plans. Not until

1931 could she resume her policy of conquest by attacking and occupying Manchuria.

In July, 1937, Japan set off the so-called China incident—the long, undeclared war that within two years led to the occupation of large parts of coastal and central China. With the beginning of the China incident, Indochina became of particular interest to Japan. As early as August, 1937, the French Foreign Office received a Japanese protest against arms shipments to China via Tongking, China's most important supply route. This was the first of a series of ultimatums which eventually left the French only one choice: to fight or to capitulate.

The Japanese, progressing rapidly in their move through China, reached Canton in October, 1938, three weeks after the West had capitulated to Hitler at Munich. With Kwanchouwan as China's only remaining port of entry, the Tongking-Yunnan railroad became vital to the Chinese armies fighting from bases in the southwest. The French, in a vain attempt at appeasement, had stopped the shipment of all arms ordered after the outbreak of hostilities and soon restricted railroad shipments to gasoline, trucks, and textiles. On February 10, 1939, the Japanese occupied the island of Hainan off the Gulf of Tongking; on March 31, they seized the Spratly Islands, which, lying 300 miles southeast of Indochina, enabled them to threaten the sea route between Singapore and Hongkong. Although the Spratly Islands were nominally French, France did not protest their seizure. The French were more concerned with Japanese efforts to strengthen the military forces of Siam (Thailand), which was known to be receiving Japanese help in its efforts to annex three Cambodian provinces. After taking Nanning, the last major Chinese city on their drive south, the Japanese reached the border of Tongking and dropped their first bombs on the Tongking-Yunnan railroad.

Although French opinion on how best to deal with Japanese pressures was divided, there was strong feeling that they should be resisted. Whether such resistance was possible and how best to prepare it became a subject of great dispute in France as well as in Indochina.

In contrast to their compatriots at home, the French in Indochina, particularly those engaged in the profitable business of shipping war supplies to China, almost unanimously favored resistance. But these realistic businessmen were unable to say how best to defend Indochina against the threat from Japan. They wanted France to send troops, ships, and planes at the very moment when France herself needed them even more desperately than they.

A much more realistic though by no means defeatist attitude was that of the man who headed the Ministry of Colonies during 1938 and 1939—Georges Mandel, a Centrist member of the Daladier cabinet, the successor to Blum's Popular Front government. Mandel and Governor General Brevié, who retained his post, supported by former Governor General Varenne and former Minister of Colonies Paul Reynaud, pushed a positive political, economic, and military program, which they hoped would improve the chances for successful resistance. They supported pacification of the native population and concessions to its elite. In view of the threat of isolation from the metropolis in case of war, essential industries were to be established, primarily for the production of munitions, pharmaceuticals, and other vital strategic goods.

Like proponents of reform everywhere, Mandel and his supporters encountered opposition and hostility. But an even greater obstacle than the enmity of colonial society was lack of time: the sins of almost eighty years could not be remedied in two.

Nevertheless, Mandel's achievement remains remarkable, if only for the scope of his actions. He succeeded in getting the principle of a Vietnamese national army accepted. A defense loan of 400 million francs was authorized; within a year, the number of indigenous recruits in Indochina's armed forces rose from 27,000 to 50,000; French military schools were opened to young Indochinese. The pathetically small Indochinese fleet (one cruiser and two gunboats) was augmented by one cruiser, two destroyers, two submarines, and three torpedo boats, but of the 200 planes promised to Indochina's small and obsolete air force, only 20 were delivered before the outbreak of the war. Mandel's decisive projects, however, had hardly been tackled when the war in Europe crippled France. Now France needed, and Mandel pressed for, a greater share of Indochina's resources. Production of rubber, rice, tea, coffee, coal, iron ore, tungsten, manganese, antimony, and other rare minerals was increased; the working day was extended; the export of certain goods to countries other than France was forbidden. But the war soon deprived France of her shipping facilities and of safe sea routes, and the Indochinese products could not reach their destination. Even before France's defeat, and in spite of a strong desire to prevent such a shift, Indochina's resources began to go to Japan instead. Indochina was inexorably drawn into the Japanese economic orbit even before the occupation, but since war and blockade had deprived them of all other customers, the French overlords had to welcome this development.

2

When Governor General Brevié was replaced in August, 1939, by the retired General Catroux, it was the first time in more than fifty years that a military man was again at the head of the Indochinese administration. Preparations for the defense of Indochina continued feverishly under Catroux. Yet no one, least of all Catroux, had any illusions about French chances in case of a serious Japanese onslaught. Moreover, those advocating appeasement of Japan were gaining. The fall of France in June, 1940, brought to a climax Japanese maneuvers to convince the French that the peaceful occupation of parts of Vietnam was the lesser of two evils. On June 19, 1940, the Japanese handed Catroux an ultimatum demanding the closing of the Tongking-China border to the export of trucks, gasoline, and other war materials. It also asked that a Japanese military mission be allowed to come to Tongking to supervise the suspension of aid to China. Catroux was given twenty-four hours in which to reply.

Catroux was neither a defeatist nor an Axis sympathizer, but he knew that he lacked the means to repel a Japanese attack. His attempts to enlist Anglo-American help had failed.[1] He accepted the ultimatum in the hope that this was all the Japanese wanted, and if not, that help from France would enable him to resist further demands. He was not a little astonished to learn that the new Pétain-Darlan government, itself hard at work to end all resistance to Hitler, frowned heroically on his surrender and with monumental bad taste relieved him of his post. He was replaced by Vice Admiral Jean Decoux, commander of the French fleet in the Far East, who was considered politically more reliable by Vichy. Catroux, upon leaving Indochina, joined the Free French.[2]

Decoux assumed his post on July 20, 1940. Less than two weeks later, it was his turn to struggle with the problem of how to keep the Japanese Army out of Indochina. Military resistance was as certain to bring them as acceptance of their new demands—free passage of Japanese troops through Tongking to China and the use of airports. The Admiral was clever enough to avoid an open rejection of the ultimatum, but he refused to take responsibility for its acceptance. With an eye to posterity, he solved his dilemma by offering verbal evidence of his willingness to fight on by waiting for his superiors in Vichy to order the surrender. But he quickly acquiesced when Pétain, on September 2, 1940, three days after the conclusion of the Franco-Japanese treaty with which Vichy recognized the "pre-eminent position of Japan in the Far East" and agreed to accord Japan "certain military facilities in Tongking for the liquidation of the China incident," signed the order to negotiate the terms for Japan's entry into Indochina.

The agreement concluded with General Nishihara in Hanoi on September 22 permitted Japan to station 6,000 men north of the Red River, and not more than 25,000 in the whole of Indochina. Haiphong was to be the port of entry for the Japanese Army, which was also allowed the use of Tongking's three major airports.

Although the Japanese had achieved their immediate aim, they decided that in order to clear the way for future negotiations they had to teach the French a lesson. On September 22, the Japanese Army in southern China, allegedly ignorant of the agreement reached that same day, crossed the border into Tongking and attacked Dong Dang and Langson. Despite strong French resistance, Dong Dang fell within twenty-four hours; Langson surrendered on September 24. The French were taken prisoner by the Japanese, who had also landed marines at a number of shore points and dropped bombs on Haiphong.

The French, fearing that the Japanese might look for an excuse to occupy all of Tongking, ordered an end to all resistance. But the Japanese, fully satisfied with the military and political results of their attack, called it an unfortunate error, released all prisoners, and eventually allowed the French to resume control of the territories they had been unable to defend.[3]

Once the Japanese had proved that the only choice open to the French was between voluntary or forced surrender, they sought French cooperation for their planned seizure of Indochina's resources. They did their best to strengthen Decoux's illusion that his government was free. Their patient diplomacy distracted from the hard fact that the French were free to govern Indochina only because, and as long as, they served the interests of Japan.

Events early in 1941, however, made it difficult for the French to maintain the illusion that Indochina was still theirs. The Japanese, who needed Thai cooperation for their planned drive toward Singapore and Burma, forced France to cede to Thailand three Cambodian provinces and Laotian lands on the right bank of the Mekong River which Thailand had been unable to wrest from the French by force. "From the moment that agreement was signed in Tokyo," wrote Bernard Fall, "it was obvious that French sovereignty over Indochina had become a farce."[4]

Two days earlier, on May 6, 1941, the first of a series of Franco-Japanese commercial treaties revealed what Japan expected to get out of Indochina, and it also showed to what extent Indochina was now economically at the mercy of Japan. All the rice, corn, coal, rubber, and minerals available for export had to go to Japan or to the Japanese forces stationed in Indochina. Indochina's export quota to Japan was set at 80 per cent of total exports; Japan was granted most-favored-nation status and Japanese firms in Indochina were put on equal footing with the French. By agreement of November 9, 1941, all Indochinese enterprises were ordered to work for the Japanese, who now reaped whatever economic benefits the prewar efforts under Mandel and Brevié had produced.

Indochina, in return for letting Japan have the bulk of her products, was to receive from Japan the goods which she was no longer able to obtain from France or any other country. But up to 1943, only meager quantities of the promised machines, tools, and particularly textiles were received. Thereafter, Japan, by now needing everything she had herself, also was prevented by Allied air attacks from shipping goods to Indochina. The exchange of goods between Indochina and Japan thus became and remained a one-way transaction. Indochina's financial plight brought on an inflation, which, together with the scarcity of food supplies and other essential goods, led to a steady decline in the living standard of the masses. While the Japanese troops paid only 25 cents for a kilo of rice, the black-market price rose to 1 piaster. When lack of shipping left the Japanese without gasoline, grain was distilled to produce fuel. When they ran out of textile fibers, rice fields were planted with jute, cotton, and ramie. And when bombings disrupted the railroad and ocean transport between north and south Vietnam, and coal from Tongking could no longer reach Cochinchina, grain was also used to produce fuel for the southern power stations.

But the worst was yet to come. In 1944–45, the north had exceptionally poor harvests; lack of transport facilities for rice from the south combined with a lack of real concern for the people led to one of the greatest catastrophes in modern Vietnamese history. Between 1.5 and 2 million people died of starvation in Tongking in 1945.

Hitler's invasion of Russia had increased Japan's freedom of action and inclination to use force. The treaty Vichy signed with Tokyo on July 29, 1941, in fact integrated Indochina into the Japanese military system. Japanese troops, under the pretext of the need for a "common defense," were stationed throughout the country, and the Japanese were allowed the use of all airports as well as of the Cam Ranh and Saigon naval bases. Cochinchina had become an advanced base for the attack on Singapore.

On the night of the attack on Pearl Harbor, the Japanese surrounded the French garrisons and handed Decoux another ultimatum, threatening that the French troops would be disarmed and imprisoned, and French "sovereignty" over Indochina abolished unless Decoux assured the continuance of French cooperation. Decoux had no choice but to yield, and Indochina became part of the "Greater East Asia Co-Prosperity Sphere," which the Japanese were just beginning to transform from slogan into reality.

As far as the outcome of the war was concerned, the resources of Indochina were hardly decisive; but there can be no doubt that Franco-Japanese collaboration in Indochina made it easier for the Japanese to arrive at the gates of India and Australia within the next five months.

3

One of the consequences of Japanese intervention was a brief resurgence of Vietnamese nationalist hopes. The Japanese had encouraged the nationalist movement between 1900 and 1907, and thirty years later, Japanese interest in Vietnamese nationalism reawakened. Prince Cuong De was back in Japan, and a number of people fed his hopes that he might possibly return to Vietnam at the head of a Japanese-sponsored national government. It was only natural that his political expectations and those of his followers should grow with the Japanese advance toward Vietnam. On September 24, 1940, nationalists, encouraged and probably armed by Japan, started an insurrection from a base in the mountainous region of Cai Kinh. Other nationalists, particularly the Communists, joined the rebellion, yet despite temporary success the insurrection ultimately failed.

French repressive measures were unusually cruel. Still, it took the French Army almost three months until the last guerrilla group, led by an old Communist, Trang Trung Lap, was wiped out. Lap was executed on December 26, 1940. The Japanese, who had freed the captured French troops on October 5, watched the slaughter of the men whose rebellion they had encouraged.

Decoux, so powerless in his dealings with the Japanese, had no trouble at all in playing the strong man vis-à-vis the Vietnamese. In November, 1940, he suspended all elected bodies in the five Indochinese states and replaced them with one "Federal Council," describing the task of this handpicked body as giving "enlightened advice to the leader who commands."

Another measure Decoux regarded as a concession to the native populations was the so-called "federalization" of the Indochinese governments. This "federalization," far from increasing the authority of local officials, became in practice a stricter centralization, with closer French control over everything except the hollow pomp of royal ceremonials. Decoux, who liked to think of himself as a man of political ideas, also conceived the abstruse notion of an "Indochinese mystique," a sort of local patriotism that was somehow never to be infected by the poison of nationalism. This mystique, which he took as seriously as he did his "federalization," proposed to mix pride in Indochina with gratitude for being part of France, a suggestion which to the peasants meant absolutely nothing and which the educated and sophisticated could greet only with sneers.

Indeed, no matter what Decoux tried to do, he could not gain the gratitude of the Indochinese. If he built roads, bridges, and hydraulic works, the Vietnamese complained that they had to pay for them directly with taxes and indirectly through the growing inflation, the result largely of Decoux's works. If he insisted that Vietnamese be promoted into higher administrative positions and paid the same rates as the French, the nationalists pointed out that he was unable to get French replacements for Frenchmen who had retired or died. Even the fact that more schools were opened under Decoux than under any of his predecessors failed to win nationalist approval.

The Vietnamese found little reason for gratitude, even when, spurred by necessity—and with poor results—local industries began to be promoted. Moreover, what was accomplished industrially was of benefit mainly to the Japanese.

Although the chief reason for Vietnamese discontent was Decoux's failure to assuage their misery, it was due also to his singularly inept native policy, a policy based on the assumption that nonpolitical concessions could reconcile the Vietnamese to his authoritarian regime. Decoux's self-deception was truly pathetic. Not only did he believe the Vietnamese to be content, but years later he still maintained that both the masses and the elite admired and even loved France.

The Decoux regime did not create the spirit of revolt that permeated the youth and the educated of Vietnam. That spirit, many decades old, merely ripened under him into the determination to free the country. Even had he foreseen the coming revolution, he could not have forestalled it. Foresight and determination no longer counted against the vehement social forces created by more than half a century of political sins.

Indeed, much of what Decoux did to appease the Indochinese people was done either in fear of or in answer to steps taken by the Japanese. Japan's toleration of nominal French sovereignty over Indochina did not deter her from doing everything possible to undermine French control over the population. One of these methods was a broad antiwhite, racist, Pan-Asian propaganda campaign directed by an information bureau attached to the Japanese diplomatic mission. This bureau merely continued more openly the work begun by the Japanese long before they moved into Vietnam. This discreet espionage bureau was headed by a businessman by the name of Matusita, whom the French had expelled in 1938.[5]

Among the people with whom Matusita had had close contacts before his expulsion were the leaders of the so-called Cao Dai. The Cao Dai, initially a rather singular religious sect, had acquired a mass following as well as political leanings that brought it into conflict with the colonial regime.

4

As a religion, the Cao Dai ranks as one of the most curious manifestations of man's hope to find an answer to the riddle of life. Caodaism is an amalgam of the traditional religious currents in Vietnam—Buddhism, Taoism, Confucianism, and a still widespread belief in spirits—and it combines these creeds with Christianity, Western philosophy, and a firm adherence to modern spiritualism. Table-rapping was, in fact, the means through which the Supreme Being of Caodaism revealed himself to man. The first man chosen to receive these revelations was an official by the name of Ngo Van Chieu, a naïve, inoffensive visionary who dreamily passed his days on an island in the Gulf of Siam communing with spirits, one of which called itself Cao Dai. This was in 1919. Later, when Ngo Van Chieu moved to Saigon, he spread his message throughout a wide circle of Vietnamese officials, who undoubtedly concerned themselves with the world of the spirits largely because concern for the world of the living was likely to get them into trouble.

Among these men was one Le Van Trung, a former government official who had become a colonial councilor after a series of bold business ventures. He recognized that Ngo Van Chieu's revelations might form the basis of a religious mass movement in Cochinchina, and in 1925, he began to organize such a movement. Ngo Van Chieu, the prophet of the new religion, was shunted aside. In November, 1926, in a series of sensational sessions, Cao Dai revealed himself not only as the incarnation of Buddha and Jesus, but also as an inspired meddler in the affairs of the new church. He chose Le Van Trung as Supreme Chief of Caodaism, and Tay Ninh as its capital. Its hierarchy was modeled after that of the Catholic Church, and its gospel was spread over most of western Cochinchina. By 1932, the new church counted 128 chapels, with 100,000 adherents; by 1938, the Caodaists claimed 300,000 followers; by 1954, the number had risen to 1.5 million. Originally restricted to government officials, landowners, and intellectuals, Caodaism became a real mass movement when the sect took root among the peasantry north and west of Saigon.

In 1935, Le Van Trung was succeeded by Pham Cong Tac. The new "pope," a former customs official, did not have Le Van Trung's interest in business deals. His passion was political power. Under him, Caodaism received its nationalist coloration. Not only did it satisfy an existing religious need, it had also begun to play the role of a substitute political party. The French soon began to treat it as such, restricting the sect to Cochinchina and outlawing it in Annam and Tongking. But the duel between Caodaism and the colonial regime began in earnest only after the outbreak of the war. Between 1939 and 1945, the French aim was to silence the Caodaists, whose mediums began to receive messages from spirits that became more and more openly anti-French and pro-Japanese.

5

Caodaism, however, was not the only religious movement that caused the French headaches. In 1939, another sect arose, this one near the Cambodian frontier of western Cochinchina, in a village called Hoa Hao, which gave the movement its name. Its founder, Huynh Phu So, the sickly son of a fairly prosperous peasant, was born in Hoa Hao in 1919. The new prophet, soon known throughout the south both as the "crazy bonze" and the "living Buddha," received his inspiration after some training by a hermit who was both a mystic and a healer.

Huynh Phu So's reform Buddhism, like the tenets of many religious innovators, was designed to appeal primarily to the oppressed and poor. He did not attempt to impress the masses with complex doctrines and spectacular ceremonies but tried to win over followers by the simplicity of his teachings. In contrast to Caodaism, the new religion had no temples and no ecclesiastical hierarchy. Its followers were said to be in direct communion with the Almighty, to whom they could appeal anywhere and any time. Thus the Hoa Hao, although a genuine and originally fervent religious movement, could not be called a church.

For the poor peasants of western Cochinchina, who responded immediately and in vast numbers to Huynh Phu So, the young prophet obviously satisfied more than purely religious longings. The young man with the mysterious gifts had come from their own ranks, was of their own flesh and blood. He knew them well, their moral and material needs; and because he was able to see that neither could be fully satisfied under existing conditions, the religious prophet became an apostle of nationalism, the saintly preacher a worldly agitator against colonialism.

In the spring of 1940, Huynh Phu So launched a major campaign throughout western Cochinchina. He made tens of thousands of converts. His prestige grew immensely as one after another of his early prophecies—the outbreak of the war, the fall of France, the coming of the Japanese—came true. The movement now also began to attract men such as Le Cong Bo, a rich landowner, who regarded it as a possible springboard for a political career, and the two men who later became the chief commanders of the Hoa Hao military forces, Tran Van Soai and Lam Thanh Nguyen, the latter one of the many converts who claimed that Huynh Phu So had healed him.

When, by the summer of 1940, Huynh Phu So's mass gatherings threatened to turn into anti-French demonstrations, Decoux decided that it was time to act. In August, Huynh Phu So was put into a psychiatric hospital under the not completely implausible assumption that he was mentally unbalanced. There the prophet soon succeeded in converting his psychiatrist. Released in May, 1941, he was forcibly confined at Bac Lieu, a town near the coast in the far south. Although a considerable distance from the sites of great Hoa Hao strength, Bac Lieu soon became "a center of pilgrimage from which [So] spread messages of religious but also of anti-French inspiration."[6] To his followers, Huynh Phu So had now become a political martyr as well. This not only made him an even more effective apostle, but it also tied his religious movement still more firmly to the national cause.

All of this was well known to the Japanese espionage and propaganda services, and in particular to Matusita, who had resumed his contacts with the Cao Dai when he returned to Saigon in 1941. Although Matusita was unable to stop the deportation of the Caodaist leadership and the internment of Huynh Phu So, he was by no means idle.

The anti-French intrigues of the Japanese were broadened considerably through the work of the Kempeitai, the Japanese political police. The Kempeitai moved into Vietnam in December, 1941, and lent effective support to efforts of the Japanese agents, particularly those of Matusita, to rally prominent Vietnamese in the south for anti-French action. In 1942, Matusita approached Tran Van An, a former leader of the Constitutionalist Party, who had just been released from a concentration camp, and persuaded him to form a clandestine pro-Japanese political group, which established itself in the fall of 1942 as the Cochinchinese branch of Prince Cuong De's Phuc Quoc (League for the Restoration of Vietnam). Another branch was organized in Tongking, where at the same time, apparently also with Japanese encouragement, the Dai Viet Cach Manh (Revolutionary Party of Vietnam) and the Dai Viet Quoc Dan (Nationalist Party of Vietnam) started their checkered political careers. Other well-known intellectuals and officials, on the whole of conservative inclination, were contacted, among them Tran Trong Kim and Ngo Dinh Diem. These men were told that the day when their services would be needed by a Japanese-supported government of Vietnam was not far off.

Vehement French protests in 1943 induced the Japanese diplomats to put a temporary halt to these schemes. But when the Kempeitai learned of impending arrests or deportation of nationalists who had shown a willingness to collaborate with them, they protected them against the French.

This was only one phase in the struggle between Sûreté and Kempeitai. Matusita, knowing that his plans required leaders who enjoyed mass support, had been concentrating his efforts on bringing the Cao Dai and Hoa Hao into the pro-Japanese camp. The deportation of the Caodaist leadership was a blow, and he was determined to prevent the Hoa Hao from suffering a similar fate. Matusita learned of a French plan to bring Huynh Phu So to Laos. On October 12, 1942, a few days before his planned transfer, the Kempeitai arranged to have him kidnaped and brought into Japanese custody to Saigon. There he lived during the next few years protected by the Kempeitai; the Japanese High Command's answer to French demands for extradition was that he was being held as a "Chinese spy." The next item on Matusita's agenda was to find a competent leader for the decapitated Cao Dai. He chose one Tran Quang Vinh, the former head of the Cao Dai mission in Phnom Penh, the capital of Cambodia, where the Cao Dai had also taken root. Protected by the Kempeitai, Vinh succeeded in February, 1943, in rebuilding the Cao Dai leadership at Tay Ninh.

In 1944, a struggle between Tokyo and the Japanese missions in Indochina over what policy to pursue gave the colonial regime a breathing spell which the French exploited to track down leaders and agents both of the Phuc Quoc in the south and the Dai Viet in the north. The chief leader of the Dai Viet, Nguyen Tuong Tam, succeeded in fleeing to China, where he went over to the VNQDD. Proof that Japanese diplomacy asserted itself against the military was that these nationalists received little Japanese help. But the Kempeitai secretly pursued their cause in the provinces, where they supplied the Cao Dai with arms.

Orders to set up armed units were issued also by the Hoa Hao. Its ties to the Japanese were not nearly so close as those of the Cao Dai, and ever since then relations between the two sects were marked by competition rather than cooperation. The need for armed bands confronted the Hoa Hao with an unwelcome necessity. Its continued temporal existence required a drastic dilution of its lofty principles. The armed bands brought into its ranks men attracted more by the prospects of pillage than by idealistic motives.

Thus, when the crucial year 1945 rolled around, the forces of Vietnamese nationalism inside the country did not offer a promising or attractive picture. The purely political organizations were largely destroyed, their leaders exiled or imprisoned. Clearly, whatever their power, the sects, by their very nature as well as by their association with the Japanese, were little qualified to speak and act in the name of a people for which the great hour of liberation was about to strike, after more than eighty years of foreign rule.

Unless better-qualified leaders were maturing elsewhere, the future national revolution would have to run its course blindly, and thus very likely be captured by forces alien to its aspirations.

6

Other forces were indeed busily preparing themselves inside the country and in China: the divided anti-Communist nationalists, as well as the tightly organized Indochinese Communist Party.

The nationalist movement was in sad disarray, with at least nine groups vying for leadership, the three most important being the old Nationalist Party of Tongking, the Viet Nam Phuc Quoc, and the Dai Viet.

As the war ran its course it became increasingly clear that Vietnam's future would be determined not by the Japanese but by the victorious Allies, with China in the best position to intervene in Vietnam. The Japanese could oust the French before the war ended, but unless Vietnamese independence became an agreed upon Allied aim, the French would return once Japan was defeated. Decisive action at this historical juncture could be expected only from China, the traditional enemy of French penetration into Vietnam. China's long-standing habit of selling out Vietnam was not forgotten, but her relative strength once the war ended might, it was thought, prevent her from making a deal with the French.

These considerations received additional weight from an awareness shared by all and admitted by none—namely, that the Communists were the only ones with an organized, active following inside the country. The fact that the anti-Communist groups had no organization in the country does not however mean that they had no followers. But they were inactive and out of touch with their exiled leaders. Moreover, they lacked a concrete political program. The Communists were the only ones with a doctrine and an answer to everything, from tactics to program.

The exiled nationalists in China responded to this danger by assuring themselves of Chinese help at the crucial moment. They had every reason to fear that without such help they would find it difficult to keep the Communists from assuming the leadership of the national revolution and keep them from turning Vietnam into a Communist state.

These early nationalist concerns were justified by the Communists' growing organizational strength in the country and by their ability to win support from abroad.

In May, 1941, the Central Committee of the Party issued a call for insurrection, but now for the first time not as spokesmen of the Party but in the name of the so-called Vietminh (Vietnam Independence League). The order to organize a supraparty alliance under Communist control (in line with the Moscow popular-front strategy) was carried to the Vietnamese Communists by Ho Chi Minh, who, after a seven-year absence, left Moscow early in 1941 for the Sino-Vietnamese border. What must be regarded as the first official announcement of the formation of the Vietminh came in September, 1941.[7] The program called for the ousting of the French and Japanese Fascists, the establishment of an independent Vietnam, the unity of all antifascist forces, and the creation of a democratic Vietnamese republic. Any group or individual subscribing to this seemingly simple program could join. But the exiled nationalists were wise enough to recognize the Vietminh as a Communist trap. True, some, believing they could not be hoodwinked, joined, but most nationalist leaders not only stayed away but fought the Vietminh from its very inception. Its leadership, though sporting a few non-Communists, was firmly in Communist hands, and Ho Chi Minh was its secretary general.

What was the purpose of the Vietminh? It was designed to

attract not the leaders but their followers, to maneuver the anti-Communists politically until they were forced to cooperate with the Party.

Because the Vietminh was based on a lie—namely that it was a multiparty, not a Communist organization—Vietnamese nationalists victimized by various Communist schemes have come to believe that in order to be successful it is necessary to be as ruthless, deceitful, and immoral as the Communists. Moralists may wish to despise the Communists, but they, having been successful, are also admired.

Such misguided admiration has been bestowed by friend and foe alike on Ho Chi Minh. Although probably a great deal more intelligent than the average Communist leader, he is not the genius that legend has made of him. He believes himself to be honest, and he undoubtedly was convinced that the struggle for independence would gain if nationalist groups worked closely together, so much so that he believed himself entirely justified in forcing all reluctant elements into a united front.

The difference between him and most other nationalist leaders was that he, through a combination of superior ability, personality, and circumstances, succeeded where all others had failed. The nationalists failed, although they were no less determined to outplay their Communist rivals and although they had the fullest support of the Chinese under Chiang Kai-shek, who had long ago broken with the Communists. The Chinese would have liked the Vietnamese to unite in a common front dominated by pro-Chinese, anti-Communist parties. The Kuomintang consequently rejected all Vietminh proposals to supply them with intelligence about the Japanese in Vietnam and to build up, with Chinese aid, a local military force for action against the Japanese. Instead, the Chinese at the end of 1941 arrested Ho Chi Minh and kept him in prison for thirteen months. They wanted that which the Vietminh was offering, but not at the price demanded.

When none of the pro-Chinese nationalists produced an espionage, propaganda, and sabotage organization against the Japanese and French in Vietnam, the Chinese decided to call a congress at Liuchow from October 4–16, 1942, to which every Vietnamese organization in southern China was invited. On October 10, a united front of all Vietnamese organizations in exile was an-

nounced. It called itself the Viet Nam Cach Minh Dong Minh
Hoi, or Vietnam Revolutionary League. The Vietminh had to be
content with being just another one of the League's ten members.
An old Vietnamese nationalist, Nguyen Hai Than, was made its
head and given a monthly allowance of 100,000 Chinese dollars.

The Chinese had hoped that the formation of the Dong Minh
Hoi would enable them to exploit the underground contacts of
the Communists in Vietnam. Before long they realized that they
had failed. The Communists never put their organization at the
disposal of the Dong Minh Hoi, whose anti-Communist leaders
remained as disputatious and organizationally incompetent as
ever. The Chinese soon realized that only the Vietminh could
give them what they had hoped to get through the Dong Minh
Hoi. When Ho Chi Minh, at the end of 1942, informed the
Chinese that he was willing to mobilize the Vietminh for cooperation with the Chinese Army, he was released from prison and
made head of the Dong Minh Hoi. Thus Ho Chi Minh almost
overnight became the recipient of the 100,000 dollars with which
the Chinese tried to buy the loyalty of the Vietnamese exiles.
It was then that the man who had entered prison as Nguyen Ai
Quoc took the name Ho Chi Minh.

7

On the whole, Communist and Vietminh activity between 1941
and 1945 had no spectacular results. Despite frequent appeals to
the people to rise up, the Communists carefully avoided risking
their own organization in local actions. Their chief aim was to
command a politically organized following when the proper moment arrived.

With Hitler's invasion of Russia, Communist propaganda
sought above all to create the impression that the cause of the
Vietminh was more or less identical with the cause of the Allies
and put forth the claim that the Vietminh was created to unite
all patriots for the liberation of their country. Another claim,
namely that the Vietminh had Allied support, was not entirely
fictitious, thanks to Chinese help through the Dong Minh Hoi,

and later also because of the contacts established between the Vietminh and officers of the U.S. Office of Strategic Services (OSS) in southern China. Various French and other sources assert that the Vietminh received not only arms but also financial help from the OSS, and thus moral and political support. After its first guerrilla group had begun to operate, the value of the Vietminh for the Chinese and the OSS increased considerably. "Thus, it was the Viet Minh that created the first anti-Japanese guerrilla forces in Viet Nam, that rescued American flyers shot down in Indochina, that provided intelligence to the Allies, that spread its propaganda among the civilian population, and that received all the credit for anti-Japanese activities during the war."[8]

The French, both the Gaullists in India and China as well as those in Vietnam who after the liberation of France had begun to embrace the Allied cause, rejected all Vietminh offers of cooperation. They were not even moved when the Communists proclaimed in March, 1945, that the Japanese had become "the only enemy of the Vietnamese revolution."[9] It is unlikely that Ho Chi Minh at this stage of the game wanted Franco-Vietnamese cooperation, which might have blurred the image the Vietminh wanted to present to the people. No matter how much Ho Chi Minh emphasized for Allied consumption that his primary aim was to fight the Japanese, at home he wanted the Vietminh to be regarded as the leading anticolonial force.

Who in Vietnam would dare to oppose a program of national independence, belittle an organization enjoying international recognition, or refuse to support such dedicated men? Even if the anti-Communists had been able to spread their views in Vietnam they would not have succeeded in destroying the reputation the Vietminh enjoyed at the end of the war.

But the Communists knew that popularity in itself was no guarantee of success. They needed a military force not only to crush the enemies of the revolution, but also to resist any attempt to undo it. The decision to create such a force was reached by the Communists immediately after the founding of the Vietminh.

They began to recruit their first native military force along the Chinese border in northern Tongking. This rough, mountainous region, which afforded comparatively easy access to agents and arms from China and offered relative safety from the French in Hanoi, was inhabited largely by ethnic minorities (Tho, Meo, Man), among whom Vietminh propaganda with its bold promise of local political autonomy was highly successful.

The man whom Ho Chi Minh put in charge of propaganda and guerrilla organization in these provinces was a young professor by the name of Vo Nguyen Giap, a veteran revolutionary and former Hanoi teacher. Giap managed to escape to China at the outbreak of the war when the Sûreté began to round up known or suspected Communists. There he studied strategy, and in particular Chinese Communist guerrilla tactics.

Within two years, Giap built up a tight organization. Though still poorly armed, his self-defense and guerrilla groups were ably led by ethnic minority chiefs and by Communist-trained Vietnamese. Toward the end of 1943, the Vietminh, openly supported by the majority of the population, controlled larger parts of the Thai Nguyen and Bac Kan provinces than the French administration. On December 22, 1944, Giap formed the first section of the "Armed Propaganda Brigade for the Liberation of Vietnam." Before the end of the war, the Vietminh was able to supply its men with arms from abandoned French Army depots, and even managed to acquire arms from Japanese defeatists. By June, 1945, six provinces between the Chinese border and Hanoi were firmly in Vietminh hands. But not until August 13, two days after Japan's offer to capitulate, did Ho Chi Minh issue his final order for a general insurrection, which, in the absence of all opposition, celebrated its first great victory on August 19 in Hanoi.

8

The Vietnam of August, 1945, was completely unlike the Vietnam over which Decoux had ruled for almost five years. Indochina was no longer French, and Decoux no longer its master. But although it was nominally independent, it was in fact ruled by the Japanese.

The checking of the Japanese advance in Southeast Asia demonstrated the material superiority of the United States. Allied progress in Europe was even more rapid once the tide had begun to turn. When the Stars and Stripes were planted on Iwo Jima in March, 1945, Allied troops had already been fighting on German soil for some months.

These events made a deep impression on the French in Indochina. In 1942, most Frenchmen in Indochina were still warmly pro-Vichy and fiercely anti-de Gaulle. A Free French movement initiated by a planter named Mario Bocquet was unable to establish functioning contacts with pro-Allied French services in China. But by the fall of 1944, after de Gaulle had moved from Algiers to Paris and MacArthur had embarked on the reconquest of the Philippines, Decoux found little support for his policy of continued collaboration with the Japanese. Not only were pro-Allied sentiments expressed openly, but an increasing number of Frenchmen began to prepare for action against Japan.

General Mordant, the head of the Indochina French Forces since late in 1940, became converted to Gaullism soon after North Africa was in Allied hands. When the Allied Southeast Asia Command at Kandy, Ceylon, established a special unit for "subversive operations" in Japanese-occupied territories, Major Langlade's proposal that French officers take charge of all operations in Indochina was accepted. Langlade, the agent of the Free French, was stationed in Calcutta. He began to cooperate closely with General Mordant and other military leaders in Indochina. With de Gaulle's approval, an "action service" was founded to prepare sabotage and guerrilla operations against the Japanese. But Langlade and his associates did not succeed in organizing an intelligence service for the Allies. For this, the Chinese, and the Americans operating in China, had to rely on their own contacts and, increasingly, on those of the Vietminh.

Information obtained through these contacts was not made available to the French. The French in Indochina were not considered trustworthy as yet, and at this point a latent conflict between Chinese, U.S., and Free French policies in regard to Indochina developed into open friction. Chiang Kai-shek did not see eye to eye with de Gaulle, to whom the future of Indochina meant a continued French presence. For the Chinese, the end of the war meant the end of French rule in Vietnam. Most Americans felt that a continuation of the colonial regime in Indochina conflicted with the aims for which the war was being fought; President Roosevelt himself had repeatedly stated that the French ought to withdraw from Indochina. The French, on the other hand, maintained that the Americans, ignorant of conditions in Indochina, were being used by the Vietminh.

The group around de Gaulle and the majority of Frenchmen in Indochina favored entering the war on the side of the Allies by leading the army in Indochina against the Japanese. In preparation for this stroke, Major Langlade parachuted into Vietnam on June 6, 1944, to confer with General Mordant and General Aymé, who soon afterward replaced Mordant as commander in chief; on September 12, de Gaulle, back in Paris, made Mordant Delegate General of the French Government to Indochina. Paris also created an Action Committee for the Liberation of Indochina, which was presided over by the Minister of Colonies, René Pleven. RAF pilots began to parachute arms, ammunitions, and French agents into Vietnam. The only real problem was to act at the right moment, neither too early nor too late.

9

The Japanese, who had no trouble finding out what the French were planning, began to take precautions. They sent a new division into Tongking, thereby raising the number of their troops to 60,000. The army under the command of General Trushihashi asked Tokyo for permission to take measures to forestall a French attack. But Tokyo, in the face of approaching defeat, began to weigh its steps with extreme care, in the hope of avoiding drastic action in Indochina. But when the French decided to protect their troops by taking them out of the cities, and even started to build defensive positions outside Saigon, the diplomats gave in to the urgent demands of the military in Indochina. On March 9, 1945, at 7 P.M., Ambassador Matsumoto handed Decoux an ultimatum demanding that the French Army be placed under Japanese command. Not having received an answer an hour later, the Japanese correctly assumed that the French had decided to reject the ultimatum. Action followed at once. Within less than twenty-four hours, most French units were disarmed and interned. French rule in Indochina had come to an end.

One of the immediate effects of the coup was the onset of a period of political humiliation for the French in Indochina for which nothing had prepared them. Having lost control of their fate, the French also lost the ability to understand it. The most important change in the lives of the French, particularly the Army, was that from oppressor to oppressed, from victor to vanquished. The garrison at Langson was completely wiped out, as were the troops at Dong Dang.

The fate of the civilians, although not quite so hard, was nonetheless not an. easy one. Almost all officials were dismissed from their posts; the Sûreté was dissolved; about 750 persons were arrested between March 10 and the end of the war, and of these, 400 died or were killed in prisons the French themselves had built.

Although the Japanese incited the population against the French, the Vietnamese on the whole behaved extremely well toward their former rulers. But the French, for so long the masters of Vietnam, did suffer in many ways. Yet this reversal relieved them of one burden: collaboration with the Japanese. Thus for many Frenchmen, the coup of March 9 was a sort of moral liberation.

The duty of serving Japan now shifted unto the shoulders of the native elite, in exchange for liberation from French rule. Vietnam could celebrate national independence on March 10. This at least was what the Japanese Ambassador came to tell Emperor Bao Dai on that day. Independent Vietnam was, of course, expected to collaborate with the Japanese within the Greater East Asia Co-Prosperity Sphere.

Bao Dai had no illusions about his country's Japanese-sponsored independence, but he saw no way of refusing collaboration. Whatever he did do was done under pressure. Bao Dai allegedly hoped that the Americans would soon land in Vietnam and take the Japanese off his people's back.

Once the Japanese decided to disarm the French, Franco-Japanese collaboration became impossible. The ousting of the French-led government forced the Japanese to turn to the Vietnamese. The administration and economy had to be kept going. But the new administration needed a government different from that which had existed under the French administration, one capable of strengthening the image of an independent Vietnam, a government composed of eminent but conservative nationalists. This should have been Prince Cuong De's moment in history. But the Japanese did not want a man whose name had been linked with revolutionary nationalism for almost half a century. Tokyo therefore advised its military leaders to retain Bao Dai and to give him a government that would serve Japan's immediate needs.

There was one man in Vietnam whose reputation as a stout nationalist was not tainted by a propensity toward radical reform: Ngo Dinh Diem. Diem, who had a score to settle with the French, agreed to head a government that, although dependent on Japan, would be able to work toward independence. He accepted the Japanese demand that Vietnam's foreign policy follow that of Thailand, namely close collaboration with the Japanese. By temporarily working with the Japanese, he no doubt planned to create a strong native administration before the French attempted to reconquer Vietnam. For a few weeks, Ngo Dinh Diem and the Japanese cooperated closely in preparing such a regime. But this government was never formed. At the last moment, the Japanese probably recognized that Diem would be too difficult to handle. In any case, Bao Dai's telegram appointing him as head of government was never delivered. It remained in the hands of the Japanese, who handled all postal and telegraphic communications.[10] What the Japanese wanted, of course, was not so much a pro-Japanese as an easily removable man. They found him in Professor Tran Trong Kim, historian, Freemason, conservative nationalist, and protégé of the Japanese ever since his persecution by the Decoux regime. His government was formed on April 17, 1945.

Kim lacked both political understanding and determination, but at this point in history no one could have succeeded. His government was "doomed in advance"; it knew that it was, yet it nonetheless tackled "its difficult and thankless task with ardor."[11] It was allowed to function only within narrow limits. Allied bombing had destroyed the railroads and halted most shipping. Road traffic was limited to Japanese military vehicles. Even the transmission of official messages depended on the good will of the Japanese. The government had no money. Its orders rarely reached the lower administrative levels, and its many reform projects were never put into effect. Kim and his colleagues were denied that freedom of action which would have demonstrated to the world that the country was truly independent.

On August 7, 1945, after four months of futility, and just one week before the Allied victory over Japan, the Kim government resigned.

10

The month of August, 1945, at last brought the revolution for which two generations of Vietnamese nationalists had fought, suffered, and died. Yet although in preparation since the turn of the century, this revolution was in the end made and won by a determined minority: the Communists at the head of the Vietminh.

In March, 1944, the Chinese had made one more attempt to mobilize Vietminh strength for an all-embracing nationalist coalition. They had convened another congress at Liuchow, at which a republican government for Vietnam consisting of all parties and groups in exile, the Vietminh included, was appointed. The Vietminh, although it had only one member in this national government, again profited. As none of the other groups was able to contradict the Vietminh, the Communists could now claim to represent not only the Vietminh and the Dong Minh Hoi, but also to speak in the name of a government-in-exile supported by all nationalist groups, a claim of enormous help in rallying non-Communist nationalists to the Vietminh.

In October, 1944, Ho Chi Minh moved his headquarters from China into the province of Thai Nguyen. By March, 1945, Vietminh strength in northern Tongking had reached a point at which French military leaders like General Sabattier began to weigh the possibility of using the Vietminh guerrillas as temporary allies against the Japanese. The Vietminh in Tongking was also strengthened by the Vietnamese Communists exiled in Madagascar, who were parachuted into guerrilla-held territory by the RAF under the assumption that this would add to the problems of the Japanese. At the beginning of August, the Vietminh stood at the height of its prerevolutionary strength.

On August 10, Japan capitulated. By then an urgent call for a "national" meeting had gone out, and on August 13, after some delay "due to transportation difficulties," the Indochinese Communist Party met in the "free zone" in Tongking for a three-day "national" conference.[12] On the very first evening the decision was reached for general insurrection and a call for immediate action. The Central Committee of the Communist Party and the General Committee of the Vietminh agreed on the need for an organization through which the country's military strength could be rallied. The execution was left to the Vietminh. On August 16, a "People's Congress" led by Ho Chi Minh himself brought sixty delegates of "all nationalities" (meaning the inclusion of minorities' representatives) and of varying political tendencies to the village of Tan Trao in the hilly province of Tuyen Quang, north of Hanoi. The Congress created the "National Liberation Committee of Vietnam," which was to form the nucleus of a provisional government, and it also transformed the Vietminh guerrillas into an "Army of Liberation." That same day, the first detachments of Vietminh guerrillas entered Hanoi.

Suddenly Vietminh leaflets appeared everywhere in the country. Mass demonstrations dominated by Vietminh speakers, posters, and slogans took place. The Vietminh boldly presented itself as the united front of all nationalists and patriots and impudently claimed that it was nothing less than the Vietnamese arm of the victorious Allied forces. The August revolution was in motion. It was a patriotic event whose irresistible drive derived from the double realization that the war had ended and that national liberation had become a possibility.

Even sober men were swept off their feet during these exhilarating days. On August 18, the imperial delegate, the emperor's representative in Tongking, resigned in favor of a citizens' committee led by the Vietminh. The next day, Vietminh military units occupied all important public buildings except the Japanese-guarded Bank of Indochina. In Hue, where the defunct Kim government had left a vacuum, Bao Dai declared his willingness to have Ho

Chi Minh form a new government, but popular sentiment expressed at a mass rally in Hanoi prevented this compromise with the old regime, though Ho Chi Minh probably would have accepted. Instead, Bao Dai was asked to resign. There is no more convincing testimony to the popular support the Vietminh enjoyed at that time than that Bao Dai gave up his throne on August 25 and expressed his support of a Vietminh regime.

His resignation was not so much an act of political generosity as an expression of his lack of interest in power. No doubt Bao Dai also regarded the Vietminh as a pro-Allied force. None of his later mistakes and irresponsible acts can quite wipe out the impression made by his explanation of his resignation. He would rather be a simple citizen of a free country, he said, than the ruler of one that was enslaved.[13]

How was it possible for the Vietminh to execute their plan in the face of strong military and police forces of the Japanese still stationed in Indochina? The Japanese, who were indeed the only ones in a position to prevent the Vietminh from taking power, remained ostensibly neutral. Thus it might be said that they made the victory of the Vietminh feasible.

Two weeks after V-J Day, the Vietminh revolution had triumphed north, center, and south. On August 29, Ho Chi Minh formed his first government. On September 2, he presented his government to the country, and before a rally of 500,000 assembled in Hanoi he proclaimed Vietnam's independence. Quoting from the Declaration of Independence and the Declaration of the French Revolution, he launched a bitter attack on French colonialism. He closed his speech with an appeal to the Allies to acknowledge the independence of Vietnam.

The greatest political hopes of the Vietnamese people seemed to have been fulfilled. The country was free and at last also united under a regime whose name held the most precious promise: Democratic Republic of Vietnam.

XI

The French Return
to Vietnam

1

THE WESTERN COLONIAL POWERS involved in the Pacific war held the conviction that the prewar order of Asia in which Europe had played such a dominant role had been stable and essentially sound. Very few Western statesmen shared the view of Asian nationalists that this order had had its day. True, its existence had been interrupted by the war, but the interested Western parties expected the old order to be re-established after the defeat of Japan.

No one believed this more strongly than the French of Indo-china. How could they have foreseen that the war would prepare Vietnam, Cambodia, and Laos for independence when they had not even recognized the need to grant these countries modest political reforms? Most of them really believed that colonialism was the best thing that had happened to the peoples of Asia, a blessing of which the contented masses should not be deprived by a few disgruntled and ambitious nationalist intellectuals.

To the leaders of Vietnamese nationalism this attitude came as no surprise. But that this position should also be taken by the new government of liberated France came as a shock. Although the French themselves had for years been engaged in a war of national liberation, they were unable to understand that liberation from foreign rule might be as important to the Indochinese as to themselves. Nor did they see that national freedom was bound to become the postwar aim of all colonial peoples. This blindness on the part of the Free French was only partly due to a desire to defend vested interests. It was the result mainly of a lack of political imagination.

After more than a year of study by a special commission, the French Government made an explicit statement about the future of Indochina within the French Community, as the colonial empire and France were henceforth euphemistically called. This was the so-called Declaration of March 24, 1945. Published exactly two weeks after the Japanese had put an end to French rule in Indochina and had allowed the Vietnamese to proclaim their independence, the March Declaration took no notice of either event. Independence was not even mentioned. In speaking of five Indochinese "states," the French made it clear that they intended to maintain the artificial division of Vietnam into Cochinchina, Annam, and Tongking. The five states, which included Cambodia and Laos (whose only tie with Vietnam was that of French rule), were to be given a federal government and even an assembly with the right to pass on the federal budget. But both assembly and government were to be "mixed," which meant they were to be composed of indigenous and French members, and the ministers were to be responsible only to the French governor general, who was to head the federation as in the past. The authors of the March Declaration revealed a truly amazing gift for being noncommittal about the governments of the five "states" in whose hands rested so much power. All they said about them was that they would be "perfected and reformed." It seemed as though Doumer's spirit had never died.

This declaration was indignantly rejected by all Vietnamese.

They believed that the impending collapse of Japan would reveal their country's independence to the world. The French, so it seemed to them, were preparing to destroy their independence just when it was about to become a reality.

Paris was completely unprepared for the possibility that Vietnam at the end of the war might in fact be controlled by the Vietnamese. This shutting out of reality was the chief reason that French preparations for a return to Indochina were largely misdirected. They were on the whole based on the conviction that the right of France to maintain herself in Indochina required merely that the French Army participate in the fight against Japan. That is why General de Gaulle was so delighted with the token resistance offered by the French after the coup of March 9, 1945. He had wanted French troops to fight "no matter how desperate their situation."[1] It apparently never occurred to him that the right of France to return had to be re-established above all in the eyes of the native population.

Faulty military and political preparations, the result of these misconceptions, ultimately led to the defeat of all French efforts and plans. The attempt to conduct a war of resistance against the Japanese similar to that waged in France against the German occupation ended in a fiasco, although it was led partly by men experienced in the French Resistance. These men paid heavily for "the error . . . in wanting to organize the Resistance in Indochina in the same manner as in France."[2] In France, they had the support of the population; in Indochina, they were surrounded by hostility.

No less wrongly inspired than the military were the political preparations for a French return to Indochina. They concerned themselves almost exclusively with removing the obstacles they suspected China and the United States were planning to erect. The future French role in Indochina was made dependent not on the elaboration of a native policy that took into account the people's longing for independence, but rather on the success of French diplomacy in Washington, London, and Chungking. It was soon to become clear that French diplomacy achieved what it had set out to do. As one vehement critic of U.S. policy in Asia put it: "With respect to Indochina, Roosevelt had once publicly intimated the possibility of a new status for that colony.

. . . But when it came down, in the wake of the war's end, to a strong Annamite rebellion against returning French power, the United States promptly concluded a credit arrangement with France for supply of vehicles and other 'relief' equipment to French authorities in Indochina. To the stunned Annamites this agreement came as a virtual American endorsement of the French reconquest."[3]

Due to the combination of military and political errors, the French never achieved complete control of Vietnam and eventually lost it entirely.

French preparations for an active role in the ousting of the Japanese from Indochina began as early as September, 1943. The two bases from which the planning for the reconquest of Indochina was conducted were Calcutta and Kunming. The only Frenchman who was fully aware of the extent to which Tongking was falling under Vietminh control and what a great political obstacle China might become for France's plans was Jean Sainteny, since spring, 1945, head of "Mission 5" in Kunming, the center of French intelligence in China. Sainteny did all he could to neutralize the Chinese, who, he feared, had imperialist designs on Tongking. He had become convinced that to gain control of Indochina it was not enough to oust the Japanese. An understanding with Vietnamese nationalist leaders had to be reached, who, Sainteny discovered, were firmly set on obtaining full independence for their country.

Torrential rains in July and early August, 1945, prevented Sainteny from meeting Ho Chi Minh before the August revolution. Had such a meeting taken place, it might have altered the course of Vietnamese history. There can be no doubt that in the course of such a meeting Sainteny would have learned that the Vietminh, if recognized as the leading political force in Vietnam, was willing to find a basis of cooperation with the French, even if this meant the postponement of independence.

It seems that Sainteny was indeed the only prominent Frenchman concerned with Indochina who understood that without a sound political program for regaining control of Vietnam, the best military preparations would fail to produce the expected result. He not only took the Vietminh seriously, but he also understood that the success of French plans required a political deal with the Chinese. He realized that without some French troops at Hanoi immediately after the Japanese surrender, the Vietminh could easily prevent the French from reassuming control of Tongking. Sainteny has said that 1,000 French soldiers in Hanoi could have prevented the Vietminh revolution.

Deeply worried by what he knew and foresaw, Sainteny rushed to Paris to impart some of his fears to the new rulers of France. The decision reached at the Potsdam Conference, of which he learned in Paris on July 26, confirmed his fears. The task of occupying Vietnam and disarming the Japanese was not given to the French but to the British and Chinese; the British were to move into southern Vietnam, the Chinese into the North. "The occupation of northern Indochina by the Chinese," Sainteny told Paris on August 13, "might be considered as the worst of all possible solutions."[4]

Seriously defective though the planning for the reconquest of Indochina was, Paris reaffirmed its determination to reconquer Indochina. On August 16, troops under the command of General Leclerc, a military hero of the European war, were ordered to proceed from France, Madagascar, and Calcutta to Vietnam. On August 17, Paris appointed Admiral Thierry d'Argenlieu High Commissioner of the new French administration for Indochina. The reconquest of Indochina turned out to be the bloodiest period in the entire history of French Indochina, proving not only that the methods of the French had not changed, but also that colonial rule could no longer be maintained by force alone.

2

The French campaign to regain control of Indochina might properly be called the second French war for Indochina, and this one, like the one after 1858, also began in the South. A brief battle for Saigon was followed by a bitter fight for Cochinchina. Most of southern Annam also was taken. At this point the military campaign came to a halt, for the French knew that they lacked the strength to take northern Annam and Tongking. Only after a one-year pause did they start the battle for northern Vietnam.

The reconquest of the South was largely a military affair, whereas that of the North had begun as a purely political struggle. The reason for the difference is to be found in the nature of the forces engaged in the struggle in the two parts of the country. The government in the North was relatively united, firmly in the hands of the Vietminh, and in command of forces capable of offering resistance. In the South the Vietminh hold on the badly split nationalist movement was tenuous; political dissension weakened the Saigon administration, which remained practically unarmed.

But the real difference between conditions in the North and South lay in the attitude of the foreign powers involved in the struggle for Vietnam. Although the French were disappointed by the Potsdam decision over Vietnam, they had every reason to be grateful that proposals that would have made their reentry into Vietnam impossible had been discarded. Roosevelt, who had opposed a French return, was dead. The Potsdam conferees also turned down a Chinese demand for sole occupation rights. Potsdam, by keeping the Chinese out of the South, opened the door for French return to Vietnam. The statesmen meeting at Potsdam had in effect agreed that it was up to the French to decide how to overcome possible Vietnamese-Chinese opposition to their return.

Under these circumstances, the first problem of the French in Saigon was what position to take on the Vietnamese revolution so long as they lacked the strength to crush it. They had only one choice: negotiations with the Vietnamese. This they did in two phases. The first, which lasted about four weeks, ended with the ouster of the Vietnamese Government from Saigon and the onset of Vietnamese armed resistance. The second, which lasted two weeks, ended after the arrival of troops under General Leclerc enabled the French to suppress the revolution throughout the South.

The chief French negotiator was Jean Cédile, the newly appointed Commissioner of the Republic for the South. He and a group of French parachutists were dropped by an RAF Dakota near Tayninh on August 22. Cédile and his party were picked up by the Japanese, who brought them to Saigon and put them up in a small house in the park of the main government building.

Two days later Cédile was allowed to establish contact with former French officials in Saigon. On August 27, some French Socialists and Communists in Saigon arranged the first meeting between Cédile and the leaders of the national revolution.

At that time, the leadership of the revolution in Saigon was in the hands of the so-called Provisional Executive Committee for the South. The story of the origin of this committee is the story of the revolutionary movement in Saigon up to the moment when it fell under Communist control.

The first nationalists to assume official positions in Saigon after the Japanese surrender were not the Vietminh but the members of a political coalition called the United National Front. It comprised the Cao Dai, Hoa Hao, the Phuc Quoc, the Dai Viet, one of the two existing Trotskyist groups, and several old and new parties of minor importance. The United National Front had been formed soon after the Japanese coup of March 9, and had moved into the positions the Japanese were about to vacate on August 16.

The United National Front led the as yet untested revolution and unorganized administration of Saigon for exactly one week. In that same week, the Vietminh effectively took power in Hanoi and Hue. A few days later, Bao Dai resigned in favor of the Vietminh regime. On August 22, the leaders of the United National Front, convinced that they would lose out in an open battle for leadership of the revolution with the Vietminh, and responding to the growing mass pressure organized by the Communists, began negotiations with the Vietminh. The Vietminh leaders adroitly played their trump card, which was that they were acceptable to the Allies while the United National Front was not. On August 23, the Front withdrew in favor of the Provisional Executive Committee for the South, seven of whose nine members were Communists. Its head, Tran Van Giau, also headed the Vietminh and the Communist Party. The Vietminh installed itself in the Government Palace and in the City Hall, appointed the Communist Duong Bach Mai as chief of the Saigon police, and proclaimed itself the southern branch of the regime that had taken power in Hanoi and Hue. On August 25, a mass demonstration such as Saigon had never before seen confirmed the change in the leadership of the revolution. From 9 A.M. until

6 P.M., thousands upon thousands marched past their new leaders, obviously content that in Saigon, too, the revolution was now being led by the Vietminh.

3

The meeting of Tran Van Giau and some of his Vietminh colleagues with Cédile on August 27 merely confirmed that French and Vietnamese views about the future of Vietnam were irreconcilable. The French were willing to discuss the future political order only on condition that their prewar rule over the country first be restored. The Vietnamese would talk about their country's future relationship with France only on condition that the French first recognize the independence of Vietnam, which Cédile neither could nor wanted to do. No nationalist leader at that time was willing to renounce independence, and most thought that an armed clash was unavoidable.

But if a war of liberation was inevitable, should the national movement wait until the French were strong enough to suppress the revolution or should the people arm to prevent French troops from entering Vietnam? The Vietnamese leaders saw only two lines of action open to them. They could either accept the inevitability of a war of national liberation and embark on one immediately, or they could adopt a course that would induce the Allies to condone Vietnamese independence and urge the French to accept a compromise. The first line of action, although widely supported by nationalists of all political shades, was consistently advocated only by the Trotskyists. The other course, which tried to save the revolution by avoiding an immediate armed conflict with the French, was that chosen by the Vietminh.

The Trotskyists of Saigon, who had suffered no loss of strength during the rise of the Vietminh, were again split into two factions—the Struggle Group and the International Communist League—and only one, the Struggle Group, had joined the United Front and later agreed to cooperate with the Vietminh. But the Struggle Group also supported many of the rival faction's radical views—i.e., expropriation of the French and the division of big landholdings in favor of peasants with too little or no land. The masses, thus given a stake in the revolution, they held, should be armed and trained for the war that was to begin as soon as French troops tried to set foot on Vietnamese soil. It was foolish, they said, to expect the Allies to pressure the French into recognizing the independence of Vietnam or to expect the French to refrain from crushing the revolution. There can be no doubt that popular sentiment strongly favored the Trotskyist policy. Yet the revolution in the South ultimately adopted the course mapped out by the Vietminh, which proved every bit as catastrophic as the Trotskyists had predicted.

Why did the nationalist movement choose the road of the Vietminh? It did so because the Vietminh policy postponed the hour of decision and thus offered at least the illusion of a chance. The Trotskyists failed to see that the attempt to prevent the return of the French would make the destruction of the national movement an absolute certainty and also eliminate the breathing spell the Vietminh policy promised to secure for the revolution.

There was no way of fighting off a French landing without also opposing the landing of the British. This would amount to an attempt by the national movement to keep the Allies out of Vietnam. The Allies had come to Indochina to disarm the Japanese, and they could not tolerate any attempt to obstruct their mission. They also had the means to break any Vietnamese resistance. Furthermore, the chance for survival of the revolution depended at least in part on the native government's ability to maintain order. There must be no violence, the Communists warned, no looting, and above all no attacks on French persons or possessions. No less important, there was to be no mistake about the nature of the revolution. It was to be a national and democratic, not a social, and certainly not a socialist, revolution. Even the demand for the immediate partition of large landholdings was denounced by the Communists as sabotage of the national cause.

For four weeks the leaders of the Vietminh in Saigon worked hard to preserve the image that the revolution, according to their strategy, was to offer to the Allies. Up to the beginning of September, order was preserved in Saigon. The breakdown of order when it came was due both to the temper of the people, daily more uncontrollable, and to the relative weakness of the Vietminh. Not only the Trotskyists but also the Cao Dai and Hoa Hao attacked the Vietminh for having entered into negotiations with the French. The struggle among the various groups for a greater share in directing the national movement was intense. The division in the nationalist movement was reflected in administrative anarchy and in the absence of a single authority whose orders all factions were willing to accept. Although the revolution had produced a government, this government was far from speaking with one voice.

The events of September 2 revealed how precarious the situation had become only one week after the Vietminh had succeeded in capturing the leadership of the revolutionary movement in Saigon. Wishing to show the unity and strength of the movement, the Executive Committee for the South organized a giant demonstration for this day. Several hundred thousand persons paraded before their leaders. But the demonstration was not a show of political unity. The various groups strongly underlined their separate identities, marching behind their own banners, shouting their own slogans, and those who had arms made it clear that these were not necessarily at the disposal of the Committee for the South. Even more distressing for the Communists than this display of disunity and opposition was the fact that there occurred the first outbreak of violence against the French. Toward the close of the demonstration shots were heard. To this day it is not known who fired these shots, but most demonstrators instantly became convinced that the French had started the shooting. Frenchmen watching the demonstration were attacked, dozens of them severely mistreated, many more dragged off to jail, and three, among them a priest, were admittedly killed.

Fully aware of the setback their policy had suffered, the Vietminh took immediate steps to repair the damage and to prevent a recurrence. On September 4, Tran Van Giau denounced the anti-French nationalists as troublemakers and saboteurs of the revolution. All arrested Frenchmen were released, the Cao Dai and Hoa Hao were asked to hand in their arms, the nationalist press was severely criticized for inciting the masses against the French, and the Trotskyist faction, which continued to call for armed resistance to the landing of the British, was dissolved and its leaders arrested.

But a week after the event of September 2, with popular sentiment responding more and more to the cries of alarm of the extremists and the fearful, the Vietminh-dominated Committee for the South found itself without much popular support at the precise moment when the impending arrival of the Allied troops was about to put its strategy to the final test. Giau and his colleagues on the Committee were no longer able to control the masses. On September 10, two days before the first units of the British Army entered Saigon, the Vietminh agreed to a drastic reorganization of the Committee, which from that day on ceased to be simply a tool of the Vietminh. The Communists succeeded in retaining only four of its thirteen members. Phan Van Bach, a prominent nationalist not affiliated with any party, replaced Tran Van Giau as chairman.

The new committee had a short life. Only thirteen days after its formation, the British and French made the move that confirmed beyond all doubt that no policy, neither that of the Vietminh or that of their opponents, could save the revolution.

4

The first British troops, a battalion of Gurkhas, arrived in Saigon on September 12. With them came the first French troops, a company from Calcutta, where the French had assembled about 1,800 men.

The British occupation troops were under the command of General Douglas D. Gracey, who regarded the right of the French to reoccupy Vietnam as self-evident. "The question of the government of Indochina is exclusively French," he said before leaving for Vietnam. "Civil and military control by the French is only a question of weeks."[5] Anthony Eden stated in his memoirs that "in accordance with the Potsdam Agreements, an Anglo-Indian force under General Gracey occupied the southern half of the country until the French were able to resume control."[6]

Gracey's views so colored his actions that he violated the instructions that the British occupation forces were not to interfere in the internal affairs of Indochina—i.e., that they were not to take sides in the developing conflict. When Admiral Mountbatten learned that these instructions were not being obeyed, he warned Gracey to stick to his job, which was to disarm the Japanese, not to take action against the Vietnamese.

Gracey did not heed these warnings. Only a week after his arrival, he took measures that enabled the French to evict the Vietnamese from the administration of Saigon. Yet it would be a mistake to assume that Gracey acted in conscious and open defiance of his government and his commander in chief. His instructions were obviously given in ignorance of the situation in Saigon. The city was in a state of utter chaos. The French troops, who immediately after their arrival had taken control of the Saigon arsenal and port, were still too weak to control the entire city. But they now felt strong enough to become aggressive and provoke the Vietnamese. The resulting tension led to numerous clashes between French soldiers and armed partisans and made it virtually impossible for the Committee for the South to curb the excited and frightened masses. The danger of open civil war, Gracey felt, was real, which meant that the lives of the French in Saigon were threatened, something which his superiors had apparently not foreseen. He could not remain passive. Compelled to intervene for the sake of civil peace, he understandably took sides. He failed to see that the French resolve to regain control of Vietnam was as responsible for the threatening civil war as was the Vietnamese wish to carry out a national revolution. He regarded the aspirations of the French as legitimate and saw the revolution as the only cause of the disorder. The idea of trying to re-establish order by supporting the Vietnamese never even entered his head. Whether or not he expected his government to vindicate his decision to intervene in the affairs of Indochina, he did so unequivocally in favor of the French.

There can be no doubt that Gracey's attitude intensified the crisis that gripped Saigon and raced toward its climax during the week of September 12–19. Gracey repeated an earlier order of the British to the Executive Committee for the South that all Vietnamese be disarmed. And he rudely reminded the Japanese commander that he had been told to use his troops to police the city and to maintain order even if this meant firing on Vietnamese.

Japanese reluctance to comply with this order has given rise to the legend of active Japanese support of the Vietnamese revolution. But in fact it was they who prevented the development of a viable native regime in March, 1945, both in the North and the South. The Japanese Army remained strictly neutral in the struggle between the national movement and the French.

What the British demanded and the French expected of the Japanese was a measure of interference in Vietnamese affairs and Allied policy which the Japanese were perfectly right to refuse. The Allied decision was that the Japanese were to be disarmed by the Chinese and the British, and that could only mean that the Japanese, after their surrender, were not to interfere in Indochinese affairs. To demand that the Vietnamese-made obstacles to a French return be removed by the Japanese was contrary to the Potsdam decision. General Gracey was therefore wrong in assuming that the French had a right to expect Japanese help, even though he was right in his assumption that the Allies did not oppose a French return. The ambiguity of the Potsdam decision would certainly have allowed him to adopt another course. If he had really been concerned only with maintaining order, he could just as well have helped the Committee for the South. Instead, he refused any further contact with the Vietnamese, treated the Committee not as a provisional native government but as the leaders of a rebellion, insisted that the Vietnamese disarm, and moved daily closer to the French position that the task of governing Vietnam was still theirs alone.

The Vietminh leaders must have realized by September 17 that their policy of compromise with the French was doomed; they called a general strike in protest against the Franco-British efforts to stifle the nationalist movement. When Cédile, on September 19, announced at a press conference that there would be no further negotiations with the Vietnamese until order was restored, the nationalists wondered what promises of help Gracey had given him to make him so intransigent. The answer came soon enough. On September 20, Gracey suspended all Vietnamese newspapers. The Vietnamese police force was made an auxiliary of the British Army. And on September 21, Gracey proclaimed martial law.

On September 22, Gracey took the last step to help the French attack the Vietnamese administration in Saigon by freeing the French parachutists whom the Japanese had captured and interned. Even more important, he armed about 1,400 French troops who had been confined to barracks near Saigon since the Japanese coup of March.

During the afternoon and evening of that same day, these soldiers bore down brutally on any Vietnamese they found in the streets. They also occupied several police stations from the Vietnamese in preparation for their move to regain Saigon, planned for the night of September 22–23. Between 4 and 5 A.M., French troops took all police stations, the Sûreté, the post office, and the treasury. Later that morning they also occupied the town hall. Scores of Vietnamese were arrested, but the members of the Committee for the South managed to escape. On September 23, a Sunday, the French disgracefully and stupidly celebrated their victory. French civilians insulted and attacked Vietnamese walking on the streets while French and British soldiers looked on. Hundreds of Vietnamese were beaten up and jailed.

This orgy of violence disgusted Cédile and infuriated Gracey, who ordered the French soldiers he had armed back into their barracks. Cédile tried to re-establish order. The paratroopers under his command finally succeeded in restoring a semblance of peace in Saigon. On Cédile's orders most of the Vietnamese arrested were released, but his hopes that this would deter the nationalists from countermeasures were shattered within twenty-four hours. The Vietminh, whose strategy had foundered, were particularly bitter, and they retaliated with a vengeance. They knew that they could recapture and retain the leadership of the revolution only by becoming the most determined war party of the entire nationalist camp, and thus they made sure that the war that French action had made inevitable would be waged under the banner of the Vietminh.

5

The Committee for the South, although not driven out of its Saigon offices until the morning hours of September 23, struck back at the French the next day. Thus, on September 24, 1945, began the Vietnamese war of national liberation against France, a war that within a few months spread over the entire South, and into Hanoi and the northern half of Vietnam a little more than a year later.

The nationalist counteroffensive opened with a paralyzing general strike which increased the chaos already reigning in Saigon. The Saigon electrical works were crippled and the central market was set on fire. This day foreshadowed the destruction, atrocities, and crimes that would become typical of the Indochina War. During the night of September 24–25, armed bands of nationalists attacked the Cité Heyraud, a French and Eurasian residential district of Saigon, killing one hundred and fifty persons, including women and children; an equal number were taken hostage.

The French obviously still lacked the strength to control the rebellious population. They could not even protect their civilians with the help of the British, whose army then numbered about 2,800. Aware of the French weakness, Gracey once more turned to the Japanese, this time determined to make them comply with his orders. For unaccountable reasons, none of the French or Indian troops in charge of patrolling Saigon on September 24 had been assigned to protect the French population, but only Japanese soldiers, who, as Gracey and Cédile should have known, could not be counted upon to act forcefully against the Vietnamese. The Japanese general in charge of the troops told Gracey that his men feared reprisals from the Vietnamese. On September 27, the British arrested the Japanese commander and threatened to hold him as a war criminal if he refused to help restore order in Saigon. From that day on, clashes between Japanese troops and armed Vietnamese became commonplace. Under Allied orders, the Japanese were now actively engaged in helping France, and with their help the French were able to strike back at the Vietnamese even before reinforcements from France had arrived. Thousands of Vietnamese were arrested and imprisoned, most of them as innocent as the slain and kidnaped French civilians.

The outbreak of civil war and the role played by the British were of great concern to Admiral Mountbatten. It seems that only the pleading of General Leclerc prevented Mountbatten from publicly disavowing the actions of Gracey and from replacing him.[7] Mountbatten summoned Gracey and Cédile to Singapore and told them again that British troops were not to be used to fight the Vietnamese. When told that the French by themselves might not be able to hold out until reinforcements arrived, Mountbatten insisted that Cédile reopen negotiations with the nationalist leaders. Thereupon Gracey arranged for a meeting between the nationalist spokesmen and Cédile, and a truce agreement went into effect on October 2, just three days before General Leclerc made his triumphant entry into Saigon at the head of the first units arriving directly from France.

The French were jubilant on October 5. But their leaders, knowing that they still lacked the strength to deal with armed resistance, and eager to gain time, continued to negotiate with the Committee for the South. The Committee demanded the disarming and removal of the French troops in Saigon. General Leclerc did not participate in the negotiations. He did not yet know that the war he was about to start could not be won by military means alone. All he was interested in was the speedy arrival of reinforcements with which to defeat the "insurgents," break the blockade of Saigon, and suppress the revolution in the provinces. More and more French troops began to pour into Saigon, and the truce threatened to break down on October 8. An appeal by Mountbatten prolonged it for forty-eight hours, but on October 11, fighting was resumed. The point had been reached when neither side was willing to observe the truce. The main forces of the Vietnamese were quickly ejected from Saigon. The Vietminh appealed to the native population to evacuate the city, and for a while it housed only Frenchmen and British and Japanese troops.

It took the French fully two weeks to break the blockade and to drive the nationalists from the city's immediate environs. In the city itself, the Vietnamese staged their last major attack as late as October 16, but as they were pitted against British and Japanese as well as French troops, their lack of adequate weapons forced them to retreat further and further into the countryside north, west, and south of Saigon. The Gurkha troops fought openly alongside the French, and the British also sent their air force against the Vietnamese. Neither the protests of the Congress Party in India nor the outcries of the Liberal and Labour press at home were able to restrain the British Army in Indochina. On October 9, Foreign Minister Ernest Bevin had concluded an accord with the French acknowledging their civil administration as the only authorized one south of the 16th parallel. The scandalous fact that the British, instead of disarming the Japanese, ordered them to help the French, was probably unknown to most members of the London government. Foreign correspondents in Saigon soon learned that the Japanese were used not only to give logistic support to the French campaign, but that they were charged with holding certain areas against the Vietnamese and with helping the French to defend vital installations in and around Saigon. This means that Japanese troops were used in open combat.

After breaking the blockade of Saigon, Leclerc prepared for the task of bringing the provinces south of the 16th parallel under French control. He thought of his campaign as a simple "mopping-up operation" which would take no more than four weeks. A ruthless application of the scorched-earth policy and incessant attacks by small guerrilla bands succeeded in slowing down the French advance. Never and nowhere were the French safe from the guerrillas. They could be fought off, but they were seldom caught and returned again and again. By the time Leclerc's troops occupied Camau, the southernmost point of Vietnam, not four weeks but four months had passed.

These guerrilla tactics had still another, more disturbing result. They made it impossible for the French to bring the country fully under their control. The confident declaration by General Leclerc in a press conference on February 5, 1946, that the conquest of the South had been completed was a short-lived delusion. A functioning administration could be set up only in and near the provincial towns. Neither tanks nor airplanes nor a steady influx of troops could prevent the guerrillas from exercising their effective control of the countryside.

The task of completing the reconquest of Vietnam, some Frenchmen began to realize, could not be left to soldiers alone.

6

The events in the South caused deep concern and anger in those parts of Vietnam which Leclerc was not yet able to overrun. This held true particularly in Hanoi, where the leaders of the Vietminh drew the logical conclusion that the French, given the opportunity, would proceed the same way in the North. With energy and skill, the Vietminh intensified its preparations for the probable showdown with the French.

The prospects for the victory of the revolution had always seemed infinitely better in the North than in the South. By September 10, when the Communists in Saigon temporarily lost control of the Committee for the South, Hanoi and most provinces of Tongking and northern Annam were firmly in Vietminh hands. The government headed by Ho Chi Minh was formed by the Vietminh alone, its right to speak for the entire people was contested by no one at that time, and it was in full control of the administration and perfectly capable of maintaining order in Hanoi. And although it conducted a violent anti-French campaign, it did not permit attacks on the French population. The friction between the Allies and the Vietnamese in Saigon brought on by disorder could therefore never have arisen in Hanoi.

However, the North was occupied by the Chinese, whose attitude toward the French and the Vietnamese national revolution was entirely different from that of the British, a factor of much greater importance for the fate of the national movement in the North than its greater unity, strength, and control of the population. The Chinese sympathized with the Vietnamese and were antagonistic toward the French. As it turned out, they too interfered in the internal affairs of Vietnam, but never on behalf of the French.

One consequence of the Chinese attitude was that the French were nonexistent as a political force in Hanoi in September, 1945. And in February, 1946, when Leclerc thought to have reconquered the South, the French still did not have a single armed soldier in the North. The few French officers who came into Hanoi in the company of Americans were stripped of their weapons, first by the Japanese and later by the Chinese. It was clear that as long as the Chinese did not withdraw their occupation forces, no French troops would be able to enter the North.

Sainteny had apparently been right when he had told his government early in August that the occupation of northern Indochina by the Chinese was the worst possible solution for France. His fears were confirmed immediately after the Japanese surrender. He knew that the position of France in Vietnam was threatened by the nationalist movement. He also knew that there was at that time not a single representative of France in Hanoi who could speak for his country and influence the Vietnamese. Being a man of exceptional self-confidence, he felt that if he were in Hanoi, he would be able to prevent developments unfavorable to France. Therefore, as soon as he learned of the Japanese surrender, he tried to get a plane to take him and a small staff to Hanoi.

As Sainteny expected, the Chinese in Kunming, unlike the British in Calcutta, showed no sympathy for French moves to re-establish their former rule over the Indochinese states. But he was not prepared for what he considered American obstructionism. The Americans in China had rendered the French what assistance they needed, and now the OSS promised Sainteny to fly him to Hanoi. But on August 16, an order of General Wedemeyer stopped all flights between Kunming and Hanoi. Sainteny's attempt to sneak out of Kunming on an RAF Dakota from Calcutta piloted by a Frenchman was prevented by the Chinese. But on August 22, he and four members of his staff were able to make the trip on an American plane with an OSS team headed by Major Archimedes L. Patti.

Sainteny was not slow to realize that Hanoi was in the hands of the Vietminh and that reinstituting French power would not be easy. But what he failed to understand was that the Vietnamese were the real obstacle to French aims, not the Allies—neither the Chinese, as he had predicted, nor the Americans, who, the French said, were coming into North Vietnam under various pretexts. He sent a radio message out of Hanoi in which he actually said that the Allies were more dangerous than the Vietminh.[8]

The small group of Americans stationed in Vietnam north of the 16th parallel consisted of five OSS teams that had been cooperating with the Vietminh in northern Tongking long before the Japanese surrender; some Air-Ground-Air-Service teams (AGAS), whose war-time mission had been the rescue of downed American fliers; members of the Joint Army-Navy Intelligence Service (JANIS); a unit of the Combat Section, South China Command; and a separate team of officers under General Nordlinger charged with the repatriation of American prisoners of war. Most of these Americans expressed strong sympathy with the Vietnamese national revolution, which under the circumstances could be interpreted as supporting the Vietminh. The French felt betrayed by an ally whose support they considered vital. French bitterness toward the Americans has given rise to the myth that the difficulties the French encountered in regaining control of the North were as much due to American hostility as to Chinese obstruction. Yet to say, as many serious French writers do, that the anticolonial sentiments of the Americans amounted to active support of the Communists is not only a crude distortion of their motives but also a ridiculous exaggeration of their effectiveness.

Indeed, Sainteny's influence in Hanoi in the fall of 1945 would not have been any greater if the Americans there, instead of committing the political error of misjudging the nature of the Vietminh, had made the historical mistake of helping the French beat down the national revolution. They could never have persuaded the Chinese to allow French troops into the North, certainly not as long as France had not paid the price China demanded for the withdrawal of her armies. That is why the Chinese prevented the French troops brought to Yunnan by the Generals Alessandri and Sabattier after March 9, 1945, from re-entering Tongking; that is why they kept the 3,000–4,000 French soldiers whom the Japanese had disarmed in semi-internment in the citadel of Hanoi, and that is why they would not allow Leclerc, after he had "pacified" the South, to proceed immediately to Tongking and northern Annam. The only French soldier to reach Hanoi with the Chinese command was General Alessandri, who, like Sainteny himself, owed his presence there to an American, General Gallagher.

The first Chinese occupation troops reached Hanoi on September 9. The very next day, Sainteny and his associates were thrown out of their offices in the building of the Government General, which the Chinese Army chiefs had chosen as their headquarters.

Installed in a small villa under the protection of Vietminh guards, Sainteny and his friends had ample time to debate whether the Vietminh, the Chinese, or the Americans were their worst enemies. Many of these men then and there developed the conviction that the OSS had come to Indochina as agents of American imperialism, and some even claimed that Gallagher approached Ho Chi Minh in the name of a "Donovan group" of business concerns, proposing that the Vietminh grant American firms all contracts for rebuilding the bombed-out railroads, airfields, and harbors of Vietnam.

Such fears must have animated Sainteny also. In 1953, when he published his book, he certainly knew how little justified these fears were, yet he was unable to overcome his anti-American bias. The fact that American shipping enabled the French to get enough troops to Saigon with which to defeat the revolution in the South seems not to have influenced his opinion. Yet this is what mattered in the long run. The anticolonial stance of the Americans in the North, from which the Vietminh derived only temporary comfort, was of short duration, partly due to misgivings Americans in Hanoi developed over the Vietminh, but largely because Secretary of State Byrnes soon let the OSS and other American agencies in Vietnam know that the United States did not oppose a French return to Indochina. If the Americans in Hanoi sinned, they did so not because they favored the Communists, but out of sympathy for the movement for national liberation.

The subject is of importance not because the pro-Vietnamese sentiments of the Americans in Hanoi influenced the course of events, which they did not, but because it leads directly to the central problem of contemporary Vietnamese history, the question of how the small Communist Party of Vietnam was able to take over the leadership of the entire national revolution and to maintain it over twenty years of brutal warfare and political maneuvering to this very day. Finding the right answer is not only of major historical interest, but very likely also of importance for the political future of the Vietnamese people.

7

There can be no doubt that the Vietminh from the very day of its formation was an instrument of the Communist Party. But it was not identical with the Party. The Party was perfectly correct in stressing in 1945 that the Vietminh was a broad national front of many political groups and parties, supported by non-Communist nationalists and accepted as the voice of the revolution. Only few knew that it was Communist-led, and none cared. The Vietminh expressed the political aspirations of the Vietnamese people as no one else did. After Ho Chi Minh proclaimed the country's independence, support of the Vietminh for years became identical with the defense of the country's newfound freedom. The Vietminh government was a reality and there existed no alternative, or at least none attractive enough.

This, and not Communist deception or political ignorance, is the secret of the support the Vietminh enjoyed. This is why Bao Dai agreed to become an "adviser" of the new regime, why some wealthy men joined the Vietminh, why a Catholic leader agreed to become Ho Chi Minh's first minister of economics, why Catholic priests came out in support of the government, and why the four Vietnamese Catholic bishops asked Catholics throughout the world to come to the aid of their "invaded country and its children, animated by pure patriotism, and decimated on the battlefield."[9]

The position of the Communists in the first Vietminh government was strong. The portfolios decisive for political control—interior, national defense, finance, propaganda, education, and youth—were in the hands of trusted Communists. Yet the cabinet presided over by Ho Chi Minh was not a Communist one. It had a non-Communist majority, and its Socialist, Catholic, and other non-Communist members were neither fools nor fellow travelers. If the future proved to some of the early Vietminh supporters that they had been mistaken, this does not mean that they had been duped. They were deceived not so much about the nature of the government they had joined as about the direction which it would take. The unwelcome development of Vietnamese national history since 1945 has deep and complex causes. To see it merely as the result of a "Communist scheme" reduces it to the level of an anti-Communist thriller.

To understand the people's political attitude toward the Hanoi government it must be remembered that the affiliations of its members offered no clue to their ultimate intentions. Anti-Communism was bound to arise sooner or later, but in 1945 it would have been pointless in the eyes of most active nationalists for the simple reason that there evidently was no Communism in Vietnam. The Communists in the government neither voiced nor tolerated Communist slogans. They spoke only as nationalists and fervently advocated the basic principles of democracy. As early as September 8, the government decreed national elections to be held in the near future on the basis of universal suffrage of all above the age of eighteen. The undemocratic councils of notables were abolished and were to be replaced by duly elected committees. On November 21, the official Vietminh paper in Hue published a government circular against the unauthorized distribution of large landholdings. The government even decreed the death penalty for attacks on private property.

More important still than the steps designed to mollify the wealthy and to win over the middle class were Hanoi's social measures. One of the first official decrees wiped out the hated opium, alcohol, and salt monopolies. It also did away with the iniquitous head tax and the land taxes of small landowners. All other land taxes, as well as interest rates on loans, were drastically reduced. The Vietminh carefully avoided a general distribution of land that might antagonize the native landlords, but the landholdings of the French, communal lands, and the lands of "traitors" who had collaborated were confiscated and given to landless peasants. The eight-hour work day became law, and workers were given the right to form unions. The government also confiscated and nationalized all public utilities. In the same spirit of national rebirth, the government attacked the problem of illiteracy, producing greater results in one year than the French had in more than sixty. Also, the University of Hanoi was reopened in November. Another achievement was in the agricultural sector. When the Vietminh came to power, famine was widespread. The Vietminh requisitioned all untilled land and gave it to anyone willing to work it. By spring, 1946, the people, though still undernourished, were no longer dying of starvation. The "Vietminh had succeeded in what the French had not been able to do: [saving] the country from famine by the unaided efforts of their citizens."[10]

This alone proved that the Vietminh had the moral authority and intellectual strength to mobilize the country's human and natural resources. The Vietminh was undoubtedly destined to remain in power.

8

The Chinese occupation of northern Vietnam was a catastrophic experience for the Vietnamese people. Although the political intentions of the Chinese were not hostile, the immediate needs of the troops and their lack of concern for the plight of the native population made them behave like conquering armies. They took what they thought they needed.

But infinitely worse than the behavior of the individual Chinese soldiers was the plunder of the country by the leaders of the army and their business-oriented associates, who tried to lay their hands on whatever they could. But as far as Chungking was concerned, the reasons for the Chinese presence in Vietnam were political. The French were chiefly concerned with the nature of China's real political intentions. The Vietnamese were equally concerned. The masses were simply antagonistic toward any foreign power; they just wanted to be left alone.

For the political leaders, Vietnamese as well as French, the problem was not nearly so simple. In fact, only those who combined intelligence with exceptional political gifts—men so different from each other as Ho Chi Minh, Vo Nguyen Giap, Jean Sainteny, and General Leclerc—reacted rationally.

Sainteny, fully aware what the pressure of the Chinese in Vietnam meant for France, knew that the real confrontation with China was yet to come. It was different for Ho Chi Minh. The arrival of the Chinese had a number of immediate and far-reaching consequences for his regime and for his own political future.

There was no doubt in Ho's mind that the Chinese had the power to oust his government if they felt this to be to their advantage.

Yet for all this, the Chinese were not a completely negative factor in Ho's political calculations. He knew that they favored Vietnam's political independence, and that they therefore would prevent the French from going north of the 16th parallel. But would they perhaps be tempted to set up a Chinese-oriented government with Vietnamese national leaders they trusted? Therein lay the real danger. For with the Chinese armies came the leaders of the anti-Vietminh nationalists—Vu Hong Khanh and Nguyen Tuong Tam of the Viet Nam Quoc Dan Dang and those of the Dong Minh Hoi. The latter under the feeble leadership of Nguyen Hai Than had shrunk into a small clique of politicians-in-exile held together only by their opposition to the Vietminh. Neither of these two groups had any organized following to speak of, and because of their late arrival had little contact with the existing weak though active national opposition to the Vietminh, which was spearheaded in Hanoi by the Dai Viet party under the leadership of the dynamic, autocratic Trung Tu Anh. The VNQDD and Dong Minh Hoi had close ties to the generals commanding the armies of occupation, and they continued to enjoy Chinese support.

Ho Chi Minh had every reason to fear that once the Chinese crossed into Vietnam, the days of his government might be numbered. As the Chinese came down from the Vietnamese border to the sea, they ousted the local Vietminh committees in a number of towns and cities and replaced them with their handpicked friends. Thus the VNQDD gained political control of a number of provinces, including much of the delta between Hanoi and Haiphong. Even control of Hanoi was divided between the Vietminh and its Chinese-installed opponents. True, the VNQDD and the Dong Minh Hoi could maintain themselves in the provinces only where Chinese units gave them effective protection against the Vietminh. But in Hanoi they became a firmly entrenched force causing much disorder and openly fighting the Vietminh. The remnants of the Dai Viet joined the pro-Chinese parties in fighting the Vietminh, as did some other small groups, like the Socialist-inspired Ngu Xa movement of Dr. Phan Quang Dan, a friend of Bao Dai, who wanted the former emperor to head a government of national union.

The Chinese could certainly have ousted the Vietminh government, and there is no simple answer to why they did not do so. It is misleading to assume, as some have done, that the Chinese tolerated the Vietminh government because it did not oppose their exploitation of the country and spent huge sums to bribe the generals. It is true that Ho had not protested against the disastrous exchange rate. There is also no doubt that the generals received handsome presents after the so-called national "gold week"—the collection, as gifts to the state, of all valuable jewelry and other gold objects. This measure by Minister of Finance Pham Van Dong to alleviate the government's financial difficulties may well have lightened its political difficulties as well. "The bulk of the money collected ended up in the pockets of the Chinese. It was the price of survival for Ho Chi Minh's government."[11] Yet this still leaves unanswered the question why the Vietminh remained in power after the Chinese left, a question that can be answered only if one examines all the forces whose political interaction constitutes the perplexing history of Vietnam during the Chinese presence in the country.

9

Of course, Chiang Kai-shek was hardly in a position to oust the Vietminh. He knew that his generals in Vietnam would ignore any order to that effect if they thought it to their advantage. He saw that Communist control of the Vietminh was a danger, but as far as he was concerned it was a French problem, not his. Besides, if French fears of the Vietminh increased, the French might be more inclined to accept the Chinese conditions for the withdrawal of their troops. But ousting the Vietminh by force would not have been easy in any case. The Chinese would gladly have removed Ho Chi Minh if overriding interests had dictated such a course. Since this was not the case, the Chinese decided to tolerate him.

Nevertheless, the Chinese generals, particularly Siao Wan, were sufficiently concerned over the Vietminh to try to curb its power. Convinced that the Communists would annihilate their opponents after the Chinese left Vietnam, Siao Wan tried to make his friends strong enough to forestall such a fate. To this end, he held negotiations with the Vietminh. But Ho Chi Minh proved again that he was a match for the wiliest of opponents. Under Chinese pressure, the Vietminh concluded an agreement with the opposition on October 25, 1945. But the VNQDD refused to accept it and the Dong Minh Hoi, which had signed it, backed down. Although Chinese pressure continued, Ho knew how to avoid a break. In order to blunt the main charge of his opponents—i.e., that the government was run by the Communists—Ho Chi Minh on November 11 took the bold step of dissolving the Communist Party of Vietnam. Ho Chi Minh always seemed able to prove to the Chinese that above all he wanted peace and cooperation with all factions, and on November 19, he concluded another agreement with the opposition. This new pact provided for a "government of national union" with VNQDD and Dong Minh Hoi participation as well as for the creation of a unified national army and a campaign for the liberation of the South. Nothing came of this agreement either. Ho's next move was to decree elections for a national assembly for December 23. The formation of the new government was postponed by the Vietminh under the pretext that it would be undemocratic not to wait until the people had had a chance to express their will.

Unable to oppose in principle elections they realized would probably be their undoing, the leaders of the VNQDD and the Dong Minh Hoi demanded that they be postponed to allow them time for campaigning. Lacking the organization to carry their election propaganda into the country and fearing that the masses would vote against them, the opposition organized demonstrations in Hanoi that led to almost daily street battles with the Vietminh. With Chinese help, the anti-Vietminh forces even succeeded in kidnaping Vo Nguyen Giap and Propaganda Minister Tran Huy Lieu. The opposition leaders again appealed to the Chinese for help, and negotiations led to another agreement on December 22, one apparently quite advantageous to the VNQDD and the Dong Minh Hoi. The elections were postponed to January 6, but irrespective of the outcome, the Chinese insisted that the opposition get 70 out of a total of 380 seats. The Vietminh was not afraid of this condition. It furthermore agreed, on December 25, that the new government was to consist of four members of the Vietminh, four of the opposition, and two "neutrals" in the posts of ministers of the interior and national defense. Another stipulation, also accepted by the Vietminh, was that Vo Nguyen Giap and Tran Huy Lieu were not to be members of the government. (They were, however, released by their captors.)

The elections, which resulted in the expected fiasco for the opposition, did nothing to hasten Vietminh compliance with the opposition demand that the new government be formed immediately. As a matter of fact, Ho Chi Minh was already more concerned with reaching an agreement with the French than with keeping the one concluded with his Vietnamese opponents. Realizing that he might be at the mercy of Leclerc's army once the Chinese left, he began in mid-January to negotiate with the French.

The expected return of the French to Hanoi profoundly affected Ho Chi Minh's tactics. Because he anticipated that the Chinese would leave and let the French in, he ceased to pay attention to the opposition. It was doomed because the Chinese were about to conclude an agreement with the French and because, as a result, Chinese troops would be relieved by French units.

A new chapter in the turbulent postwar history of Vietnam was about to open.

10

Franco-Chinese negotiations began in earnest early in January, 1946. Leclerc had tried earlier to get Chinese agreement to move some of his troops north, but he was told that this would have to be part of an over-all agreement between Chungking and Paris. A sign that agreement was imminent was Chungking's recall, on February 23, 1946, of Siao Wan, the anti-Vietminh and also very anti-French political spokesman of the Chinese occupation forces.

The Franco-Chinese treaty concluded on February 28 was a political victory for the Chinese. With it France relinquished her old concessions in Shanghai, Tientsin, Hankow, and Canton, and also renounced the territory of Kwanchouwan, which she had annexed in the 1880's. China was given a free port at Haiphong and granted custom-free transit of all goods from her borders to the port. The treaty also provided for the sale of the Yunnan railway to China, and for a substantial improvement of the status of Chinese nationals residing in Vietnam. All these sacrifices the French made for the sake of only one Chinese concession: that French troops were to relieve the Chinese armies of occupation between March 1 and 15, 1946.[12]

For the Vietnamese, the treaty was just another betrayal of the Vietnamese national cause. No other event in 1946 could have altered more profoundly the circumstances on which the survival of the Hanoi government depended. The British, too, had just announced that after March 4, their army would leave Vietnam and that the country south of the 16th parallel would again be under the sole authority of the French. Now at last the French had removed the main obstacle to their return to the North.

None of this came as a surprise to Ho Chi Minh. Long before the signing of the Franco-Chinese treaty, the prospect of a French military reoccupation of Tongking had become a weighty element in his tactical calculations. The hopes he may once have pinned on the Americans were dead. The Chinese had just given evidence that they no longer cared whether Vietnam was free or again became a French colony. Not even the Soviet Union had so far bothered to extend official recognition to Ho's government. In this new phase in the life of the Vietminh, everything therefore turned around the question whether the Vietminh would be forced to wage the kind of devastating war that the return of the French had unleashed in the South. This question forced the Vietminh to make an agonizing choice between negotiating the peaceful return of some French units or resisting French re-entry. Ho never had any doubts as to the course he would adopt: He would negotiate, and he would resort to armed resistance only if all else failed.

Feelers to ascertain what concessions the French were willing to make had been sent out almost immediately after Sainteny's appearance in Hanoi. The first meeting, on August 27, arranged by Major Patti, brought Sainteny together with Giap, then minister of the interior. Ho Chi Minh himself began to take part in the negotiations after September 28. He met with General Alessandri and Léon Pignon, political counselor to Sainteny.

As the months went by and Chinese pressure on the Vietminh increased, Ho became more and more cordial toward the French. The Chinese and their Vietnamese allies knew that a Franco-Vietminh *rapprochement* was likely to strengthen Ho. In order to prevent this, they mounted an intensive anti-French hate campaign. Bands of hoodlums organized by the Chinese attacked Hanoi's French population. These attacks, most of which occurred on January 10 and 11, were sharply condemned by the government, which ordered the police to protect the French. From mid-February on, the Vietminh press also began to moderate its criticism of the French and to speak of the need for better Franco-Vietnamese understanding.

The French knew that the Vietminh was in a position to destroy everything before the French Army could reach Hanoi, and that it would therefore be futile to ignore it. Only through a political accord with Hanoi could that danger be averted.

On February 16, 1946, Sainteny learned Ho Chi Minh's conditions for the return of the French Army. He found them acceptable and went to Saigon to report to Leclerc, who agreed with him and persuaded Paris to make the concessions. The actual agreement was not signed until March 6, but the stage for the return of the French to the North had been set. Leclerc left Saigon for the North on March 1, the day after the signing of the Franco-Chinese treaty, of which he was informed by a wire from Chungking which said: "Agreement signed. The fleet can leave."

While Ho Chi Minh and Sainteny were busy hammering out the political and military provisions of the agreement, Ho, deeply concerned over popular reaction to a treaty allowing French troops into the North, resumed negotiations with his nationalist enemies. Rightly afraid that they would exploit popular dissatisfaction with the agreement, he felt that this could be prevented only if the opposition was made a party to it. He therefore invited the opposition leaders to join his government, offering them all they had asked for and that had been granted them on paper on December 22. The opposition, apprehensive over the prospect of being implicated in a deal with the French, now had to be coaxed into accepting what they themselves had previously demanded. But Sainteny spoke to Siao Wan, and the Chinese general for the last time took a hand in Vietnamese affairs. He urged his Vietnamese friends not to miss this chance at sharing in the exercise of power.

On February 24, a new government was formed, composed exactly along the lines the opposition and the Chinese had requested two months earlier. Four ministries went to the Vietminh, four to the opposition. But the new government did not represent a shift in real power. Ho Chi Minh was able not only to maneuver the opposition into having to defend what they until then had denounced as treason, he could actually do so without any risk to Vietminh control of his government. Frightened by the realization that he had to share responsibility for a deal with the French, Vice-President Nguyen Hai Than, the Dong Minh Hoi leader, left the country a day before the new government was presented to the National Assembly. The aggressiveness of the VNQDD was effectively curbed after Ho Chi Minh implicated their minister of foreign affairs in his negotiations with the French. Of the two "neutrals," the ministers of the interior and of defense, one was a secret ally of the Vietminh, the other a sympathizer. Moreover, the creation of a "Superior War Council" placed control of the army in the hands of Giap, who although not a member of the government, became a more powerful figure than anyone in it with the exception of Ho himself. The VNQDD agreed to this arrangement because their chief, Vu Hong Khanh, was made vice-president of this new council, a position the Vietminh very much wanted him to have. As the Superior War Council had to sign the military provisions of the treaty with the French, Vu Hong Khanh and the VNQDD would also be forced to defend Ho Chi Minh's decision to accede to the entry of French troops into the North.

On March 2, the National Assembly voted the new government into office. It also accepted the seventy opposition members who had not been elected but agreed upon as a minimum representation of the opposition. To sugarcoat the decision that the idea of armed resistance against the French was about to be shelved, the new government was called a "government of resistance." The four days that followed, probably the most difficult ones in the political career of Ho Chi Minh, were filled with hectic negotiations between Ho and Sainteny.

The main provisions of the treaty signed on March 6 were French recognition of Vietnam as a "free state with its own government, parliament, army, and finances," and Vietnamese agreement that their country was to form "part of the Indochinese Federation and the French Union."[13] A referendum to be held in Cochinchina was to decide whether the three "states" of Vietnam should be united under one national government. Since its outcome was a foregone conclusion, this too was a French concession. In the military appendix to the agreement the number of troops to be stationed by the French in Vietnam was fixed at 25,000, of which 15,000 were to be French and 10,000 Vietnamese under French command. But France promised to withdraw her troops in five annual installments, which would have meant the end of French military occupation in 1952. The Vietnamese pledged to end the war their guerrillas were conducting in the South.

The agreement signified above all that in the postwar struggle for Indochina the Vietnamese and the French were at last facing each other directly, and it brought to the fore sharp divisions on both sides. French dissatisfaction was particularly strong among the military, who regarded the projected gradual evacuation of Vietnam by the French Army as a sellout. Their attitude and that of the many administrators who failed to receive coveted jobs was forcefully expressed by Admiral d'Argenlieu, who had been in France during the final negotiations. He expressed his amazement over the agreement. "Yes," he said, "that is the word, my amazement that France had such a fine expeditionary corps in Indochina and yet its leaders prefer to negotiate rather than to fight."[14]

Vietnamese dissatisfaction also ran high, not only in the anti-Vietminh parties but within the cadres of the Vietminh as well. As a matter of fact, opposition to it was so strong that a lesser leader than Ho Chi Minh might not have been able to master it. The Vietminh leaders had to overcome a deep crisis of confidence. In facing this crisis, Ho Chi Minh and his more prominent colleagues proved that they were eminently qualified to lead the national revolution.

On March 7, Giap in a speech blending passion with cold political logic defended the agreement before an estimated crowd of 100,000 gathered in front of the Hanoi Municipal Theatre. "In this agreement," he said, "there are arrangements that are satisfactory to us and others that are not. . . . Liberty . . . is not yet independence. Once liberty is obtained we will go toward independence, toward complete independence." Giap was frank in stating why negotiations were preferable to armed resistance. The country was not yet ready for a long-drawn-out war and the French were too strong for a short war. "We negotiated above all to protect and reinforce our political, military, and economic position."[15] Ho Chi Minh also addressed the meeting. In his short speech he solemnly told his followers that he had not sold them out. He concluded by saying: "You know that I would rather die than sell our country."

He has kept his word.

XII

The Road to War

1

THE EFFECTS OF THE AGREEMENT of March 6, 1946, were profound. Not only could the events it set in motion not be halted, but—and this could not easily have been foreseen at the time—its consequences were bound to be calamitous in every way. The agreement raised hopes for the resolution of Franco-Vietnamese differences, yet in effect it served to destroy any chance for a peaceful settlement.

According to propaganda proclamations, what was to emerge in the end was a self-governed, united Vietnam in which the French would retain much of their old economic power and cultural influence. However, the concessions the two sides made in the agreement were so incompatible with the stated objectives that insistence on the aims was bound to end in war. This was one of those rare compromises in which the advantages accruing

244

to the contracting parties outweighed their losses. The French recognized Vietnam's independence, but they won the entry of French troops into the North, a matter well worth even greater sacrifices, for it gave them the means to revoke what they had conceded once the time was ripe. The Vietminh won time to build up its military forces and to consolidate its political control of the country. And most important, France, by recognizing the "Free State" of Vietnam had granted Hanoi *de facto* recognition as the only legitimate native regime for the entire country.

The agreement was made for tactical reasons dominated by military considerations. It was in fact merely a truce in a war that had already begun. And in this limited sense it served its purpose, for the French as well as for the Vietminh.

What, however, were the actual intentions of the men who concluded this treaty? Was it simply a Machiavellian deal in which the two parties tried to outmaneuver each other to gain time? But the charge of Machiavellianism, brought by both sides, is a poor substitute for political analysis. It assumes that people engaged in complex political maneuvers are always dishonest, always fully aware of their own motives, always able to control their every move, and able to foresee the effects of their actions.

These considerations have particular relevance to Ho Chi Minh. There are those even among his enemies who believe that he labored honestly to avert the war, and there are others who hold that his tactics merely served to camouflage a policy that made war inevitable. Yet the truth is perhaps simpler than it would appear. Ho's policy both before and after the conclusion of the agreement was largely dictated by circumstances. The fact that he talked peace while preparing for war was neither contradictory nor deceitful. He may have doubted that a peaceful settlement was possible, but it would be hard to prove that he did not want one. The charge of duplicity also cannot easily be sustained. He always said that the alternative to independence through agreement was war, and if there was a war it would be bitter and long.

The French, too, talked peace and prepared for war, and it was they, not Hanoi, who first broke the agreement soon after their High Commissioner, Admiral Thierry d'Argenlieu, denounced it. Not only were the French determined to prevent Hanoi from extending its authority to the South, but they took steps to curtail

Ho's sovereignty in the North. In their campaign against the Hanoi government, the French applied growing pressure on Ho Chi Minh. When he reached the point where one more step backward would have made him a captive of French power, he decided to strike back. It is to his credit that in this hour he as the leader of the movement for national independence was not entirely unprepared.

In order to judge fairly the roles played by both protagonists one must remember that this was a confrontation of deeply rooted, hopelessly entangled historical forces. Both camps encompassed people who honestly strove to observe the truce, but even they believed that in order to avoid war they had to prepare for it, and this dilemma was most sharply reflected in the actions of Ho Chi Minh. An air of ambiguity beclouds the role he played in 1946, perhaps because in 1946 even the honest efforts of either side must have seemed deceitful to the other.

But Ho Chi Minh was not only a national leader, he was also the leader of a party. And while his methods in the struggle for independence were hailed throughout the country, his reasons for winning a monopoly of power for the Communist Party divided his people and damaged his reputation as a man dedicated to the liberation of his people.

2

In the Franco-Vietnamese contest between March and December, 1946, when the war broke out in the North, the man most firmly opposed to further French concessions was High Commissioner d'Argenlieu.

The Admiral had served in World War I, and had retired in 1920 to join the Carmelite Order. He left his monastery when World War II broke out and resumed his naval career. Captured by the Germans after the fall of France, he escaped and joined the Free French in London. Before his appointment to Indochina in August, 1945, he served in the French government-in-exile and in the first government of liberated France. He was close to de Gaulle, with whom he shared "a rigidity of mind and a preference for authoritarian methods."¹ But he owed his appointment as High Commissioner largely to the new Catholic party of postwar France, the MRP, which, under the leadership of Georges Bidault, soon became a new rallying point as well as an effective lobby for what the French have traditionally called the "colonial party." This group warmly applauded d'Argenlieu's belief that it was "the sacred duty of France to re-establish order"² in Vietnam, and approved wholeheartedly his telling the Vietnamese that "France has come guided not by material or financial interest but by humanitarian goals."³

D'Argenlieu is said to have arrived in Indochina full of generous political intentions, which he had planned to make known in speeches prepared but never delivered. Yet it would be an insult to the man to say that the colons, administrators, and military men who surrounded him in Saigon had induced him to change his mind. He fully shared their views before ever meeting them. While still in Paris he may have thought that "French greatness" in Indochina was compatible with Vietnamese national interests. Like so many Frenchmen, he was unaware of the force and purpose of the national movement. But once in Saigon, he realized that his mission was bound to fail unless the national rebels were defeated. His policy throughout his entire term was to deny the demands of the Vietnamese nationalists and to undo their gains.

D'Argenlieu had no quarrel with the French policy of force being used in Cochinchina. As a matter of fact, he was a fervent believer in the use of force, North as well as South. At the risk of being recalled, the Admiral set about to retract the concessions France had made. His first move was to prevent the implementation of the March agreement's provisions calling for joint Franco-Vietnamese efforts to end hostilities in the South and for a referendum on whether Cochinchina would reunite with the North. Since the outcome of this referendum doubtlessly would have meant the extension of Hanoi's authority over Cochinchina, it must be assumed that the French agreement was made in bad faith. Hence it does not come as a surprise that the scheme d'Argenlieu devised was supported by Paris as well as by the French in Indochina.

On March 12, Commissioner Cédile had assured colonial society in Saigon that the agreement did not apply to Cochinchina.

He had called it a "regional arrangement" between Hanoi and the French Commissioner for Tongking and northern Annam. Cochinchina, he said, would remain a separate "state" within the Indochinese Federation.[4] Two days later, Marius Moutet, the Socialist Minister for Overseas Territories, sanctioned this open breach of the agreement by confirming that Cochinchina would be treated as a separate "free state."

Transforming Cochinchina into a free state while simultaneously retaining control called for complicated maneuvering. The instrument employed by the French was the Advisory Council for Cochinchina which had been created on February 4. All its members, four French and eight Vietnamese, were French-appointed. The Advisory Council was proclaimed the authorized voice of the South. Under French instruction it assumed its new function by demanding, on March 26, the formation of a provisional autonomous government for Cochinchina.

D'Argenlieu justified his refusal to prepare for the stipulated referendum in Cochinchina by saying it could not be held as long as the fighting in the South continued, and to make sure that peace, should it come, would not find him unprepared, he pushed his plan for Cochinchinese "autonomy," and with equal tenacity he denied Hanoi a voice, saying that the cessation of hostilities was not a proper subject for negotiations. Emissaries sent by Hanoi to arrange for a cease-fire were arrested by the French. A price was put on the heads of resistance leaders who refused to surrender unconditionally by March 31. As a result, the fighting which the agreement was to have halted grew more savage. The nationalists stepped up their attacks and the French retaliated with increasing brutality.

None of the agreement's provisions was ever implemented in Cochinchina. Clearly the French had never intended to retreat from their position of strength in the South.

The French idea of a free state was not necessarily one without a native government. They were quite willing to accept such a government provided it was "friendly." The reason the French insisted in bringing their army into Tongking was not so much to prepare for the overthrow of the Hanoi regime but to impose their version of a free state. The French, unlike the Vietnamese, were in no hurry to hold the treaty conference that would put Vietnam on the road to independence, but they could not very well post-pone it forever. They finally agreed, but they made sure that it would deliberate endlessly without producing any results.

With an eagerness that betrayed his illusions about the "new France," Ho Chi Minh asked that the conference be held in Paris. He feared that in Vietnam the French participants would be ex-posed to the pressures of colonial society, and he also hoped that the Vietnamese cause would receive a better hearing in the more liberal atmosphere of the French capital. D'Argenlieu rejected Ho's request for those same reasons. Rather than wait, Ho agreed to a preliminary conference at Dalat, the resort town and hunting ground of Bao Dai and of wealthy colonials.

The Dalat conference opened on April 17 and lasted until May 11. D'Argenlieu presided over the opening session, then handed the conduct of the meetings over to Max André, head of the French delegation, who, as a former director of the Franco-Chinese Bank, had close ties to the Bank of Indochina. The French dele-gation consisted mainly of colonial administrators and technicians. It did not include a single person authorized to speak for France or conclude any kind of political agreement. The Vietnamese dele-gation, on the other hand, although it did not include Ho Chi Minh, was primarily political. It was formally headed by Foreign Minister Nguyen Tuong Tam, a VNQDD leader, and of its ten most important delegates, only two—Vo Nguyen Giap and Duong Bach Mai—were Communists.

The conference ended in profound disagreement.[5] The French delegation declined to discuss the fundamental questions of a cease-fire in the South, the referendum in Cochinchina, and the scope of Vietnamese sovereignty within the French Union. Their position was that these issues would be taken up at a later confer-ence, one which the French Government had in fact already promised to hold in France. But after the experience of Dalat, this promise seemed of little value.

The Vietnamese delegates allegedly left the conference in tears. Giap, who had emerged as the strong man of the delegation, seemed more upset than his colleagues. It may well be that at Dalat he became convinced that war had become a certainty. In any case, he now saw to it that his government would be prepared. That is why the French henceforth regarded him as the leader of a radical Vietminh faction opposed to further compromise and concerned only with preparing his party and government for war.

3

In contrast to Giap, Ho Chi Minh was then generally thought of as a moderate. But both knew that if negotiation failed, war was inevitable. The roles of Ho, the born diplomat, and Giap, the gifted military leader, were therefore only two complementary aspects of a well-integrated strategy.

As the negotiations were about to enter their decisive phase, it was Ho Chi Minh who for the next few months stood in the limelight of history. He left for the conference in Paris on May 31. His thoughts on the prospects of his mission will never be known. True, the French had finally agreed to negotiate in Paris, and that in itself was progress, and there was widespread sympathy for the Vietnamese national cause in the French capital. But on the other hand, the fighting in the South continued and d'Argenlieu persisted in his maneuvers to formalize Cochinchina's separation. Furthermore, only three days before Ho's departure, the French had proclaimed the highlands of central Vietnam, inhabited largely by ethnic minorities, an "autonomous region," to be administered by a French-staffed Commissariat for the Mountain Population. Still more was to come. On June 1, only twenty-four hours after Ho left for Paris, d'Argenlieu "recognized" the Republic of Cochinchina in the name of France, neglecting to mention that this clear violation of the March agreement had not been authorized by Paris. Ho Chi Minh, on hearing the news, remarked that there must be some misunderstanding. His chief concern was to save the conference, which d'Argenlieu was obviously determined to wreck.

The next disappointment came when Sainteny greeted Ho Chi Minh at Orly airport with the announcement that the conference would have to be postponed for a month or so. Elections were to be held on June 2, and the conference would have to wait until a new government could be formed. The Vietnamese delegation was sent to Biarritz, lest while in Paris they gain support for their cause.

Only after Georges Bidault, the MRP leader, became head of the new government on June 19, was Ho Chi Minh allowed to come to Paris in his capacity as head of the "free state" of Vietnam. Before the conference opened on July 6, the Vietnamese had to swallow two more disappointments. The conference was shifted from Paris to Fontainebleau, and, worse still, the French delegation, which did not include a single cabinet member or prominent political personality, was, as at Dalat, composed largely of colonial officials and again headed by Max André. Three rather obscure deputies were also part of the delegation, but one of them, the Socialist Paul Rivet, resigned before the conference got under way. He became convinced at a strategy meeting that the negotiations would be deliberately conducted so as to lead to an impasse and the blame put on the Vietnamese.[6] Without doubt, the absence of any member of the French Government at the conference table reflected a determination to leave basic political differences unsettled—i.e., to proceed as if there had never been any March agreement. The French felt that they could treat the agreement as the truce it was, one that had served its purpose but was about to expire.

Ho Chi Minh, in a far more positive spirit, had selected a team that included not only members of his government, among them the foreign minister, the ministers of national defense, finance, and agriculture, but several vice ministers, former ministers, and leaders of all parties and groups cooperating with the Vietminh. There were also representatives of the anti-Vietminh parties that had joined the government before the conclusion of the March agreement. Even a member of the former royal family had been added to the delegation. It was an impressive array, "among the best that Viet Nam could offer."[7] Ho Chi Minh, after finding out how the French were slighting the conference, wisely decided to stay away also.

A glance at the two delegations sufficed to show that Fontainebleau was not a confrontation between French democracy and Vietnamese Communism, but rather a meeting at which the representatives of French colonialism were pitted against the authentic spokesmen of the Vietnamese movement for national liberation.

Meanwhile, d'Argenlieu made another provocative move by sending troops into the provinces of Kontum and Pleiku in central Annam, under the pretext that the "autonomy" of the mountain populations had to be protected. Thus French control was extended to yet another part of Vietnam.

Negotiations had been going on for almost three weeks when d'Argenlieu took one more step to forestall a possible *rapprochement*. He declared that relations between France and the Indochinese people could not be settled at a conference attended by delegates only from Hanoi. He called what can only be considered a counterconference for August 1 at Dalat. At this second Dalat conference, which was to decide how the Indochinese Federation was to be organized, Hanoi was not represented at all. D'Argenlieu had invited delegates from French-controlled Cambodia and Laos, and no less than three Vietnamese delegations: one from the "Republic of Cochinchina," one from the "autonomous region" of the mountain populations, and one from an administratively nonexistent entity called Southern Annam.

This crude maneuver almost brought the Fountainebleau conference to an abrupt halt. When Paris, although deeply embarrassed, again failed to disavow its High Commissioner, the Vietnamese delegation was ready to pack up and leave. Ho Chi Minh dissuaded them, and negotiations continued through August. Tentative agreements on a number of economic and financial questions were drawn up, but the adamant refusal on the part of the French to make even the slightest political concessions rendered these agreements worthless to the Vietnamese. Pham Van Dong, the head of the Vietnamese delegation, repudiated them on the night of September 9–10, after his final appeal that the conference take up the question of the Cochinchinese referendum was rejected. "This incident concluded a conference which had served only to show that no basis for negotiations existed."[8]

In the acrimonious debate that followed, French liberals and Socialists blamed d'Argenlieu for the failure of the conference. But if the French Government had really wanted to arrive at a lasting understanding with the Vietnamese national movement, it could easily have replaced d'Argenlieu. There can be only one reason why Paris did not recall him immediately after his un-authorized "recognition" of the Cochinchinese republic: Paris, though deploring his methods, was in basic agreement with his objectives.

After Fontainebleau, the French gravitated more and more toward a solution by force—the policy of unilateral steps adopted in Saigon in September, 1945, and subsequently pursued by d'Argenlieu. For the Vietnamese nationalists this meant that they had to get ready to fight.

Such was the mood on September 13, when the Vietnamese left Paris to sail from Toulon to Haiphong. The outbreak of war was now considered only a matter of time.

It was at this moment that Ho Chi Minh took a step no less bold than his decision to conclude the March agreement. To everybody's surprise, he reversed the position taken by his delegation and renounced the objectives for which it had fought at Fontainebleau. At about midnight on September 14, after an evening of stormy negotiations, he and Marius Moutet signed a *modus vivendi* which gave the French everything they had demanded first at Dalat and then at Fontainebleau. The chief purpose of this *modus vivendi* was to bring about a resumption of French economic and cultural activities in the North, as well as a further improvement of their military position.[9] As to the political issues vital for the Vietnamese, the *modus vivendi* was silent: nothing was said about the promise of ultimate independence. The French flatly refused to reconfirm their recognition of Vietnam as a "free state." All Ho Chi Minh received was another promise of negotiations for a "final treaty," to start no later than January, 1947.

Whatever Ho Chi Minh's reasons for signing the *modus vivendi* —whether a desire to avoid war at any cost, a belief that the elections in France to be held in November might produce a government dependent on Communist support and more inclined to make concessions, or the simple necessity to gain a few more months during which preparations for the war could be completed—he paid a heavy price for upholding the truce.

4

Ho Chi Minh left Paris on September 16. He returned home aboard a French warship, arriving in Haiphong on October 20, after an absence of almost five months. His delegation had arrived home on October 3 and been given a tumultuous welcome. He must surely have wondered how he, having reversed their position, would be received. He was given the answer almost the moment he set foot on his native soil. In a chain of popular demonstrations extending from Haiphong to Hanoi, he was greeted even more enthusiastically than the delegation.

He was pleased to find that in his absence his lieutenants had destroyed the pro-Chinese parties and widened his organizational basis. What disturbed him was the progress by the French in strengthening their military position. French efforts toward that end had begun right after the signing on April 3 of the military appendix to the March agreement. The Vietnamese soon accused the French of stationing more troops in the North than the agreement allowed. The occupation of Pleiku and Kontum and the strengthening of the garrison at Tourane were instances of unauthorized French acts, as were the use of military installations, the occupation of public buildings, troop movements, and the recruiting of "coolies" for military construction work.

Evidence that the overthrow of Ho Chi Minh's government was the French aim was contained in a circular issued on April 19, 1946, by General Valluy, who, after Leclerc's voluntary resignation, became commander in chief of the French troops in Indochina. Valluy directed the French garrisons in Vietnam to undertake "the study of measures which would have the effect of progressively modifying and transforming the plan of action, which is that of a purely military operation, into a plan of action for a *coup d'état.*"[10]

When Valluy issued his circular, the moment for French military action was still far off. The French needed more time, and so did the Vietminh. Ho and Giap knew that the only way they could win was by conducting a "people's war" which enjoyed the fullest support of the entire population. To achieve the requisite control of the masses, the Vietminh had a choice between two possible courses: a coalition of all parties and political groupings, or the elimination of all groups opposed to Vietminh leadership and control. The Communists chose the latter.

The prospect that the conflict in the South would turn into a national war against the French vastly improved the chances of the Communists for retaining the commanding position they had gained in the August revolution. They did not want to share control of the national movement with anyone. They were not interested in a free Vietnam dominated by their political enemies in the nationalist camp. The fight for independence was for them only a vehicle for the conquest of power.

Their efforts to retain leadership had been remarkably success-ful in 1945. But by the spring of 1946, the honeymoon of the national revolution came to an end. The peaceful method of gathering support around the Vietminh failed to produce the earlier successful results. Some prominent national figures ceased their support of the Vietminh and still others turned into out-spoken critics. In February, Ho Chi Minh brought the Catholic leader Ngo Dinh Diem from his confinement in a Tongkingese mountain village to Hanoi and invited him to join his "govern-ment of national resistance." Diem refused.[11] On March 18, Bao Dai left the country, thus putting an end to his association with the Vietminh.[12]

When the Communists began to realize that they could no longer get the support of prominent non-Communists, they con-centrated on perfecting their direct organizational control of the masses. One of the steps they had taken was the creation, on May 27, just before Ho Chi Minh's departure for France, of the Lien Viet, or Popular National Front, into which they pressed every legal political party, dozens of Vietminh-inspired ethnic groups, and all cultural, religious, and professional organizations. The vital center of the Lien Viet was of course the Vietminh. In fact, the Lien Viet was nothing but a kind of super-Vietminh. Those who refused to join were denounced as enemies of independence and democracy and as "reactionaries," which was almost tanta-mount to being designated for assassination. To escape this stigma, many nationalists joined the Lien Viet by forming separate groups, among them the Vietnamese Socialist Party, which joined the

Lien Viet in July. Its leader became so loyal a supporter of Ho Chi Minh that he later was made minister of foreign affairs.[13]

5

Although the VNQDD and Dong Minh Hoi had subscribed to the March agreement, they never ceased their propaganda against a temporary truce with the French. Exploiting the very real popular discontent with the agreement was their only weapon against the Vietminh. They sought to discredit the Vietminh in order to provoke an armed clash between the government and the French. The trouble they stirred up strained Franco-Vietnamese relations almost to the breaking point. Both the French and the Vietminh decided that something had to be done.

There can be no doubt that had it not been for the presence of the Chinese, the Vietminh would have wiped out the VNQDD and Dong Minh Hoi long before. No sooner had the Chinese left when the Vietminh struck. The French immediately responded to the invitation for joint action against the "enemies of the peace." Joint Franco-Vietminh patrols were set up to maintain order and prevent further violence. But this was only a beginning. The steps taken showed that the Vietminh saw this as an opportunity to crush the pro-Chinese parties, and the French, who preferred a cooperative Communist to an uncompromising nationalist, supported the Vietminh.

Giap sent his troops into VNQDD and Dong Minh Hoi territory. The French equipped Giap's troops and also sent their own as reinforcements. In the Hongay mining district, where the Dong Minh Hoi had set up an insurgent "government," the French went even further, ejecting the Dong Minh Hoi and handing the administration over to the Vietminh. In some regions of the Red River Valley controlled by the VNQDD, this campaign lasted until October—as a matter of fact, Lao Kay, on the Vietnam-Yunnan border, was not "liberated" until November 2—but on the whole, the pro-Chinese parties were with French help eliminated from the political scene before the end of July. As was to be expected, after their defeat some of the leaders rallied to the

Vietminh, and under the leadership of Nguyen Van Xuan, the VNQDD was "reorganized." The old leaders were charged with having betrayed the ideals of the party; and in July, the new VNQDD joined the Lien Viet.

The conduct and fate of Vietnam's anti-Communist movements in 1946 augured ill for the future. The country lacked that which it needed most: anti-Communist leaders morally and politically superior to the leadership of the Vietminh.

6

When Ho Chi Minh resumed the presidency on October 20, the double task of eliminating the opposition and of herding both the willing and reluctant into the Lien Viet was virtually completed. Credit for this was due largely to Giap, who in Ho's absence had proved a strong leader.

The shift in power produced by Giap's measures had to be formalized and the newly forged "unity" of the nation in the Lien Viet made manifest in the country's political institutions. Always careful to observe formal democratic procedures that helped to tighten Party control over the state, the Communists decided to call the National Assembly into session. It convened on October 28 to elect a new government and give the country a constitution.

The government that had been formed at the end of February resigned. As expected, Ho Chi Minh was charged with forming the new government, which the Assembly approved on November 3. The main difference between the old and the new was the elimination of the unregenerate opposition members and greater direct Communist participation. In addition to the presidency, Ho Chi Minh took over the ministry of foreign affairs, but he appointed a close friend, Hoang Minh Giam, the head of the Socialist Party, as his deputy. Giap became minister of national defense. Two Communists, Nguyen Van Tao and Le Van Hien, held the ministries of finance and labor. Although by far the smallest group in the Assembly, the Communists were now by far the strongest in the cabinet.

But no one knew better than Ho Chi Minh that the struggle

for independence could not be conducted under the banner of Communism. The establishment of an open Party dictatorship would only have brought about the collapse of the ingenious political edifice through which the Communists dominated the nationalist movement. The more the regime evolved toward one-party rule, the greater became the need for democratic rhetoric and ritual and for a splendid façade of democratic institutions. The constitution submitted to the Assembly was designed to meet this need. It was adopted on November 8, with 240 against 2 votes, and its only lasting achievement was the solemn confirmation of the name of the new state: Democratic Republic of Vietnam (D.R.V.N.). It proclaimed that the country, "one and indivisible," consisting of three parts—Bac Bo (north), Trung Bo (center), and Nam Bo (south)—was to be ruled by a single chamber, the People's Parliament, elected every three years by direct, secret, universal suffrage of all Vietnamese over eighteen years of age. The constitution guaranteed equal rights to members of the ethnic minorities and women. It granted the citizens of Vietnam freedom of speech, assembly, association, religion, residence, and travel; it made primary education compulsory and free and stipulated state support for the aged and infirm. But it contained no social-welfare provisions, said nothing about economic planning, and placed no specific restrictions on private property. On the contrary, it guaranteed to all Vietnamese the rights of property and ownership.

The National Assembly did not meet again until December, 1953. The constitution remained stillborn. Its lofty principles had no influence on the political evolution of the Hanoi regime. Even before the armed conflict blanketed the entire country, the Communists felt perfectly justified in equating opposition to the Vietminh with antistate activities. Though the Communists introduced radical democratic reforms, they had no compunction about imprisoning or even murdering those who tried to use these reforms to oppose them. During the first weeks of the revolution, scores of nationalists were murdered; others, tried by "people's courts," were sentenced to death as traitors. "Whatever represented political opposition," admits Le Thanh Khoi, a pro-Communist Vietnamese, "was eliminated without mercy,"[14] and Truong Chinh, in his official *August Revolution* expresses regret that the repression was not carried out "fully within the framework of its possibilities."[15]

But these political murders were not confined to the first chaotic weeks of the revolution, nor were they restricted to "collaborators" and "reactionaries." The Stalinists saw to it that anyone who might have dimmed their own luster was eliminated.

Tran Van Giau was convinced that a unified command for the war in the South was possible only if all nationalists who refused blind allegiance were eliminated. Next to the Trotskyists, whom he wiped out, he feared the well-organized political sects most. So hated did he make himself among other anti-French nationalists that he was recalled to Hanoi in January, 1946, and replaced by Nguyen Binh. But Binh, though more subtle, was equally ruthless. He succeeded in temporarily uniting the badly split resistance movement in the South, but before long the various factions began to fight again among themselves, until Communist terror gradually drove many of the anti-Communists into the French camp.

In the Hoa Hao this fateful shift did not take place until May, 1947, after a year and a half of alternating open warfare and uneasy coexistence with the Vietminh. When Nguyen Binh became convinced that Huynh Phu So, the Hoa Hao leader, would never knuckle under to the Vietminh, he led him into a trap in April, 1947, and subsequently had him executed.

Except for brief intervals of concerted anti-French action, the battle between the Vietminh and the sects, one of the most terrible chapters in the history of the anticolonial movement, continued throughout the entire Indochina War. This is true not only of the Hoa Hao, but also of the Cao Dai and Binh Xuyen. They might have ended up by making peace with the French even without being impelled by the Vietminh, but from a national point of view, Communist policy toward the sects was no less criminal than the assassination of opponents.

The Binh Xuyen was the first to respond to Vietminh terror with counterthreats of negotiations with the French. A small group joined the French in fighting the Vietminh in June, 1947, and the sect's entire army followed a year later. The Binh Xuyen became more stalwart allies of the French than either the Cao Dai or Hoa Hao. The transition of the Cao Dai from resistance to collaboration was accelerated by the Vietminh's treatment of the Cao Dai chief, Tran Quang Vinh. After his escape from the Vietminh, Vinh persuaded his followers to come to terms with the French. A small group rallied to the French in June, 1946, and a larger one in November, after the French permitted the Cao Dai pope to return from exile. Because of the strong anti-French feeling in its ranks, the Hoa Hao did not break with the Vietminh until May, 1947, despite armed clashes between the two as early as September, 1945. The brutality of some of the Hoa Hao units in fighting the Vietminh has remained unmatched in the bloody post-1945 history of Vietnam.

7

Despite the intensive warfare between the Vietminh and the sects, the guerrilla war in the South continued unabated. On October 30, 1946, when the cease-fire agreed upon in the *modus vivendi* was supposed to become effective, the Vietminh controlled more territory, was stronger, and more firmly dominated the resistance movement than at the beginning of the year. The man credited with this achievement was Nguyen Binh, whose energy, boldness, and organizational talents helped to perfect guerrilla tactics. The French response to the stepped-up guerrilla tactics was to increase their terrorization of the population and to pillage and burn villages from which they had been fired on, thus turning thousands of lukewarm nationalists and even people friendly to them into bitter enemies.

French intransigence became something like a secret weapon for the Communists. It facilitated the application of their methods. Extremists often have in common a reluctance to work toward their goals by compromising with intermediate political forces. The French insisted on "collaboration" under conditions that made native self-rule a farce, and the Communists insisted on "unity" under conditions that forced all other resistance groups to give up their identities and become satellites of the Vietminh.

The French desired a Communist monopoly of the national resistance movement as ardently as the Communists themselves; their wish that there should be none left whom to fight except the

Communists soon led them to believe that this had become the case. The Communists, though they did not share the French view that only they were fighting the French, shared the French wish that none should be left to conduct the struggle for independence except the Vietminh.

The temporary alliance between the Vietminh and the French against the pro-Chinese parties ended as soon as the VNQDD and Dong Minh Hoi were destroyed. Between June and November, 1946, Giap doubled the strength of his regular army from 30,000 to 60,000. In addition, the Vietminh continually recruited young men for its paramilitary formations. When the war broke out, the organized military strength of the Vietminh was about 100,000 men.

Not only did both sides intensify their military preparations, but they also sabotaged whatever provisions of the March agreement they considered obstacles to the achievement of their aims. The French persisted in their refusal to negotiate a cease-fire in the South and to make the concessions needed to validate their recognition of Vietnam as a free state. The Vietminh used this refusal as an excuse for not cooperating in forming a joint military force under French command. Neither the *modus vivendi* nor Ho Chi Minh's conciliatory words after his return to Vietnam were able to reduce the existing antagonisms.

A basic inability to conclude further compromises created mutual vexations over matters both trivial and important. The trivial included such Vietnamese ceremonies as the public destruction of all French decorations and diplomas and the refusal of the Vietnamese Army to take part in the French armistice celebrations. More serious were the strikes that broke out at factories that had been returned to the French, or the refusal to handle food shipments to French garrisons.

The list of Vietnamese grievances was headed by the nonobservance of the cease-fire agreed upon in the *modus vivendi*. While the French refused to respect the *modus vivendi* in regard to the hostilities in the South, they acted as if some of its provisions gave them governmental authority in the North. Without prior agreement with Hanoi, they arrogated to themselves the right to impose taxes on French nationals, in particular on French-owned factories. This was a breach of the *modus vivendi*. Equally provocative was the institution by the French of a federal postal service in Hanoi. Moreover, on October 27 the French promulgated a constitution for the French Union without consulting any of the Indochinese states.

Yet these matters were of secondary importance compared with the conflict over the questions of currency and customs. The *modus vivendi* stipulated that joint commissions work out how and by whom the country's currency should in future be issued, and how and for whose benefit the customs duties should be collected. The French, who continued to issue the old piaster through the Bank of Indochina, were in no hurry to start negotiations to abolish a system that suited them well. On the other hand, they had compelling reasons for changing import controls and the collection of customs duties. The French view was that there should be only one customs service for the whole of Indochina, i.e., that customs should be taken out of the hands of the states and administered by the French alone. The Vietnamese not only rejected interference with their right to import what they needed and tax whatever entered their country, but they also wanted to alleviate the government's financial plight through the collection of customs duties. The Vietnamese, not at all anxious to relinquish their border control and the income derived from it, or even share it with the French, did nothing to hasten compliance with the *modus vivendi* in regard to customs. This only strengthened the resolve of the French to settle the matter unilaterally. It also gave them an opportunity for a show of strength.

On August 29, two weeks before the signing of the *modus vivendi*, French Army units at Haiphong expelled the Vietnamese from their customs house at Haiphong, under the pretext that Chinese merchants were being forced to pay import duties in violation of the Franco-Chinese treaty that stipulated duty-free entry of Chinese goods into Indochina—a treaty to which the Vietnamese Government was not a party. The incident had barely been settled through the personal intervention of Giap when General Morlière, commander of the French troops in the North, announced on September 10, four days before the *modus vivendi* brought up the question of customs for negotiations, that the French would take full and sole control of all imports and exports in Haiphong on October 15. The order was not canceled after the signing of the *modus vivendi*, and a protest by Ho Chi Minh to Paris on November 16 went unanswered.

Although Ho Chi Minh continued to appeal publicly for negotiations, his government began to act in precisely the same spirit as the French. The constitution adopted by the Assembly made no reference to the French Union, nor to the Indochinese Federation of which Vietnam, according to the March agreement, was to be a member. On November 6, the Assembly voted a new currency for Vietnam, the so-called Ho Chi Minh piaster. On November 8, it protested against the infringement of national sovereignty by the French border controls at Haiphong. Propaganda and military preparations became more hectic. When the Assembly adjourned on November 14, the stage was set for the great drama which began to be acted out in Vietnam a week later.

8

November 20 is a day to remember. It saw two armed collisions, of which the one at Langson was settled within twenty-four hours, with a clear victory for the French. The other clash occurred at Haiphong, the very center of the war of nerves that preceded the outbreak of hostilities in the North.

Were it not for incontrovertible evidence that the events that started at Haiphong on November 20 actually did take place, one would hardly believe this incredible tale. Strangely enough, at that time neither France nor any other country had newspaper correspondents in North Vietnam. The reports on which the story is based were written by French participants in the events, men interested in proving that they were not to blame for the horror caused by their faulty judgment, their lack of concern for human lives, and their stupidity. Although this makes a satisfactory explanation of the chain of events between November 20 and 23 impossible, it at least permits a reasonably accurate account.

In the early morning hours of November 20, a French patrol boat in the harbor of Haiphong seized a Chinese junk carrying "contraband" cargo. The Vietminh militia (Tu Ve) intercepted the French boat and took its three-man crew prisoners. This action was accompanied by a number of minor clashes in and around the harbor, during which another three French soldiers were taken prisoner. The local French commander, Colonel Debès, thereupon decided to free the six by force. The intrusion of French troops into the Vietnamese quarters led to serious fighting. The Tu Ve erected barricades and frustrated French attempts to free their men. The French, angered by their failure, attacked and expelled the Vietminh guards stationed in the town's French quarter. French troops were soon in control of most of the city, including large sections of the Vietnamese quarter. While fighting continued, the local permanent liaison commission, which included two level-headed Frenchmen, met at 11 A.M. to try to settle the matter. The attitude of the Vietnamese was conciliatory; the French prisoners were released. The Vietnamese also accepted a French demand that all barricades be removed before 2 P.M. and agreed to a cease-fire, although the French rejected their demand that both parties return to their original positions. The French remained in the Vietnamese sections but did not permit the Vietminh to return to their posts in the French part of the city. At 2 o'clock, however, when the French demand that all barricades be razed had not been fully complied with, French troops moved into the Vietnamese quarter with bulldozers and armored cars. The fighting resumed immediately and with increased fury.

The incident was settled and the fighting stopped on November 21, after the respective commanders at Haiphong had been ordered to observe the cease-fire. But Saigon's intervention, with Paris approval, shattered not only the precarious local cease-fire but simultaneously all hopes of arresting the drift toward hostilities in the North.

On November 18, a French civilian delegation from Saigon headed by M. R. Lacharrière had come to Hanoi to find out whether the mixed commission that was to deal with the problems of customs and foreign trade could at last begin its work. On November 20, while blood was being shed at Haiphong, Lacharrière dined with Ho Chi Minh, who agreed to an immediate opening of talks at Hanoi. But in Saigon the desire to settle these problems had vanished as soon as the news of the Haiphong fighting reached the offices of the commander in chief, General Valluy, who, in d'Argenlieu's absence, acted as high commissioner. Valluy immediately saw that this was his chance for achieving one of his most important tactical aims: complete French control of the Haiphong harbor. He therefore informed both General Morlière and Lacharrière that Ho Chi Minh's proposal for negotiations was acceptable only under two conditions: the immediate evacuation of all Vietnamese troops from Haiphong and complete French military control of the Haiphong area.

General Morlière, who knew that total capitulation at Haiphong was unacceptable to the Vietminh, did not even bother to submit these demands to Ho Chi Minh. Instead, he reassured Saigon that the incident was settled. Valluy, having foreseen that General Morlière might not share his views, ignored hitherto sacred procedures and issued direct orders to the local commander at Haiphong, who had almost been persuaded to honor the cease-fire. On November 22, Colonel Debès received another message from Valluy persuading him that he could act even without the approval of his immediate superior, General Morlière.[16] What had led Valluy to insist on breaking the cease-fire was a message from Admiral d'Argenlieu, who had succeeded in gaining Bidault's consent that the French use the Haiphong incident to teach the Vietnamese a lesson. In his fateful if not entirely truthful message to Debès, General Valluy instructed the commander of Haiphong to use all the means at his disposal "to make yourself complete master of Haiphong and so bring the Vietnamese Army around to a better understanding of the situation."[17]

On November 23, Debès transmitted Valluy's request to the local Vietnamese authorities as an ultimatum demanding that the Vietnamese troops evacuate Haiphong within two hours under the pretext that Vietnamese troop movements constituted a breach of the cease-fire. Two hours later, the Vietnamese replied that they had asked Hanoi for instructions and that they had not violated the cease-fire. Debès gave them another forty-five minutes before deciding that his ultimatum had been rejected and that the attack could begin.

The French threw everything they had into the battle for Haiphong—infantry, tanks, artillery, airplanes, and even naval guns, which fired at Vietnamese sectors where there was no fighting at all. Even civilians who had managed to reach open terrain outside the town were fired upon by the naval guns because they were mistaken for soldiers massing for an attack.

The controversy about the number of Vietnamese killed in this brutal action remains unresolved. There was no one left in Haiphong in a position either to count the dead or interested in doing so. The Vietnamese claim that the number of victims was close to 20,000 is disputed by the French. "No more than 6,000 killed, in so far as naval bombardment of fleeing civilians was concerned," Admiral Battet later told Paul Mus.[18]

On November 24, Admiral d'Argenlieu had the bad taste to send a message to Valluy whose barbarity of style reflected the character of the man: "I have learned with indignation of the recent attacks at Haiphong and Langson. Our troops were once more victims of criminal premeditation. I bow down before our great, dead soldiers. I salute the wounded. . . . The Government of the Republic and the whole country, profoundly moved . . . realize the extraordinary difficulties you have met. . . . You have my esteem and my confidence. We shall never retreat or give up."[19]

The battle for Haiphong lasted several days. Vietnamese resistance was strong, but their arms were inadequate. By November 28, the Tu Ve had lost its foothold in the town, the harbor, and at the nearby airport.

9

Despite the shock the French action had produced in Hanoi, the government still clung to the hope that a return to the situation that had prevailed before the attack was possible. Ho Chi Minh appealed to the people to remain calm. Giap asked to see General Morlière on November 27 to discuss measures for easing the tension. He was granted an audience two days later, but the instructions Morlière communicated to Giap were nothing less than another ultimatum. Talks about any new accord, General Valluy had ordered, could be considered only if the government formally agreed that the French exercise full control of Haiphong and its surroundings, and of all roads connecting their garrisons, especially the routes between Haiphong and Hanoi. These demands, Morlière told

Giap, were not subject to negotiations; they had to be accepted before the French would agree to any further talks.

It may be assumed that now Ho Chi Minh, in spite of his untiring efforts to keep peace talks alive, had become convinced that war had become inevitable. In any case, he did not interfere with Giap's final military preparations, nor did he stop the Central Committee of the Vietminh from issuing belligerent appeals asking the people to be ready if the government should give the order to rise.

Giap's most significant step was the removal of his regular troops from Hanoi and other large cities. He concentrated the bulk of his army in the provinces of Bac Kan, Ha Giang, Tuyen Quang, and Thai Nguyen, a vast area north of Hanoi known as the Viet Bac. Other preparations included the setting up of roadblocks between Haiphong and Hanoi. In Hanoi itself, the Vietminh began to erect barricades, dig trenches, fell trees, and bore tunnels for safe passage between their various strongholds. Large numbers of people, frightened by the events at Haiphong and by the increasingly aggressive behavior of the French, fled Hanoi; the more radical as well as the merely impatient and excited elements of the Vietminh, in particular the Tu Ve, began to shed their former restraint. Some needed little provocation to attack French soldiers or even civilians, and not a day now passed without shooting in some part of the city.

Once again it was Sainteny who, after his return to Hanoi on December 2 as Commissioner for the Republic, sought to intervene in behalf of peace through a resumption of his contacts with Ho Chi Minh. The fact that the two men tried up to the last minute to preserve the peace may be proof only of their desire to lessen their personal responsibility for the impending catastrophe rather than of a belief in the success of their efforts. Ho Chi Minh missed no opportunity to appeal to public opinion in France and to seek intervention by Paris "against certain Frenchmen in Indochina," as he put it. He did so in a moving broadcast appeal to the French National Assembly on December 6, and again in an interview in *Paris-Saigon* on December 7. "We want peace," he kept repeating. "Neither France nor Vietnam can afford the luxury of a bloody war." However, he added, the Vietnamese "would do anything rather than renounce their liberty."

From Paris came a friendly echo on December 10. The Socialist leader Léon Blum wrote in *Le Populaire* that there was only one way for the French to maintain their prestige and their cultural and political influence in Indochina: a sincere agreement based on independence for Vietnam. Two days later, Blum formed an all-Socialist caretaker government, which, on December 17, received a vote of confidence from the Chamber of Deputies. On December 18, the Council of Ministers decided that Marius Moutet, the Minister for Overseas Territories, was to go to Saigon to make a supreme effort on behalf of peace.

It was too late. Neither the French nor the Vietminh were any longer able to check their preparations. The attitude of the French became daily more aggressive, the reaction of the Vietnamese increasingly uncontrollable. On December 15, aware that time was running out, Ho Chi Minh in a cabled appeal to Léon Blum again stressed his government's desire to work with the French.[20] His message contained absolutely fair and concrete proposals for breaking the impasse. In view of its reasonableness, it is not surprising that Saigon censorship held up the message. It reached Paris only on December 26, a week after the outbreak of hostilities in the North.

On December 17, General Valluy paid a surprise visit to Haiphong to tell the local commanders to be ready for the imminent showdown. On the same day, an incident in Hanoi showed that Sainteny could be as savage as any committed nationalist. In revenge for an attack by the Tu Ve on a French truck in which several soldiers were killed, he ordered the "liquidation" of a nearby Tu Ve post. The houses around the post were set on fire and fifteen Vietnamese slain in cold blood. The next day, Sainteny requested that the government order the removal of all barricades in Hanoi. Without allowing time to do so, he sent bulldozers to clear the city streets. That same day, the French occupied the Ministries of Finance and Communications under the pretext that they had been fired on from these buildings. Finally on the morning of December 19, General Morlière demanded that the Tu Ve be disarmed immediately and all security duties in Hanoi turned over to the French.

The Vietnamese considered this a call to surrender. Ho Chi Minh pleaded with Sainteny not to insist on this demand. His foreign minister, Giam, asked for an audience with Morlière, which was refused. The French ordered all soldiers to their barracks, a move that Giap took as a sign that they were ready to attack and disarm the Tu Ve. Giap appealed to Morlière to rescind the order. The French version holds that they heeded Giap's appeal and actually permitted their troops to leave the barracks. But at 6 P.M., so goes the story, a Eurasian agent engaged by the French to work with the Vietminh reported that an attack was being prepared by the Tu Ve for that same evening. The attack on French posts and residential districts took place right after the central electrical works were put out of operation at 8 P.M.—the hour at which, according to the French, the Indochina War officially started, to the great satisfaction of General Valluy and Admiral d'Argenlieu, who at last were able to conduct the war they had so assiduously prepared while maintaining that the Vietminh was the aggressor.

The French occupied Ho Chi Minh's residence in the afternoon of December 20, but he and all his close collaborators had managed to escape. The Vietminh launched a number of strong attacks in various cities, but at no important location were its men able to hold out for any length of time against the superior equipment thrown against them by the French. Still it took the French almost three months to establish their control over the principal towns of Tongking and northern Annam. However, as in the South, the countryside was and remained under effective Vietminh control.

A curious detail, which does not quite fit in with the theory of a premeditated Vietminh attack, is the apparent lack of co-ordination that characterized the entire action of December 19. Giap's order for a general uprising was issued only at 9:30 P.M., after the fighting in Hanoi had already been going on for over an hour. In most major cities action began at various hours; at Hue, for instance, it did not begin until 2 A.M. of December 20. Was the action premeditated but ill-planned, or is there truth in the theory that the tragic events of that day were triggered accidentally?

Ever since the day the fighting spread throughout the North, the question of who was responsible for the outbreak of the war has agitated both the French and Vietnamese. Merely to determine who fired the first shot cannot furnish the answer. Those who believe that the war began on December 19, 1946, in Hanoi say that it was started by the Vietminh. This contention, unconvincing even from a purely technical point of view, moreover is politically irrelevant. Those who fire the first shot do not always bear sole responsibility for the outbreak of a war. Fighting starts once political decisions that make war inevitable have been taken. On this level, the French can say that there would have been no war if the Vietnamese had settled for less than full independence. And the Vietnamese can counter that there would have been no war if the French had not insisted on re-establishing the colonial rule after World War II that a Vietnamese national revolution had liquidated. In this political sense the French unquestionably were the aggressors and primarily responsible for the war. The action of the Vietminh on December 19 can be likened to that of a man who, while being hanged, cuts the rope he knows is about to strangle him.

Yet the question of responsibility must be raised on still another level, in relation to the dominant historical trends of our time, among them the spread of nationalism. Although the motives of the Communists were as questionable and their methods as odious as those of the French, the cause for which the Vietminh fought was a nobler one than that of the French, which was out of tune with the forward movement of history and violated the very principles on which France herself bases her political existence.

On this historical level, responsibility for the Indochina War rests primarily with the leaders of the so-called Free French, and in particular with General de Gaulle, who in 1945 had the power to foil the schemes of his country's colonial party. His failure to do so was probably the most serious error of his political career. Although no longer in power in August, 1946, he remained the most influential voice of France. He contributed to the failure of the Fontainebleau conference with a speech in which he said: "United with the overseas territories which she opened to civilization, France is a great power. Without these territories she would be in danger of no longer being one."[21]

On August 18, 1945, Bao Dai had addressed a moving appeal to de Gaulle on behalf of Vietnamese independence, in which he prophesied that "even if you were to . . . re-establish a French administration here, it would no longer be obeyed; each village would be a nest of resistance, every former friend an enemy, and your officials and colonists themselves would ask to depart from this unbreathable atmosphere."[22] De Gaulle never replied, and his public statements still are devoid of any awareness that his Indochina policy was catastrophic. Indeed, if this flawed national hero could have risen above the tragic mediocrity of his country's political leadership after World War II, France and Vietnam would probably have been spared the ordeal of the Indochina War.

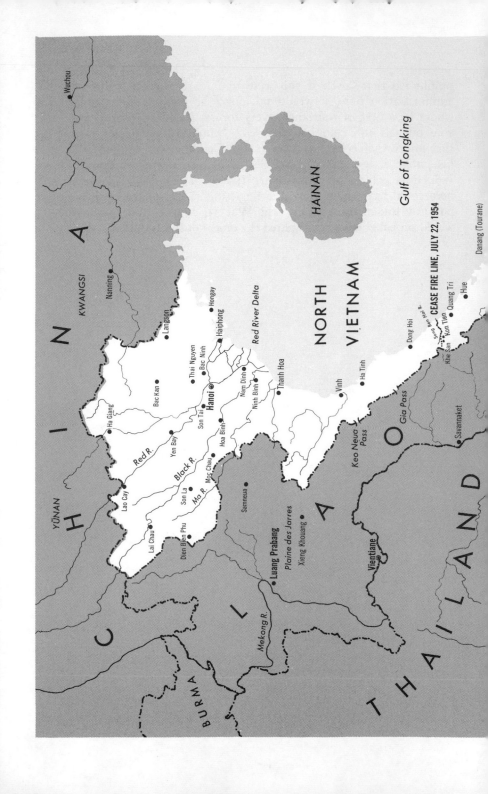

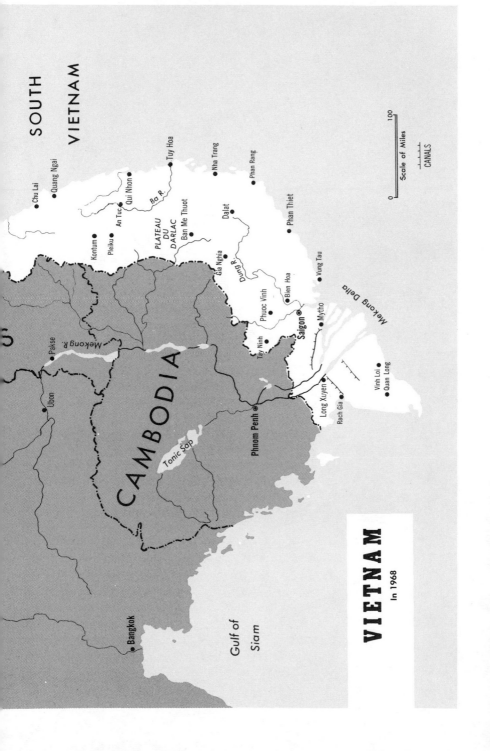

SOUTH
VIETNAM

• Chu Lai
• Quang Ngai

• Tuy Hoa

• Qui Nhon
Ba R.
• An Tuc
• Nha Trang

• Kontum
• Pleiku
PLATEAU
DU
DARLAC
• Ban Me Thuot
• Phan Rang

• Dalat
Gia Nghia •
Dung R.
• Phan Thiet

Pakse •
Mekong R.
Phuoc Vinh •
Bien Hoa •
Vung Tau •

• Ubon
Tay Ninh •
Saigon ◉
Mytho •
Mekong Delta

CAMBODIA
Long Xuyen •
Vinh Loi •
• Quan Long
Phnom Penh ◉
Rach Gia •

Tonic Sap

Gulf of
Siam

• Bangkok

0   100
Scale of Miles

------ CANALS

VIETNAM
In 1968

Part Three

Vietnam at War

XIII

The "Bao Dai Solution"

1

OF THE MANY ARMED CONFLICTS of this century, none has lasted as long as the struggle for Indochina, and none compares in political complexity and unresolved consequences.

What were the issues in the war? Why did it last so long? And why, when it did end, did the struggle for Vietnam not end also? Satisfactory answers can be found only if the controversy over the date when the Indochina War actually did begin can be settled.

If war is the use by two or more nations of military means for political ends, then the war began in September, 1945, when the French with British help ousted the Vietnamese administration installed by the Provisional Committee for the South in Saigon. Thus Vietnamese opinion holds almost unanimously that the war resulted from French aggression. The official French version clings to December 19, 1946, as the date when war began as a result of Vietminh action in Hanoi. But if peace reigned officially until then, war nonetheless had become a fact of life. It had been raging almost uninterruptedly in the southern half of the country for more than a year. Hence December, 1946, marks not the beginning of war but merely the collapse of efforts to prevent it from spreading.

In their attempt to deny responsibility for the war that they had caused in the South, the French not only clung to their contention that it had been brought on by the Vietminh in December, 1946, but they also claimed that they were fighting solely to prevent Vietnam from falling under a Communist dictatorship. France, it seems, was sacrificing her wealth and her manpower to save Vietnam for the "free world." It was a conflict between Democracy and Communism. "Not since the Crusades," said General Jean de Lattre de Tassigny in July, 1951, "has France undertaken such disinterested action. This war is the war of Vietnam for Vietnam."[1]

If the war had really started only in December, 1946, it might be proved more easily that not the French but the Vietminh were the aggressors, and that the French were not conducting a colonial war. France could not deny that the fighting had started in September, 1945, but because it remained confined to the South, it was not really a war but a temporary state of disorder caused by local rebels.

Once the entire country was engulfed in war, the evidence that it was a war of colonial reconquest brought on by the French became overwhelming. To prove that they had not sought the war, that they were merely defending themselves against a Vietnamese attack, all the French had to do was to indicate interest in working out terms for the restoration of peace. But the men responsible for French policy in Indochina firmly refused to seek peace through negotiations. The military welcomed the war, Paris hypocritically deplored its extension, and both were united in their refusal to negotiate, for they knew that negotiation meant recognition of Vietnam's independence, and this the French were unwilling to grant.

2

In 1945, the French people, although fairly united behind a policy of "French presence" in Indochina, were not at all of one mind about the purpose of this presence, let alone about the methods of maintaining that presence.

Of these divisions in French opinion, the one most talked about was that between the French in Indochina and the men in France engaged in colonial affairs. The old colonialists failed to see that Vietnam was going through a genuine national revolution. The radical leaders of colonial society put the blame for the growing strength of the Vietminh and French inability to defeat the rebels in the South on Paris' "soft" policy toward the nationalist movement, as exemplified by Cédile's negotiations with the rebels in Saigon, the recognition of the Hanoi regime in the March agreement, and subsequent attempts to reach a compromise with the Ho Chi Minh government at Dalat and Fontainebleau.

However, the differences between these die-hards and the "new men" in metropolitan France were merely apparent, not real. They concerned means, not ends. The astonishing truth is that after World War II, all Frenchmen, including the Communists, agreed that Indochina ought to remain within the French colonial empire. The difference between the Left and the Right concerned methods. The Left, at least up to December, 1946, favored bona fide negotiations with Hanoi. After that date, the quarrel between the two camps revealed a deeper division, though it still did not focus on aims but on methods. The Left (except the Communists, who wanted negotiations with no one except Ho Chi Minh) began to see the advisability of negotiations with nationalists other than the Vietminh, and even to accept the necessity of promising independence to a non-Communist Vietnam; the Right, including the Rassemblement Populaire Français (the new formation behind de Gaulle), opposed not only negotiations with Ho Chi Minh but the granting of independence to any Vietnamese regime. In this alignment of forces, which lasted to the end of the Indochina War, the Frenchmen in Indochina acted merely as the radical wing of the parties of the Right and Center, both of which supported a military solution. And when France, haltingly and much too late, began to make concessions toward eventual independence, colonial officialdom sabotaged them. It was the systematic undoing, in Saigon and Hanoi, of concessions made by Paris that lent French policy its aura of duplicity. But in this respect, too, colonial society acted as a faction of the colonial party of France. Its sabotage could have been broken by Paris only if the Left had advocated a consistent anticolonial policy for Indochina and thereby had succeeded in defeating the imperialist position of the Right.

The quarrel over Vietnam that tore France apart politically between 1945 and 1954 was bogged down in a number of subdisputes, not all of which have been resolved. These disputes not only divided the Left and Right, but also the Left itself. Furthermore, on the issue of Indochina the parliamentary "Center," represented in all postwar French governments, always threw its weight to the Right. The main Center group was the Catholic MRP (Mouvement Republicain Populaire), which on domestic policy usually sided with the Left. These divisions and disputes, plus the fact that France during this period had fifteen governments, account for the indecision and vacillation of French policy in Indochina.

During the early months of 1947, the chief dispute in regard to Vietnam was whether the conflict should be settled through negotiations or purely militarily. The Left, except for the Communists, temporarily adopted the position of the Right, which was that there could be no negotiations before "order" had been restored. When the expectation of a quick military decision had to be relinquished, Right and Left again moved apart. The new split, which opened up in the spring of 1947, at first concerned only the question of whether France should again negotiate with Ho Chi Minh. The Right unanimously opposed such negotiation; the Left, which headed the government, was badly split. The Communists, who stayed in the government until May, and most Socialists, advocated negotiations; the MRP and most Radicals firmly opposed them. Consequently no negotiations took place. The question of whether the Vietminh was a truly representative national coalition or merely an instrument of the Communists in turn posed the problem of whether one ought to refuse to negotiate with the Communist-dominated Vietminh because it was not sufficiently representative of the Vietnamese national movement. This by and large was the position taken by the non-Communist Left. The Center, in particular the MRP, sided with the non-Communist Left. The refusal to negotiate with Hanoi gave rise to the question with whom to negotiate, and out of the rather arbitrary decision that the Vietminh was not really representative of the people arose the further question whether, for the purpose of negotiation, any other government could be created. And if such a government were to become capable of taking the wind out of the sails of the Vietminh, would it not have to obtain what the Vietminh tried to achieve—full independence?

3

Why did the French fail to realize, as did the British and eventually the Dutch, that the age of Western domination of Asia was coming to an end? Although all the major French parties, including the Communists, must share the blame for the failure to prevent the war, the group chiefly responsible is the non-Communist Left. It was they who ruled France during the first crucial postwar years; it was under them that the fateful decisions that made this war inevitable were made. It was they who tolerated d'Argenlieu's sabotage of the March agreement, condoned General Valluy's provocations, and by their pettiness at the conference table destroyed the chance for a more lasting agreement at Fontainebleau. It has been said that at the time when a solution short of war was still possible, France had no Indochinese policy at all. The truth is that there was a policy, the policy of colonial reconquest, and that the Left, in control of the government but lacking a policy of its own, adopted the catastrophic course advocated by the Right.

Most significant for the failure of the Left to impose the liberal intentions it frequently voiced toward Vietnam was the role played during these years by the Socialist Party of France. The statements by men like Léon Blum and Guy Mollet, and resolutions adopted by the party between 1945 and 1954, prove that from 1945 on, of the major political groups only the Socialists had a workable answer to the problems created for France by the Vietnamese national revolution, and they consistently opposed d'Argenlieu's sabotage of the March agreement. After the war had spread, Léon Blum, as temporary premier, recognized the right of the Vietnamese to national freedom and, speaking in the French Assembly on December 23, 1946, openly stated that the old colonial system was finished.[2] But while the Socialists throughout 1947 and 1948 continued to demand that the government enter into peace negotiations with Ho Chi Minh, and gradually came to embrace the concept of total independence for Vietnam, the Socialist cabinet members who codetermined and even directed French policy toward Indochina consistently acted contrary to their party's enlightened views. Well-disposed critics therefore called the Socialists prisoners of the colonial party; angry Vietnamese accused them of being accomplices. It has been said in extenuation that the Socialists acted as they did for compelling innerpolitical reasons, that they looked upon participation in the government as an obligation toward the electorate which they could not disregard.

This holds true for most leading Socialists—men like Felix Gouin, Paul Ramadier, and Jules Moch—for the simple reason that France was closer to them than was Vietnam. Theirs was a position of painful compromise; they themselves regarded it as a necessary sacrifice but did not feel that it was a betrayal of Vietnam.

This defense cannot be made of the Socialist Minister for Overseas Territories, Marius Moutet. He no doubt believed that French policy in Indochina, although steadily moving toward the inevitable colonial war, would be less disastrous and less reprehensible if presided over by a known friend of the colonial peoples. Thus Moutet became a prisoner of the colonial party, and once he had allowed this to happen, he could act and defend his actions only as an accomplice of that party. Even Léon Blum, who had the misfortune of heading the all-Socialist caretaker government when hostilities broke out in Hanoi, in a speech on December 23, 1946, based his justification of a policy of force on the dubious assertion that responsibility for the outbreak of the war lay entirely with the Vietminh. When he spoke thus he did not know that Saigon was holding back the peace proposals that Ho Chi Minh had addressed to him on December 15. He spoke movingly and with a heavy heart, reiterating that in the end Vietnam had to be given her freedom and that only negotiations could produce lasting and friendly relations between France and Vietnam. But he failed to see that what had produced the war were the official aims of France as proclaimed in 1945 and firmly pursued in 1946. His failure to see that these aims called for the methods that were applied also made him a prisoner of the forces that determined French policy in Indochina after World War II.

It is therefore wrong to say, as the Left in France still does, that the war broke out because the nobler intentions of France were continuously thwarted by the advocates of force who held strategic positions both at home and in Indochina. In a speech in the Chamber of Deputies on March 18, 1946, Marius Moutet himself destroyed the myth that d'Argenlieu was out of step with Paris. Replying to critics who blamed the Admiral for the failure of the negotiations between March and December, 1945, Moutet stated: "What I reproach Admiral d'Argenlieu for is not that he did not follow the directives of the government. I reproach him for having anticipated them."[3]

Whatever differences may have existed between Paris and Saigon in 1946 were wiped out by the events of December. Moutet, sent by Blum to Indochina on a mission which Hanoi hoped was one of seeking peace, arrived in Saigon on December 25. Two days later he made statements that differed only in tone from the belligerent ones d'Argenlieu was making in Paris before his return to Saigon. D'Argenlieu's statement of December 27 that France would not relinquish her hold on Indochina but "was determined to maintain and develop her present influence" was echoed that same day by Moutet, who in Saigon spoke of "the necessity of maintaining the presence of France [in Indochina]." At a dinner given by the Cao Dai leader Le Van Hoach, who had served the Japanese as a high police official and now served the French as head of the separatist government of Cochinchina, Moutet warmed the hearts of all who had so successfully sabotaged the March agreement by placing the blame for the outbreak of the war entirely on the Vietminh. Instead of going to Hanoi to see what had really happened and whether there was still a chance of stopping the fighting, Moutet paid a leisurely visit to Cambodia and Laos, both firmly in French hands. When, on January 3, 1947, he finally did go to Hanoi (where the French had proclaimed martial law on December 23), his chief concern was to prevent any member of his mission from contacting representatives of the Vietminh government. Later, when Moutet came under attack for his failure to explore the chances of a cease-fire while in Hanoi, he defended himself by denying, despite testimony to the contrary, that any member of his mission had received any peace proposal from representatives of the Vietminh.[4] But on leaving the still-embattled city, he made it clear that such proposals were not welcome to the French Government, in whose name apparently he personally decided that negotiations with the Vietminh were out. "Before any negotiations," he told *Le Monde* on January 5, 1947, "it is necessary to have a military decision. I regret," he added, "but one cannot commit the sort of acts of madness the Vietnamese have done with impunity."

The men of war had won a total victory: Official France, under an all-Socialist government, now openly accepted the demand that the Franco-Vietnamese conflict be resolved through a "military decision."

A deeply disturbed Léon Blum, in his efforts to find a way out of his predicament, turned to the man who had played a decisive role in getting France to accept the March agreement. He asked Leclerc to return to Indochina, over the objections of d'Argenlieu, who regarded Leclerc as an appeaser of the Vietminh.

But Leclerc, who went to Indochina on a brief inspection tour, refused the posts of commander in chief and high commissioner offered him a few weeks later, not because d'Argenlieu disapproved of him or de Gaulle advised him against accepting either; nor was his reluctance to return to Indochina based on his knowledge that no government would grant him the well-equipped army of 500,000 men which he considered the minimum required for military success. His reasons were deeper: He knew that this was a war that could not be won. "In 1947," Leclerc said, "France will no longer put down by force a grouping of 24 million inhabitants which is assuming unity and in which there exists a xenophobic

and perhaps a national ideal." And in sharp contrast to d'Argenlieu and General Valluy, who now concentrated all their efforts
on a quick military solution, Leclerc stated: "The major problem
from now on is political."[5]

In Indochina, Leclerc's warnings fell on deaf ears, but not so
in Paris. There the new coalition government of the MRP, Socialists, Radicals, and Communists, headed by the Socialist Paul
Ramadier, which had come into power on January 21, was greatly
disturbed by Leclerc's forecasts.

Embarrassed by Leclerc's appeal for negotiations "with all factions of the Vietnamese people," the spokesmen of the French
Government tried to convince public opinion that not the French
but the Vietminh refused to seek peace through negotiations.
The Vietminh broadcasts asking for peace talks, it was said, could
not be regarded as official proposals. The attempt to reach Moutet
in Hanoi through members of his mission was brazenly denied.
When the government finally had to admit that it had received
written peace proposals, Premier Ramadier simply claimed that
according to expert opinion, Ho Chi Minh's signature on the document was not really his. Even the Communist cabinet members
did not make their demand for talks with Ho a condition for
remaining in the coalition, and when they did resign in May,
they did so over a question of internal policy, not over Indochina.

However, when, after two months of fighting, it became evident
that prospects for a quick military solution were anything but
good, Leclerc's belief that the main problem in Vietnam was
political rapidly gained ground in the more enlightened circles
of the Left and Center. While the military leaders in Indochina
remained ludicrously optimistic, the government began to concern itself with possible political steps to improve the position
of France in Vietnam. Ramadier spoke of the necessity of entering into a new "constructive phase" of policy for Vietnam. To
determine what this was to be was not easy, since both the legislature and the cabinet were deeply split over the issue of negotiations.

Negotiations, yes, but with whom? With Ho Chi Minh, said
the Communists; with all factions of the Vietnamese people,
including the Vietminh, said the majority of the Socialists and
some Radicals; with all factions except the Vietminh, said the

majority of the Radicals and some Socialists, above all the influential MRP. Who these factions were was hard to say. Could they be found among the followers of the VNQDD and the Dong Minh Hoi? Who else was there with whom an anti-Vietminh movement could be created for the purpose of Franco-Vietnamese negotiations?

Gradually, a plan emerged whose outlines had existed in d'Argenlieu's mind for some time. The basic feature was to unite all anti-Communist nationalist forces behind the former Emperor Bao Dai, to create a government headed by Bao Dai, and to negotiate an acceptable settlement with this government. The expectation was that this would reduce the Vietminh from its position of leading nationalist force to one of a "faction." After thus being decisively weakened, the Vietminh would either have to come to terms with the French, on a basis short of full independence, or be defeated by the combined forces of the French and the new government of Vietnam. If the Vietminh refused to submit, the war would continue. But now it would no longer be a colonial war. It would become a war between two Vietnamese governments, a civil war, a war between "Communism" and "anti-Communism," in which the role of the French would merely be to support the "anti-Communist" regime against the Vietminh.

Once this course was decided upon, the French line of conduct was set for the entire duration of the Indochina War. The policy of force was now combined with political intrigue. Vietnamese nationalism was to be used to defeat Vietnamese Communism, under the false assumption that Communism, not nationalism, was the force that strove to prevent the "presence" of France in Vietnam.

But the fundamental problem of the French could not be solved by political intrigue. The success of the Bao Dai scheme depended on the fulfillment of conditions which would make the plan useless for the French, for only a truly nationalist government could gain popular support. No regime that failed to fight for independence could ever become a viable anti-Communist force.

Again it was Leclerc who, looking further ahead than most of his compatriots, succinctly formulated the problem: "Anti-Communism," he said, "will remain a useless tool as long as the problem of nationalism is not solved."[6] His warning was not heeded: anti-Communism became official French policy in Vietnam for the next seven years.

4

In March, 1947, the leftist government of France finally took the action it should have taken in March, 1946: the recall of d'Argenlieu. This was a gesture designed chiefly to impress the Vietnamese. They could not possibly be expected to believe in new and better French intentions as long as d'Argenlieu remained in his post.

D'Argenlieu was replaced as high commissioner by Emile Bollaert, a member of the Radical Party, which had long demanded a greater role in the shaping of French Indochinese policy. In assuming his post, Bollaert promised not to take any decisive step without prior consultation with Paris.

What Ramadier had called the "constructive phase" of French policy began with Bollaert's arrival in Saigon early in April, 1947. He lifted the censorship in Saigon and the state of siege in Hanoi and Haiphong. He also replaced d'Argenlieu's political adviser, Léon Pignon, with Paul Mus, a man known for being sympathetic to Vietnamese national aspirations. Nothing else either new or striking was done, except that Bollaert introduced a change of reasoning, in preparation of French plans for Bao Dai. Instead of insisting, as Moutet had done, that the aggressors had to be defeated before the French would agree to talks, it was now emphasized that the Hanoi regime was not sufficiently representative of the Vietnamese people. The Vietminh was controlled by the Communists, who constituted only a small faction of the nationalist movement. France was willing to negotiate and make concessions, but only to a truly representative government, one willing to agree that the free state of Vietnam remain a member of the French Union. Bollaert advised the leaders of Vietnamese nationalism to cooperate with him in preparing such a government.

But Bollaert soon ran into the main obstacle to his plans: the refusal by well-known anti-Communist leaders to cooperate in this scheme. Every respected nationalist recognized the attempt to form an anti-Vietminh government for what it was—a maneuver to avoid making the concessions the people wanted. Among the men whom Bollaert approached were the Catholics Ngo Dinh Diem and Nguyen Manh Ha. Diem had once publicly broken with the colonial administration, and in 1945, the Japanese had found that he was too independent for the role of head of a Japanese-sponsored government of a "free" Vietnam. Later, he turned down an invitation of Ho to join the Hanoi government. Nguyen Manh Ha, although certainly not a Communist, had served as Ho Chi Minh's economics minister until December 19, 1946; when Ho's cabinet fled from Hanoi, he stayed behind. The refusal of both Diem and Ha to join a French-sponsored anti-Vietminh government was not only an act of personal political integrity, but also an expression of the national mood. Once the war spread to the North and Ho Chi Minh called the nation to arms, even the exiled anti-Vietminh leaders of the VNQDD and the Dong Minh Hoi appealed to the people to join the fight against the French. Their hatred for the Vietminh was undiminished, but, like the anti-Communist leaders at home, they knew that to condemn the Vietminh at the moment when it proclaimed a war of national liberation would have been regarded as siding with the French. For the time being, and indeed for a long time to come, the Hanoi government symbolized the people's refusal ever again to submit to any form of foreign domination. But Bollaert's efforts to enlist men of unblemished political repute were merely preparation for France's plans for Bao Dai; his failure therefore was not considered critical.

Bao Dai had been residing in Hong Kong since disengaging himself from the Vietminh in March, 1946. He had learned of the French plan of using him against the Vietminh back in January, 1947, from an emissary of d'Argenlieu. Ever since then, and particularly after Bollaert's arrival in Saigon, messengers and old collaborators of the French had been going to Hong Kong, only to confirm to Bollaert what d'Argenlieu had learned before: Bao Dai, his will strengthened by cautious advisers, was remaining aloof. As Bao Dai told Paul Mus in Hong Kong in May, if the French wished to win his cooperation, they would have to offer him at least as much as Ho Chi Minh demanded: the disolution of the Cochinchinese government, the reunification of Vietnam under one government, and, of course, independence.

Bao Dai's demands came as a surprise to the many Frenchmen who looked upon him as nothing but a playboy. They did not realize that his flight into dissipation was in part due to despair over the undignified role the French expected him to play. His seemingly "natural diffidence and indolence" on public affairs stemmed largely from his unwillingness to be an active tool of the French. In approaching him in the spring of 1947, the French were ignorant of Bao Dai's dormant political abilities and astonished to see that the "playboy," if he cared, could himself turn into a schemer, determined to outwit his opponents.

Indeed, in the spring of 1947, Bao Dai not only cared but was fully aware that the French were trying to circumvent the necessity of granting Vietnam independence by reducing the problem of nationalism to a simpler question, namely how he and other respectable national leaders could be lured into cooperating with the French. And Bao Dai conjectured, even before the French themselves fully realized it, that in this game, talks between the French and the Vietminh might very well become necessary at some point, if only as a means of applying pressure on him. He also anticipated that the French might use the threat of forming a "legal" Vietnamese government under him, and the even greater threat of granting this government independence, merely as a means of pressuring Ho Chi Minh into a new compromise, in which case his role would once more have been that of a French pawn.

Such were indeed the intentions of some of the policy-makers in Paris. Bollaert, however, was not one of them. His idea was to use talks with Ho Chi Minh only as a means of putting pressure on Bao Dai. By that time, French policy on the question of negotiations with Ho Chi Minh had in fact become less dogmatic. A secret agreement to allow such talks, if Bollaert considered them useful, had been concluded before Bollaert's departure. In part, this was the price for the support the Communists gave to the Ramadier cabinet and its Indochina policy. The Communist cabinet members voted for the credits needed to conduct the Indochina War; in the Chamber vote, the Communist deputies simply abstained. But a more important reason for secret talks with Ho was the awareness, at least on Bollaert's part, that in his dealings with Bao Dai his hands would be tied if talks with Ho Chi Minh were ruled out entirely.

Bollaert and his supporters who really saw in Bao Dai the solution to the conflict conceived of talks with Ho Chi Minh essentially as a maneuver, while another faction, mostly Socialists and Radicals skeptical about Bao Dai's usefulness as an anti-Vietminh force, nursed the illusion that a new compromise could be worked out in negotiations with Ho. They, too, approved of talks with Bao Dai, but merely as a means of frightening Ho Chi Minh.

5

In the three-sided tug of war staged by the French, the Vietminh, and Bao Dai, each party took a demonstratively firm stance. Bollaert, in a statement to *Le Monde* on May 17, 1947, said: "France will remain in Indochina, and Indochina will remain within the French Union." But he added: "Let the representatives of *all* parties come to us" (italics added). Bao Dai made clear to Paul Mus that he would negotiate only on the basis of unity and independence. Ho's position was of course known. Why, then, did Bollaert bother to send Paul Mus on a perilous journey to Ho Chi Minh's headquarters with proposals that amounted not only to a virtual ultimatum to surrender, but also demanded conditions which, in Ho Chi Minh's words, only a man without honor and a coward could have accepted? The three main conditions relayed by Mus were "return of prisoners and hostages taken, delivery of a large part of the arms and ammunitions, free entry of French troops to all territories under Vietminh occupation."[7] Mus, who knew Ho Chi Minh well, admitted later that the French "requests for guarantees" were "equivalent to surrender," and he agreed that in Ho Chi Minh's place he, too, would have rejected them.[8]

The Mus mission, one of the most extraordinary episodes in Franco-Vietnamese relations, demonstrated the breadth of Bol-

laert's drive for the support of all shades of French opinion. In
conceiving the mission, Bollaert tried to satisfy the Socialists in
the government by establishing contact with Ho Chi Minh without arousing his own party and the MRP by opening too wide the
door for negotiations. Strengthened by the expected arrival of
massive reinforcements from France, not only General Valluy,
who believed he could defeat the Vietminh, insisted that Bollaert
demand surrender; the minister of war, Paul Coste-Floret, a member of the MRP, was of the same opinion. After returning from
an inspection tour in Indochina lasting from April 26 to May 3,
1947, Coste-Floret said that there was no longer any military
problem in Vietnam; the success of the French arms, he asserted,
was complete (even though, as he himself admitted, "the greater
part of the country remains in the hands of the Vietminh").⁹ Although Bollaert did not share Valluy's and Coste-Floret's unfounded optimism, he gave in to the combined pressure of the
military, colonial society, and the French Right. In retrospect it
is not difficult to see that a peaceful solution was possible only
if France agreed to withdraw from Vietnam. The continuation
of the French presence demanded force. An inner conviction that
this *might* be the case broke the will of many an honest "man
of peace," and the fact that it *actually* was the case made all efforts
to mitigate the policy of force ineffective. This alone can explain
why the Mus mission came about, a mission that Bollaert should
never have ordered and Mus should never have undertaken.

The attempts to persuade Bao Dai into collaboration and to
threaten Ho Chi Minh into surrender had failed. Not willing to
accept defeat, Bollaert himself now went to Hong Kong, trying
to squeeze some benefit out of the failure of the Mus mission
by assuring Bao Dai that his fears of a new Franco-Vietminh deal
were unfounded and warning him against the dangers of a course
that looked as if he wished to make common cause with the Vietminh. But Bao Dai persisted in his refusal to play the role the
French had assigned to him unless given a promise of unity and
independence for Vietnam. He even refused to take a public
stand against the Vietminh, to which he frequently referred as the
"resistance," thus emphasizing that he did not regard all nationalists who had taken up arms against the French as Communists. In July, in an interview for a Saigon newspaper, Bao

Dai went so far as to state that he was "neither for the Vietminh nor against them. I belong to no party."[10] However, on the advice of his counselors, he rejected an offer by Ho Chi Minh, submitted by a non-Communist emissary by the name of Ho Dac Lieu, to negotiate also on behalf of the Vietminh government, an offer which clearly indicated that the Vietminh, unafraid of negotiations, no longer insisted on excluding other nationalist forces from a new Franco-Vietnamese deal.

After his return from Hong Kong, Bollaert decided that the impasse into which he had maneuvered himself could be broken only by a bold political step. Always eager to have the support of his government, he went to Paris to obtain authority for a new plan with which to shake Bao Dai out of his rigid stand. How the French cabinet, which was as divided as ever, was brought around to authorizing Bollaert's plan remains a secret. He himself felt that he had the needed backing. Back at Saigon, he startled the Vietminh more than Bao Dai by saying that France wanted a truce without victors or vanquished, and that he was ready to talk to all Vietnamese parties and groups.

Bollaert's new plan was based on the assumption that the Vietminh was keenly interested in ending hostilities and beginning negotiations with anyone the French chose so long as Hanoi was not excluded. Consequently Bollaert ordered a cease-fire without prior agreement with the Vietminh. It was to become effective on August 15, 1947, the date of the scheduled transfer of British sovereignty in India. Sealed orders to this effect were transmitted to all commanders in the field. On the same day, Bollaert planned to make a speech in which a representative of France, in speaking of the future status of Vietnam, was for the first time to utter the word "independence."

The events of the next few weeks demonstrated once more that military reconquest remained the one firm French line in Vietnam. Colonial society, fully supported by General Valluy, who claimed that the offensive he had prepared for the dry season would once and for all destroy the Vietminh, was in an uproar. Now it was Valluy's turn to rush to Paris to rally the country and the government against Bollaert's untimely cease-fire. War Minister Coste-Floret and former Premier Georges Bidault vigorously supported the General by denouncing the idea of seeking peace when the long-expected "military solution" at last was at hand. They won over the majority of the cabinet, and the Socialists, unwilling to risk the life of the government, concurred. Premier Ramadier called Bollaert to Paris. The projected cease-fire was called off, and the speech in which France was to hold out the prospect of independence for Vietnam within the French Union was never delivered.

After this sorry episode, French policy toward Ho Chi Minh reverted to what it had been before Bollaert came to Indochina. The idea of negotiations with the Vietminh was buried. It became Bollaert's rather degrading and unpromising task to pressure Bao Dai, or if necessary buy him or maneuver him into playing the game of the French. The military counterpart of this "policy" was the expected destruction of the Vietminh.

On September 10, Bollaert in a speech at Ha Dong submitted the "new" French policy to the Vietnamese "parties and groups" whose cooperation against the Vietminh he sought to enlist. The truce, which some weeks ago he had regarded as essential for successful negotiations, was never mentioned. Instead of independence, he offered "liberty within the French Union."[11] "Liberty" meant that the army, diplomacy, the "federal services," and the federal budget would remain in French hands. The ethnic minorities were to have a "special status," which meant that the regions they inhabited would remain under direct French rule. Bollaert made much of what he considered a generous concession: Vietnam would regain her unity if the people of Cochinchina desired to rejoin Annam and Tongking—a promise already made in the March agreement; but even this concession was robbed of any possible value by the stipulation that the high commissioner for Indochina would act as the "arbiter" between the local governments of the three "regions" of Vietnam. And with an arrogance that revealed the depth of French ignorance about the real mood of the Vietnamese people, Bollaert proclaimed that negotiations could not modify the French position. France's offer was final; the Vietnamese had only one choice: Take it or leave it.

Bollaert's speech taught all Vietnamese, whether pro- or anti-Vietminh, an unforgettable lesson, namely that French determination to remain masters of Vietnam, and not Ho Chi Minh's Communism, was the cause of the Indochina War.

6

The first group to express its disappointment over Bollaert's speech was the Vietminh. Its dissatisfaction was due largely to the obvious inference that all ideas of talks with the Vietminh had been dropped. But the exclusion from all further Franco-Vietnamese negotiations was just another of several disappointments for Ho Chi Minh. The year 1947, the first of the seven and a half years of all-out war, had so far been one of great personal hardship and political setbacks. Driven from Hanoi, Ho Chi Minh and his government had retired into the old rebel country known as the Viet Bac, as inaccessible to the French for the time being as were the large Vietminh-held territories in northern Annam and their mountainous retreat south of Hue. There, in the Viet Bac, the revolutionaries lived primitively, changing their headquarters frequently to escape capture. (Once French parachutists almost succeeded in taking the government prisoner.) But what made life difficult for these men was not the hardships they had to endure but the reverses they suffered.

Ho Chi Minh's main disappointments of the year 1947 were not in the military field. He had anticipated that the struggle would be long and difficult. The loss of cities and surrounding areas did not dishearten him. "We shall temporarily lose terrain," he stated soon after the outbreak of the war, "but we are determined not to lose the heart of the people."[12] But developments in the political field blighted a great many Vietminh hopes. The war failed to arouse pro-Vietnamese sentiments in France; public opinion echoed press reports, which were fabricated almost exclusively by colonial officials in Hanoi and Saigon. Not only the Socialists, but the Communists also abstained from making Vietnam a central issue of French politics.

Equally distressing for Ho Chi Minh was the total lack of international recognition and support for his regime. Although the United States was not yet actively siding with the French —the defense of Southeast Asia had not yet become a pressing U.S. concern—Washington abstained from criticizing French policy in Vietnam, or from supporting the nationalist cause, as it did in the case of Indonesia. A number of American journalists tried to convey their misgivings over the French policy of recon-quest in Vietnam, but it seemed that no strong anticolonial feel-ings could be aroused against the French among the American people, nor any sympathy for a country of whose problems very few Americans had any knowledge. Nor did the Vietminh, already widely suspected of being Communist, receive the slightest en-couragement from Labourite Britain. On the contrary, Foreign Minister Bevin told the House of Commons on February 12, 1947, that the problem of Indochina was the concern solely of the French.

Recognition by the Soviet Union might have been a doubtful blessing for the Hanoi regime in 1947, but the absence of all Soviet support, moral or material, was a bitter pill for Ho Chi Minh. At that time, Stalin indeed was still more concerned with not antagonizing the French than with currying favor with the nationalists of a remote and apparently unimportant country, and more interested in strengthening the French Communist Party than in supporting an anti-French Vietnamese revolution. Contrary to her position on Indonesia, the Soviet Union even abstained from putting the war in Vietnam before the United Nations.

On the home front, Ho Chi Minh also suffered several disap-pointments, all related to the one problem for which despite his resourcefulness he could find no solution. No matter how many concessions he made to the non-Communist elements in the Viet-minh, he could not remove the stigma of Communism from his government. Not that this diminished his popularity among the people, but it severely limited his chances of mobilizing the entire nationalist movement. During July, 1947, when it looked as if Bao Dai might be persuaded to cooperate with the Vietminh, Ho Chi Minh drastically altered the composition of his govern-ment in favor of its non-Communist component. The two most prominent Communists next to Ho Chi Minh, Vo Nguyen Giap and Pham Van Dong, were dropped from the cabinet. The So-cialist Hoang Minh Giam was promoted to foreign minister, the Oxford-educated "independent" Ta Quang Buu became minister of national defense, a non-Communist Catholic was made min-ister of veterans, and the important post of minister of the in-terior was given to the former imperial delegate for Tongking,

Phan Ke Toai. In Cochinchina, too, the Committee for the South gave important functions to "official" Catholics, Buddhists, "independents," and dissident sect leaders who claimed to represent substantial Hoa Hao and Cao Dai groups. Ho Chi Minh even had Bao Dai reconfirmed as supreme counselor of the government. It was all in vain, since both the French and Bao Dai, although using the threat of negotiations with the Vietminh against each other, were quite determined not to make common cause with Ho Chi Minh.

By accepting the French view that Ho Chi Minh's government had ceased to be the authorized spokesman for the country, the anti-Communist nationalists made their most serious political mistake. Bao Dai and his followers knew quite well that total Communist control of the armed resistance movement was as yet not a fact. However, by denouncing all resistance as Communist, they implicitly condemned all non-Communists fighting with the Vietminh. Faced with the alternative of renouncing armed resistance or continuing to fight, these nationalists moved closer and closer to the Communist leadership of the Vietminh, which ultimately did indeed achieve complete control of the entire resistance movement. Once again anti-Communism turned more nationalists into Communists than did Communist propaganda.

In 1947, this transformation of nationalists into Communists might still have been prevented by the creation of a non-Communist movement as firmly nationalist and anticolonial as the Vietminh. Contemporary history offers no clearer proof of the political ineffectiveness of anti-Communism as such than the failure of Bao Dai and his advisers to be as convincingly nationalist as the Vietminh. The only effective way of fighting Communism in Vietnam was to fight the French.

Bao Dai would very much have liked to force the French into granting Vietnam independence, thus depriving Ho Chi Minh of the glory of fulfilling his country's manifest destiny, but he lacked the talent. He was an adroit tactician, a frequently eloquent spokesman for his country, and for a long time sincerely involved. But being neither politician nor determined fighter, he was unfit for the tough job of leading his people in their struggle for national liberation.

7

Although Bollaert's speech of September 10 accepted none of Bao Dai's conditions, Bao Dai's rejection of the French offer was couched in surprisingly mild terms. The reason for this was not merely Bao Dai's lack of firmness. The disoriented and bitterly divided forces of anti-Vietminh nationalism were beginning to look toward Bao Dai as the man to lead them out of their political isolation. Men as mutually antagonistic as the collaborator Le Van Hoach and the stubborn dissident Ngo Dinh Diem went to Hong Kong in the hope of winning Bao Dai over to their proposals for dealing with the French and the Vietminh.

A few dozen ambitious men, many of whom claimed to represent "parties," offered their support to Bao Dai, some urging him to stand firm, but more pleading with him to grasp any opportunity for action. All jumped on his bandwagon before it began to roll, giving conflicting advice to a man reluctant to command.

Bao Dai's defects as a leader were soon made obvious by the caliber of the men who rallied around him. The first to prepare themselves for a return into officialdom under him were the exiled spokesmen of the moribund VNQDD and of the Dong Minh Hoi. At a conference in Nanking in February, 1947, they founded a United National Front; at another conference at Canton in March, they voted to withhold further support from the Vietminh government and to place themselves under Bao Dai's direction, thus indicating their willingness to cooperate with the French who, only six months earlier, had helped the Vietminh eliminate them. Cooperation was, of course, made dependent on "equality and independence," which, however, could not be theirs until the French were defeated. Therefore the few remaining adherents of these two groups inside Vietnam continued to fight the French through many local nationalist authorities over which the Vietminh had no control and who, without direction from any anti-Vietminh national leadership, defied both the Vietminh and the French.

The United National Front of these exiles was a poor beginning for an organized popular movement behind Bao Dai, but at least it was composed of men who had so far refused to collaborate with the French. Soon afterward, another United National Front arose in Cochinchina, this one promoted chiefly by men who either were, or were preparing to become, French collaborators. Its guiding spirits were Nguyen Van Sam, head of a "Social Democratic" group sponsored chiefly by members of the Hoa Hao sect, and Tran Van Tuyen, former chief of cabinet for the VNQDD leader Nguyen Tuong Tam while the latter was foreign minister under Ho Chi Minh. This United National Front consisted of the Cao Dai and Hoa Hao, most of whose factions had by that time completed their transition from resistance to cooperation with the French; of the small remaining VNQDD groups (the Dong Minh Hoi had virtually ceased to exist in the country); of some Buddhist sects, and the usual number of ephemeral national "parties." On August 18, a conference of this United National Front held with French blessing sent a telegram to Bao Dai asking him to return to Vietnam. But as a "voice of the people," this organization based mainly on the sects carried little weight with Bao Dai, who knew that most sect leaders were questionable exponents of the national cause.

Bao Dai's most loyal supporters were the royalist mandarins of Annam and Tongking, the most prominent of whom had been led into collaboration with the French by their hatred for the Vietminh. Their spokesmen actually headed the Administrative Committees of Annam and Tongking set up to camouflage direct French rule. In Tongking, this was Truong Dinh Tri, formerly a VNQDD member in Ho Chi Minh's cabinet; in Annam, it was the well-known Catholic Tran Van Ly. Outside of Cochinchina, these two men, who consistently opposed talks with the Vietminh, were the most active champions of a national government headed by Bao Dai. Others in Annam and Tongking, less inclined toward collaboration, listened to the advice of Ngo Dinh Diem, whose chief concern was to keep Bao Dai from abandoning his firm nationalist position. Diem spoke for the majority of Vietnam's Catholics, who had so far refused to be drawn into either collaboration with the French or aggressive opposition to the Vietminh.

But these restraining influences were countered by the mounting pressure of the collaborators and would-be collaborators, including 'the discredited separatists who had helped d'Argenlieu create the Republic of Cochinchina. Outstanding among these gravediggers of anti-Communist nationalism were two leading separatists, Le Van Hoach, still head of the Republic of Cochinchina, representing the Cao Dai, and Nguyen Van Xuan, whom the French had since promoted from colonel to general—the first Vietnamese to be so honored. As soon as it became clear that the French considered dropping Cochinchinese separatism in favor of a national anti-Vietminh regime, Xuan returned to Saigon, and in a repulsive display of opportunism transformed himself from separatist into nationalist. Then he rushed to Hong Kong, where he had been preceded by his rival Le Van Hoach, who was also trying to become a national leader even though still the official spokesman of separatism. Xuan was able to exploit Hoach's somewhat embarrassing position. He forced his rival to resign from the government, and after proclaiming himself president of the Republic of Cochinchina on October 1, offered to Bao Dai to liquidate separatism in exchange for a leading role in a national government. His first move was to drop the name "Government of the Autonomous Republic of Cochinchina" in favor of "Government of South Vietnam."

After his ouster, Le Van Hoach devoted himself to organizing a "popular base" for a national government. The National Union which he founded at the end of 1947, and which absorbed the various national fronts that had preceded it, exerted no greater popular appeal than had its constituent members before they united behind Bao Dai. They were the Hoa Hao and Cao Dai, the remnants of the VNQDD, the deeply divided Dai Viet, and some loosely organized Buddhist and Catholic groups. Even Ngo Dinh Diem, "for the first and only time, joined a party of which he was not the founder."[13]

But even before this fragile coalition of discredited collaborators, ambitious masterful intrigants, and incompetent sectarians, plus a smattering of honest leaders without a following had created this "popular base," Bao Dai, in a moment of weakness he soon came to regret, took the first step on the slippery road of capitulation.

8

In order to understand the French resolve to refuse Bao Dai even the prospect of eventual independence one must recall that General Valluy's offensive was then in the last stages of preparation. Even the least sanguine Frenchman expected it to produce a marked improvement of the French position.

In three interviews given to the Saigon press in August, 1947, Tran Van Tuyen, a spokesman for Bao Dai, said that the former emperor would agree to head an anti-Vietminh government only if the French accepted his demands for unity and independence. Bao Dai and his supporters knew that they were the instruments of a French scheme, but they were divided on how this scheme could be turned to their advantage, how to inject life into Bao Dai's movement, and whether or not to compromise. They were divided not by differences over doctrine; theirs were differences of temperament, ability, ambition, and skill. In vying for places in a future government, the anti-Communist nationalists once again displayed their tragic inability to subordinate their conflicts to the national cause.

When Bollaert made his speech, a great many of these anti-Communist nationalists were gathered at Hong Kong around Bao Dai. For obvious reasons they were not nationalists of the purest water: those who came from Vietnam had to have passports and money issued to them by the French. Yet among them were some well-known nationalists, such as the head of the National Front, Nguyen Van Sam, the Cao Dai leader Tran Quang Vinh, and the journalist Nguyen Van Long, all three from Saigon; there also were the heads of the Administrative Committees of Annam and Tongking, Tran Van Ly from Hue and Truong Dinh Tri from Hanoi, the former speaking for the Catholics, the other for the VNQDD, whose exiled leaders Nguyen Hai Than and Nguyen Tuong Tam had come from China and also were there. In addition, there were Bao Dai's counselors Dinh Xuan Quang and Phan Huy Dan (the latter better known in later years as Dr. Phan Quang Dan), who had proposed a Bao Dai government against the Vietminh long before the French took up the idea. It was a gathering which still had "the means of limiting the power of the Marxists, provided they were given a chance to prove that a policy of understanding with France was possible and worthwhile."[14]

Since these men realized that Bollaert's proposal denied them this chance, their immediate reaction was deep disappointment. The men in exile, their hopes defeated, returned to China; Nguyen Van Sam's National Front at Saigon promptly decided to reject Bollaert's ultimatum. Only the moderate nationalists around the former emperor, sworn enemies of the Vietminh, rejected Bollaert's conditions without entirely renouncing the idea of a political mission for Bao Dai. Upon their advice, Bao Dai on September 18 issued a proclamation in which he stated (under the pretext of complying with a request of the Vietnamese people to arbitrate the conflict) his willingness to enter into talks with the French. True, he repeated his demands for unity and independence, but his failure to slam the door in the face of the French was the first crack in the armor of his resistance.

The leaders of the Bao Dai movement now found themselves in a serious predicament. Their difficulties increased when Valluy's anti-Vietminh offensive had some initial successes in October. The anti-Communists wanted to see a Vietminh defeat, but knowing that the French needed them only so long as the Vietminh was strong, they also wanted the French offensive to fail.

This predicament naturally paralyzed the honest nationalists in the Bao Dai camp more than the opportunists, who now became more active. Spearheaded by Le Van Hoach and Nguyen Van Xuan, the clique of hardened collaborators battled in Hong Kong to win over Bao Dai, while in Tongking the French fought to defeat Ho Chi Minh. Bao Dai, after some hesitation, gave in and agreed to meet Bollaert aboard a French warship in the Bay of Along on December 7. Bao Dai had been advised by his counselors only to listen and under no circumstances to sign any binding document without a firm French promise of independence. However, what he did do was to sign a "protocol" specifying the conditions for collaboration. The conditions Bao Dai accepted were such that even his most uncritical supporters let him know that in doing so he had seriously jeopardized his cause. Since he was no fool, nobody quite understood why he had signed a statement that was denounced not only by Ngo Dinh Diem but also by so shrewd a collaborator as General Xuan, a man quite ready to sell out, but not for nothing. It is not likely that Bao Dai was already "bought" at this early stage, since he regretted his act and in fact did not live up to his commitment.

Ngo Dinh Diem and Tran Van Ly persuaded Bao Dai to extricate himself from this embarrassing situation by raising new demands, such as the immediate dissolution of the Cochinchinese government in favor of an Administrative Committee for the South as a first step toward reunification.

Incredibly enough, the French lacked the sense to comply with this simple request and thereby keep Bao Dai in the net in which Bollaert had caught him. And since no other concessions were made either, Bao Dai, in order to avoid being held to his commitment, decided to remove himself from the scene. At the end of December he left Hong Kong for Europe and began his wanderings, a combination of pleasure trips and flights. He went first to Geneva, with Bollaert right on his heels, and soon afterward to Paris. There, the difficulties the French, and in particular Bollaert, had in catching up with him increased with the number of places of amusement he visited. (It is still not known who was paying his expenses.) Bollaert arranged for a new meeting on February 13 at the Bay of Along, but Bao Dai simply did not show up. It was then that he acquired the epithets "unreachable mediator" and "night club emperor,"[15] the latter a misnomer. Bao Dai had not only voluntarily abdicated as emperor; one of his reasons for seeking amusement in Paris was his refusal to accept the French conditions for again making him emperor.

Bao Dai's undeniably compulsive quest for pleasure was not the main reason for his presence in Paris and his continued reluctance to negotiate with the French. He had gone there chiefly to find out for himself what forces determined French policy in Indochina and what chances they offered for cooperation under conditions he could accept. He did not like what he found. In November, 1947, France again got a new government in which the shift to the Right that affected Indochina became evident in the leading positions held by the procolonial MRP. Both the new Premier (Schuman) and the Minister for Overseas Territories (Coste-Floret) were members of the MRP. There was also talk of a further increase of rightist strength in new elections. General de

Gaulle's Rassemblement Populaire was expected to form the next government. Holding an ultracolonial position, it recommended the rejection of any agreement made by its predecessors that undermined the position of France in Indochina. Although the Schuman government was definitely committed to what came to be known as the Bao Dai solution, the man on whose consent the solution depended had little hope when he left Paris for Hong Kong in March, 1948, that this solution, if it ever came about, would be a decisive step toward the liberation of Vietnam.

During Bao Dai's stay in Europe his followers had by no means been idle. Le Van Hoach proceeded to put together the National Union, which was a step forward in that, although primarily an anti-Vietminh grouping, it gave little comfort to the French. The groups inside the National Union competed with one another and with the Vietminh in verbal expressions of nationalist militancy. Even such separatists as Xuan and Hoach now proclaimed that territorial unity of Vietnam was an absolutely indispensable condition for any kind of Franco-Vietnamese collaboration.

In March, after Bao Dai's return to Hong Kong, the feeling that one could not wait until the French were ready to grant full independence began to dominate the thinking of Bao Dai's followers. On the French side, too, a desire to break the deadlock was transmitted to Bao Dai by an increasingly impatient Bollaert. A full year had passed since the French had decided to use Bao Dai as their chief political weapon against Ho Chi Minh, but no visible progress had been made in the realization of this scheme. The matter was now the more urgent, since the first great attempt to destroy the Vietminh militarily was known to have failed.

But the key to a solution was Bao Dai. Exposed again to pressures from the French and to appeals from his countrymen, he could hardly continue to defer a decision much longer. The hour to prove himself, and to demonstrate that he was ready to fight both colonialism and Communism, was now at hand.

9

The year 1948 brought the gradual erosion of Bao Dai's resistance; 1949, its collapse. It is possible that the task history required of him was beyond the powers of any human being. He was intelligent enough to realize that he was being used, yet to say no and prevent the exploitation of his name required far greater strength than nature had endowed him with. Throughout 1948 and up to the spring of 1949, Bao Dai continued to fight, sometimes bravely and skillfully, only to give up the struggle, in a mood of self-destructive resignation, by capitulating to the French and the collaborators in his camp.

The taming of Bao Dai went through three stages. First, soon after his return to Hong Kong, he endorsed the formation of a national government without having obtained independence. Second, on June 5, 1948, he approved the Bay of Along agreement concluded with High Commissioner Bollaert. And third, in spring, 1949, he consented to return to Vietnam as head of state, although he recognized that the independence France had by then twice formally granted was a blatant deception.

The French obtained Bao Dai's endorsement of an anti-Vietminh government by a move that can be described only as shady. They sent Louis Caput, a French Socialist known as an opponent of the Bao Dai solution, to Hong Kong and leaked the "information" that he was about to establish contact with the Vietminh. No negotiations were intended, and Caput never even saw a representative of Ho Chi Minh's government. The sole purpose of his trip, of which Caput himself apparently was ignorant, was to frighten Bao Dai and his supporters, a maneuver that proved highly successful. The Bao Dai camp was gripped by fear of a new Franco-Vietminh deal that would put an end to its own political aspirations. Instead of fighting back by threatening to make common cause with the Vietminh, most Bao Daists began to look for a way out of the impasse created by their rejection of the "protocol" of December, 1947, the one Bao Dai had signed but later disavowed. Still unwilling to commit himself on this basis, Bao Dai tried to obtain better conditions for collaboration from the French, but Ngo Dinh Diem, whom he sent to Saigon on March 30, 1948, to negotiate with Bollaert, returned empty-handed.

Bao Dai's more impatient supporters hit upon a strategy designed to allow them to act without initially involving the ex-emperor. At a conference in Hong Kong on April 29 it was decided, in the presence of the heads of the Administrative Committees of Tongking and Annam and of the government of Cochin-china, to form a provisional central government to initiate the liquidation of Cochinchinese separatism. Bollaert agreed to seek Paris' consent for this project, but he insisted that Bao Dai endorse such a government and countersign any agreement between it and the French, who by then had decided to the use of the term "in-dependence" to describe the status of Vietnam vis-à-vis France. The real content of such an agreement, however, was still to be the formerly rejected "protocol," which the men who insisted on forming an anti-Vietminh government were now obliged to ac-cept. They had thus maneuvered themselves into the ridiculous situation of having to obtain French consent for what Bollaert had urged on Bao Dai for a full year.

A government formed under these conditions could not possibly be headed by upright anticolonialists. Men like Ngo Dinh Diem refused not only to join but even to endorse it. With Bao Dai's blessing, General Xuan, the most notorious of all collaborators in the anti-Vietminh camp, became its head, after obtaining his "mandate" from a "congress" of about forty men whom he had managed to assemble in Saigon and to whom he showed a letter from Bao Dai asking him to form a provisional central govern-ment. On May 27, he presented his government to Bao Dai in Hong Kong.[16] Paris only "took notice" of its formation, and Bao Dai, without whose consent the Xuan government could not have come into existence, began to have second thoughts. He issued a declaration that this government could not act in his name, and he continued in his refusal to return to Vietnam.

Bao Dai would also have liked to avoid involvement with the treaty on which the French and the Xuan government based their collaboration. But this Paris and Bollaert would not permit. On June 5, 1948, the High Commissioner and General Xuan met in the Bay of Along in Bao Dai's presence to sign the agreement through which France, publicly and "solemnly," recognized the independence of Vietnam. However, the solemnity of the promise in no way compensated for its hollowness. The armed forces and foreign policy were to remain in French hands, while the transfer of governmental authority in other fields was envisaged only on the basis of separate accords still to be concluded. The protocol containing the stipulations which made this independence a gesture devoid of practical significance remained secret.

Bao Dai, loath to enter into any further commitments, again removed himself from the scene. On June 5, he hurriedly departed for Europe. In a letter to Bollaert dated July 11, he dissociated himself from the Bay of Along agreement, saying that he had merely "witnessed" its signing, and that the agreement could not serve as a basis for a lasting Franco-Vietnamese understanding. Bollaert's inability to enlist Bao Dai against Ho Chi Minh without meaningful concessions became evident in a final interview between the two men at Saint-Germain on August 25. The ex-emperor once more stated that he would return to Vietnam only after the liquidation of the separatist regime in Cochinchina and after receiving adequate guarantees of real independence.

Had the promise of independence in the Bay of Along agreement been kept, this document might have become the hoped-for turning point. For a while it looked as though the Communists had good reason to fear that their hold over non-Communist nationalists would be broken. Thanks to the duplicity of the French, this fear was short-lived. The central government was a government without moral authority, without funds, and without an army. Hence, although a French tool, it was politically useless to the French and of no value whatsoever to the Vietnamese cause. Ho Chi Minh rightly denounced the Xuan government as a French tool. The Vietminh tried Xuan and sentenced him to death, but because the discredit he brought on anti-Communist nationalism benefited the Vietminh, no effort was made to carry out this sentence.

The unwillingness of the French Government to abide by the Bay of Along agreement, and a rightist campaign against "betraying the interests of France in Indochina," gave encouragement to those determined and in a position to sabotage both the transfer of authority to the Xuan government and the liquidation of the separatist regime of Cochinchina. Under the leadership of Tran Van Huu, Xuan's old rival and successor as head of the separatist government, they effectively opposed all attempts to extend the central government's authority over Cochinchina. The French enclaves of Hanoi, Haiphong, and Tourane (now Danang) were to remain outside of Vietnamese control, and the "autonomous" montagnard regions of the South were French-administered. More-over, in March, 1948, the French established an "autonomous" federation of the Thai peoples in the North over which the Xuan government had no authority either. No wonder that Xuan had trouble recruiting ministers, that many resigned soon after joining him, and that no respected nationalist would join any of the governments created later in the name of Bao Dai.

10

The Xuan government, although useless to the French and detrimental to the anti-Vietminh, was allowed to survive for a full year, the second year in which the French made no progress in the war against the Vietminh.

Behind the delay in bringing about the Bao Dai solution lay widespread doubt about its effectiveness. The manner in which the French treated the government they wanted to use against the Vietminh discouraged all true nationalists and even some of the more intelligent collaborators and cooled their ardor for the Bao Dai solution. In Saigon, Nguyen Phan Long published a strong attack on the Xuan government and said that Xuan would fail to bring about peace. In Paris, Buu Hoi, claiming to speak for the entire royal family, warned the French early in 1949 against erecting and supporting "artificial governments"; it was idle to expect that they could attract popular support.

On the French side, doubts and reservations about the Bao Dai solution began to be heard. The Socialists rejected it on the grounds that the ex-emperor did not enjoy authority in the country, and the Right opposed him because of his rigid insistence on unity and independence. Caught in this crossfire, the government now headed by Henri Queuille chose the familiar road of indecision. In trying to force Bao Dai's hand and to justify their refusal to unify Vietnam, the French continued to say that no decisive steps would be taken before Bao Dai's return as head of government. Hardly a day passed without the press urging him to return. His answer was to spend more and more time on the Riviera.

One consequence of the new impasse was that Bollaert was replaced by Léon Pignon, the old colonial official whom Bollaert had removed from Indochina in April, 1947. The return of Pignon presaged a hardening of the French position. Yet even he realized that efforts to generate a politically effective anti-Vietminh regime friendly to France could not be abandoned.

In January, 1949, the Chinese Communists took Peking. With a Communist China in the rear of the Vietminh, the struggle for Indochina more and more took on the appearance of being just one part of the East-West conflict.

The United States could hardly remain indifferent if a Communist victory in Vietnam were to open the door to the subjugation of Southeast Asia to Communist China. Sooner or later Washington would feel obliged to extend aid to a France engaged in containing Communism. But such an internationalization of the conflict was possible only if the United States could be persuaded that support of the French was in the vital interest of the "free world." This, however, presupposed that the Vietnam that was to be kept out of Communist hands was an independent, not a colonial country, that its government was not headed by a French puppet, and that anti-Communism ceasc to be a device for maintaining French rule. Once the United States felt compelled to support the French, which was likely to happen if the Communist powers came to the assistance of Hanoi, the prospects of genuine French concessions to anti-Communist nationalism were bound to improve. American aid, Bao Dai reasoned, could not be obtained for the purpose of saving colonialism. The French, therefore, could not forever prevent the emergence of a free Vietnam; an anti-Communist government under Bao Dai would make sense only if it was not merely "a screen for the French administration."[17]

These were the hopes and fears that led the two sides to reconsider their positions. After long negotiations in January, 1949—Pignon even went to Cannes to talk to Bao Dai—a new accord was concluded on March 8. It took the form of an exchange of letters between Bao Dai and President Vincent Auriol and became known as the Elysée agreement. This new accord reconfirmed the independence of Vietnam and her status as an associated state of the French Union, but it was notable chiefly for its provisions about the unity of Vietnam. For the first time the French, going beyond the mere promise of liquidating Cochinchinese separatism, spelled out the steps to bring this about. They also relinquished the administration of Hanoi, Haiphong, and Tourane. But they still refused to return the "autonomous regions" of the montagnards in the South and the Thai people in the North.

More important, however, than this flaw were the limitations of sovereignty to which Bao Dai agreed. Defense and foreign relations remained in French hands. But since the French needed native help to combat Vietminh-led resistance, Vietnam was to be allowed its own police force and granted the right to appoint some ambassadors and delegates to the Assembly and High Council of the French Union, two bodies distinguished for their total lack of influence on policy-making. In matters of real importance, the agreement either permanently restricted the exercise of sovereignty or made it dependent on separate, yet-to-be-concluded accords. Independence, in other words, would become a reality only when the French felt ready, and only to the extent to which they were willing to relinquish control.

Only his belief that France, eager for American aid, would therefore honor its new promises can explain the optimism Bao Dai voiced over the agreement. But he was far too intelligent really to believe what he said. Holding on to his one remaining weapon, he delayed his return until the promised steps toward unity had been taken.

It turned out that this was no simple matter. Provisions in the constitution of the French Union for such a change had to be observed. They called for the creation of a territorial assembly for Cochinchina to decide on whether this part of Vietnam was to be returned to centralized rule. But permission for the creation of such an assembly had to be given by the French parliament, and once constituted, the decisions it reached also required approval by the French legislature.

On March 12, 1949, France authorized a Cochinchinese assembly. The Socialist proposal for direct, popular elections was rejected in favor of indirect elections by local bodies and provincial councils and by the French chambers of commerce and agriculture. But many of the local councils had ceased to function, and so their membership was replenished by administrative appointees. At least forty of the sixty-four members of the new assembly (sixteen were to be French) were elected by administration-picked people. The "elections" were held on April 10 amid general indifference. Only some seven hundred of the five thousand Vietnamese eligible to vote availed themselves of their right.[18] Worse still, many of the sixty-four regarded their votes as a commodity to be sold to the highest bidder. Twenty million francs were allegedly distributed by General Xuan himself before the assembly met on April 19. The votes needed to end Cochinchinese separatism were also obtained through pressure, including threats of death.[19] Even so, it took four days before the assembly, on April 23, voted that Cochinchina would rejoin Vietnam.

Bao Dai had promised to return as soon as the assembly made the expected decision, and this he did on April 25, after an absence of more than three years. But he did not immediately take over the government. Instead, he went to Dalat, where he waited until the French Assembly also voted for Cochinchina's rejoining of Vietnam. The bill to this effect became law on June 4. On June 13, Bao Dai went to Saigon under heavy French guard, displaying a lack of enthusiasm matched only by the total indifference of the population. At the end of the month he was handed the formal resignation of the Cochinchinese government. Separatism had at last come to an end.

But without true independence, the unity extracted by Bao Dai was of little value to the Vietnamese. Realizing this, Bao Dai used both persuasion and pressure on the French to speed up the realization of independence, with complete lack of success. About a dozen separate accords were signed on December 30, 1949, and progress, at least on paper, was made at the Pau conference meeting from June to November, 1950, at which the three Associated States of Indochina tried to settle their differences with France. One of the agreements reached at Pau fixed the exchange rate between the piaster and the franc. On May 11, 1953, the French Government, in open violation of this accord and without prior consultation with the Associated States, reduced the rate from 17 to 10 francs to the piaster.

As if admitting that the promise of the Elysée agreement had not yet been fulfilled, the French Government, on July 3, 1953, stated that the time had come "to perfect the independence and sovereignty of the Associated States of Indochina." But the new negotiations that, on April 28, 1954, resulted in a declaration of "total" independence did not get under way until March. Thus, in the words of some, the independence won in 1949 was a shabby independence, and the Bao Dai solution a bastard solution.

11

Those who most effectively aided the Vietminh by allowing themselves to be used by the French were the members of the several governments under Bao Dai and Bao Dai himself. Bao Dai was largely a victim of circumstances, yet his grievous political fate failed to arouse pity. He himself headed the first cabinet after his return. Although he "retained" the title of Emperor, he called himself only chief of state. He said it was not for him to decide whether Vietnam should be a monarchy or a republic, and he solemnly proclaimed that the future constitution of Vietnam would be decided by the people who had fought so heroically for the independence of their homeland.

This sort of declaration was one of the frequent gestures with which Bao Dai and some of his adherents tried to lure the non-Communist resistance leaders into their camp. But Ngo Dinh Diem, who for tactical reasons carefully avoided public attacks on the Vietminh, told Bao Dai that as long as the French prevented the fulfillment of Vietnam's national aspirations these wooings were pointless; resistance fighters could only regard them as an invitation to collaborate. Diem himself declined an offer by Bao Dai to head his first cabinet. He would agree only after the national aspirations of the Vietnamese were satisfied, which meant for him "the day when our nation obtains the same political status which India and Pakistan enjoy."[20]

Ngo Dinh Diem did not expect the day when Vietnam would be as free as India to arrive soon. Unable to support either the French or the Vietminh, he left Vietnam during 1950, as did many other prominent nationalists. The only people left to Bao Dai for his several governments between 1949 and 1954 were known collaborators and unprincipled, self-serving demagogues.

In what seemed a last attempt to assert himself against the French and to rid himself of the taint of all-out collaboration, Bao Dai gave the premiership to Nguyen Phan Long, who was known not only for his insistence on greater French concessions, but also as the earliest advocate of a policy built on the expectation that U.S. pressure would eventually force France to drop her opposition to genuine Vietnamese independence. He asked for American military and economic aid to the Vietnamese without French intermediation. The idea that he could strengthen his regime against the French with direct American aid was only one of many mistaken notions. When the French decided that they had to get rid of him, no one stood up in his defense. Bao Dai dropped him after only three months in office.

The next head of Bao Dai's government, Tran Van Huu, was a rich landowner engaged in financial speculations, a French citizen, and a separatist who, as governor of Cochinchina, had obstructed the transfer of this administration to the central government up to May 6, 1950, when he himself became prime minister. His usefulness to the French is beyond doubt, since he was able to hold on to his position until June, 1952. The Huu government was allowed to appoint a great many ambassadors and ministerial and other high officials, appointments that swelled the rolls of those willing to be corrupted. One instance of the use of public office for personal gain (an art in which Huu himself displayed consummate skill) was the case of Phan Van Giao, governor of Central Vietnam, who, alone in the months of January and April, is rumored to have transferred the sum of 84 million francs to France.[21]

The Huu government was also allowed to recruit more and more Vietnamese troops, but its army remained under French command. Only in one government department were the Vietnamese given almost complete autonomy—the Department of Public Security, which persecuted nationalists who fought the French and their Vietnamese tools. It was headed by one Nguyen Van Tam, who had acquired renown for his loyalty to the French and his fierce anti-Communism long before the war and the Japanese occupation. A well-known separatist, he had headed the Department of Public Security under the Cochinchinese governments of Dr. Trinh and Le Van Hoach, in preparation, as it were, for the task of arresting, "questioning," imprisoning, or killing persons known to be or suspected of being Vietminh adherents. And this was the man who was to become the next prime minister of "independent" Vietnam. However, all Bao Dai governments were politically ineffective, and since they failed to split the non-Communist resistance from the Vietminh, therefore also useless to the French. The nationalists who opposed the Vietminh remained as weak as ever. Moreover, in order to maintain a minimum of popular support, their reluctance to support Bao Dai's French-sponsored governments changed into open opposition and even into occasional rebellion. This was true in particular of the politically capricious, divided, and armed Cao Dai and Hoa Hao sects. The nationalist mood of their followers compelled them to raise demands which neither Huu nor his successor Tam could meet. Both antagonized the sects when they tried to extend the central government's authority over sect-held territories and to force the military units of the sects into the national army. The opposition of the sects and the parties forced Tran Van Huu to form his second cabinet, installed on February 21, 1951, with only "technicians" and political "independents."

Two of the men who refused to join Huu's second cabinet were the Dai Viet leader Nguyen Huu Tri and the Dai Viet sympathizer Phan Huy Quat. The Dai Viet, although as badly split over the issue of support or opposition to Bao Dai as all other nationalist groups opposed to the Vietminh, was at this time the strongest and best organized of all anti-Vietminh factions. In the eyes of many, its firm anti-Communism and extreme nationalism, combined with the ambition and vitality of its leaders, predestined the Dai Viet to play a decisive role in a government subject neither to Communist nor French control. The Dai Viet entered Bao Dai's government in June, 1949, only to leave after realizing that in the absence of true independence, collaboration could not become a road to power.

To refurbish its soiled image, the Dai Viet's leaders began to intensify their propaganda for true independence, attacking not only the Huu government but also Bao Dai and the French, who decided to oust Dai Viet members from their administrative positions. The Dai Viet had in fact successfully "infiltrated" the administration, particularly in the North; the governor of Tongking, Nguyen Huu Tri, the mayors of Hanoi and Haiphong, and many

314 • *Vietnam at War*

provincial administrators were Dai Viet members. The pretext for their removal, and for the suppression of the Dai Viet's legal activities, was a conflict that arose when Governor Tri attempted to do away with the administrative autonomy enjoyed by the two Catholic provinces of Phat Diem and Bui Chu, where, under Bishop Le Huu Tu, the Catholics not only ruled but also defended their domains with their own troops. Security Minister Tam conducted the elimination of the Dai Viet with his customary ruthlessness on direct orders from General de Lattre, who, on December 10, 1950, had become both commander in chief of the French armies and high commissioner of Indochina. Instead of hitting the Vietnamese politically by giving nationalists like Nguyen Huu Tri a freer hand, de Lattre insisted that the Huu government remove them from office and silence the Dai Viet.

As a result of this policy, the Huu government became a political liability to the French as well as to Bao Dai. The sects disliked it, the Dai Viet fought it, the Vietminh denounced it, and the population despised it. Sooner or later, Huu had to go. In trying to save himself, he chose methods that only hastened his downfall. Huu attempted to win greater popularity by posing as a more ardent patriot than Bao Dai and by expressing nationalist sentiments embarrassing to the French, without whose approval his government could never have come into existence.

Although antagonized by Huu's behavior, Bao Dai hesitated a long time before yielding to French pressure to dismiss him. Totally disillusioned and increasingly dependent on the revenues he derived from his position, Bao Dai finally consented to replace Huu with Nguyen Van Tam, the only prominent Vietnamese who was known as being "entirely devoted to the French."[22]

When Tam was made prime minister in June, 1952, every nationalist knew that the Bao Dai solution was dead.

XIV

Political Failure and
Military Decline

1

AFTER THE "FRENCH PATRIOT" Nguyen Van Tam was appointed prime minister of Vietnam, there remained no doubt in the minds of anti-Vietminh nationalists that Bao Dai and his government were French tools, and that preventing independence was the real objective of the Bao Dai "solution." To expect this regime to become a politically effective anti-Vietminh instrument was to delude oneself. On the contrary: It was bound to strengthen Ho Chi Minh by supporting his claim of being the sole fighter for national independence. The Vietminh must have welcomed Tam's appointment.

The French, whose ability for lucid political thought continued to erode, also were pleased that Bao Dai had finally chosen a true, reliable anti-Communist, a man who would neither curry favor with the Vietminh nor make unreasonable demands. Tam would accept the limitations on Vietnamese sovereignty imposed by the requirements of war. And he was a man who would "get things done."

One of the things he was expected to "get done" was the creation of a Vietnamese national army. The war was in its sixth year; the French-controlled territory had grown smaller; the Vietminh had begun to conduct large-scale offensives. After five years of costly and arduous effort, the French were farther from their goal than they had been at the outbreak of hostilities.

At first the war had gone badly for the Vietminh. They had lost not only Hanoi, Haiphong, and Hue, but by the end of March, 1947, they had also lost almost all towns in Tongking and northern Annam and many of their lines of communication. The Vietminh army, which had remained largely intact, was moved into the Viet Bac, the mountainous region north of Hanoi, and for the duration of the war the Viet Bac remained the training ground, supply base, and command center of the armed forces, as well as the governmental and organizational headquarters of the Vietminh.

The Vietminh leadership, knowing that it would take years before they could hope to defeat the French, for over three years refused to engage in open, large-scale armed encounters with the French. Ho Chi Minh apparently meant it when he said that the war might last ten to fifteen years. But by the fall of 1950, when Giap decided to oust the French from their positions between Hanoi and the Chinese border, the Vietminh disposed of a well-trained, well-equipped regular army of at least 60,000 men grouped in five divisions of 12,000 each, all but one of which, the 320th, were stationed in the Viet Bac.[1] The cautious Vietminh policy led the French to underestimate the strength and ability of the Vietminh forces, a miscalculation for which they were to pay their first heavy price in October, 1950.

More immediately detrimental to the French cause was their inability to occupy the entire country and control the thousands of villages housing the vast majority of the population. This failure gave early evidence to all but the closed minds of the French that the struggle for Indochina was likely to end in a Vietminh victory. In 1940, the French managed to control all of Vietnam with only a fraction of the troops at their disposal in 1947. If now they failed it was because control of the countryside was being denied them by the very people they thought to have defeated: the armed Vietnamese guerrillas and the so-called regional forces of the Vietminh, which in size, training, and equipment ranked between the small guerrilla units and the regular army. The existence of the guerrillas and regional troops was evidence that the people themselves, not only the army, were actively fighting the French.

The strong nationalist and anti-French sentiment of the population explained the widespread support enjoyed by the Vietminh fighting units. This support made it possible for them to assemble without fear of discovery, to replenish their ranks, and to create an intelligence network that kept them informed about the strength, movement, and even the plans of the French.[2]

Vietminh strategy between 1947 and 1950 called for keeping the French out of regions vital to the Hanoi government as sources of food, manpower, and minerals, and for harassing the French wherever they had established themselves. Though the Vietminh fighters, as ubiquitous and persistent as the country's mosquitoes and leeches, did not succeed in expelling the French from their positions, they did succeed in immobilizing the men needed to hold them. Consequently the French came to recognize that they had to limit their military occupation to strategically and economically vital regions from which the Vietminh could not as yet oust them. There the guerrillas and regional forces carried on their fight chiefly by night, blowing up bridges, building road blocks, ambushing patrols and convoys, assassinating collaborators, and attacking lookouts. Many French-controlled regions became Vietminh territory after dark.

The Vietminh was eminently successful. When General Valluy began his fall offensive against the Vietminh forces in the Viet Bac, at least half of Vietnam was under full Vietminh control, and still more was theirs at night, particularly in the north and center. Even before starting its offensives in 1950, the Vietminh controlled more than half of Tongking fully and great portions of the other half partially. The French were determined to hold on to the rich, thickly populated Red River Delta, from about 50 miles north of Hanoi down to the sea. Until October, 1950, they also maintained increasingly isolated outposts along the Chinese border in the northwest, including the towns of Caobang and

Langson (along Colonial Route 4, which was destined to become the first road of disaster for the French); and they loosely controlled most of the northwestern highlands between the Red and the Black Rivers, inhabited chiefly by Thai minorities and bordering on China in the north and Laos in the west. They kept a tenuous hold on the south and center of this region and maintained themselves precariously in the more distant northwestern Thai provinces. All other Tongking provinces were held by the Vietminh and administered by agents of the Hanoi government, which was master not only of the entire country northeast and east of the Red River and Hanoi, but also of the vast fertile provinces south of the Red River Delta down to northern Annam. In northern and central Annam, Vietminh domination of the countryside was even more extensive. Between the towns of Vinh and Qui Nhon, approximately 450 miles to the south, the French held only a narrow coastal strip. The former capital city of Hue was in French hands, but the French did not succeed in wresting the wooded, hilly land a few miles west of Hue up to the border of Laos and the hinterland of the central Annam coast from the Vietminh. Apart from the vast but thinly populated highland held mostly by the French, it is safe to say that close to 80 per cent of both land and people of northern and central Annam were under Vietminh control and remained in Vietminh hands to the end of the war.

The situation in southern Annam and Cochinchina was somewhat different. There the French reconquest had begun back in October, 1945, fifteen months before the start of the war in the North. In the South, French control, although far from being either total or secure, was much firmer. Most routes between the cities, although never safe, could be kept open. The French, understandably, spared no effort to keep control of the Cochinchinese and Cambodian rubber lands. But the Vietminh guerrillas in the South did succeed in gaining complete control of some regions and in making French control in many others extremely fragile. In fact, the entire region beyond the Bassac River, a western arm of the Mekong, was largely guerrilla-controlled, as was the Plain of Reeds to the west of Saigon and great portions of the provinces of Tay Ninh to the north and Baria to the southeast. In addition, the Vietminh maintained bases throughout the South.

The French could never spare enough troops to wipe out these enclaves, from which the guerrillas staged their attacks and by night dominated country nominally under French control. Thus the guerrillas were able to levy taxes, recruit soldiers, collect rice, indoctrinate the population, spread their net of informers, and if necessary terrorize villages considered hostile. This French inability to eliminate the Vietminh pockets and to deal effectively with the guerrillas was mainly responsible for France's losing the war. Whenever the French, after long preparation, moved against their elusive foe, he disappeared, and the French found that they had conquered empty marshes, jungles, and mountains. The guerrillas meanwhile, having dispersed, would reassemble at another base some distance away and repeat their maneuver. Sooner or later the pursuing French, far away from their own bases, out of supplies and ammunition, were left no choice but to return to their base, usually followed closely and harassed by the reappearing guerrillas. It would have been pointless for the French to occupy permanently sites which they had won, for wherever they did so, it meant that a contingent of their army was pinned down in a hard-to-supply, isolated outpost, doomed to inaction, and in control of only a small surrounding area. The immobilization of as many French troops as possible was precisely the objective of the Vietminh.

Evidence of the success of this strategy soon became abundant in the region the French considered important enough to hold at any cost in men and equipment: the Red River Delta. Its fertility, its 6 to 7 million inhabitants, its industrial centers, its vital communication links, especially between Haiphong and Hanoi, made the delta by far the most valuable prize of the war. Consequently, the duel for the delta, which ended only on the very last day of the war, produced the longest, bloodiest, and most bitterly fought engagement before the battle of Dien Bien Phu. Had the Vietminh been wiped out in the delta, they might not have been able to survive, since it would have meant not only the loss of a vital source of manpower, rice, and taxes, but also would have freed a substantial part of the Expeditionary Corps for offensive action. For the French the stakes were at least as high. Expulsion from the delta would have meant the loss of the entire North from the Chinese border down to Quang Tri or

Hue. This sense of urgency about the delta was responsible for some of the greatest military blunders of both the Vietminh and French.

Early in 1951, Giap, now in possession of a strong, well-equipped regular army, made a number of ill-advised attempts to drive the French out of Hanoi and Haiphong. The French defeated him in these first great battles of the war. Thereafter, the Vietminh contented itself with minor operations inside the delta conducted by local guerrillas, regional troops, and some regular army battalions. These tactics proved so effective that French control was reduced to one half of this important region, and, by 1953, to one third. The famous de Lattre Line of watchtowers and small fortifications built in 1951 to stop further infiltration was about as effective as a sieve. The subversion of French control behind the line was called the "rotting away" (*pourrissement*) of the delta.[3]

Guerrilla control of territories in the south, center, and delta region, which nailed down increasing numbers of French troops, rather than political acumen was the reason that de Lattre, Salan, and Navarre, the generals commanding the Expeditionary Corps between 1950 and 1954, insisted on the creation of a Vietnamese national army. Only if a Vietnamese army could free their troops from the task of defending and pacifying French-held territories would they be able to dispose of the manpower necessary for invading Vietminh-held territory, destroy Giap's army, and thus end the war.

2

In October, 1947, when General Valluy launched his first offensive to "wipe out" the Vietminh, the French were largely unaware of the advantages their opponent enjoyed—mountains in which to set up secret bases, jungles and marshes favoring the guerrillas, seemingly inexhaustible reserves of manpower, skill, and aggressiveness, and, above all, widespread popular support. Only slowly did the French gain awareness of these Vietminh assets, and of several others as well.

Valluy started his offensive with an army of 30,000. His objectives were to penetrate the Viet Bac, destroy Giap's regular army, and capture the Vietminh leaders. He hoped to achieve these goals by first encircling and then attacking the Viet Bac. All that the French possessed in modern arms and heavy equipment was employed in what was undoubtedly the greatest military action in French colonial history.

This colossal effort bore bitter fruit. With their vehicles, tanks, and heavy artillery, the French became "prisoners of the roads," as they themselves came to realize. Roads were few and poor, and none led into the depths of the Viet Bac mountains. Instead, they led through narrow, densely wooded passes and jungles which it was both difficult and senseless to penetrate in search of an invisible army. French columns traveled for weeks without meeting a single Vietminh soldier. Yet the French knew that the enemy was all around them, close by, and the evidence of his presence was much more distressing than the expected and longed-for military encounter. The villages the French passed were burning, the towns they reached were destroyed, the bridges of the many small rivers were blown up, and the roads they were forced to travel were made impassable by mines, ditches, and ingenious barriers built by men who watched their slow removal from the unstirring jungle no more than 50 yards away, patiently biding their time.

When the French reached the ruined, empty towns around the Viet Bac, they were low in fuel, their rations were depleted, and even worse, their confidence was shattered. If now they ventured out from their main positions, they were ambushed and attacked by the Vietminh. The jungle was the ally of the Vietminh, allowing them to prepare ambushes and condemning pursuit to failure. Soon the chief concern of the French was not how to reach and destroy Giap's regular army, but how to prevent the Vietminh from cutting French lines of communication, and the French found that they had to devote their strength to the protection of supply convoys and other purely defensive actions. Lacking the courage to admit failure, Valluy kept postponing the inevitable decision to withdraw, thereby adding to his losses and rendering more difficult the task of extracting his army from a hopeless situation. Early in 1948, the position of the French outside the delta was again what it had been a year before. All the French had gained from their gigantic effort was greater understanding of the peculiar nature of this war. However, only the soldiers, not the generals or politicians, had a premonition that France had lost the Indochina War then and there.

That the strategy of destroying the Vietminh with one giant stroke had failed, at least for the time being, was clear to the military and political leaders. Both, therefore, had to adapt their thinking and tactics to the reality of the situation created by this failure. Bollaert intensified his wooing of Bao Dai, but the generals were temporarily without any plan whatever. They still saw the war primarily as a military contest, and consequently they failed to grasp all the implications of their failure. However, by the spring of 1948, even official optimism could not ignore that Vietminh resistance had fought the French armies to a standstill and that new methods had to be devised for dealing with an enemy who refused to fight according to tested military methods.

Making a virtue of necessity, French military cerebration produced what was pompously presented as an entirely new strategy. Its guiding idea, a simple one, indicated that the French had little choice. Instead of attacking and destroying the main enemy forces in the Viet Bac, the French planned to cut them off from all other Vietminh regions and concentrate on "pacifying" them —i.e., bringing them under their full control. Thus isolated from the rest of the country and deprived of their supplies of food, raw materials, money, and manpower, the Vietminh, the French believed, would then be left with only one alternative to surrender: to move out of its stronghold, face the French in open battle, and suffer defeat.

The main drawback of such a strategy was that it would take time, and time was not working for the French. Whatever gains the French made during 1948 were temporary, since to preserve them would have meant using the entire army for static and defensive tasks. The French simply lacked the enormous number of troops needed to pacify and hold the country. The more territory they tried to occupy, the less effective was their control of what they already had, and the dimmer grew their prospects of ever building up a mobile force with which to strike out against the Vietminh.

The year 1949 also failed to produce a change in the new pattern of the war. It brought the French not one step nearer their goal. Innumerable short and brutal small actions were fought all over the country, imposing on the soldiers of both sides a burden of suffering that no human being should be forced to bear. The Vietminh continued to infiltrate delta territory and to reduce the number of villages under French military and Bao Dai administrative control. (This process of *pourrissement* accelerated as the war went on. At the end of 1953, the Vietminh was said to have had 80,000 fighting men in the delta. In 1952, the Vietminh controlled more than 600 of the 2,700 villages in the four major delta provinces; by July, 1953, that figure had risen to 1,486—more than half.[4]) The guerrillas repeatedly threatened to cut the vital French line of communication, the road between Haiphong and Hanoi. The French, on the other hand, never succeeded in blocking the roads, paths, and waterways connecting the rich provinces south of the delta with the Viet Bac. During this theoretical period of pacification, the French hold on Tongking became even feebler, particularly after they had been forced, in August, 1948, to relinquish Bac Kan, taken by paratroopers at the beginning of Valluy's offensive. This removed the last threat to the back door of the enemy's training base and headquarters.

In May, 1949, France, disturbed by the lack of progress in the war, sent Chief of Staff General Revers to Indochina. In a secret report, General Revers recommended the evacuation of the isolated garrisons along the Chinese border, which, he said, constituted a drain on French resources and probably would be unable to withstand a serious attack. He also maintained that before another offensive against the Viet Bac could be undertaken, the delta had to be completely pacified and its defense turned over to a Vietnamese army. He realized that without a strong Vietnamese army to support the French, victory over the Vietminh would be difficult to achieve, and he also understood the political conditions that would make such an army effective. In this war, he said, "diplomacy" must take precedence over military considerations.

The Revers report, the first of a long series of recommendations by special commissions, shared the fate of most later ones: being misunderstood or disregarded. Not only did "diplomacy" fail to create the political conditions for a fighting Vietnamese army, but not even the suggestions to liquidate obviously untenable military positions were acted upon.

A hint of the turn military events might take during 1950 came early in the year, when the Vietminh began to move in strength along the Red River against the city of Laokay on the Chinese border. Giap, with five regular army infantry battalions supported by 81-mm. mortars, attacked the French at Laokay. The mortars, obtained from the Chinese Communists, were the forerunners of vastly greater Chinese aid to come. The French, greatly outnumbered, were defeated after a brief struggle. This was in February. On May 25, Giap attacked and took the post of Dong Khe, some 15 miles south of Caobang, but lost it again to French paratroopers two days later. The rainy season prevented major operations for almost four months, but on September 18, the Dong Khe garrison of 800 was overwhelmed by the Vietminh.

This attack was the prelude to an all-out Vietminh effort to clear the Sino-Vietnamese border area of all French-held positions. The most distant French garrison, at Caobang, was entirely cut off by the fall of Dong Khe. The French had no choice but to attempt a retreat toward Langson. They started out from Caobang on October 3 with 1,600 regulars, 1,000 partisans, and numerous civilians who feared for their lives. With a column of 3,500 men, mainly Moroccans who had been stationed further south at That Me, the French tried to protect the retreat of their Caobang garrison. But both groups, ambushed and attacked by six Vietminh battalions, were forced to abandon their vehicles and driven into the hills. There, tracked down and outnumbered, they were either killed or taken prisoner by the Vietminh. A paratroop battalion sent in to cover the now chaotic retreat was practically wiped out. Langson, in immediate danger of being overrun, was abandoned on the night of October 17–18, but the arms, ammunition, and vehicles stocked there had to be left behind. "By October 19, this disastrous phase was over. The French had been completely driven out of northern Tongking, from the sea to the Red River, and a huge slice of territory adjacent to China was now completely under Vietminh control."[5] In addition to the vast amount of equipment they had to abandon, the Expeditionary Corps lost 6,000 men. The Vietminh, without themselves suffering many casualties, inflicted on the French what until then was the greatest military defeat in France's colonial history. According to Bernard Fall, the abandoned stocks alone were enough to equip a whole Vietminh division.[6] On November 6, the French, wiser now but too late, began to evacuate the town of Hoa Binh, gateway to the hilly Muong country along the northwestern border of the Red River Delta. This meant not only extending the Vietminh supply route to the Viet Bac, but it also brought the Muong minority population, which was not too friendly toward Hanoi, under Vietminh control.

Time, the French came to realize, was not on their side. A shift in the relative strength of the two sides in favor of the Vietminh had taken place, and this shift had brought about a new kind of war engaging larger units in open battle. In addition, the guerrilla war throughout the country was being pursued relentlessly in the northern delta, in central Vietnam, and with renewed vigor in the South. On the fourth anniversary of the outbreak of the war in the North, French morale was understandably low, whereas the Vietminh radio confidently began to predict the early return of Ho Chi Minh to Hanoi. Indeed, Giap believed that his victories were the first waves of a great tide that would ultimately sweep the French out of the delta itself.

Although the war conducted by the Vietminh may have been unorthodox by Western standards, they did fight according to the book. Their canon, a modified version of the laws of revolutionary warfare laid down by Mao Tse-tung, stated that the war would have to go through three stages not divided by fixed points in time. These stages, though overlapping, would be distinctly different from one another. They were described in a mixture of propagandistic exhortations and pedantic theorizing by Truong Chinh (alias Dang Xuan Khu), the then chief theoretician of Vietnamese Communism. Truong Chinh's booklet, *The Resistance Will Win*, which appeared in June, 1947, expounded this theory on the three stages of the war. Initially, it held, the Vietminh will be weak and the enemy strong. The Vietminh therefore will be on the defensive and the enemy take the offensive. In this first phase, the Vietminh had to preserve its forces, withdraw into safe territory, and be content with harassing enemy convoys and bases. In the second phase, that of the "equilibrium of forces and of active resistance," the enemy will no longer be able to make headway, but the Vietminh will not yet be able to regain lost territory. The military task during this period consists of engaging, tying down, and, if possible, exterminating enemy units through guerrillas and regional troops, and of sabotaging the enemy's economic activities. This second phase promises to be the longest of the three. It will end when the Vietminh has built up enough strength to open its own counteroffensive, beginning with a war of maneuver, passing through a war of large movement, into a war of position, and ending with the victory of the Vietminh.

As far as the Vietminh was concerned, the war thus far was proceeding according to the book. The first phase had come to an end with Valluy's failure to reach and destroy the Vietminh forces in the Viet Bac. The following three years, up to the defeat of the French on Colonial Route 4, were the second phase. Elated but also misled by his victories at the end of 1950, Giap believed this phase to be over as well and considered Vietminh strength as sufficient for a war of movement and large-scale attacks on the French. He therefore launched three such attacks early in 1951. For the first time in the war, Giap's regular army moved out of the Viet Bac.

The first of these offensives was begun on January 13 and aimed at Hanoi. On a 12-mile front north of Hanoi, between Viet Tri and Luc Nam, Giap attacked with eighteen of his best battalions whose logistic support was organized primitively yet effectively by an army of 180,000 porters. The battle lasted four days. Wave after wave of attackers were mowed down by the French; the Vietminh troops were unable to break through the main French defenses. After losing at least 6,000 of his best men, Giap retreated to the Viet Bac with his battered army.

On March 24, he began his second offensive, moving from Langson in the direction of Dong Trieu. He planned to cut off the coal region of Moncay and then overwhelm Haiphong. Had he succeeded, the French would have been forced to evacuate Hanoi and perhaps the entire delta. But after eight days of fruitless and costly battle, Giap once more had to accept defeat. French fire and air power stopped the Vietminh at the village of Mao Khe after inflicting another 3,000 casualties.

But a determined Giap launched a third offensive. This time he tried to force the French out of the delta by attacking from the south. This battle, which has become known as the Battle of the Day River, began on May 29. The Vietminh had succeeded in building up an entire division (the 320th)—the only one formed, trained, and equipped outside of the Viet Bac—in Than Hoa Province. In a remarkable logistic achievement, Giap brought two more divisions (the 304th and 308th) all the way down from the heart of the Viet Bac, over a distance of more than 150 miles.

The Vietminh attacked first at Phu Ly and Ninh Binh some 50 miles up from the coast. Giap's strategy was to force the French commander to bring his reserves from the delta into this area; Giap then sent his 320th Division, stationed farther south, over the Day River into the delta. The French held fast without committing many of their mobile reserves. The Vietminh pushed deep into the heart of the Catholic Phat Diem Province, attempting to link up with two regiments already operating in the delta. But popular support, so vital to the Vietminh, was conspicuously lacking in the Catholic regions. Moreover, the French Navy was able to move enough attacking craft up the Day River to cut Giap's supply lines; the French also used napalm bombs on an enemy who for the first time had left the protection of the jungles. After being battered and stalled for ten days, Giap realized that to continue would merely increase his losses and demoralize his men. It took him a full week to pull his troops back behind the Day River. He had lost a third of his army.[8]

Thus, in the fifth year of the war, the contestants were back where they had been before Giap prematurely embarked on a mobile war. The French attempted to exploit Giap's setback by launching fierce attacks at the western edge of the delta, but the over-all situation remained stalemated. The French were no longer able to make progress and the Vietminh was not yet able to win the battles into which it had rushed precipitately.

3

The outcome of the battle for Route 4 had had an extremely sobering effect on the French. Scapegoats were needed. The first, General Alessandri, was relieved of his post as commander of the French Army in Tongking. The commander in chief of the Expeditionary Corps, General Carpentier, and the high commissioner for Indochina, Léon Pignon, were also recalled. The French Government decided to put all civilian and military power into one hand. It offered both vacant positions to General Jean de Lattre de Tassigny.

De Lattre, who had gained renown during World War II, was a highly controversial figure. His excessive exercise of personal power combined with the "artistic" features of his temperament struck terror into the hearts of his men. His personality was forbidding; the only relationship he accepted was that of subservience to his authority. Donald Lancaster, who served at the British Legation when de Lattre took over on December 17, 1950, says that the General had a "legendary capacity for volcanic expressions of displeasure," an "overbearing manner," and a "disregard for normal civilities" that was only occasionally mitigated by a "considerable ability to charm." In the "frequent excesses of his autocratic temperament," de Lattre committed many "injustices." He humiliated his most loyal collaborators and imposed unnecessary hardships on soldiers and civilians.[9]

De Lattre's life ended tragically. He died in Paris of cancer on January 11, 1952, after less than a year's service in Indochina. But grief befell him long before he was stricken by disease. Only a few months after assuming his command, on May 30, 1951, he lost his only son, Bernard, in the defense of Binh Dinh, a position he himself had ordered held at all costs. But neither grief nor physical suffering could break de Lattre's pride. It is reported that the dying man, on hearing that his government had decided to make him a Marshal of France, demanded assurance that he was the only one to be thus honored.[10]

His soldiers could not be said to have loved de Lattre, but they did admire him. If his excessive pride, boundless self-esteem, and crude authoritarianism were destructive of decent human relations, they were at the same time evidence of an explosive energy and thus capable of instilling confidence into men longing to leave the dismal road of defeat. This he achieved, at least briefly. It was his skillful and courageous leadership that thwarted Giap's attempts to expel the French from Hanoi and the delta. When the tide once more turned against the French, de Lattre was already dead. His leadership probably averted a major disaster for the French in 1951, but "his failure to effect any basic change in strategy . . . makes it unlikely that the Expeditionary Corps was deprived of final victory by his death."[11]

The one course that might have helped the French check the growth of Vietminh strength could not even be considered: interrupting the rising flow of Chinese aid for the Vietminh by reoccupying the positions along Route 4 lost in October, 1950. There can be no doubt that de Lattre thereby "tacitly admitted that a military victory at this stage was beyond the grasp of the Expeditionary Corps."[12] He recognized that offensive action broad enough to promise success was possible only under three conditions: the securing of the delta; the strengthening of the Expeditionary Corps and relieving it of its static, purely defensive duties; and convincing the United States to help France carry the mounting burden of the war.

The attempt to make the delta safe led to the construction of the so-called de Lattre Line—fortified concrete strongholds built in groups of five or six, 1 or 2 miles apart, all around the delta; the desire for a larger mobile offensive force impelled de Lattre to urge Bao Dai to speed up the formation of the embryonic Vietnamese National Army; and in his effort to mobilize help, de Lattre went to Washington in September, 1951, to plead for massive military aid.

In all three respects de Lattre was only moderately successful. He asked Washington for aircraft, trucks, tanks, amphibious vehicles, automatic weapons, artillery, etc. But the United States was still involved in Korea, and although he obtained a promise of increased aid, the quantities he desired were not forthcoming.

A recommendation to construct fortified posts around the delta had already been made by General Revers in his report, but the weak towers that had been built proved not so much an obstacle to Vietminh penetration as a target for guerrilla attacks. A line of strong and continuous fortifications was a tremendous undertaking, but de Lattre embarked on it without a moment's hesitation. Unfortunately, this line of defense did not serve its purpose too well. Although the roads between these static defense positions were patrolled by small armored units, infiltration nonetheless could not be prevented. As a result, the Vietminh forces operating inside the delta were stronger after the completion of the line than before. Furthermore, the manning of the 1,200 strong points and the patrolling of the area nailed down a substantial portion of the available troops, leaving de Lattre with insufficient forces for offensive action.

These factors, not great political insight, were the compelling military reasons that induced de Lattre, and later Salan and Navarre, to demand a Vietnamese national army large enough to free the Expeditionary Corps for offensive action.

The Vietminh had an advantage over the French in all respects except in the number of regular troops and amount of heavy equipment. The Vietminh had few cities to garrison and defend, no posts or blockhouses to guard and hold, and except for the Viet Bac, which was practically impregnable, few territories so vital that they could not be temporarily abandoned if defending them proved too difficult or too costly.

The great disadvantage of the French, loudly deplored by de Lattre in 1951, Salan in 1952, and Navarre in 1953, was that with an organized, well-equipped fighting force almost twice the size Giap's regular army, fewer troops were available to them for offensive action than to the Vietminh. Navarre estimated that of the 190,000 men in the Expeditionary Corps, at least 100,000 were tied down in static defense. Lacouture and Devillers claim that of the 500,000 soldiers of which the French disposed after the buildup of the Vietnamese National Army in 1953, no less than 350,000 were engaged in static duties. The Vietminh battle corps consisted of six divisions; the French had the equivalent of only three, including their eight parachute battalions.[13] The other 350,000 men were assigned to the defense of cities, to holding isolated strong points, escorting convoys, patrolling highways, and conducting punitive actions against villages suspected of hiding and supporting guerrillas.

The French command became one of the most determined promoters of a Vietnamese national army. It was de Lattre who broke French opposition to such an army, a resistance apparently led by High Commissioner Léon Pignon. The majority of French officers in Indochina opposed a native army not under complete French control. De Lattre's authority was instrumental in changing this attitude. Much too late, French military leaders agreed that a Vietnamese national army should be under the command of Vietnamese nationals.

At the urging of de Lattre, conscription was introduced in July, 1951, but because of the shortage of trained officers only a token number was called up. To avoid conscription, many young men in the South joined the Cao Dai and Hoa Hao militias. Those who enlisted during 1951 were poorly trained and equipped, but the major deficiency then and for a long time to come was the lack of qualified officers. The best elements of the educated middle class had no desire to fight in an army still under over-all French direction for a regime they despised and against people who, even if Communist-led, were fighting for national independence. For these political reasons, which the colonial French mind failed to grasp, the Vietnamese National Army never became much of a fighting force. It remained indifferently trained, poorly led, and unmotivated. Although at the end of the war the French had at their disposal a 300,000-man Vietnamese force, not one additional square mile of territory had been pacified and few French troops had been freed for offensive action.

The contention that the Vietnamese were incapable of becoming good soldiers was one of the many self-deceptions with which the French propped their belief in their Indochinese policy. The contrary was proved not only by the extraordinary valor and skill of the Vietminh, but also by the Vietnamese in the Expeditionary Corps, who usually fought well and whose casualty rate was higher than that of any other French-led group. A Vietnamese national army could have been of military value only in fighting for or defending independence. But since it was an instrument of the Bao Dai regime, no amount of training or propaganda could produce the officers or men willing to risk their lives. For a long time even Bao Dai was reluctant to push the build-up of his army. "It would be dangerous," he told one of his advisers, "to expand the Vietnamese Army, because it might defect en masse and go to the Vietminh."[14] In fact, a few companies did desert; others refused to go out on patrol or move from their home districts.[15] Nguyen Van Hinh, a French citizen and French officer, who became its general and chief of staff, said it would take seven years before the National Army would be ready to relieve the Expeditionary Corps of its static duties and take part in offensive operations against the Vietminh. But in a different political climate, the National Army might have been turned into an efficient and inspired fighting force in less than three years.

De Lattre thought he had not been able to regain territory and start an offensive because he did not have a Vietnamese army. But Salan and Navarre later had such an army, yet they too failed, because, as Lacouture and Devillers have pointed out, the condition for military success—the creation of a unified, independent, truly democratic Vietnam—was never achieved.[16]

4

The "secret weapon" of the Vietnamese Communists, if one might call it that, was their ability to organize, indoctrinate, and lead the masses. A couple of hundred gifted men, rich and poor, had learned and adapted to Vietnamese conditions the techniques of mass propaganda and organization developed by the European labor movement and by the Bolsheviks.

But Vietminh propaganda was not aimed at filling the people's minds with Communist ideas. The Vietminh, as long as it existed as an instrument of the Communists, concentrated on achieving national liberation and a "progressive," "democratic" state. To say that the Vietminh leaders, being Communists, merely pursued their Party's aims is politically misleading, for it implies that their nationalism was fraudulent, that they "used" nationalism to advance their cause.

Unless one understands this point one cannot possibly understand how the Vietminh could become the vehicle through which the Vietnamese Communists achieved their victories. To say that the Communists "used" nationalism is true only in so far as all nationalists "use" nationalism. Nationalism was an integral part of the Vietnamese Communist cause, not merely a cover for their real aims. The truth is that being Communists did not prevent the Vietminh leaders from being authentic nationalists, as extreme and determined as any the anticolonial movement had produced. In fact, the Vietnamese Communists could become effective only by being nationalists first and Communists second. This was true in more than just the chronological sense imposed on them by obvious strategic considerations, since the ultimate aims of the Communists could become objects of policy only after the triumph of the people's national aspirations. For this reason the national aspirations of the Communists were as genuine as those of any non-Communist in or out of the Vietminh.

The evidence that the Vietminh leaders were talented, energetic, and devoted can be ignored only at the risk of failing to grasp the reasons for their success. Their propaganda reached every corner of the country; they mastered the art of organizing great masses openly and clandestinely both in their territory and in French-controlled regions; they battled starvation and overcame the crippling shortages of agricultural tools and essential drugs. The tasks that faced them were gigantic. At the beginning of the war they possessed virtually no means of transportation, no heavy weapons, not a single plane, and they themselves had de-stroyed most of the roads, railroads, and bridges to block the French. Their soldiers had no shoes, their children no clothing, they had no soap with which to wash the one garment they owned, and their diet was not varied enough to sustain soldiers and civilians in the tremendous effort demanded of them. That the Vietminh ultimately won the war stands as a truly extraordinary achievement.

The chief problem of the Hanoi government was how to feed its people and equip its soldiers. No outside help could be ex-pected, and in fact none was received during the first four years of the war. The Vietminh survived on what could be produced or procured locally.

The country's economic resources were mobilized chiefly through the intensified use of human working capabilities. Land rents were lowered to 25 per cent of the crop, but the larger landholdings were neither divided nor expropriated. The govern-ment concentrated on achieving self-sufficiency in basic foods by improving production methods and increasing yields. Dams and dykes were maintained and new ones built to win new arable lands. In meetings, on posters, in songs, plays, and poems, the people were exhorted to work harder. The rice field was called a battlefield, the hoe and plough weapons, and the working population urged to compete with the soldiers. Since the rich food-producing areas were largely in French hands, rice was collected at night and carried by teams of porters from the delta region into the Viet Bac, or by sampans and junks from the Mekong region to the coast of central Annam.

Yet despite the tremendous efforts of the people, Hanoi's food supplies were never adequate. Although production rose, it could not keep pace with the mounting civilian and military needs. Periods of scarcity were common even for the army, and pockets of starvation existed at least until 1952.

One of the gravest problems of Hanoi was that it was cut off from the country's industrial production. Nor did it have free access to markets abroad. Radio receivers for field communication and drugs for the wounded and ill were among the most serious shortages. Consequently, medical care, both civilian and military, was poor. But the Vietminh managed to avoid catastrophe by using substitutes for unavailable goods or eventually producing them.

Priority was of course given to arms production, and, significantly, to paper. The Vietminh regarded its papers and other propaganda materials as essential to victory as guns. Lack of machinery limited industrial production largely to goods that could be produced with the available handicraft skills and equipment. Thanks to the French policy of preventing industrialization and of keeping the peasants too poor to buy imported goods, these skills had survived. Small establishments turned out textiles, soap, paper, sugar, metal, and simple agricultural implements. Some vitally important articles, such as mechanical pumps, were made from the motors of captured vehicles. The French air force had difficulty in knocking out the many production sites, few of which could rightly be labeled factories. They were well hidden in dense jungles, and many operated either underground or in caves.

Organization coupled with some pressure and a great deal of propaganda was the key to this achievement and also to the mining and export of phosphorus, tungsten, tin, lead, and other minerals. All mines were nationalized. The shipment of these minerals to the coast for sale abroad was a most complicated organizational task. Poppy seed from northern Tongking and Laos, pepper from

Cambodia, and even rice from the Mekong Delta were exported to obtain foreign currency (the Ho Chi Minh piaster had become worthless, even in Vietminh-controlled territory). The income from these sales was used for the purchase of arms, radios, drugs, and machinery in Hong Kong, Singapore, and the Philippines—mostly U.S. Army surplus. Both overland and sea transport of these cargoes was extremely hazardous, and the losses suffered were great—as high as 50 per cent according to some estimates.

Despite these overriding problems, the Vietminh always had people to spare for work in other fields as well. For example, the campaign against illiteracy continued throughout the war. Combating illiteracy of course had a political purpose. The people had to be indoctrinated and propaganda spread not only by the spoken word but also by the more enduring printed word.

Technical education was stressed, but other branches of higher learning were not neglected. For the Party elite, intensive courses in Marxism were conducted with as much zeal as the training of officers in military academies. Officer training was of course also largely political, and if these men were not as knowledgeable in military science as the French, field practice and combat experience made them superior leaders, at least in the type of small-scale "revolutionary warfare" that dominated the fighting. In the preparation of ambushes, in attacking isolated posts, and in the arts of dispersion, reconcentration, hiding, and camouflage, the Vietminh military leaders developed a degree of perfection that never ceased to astonish the French.

It was the total mobilization of the entire people (which led to organized control of thought and action) and the integration of military and political life that made the Vietminh leadership such a formidable and invincible opponent. In one way or another, the entire nation, children included, was engaged in the war, working and fighting on all fronts—economic, political, cultural, and military. This total integration of all aspects of life with the multiform military steps devised for winning the war is probably the only new political phenomenon since the end of World War II; it was certainly the key to the victories won by the Communists in Vietnam.

The scope of the political indoctrination of the people was truly fantastic. The different local and national groups that composed the Lien Viet (National Front) claimed a membership of 8 million. The variety and separate activities of these organizations, their ritualistic "election" of leaders, gave the impression of an autonomous and highly decentralized existence, but control over them was total, even though it was discernible only to the trained political eye. All leading positions in all organized bodies and on all vital economic, cultural, or military fronts were in the hands either of Communist Party members or their proven allies in the Vietminh. The Communist Party, officially dissolved on November 11, 1945, but leading a clandestine existence, counted 5,000 members in 1945. In 1946, membership jumped to 210,000, and a year later to 365,000. These 365,000 became the founding members of the Lao Dong (Workers Party), the name under which the Communist Party was officially re-formed on March 3, 1951. Never in the modern history of Vietnam, either before or after the Indochina War, did any other Vietnamese political party succeed in gaining even a fraction of this organized strength. It is safe to say that the Hanoi government maintained some kind of functioning administration in all of French-held Vietnam, and that its agents, partly because of the mounting fear of a Vietminh victory, were able to collect large sums in "taxes" even from the rich. The peasants were persuaded, sometimes by threats, to make "voluntary contributions." Taxes from them were collected in goods, chiefly rice, which in fact became the official currency of the Hanoi regime. Even its budget was drawn up in kilos of rice, and its officials and high-ranking officers were paid in rice. Needless to say, these men, unlike their counterparts in the Bao Dai regime, did not live in luxury and did not enrich themselves at the expense of the people.

An erroneous opinion that gained currency soon after the outbreak of the Indochina War holds that the defeat of the French was due to their alleged ignorance of Vietminh military theory and Vietminh ingenuity in mobilizing the population. But the French knew a great deal more in 1952 than the Americans had learned by 1965. They failed militarily for basic political reasons which they could not have overcome even if, instead of napalm, they had made more extensive use of their own counterguerrillas.[18] Nor was the French defeat due to massive outside (Chinese) aid to the Vietminh, despite the claims of Western propaganda. The

French were losing long before Chinese aid became effective. And since Chinese aid resulted in vastly greater and speedier U.S. assistance, it is safe to say that the Vietminh would have defeated the French also without Chinese aid. The victory of Communism in China, however, had far-reaching political effects on Vietnam. It led to the recognition of the Ho Chi Minh regime by China, the Soviet Union, and the East European Communist states, and it led the West to recognize the Bao Dai regime as the legitimate government of a nominally independent Vietnam.

The effect of these developments on the Vietminh regime was a slow and not entirely voluntary changeover toward a so-called people's democracy, or a more or less overtly Communist state. It would be hard to prove that this course was historically determined the moment the Vietminh regime was formed. Since French policy between 1947 and 1950 ruled out a peaceful settlement, and thus a compromise between the Vietminh and the forces around Bao Dai, Hanoi, in spite of verbal assurances to the contrary, became interested chiefly in military victory. This meant not only that Ho had to depend increasingly on Chinese aid, which he knew had strings attached to it, but it also affected his internal policy. Since Ho had gained nothing by trying to please the West and the pro-Western forces around Bao Dai, he put his regime, hesitantly but unmistakably, into the Soviet and Chinese camp.

One step in that direction was the emergence of the Communist Party as the Workers Party; another was the installation of Party members and reliable allies in crucial administrative and command positions. Critical observers had always been convinced that Hanoi would turn into a people's democracy, but before 1950, more than just a façade hid its tendency toward becoming a Communist state, not because the Communists would ever renounce their ultimate aims, but simply because it was theoretically still possible to mobilize the non-Communist forces inside and outside the Vietminh for a different solution. Before 1950, the "Democratic Republic of Vietnam" was a rather "modern" state, with a new "civil code" and a progressive educational system, and outside the political arena it promoted all kinds of "freedoms" formerly unknown in Vietnam. And in regard to political freedom, the people were hardly any less well off than the population under the French-sponsored Bao Dai regime. There was as little democracy on the side that claimed to be fighting for freedom as there was in the regions administered by Hanoi.

The most far-reaching change after Hanoi's proclaimed solidarity with the Soviet and Chinese camp and the founding of the Lao Dong was the gradual purging of all leaders and officials not sufficiently subservient to the Communists. In the course of this process, the Vietminh was merged with the Lien Viet, for the rise of the Lao Dong and its control of the Lien Viet made the Vietminh superfluous as a separate instrument of Communist domination. After February, 1951, the Vietminh ceased to exist. In line with their new course, the Communists, after much hesitation and long preparations, at last began a land-reform program. This reform, aimed at the "total liquidation of the old feudal regime" and conducted with great circumspection, was announced by Ho Chi Minh in a speech on December 19, 1952, the seventh anniversary of the outbreak of the war in Hanoi. In this speech Ho admitted, at least by implication, that the peasants lived "more than ever in misery." He said that the peasants, who constituted 90 per cent of the army, regional forces, militia, and guerrillas, had "made the largest contribution to the resistance and accepted the greatest sacrifices, and meanwhile they are still among the poorest of our people because they lack land."[19] But the land reform took shape only with the decrees of April 12, 1953, and was given its final form in a law adopted by the rump National Assembly on December 4, 1953.

Thus, when Giap and Navarre, in 1953, were preparing for the final phase of the war, the conflict, though still a colonial war, had definitely taken on two new aspects. The existence of a Vietnamese national army under Bao Dai added an element of civil war, and the growing involvement of the Communist powers on the one side and the United States on the other turned it more and more into an international conflict.

5

The war brought misery for the mass of the people on both sides, but life was harder in the Vietminh-ruled regions than in the territories under firm French control. The people in the

French regions, which encompassed most of the cities into which refugees from the war-torn countryside had fled, lived in extreme poverty, but at least they were no longer exposed to the ordeals which the countryside was suffering. There was less hunger in the French-controlled areas, more doctors and drugs, and probably fewer demands for the sort of extreme physical exertion the Vietminh imposed on its own people.

For the people who enjoyed the privileges of wealth or who held important political and administrative posts, life under the French was entirely different from life under the Vietminh. The top people in the Vietminh camp led a truly Spartan existence. True, they did not suffer hunger and had adequate medical care, but most lacked many bare necessities and none had luxuries. Not even their worst enemies have accused the Vietminh leaders of corruption, and if none was corrupt it was not for lack of opportunity. They were a breed of men entirely different from those on the other side, who had either long collaborated with the French or had risen to eminence since the Bao Dai solution.

If the people around Bao Dai lacked some of the faults that revolutionary fanaticism is likely to breed, they also lacked the virtues of their adversaries: devotion to a cause and personal disinterestedness. The models for most Bao Dai ministers and high officials were the French and Vietnamese war profiteers who led luxurious or at least very comfortable lives while their countrymen starved and died. Corruption flourished. Bao Dai officials sold high positions that offered opportunities for "second-line corruption" for fantastic prices. The eagerness to grab the benefits of power was greatly enhanced by the cynical attitude of top officials toward a war supposedly being waged for the "defense of the free world." Since paying lip-service to this belief did not in the least interfere with the flow of funds into their own pockets, some of the worst grafters and extortionists posed as the most determined defenders of freedom. The soldiers of the Vietnamese National Army, in so far as they really believed they were serving a good cause, were shamelessly betrayed by their leaders, though no more so than the French officers and men who fought, suffered, and died, supposedly for their country. They, too, were sacrificed in cold blood for the gains of their speculating and profiteering countrymen in Indochina and at home.

One way of making money was to traffic in piasters. The 17 francs per piaster rate of exchange was more than double the piaster's real value measured in purchasing power (or its black market price). Piaster deals became one of the greatest financial scandals in the entire history of colonial Indochina. Anyone with say 10,000 piasters to spare could enter the piaster trade. All that was needed was permission to transfer the money to France at the official rate of exchange. With the right connections, permission could be obtained from an office controlled by the Bank of Indochina. "The operation took place in a dusty and lamentable building in Saigon called the Office of Exchange, which, rather than the Office of the High Commissioner or of the Army Chief of Staff, was the real center of Indochina."[20] But permission for the transfer was only the beginning of the operation. The 170,000 francs realized from the conversion of 10,000 piasters were now used to acquire piasters at their real value of 7 or 8 francs per piaster. This could be done legally by importing goods into Indochina, or illegally by changing the francs into dollars and with these dollars buying cheap piasters on the black market. The 10,000 piasters had thus been turned into 20,000–25,000, and if retransferred to France, to 250,000–300,000 francs, four times the piasters' actual value. Theoretically, this operation could go on forever, and in fact went on long enough to produce quite a number of new French and Vietnamese multimillionaires at the expense of the French treasury, which bought piasters sold for 7 or 8 francs for 17 francs.

The piaster traffic went on for years, although it was known that one of its scandalous by-products was aiding the war effort of the Vietminh. Piasters collected by the Hanoi government in the form of taxes or as "voluntary contributions" were sold on the black market for dollars that came from the speculators on the French side, dollars the Vietminh desperately needed to purchase arms and equipment that could not be produced at home.

The piaster had not been overvalued when its exchange rate was fixed in December, 1945. But the devastations of the war had caused it to fall more quickly than the franc. What was the French Government to do when the piaster was becoming a drain on its treasury? It could not cut off the piaster from the franc without cutting off Indochina from France economically.

It would have meant giving up French economic control of Indochina. And France's unenlightened political leadership after World War II had allowed itself to be pushed into the Indochina War by the powerful colonial interests precisely in order to maintain this control. As long as France hoped to win the war, she could not very well devalue the piaster, for this would have destroyed the modicum of economic stability that existed in Indochina. Maintaining the 17 to 1 franc-piaster exchange rate meant maintaining the purchasing power of the Indochinese states, and thereby enabling them to buy the goods they needed from France. Prime Minister Nguyen Van Tam was well aware of the French interest in maintaining the high rate of the piaster. In a speech in Paris on November 27, 1952, he said that imports from France had never been as great as in 1952, when they were expected to reach a total of 222 billion francs. And he reminded his audience of the role French exports to Indochina played in the economic stability of France.

These exports obviously were possible only because France, by maintaining the exchange rate, was giving desperately needed assistance to the Indochinese economy. Without this assistance, the economy of the so-called Associated States of Indochina would have collapsed. However, the billions earned by the traders in French goods represented only a fraction of the money which the French taxpayers (soon to be joined by their American fellow victims) had to supply to keep Indochina in the French Union. Businessmen and speculators were the only ones to benefit from this situation, at the expense of the French people. Now more than ever, French privileges in Indochina were profitable for a select few and costly for the mass of people.

It came as a terrible economic, political, and psychological shock when France, on May 11, 1953, devalued the piaster to 10 francs—political because this unilateral action made a mockery of the "national sovereignty" of the Indochinese states, psychological because it seemed to imply that France was no longer either able or willing to carry the heavy costs of the war. Furthermore, since the devaluation "took place after French financial and commercial interests had completed the transfer of their capital and activities to other parts of the world,"[21] Vietnamese nationalists concluded that the French engaged in Indochinese business, and the Bank of Indochina in particular, no longer believed in a military solution.

The economic impact of the devaluation compounded its political and psychological effects. Almost from one day to the next, prices, including those of rice and other local products, rose by 50 per cent. In an impoverished country this was bound to have severe political repercussions more disastrous than a major military defeat. Even people who had believed themselves unaffected by the political maneuvering between the French and the Bao Dai nationalists suddenly realized that independence was not a theoretical matter that concerned only a political elite. In the absence of true independence, the French Government had been able to cut the purchasing power of the Vietnamese people in half. Independence had obvious moral and spiritual values, but it was also of great practical and material importance. Those keen enough to anticipate the trend of events rightly concluded that a France unable to preserve the abysmally low standard of living of the Indochinese people would not be able to continue the war much longer. And since France had not complied with even her limited promises regarding the sovereignty of the Indochinese states, most people also concluded that independence could become real only after the French were made to leave. The popular mood was such that even Nguyen Van Tam felt obliged to speak out not as a French but as a Vietnamese patriot. In a broadcast on June 8, 1953, he stated: "Our relations with France have recently been burdened. The frailty and inadequacy of the agreements of March, 1949, and of 1950, have become clear. If the principle of our adherence to the French Union is to be upheld, it must be recognized that the constitution established by France in 1946 no longer conforms to the needs of the nations asked to adhere to the Union. It is important that we no longer remain in this Union as tenants of a house built without us."

It had become evident that the permanent crisis of Bao Dai nationalism had entered its final, climactic phase. There no longer existed any hope of arousing a fighting spirit against the Vietminh either in the army or among the population. The morale of the army was shattered. Those who joined in 1953 did so largely to escape their poverty. The Bao Dai regime was rapidly deteriorating.

The one predictable outcome was the fall of the government of Nguyen Van Tam.

To forestall this, Tam made a rather bold political move. In an attempt to improve his image, he demanded greater independence and introduced a number of social and political reforms—mostly on paper. This brought him into conflict not only with the French, but also with those Vietnamese whose support was vital to his survival: Bao Dai and his conservative counselors, the rich Vietnamese in the cities, and above all the large landowners whose privileges Tam was threatening, "not out of conviction but for tactical political reasons."[22]

The "era of reform," one of the many abortive attempts to gain popular support, began on November 16, 1952, with Tam's proclamation of freedom for trade unions. Although this aroused the violent opposition of the conservative elements, it failed to create support for the regime among the workers. On the contrary, the unions, although largely under "Christian" influence, served as a vehicle through which the "socialist" tendencies of the masses and their hostility against the Bao Dai regime could be expressed more overtly.

On January 25, 1953, municipal elections were held, the first step toward keeping a promise already made by Tran Van Huu. But these elections could be held only in French-controlled territory, about 25 per cent of the country housing 50 per cent of its population. In most areas only one out of three villages was considered sufficiently pacified to be allowed to vote, and in the vital and critical Red River Delta the proportion was not even that high. Of the 7,000 delta villages, 687 took part in the elections. This meant that no more than 1 million out of a total population of 27 million (or of the 13 million under French and Bao Dai rule) were allowed to vote. Yet despite these precautions, candidates openly critical of the regime won the majority of votes. In Hanoi, an antigovernment list headed by one Nguyen The Truyen, a former associate of Ho Chi Minh, received 60 per cent of votes cast, thanks to the open support not only of the Dai Viet but also of the Catholics and several other anti-Vietminh groups. (The Vietminh had called upon the people to boycott the elections.)

The results of the municipal elections killed the idea of provincial and national elections, which had been promised for October, 1953. Tam, although still in the fight, knew that the day when Bao Dai and the French would drop him was not too far off. Not even his most masterful move, a land reform decreed in June, 1953, could avert his downfall.[23] As a matter of fact, it may very likely have hastened it, as did his flirtation with "democracy" and his demand for true independence, for now landlord opposition to Tam grew as fast as French disenchantment and the fear of radical reforms in the circles around Bao Dai.

Whether Tam was on the right track will never be known, for his too timid reforms had no time to bear fruit.[24] Opposition against them was too strong, and Tam was not able to mobilize the political forces needed to overcome it. Even those who had once supported him, including Bao Dai, no longer trusted him. While the iron grip of the Lao Dong on the Lien Viet strengthened and unified the Hanoi regime, the Bao Dai regime was disintegrating. Tam's government included only the most discredited elements of the VNQDD and the Dong Minh Hoi, old *émigrés* who had returned to Vietnam late in 1949 with the remnants of Chiang Kai-shek's retreating army. (The Vietminh wisely let them pass through into French-held territory.) Only insignificant factions of the badly split Dai Viet were on-and-off supporters of Bao Dai. Tam also lost the support of the religious-political sects, not so much because of his vain effort to integrate their troops into the National Army, but because of popular discontent. The sect leaders assumed an increasingly rebellious attitude toward the Bao Dai regime. The two major sects, especially the Hoa Hao, were deeply split politically. Substantial groups of both the Cao Dai and the Hoa Hao withdrew from the fight against the Vietminh. Trinh Min The, the Cao Dai chief of staff, was the first of a number of sect leaders who attempted to form a "third" political force between the Vietminh and the Bao Dai regime. The more conservative elements of the sects, particularly among the Cao Dai leaders, withdrew their support from Tam because they feared that a liberalization of the Bao Dai regime might threaten their privileged positions.

The role played by the Binh Xuyen in the maneuvers that led to the fall of Tam differed from that played by the other two sects. The Binh Xuyen also indulged in nationalistic propaganda and cared little about the fate of Tam; but they had learned that it was to their advantage to remain loyal to Bao Dai. Bay Vien, alias Le Van Vien, the undisputed chief of the Binh Xuyen, was tied to Bao Dai with the strongest possible bond: mutual financial interests. From his headquarters in Cholon, Le Van Vien controlled gambling and the no less remunerative houses of prostitution. Opium remained another safe source of his income as long as he handed a portion of his profits over to Bao Dai. This was indeed the lowest point to which the ex-emperor had sunk, a steep descent from the time when he had enthusiastically attempted to introduce reforms and fought for a measure of independence for his country. The least objectionable of his interests now were big-game hunting, yachting, and cars, and his main fear was that he might lose the position that made it possible to indulge his expensive tastes. Social and political reforms seemed to threaten not only the privileges of the rich but also the monarchy itself. Since Bao Dai had become a disgrace to the monarchy, some conservative leaders openly advocated that Bao Dai abdicate in favor of his son Bao Long.

The depth of the crisis in the camp of anti-Vietminh nationalism became apparent during two national congresses held in September and October, 1953. The first one, which took place in Cholon on September 5, was intended as a demonstration of all major anti-Vietminh factions against the Tam government, Bao Dai, and the French. But since the participants lacked not only a doctrine, but also a program taking up the most pressing needs of the people, their well-intentioned refusal to work with the French became mere inactivity accomplishing nothing. They proved once again that the Vietnamese anti-Communist intellectuals lacked both political originality and the skill to organize and lead the masses. Sensing the mood of the people, they fell back on their easiest demand, which was that the French leave, a call supported even by the Catholic bishop of Phat Diem. "As if without us," a Frenchman observed sarcastically, "nationalist Vietnam could survive."[25]

The September congress marked the appearance on the political scene of Ngo Dinh Diem's younger brother Ngo Dinh Nhu, who masterminded this phase of the rebellion against Bao Dai, the French, and Tam. Nhu had gained some prominence as the organizer of a Catholic trade-union movement modeled on the French Force Ouvrière. With ideas largely borrowed from France, and aided in their articulation by Father Parrel, a Dominican priest, Nhu embellished his passion for power with the presumption of an original political philosophy—the creed of the French "personalist" group organized around the periodical *Esprit*, but deprived of its meager relevance by its transplantation from Europe to Asia. Nhu's only real talent was for political behind-the-scenes manipulation, in whose exercise he consistently disregarded the principles he professed.

Nhu's aim in the late summer of 1953 was the creation of a "national union for independence and peace" in support of a new government to be headed by Diem. For his congress on September 5, Nhu gained not only the support of the Cao Dai and Hoa Hao leadership, but also the active help of Le Van Vien, at whose headquarters in Cholon the meeting was held under Binh Xuyen military protection. However, the mood of the congress, violently anti-French and anti–Bao Dai, disregarded the sect leaders' need for caution. This prompted them to send a loyalty message to Bao Dai after the proceedings had become so tumultuous that Le Van Vien ordered his guards to clear the hall. Some speakers had demanded not only total independence, radical reforms, and free elections, but also the establishment of a republic. Ousting Bao Dai was one of Nhu's aims, but his too-open pursuit of it before the time was ripe was one of the reasons that his movement for independence and peace failed to mobilize the anti-Vietminh nationalists for united action.

But the September congress, although a failure for Nhu, nonetheless dealt a hard blow to Bao Dai. Realizing how quickly the coalition on which his regime rested could fall apart, he and his advisers decided to wipe out the impression of disunity and opposition created by the meeting. This was to be accomplished through another congress, one they claimed would be truly representative of the entire nation. Bao Dai summoned his cousin, Prince Buu Loc, Vietnam's representative in Paris, to Saigon to organize this congress, which opened on October 12 and was attended by about two hundred delegates. Although officially controlled, this meeting revealed that even the mildest of nationalists considered any further dependence on France politically intolerable. A resolution demanding the withdrawal of Vietnam from the French Union was adopted on October 16. Under official pressure this was amended a day later to read that Vietnam could not stay in the French Union "in its present form," but this was not much of an improvement as far as France was concerned. And in a move clearly directed against Bao Dai and the Tam government, the congress requested that a permanent committee of a provisional assembly formed by the congress before elections could be held take part in all future negotiations between Vietnam and France.[26]

By the end of 1953, all avenues for maintaining Franco-Vietnamese cooperation without full independence had obviously been exhausted. Tam tried to save himself by insisting on his reforms and by adopting some of the demands of the October congress. This was too much for the people who, at least secretly, wanted Franco-Vietnamese cooperation to continue: the rich landowners, profiteers, and staunchly monarchist, antidemocratic circles around Bao Dai. They urged him to drop Tam, and on December 17 he gave in. Bao Dai then charged Buu Loc with forming a new cabinet. This turned out to be the last Vietnamese government before the ending of the war brought unexpected forms of "total independence."

6

The consolidation of Communist control on the one side and the disarray of the nationalist camp on the other were bound to be reflected in the further course of military events. Despite some displeasure over the growing Communist domination of the "resistance," Hanoi's military strength increased, whereas the expectations attached to the formation of a Vietnamese national army never materialized.

The initiative was now clearly on the side of the Hanoi regime. During the last third of the war, the French no longer attempted to break Vietminh resistance but rather tried to deal with the enemy's growing power and aggressiveness. Clear heads in the nationalist camp foresaw that France would lose Vietnam even though she might still win the war. On the Vietminh side, mounting hopes based on steady military progress, Chinese aid, and the political ineptitude of the opponent gave rise to the conviction that a favorable military outcome was not an unrealistic expectation.

Giap embarked on what turned out to be the last phase of the war in October, 1952. He assembled three divisions east of the Red River, between Phu Tho and Yen Bay. The French, not knowing what to expect, prepared themselves to repel another attack on the delta. But Giap, crossing the Red River by night, turned his back on the delta and moved west and north into the region of the Red and Black Rivers, an area inhabited largely by the Thai, Vietnam's largest ethnic minority. Giap's long-term strategy had two aims: the conquest of northwestern Tongking and a further dispersion of French forces for purely defensive operations. The French might decide to thwart the first objective by holding on to their fortified positions in northwestern Tongking in order to block a Vietminh invasion of Laos, but even if they succeeded, Giap felt he would achieve his second aim, since the French could stop him only by employing most of the mobile reserve units being built up for future offensive action. Furthermore, these reserves had to be flown into northwestern Tongking and Laos, where they could be supplied only by air. Thus the air force would also be tied down in a purely defensive operation. Giap achieved both his aims, even if not simultaneously. The French were thrown out of northwestern Tongking. By the end of 1953, a military situation had developed whereby the French efforts to win the battle for Laos were leading up to a French defeat in the Indochina War.

In the night of October 17, 1952, the Vietminh attacked Nghia Lo, a French stronghold between the Red and Black Rivers, some 25 miles west of Yen Bay. Just a year earlier, Giap had failed to expel the French from Nghia Lo; now he captured it in one night, taking many prisoners and forcing the French to evacuate numerous smaller posts west of the Red River. The French garrisons fled toward the Black River, closely pursued by the Vietminh, who wiped out most of the paratroops dropped by the French to cover their retreat.

The French hastily reinforced their garrisons at Na Sam and Son La west of the Black River, in the mistaken belief that they could block further Vietminh penetration north and west. In addition, Salan decided to use his entire mobile strength in an attack on the Viet Bac, expecting Giap to withdraw his divisions from the Black River Valley to defend his main Tongking base. Salan's offensive—Operation Lorraine—began on October 29. The French started out from Trung Ha and Viet Tri, two points at the northern confines of the de Lattre Line. They did not reach Phu Tho, 15 miles north, until November 5; on November 9, they dropped paratroops on Phu Doan, 20 miles farther north; an armored column arrived there that same day. The French plan was to move from Phu Doan up the Clear River toward the Viet Bac. By pushing up the Clay River more to the west, they hoped to intercept the divisions that Salan confidently expected Giap to rush to the defense of the Viet Bac.

Operation Lorraine, into which Salan threw 30,000 troops and his best heavy equipment, was an even greater disaster than Valluy's 1947 fall offensive. The French did not penetrate the Viet Bac, and Giap did not withdraw his three divisions from the Black River Valley. He correctly assumed that Operation Lorraine would collapse of its own weight. On November 14, sixteen days after it had begun, the operation was halted. It took the French a full week to retreat behind the de Lattre Line. In fact, the withdrawal proved more difficult and costly than the advance. An ambush on November 17 in the Chan Muong Valley underlined the dangers to which the French would have exposed themselves if Salan had tried to hold on to Phu Doan.[27] Although Giap had refused to give battle and had engaged no major units, the French suffered 1,200 casualties. They had also lost their positions at the southern end of their defense line along the Black River Valley. As soon as the French had wound up Operation Lorraine, Giap took these positions by moving south with one of the divisions he had kept in the Thai country. The lesson of these events was clear: the time for successful offensive operations by the French was not yet.

Elated and overconfident, Giap now tried to throw the French out of their remaining strong points in the Black River Valley. Apparently uninformed about the size of the reinforcements the French had brought in by air, Giap attacked Na Sam on November 23. The attack was repulsed, but only after repeated attempts on November 30 and December 1 was Giap persuaded that Na Sam would become merely another name on the list of his major defeats if he persevered. It was small consolation for him that his 312th Division, moving farther north toward Laos, had on November 30 taken a rather unimportant and poorly garrisoned town by the name of Dien Bien Phu. Giap now decided to move southwest from the Black River toward Laos. He had no trouble overrunning the weak border posts and entering the Houa Pham Province of northeastern Laos. But the difficulties of supplying his fast-moving troops forced him to give up his plan of taking the provincial capital Sam Neua. He withdrew into Thai country, and between December, 1952, and March, 1953, engaged only in minor skirmishes. Giap used this period to reorganize his supply service. This was done largely with outside manpower, since the Thai population of northwestern Tongking remained uncooperative. Giap considered it unwise to enlist their services by force. The Vietminh built up a new supply center for the divisions in the Thai country at Moc Chau late in 1952, and also took the important political step of setting up an autonomous government for the Thai regions.

On April 9, 1953, Giap resumed his war of movement from the Thai country into Laos. He marched directly west into Laos, containing the French at Na Sam with one regiment of his 308th Division. From the north, the 312th Division stationed at Dien Bien Phu descended along the Nam Ou River Valley toward Luang Prabang, while Giap's third division, the 316th, aimed at the same objective on a route farther south that led from its base at Moc Chau to Luang Prabang via Sam Neua. Although the French flew reinforcements to their positions, they had to abandon Sam Neua on April 13, and sustained heavy losses in their retreat.

This first Vietminh invasion of Laos did not lead to any major battles, but it nevertheless had serious implications, for it proved that the French were unable to prevent northern Laos from being overrun by the Vietminh. A strong garrison at Muong Khoua under French command, surrounded and totally isolated, had to be supplied by air. By April 30, Luang Prabang had been invested by the 313th Division. The 308th Division continued to move south, apparently aiming at Vientiane, the administrative capital of Laos. In order to block the direct road to Vientiane, the French gave up a position at Xieng Khouang in favor of one farther west in the Plaine des Jarres, which they strengthened by flying in five additional battalions from the delta. Both the 308th and 316th Divisions now turned toward the Plaine des Jarres, and by April 23 the French were surrounded. Now this position also had to be supplied by air. The entire French air transport was thus engaged in maintaining the French outposts in the Thai country and northern Laos, positions which could do nothing to prevent the Vietminh from roaming freely over these regions. The Vietminh recruited guides, established cooperation with small "Free Laotion" (Pathet Lao) guerrillas under the pro-Communist Prince Souphanouvong, and harvested the valuable opium crop before unexpectedly retiring to northern Tongking on May 7. Only small forces remained behind to contain the French and furnish the Pathet Lao with military and political advice. Giap had once more achieved his aim, which was to absorb all the reserves of the French and to nullify their efforts to build up offensive strength. The action had also served to train the Vietminh in moving and supplying large armies over great distances. But Giap had achieved something else, something he himself did not as yet realize: He had frightened the French into believing that the defense of Laos justified an exceptional military effort. It was this belief that led to the fatal French decision to retake Dien Bien Phu and build it up into a fortress capable of blocking any new Vietminh attempt to invade Laos.

The man later blamed for this decision was General Henri Navarre, who on May 8, 1953, was appointed to succeed General Salan. Navarre was considered a brilliant strategist, but knew nothing about Indochina. He assumed his post on May 20. After studying the military situation, he updated some of de Lattre and Salan's plans and submitted them to Paris, where they won the unenthusiastic approval of his military and political superiors. The "Navarre Plan" aimed at a slow build-up of military strength sufficient for large-scale action against the Vietminh, but it did not advocate a merely defensive attitude while this goal was being pursued. On the contrary, Navarre favored vigorous and continuous offensive action, even if the means at his disposal limited the scope of his operations.

Navarre also submitted his ideas to Washington, where he

sought increased military aid. The military were highly critical of the French performance in Indochina, but the political leadership, particularly Secretary of State Dulles, welcomed and believed in the Navarre Plan. The lack of enthusiasm that greeted the plan in France was largely due to Navarre's request for reinforcements before December 1, 1953. In describing French official reaction to the plan, Premier Joseph Laniel wrote that Navarre was informed of the government's intention to engage in negotiations on a cease-fire as soon as the conclusion of the armistice in Korea would render conditions favorable to such an attempt.[28]

Navarre began his operations on July 17 with an attack by three paratroop battalions on Langson. Operation Hirondelle, as this attack was called, might be considered a success, since the para-troops destroyed large Vietminh stockpiles and returned safely to the delta. Operation Camargue, however, which started on July 28, was a failure. It aimed at clearing Highway 1, between Hue and Quang Tri, of the Vietminh regional units that had turned this important road link into a "street without joy" for the French. A large armored force succeeded in surrounding the guerrilla-infested area but failed to capture any of the Vietminh fighters. The action was called off on August 4. Superior force and heavy arms alone apparently were unable to prevent the Vietminh from escaping from even the best-laid traps. The French press called the operation a total success.

Navarre's next important operation, which the French also listed as a success, was the evacuation on August 8, 1953, of Camp Na Sam. This meant that the lower center of the Thai country was no longer considered defensible. The French had to destroy much of their equipment, but they did manage to save their troops. After the evacuation of Na Sam, the only French position in northwestern Tongking was the distant camp at Lai Chau. It was easy to foresee that sooner or later this position too would have to be given up. This was done two weeks after the French had retaken Dien Bien Phu in Operation Castor on November 20, 1953. The Vietminh promptly moved into Lai Chau. They wasted no time before starting a strategic project vital for the action they planned in case the French should attempt to turn the defense of Laos into a major clash. This project was the construction of a road from supply depots at the Chinese border via Lai Chau to

Tuam Giao, a new Vietminh major supply center a bit northeast of Dien Bien Phu.

The fate of all other operations staged by the French during 1953 underlined the inadequacy of their military means as much as their inability to deal with the tactics of the Vietminh. Punitive action against villages suspected of hiding guerrillas had always been conducted in a manner that made it impossible to protect people not engaged in the fighting. Any man under fifty risked being looked on as a Vietminh fighter, and being shot or captured and "interrogated" by the French. Many decided that the best way to escape this fate was to join the guerrillas before being forcibly recruited by them. Moreover, the Vietminh made sure that no one who refused to work with them survived in a contested village. They would send a few snipers into a village with orders to kill a few of the advancing French. When that happened, the French usually slaughtered all able-bodied men they found when they entered the village. The snipers, of course, disappeared. Even when they were not attacked, the French arrested the entire male population between the ages of fourteen and sixty as prisoners of war. That is why, toward the end of the war, most Tongking villages were populated only by old men, women, and children. Like all his predecessors, Navarre had failed to come up with ideas for a strategy less destructive of the people, less disastrous to the reputation of France, and less effective in strengthening the ranks of the Vietminh.

After the signing of the Korean armistice, on July 7, 1953, Chinese aid to the Vietminh—trucks, heavy artillery, and anti-aircraft guns—became massive. As soon as Giap realized that the French had decided to defend Laos and to this end would give battle to the Vietminh at Dien Bien Phu, he began to direct this equipment toward Tuam Giao and other nearby supply centers. In trucks and on the shoulders of a vast army of porters, these supplies were carried over distances of hundreds of miles toward the hills surrounding Dien Bien Phu, in preparation for the long siege that led to the most famous battle of the Indochina War.

XV

The End of French Indochina

1

AFTER SEVEN YEARS of fruitless military and political effort, the French people had good reason to question the course chosen by their leaders in Indochina. The desire to put an end to the Indochina War, so costly in money and lives, grew stronger with each passing year.

The cost of the war not only put a heavy burden on the French people but was also largely responsible for France's lagging economic recovery after World War II. Even in 1953, when the United States defrayed close to half the cost of the war (270 billion francs), the expenses shouldered by the French remained nearly as high as those of the preceding year. The widespread belief that the war was being paid for by the United States, even if true, in no way invalidates the belief of a growing number of French legislators that after 1952 France could no longer afford

354

to carry the crushing burden of the war. People whose patriotism was beyond question began to use the Communist epithet for the Indochina War: *la sale guerre* (the dirty war).

Opposition to the war was most vigorously articulated by the intellectuals. To what extent this opposition might have been influenced by Communist propaganda soon became secondary. What mattered was that more and more people began to believe that the Communists were right in their opposition to the war, since to continue it was nothing but an attempt to "preserve what was already lost."[1]

France's political leaders, themselves mostly intellectuals, listened to the many voices of writers, students, professors, and artists who were demanding an end to a war that saw so many "profitable deals on the one side and so much useless heroism on the other."[2] They were aware that the intellectuals wielded little political influence, but they also recognized their protests as an expression, possibly premature and overstated, of a growing popular mood. Since the Socialist Party no longer supported the policies of Marius Moutet, the working class now solidly backed the demand for a negotiated peace, a demand that was also being raised with growing force by some leaders of the Radicals and MRP.

A study of the parliamentary debates on Indochina from 1947 on shows how the refusal to talk to Ho Chi Minh, based on the expectation of a quick military solution, was slowly being undermined, until on March 9, 1954, the Assembly agreed to negotiations with Hanoi at Geneva. Resistance to negotiations with Ho Chi Minh broke down only after it had become evident that Navarre's plans and operations, far from improving the French military position, had only helped to worsen it.

On December 20, 1953, two Vietminh regiments moved from the neighborhood of Vinh westward along mountain paths across Annam into Laos, where, on December 25, they reached and occupied the town of Thakhet on the Mekong River. This meant that communications between North and South were cut both in Annam and Laos. On January 20, 1954, Navarre began his much-advertised and later much-criticized Operation Atlante. Its object was to drive the Vietminh from the coastal areas of southern Annam, where they had been roaming about rather freely ever since the beginning of the war. In this operation the French for the first time relied heavily on units of the Vietnamese National Army. A large Franco-Vietnamese force moving northward from Nha Trang along the coast initially met little resistance, but was slowed down as soon as the Vietminh went into action. Giap used only local Vietminh troops in Operation Atlante. The French reached the coastal town of Qui Nhon, less than 100 miles to the north of Nha Trang, only after more than six weeks of rather pointless efforts. The territory between Nha Trang and Qui Nhon was still in Vietminh hands when Operation Atlante was called off at the beginning of March. The troops engaged in it might indeed have been used to better purpose in the mountain plateau of Annam, where the Vietminh, in spite of their preoccupation with the siege of Dien Bien Phu, were strong enough to carry out major offensive actions against all French positions north of Ban Me Thuot. Kontum had to be evacuated on February 7, and soon afterward the Vietminh completely invested Pleiku, turning it into yet another French outpost that had to be supplied by air. The struggle for control of the highlands of southern Annam, although overshadowed by the battle of Dien Bien Phu, was one of the most gruesome episodes of the entire Indochina War. Some of the less fortunate French units were engaged in it beyond the signing of the armistice on July 21; Mobile Group 100, one of the bravest and most seasoned French fighting groups, was completely wiped out in a series of harrowing battles.[3]

Even before Navarre started his Operation Atlante, the Vietminh had completed the encirclement of Dien Bien Phu, a large village in the center of a prosperous opium-growing district set in a flat, heartshaped, paddy-field basin, measuring about 12 miles north to south, and about 8 miles east to west, and fringed by low but rather steep, heavily wooded hills. Dien Bien Phu had little strategic significance in itself, but it was located only 10 miles from the Laotian border and at the junction of three routes: the northern route to China, the northeastern route to Tuam Giao, and the southern route to Laos.

The French knew that Giap had assembled the equivalent of four full divisions around Dien Bien Phu, including the 351st, which the Chinese had supplied with 105-mm. guns. These, and sixteen Chinese 37-mm. anti-aircraft guns, were placed singly in caves dug into the hills east and north of the French position, well concealed by dense foliage. In fact, the entire Vietminh force of 40,000 men was invisible, not only to the besieged garrison but also to the French reconnaissance aircraft.

Before the great battle started early in March, the French had concentrated twelve well-armed battalions at Dien Bien Phu. Six fighter bombers stood on the airstrip; ten light tanks had been flown in and assembled on the spot for counterattacks the French planned to launch after beating back the first Vietminh assaults. In the course of the battle, six more paratroop battalions were flown in from the delta. The French fighting force was less than half the size of the besieging army, but both officers and men considered their equipment, artillery, and air support sufficient to repel any Vietminh attempt to storm their strongly fortified positions. The enemy, they believed, would have to come out of the hills into the open, where the superior firing power of the garrison would prevent him from reaching even the outer defenses. French overoptimism was shared by official American spokesmen up to the fall of Dien Bien Phu.

What French intelligence reports failed to tell was that the artillery assembled by the Vietminh in the hills was in fact superior to their own, and what the French failed to foresee was that the Vietminh gun emplacements were too well camouflaged to be bombed out of existence; that these Vietminh guns would put the airstrip out of operation; that morning fogs and afternoon rains would limit the use of aircraft; and above all they did not foresee that the Vietminh porters would be able to bring in enough ammunition to sustain an almost continuous artillery barrage and massive infantry attacks. The French had assumed that the Vietminh would run out of supplies after at most four days of heavy action.

These mistaken assumptions explain the optimism with which the French looked forward to a battle for Dien Bien Phu and their hope that Giap would launch his attack soon. They were disappointed, and also rather perplexed, as weeks went by during which there were only minor clashes when their patrols met up with Vietminh forces. They learned that the ring the enemy had thrown around them was both narrower and tighter than they had assumed. The French had expected the attack as early as January 25, but Giap apparently was not yet ready and decided to use the

interval to invade Laos once more, forcing the French to withdraw still more of their already depleted reserves from the delta.
On their new descent toward Luang Prabang, the Vietminh overwhelmed the French position at Muong Khoua. On February 7,
units of the 316th Division sighted Luang Prabang, for whose defense, as Giap had expected, Navarre flew in five battalions. However, on February 23, the Vietminh forces suddenly turned back
and joined Giap's army around Dien Bien Phu. Since the strong
French garrison established there to prevent another invasion of
Laos had proved no obstacle to Giap's renewed tactical threat
against Luang Prabang, some French leaders began to question
the wisdom of Navarre's decision to engage his best forces in the
defense of an isolated outpost of doubtful strategic importance.

The battle of Dien Bien Phu was begun by the Vietminh on the
night of March 13, 1954. Its first phase lasted five days, by which
time the fate of the French garrison was sealed.

Giap's first success at Dien Bien Phu was largely the result of
unexpectedly strong artillery fire followed by waves of suicidal infantry attacks. The French estimated that these victories cost the
Vietminh 2,500 dead. But when, on March 28, the Vietminh succeeded in subjecting the airstrip to constant, well-aimed shelling,
the French knew that the task of holding Dien Bien Phu had
become hopeless.

It was at this point that two developments in the diplomatic
area opened up two conflicting prospects for the French. One was
the possibility of a cease-fire before complete military collapse
made Hanoi the master of Vietnam. Everyone in France willing to
negotiate and compromise with the Vietminh looked toward the
conference that was to meet at Geneva on April 26, and which
had been agreed to by the United States, the Soviet Union,
France, and Great Britain. Officially summoned to find a solution
to the East-West conflict over Korea, it had in fact been called
primarily to find a compromise to end the Indochina War.

But there were those in France who still failed to realize that
Indochina was lost, and they desparately searched for new military
means to save a situation obviously beyond salvage. Since the
means that France possessed or was willing to supply were either
insufficient or not readily available, these men asked the United

States to intervene militarily to save the French garrison at Dien Bien Phu and prevent the Vietminh from pushing France out of Indochina.

2

At the outbreak of the Indochina War, France was too important an ally in Europe to be officially rebuffed by Washington for her Indochinese policy, and American fear that a compromise with Hanoi might bring about a Communist Vietnam was even then great. Washington felt it could not urge France to seek such a solution. But when developments killed all hope for an early peace, Washington was gradually induced to drop its officially "neutral" stance and take an active part in the struggle for Indochina.

Washington's new active role in Indochinese affairs was not unanimously applauded, but nobody could foresee where the first modest steps would ultimately lead. The men who formulated U.S. policy over the next few years were convinced that they were being faithful to American ideals of political pragmatism. Not even the fiercest enemies of French colonialism denied that the rise of a new Communist state in Asia would upset the existing balance of power in the world and had to be prevented. The practical question was how this could be done without actually helping French colonialism, which some at least knew to be one of the reasons for Communist strength in Vietnam.

The first attempt, still unofficial, to outline a U.S. policy on the Franco-Vietnamese conflict was that of former Ambassador William Bullitt in an article in *Life* magazine of December 29, 1947, entitled "The Saddest War." Bullitt recognized that "all decent Annamites want independence," that "not one in a hundred is a Communist," and that "Ho Chi Minh, the Communist leader of the Annamite fight for independence, is followed by millions of Annamites who disagree with his political views because he is the symbol of resistance to France."

Bullitt, though apparently ignorant of recent Indochinese history, could easily have drawn some obvious conclusions, such as that the Vietnamese followed Ho Chi Minh because the French denied them independence and that they would cease to do so if a non-Communist leadership were to fight for their country's independence with equal determination. But Bullitt had a more idyllic view of the conflict. "The nub of the problem in Vietnam," he wrote, "is the establishment of cooperation between the French and the Annamite nationalists for the elimination of the Communists." Bullitt's proposal for ending the conflict was indeed simple: a French promise of eventual independence to Vietnam. And his assumption that France would keep such a promise was even simpler.

What makes these naïve pronouncements memorable is that Bullitt's misconceptions and false hopes were to become the basis of official U.S. policy up to the fatal battle of Dien Bien Phu. Not only did the United States subscribe to the view that since Communism had to be defeated there must be no negotiations with Ho Chi Minh, but it also accepted the French contention that this required a military victory over the Vietminh, and that if France lacked the means to achieve this victory she had a right to ask the "free world" for aid. This meant that military aid would soon be extended for the fight against Vietnamese Communism, as the entire anti-French resistance movement came to be called, and that this aid was given not to an independent anti-Communist government, which did not exist, but to the French. It also meant that Washington embraced the Bao Dai solution and accepted "independence within the French Union" as the answer to the problem of Vietnamese nationalism. However, overt U.S. support was still slow in coming. It became official policy only after the victory of Communism in China.

Now the Indochina War ceased to be regarded as a colonial war. It had become a war between Communism and the "free world," and the independence of the Associated States was said to be approaching realization. This at least is what Secretary Dulles stated in July, 1953, six months after General Eisenhower became President. Dulles went even beyond the claims of French propaganda by comparing the French Union with the British Commonwealth, asserting that it "offers a possibility of free association of wholly independent and sovereign nations."[4]

An informed and articulate minority of Americans, including

legislators, political analysts, and military leaders, were opposed to aiding France as long as the Associated States were denied full independence, but no serious pressure to bring about a change in French policy was ever applied. The failure to do so had a deep and consequential reason, one that could not be publicly admitted, for it had not yet become a fully conscious motive of U.S. foreign policy. The great question facing Washington was whether France would continue the war if, as seemed likely, she lost control over Vietnam, Cambodia, and Laos, even if American aid were to enable the Expeditionary Corps to defeat the Vietminh. The answer, unacceptable to the United States, was that France would not. The French, no matter what they publicly stated, would continue the war only so long as there was hope that the French "presence" in Indochina could be maintained. But Washington's interest in Indochina was to contain Communism, not to preserve a modified form of French rule. However, for the sake of staving off another Communist victory in Asia, Washington decided that continued French domination of Indochina was the lesser of two evils. Thus the Vietnamese, though French-ruled, were promoted to the status of a "free people" resisting "subversion by armed minorities or by outside pressure."[5] Indeed, all the clichés that ten years later would be used to justify U.S. policy in Vietnam, including the famous domino theory, were already coined when Washington decided to extend political and military support to the French in their war. Ignoring the fact that Communist strength in Vietnam was a unique and isolated phenomenon, this theory assumed that a refusal to defend French Indochina would necessarily lead to the triumph of Communist aggression throughout Southeast Asia. The wish to contain Communism was infinitely stronger than the desire to see colonialism end, and as early as February, 1950, it produced the most dubious and yet most enduring of all propaganda claims—namely that the war was "fostered from the outside."

This American attitude explains why U.S. participation in the struggle for Indochina generated not a single new idea for a political solution, why it in no way modified the course pursued by the French, and why it contributed nothing to a better understanding of the political conditions for reducing Communist strength. On the contrary, it soon became evident that U.S. intervention multiplied the obstacles to a political settlement of the war. When, after eight years of futile effort, the French were ready to seek peace, if necessary through negotiations and compromise with Ho Chi Minh, the United States was the only country of all concerned that sought to prevent a conference toward this end, and at the conference, which came about against U.S. wishes, Washington refused to play an active role.

3

Overcoming the obstacles to a compromise solution was a task for which contemporary diplomacy, debilitated by the constraints of the Cold War, was not too well equipped. It almost failed in taking the first hurdle to a negotiated settlement—convening a conference to discuss the conflict. The idea of "compromising with Communism" was abhorrent to the Republican Administration. Bao Dai as well as the stanchly anti-French nationalists rightly feared that in a deal with Ho Chi Minh they would be sold down the river; and there were indications that the Hanoi regime was also unhappy about the prospect of a negotiated peace. The Vietminh leaders, who for years had pleaded for such a settlement, now were looking toward total victory.

On November 29, 1953, the Swedish newspaper *Expressen* published a statement by Ho Chi Minh expressing his willingness to study proposals for a cease-fire. Why, since Ho knew that the French were tired of the war and indirectly were admitting the possibility of a Vietminh victory, did he indicate a readiness to consider a cease-fire?

Two days before Ho's statement was made public, the Kremlin had accepted an old Western proposal for a conference of the Big Four, which opened in Berlin on January 25, 1954. Ostensibly called to seek a solution to the East-West conflict over Germany, shrewd British and Soviet diplomacy steered the meeting into exploring the chances for a settlement of the Indochina War. The Kremlin had become convinced that France was at last ready for peace talks and probably also willing to pay the price Russia asked for persuading the Vietminh to accept less than total victory: staying out of the European Defense Community and accepting Communist China at the conference table.

Did Ho, then, in agreeing to talks for a cease-fire just when Giap was victorious on all fronts, merely lend himself to a diplomatic maneuver by Moscow and Peking? There can be no doubt that the Vietminh was not happy over the decision to call a conference that might also discuss terms for settling the Indochina conflict. Vietminh broadcasts "tended at first to discount the prevalent rumors of impending negotiations, but when these rumors proved to be well-founded, incredulity gave place to anger and dismay."[6] But whether the Vietminh leaders changed their minds under Sino-Soviet pressure or whether they recognized that no compromise could in the end deprive them of a political victory they had won long ago, they knew that a decisive defeat of the Expeditionary Corps before the start of negotiations would greatly enhance their position at the bargaining table. Dien Bien Phu offered them an opportunity for it. There is in fact reason to believe that Giap's conduct of the battle of Dien Bien Phu was largely influenced by political and diplomatic considerations. He intended to produce conclusive evidence that the military position of the French was collapsing on the very day the talks on Indochina were scheduled to open.

The displeasure of Hanoi over the proposal to settle the war at an international conference may have been only tactical, but the strong reaction in Saigon was not. There the negative response hardened into a decision never to accept a compromise that would recognize Hanoi's authority over any part of Vietnam. The anti-French, anti-Vietminh nationalists feared being sold out by France, and this fear soon gripped the confirmed collaborators as well. They, and Bao Dai himself, realized that a compromise solution might well leave them at the mercy of the Vietminh. Some, concerned for their political future or even their very lives, now claimed that they had always sympathized with and secretly supported the "resistance." All of them loudly demanded "total independence." Above all, they clamored for a new government, one genuinely nationalist and not subject to any French control whatsoever. The formation of such a government was most urgently requested by Ngo Dinh Nhu's Movement for National Unity and Peace. But the demand never generated popular en-

364 • *Vietnam at War*

thusiasm and the movement's support dwindled. Yet matching the nationalism of the Vietminh was the only weapon left to the spokesmen of anti-Vietminh nationalism, and even Bao Dai and his counselors decided that the demand for total independence offered the only chance for the survival of their state. Bao Dai went to Paris on April 10, but not even he was able to persuade the French that they had to save anti-Vietminh nationalism by granting freely to him what their military weakness would soon compel them to grant to Ho Chi Minh: true independence. The French, already thinking of partition as the basis of a compromise with the Vietminh, of course knew that one half of Vietnam could not be salvaged. But they still nourished the hope of maintaining a measure of control over the other part.

4

Although the idea of partition was violently rejected by all spokesmen for Vietnamese nationalism, it nevertheless began to be recognized as a possible condition for a peace. Rejected on principle by all, partition was nevertheless the only remaining hope for political survival of all anti-Vietminh nationalists untainted by collaboration with the French and uncorrupted by the Bao Dai regime. Their despair over their country's moral and political bankruptcy and its probable fate after a Franco-Vietnamese deal was cushioned by the hopes they pinned on the growing involvement of the United States in Franco-Indochinese affairs. There was no shortage of pronouncements from Washington to nourish such hopes. The "anticolonial" tenor of these statements was understood to mean that if the United States were to interfere militarily to thwart a Communist victory, it would do so only on condition that all traces of French colonial rule were wiped out.

At the Berlin conference, Secretary Dulles forcefully voiced U.S. opposition to a settlement involving concessions to "Communism" and opposed any conference attended by Communist China. Eden and Molotov finally succeeded in getting Washington to participate in the forthcoming Geneva meeting. But the differences between the United States and its main allies, Great Britain and France, exploded into an open conflict shortly before the conference. They were not resolved during the conference and they remained latent until the "American" Indochina War reactivated them ten years later.

The first great crisis over conflicting allied aims in Indochina, which the boorish diplomacy of Dulles did nothing to mitigate, reached its climax in the spring of 1954. On March 20, about a week before the first blows against the garrison at Dien Bien Phu, General Paul Ely arrived in Washington to make clear the full plight of the French Expeditionary Corps, to press for immediate additional supplies, above all bombers, and auxiliary American personnel to support the French air arm. But Ely was also instructed by his government to leave no doubt about French reluctance to continue the war. The purpose of the requested military help was to keep the Expeditionary Corps in the fight until the Geneva conference had produced an acceptable settlement.

Official reaction to Ely's rather modest demands and to his surprising pessimism was understandably mixed. Those opposed to any steps that might involve the United States in another Korean-type war in Asia—i.e., the vast majority of the Congress and even of the Joint Chiefs of Staff—were relieved. So was President Eisenhower, who gave Ely assurances of speedy compliance with his requests for aid. But those who had expected American aid to help the French defeat the Vietminh were shocked by France's willingness to compromise. Not only the so-called China Lobby and the Republican majority leader, Senator Knowland, denounced the idea of a compromise solution as another betrayal of the cause of freedom. Vice-President Nixon, Secretary Dulles, and the Chairman of the Joint Chiefs of Staff, Admiral Radford, also took the position that such a compromise must be avoided, if necessary through direct U.S. military intervention.

The maneuverings of these three powerful men, which, in the absence of Presidential leadership, remained uncoordinated throughout, are among the saddest chapters in U.S. diplomacy. The first one to act, entirely on his own, to bring about direct American military intervention, was Admiral Radford. He induced Ely to postpone his departure for Paris, scheduled for

March 25, for twenty-four hours during which he persuaded the receptive French general that a massive U.S. airstrike could still save the French garrison at Dien Bien Phu. Radford assured Ely that Eisenhower would approve such a step. The plan, which became known as Operation Vautour (Vulture), envisaged the use of planes based in the Philippines and on aircraft carriers in the Far East, which were later ordered to move into the Gulf of Tongking.

Ely submitted Radford's offer to the French Government on March 27. On April 2, the government was informed of Navarre's belief that such an airstrike could destroy the Vietminh artillery positions around Dien Bien Phu and probably save the garrison, which otherwise would certainly be lost. The French Government thereupon decided on April 4, not without some misgivings, officially to request the intervention proposed by Admiral Radford.

If there is one specific day when the policy that would govern U.S.–Vietnamese relations for more than a decade was decided, it was April 5, 1954, the day Ambassador Dillon transmitted Washington's answer to the French request. It was a downright refusal.

The French Government, surprised and shocked, learned only much later what had happened. It seems that immediately after Ely's departure, the initiative for shaping policy on Indochina had passed from Admiral Radford to Secretary Dulles, and Dulles had an entirely different concept of the U.S. role at this historical juncture. But Dulles' concept could be pursued only with full Congressional support. Dulles did not want a one-strike American intervention to save the French at Dien Bien Phu. He wanted Indochina—all of it—saved from Communism. Dulles was not interested in having the United States intervene merely to improve the French position at Geneva. He was opposed to any compromise. He wanted the war to continue until Communism was defeated, and he did not want this war to be conducted under the tainted banner of French colonialism. The war had to be internationalized and the French replaced by a Western coalition under U.S. leadership.

With Eisenhower's consent, Dulles killed the Radford plan, which neither Congress nor the Joint Chiefs of Staff seemed inclined to endorse. Dulles' thesis that the United States should act only as the leader of a "democratic" and "anticolonial" front was accepted by a meeting of Administration spokesmen and Congressional leaders.

There is, however, another side to the story of Dulles' readiness to drop the plan for immediate American intervention to save the garrison at Dien Bien Phu. He simply did not believe that the French military situation was as desperate as described by Ely. He thought that even if Dien Bien Phu fell, the French would still be able to continue the war, particularly if prospects for Western "united action" existed. As late as March 22, more than a week after the first French debacle at Dien Bien Phu, Dulles said that the Navarre Plan need not be abandoned, for according to his own military judgment it still promised victory within a year.

The one notion that dominated Dulles' thinking was that no time must be lost in preparing "united action," and that at least the threat of such action had to become real before the start of the Geneva conference. Preventing the conference had been his aim at Berlin; torpedoing it was his ill-concealed intention now. But French and British determination to steer clear of anything that might wreck the conference was precisely why Dulles' project failed. On April 6, the French cabinet, fearful that a pact threatening military intervention in Indochina would endanger chances for a compromise settlement, rejected the Dulles proposal, as did the British cabinet one day later.

During the next two weeks there developed what can only be described as the greatest crisis to date in U.S. relations with Great Britain and France. Dulles went to London on April 11, only to learn that both Churchill and Eden (supported by the Labour Party) were adamant in their refusal to agree to any allied united action before the chances of a settlement at Geneva had been explored. In a joint statement on April 13, Eden agreed to an "examination of the possibilities" for such action. Dulles interpreted this as an acceptance of the substance of his plan and invited the ambassadors of nine countries to a conference in Washington April 20. British reaction, quick and sharp, taught Dulles that there had been a "misunderstanding." The British

Government ordered its ambassador to stay away from the meeting.

Dulles' subsequent behavior supports the view that his anger over the rejection by Paris and London was one of the main reasons that American military intervention during the battle of Dien Bien Phu never materialized. Fearing that without massive air support Dien Bien Phu would soon fall, the French Government on April 23 and 24 asked Dulles to reconsider his government's refusal of April 7 and authorize Operation Vautour. Dulles, after consultations with his military advisers, decided that Dien Bien Phu could no longer be saved. Yet although he believed that airstrikes could not save the garrison, he was nevertheless willing to recommend them provided the French Government agreed to a statement on united action and obtained London's consent.

The desperate French capitulated. But their efforts to persuade London were of no avail. Eden, supported by Churchill, held fast to the position that the chances for an accord at Geneva and for a general easing of tension in Asia must not be thrown away. This meant that Dulles' project was dead.

During the tense weeks between Ely's visit to Washington and the opening of the Geneva conference on April 26, Vice-President Nixon had come out openly with proposals that neither Radford nor Dulles were willing to embrace. In a brazen display of cynicism designed to mislead an uninformed public, Nixon in a speech in December, 1953, had said that were it not for the existence of Communist China there would be no Indochina War. He was on safe ground, for how many people in the United States knew that France had been fighting the Vietminh for four years before China became Communist? It was Nixon's view that if Communism was to be stopped in Asia, the United States had to act in Indochina, not only with airstrikes, but "by putting our boys in"; and not only in support of French or allied action, but, if necessary, alone—"regardless of allied support."[7] Nixon's notion that "the United States would have to replace [the French] if necessary, to prevent a Communist conquest of Southeast Asia"[8] anticipated the future, but in April, 1954, the time was not yet ripe.

President Eisenhower during most of this critical period both supported and opposed military intervention to save Dien Bien Phu, for whose fate he showed a deep concern. What he said seemed to depend chiefly on whom he had last spoken to. He had both endorsed and helped kill the Radford-Ely plan. He pointed out the danger of intervention[9] but would no doubt have approved of it if Dulles had managed to enlist British support. At a press conference on April 29, he denied that there had ever been an American proposal to intervene with massive air attacks, but in his book he states that he was "disappointed" when "our efforts for a satisfactory method of allied intervention failed."[10]

While the statesmen were bickering, the soldiers in and around Dien Bien Phu fought and died. Vietminh artillery had put the airstrip out of commission; the wounded could no longer be evacuated; supplies had to be parachuted into the camp. Digging a complex network of trenches within yards of the French defenses, the enemy encircled the garrison and the French were unable to break through. Rain turned the camp into an ocean of mud and the trenches into coffins of mire for thousands of Vietminh soldiers. Dien Bien Phu was hell long before the new general assault in the night of May 1–2 brought the besiegers, at an enormous cost in lives, right to the edge of the main French positions. The final attack was undertaken on the night of May 6, and the garrison was overwhelmed on May 7, the day before Indochina was on the agenda at Geneva.

For the statesmen at Geneva, for the people of France, but above all for the soldiers of the Expeditionary Corps, the fall of Dien Bien Phu signaled the imminent collapse of the French military effort in Indochina.

5

The Geneva conference, attended by delegates from France, Great Britain, the United States, the Soviet Union, the People's Republic of China, Cambodia, Laos, Bao Dai's State of Vietnam, and Ho Chi Minh's Democratic Republic of Vietnam, met from April 26 to July 21, 1954. On May 8, twenty-four hours after the

French High Command received the last somber message from its doomed garrison at Dien Bien Phu, the conference turned to the problem of Indochina.

From the very outset, Great Britain was the only Western power wholeheartedly working for the success of the conference. Eden was the only Western statesman who consistently tried for an accommodation of the widely conflicting views. Because Britain, unlike France, did not have to pay the price of compromise, and because it did not share the American obsession with the danger of Communism in Asia, it possessed the necessary freedom of action to match the tactical flexibility of the Communist delegations. The threat of U.S. military intervention in case the war continued may at one time have strengthened the weak French bargaining position, but at no time did there exist that minimum of diplomatic coordination between Paris and Washington that might have enabled their delegations to use this threat as a weapon. Nor were the French prepared to face the consequences of their crumbling military position and assist Eden in his search for an acceptable solution. Like Dulles, who acted as though the Chinese delegation did not exist, Bidault refused all contact with the head of the Vietminh delegation. He was the only Western spokesman who lacked the good sense to refrain from the sort of historical recriminations and propagandistic accusations in which the Communist delegations indulged. Bidault's conduct betrayed that he was quite cool toward the proposals for a cease-fire that he himself had submitted in the name of his government. The French Assembly could muster a majority of only two votes when, on May 13, it expressed its confidence in the government's handling of the Geneva negotiations. France was evidently getting ready to accept a compromise solution in Indochina by making concessions to the Vietminh. Vietminh prospects at Geneva improved greatly after May 13, when the National Assembly almost overthrew the Laniel government for its apparent lack of zeal in seeking a compromise.

Western disunity and irresolution were even more glaringly displayed by the U.S. spokesmen. During the entire Geneva period, the diplomacy of the Eisenhower Administration was never anything but wildly incoherent. It helped neither Eden's conciliatory stance nor Bidault's belligerence. Washington, inconsistent throughout, failed to strengthen the French position by upholding and making believable the threat of U.S. intervention in case the Communist bloc insisted on the unacceptable demand of Vietminh control of all of Vietnam. On the contrary, Dulles publicly retreated from his interventionist position. This deprived Bidault of the only effective weapon in his attempt to prevent a compromise that was in fact a victory for the Vietminh. Dulles, still interested only in united action, stubbornly continued his efforts for a Western alliance against the Communist threat to Southeast Asia. But a few days later, on May 11, both Dulles and Eisenhower indirectly indicated that Washington had become reconciled to a settlement of the war. Had the American people been truly concerned about the conduct of foreign affairs by Eisenhower and Dulles, they would have been no less upset during these weeks than were Washington's European allies. On April 9, Eisenhower had said that the loss of Indochina would cause Southeast Asia to fall like a set of dominoes,[11] but barely five weeks later both he and his secretary of state stated flatly that the retention of Indochina was not essential for the defense of Southeast Asia. When were they right?

But more was yet to come. Allied disunity reached a really dangerous level when France, under U.S. pressure, agreed on May 17 to discuss a treaty aiming at united action without the participation of Britain. The French had gone along in hopes that such a threat would induce the Communist powers to reduce their demands. But the only ones who worried over it were the British. Eden protested angrily when he learned from Swiss newspapers that Franco-American talks on united action were being conducted. It was then that Churchill decided that only his personal intervention could prevent further deterioration in U.S.-British relations and secure a minimum of American cooperation in the efforts to bring peace to Vietnam.

6

Unlike the Western allies, the Communist powers at Geneva appeared solidly united. They seemed to know what they wanted, coordinated their tactics, and concealed the differences that in fact did exist among them.

The Soviet Union and China did not differ on the purpose of the Geneva conference. The Chinese had persuaded themselves, or been persuaded by their Russian friends, that they had to settle for less than Communist control of all of Indochina. They, like the British, were guided by a desire to end the war and by the knowledge that this required a willingness to compromise. Throughout the negotiations, the Chinese delegation accepted every one of Molotov's compromise proposals. It was Molotov's tough bargaining which kept the way open for a final settlement. In fact, the most constructive proposal after more than five weeks of desultory negotiations came from Chou En-lai, who on June 16 agreed to the withdrawal of all Vietminh troops from Laos and Cambodia and who persuaded the Vietminh to drop their request for participation of shadow governments of the Communist Khmer Issarak and Pathet Lao rebels in the conference.

The settlement Russia and China were willing to accept and ultimately made possible by a step-by-step retreat from their original position indeed did not meet the expectations of the Vietminh delegates. They regarded the cease-fire demanded by the French as just a step toward the withdrawal of the Expeditionary Corps, to be followed by elections within a few months. These elections, which they were certain they would win, would then make them masters of the whole of Vietnam.

It was not entirely unrealistic for the Vietminh to believe in the possibility of such a peace. French military resistance was likely to collapse. The French themselves recognized the hopelessness of their position after the fall of Dien Bien Phu. Most French military experts expected a Vietminh attack on Hanoi in the middle of June. The route between Hanoi and Haiphong could not be kept open after nightfall, and on most days it remained closed in the morning hours as well to permit the removal of the mines planted and the barricades erected by the Vietminh. Everywhere isolated French posts fell to the Vietminh, who knew that the French no longer had the reserves needed to interfere with their concentrated and determined attacks. And although the French had strengthened the Vietnamese National Army, they had been unable to raise its morale. After the fall of Dien Bien

Phu, most Vietnamese units were no longer combat-ready, and the number of its soldiers who chose to join the Vietminh rather than fight them grew with the mounting evidence of an early French collapse.

The demands raised by Foreign Minister Pham Van Dong at the beginning of the conference confirmed the impression that the Vietminh, confident that they would defeat the French, were not at all interested in a peace at the price of concessions. There can be no doubt that when they reluctantly accepted the final compromise, they did so not in deference to the judgment of their allies but because they had no choice. According to *The New York Times* of July 25, 1954, members of the Vietminh delegation openly stated that Russian and Chinese pressure forced them to accept less than what they thought they should have obtained. A last-ditch effort to throw the French out of Indochina could succeed only with Chinese consent, since it required continued and even increased Chinese aid. Whatever the Chinese motives for supporting a compromise solution, the fact that the Vietminh leaders were compelled to accept it proves that they lacked Chinese consent for wrecking the conference and for continuing the war.

7

Another party that was surprised and antagonized by China's willingness to compromise was the United States as represented by the diplomacy of John Foster Dulles. To be sure, this diplomacy was far from consistent. It wanted a settlement without concessions to the Vietminh, and it expected the French to give up control of Indochina yet continue the war.

These contradictions explain both the vacillation and capricious rationalizations of U.S. policy during this crisis. Washington agreed to the Geneva conference yet refused to cooperate in achieving its stated purpose; it accepted China's presence but ignored its delegation; it promised military intervention but backed down when Britain and France refused to conclude an agreement that would have wrecked the conference before it ever opened. Washington even denied that intervention had ever been planned. Yet the threat of intervention was repeated firmly enough for French Foreign Minister Bidault to make it the cornerstone of his strategy at Geneva, only to have it destroyed when Dulles, on June 8, categorically declared that he did not intend to ask Congress to authorize U.S. intervention in Indochina. It had been stated repeatedly that defeat in Indochina would lead to the loss of Southeast Asia, but when the refusal to act had to be justified it was suddenly found that Southeast Asia could be defended even if Indochina were lost. To top it all, Dulles continued to describe the search for a compromise at Geneva as "appeasement" although he had secretly become reconciled to a compromise based on partition.

Washington's endorsement of partition was the result of meetings between Churchill, Eden, Eisenhower, and Dulles from June 24–29. It was contained in a secret seven-point Anglo-American memorandum which offered a surprisingly accurate outline both of the formal agreements reached at Geneva and of the manner in which the United States would later interpret these agreements. The seven points promised (1) to preserve the integrity and independence of Laos and Cambodia by ensuring the withdrawal of the Vietminh forces from these two countries; (2) to preserve the southern half of Vietnam and if possible also an enclave in the Tongking Delta, with the line of demarcation not to run south of Dong Hoi (north of the 17th parallel); (3) to impose neither on Cambodia nor Laos nor on the part of Vietnam that was preserved any restrictions on their ability to maintain stable non-Communist governments; (4) to refuse to accept any stipulation that might lead to the loss of the free zones for the benefit of the Communists; (5) not to rule out the possibility of the ultimate unification of Vietnam by peaceful means; (6) to allow the transfer of all who wished to move from one zone of Vietnam to the other; (7) to establish an effective system of international controls.[13] Thus Dulles found a compromise based on partition acceptable under two conditions: that the part of Vietnam denied to the Vietminh (and Cambodia and Laos) be allowed to arm against internal and external aggression, and that the agreement reached contain no stipulations that would enable the Communists to gain control of the entire country. In other words, the United

States must be free to arm the non-Communist half of Vietnam, and no elections were to be held as long as a Communist electoral victory seemed a certainty. Dulles was determined to deny approval to any agreement that failed to meet these conditions. With this decision, the vacillation that had characterized American diplomacy since the Berlin conference came to an end.

In the meantime, progress toward solving the technical problems involved in a cease-fire had been made in talks between French and Vietminh officers. But a more important development was the fall of the Laniel government on June 12. This removed Bidault, whose tactics had convinced Molotov that the Laniel government was an obstacle to a compromise solution, from Geneva. Pierre Mendès-France, the best-known advocate of direct peace negotiations with the Vietminh, became the new head of government. "I am ready to resign," he said on June 17 in presenting his government to the Assembly, "if by July 20 I have not obtained a cease-fire in Indochina."

Mendès-France tackled his task with energy and skill, a task which in the eyes of many was made doubly difficult by the thirty-day limit he had imposed on himself. Had he not thereby handed the Communists the tools to overthrow him if he refused to accept their conditions? Mendès-France, however, considered this a necessary risk. It would reveal whether the Communists were really willing to accept a compromise solution, for his failure could only result in a government bent on continuing the war. Mendès-France made clear that he would support such a policy by announcing that his last act before resigning would be a request for additional troops to Indochina.

Under Mendès-France, allied strategy at Geneva at last became reasonably coordinated, above all between Paris and London, but to some extent also between France and the United States. And in Geneva he also established direct contact with the heads of the Chinese and Vietminh delegations. In endless days of sparring with Molotov, and only hours before the expiration of his self-imposed deadline, he extracted two important concessions: the 17th parallel instead of the 13th as the provisional boundary between the two Vietnamese zones, and a two-year delay in the projected elections.

8

The only government that reacted with shock, dismay, and violent opposition to the developments at Geneva was Bao Dai's Vietnam. The thought that the French, who had always used them as political pawns in the struggle against the Vietminh, would now sacrifice them in a deal, caused panic and deep resentment among the anti-Vietminh nationalists and a determination never to become a party to this political "betrayal."

But how could the Bao Dai regime, a creature of the French, fight this threat when its very existence depended on the willingness of the French to defend it against the growing power of the Vietminh? Caught in a dilemma from which no belated surge of political wisdom could have found a way out, the reactions of the men around Bao Dai merely confirmed that in the world of politics the prospects of doom rarely improve the capacity for sound judgment. The spokesmen for the Bao Dai regime and Bao Dai himself fully realized the hopelessness of their position, but not one of them possessed the strength of character and the courage needed for the awesome tasks that would have been theirs had they faced up to their political dilemma. Since they knew that it mattered little whether they gave or refused their consent to the compromise that was likely to emerge, they decided to be for once men of principle and oppose even the slightest concessions to the Vietminh, including the one that offered them the only chance, however slight, of political survival: partition. On May 12, Foreign Minister Nguyen Quoc Dinh, the head of Bao Dai's delegation, accordingly submitted a plan for a settlement designed to save a regime which the French could no longer defend. Dinh contended that there existed only one Vietnamese state authorized to speak for the country, that of "His Majesty" Bao Dai; that the country had only one army, that of the State of Vietnam, into which the Vietminh soldiers should be integrated; that elections under U.N. auspices should be held "within the framework and the competence of the State of Vietnam" as soon as that state had established its authority over the entire country; and that after these elections, a representative government under Bao Dai be formed.

Everybody knew that Bao Dai's state, if dropped by the French, would collapse overnight under the weight of Vietminh military and political power. Only the American delegation felt compelled to give open support to Dinh's fantastic proposals.

But did the partition of Vietnam, even if only temporary, necessarily mean the end of anti-Communist nationalism? At least two parties involved in the struggle over Vietnam denied that this was so provided that certain obstacles were removed. One of these parties was the United States. In the optimistic view of Dulles, united Western action to protect Southeast Asia against Communism could also defend whatever portion of Vietnam was denied to the Vietminh. The other group was composed of Vietnamese nationalists who had rejected collaboration with the French, and their increasingly active opposition to Bao Dai could be taken as evidence that between the extremes of collaboration and the Vietminh a "third force" might possibly emerge. These two parties agreed that such a development was possible if a substantial part of Vietnam remained outside Vietminh control, if all traces of colonialism were wiped out, if Vietnam was given a nationalist government untainted by collaboration, and if the United States assumed the burden of making the nationalist regime in a divided Vietnam viable and capable of defending itself against Communist subversion and aggression.

Even before partition had become an avowed objective at Geneva, steps toward at least a partial meeting of the conditions for a survival of a mutilated but non-Communist Vietnam had been taken. On June 3, representatives of France and Bao Dai initialed a treaty which at last recognized Vietnam as a "fully independent and sovereign state." Two weeks later, Bao Dai took a step of the most far-reaching consequence for himself and the future of Vietnam: He accepted the resignation of his cousin Prince Buu Loc. On June 16, he invited the most prominent of the nationalists who had opposed the "Bao Dai experiment," Ngo Dinh Diem, to form a new government. These steps which, if taken eight years earlier, might have checked the growth of Vietminh strength, were now being imposed by circumstances on the French and on Bao Dai.

In the meantime, the Geneva conference had arrived at a point at which a settlement based on partition had become a virtual certainty. The French had to tell their Vietnamese protégés how the political fate of Vietnam was about to be decided. Bao Dai, who was informed early in July, neglected to forward this information to Saigon. Diem was given the bad news by U.S. Ambassador Donald Heath together with a reassuring message from President Eisenhower.

The news could hardly have come as a surprise to any anti-Communist with a realistic view of Vietminh military and political strength, but they reportedly came as a shock to Diem. The role into which Dr. Tran Van Do, Saigon's new foreign minister, had been cast at Geneva was not an enviable one, but the dignified manner in which he discharged his task earned him respect. When the armistice was finally concluded, he knew that all he could do was denounce it in the name of his government. He did, calling it "catastrophic and immoral." His demand that his government's reservations be included in the Final Declaration of the conference was brushed aside by Mendès-France and overruled by Eden as chairman.

The Geneva agreements consisted of two parts. The first was a lengthy document dealing solely with the implementation of the cease-fire and the regrouping of the French and Vietminh forces in their respective zones. The cease-fire agreement was the only document actually signed at Geneva. It provided for Vietnam's provisional division along the 17th parallel, and for the regroupment of the French Union forces and Vietminh forces south and north of this line, respectively. Regroupment was to be completed within 300 days. The agreement also stipulated that any civilian wishing to move from one zone to the other be allowed to do so before May 18, 1955. Both parties pledged to refrain from reprisals against persons or organizations for acts committed during the hostilities and agreed to a ban on the introduction of fresh troops, military personnel, arms, munitions, and military bases. The cease-fire was to be supervised by an international commission composed of representatives of India, Canada, and Poland.

The second document was the so-called Final Declaration. This agreement, in addition to being a formal endorsement of the stipulations for ending hostilities, attempted to spell out the existing political differences, in particular the question of how and when the partition of Vietnam as set forth in the cease-fire agreement should come to an end. The document essentially contained the concessions on which the Communist powers had insisted as conditions for agreeing to a cease-fire, the most important of these being that the military demarcation line was to be provisional and not to be considered a political or territorial boundary.

The section dealing with the projected elections was both a political surprise and a semantic monstrosity. The Vietminh had demanded that elections be held a few months after the cessation of hostilities, but Molotov, to the astonishment of the French, who had not expected this concession, proposed a two-year waiting period. The obscure phrasing of this issue defies logical analysis. It stated that elections shall be held "in order to insure that sufficient progress in the restoration of peace has been made, and that all the necessary conditions obtain for the expression of the national will"—which probably meant, at least to the Communists, that elections would produce a Saigon government ready to express the "national will" by uniting the South and the North. The date for general elections was set for July, 1956, with "consultations to be held on this subject between the competent authorities of the two zones from July 20, 1955, onwards." Since the State of Vietnam was not mentioned in this context, the matter of who these "competent representative authorities" might be remained open. Was it the French, the only non-Communist party to have signed anything at Geneva, or was it the government south of the 17th parallel, which had vigorously opposed the Geneva agreements? This unresolved question was only surpassed by the expectation that the powers that concluded the agreement on elections would consider it binding although it remained unsigned.

American rejection of some of the stipulations of the Geneva agreements cannot, however, be justified by asserting that the United States was not a signatory to these agreements. Except for the cease-fire accords signed by the French and Vietminh High Commands, nobody signed anything at all at Geneva. The other stipulations were accepted by a voice vote by all participants, and this was followed by declarations of various delegations wishing to state reservations and offer their own interpretation of certain points, among them the U.S. delegate, General Walter Bedell Smith. (Secretary Dulles had left Geneva on May 5.) His government, Smith said, was not prepared to join in a declaration by the conference such as had been submitted, but it would refrain from the threat or use of force to disturb the agreements. However, the warning he addressed to the Communists—i.e., that his government "would view any renewal of the aggression in violation of the aforesaid Agreements with grave concern and as seriously threatening international peace and security"—could be interpreted as a qualified endorsement of the agreement. Concerning the elections, Smith repeated a declaration made by Washington on June 29: "In the case of nations now divided against their will, we shall continue to seek to achieve unity through free elections supervised by the United Nations to insure that they are conducted fairly."[14]

The only unambiguous protest came from Foreign Minister Tran Van Do. In a cable to Premier Diem dated July 22, he said: "We fought desperately against partition and for a neutral zone in the Catholic area of North Vietnam. Absolutely impossible to surmount the hostility of our enemies and the perfidy of false friends. We express our deepest sorrow in this total failure of our mission. We respectfully submit our resignation."[15] On July 23, Diem, broadcasting from Saigon, voiced "a most solemn protest" against the "iniquity which hands over to the Communists the entire North of the country and more than four provinces of the Center." All flags were ordered flown at halfmast for three days.

More important, however, for the future relations between South Vietnam and North Vietnam was a statement made by Tran Van Do in the name of his government before the conclusion of the conference. "Vietnam," he declared "reserves to itself the entire freedom of action to safeguard the sacred right of the Vietnamese people to territorial unity, independence, and freedom."[16] This was a formal announcement of nonconcurrence with the Geneva agreements on the part of the Diem government. Although even in the South it was a government in name only, on August 3 it called on the people of the North "to rally to the South in order to continue the struggle for independence and liberty."[17]

Dulles, too, offered a postscript to Geneva at a news conference on July 23. What he said was of infinitely greater significance than Diem's empty threat. Dulles stated that "military developments in Indochina" and the disinclination of the French people "to prolong the war" led to a settlement containing "many features which we do not like." But "the important thing" was "not to mourn the past but to seize the future opportunity to prevent the loss in northern Vietnam from leading to the extension of Communism throughout Southeast Asia and the Southwest Pacific." Dulles implied once more that French colonialism had been an obstacle in the fight against the Vietminh. "One lesson is that resistance to Communism needs popular support, and this in turn means that the people should feel that they are defending their own national institutions." Dulles went so far as to speak of the "good aspects" of the Geneva conference, one of which was "that it advances the truly independent status of Cambodia, Laos, and Southern Vietnam." And he added: "The evolution from colonialism to national independence is thus about to be completed in Indochina, and the free governments of this area should from now on be able to enlist the loyalty of their people to maintain their independence as against Communist colonialism."[18] In fact, there is some evidence that Dulles was not at all unhappy over the French defeat in Indochina. "We have a clear base there now without a taint of colonialism," he is reported to have said, adding: "Dien Bien Phu was a blessing in disguise."[19]

The obstacles to "united action" had at last been removed. "Prompt steps will be taken in this direction," he announced after having secured British and French consent to proceed in the preparation of what, via the so-called Manila Pact, became the Southeast Asia Treaty Organization.

The response in France to the Geneva agreements was one of undisguised relief. The settlement was unquestionably a political triumph for Mendès-France. There was a general feeling that France had fared better than had been hoped. Still, Geneva was a great blow for the French, and no one knew this better than Mendès-France. "I want no one to have any illusions about the contents of the agreements that have just been signed at Geneva," he said with his customary frankness. "Much of what they say is cruel, since they consecrate cruel facts. It could not have been otherwise."[20] The French Chamber overwhelmingly voted to accept the agreements.

In spite of Vietminh dissatisfaction, the Communists had every reason to be content with the agreements reached: a Communist-led national movement of armed resistance had defeated the armies of one of the oldest and greatest Western colonial powers; France, as Ho Chi Minh had predicted, had lost the war; and the West was forced to become reconciled to the existence of yet another Communist state.

9

Whatever the shortcomings of the Geneva agreements, their great historical importance is beyond dispute. They put a stop to the longest and most senseless attempt of this century to defeat an anticolonial movement of national liberation by military means, they ended almost one hundred years of French colonial rule in Indochina, and they produced the two Vietnams.

This division of Vietnam into two states with hostile regimes received a measure of international sanction from the powers that concluded the Geneva agreements. But as to the conflict between the Vietminh and their nationalist opponents, the Geneva conference failed to come up with a workable solution. The promise of national unity was destined to remain unfulfilled, and it therefore could have been foreseen that the peace that Geneva brought would not be a lasting one. It was to be expected that the hostile governments in Hanoi and Saigon would continue to move further apart. Since, under the prevailing conditions, the regime in the South could not have survived a general election, it was predictable that it would oppose the holding of such elections, while the Communists, deprived of this peaceful extension of their rule would again resort to force. When they unleashed their insurrection against the regime of Ngo Dinh Diem, a troubled world was reminded of how dangerously imperfect the settlement reached at Geneva had been. Ten years after Geneva, a new armed conflict reached dimensions and produced international involvements that posed an even greater threat to world peace than that posed by the first Indochina War.

Finally, the Geneva settlement, along with its failure to bring unity and lasting peace, also failed to open the road to political freedom both North and South. In the North, the struggle for economic survival and industrial progress blocked any retreat from the harsh Communist dictatorship into which Ho Chi Minh's regime had turned during the last years of the war. In the South, civil war reinforced the government's innate tendency toward authoritarian rule. The anti-Communist regime also turned into a ruthless dictatorship, without however producing what was supposed to be its *raison d'être*—administrative efficiency and military strength. Ten years after achieving independence, the people of Vietnam still did not have free institutions, were still deprived of national unity, and were once more in danger of losing what they had fought for throughout the entire colonial period: a truly independent national existence.

XVI

Independence Without Unity or Freedom

1

Ngo Dinh Diem, the man called on by Bao Dai on June 16, 1954, to form a new government, was not universally beloved. Bao Dai himself had never liked him; the French would hardly have chosen him had they still possessed the power to install a puppet; those who had collaborated with the French, including the sect leaders, distrusted him; and the Vietminh, who in the past had denounced him for his "contacts with the Japanese Fascists," now called him "the man of the U.S. interventionists."

The open enmities and secret intrigues against Diem may have helped to enhance his stature as an uncompromising nationalist, but there was legitimate cause for concern about his qualifications as a leader. A devout Catholic, Diem was very different from the majority of the people and the educated elite. To some extent his Catholicism also gave rise to political misgivings. Vietnam's Catholic community, a minority of 10 to 15 per cent of the population, had generally remained aloof from the nationalist and antiforeign sentiments that inspired the non-Catholic majority, in particular the mandarins and scholars who articulated these feelings.

More important, Diem's temperament, social philosophy, and political behavior seemed to preclude any prospect of his ever becoming a popular hero. He did not ask for love, but for the respect and obedience he considered his due as head of state. Since he considered it demeaning to try to win this respect by ingratiating himself with the people, Diem was known only to a small, politically active circle. His name did not arouse enthusiasm. After all, he had been away from Vietnam for almost four years and had not played an active role in the nationalist upsurge that led to the disintegration of the Bao Dai regime.

Diem had left Vietnam in August, 1950, together with his brother, Bishop Ngo Dinh Thuc, to attend the Holy Year celebration in Rome. He went to Rome via Tokyo, where he met with Americans who advised him on possible contacts in Washington. He spent the months of September and October in the United States, and there came into contact with a small group of men concerned about Vietnam but unfamiliar with the complexities of the military and political conditions in Indochina. Diem's thesis combined appealing simplicity with compelling logic: if colonialism were ended and Vietnam be given a truly nationalist government, then the Vietminh could be quickly defeated. Cardinal Spellman, to whom Diem was introduced by his brother, was probably the first American to entertain the idea of a Vietnamese government headed by the Catholic Ngo Dinh Diem.

After a brief stay in Rome, Diem visited Switzerland, Belgium, and France, where he talked with prominent exiled Vietnamese. He returned to the United States in 1951 and spent two years at Maryknoll seminaries in Lakewood, New Jersey, and Ossining, New York. He lectured at various Eastern and Midwestern universities and made a number of trips to Washington, where he found many sympathetic listeners, among them Senators Mike Mansfield and John F. Kennedy, Representative Walter Judd, and Justice William Douglas. But the pleas of these men to support the cause of Vietnamese independence influenced neither the Truman nor Eisenhower Administrations, both of which continued to grant unconditional aid to the French.

At the urging of exiled Vietnamese Catholic leaders, Diem left the United States for Paris in May, 1953, and from there went to Belgium and the Benedictine Monastery of St. André les Bruges. But the month of May, 1954, when the fate of Vietnam was being decided at Dien Bien Phu and Geneva, found Diem back in Paris. During the ensuing weeks of consultations in Paris, Diem, who did not know how to deal with the shallow political sophistication of Paris, was guided by his younger and more worldly brother Luyen.

The most important talks Diem held during his stay in Paris were those with Bao Dai, who finally decided to ask Diem to form a new government. In view of Bao Dai's well-known disapproval of Diem, and that of the French also, this decision gave rise to the still widely accepted myth that the choice of Diem was engineered by strong U.S. pressure on Bao Dai and the French, and by the intervention of Cardinal Spellman via the Catholic MRP. This does not mean that Dulles and Cardinal Spellman did not favor a Diem government. They did, although evidence suggests that Dulles was not overenthusiastic. The point is that there was no need for American pressure. The French Government did not oppose Diem's appointment. The person of the next Vietnamese prime minister was the least of its concerns. There was, furthermore, surprisingly little opposition against Diem among Vietnamese leaders who had collaborated with the French and who hated him. Many of them, and perhaps Bao Dai also, believed that anyone foolish enough to want to govern the truncated, demoralized country likely to emerge from Geneva was courting political doom—a fate they all wished on Ngo Dinh Diem.

The fact remains, however, that neither Vietnamese, American, Catholic, nor French promoters cleared the road to power for Diem. He was carried into office by the tide of events. A new government at this juncture could not possibly have been headed by a known French collaborator. There was no need for Washington to tell Bao Dai that without American support Vietnamese anti-Communism did not have the slightest chance of stemming the Communist tide. Washington and the Vietnamese anti-Communists were also of one mind in firmly rejecting a course advocated by some former collaborators—i.e., to swim cautiously with the Communist tide in the hope of being carried to safe shores.

That is why Bao Dai resisted pressure to reappoint former Prime Minister Tran Van Huu, the first prominent Vietnamese to accept the Geneva agreement and to advocate what was to become known as a "neutralist" solution.

There was no serious competitor for the office of Diem's stature and political acceptability. Meanwhile in Saigon, Diem's brother Nhu had, on May 27, formed another coalition of all active political forces called the Front for a National Salvation. It was composed of the sects, the organized Catholics, the Dai Viet, and other nationalist groups. The Front demanded a new regime to fight Communism, and groups that Diem soon afterward moved to destroy now demanded that he be called upon to head this new regime.

Diem accepted his appointment on June 19, after persuading a reluctant Bao Dai to confer full civilian and military powers on him. Nhu, obsessed with shaping his brother's political destiny, immediately sent one of his closest collaborators to Paris to prepare Diem for his return to the country he was to rule. The man Nhu chose was Tran Chanh Thanh, a lawyer formerly associated with the Vietminh, and later Diem's minister of information.

Diem left Paris for Saigon on June 24, accompanied by his brother Luyen, Tran Chanh Thanh, and Nguyen Van Thoai, a relative and the only prominent exile willing to join Diem's cabinet. Others whom he tried to recruit rejected his concept of government, which clearly aimed at one-man rule. Nor did they share Diem's illusions about the chances of preventing a settlement at Geneva favorable to the Vietminh. Diem apparently believed that a national army fighting for an independent government could defeat the Vietminh.

Diem's arrival in Saigon on June 26, 1954, caused little stir and no popular joy. Diem was not received like a returning national hero who had fought for his country. Clearly his name sparked no fire in the hearts of the masses. The five hundred persons gathered at the airport were mostly elderly mandarins, Catholic dignitaries, and government officials. The men who had come to greet him as the country's new leader could not, of course, anticipate that in stepping off the plane Diem was setting foot on a road that would lead him to brief glory, despair, and premature death.

2

The powers Bao Dai had conferred on his new prime minister theoretically made Diem the most powerful man in the country, but within a few short weeks Diem realized that in fact he held no powers at all. Power in the State of Vietnam did not rest with the government. As in the past, it remained fragmented and rested in the hands of fiercely competing factions. The interests of the groups among whom it was divided were compatible with those of the French, whose domination had been built on the age-old principle of divide and conquer. But these interests, and the absence of a central authority, conflicted sharply with the political needs of an independent state engaged in a struggle for survival.

In addition to chaotic political conditions inherited from the colonial regime, Diem faced equally discouraging tasks on a number of other fronts. The country was in ruins. Bridges, dykes, canals, roads, railways, telephone and telegraph services were either destroyed or in disrepair; vast rice-land areas were uncultivated; innumerable peasants who had fled the countryside found themselves unemployed in the cities. And an insolvent administration run by an incompetent, politically hostile, disintegrating civil service was called upon to provide the human and material resources for looking after the stream of refugees from the North.

Diem was faced with the problem of how to overcome the obstructionism of the many hostile or indifferent factions and forces. He was opposed by the Army and disobeyed by the police and secret service, and the French and Chinese circles who controlled major portions of the economy were hostile because they feared that a strong national regime would curtail their powers. This was true also of the Vietnamese landlords, who feared that Diem's call for a national "revolution" implied radical agrarian reforms. The old collaborators in and outside the administration sabotaged his every step, and the old *attentists* refused to support him out of fear that his regime would collapse and the South be taken over by Vietminh. Such a possible takeover was indeed the greatest of dangers threatening Diem and one of the main reasons that the chances for his survival were thought to be nil.

The Vietminh did not withdraw its political cadres from the South, and although the overthrow of Diem was not their immediate assignment, their activities constituted the greatest challenge Diem had to meet, because once again the masses were receptive to Vietminh propaganda. Hanoi's triumph over the French had impressed the entire population. The great patriotic demand for freedom from foreign rule had become a reality as the result of the armed struggle led by the Vietminh. After almost fifteen years, peace was at last returning to their ravaged land, and all because the Vietminh had beaten the French. The Vietminh, to be sure, was Communist-controlled and the masses were anything but Communist. But to denounce the Vietminh as Communist was completely pointless. If the Vietminh was Communist, then the Communists had to be given the credit for having liberated Vietnam. Except for the well-indoctrinated Catholic minority, which had its special reasons for opposing Communism, the people therefore could not be expected to be openly hostile to the Vietminh or to be enthusiastic about the implacable anti-Communism of the new regime. At best they could be expected to remain neutral, which in fact was the attitude of the majority toward Diem. Realizing that the country had arrived at a turning point, they stood ready to measure Diem's accomplishments against their needs rather than against Vietminh propaganda claims.

Here lay the chance for the survival of a non-Communist Vietnam, the chance to break the hold the Vietminh had gained over the people, the chance to find an answer to the problem of establishing contact with the broad masses, of setting up a regime to which the people could respond. Would those who opposed Diem, who had already contributed so much to the failure of anti-Communism, allow him to take the necessary steps to reverse this trend? And more important still: Did Diem realize that this required a break with those institutions and practices of the past that formed a wall between the government and the people? Did he know enough about the longing of the masses for justice and dignity, of their desire to enjoy the fruits of their labor? And if so, was he ready to institute drastic reforms, changes tantamount to social revolution?

There is little evidence that Diem was equipped for such a

task. His radicalism found expression in nationalist intransigence, not in demands for social and political reform. And a government that lacked mass support and was opposed by the country's police and army was obviously not equipped for the execution of reforms bound to hurt the interests of entrenched social and political groups. It was Diem's plausible contention that he first had to overcome the paralyzing conditions afflicting his government, and the choices at his disposal were not very great. But was not one of the means the support of the masses against his enemies, and was not immediate response to the need for social reforms the precondition for popular support? Diem, it has been argued, could have won over the peasants by reducing land rents (as a first step toward a radical land reform), by proclaiming that the recipients of land distributed in Vietminh-held territories would be recognized as the legal owners, and by ordering a temporary moratorium on all peasant taxes. The big landlords would of course have violently opposed such measures, but they could have been compensated for their losses. American aid, already considerable, could have been extended to cover the cost of such reforms, with enormous political benefits to the "free world."

Diem did not choose this way out, and not merely because he was by temperament and philosophy a conservative. The difficulties and obstacles he would surely have encountered might have frightened even a radical social reformer. Diem could have decreed such reforms but he could not have implemented them. Not even a cut in land rents could have been carried through because the government lacked the personnel to enforce such a measure at the local level. The provincial, regional, and local chiefs were appointees of the old, corrupt governments. They cooperated with the landlords in exploiting and terrorizing the peasants. If an order to suspend peasant taxes had gone out, the taxes would still have been collected, but instead of going to Saigon they would henceforth have gone into the pockets of the local officials.

Diem knew that these things had to be changed, but the measure he decided upon—replacing local officials with his own appointees—was neither of immediate help nor did it get at the roots of the evil. The means for changing this system—the creation of elected local institutions responsible not only to the government but also to the people—were, however, not available to

Diem, at least not at that time. Even if Diem had wished to pursue such a course he could not have done so in the summer of 1954. Local elections would have given the Vietminh control of most of the rural communities.

Similarly, popular enthusiasm for the regime, even if it could have been generated, could not have been channeled into freely constituted organizations and parties. Here, too, the regime lacked the necessary trained personnel. Vietnam in 1954 was still dominated by the issues of the immediate past that had led to the Vietminh victory, and the consequent Communist strength could not be overcome in a few short months. Freely constituted organizations would also have been captured by the Vietminh. Communist-inspired "democratic fronts" began to be active throughout the South immediately after the Geneva settlement. It would have been suicidal for Diem to let such groups develop freely. He had to fight them, but he was able to do so only by suppressing all unauthorized political activities, including the arrest of people suspected of conducting clandestine activities. The regime's inherent political weakness thus manifested itself in an inability to permit the workings of democracy, since democracy in action seemed to benefit its enemies. This meant that Diem could not even marshal the existing potential of mass support for his regime, which may have been considerably greater than was generally assumed.

This lack of organized support and the growing hostility of all groups and factions opposed to Diem led to the widely held conviction in Vietnam and abroad that Diem, in order to survive, had to share his powers with his anti-Communist opponents: the pro-French military leadership, the sects, and even some members of Bao Dai's former government who had collaborated with the French. But Diem, for all his shortcomings, knew that in the long run such a course would fatally impair South Vietnam's chances of survival. His sense of history, however defective, warned him against retreating from his position of uncompromising nationalism. Without this one weapon, all others that he might later try to forge against the threat of Communism would remain ineffective. Diem was not deceived by the "unity" that this policy was supposed to produce. There are times in the life of a new state when all groups and factions, no matter how hostile, must unite to save the country, but there are other times when unity can be brought about only by eliminating the elements incompatible with it.

After Geneva, a politically unified state and single administrative authority in South Vietnam was possible only by setting the government above the Army, by taking control of the police away from a private armed group, and by incorporating all regions controlled by the religious-political sects into the national administration. This meant that the openly dissident Army leadership had to be replaced, that the Binh Xuyen, if it refused to give up control of the police, had to be destroyed, as would the Hoa Hao and the Cao Dai if they refused to incorporate their forces into the country's Army and if they refused to accept the central administrative authority of Saigon. Diem understood this better than any other nationalist leader.

But having decided that the Army and the sects must not be appeased, how could Diem eliminate them? He held a mandate without any real power. The hopelessness of his situation was glaringly underlined when the Binh Xuyen–controlled Saigon police brutally dispersed a pro-government demonstration staged by Diem's Catholic supporters. It was no surprise, therefore, that the fall of Diem was predicted daily in Vietnam and abroad even before his clash with the sects in the spring of 1955 almost made it a fact.

Diem remained impervious to all proof of his political impotence and deaf to all voices of despair. Looking upon himself as a man with a mission that could not be abandoned, Diem resolutely took the only road open to him: short-term political maneuvers to divide and neutralize his enemies, and even to buy their temporary cooperation—until he gained enough strength to smash them separately. He made concessions, played one side against another, and was determined at the opportune moment to take back what he had granted. In what can be described only as a ruthless and unscrupulous game of many-sided intrigues, he dealt separately with his opponents, and deepened and then exploited the conflicts between them. With the able assistance of his brother Nhu, who regarded the crooked paths of intrigue as the only sure road to power, Diem succeeded with these methods, but only because his enemies were not only venal and divided but also politically bankrupt, and because he enjoyed the political, moral, and financial backing of the United States.

3

The bankruptcy of Diem's opponents and the importance of U.S. support were first revealed in the struggle for control of the Army, a struggle that led to a crisis lasting almost three months. It began early in September with public attacks on Diem by the chief of staff, General Nguyen Van Hinh. Demanding that the country be given a "strong and popular" new government, Hinh openly admitted that he was preparing a *coup d'état* and boasted that he could overthrow Diem merely by picking up the telephone.

Accepting the challenge, Diem on September 11, 1954, ordered Hinh to take a six-week "study vacation" in France, to begin within twenty-four hours. Hinh showed his defiance by riding through the streets of Saigon in shirt sleeves on a motorcycle. On September 19, Hinh released a statement to the press explaining his stand, together with the text of a cable to Bao Dai asking him to intervene. That same day Diem publicly accused Hinh of rebellion, whereupon Hinh, quite unnecessarily, barricaded himself in his home. A few days later he stationed tanks around Norodom Palace (now Independence Palace), the former seat of the French High Commission, which General Ely had handed over to Diem on September 7. The police guarding the Palace was under the command of Diem's sworn enemies in the Binh Xuyen. In order to defend himself against his "protectors," Diem brought militia units from Annam into Saigon. The Binh Xuyen, together with the Hoa Hao and Cao Dai, had by that time openly come out for General Hinh against Diem. In a joint manifesto issued on September 16, the warlords, gangsters, bordello owners, and dishonest sect leaders speaking in tones of high virtue demanded a new government. Their demand was transmitted to Bao Dai by the Binh Xuyen leader Le Van Vien. On September 20, nine of the fifteen members of Diem's government resigned, apparently convinced, like most local and international prophets, that Diem was doomed.

Diem, however, rightly assumed that his opponents, planless and divided, had rallied to Hinh chiefly in order to raise the price of their neutrality or collaboration. He was not dismayed by the resignations of men he sooner or later would have dropped anyway. Diem now began to limit his cabinet to members of his family and close personal friends. Furthermore, the resignation of the nine ministers enabled Diem to offer the vacant posts to sect leaders ready to sell out. While Hinh was waiting for Bao Dai's permission to execute his coup, Diem's negotiators, armed with American funds, went to work. Under the pretext of having to prevent a Communist move to exploit the crisis, Hinh kept the Palace surrounded with his troops. Le Van Vien, just back from his visit to Bao Dai, had begun to negotiate with the Hoa Hao and Cao Dai to form a government headed by himself. But Diem had not been idle. The Hoa Hao and Cao Dai leaders suddenly informed the Binh Xuyen chieftain that he was not acceptable to them as head of a new government and that they also opposed Bao Dai's return to Vietnam: On September 24, forty-eight hours before the projected joint action of the sects against Diem, four Hoa Hao and four Cao Dai leaders joined the government they had been plotting to overthrow. This maneuver was underwritten by the American taxpayers to the tune of millions of piasters that went into the coffers of the two sects.

Diem's "uncanny ability to divide his enemies by a series of intricate maneuvers"[1] helped him enormously in his struggle against the Army leadership enjoying the support of Bao Dai and influential French circles in Vietnam. But these talents would not have saved him had it not been for international developments that proved decisive for his political fortunes. A three-day Franco-American meeting in Washington between September 27 and 29 produced clear evidence that henceforth the survival of a non-Communist Vietnam would depend on the United States, not on France. The course of events before Geneva, particularly growing French dependence on U.S. aid for the war in Indochina, had laid the groundwork for this shift, and it was this change that propelled Diem in his struggle for supreme power. Remnants of colonialism still survived in the Army, the sects, and more remotely in the French-created "legitimacy" of the chief of state, Bao Dai. By the end of September, 1954, it had become evident that all this had to go. Washington was footing the bill in Vietnam, and confident that it knew better than Paris how to stop Communism in Asia, it was determined to call the tune. France had no choice. She had already agreed to join SEATO. Now the French delegation at Washington agreed to the steps that would, as General Ely had put it on August 30, achieve "total independence." Responsibility for the administration of justice, police, security, public safety, and civil aviation had, at least in theory, been turned over to the Diem government on September 11. The next step, agreed upon in principle at Washington, was permission for Vietnam to issue her own currency, which in fact meant the liquidation of the Bank of Indochina. January 1, 1955, was the date set for this momentous change. The French further agreed to the abrogation of the Pau agreements, through which France had exercised effective control over the economy, commerce, and finances of Vietnam; to the transfer of the over-all command of the National Army to the Vietnamese Government; to handing over responsibility for the training of the Vietnamese Army to the U.S. military mission; to give the Vietnamese Government full control over all aid funds from the United States; and, finally, to withdraw the Expeditionary Corps upon request of the Vietnamese Government.

That these steps had been agreed upon in Washington in September did not become known until after Mendès-France's visit to Washington on November 20. During the subsequent debate in the French Chamber, Mendès-France was accused of having sold out the interests of France by his acceptance of the "American solution." This was denied by Guy La Chambre, the Minister for the Associated States, who asserted that the Washington agreements aimed at Franco-American cooperation in Indochina. Vietnam and the United States, he said, had given firm assurances not to interfere with French economic and commercial interests.

La Chambre was on fairly safe ground. The United States was not interested in replacing France economically in Indochina. Washington was motivated by strategic and political rather than by immediate economic considerations. Moreover, French business interests for the time being were not threatened. On December 30, 1954, and again on March 30, 1955, Diem concluded economic agreements safeguarding French business interests in South Vietnam. Diem's motives also were primarily political and military. He wished to create the conditions that would make successful resistance to Communism possible. One of these conditions was having the United States assume the military protection of South Vietnam; another, and this seemed of more immediate significance, was to have France relinquish her political hold on Vietnam, which Diem had always regarded as the chief stumbling block to Vietnam's struggle against Communism.

A great deal of friction and a number of dramatic confrontations were still to be expected before the French in Indochina would become resigned to giving up their positions of control, but in the long run American, not French, influence would determine the political fate of South Vietnam.

Diem anticipated this development, and therefore he was never really in doubt about the outcome of his duel with General Hinh. He ignored Bao Dai's advice on October 1 to take Hinh, Le Van Vien, and Nguyen Van Xuan into the cabinet. All later appeals by Hinh to Bao Dai for support against Diem failed to elicit any response whatever. Only a few people knew the reason for Bao Dai's caution, namely that on October 2, General Ely, back from the talks in Washington, had told Bao Dai what had been agreed upon and why France was obliged to go along with U.S. support for Diem. After a stalemate of more than six weeks, during which Diem refused to discuss any kind of compromise, Bao Dai gave in. On November 13, he called Hinh to France for "consultations," and on November 29 he announced Hinh's dismissal, on the grounds that he had made "ill-advised statements."[2] Bao Dai also remained deaf to all further demands by his supporters to to involve himself personally and return to Vietnam with Hinh. Washington had let it be known that it would not stand idly by if Diem were ousted. A report submitted on October 15 to the Senate Foreign Relations Committee by Senator Mansfield sharply objected to any plans to replace Diem. If Diem should be overthrown, Mansfield said, "the United States should consider an immediate suspension of all aid to Vietnam and the French Union forces there, except that of a humanitarian nature."[3] On October 24, President Eisenhower sent an encouraging open letter of support to Diem reaffirming earlier promises of aid and informing him that as of January 1, 1955, all American aid to Vietnam would be given directly to his government. (This letter became a point of dispute between Eisenhower and President Johnson, who maintained that it initiated the policy the United States was now pursuing in Vietnam. Eisenhower claimed that he had spoken only of economic aid and that the letter did not constitute a commitment to the military defense of Vietnam by the United States. The text of the letter would indicate that the truth, as usual, lies halfway between these two assertions. Certain of its passages lend themselves to either interpretation, e.g.: "I am, accordingly, instructing the American ambassador to Vietnam to examine with you in your capacity as chief of government, how an intelligent program of American aid given directly to your Government can serve to assist Vietnam in its present hour of trial, provided that your Government is prepared to give assurances as to the standards of performance it would be able to maintain in the event such aid were supplied. The purpose of this offer is to assist the Government of Vietnam in developing and maintaining a strong, viable state, capable of resisting attempted subversion or aggression through military means.")

Thanks to such strong support, Diem was able to survive his first major test in his struggle to create an effective, independent government for South Vietnam. By the end of 1954, he was ready for the next campaign, the battle to oust the sects from the political life of Vietnam, and thereby almost undid what he had so far achieved.

4

Diem launched his war against the sects with an apparently unpolitical move against the head of the Binh Xuyen: he refused to renew Le Van Vien's license for the gambling establishment Grand Monde. The Hoa Hao "Generalissimo" Tran Van Soai, extortionist, gambling profiteer and cabinet member, could easily match Le Van Vien's immorality, but Diem could not afford to tackle all three sects simultaneously. Besides, Binh Xuyen control of the Saigon-Cholon police and security service posed a more immediate threat than Hoa Hao activities in more distant regions. Next to obtaining control of the Army, Diem's most important objective at this time was to gain control of the capital's police.

Thanks to his victory over Hinh, and even more because of the promulgation of measures on behalf of Vietnamese sovereignty, Diem in early 1955 was in a much stronger position than he had been earlier. The foreign-controlled activities of the Bank of Indochina were brought to an end, and by decree of December 3, a National Bank of Vietnam was established, rather hastily, since it had to be in operation by January 1, 1955, the date on which American aid was to go directly to the Saigon government. On January 12, the government formally took over the administration of the port of Saigon from the French. There can be no doubt that these and later measures enhanced Diem's prestige as a nationalist determined to eradicate all traces of colonialism.

The fact that direct American aid also comprised aid for the Vietnamese armed forces was decisive for Diem's power struggle, for it meant that the Army was now dependent on the government rather than on the French. It also gave Diem another lever against the sects, since the French had stopped their subsidies to them on February 11. An agreement signed on that day between the French General Agostini and the new chief of staff, Le Van Ty, marked another big step toward national sovereignty. The French command transferred all responsibility for the Vietnamese armed forces to the Vietnamese Government. Though not many officers were completely loyal to Diem, most now moved closer to the regime, since they knew that the training and organization of the Army was going to be taken over by American officers, most of whom were definitely pro-Diem. Also, Diem had replaced Hinh by a man whom he considered loyal: General Le Van Ty. But Diem's victory over the Army was incomplete, since he had gotten Ty only by agreeing to the appointment of a pro-French, pro-Bao Dai inspector general of the armed forces: General Nguyen Van Vy. The Generals Ty and Vy became central figures in the struggle against the sects, but two other French-educated officers, Colonel Tran Van Don and Colonel Duong Van Minh ("Big Minh") were to play a more fateful role in the life of Diem and in the political evolution of South Vietnam. Early in 1955, however, they were simply two among many young officers whom prospects of promotion turned into patriots and eventually into supporters of Diem.

Obviously convinced that a virtuous man is justified in combating evil with means considered immoral if employed by his enemies, Diem set about weakening the sects by exploiting the venality of their leaders. On January 14, he succeeded in luring an important Hoa Hao officer, Colonel Nguyen Van Hue, the chief of staff of Generalissimo Tran Van Soai, into his camp. Hue brought with him 3,500 men who were eventually integrated into the National Army. Another officer, Major Nguyen Day, a few weeks later brought another 1,500 Hoa Hao soldiers. After pocketing their reward for betraying Soai, who incidentally was still in Diem's cabinet, Day and Hue accused Soai of greed and of having betrayed his nation. At the end of January, the Cao Dai leader Trinh Minh The, who had already rallied to Diem the preceding November, did so again, perhaps only as a demonstration of growing governmental strength. He was rewarded by a promotion to general. Shortly thereafter, The brought his 5,000-man army into Saigon. After Diem had thus secured the one Cao Dai faction that had long been the nucleus of a "third force" between Communists and collaborators, another shifty Hoa Hao "general," Nguyen Gia Ngo, announced his intention to rally; however, he waited until he was sure that Diem had definitely gained the upper hand before transferring his troops.

While Diem's military potential continued to grow at the expense of the sects, conflicts between the Hoa Hao and Cao Dai, as well as dissension within the sects, continued to erode their ability to prepare their resistance against the expected strikes by Diem. The Binh Xuyen, Diem's first target, was solidly united behind its leader, but their interests were too specific, too local, too opposed to national goals, to qualify them for the leadership of a coalition aspiring to govern the whole country. Old rivalries between the Hoa Hao and Cao Dai were intensified when both tried to extend the boundaries of the regions they controlled by taking over former Vietminh territory. Yet these political gangsters knew that Diem would destroy them one by one unless they united, but their flashes of insight were the products of the fear of losing the power to safeguard their sources of income, and thus the sect leaders were not given to rational action. Since so many of them competed in plundering the nation's resources, fear of losing part of their loot only fed their dissensions. This explains why so many sect leaders, once Diem decided to buy them, were willing to act against their own interests, which lay in common action.

It took Bao Dai, who saw a chance of blocking Diem's quest for real power, to bring about a truce among the sects. On March 3, the Binh Xuyen, Cao Dai, and Hoa Hao concluded a "nonaggression pact" and formed a "spiritual union" of the three sects, designed "to protect the country and to serve the people." On March 4, the leading political shark of this shady coalition, Pham Cong Tac, the Cao Dai "pope," demanded a strong democratic government "composed of honest men."[4] The coalition was joined by several anti-Diem nationalist groups for a variety of reasons. Some, like the Dai Viet leader Nguyen Ton Hoan, joined because Diem had rejected his demand for a role in the government; others, like the "Democratic Party" leader Phan Quang Dan and the former Trotskyist Ho Huu Tuong joined because they thought, mistakenly, that the sects could be used to bring about a true coalition government of all reputable nationalist personalities. What was even more surprising, and no doubt came as a shock to Diem, was that the newly promoted General The also joined this front—for a few days only, as if to prove once more his rather insolent independence. He returned to Diem on March 7, probably for another cash payment. Not to be outcrooked in this scramble for power and riches, Bao Dai covered up his scheme to unseat Diem by expressing satisfaction with Diem's performance.

Since time was unlikely to work in favor of the sects they had to act. On March 21, they issued an ultimatum requesting the formation of a national government within five days. Diem, who had no intention of complying, was nevertheless cautious in his rejection of the ultimatum. He held out vague hopes for integrating the sect armies into the National Army under conditions acceptable to the leaders. Dissatisfied, and realizing that once again they were being held off by a maneuver, they decided to withdraw their representatives from the government. But the overthrow of Diem would have required solidarity among the sect leaders, courage to stake everything on one card, and the conviction that their combined strength could match Diem's—all of which the sects lacked, particularly solidarity. The Binh Xuyen fortified themselves in the police and security-service headquarters and in other buildings in Saigon and Cholon; the Hoa Hao, which controlled much of the river traffic in the Mekong Delta, began to hold up food supplies for the capital; and the Cao Dai, weakened by The's final defection, did nothing, or rather worse than nothing: some of its leaders entered into secret negotiations with Diem.

While his adversaries were busily preparing for a united action which never came off, Diem took military and political measures that would enable him to take the initiative in the case of civil war. He reinforced the Army in Saigon with militia and paratroops from other areas and also fortified his position politically. In a television address on March 8, Secretary Dulles assured Diem of unwavering American support, and a letter sent by President Eisenhower to Bao Dai on March 9 might be construed as a warning to the chief of state to stop making difficulties for Diem.[5]

Diem disregarded an appeal by Bao Dai on March 25 for "unity" with the sects; instead, in his dealing with them he decided to rely once more on the lure of the dollar and on his growing military strength. With "swift moves that left each sect chief wondering whether his sworn ally of yesterday had not sold him out for a substantial sum,"[6] Diem dealt the "unity" of the sects another blow. On March 29, he succeeded in buying the commander in chief of the Cao Dai forces, General Nguyen Thanh Phuong. On March 31, exactly four weeks after having demanded that the Diem government be replaced by one of honest men, Phuong publicly proclaimed his loyalty to Diem.

By March 31, Diem had burned all bridges to the sect leaders, both to those who had refused to strike another bargain and those whom he had always wanted to destroy—the Binh Xuyen. On March 27, Diem, certain of Phuong's readiness to defect from the sects' front, ordered his paratroopers under Colonel Tri to occupy the Binh Xuyen–held police headquarters and security building on the Boulevard Gallieni, the road connecting Cholon with Saigon. The Binh Xuyen retreated from the police headquarters but refused to evacuate the security building. Diem, convinced that compromise was no longer necessary, decided to use force. On March 28, he ordered Colonel Tri to occupy the building. But before the attack got under way, General Ely intervened. Diem reluctantly acceded to Ely's pressure. But in the night of March 29–30, it came to a clash between government troops and Binh Xuyen near the security building, and both sides sustained casualties.

At this juncture Diem was temporarily checked in his race for undisputed control. Fear of a civil war, entirely unfounded according to Diem, provoked strong reaction on the part of General Ely. As long as the French Army was in the country, its commander in chief felt responsible also for the safety of the European population. He could hardly stand idly by if Saigon and possibly other cities were turned into battlefields. Moreover, many Frenchmen who sided with Bao Dai and the sects did not want Diem to fight a battle he might win and therefore chose to oppose the use of force to settle a political conflict. Since it was Diem who proposed to use force it was against him that the French, for the first time since his appointment, now threw the full weight of their diminishing influence.

5

Diem and the U.S. support he enjoyed had been under attack by the French press long before the sect crisis came to a head. Quite a few had been predicting Diem's imminent fall for months. The hopes of these Frenchmen for a government more to their liking could be kept alive only if Diem could be prevented from eliminating the sects, and hence the campaign against him grew more intense. In this French campaign, which evoked an extraordinary international response, Diem was called "inept" and "rigid" and much was made of his "inability to compromise," with complete disregard for the fact that the compromises asked of him would inevitably have resulted in the disintegration of all governmental authority in the country.

This campaign must be seen as a final attempt on the part of some Frenchmen to turn the tide of the anticolonialism, which under Diem was clearly running counter to a future French presence in Vietnam. Businessmen sympathized with Diem's opponents, as did military officers, former administrative aides, and the many members of the various "special services" created during the war years. The most important member of General Ely's staff,

Assistant High Commissioner Jean Daridan, became an authoritative spokesman for these defenders of a lost cause.

Ely had accepted the need for a complete French withdrawal from Vietnamese political life and became reconciled to the replacement of French political, economic, and military advisers by American personnel. But at the end of March, 1955, he felt it his duty to stand up against Diem. Ely would have tolerated both Diem's lack of graciousness and his intemperate demands had he been convinced of his ability to master the chaotic political situation. But he was not convinced, and when Diem decided to send his troops against the Binh Xuyen, Ely decided to step in. There was genuine fear among the French nationals that a wider civil war would lead to the breakdown of all established authority, arouse chauvinistic feelings, and endanger their property and lives. Ely shared these fears.

It was for these reasons that Ely, although no friend of the sects, stopped Diem from crushing the Binh Xuyen. Not being a Vietnamese concerned with his country's political regeneration, Ely could hardly be expected to see that if the country was to have a united and strong regime, the corrupt sects had to be suppressed, and he also failed to see that at this stage a man like Diem was precisely what South Vietnam needed in order to survive. In fact, some of Diem's shortcomings may have made him far better suited to the task at hand than if his had been a broader and more generous political mind. Ely believed that he had to arbitrate the conflict between Diem and the sects. Moreover, he wanted to make peace between Diem and the Frenchmen with vested interests in Vietnam. Still another of his concerns was the growing friction between the French and Americans in Saigon.

This Franco-American conflict was of serious concern also to President Eisenhower's special envoy to Saigon, General Collins. His predecessor, Ambassador Heath, had never been fond of Diem, nor had he been convinced of the wisdom of Diem's policies. He carried out his instructions with excessive concern for the sensibilities of the French. But Collins, too, began to have mixed feelings about this stubborn man with whom it was so difficult to establish contact and who seemed not to know what was meant by an exchange of views. Collins ended up by advising Washington to drop Diem. By mid-April, when it had become evident that Diem would sooner or later renew his attack on the Binh Xuyen, Collins became almost emphatic in his opposition to Diem.

If Diem had been unaware earlier of how Collins felt about his attitude toward the sects, all doubts were erased after March 29, when Collins unequivocally supported the measures of the French to stop the attacks on the Binh Xuyen. The French High Command imposed a cease-fire on the government forces, granted the Binh Xuyen troops permission to fortify their positions in and around Saigon, and declared a number of sectors of Saigon, including those held by the Binh Xuyen, off limits to the National Army. The French, who still controlled the supplies for the Vietnamese Army, withheld the ammunition needed to continue the operation against the Binh Xuyen. Collins strongly urged Diem not to resume the attack.[7] "Our hands have been tied by the intervention of General Collins," claimed a government spokesman on April 7.[8]

In his long struggle to gain and later to preserve power, Diem went through a number of periods of agonizing uncertainty. But it may be assumed that not even the weeks before his downfall and death in 1963 were more anguish-filled than the month of April, 1955. He no longer had a government; all sect ministers had resigned at the end of March. A still greater blow was the defection of his respected foreign minister, Tran Van Do, together with Ho Thong Minh, the minister of defense, whose appointment had brought on the first disagreement with Collins. The government was replaced by a junta consisting of three Ngo brothers—Diem, Nhu, and Luyen—and a nephew by marriage, Tran Trung Dung. Another relative, Nguyen Van Thoai, resigned from the government—spectacularly—by announcing his step while serving as the head of the Vietnamese delegation to the Bandung conference. Many high officials, most of them French appointees, left the government—the proverbial rats leaving the sinking ship. The countryside remained sect territory or Communist-controlled, even after the evacuation of the Vietminh troops. Diem did not have enough loyal provincial administrators and enough military forces to establish control over these regions. The few Army units willing to fight for the government were needed in Saigon to protect the government against the Binh Xuyen. Diem's efforts to have a few more battalions transferred from central Vietnam to Saigon were frustrated by the French, who continued to prevent troops loyal to Diem from circulating freely in Saigon but did not interfere with the movement of the Binh Xuyen, which still controlled the capital's police force. Growing bolder by the hour, the Binh Xuyen occupied more and more strategic positions in the Saigon-Cholon area.

It was not surprising that during these critical weeks Bao Dai's interest in his country revived. He may no longer have possessed the power to shape his country's political course, but his attitude was a significant barometer of the force of the storm that was descending on Diem. Bao Dai knew better than anyone else that Diem could not survive without unqualified American support. His keen political instinct told him that Washington had begun to entertain serious doubts about Diem's ability to lead the country out of chaos. He also knew that Collins, called to Washington on April 23, was advocating what had become the French position—namely, to replace Diem.

Bao Dai was already casting about for a new prime minister when he received a request from Diem to dismiss the head of the security service, a Binh Xuyen chief whom Bao Dai had appointed early in 1954. The request was refused. Instead, Bao Dai demanded that Diem cooperate with the sects. Urged on by the French, Bao Dai issued a decree making the pro-French General Nguyen Van Vy head of the Army. Next he invited Diem for "consultations." Diem replied that he could not leave the country. Thereupon Bao Dai ordered him to France and to bring with him General Ty, the Army head whom Bao Dai had just replaced with his own man.

Toward the end of April it seemed to most observers that Diem was through and that only his deplorable "lack of imagination" prevented him from realizing this. Every foreign newspaper announced that his days were numbered. The French press, openly hostile, stated that his departure would be a blessing for South Vietnam; the British press, more aloof, regretted his shortcomings but felt that they made his replacement inevitable; and the American press, although only in part hostile, was almost unanimously pessimistic about his chances of survival. Most American papers, even those friendly to Diem, were resigned to this sad and probably disastrous probability, since civil war and the fall of Diem would undoubtedly open the door to Communism. South Vietnam, according to Graham Greene, was "about to retire behind the iron curtain."[9]

6

On April 23, when almost everyone expected Diem to announce his resignation, he instead announced that general elections would be held within three or four months—a first indication that Diem would henceforth employ political demagogy as well as force and bribes to maintain himself in power. Everyone knew that conditions in South Vietnam ruled out the holding of genuine elections.

Diem, confident that it would be in his favor, decided that the time had come to force a decision. After urging Washington to bring pressure on the French to stop protecting the Binh Xuyen, Diem informed Ely that no amount of French obstructionism could prevent him from asserting the government's authority against the Binh Xuyen chief of the security service by replacing him with Colonel Nguyen Ngo Le, a loyal Catholic. On April 26, all members of the security service who failed to report to Colonel Le within forty-eight hours were threatened with court-martial. On April 27, the government announced that after the expiration of that time limit, the Binh Xuyen troops would be forbidden to circulate in Saigon-Cholon.

The Binh Xuyen, not at all intimidated, became more aggressive. Clashes with government troops in various parts of town followed. But it was the Army that set off the real battle. At around noon on April 28, two truckloads of paratroopers fired at a building on the Boulevard Gallieni occupied by a Binh Xuyen commando. The Army then moved four battalions of paratroopers and one armored unit against other Binh Xuyen strongholds between Saigon and Cholon. At 1:15 P.M., the Binh Xuyen fired four shells into the grounds of the Presidential Palace, an incident later cited by Diem, in an unnecessary embellishment of historical truth, as the reason that "peace was lost in Saigon."[10] After only a few hours of fighting, civilian casualties were running well into the hundreds. An estimated twenty thousand were made homeless.

In the course of the afternoon, General Ely tried once more to arrange a cease-fire. But Diem would have none of it. On May 1, Ely ordered 400 French tanks to ride through the streets of Saigon, a final gesture of French power through which Ely reminded Diem that he could easily have frustrated his plan to oust the Binh Xuyen from Saigon. By May 1, however, the battle for control of the city was already over. The paratroopers had proved superior to the Binh Xuyen, whose fighting spirit turned out to be surprisingly low. The last units of Le Van Vien, who had fled from his head-quarters on April 29, retired from Cholon before dawn broke on April 30. They and the reserves that Le Van Vien had failed to throw into the battle regrouped outside the city. The Binh Xuyen had apparently counted on the French to save them. During the next few days they were again defeated outside the city by the Army and Cao Dai units under General The and driven into the marshes of Rung Sat, 10 miles south of Saigon.

The period during which the government forces were expelling the Binh Xuyen from Saigon was marked by hectic activity, both on the political home front and in the diplomatic arena. Bao Dai's summons of Diem and his chief of staff to Paris came on April 28, just after the fighting had broken out. April 29 brought not only a statement by Premier Faure calling Diem unfit for his job,[11] but also another display of French hostility to Diem and support for Bao Dai: French official recognition of Bao Dai's appointee, General Vy, as head of the Vietnamese Army.[12] Bao Dai, no doubt urged on by the French, sent General Hinh back to Saigon to help the sects in their battle against Diem.

The news from Saigon on April 29 may have been bad for the French and Bao Dai, but Washington was relieved that Diem seemed to be gaining the upper hand and immediately began to recover from its "grave apprehensions"[13] concerning Diem and to express its displeasure over the attempts to unseat him. On the same day that Faure denounced Diem, Dulles warned Ambassador Couve de Murville against further moves to unseat Diem,[14] and Ambassador Dillon did the same in Paris in an audience with Premier Faure. The most conspicuous indication of the revival of American support for Diem came in a demand to the French to furnish the Vietnamese Army with the supplies needed to fight the rebellious sects; after all, the United States was paying for these supplies. Encouraged by the American support and by the success of troops in fighting the Binh Xuyen, Diem felt on safe ground in refusing to obey Bao Dai's April 29 summons. Twenty-four hours later, Diem received a cable from Washington assuring him of continued U.S. support.

In other tenebrous phases of these power struggles in South Vietnam, the truth can be glimpsed through the tightly woven screen of intrigues. This is not the case in the chain of events that began in the afternoon of April 30, 1955, when a gathering of some 200 persons at the Saigon town hall constituted itself as a General Assembly of Democratic and Revolutionary Forces of the Nation. Although the outcome of these events is known, what actually happened at various critical stages is not. The picture that emerges from the available conflicting reports is that of a weird kaleidoscope made up of hate, lust for power, greed, cowardice, and treachery.

The apparent and immediate purpose of the town hall meeting was to provide evidence of popular support for Diem. The General Assembly was composed of eighteen political "parties," none representative of more than a handful of persons, and of the Cao Dai leaders who had gone over to Diem. After the symbolic act of tossing Bao Dai's picture out a window, the meeting decided that the former emperor had to abdicate and a new government be formed under Ngo Dinh Diem, in order to restore order, ensure the early departure of the French Expeditionary Corps, and prepare elections for a national assembly. The meeting culminated in the election of a thirty-three-member Revolutionary Committee, which promptly submitted the demands of the General Assembly to Diem.

Although all this had been prearranged—the scheme was generally thought to have been the brainchild of Ngo Dinh Nhu—there were indications that Diem was not altogether happy with the way things were going, since some of the men called upon to act at this new stage refused to be manipulated. The strongest members of the committee were the two Cao Dai leaders who had rallied to Diem, General The and General Phuong. Both still commanded the loyalty of some thousands of armed followers, and The had already caused some uneasiness at the Palace when he stationed groups of his soldiers in Saigon immediately after the paratroop attack on the Binh Xuyen on April 28. Both The and Phuong could be expected to use the committee for aims not necessarily identical with those of Diem. Of the other committee members, two were former Vietminh political commissars, some were known for their contacts with French left-wing circles, and others for their predilection for expressions of extreme nationalism and demands for radical reforms.[15]

No reliable report on the next twenty-four crucial hours exists, but the following account, although based on conflicting testimony, is probably essentially accurate. When the Revolutionary Committee arrived at the Palace at about 6:15 P.M., Diem was in conference with the Generals Ty and Vy, the former said to be for him and the latter known to be against him. On that evening both affirmed their loyalty to Bao Dai, in whose name Vy was to assume command of the Army. Neither of these two men was a hero, and both were at least twenty-four hours behind the decision of history. The appearance of the Revolutionary Committee put an end to Diem's "negotiations" with Ty and Vy. An attempt by one committee member to kill Vy allegedly was thwarted by Diem, who, according to some informants, said that he did not wish to have blood spilled on his Chinese rug.[16] According to another version, Vy was saved by Colonel Cao Van Tri, a fellow paratrooper who had just defeated the Binh Xuyen. Tri allegedly called Diem and threatened to storm the Palace unless Vy was released.[17] What remains certain, though, is that foreign correspondents called to the Palace at 9:30 P.M. found a trembling Vy, guarded by The and Phuong, ready to read a statement repudiating Bao Dai and supporting the Revolutionary Committee's demands for an end of French interference in Vietnamese affairs.[18] Having read the statement, they were released. Once again, the Diem government, "after tottering on the brink of dissolution,"[19] was saved.

Diem's victory over the Binh Xuyen was now nearly complete, yet he still had not won that total freedom of action which he considered necessary and his due. The Revolutionary Committee installed itself in the Palace with the obvious intention of directly influencing official policy. The radical and demagogic nationalism of many of its members threatened to tarnish Diem's self-made image as the true and only liberator of his country from colonialism, and their demand for the immediate ouster of Bao Dai interfered with Diem's own strategy for achieving this end.

The only member of the Revolutionary Committee who might possibly have become a rival for Diem was General Trin Minh The. Well-known as an ardent nationalist for years, General The presented himself as a champion of the people and a fighter against corruption. What remains certain is that he was a man of ambition and strength. But fate prevented him from matching his talents in a competition for leadership with Diem. On May 3, while fighting against the Binh Xuyen, The was killed. His death occurred "under mysterious circumstances,"[20] giving rise to rumors of murder, but by whom and why has remained a matter of dispute. Circumstantial evidence seems to rule out one of the theories advanced, namely that he was killed on orders by Diem.[21]

After The's death, Diem gradually pushed the Revolutionary Committee out of the Palace, and to demonstrate that he no longer needed them he staged a new and firmly government-controlled show of popular support: a national congress held in Saigon on May 5, attended mainly by docile civil servants and hand-picked supporters. The resolutions of this congress, though milder than the demands of the Revolutionary Committee, nevertheless made it clear that the regime wished to get rid of Bao Dai. A rival meeting called by the Revolutionary Committee for the same day merely proved that men who permit themselves to become tools rarely possess the skill for independent action, and can, once their usefulness has come to an end, be traded in for other pawns. The Committee's only possible source of strength were the Cao Dai troops of the generals who had rallied to Diem, and which were ultimately bound to be loyal to the man who paid them.

In forming his new cabinet on May 10, composed of trusted followers and a handful of obscure administration officials, Diem could safely ignore the demands of the Revolutionary Committee. When its chairman resigned in protest against Diem's authoritarianism and left the country, the government accused him of having embezzled the committee's funds. When Diem, in October, 1955, asked that the committee be dissolved, its remaining members acquiesced. Neither Diem's enemies nor the people willing to accept him as the country's leader seemed able to compete with this determined man for a share in governmental power.

7

More important, however, than the elimination of inconvenient allies were two other by-products of Diem's victory over the Binh Xuyen. He convinced Washington that in order to save South Vietnam the United States had to support him, and he at last put an end to French interference.

After their failure to oust Diem, the French under U.S. pressure became reconciled to liquidating all remnants of colonialism. The steps toward this end were agreed on in a Franco-American meeting in Paris from May 7–12. Dulles no longer hesitated in his support for Diem. By defeating the Binh Xuyen and proving his ability to survive, Diem had at last also conquered the growing doubts of his American protectors. Dulles obviously enjoyed the opportunity of taking a firm stand against French colonialist intrigues in favor of Washington's brave and clever protégé at Saigon. He extracted concessions ranging from the recall of Frenchmen who had actively opposed Diem to the early and complete withdrawal of all French troops should Diem so desire. French acceptance of these demands was made easier when Dulles agreed to Washington's recall of officials who had caused friction with the French, a condition which, incidentally, Washington never fulfilled. As a matter of fact, the only American withdrawn from Saigon was the man who had consistently tried to reduce Franco-American friction—Ambassador Collins. Washington's renewed confidence in Diem was unequivocally expressed by its new ambassador, G. Frederick Reinhardt, who said on May 27 that he had come to carry out U.S. policy in support of the government under Premier Ngo Dinh Diem.[22]

French representation in Saigon was also due for a change. On May 20, General Ely demanded to be relieved. He left Saigon on June 20. Diem took this opportunity to insist that henceforth France be represented not by a high commissioner but by an ambassador acceptable to his government. Paris, still not reconciled to "total independence," long resisted this reasonable demand.

Another year elapsed before the departure of the Expeditionary Corps removed the last vestiges of French "presence" from Vietnam. On May 20, 1955, the French command agreed to retire its troops from the Saigon-Cholon area. On July 2, 1955, the dependence of the Vietnamese Army on the French High Command at last came to an end. By then, the Expeditionary Corps, now concentrated in the vicinity of Cape St. Jacques, had been reduced from 175,000 to 30,000 men. Negotiations held in August, 1955, failed to produce agreement on the early withdrawal of all French troops, but finally the French did agree to honor the promise made at Geneva. The last French soldier left South Vietnam on April 28, 1956, the day on which the French High Command for Indochina was officially dissolved.

Direct and effective French interference, however, had already ended in May, 1955. This meant that the remaining sect forces, deprived of French support, either had to submit or fight and risk total defeat. Having learned that submission was the road to political limbo, they decided to stake everything on the slim chance that armed resistance might still bring about Diem's fall. Diem dealt with them separately. Since most of the military contingents of the Cao Dai had joined the government with the Generals The and Phuong, the problem of how to end the Cao Dai's political autonomy, although a delicate one because of its religious implications, required caution rather than strong military action. On October 5, 1955, General Phuong with some of his former military units went to the Cao Dai headquarters at Tay Ninh and disarmed Pham Cong Tac's 300-man papal guard, arrested his two daughters on charges of corruption and exploitation of the people, and some days later announced that he had deposed the Cao Dai pope. In February, 1956, Tac fled to Cambodia, where he died soon afterward. As was to be expected, Diem eventually rid himself of Phuong also, thereby eliminating the military leadership of the Cao Dai as well.

The liquidation of the Hoa Hao turned out to be a tougher problem. Diem, before sending out his army to fight the Hoa Hao, made one more attempt to buy its leaders. Its four rival chiefs—Generalissimo Tran Van Soai, General Lam Thanh Nguyen, General Nguyen Gia Ngo, and Bacut (Le Quang Vinh)—were not all of one mind when, on May 24, they received an offer of 100 million piasters (about $1.2 million at the black-market rate) to rally to Diem. But the offer was rejected, not without misgivings on the part of some. The Hoa Hao leaders declared war on the government, but knowing that they were no match for the National Army in open battle, they abandoned their posts and bases after setting fire to their huts and stores and prepared for guerrilla warfare. The government's troops started their offensive on June 5. Five Hoa Hao battalions surrendered immediately, and on June 18, General Nguyen Gia Ngo once again rallied to the government, this time for good—that is, until he joined the officers' conspiracy that overthrew Diem. Generalissimo Soai massed his troops near the Cambodian border, where he was joined by the Generals Hinh and Vy. But the government troops dispersed the Hoa Hao forces, and on June 19, all three generals fled to Cambodia. Their colleague Lam Thanh Nguyen decided to surrender. Hoa Hao resistance was reduced to guerrilla operations conducted by bands of the fanatical Bacut, but these ended when Bacut was trapped and arrested in April, 1956. He was publicly beheaded at Cantho on July 13, 1956.

The end of the Binh Xuyen had already come in October, 1955. After months of leeches and mosquitoes in the marshes and tidal waters of Rung Sat, and of growing despair, Le Van Vien's troops, surrounded and weakened, were attacked by the Army and wiped out in a campaign that lasted four weeks. The Binh Xuyen soldiers who survived were captured or dispersed. Their chief succeeded in escaping to France, where he settled down to enjoy the riches he had amassed while serving the French and Bao Dai. Thus ended the military history of the political-religious sects of Vietnam.

8

October, 1955, was also the month when another rotten relic of Vietnam's past—the monarchy, together with its last, unworthy representative, Bao Dai—was thrown on the junk heap of history. Bao Dai's fate was sealed when it became clear that the French no longer guided the destiny of Vietnam. Bao Dai knew that the Americans, at best willing to tolerate him as an absent and nominal ruler, would never defend him if Diem decided that he must go.

If Diem had not already decided in June, 1954, that he would one day remove Bao Dai, he certainly made up his mind after April, 1955. Diem lost no time and used every trick he knew in his campaign against Bao Dai. On May 15, he abolished the Imperial Guard; its 5,000 men became the 11th and 42nd Infantry Regiments of the National Army. Next, Diem deprived Bao Dai of his extensive crown lands. Then, on June 15, Diem got the archaic Council of the Royal Family at Hue to strip Bao Dai of all prerogatives and to propose that Diem be elected president. On July 7, the first anniversary of his installation as prime minister, Diem announced that a national referendum to decide the future form of government would be held on October 23, 1955.

The one-sided "election campaign" that followed and the methods employed to assure an almost unanimous vote for Diem showed "such cynical disregard for decency and democratic principles that even the Viet Minh professed to be shocked. . . . The government-controlled press proceeded to overwhelm [Bao Dai] with scurrilous abuse. . . . In addition police agents and canvassers went from door to door explaining the unpleasant consequences which failure to vote would be likely to entail."[23]

No one doubted what the outcome of the referendum would be. On October 22, Bao Dai even boasted that he could predict the number of votes that Diem had decided would be his.[24] But even Bao Dai did not foresee that the votes cast would in some cases exceed the number of names on the electoral roll.[25] Thus the 450,000 Saigon voters cast 605,000 votes, which the authorities explained by saying that the people of adjacent communities had voted in Saigon. Diem received 98.2 per cent of all votes cast (5,721,735), and Bao Dai 1.1 per cent (63,017). As one Western observer remarked, "the referendum was not, and was not intended to be, an exercise in democratic procedures," but "a collective demonstration of loyalty to the ruling authority."[26]

The mass of the people had no reason to defend or commiserate with Bao Dai; the forces that surrounded him were totally discredited. France was no longer in a position to lend him support, and the United States was just beginning to praise Diem as a new hero of the "free world." Because Bao Dai knew all this, he had reacted to Diem's maneuvers too late and like a man weary of fighting a futile battle. He protested the holding of the referendum on October 15 and asked France, the United States, Great Britain, India, and even the Soviet Union not to support the Diem regime, indicating that it was an obstacle to the peaceful reunification of Vietnam called for in the Geneva agreements.[27] On October 18 he made the vain gesture of dismissing Diem. The next day he denounced the "police methods" of Diem's "dictatorship" and warned the Vietnamese people, somewhat prophetically, "against a regime that was bound to lead them to ruin, famine, and war,"[28] a message which, like Bao Dai's dismissal of Diem, Saigon censorship kept from the Vietnamese people. Ultimately Bao Dai resigned himself to the loss of his position and settled for the unhampered enjoyment of life, which was probably all he had ever wanted.

Diem, too, had achieved his goal—total fulfillment of his political aspirations. On October 26, 1955, he was proclaimed President of the new Republic of Vietnam. Supreme power was all he had ever asked of life. Having achieved it neither surprised him nor made him humble. He was apparently convinced that his rise to power was simply a case of virtue and merit being justly rewarded.

But what did his victory portend for the future of Vietnam? By overcoming the opposition of the French, the Army, the sects, and Bao Dai, Diem had done nothing more than lay a foundation and gain time for building a viable state. The more difficult task still lay ahead of him. Success or failure in building a state able to win the allegiance of the people would decide the fate of South Vietnam when the expected attempt to unify the country under the sign of Communism got under way. Now Diem had to show whether anti-Communist nationalism had at last found a leader who was a match for Ho Chi Minh.

9

Ho Chi Minh had returned to Hanoi in October, 1954, after an absence of almost eight years spent in the jungles and mountains of the Viet Bac as the leader of a revolutionary war. But these long, hard years had not broken him, nor had they weakened his hold on his government and the people. In returning to Hanoi, Ho Chi Minh faced none of the difficulties of his antagonist in Saigon. There was no one to question Ho's right to supreme leadership and no real opposition. His control of the military, police, administration, and mass organizations was near total. There were no sects in the North to threaten the regime. The Catholic militias that had fought the Vietminh had disbanded and joined the exodus to the South; the French who caused Diem such trouble in Saigon were out of Hanoi before Ho's return.

The last French troops left Hanoi on October 9. Both the transfer of governmental authority and the replacement of the French garrison by Vietminh troops were effected without friction. Vietminh civil guards had begun to arrive in Hanoi on October 3, and Ha Dong, adjacent to Hanoi, had been handed over to detachments of the 308th Vietminh Division on October 6. These and other troops were assembled in the suburbs of Hanoi on October 9. They marched into the city on October 10, and in an impressive display of military strength celebrated their victory over the French. But there were no frenetic outbursts of joy. Peace was welcome to all, but too many of the people had reason to fear the future.

Like the Catholic provinces in the southern delta, Hanoi also witnessed a mass exodus of persons who feared for their lives under a regime that no longer disguised its Communist orientation. These refugees included not only collaborators and profiteers but also officials, professors, and students, journalists and artists who had voiced anti-Communist sentiments, businessmen who had the wisdom to foresee their eventual expropriation, and the many dependents of National Army personnel. Yet many members of the native middle class—shopkeepers, small merchants, lawyers, doctors, and other professionals—stayed rather than give up their established lives.

No organized festivities greeted the returning Vietminh leaders. They arrived in Hanoi unannounced and unseen. The first one to appear publicly was Giap, who, on October 12, inspected the Vietminh garrison that had replaced the French at the citadel. The next leader to be heard of, although he was not seen by the public, was Ho Chi Minh himself, who, on October 17, greeted the first official visitor to his "liberated" capital, Indian Prime Minister

Nehru, who stopped over briefly at Hanoi on his way to Peking. Not until January 1, 1955, did Ho Chi Minh show himself to the people, when for five and a half hours he watched one of those interminable parades which seems to instill Communists with a special sense of power. Throughout it all, Ho never stopped waving to the marchers and the applauding crowds estimated at two hundred thousand. It was the best show the Party had ever staged, but it was also the last for a long time to come at which waves of popular enthusiasm rolled so spontaneously toward the assembled dignitaries.

Hard times lay ahead for the people of North Vietnam. Though colonialism was dead, misery and unfreedom continued to be their lot. And amid the political conflicts that these conditions were bound to produce, terror remained the chief official weapon against popular discontent.

Some of the problems of the country no doubt were the results of eight years of war and of the partition of Vietnam. The North would henceforth be deprived of the vital food reserves of the South. There is no doubt that the Communist leaders of the North had the intelligence and courage to attack the staggering problems they had inherited, and it would be ridiculous to say that they were not concerned about the material conditions of the people. But their desperate efforts to secure enough food were subordinated to their chief concern—the radical transformation of society according to what both they and their enemies called the "Marxist" blueprint. Regardless of all suffering and terror, North Vietnam had to be turned into a "socialist" state immediately, one in which neither economic difficulties nor social discontent would ever challenge the power of the ruling political group, the Communist Party.

10

The problems Ho Chi Minh faced after his return to Hanoi were not the petty ones that forced Ngo Dinh Diem to devote himself for one whole year to the negative task of mere survival. The troubles that began to bedevil Hanoi, far from being caused by a lack of strength, were the result of an excess of power, which in October, 1954, was nearly total.

The rebuilding of the country—the North had suffered more destruction than the South—demanded superhuman sacrifices. The railroad between Hanoi and the Chinese border, for instance, was rebuilt in less than six months, a gigantic task involving the recruitment of 80,000 workers. The conditions under which this "voluntary" work force labored were in many respects as bad as those of the "coolies" of the colonial era. The superhuman sacrifices and suffering demanded of the people were due to the excessive power and ambition of the leaders, which led them to look on rapid reconstruction as only a first step toward their real goal— nothing less than the immediate transformation of the country's social structure, of a nation's way of life. This economically underdeveloped country whose mainstay was its peasantry was to be turned into a modern industrial state. The Vietminh leaders intended to accomplish in a few years that which in more advanced nations had taken decades.

Treading in the bloody footsteps of the Soviet revolution, the Hanoi regime turned on the peasants, taking from them more than they could spare, keeping them overtaxed and undernourished. None of the meager imports the country could afford and little of the foreign aid it received went to alleviate the misery of the masses. Industrial equipment took priority over such badly needed things as drugs and textiles and even food. The regime felt fully justified in maintaining the lowest possible living standard for the sake of getting industries built as rapidly as possible. Once again, the end justified the means.

If this were the whole story, the course chosen by the leaders of the North, although certainly not above criticism, could not be wholly condemned. The truth, however, is that other approaches were available. There was little sense in trying to industrialize rapidly. Factories could have been built at a slower rate. Industrialization at the expense of the people was not dictated by circumstances. It was imposed by the leadership's political philosophy and by its preoccupation with power. They wanted to create social conditions on which their power monopoly could rest securely. This meant that old classes had to be abolished and new ones created through the systematic intervention of the state in the country's economy.

With a touch of megalomania which was in no way diminished by their victory over the French, the Vietminh leaders embarked upon their self-imposed task, a truly monstrous one, since even its partial realization required inhuman methods. The blueprint called for control of the economy by the same men who controlled the state. Mines, factories, new industries, small private enterprise, handicraft production—all had to be nationalized or turned into "cooperatives."

The extent to which this economic policy was motivated by a desire for absolute political control became apparent in the measures in agriculture, which made no economic sense. The chief purpose of the so-called agrarian reform in North Vietnam was to bring all agricultural production under state control. This was achieved mainly through terror and produced the first and only serious wave of popular opposition against the regime. At the end of 1956, when it seemed as if Diem had at last cleared the way for positive action, Ho was in deeper trouble with his people than at any time since his coming to power in 1945. And his troubles, unlike Diem's, were entirely of his own making.

11

Ho's pitiless exploitation of labor could not solve all problems of reconstruction, among them one dealt by the parting blow of the retiring Franco-Vietnamese administration. Under the direction of Diem's Committee for the Defense of the North, everything movable of any value, both public and private property, was shipped from Haiphong to the South. Broadcasting stations, railroad repair shops, and harbor installations were dismantled, post offices, libraries, and laboratories were stripped, radium was removed from X-ray machines, factories were cleaned of machinery, tools, raw materials, and finished products. The anti-Communist Vietnamese authorities did not feel obliged to honor the pledge of the French at Geneva that all public institutions and services were to be handed over to the Hanoi regime in working order. The French Government, however, did honor it, and subsequently paid Hanoi the sum of 265 million francs in reparations.[29]

The Vietnamese who fled to the South may have felt that the removal of goods was justified, since they themselves left behind everything they owned. But the authorities in the South never even attempted to use their spoils to compensate individuals for the losses they had suffered.

The number of those who lost almost everything was staggering. Most of the 900,000 persons who came to the South must be regarded as genuine political refugees. Official statistics say that of the total number, 794,000 were Catholics. Although it is impossible to determine their exact number—it may have been as low as 600,000[30]—there is no doubt that they accounted for more than 60 per cent of the total. The Communists have claimed that going to the South was not a personal decision for many of the Catholics, that they left under pressure of the community and as a group. The priests were accused of having spread the word that God had gone South, that those who remained in the North would risk losing their souls and probably also their lives, since the North would be destroyed by American bombs. If these Communist charges and the instructions by Hanoi to treat the Catholics with prudence proved that the regime was embarrassed by the mass exodus, there is nevertheless reason to believe that Communist discomfort was mixed with relief. The regime was thus rid of a great many implacable enemies.

The mass exodus had also made available close to half a million acres of excellent rice land, which was promptly distributed. Still rice production declined. And although the Soviet-bloc countries began to replace much of the equipment "stolen" by the authorities of the South, it took from one to two years before many of the public services began to function normally.

As Communist control over the economy and the people was being consolidated, the regime, in its efforts to extend this control over French-owned property, proceeded with great circumspection. In 1954, about 150 French-owned companies were still operating in the North, including coal mines in Hongay and Campha, cement and glass works in Haiphong, cotton mills at Nam Dinh, breweries and distilleries at Hanoi, and ship yards and port services at Haiphong. The water and electricity works of both Hanoi and Haiphong were French-owned, as was the Yunnan Railway and all public transportation.

In a letter to the French Government written immediately after the end of the Geneva conference, Foreign Minister Pham Van Dong gave assurances of the unhampered operation of French economic enterprises and cultural institutions, but he was ambiguous about French interests in cases of requisition or expropriation.[31] The efforts to safeguard private French business interests and to maintain a maximum of economic cooperation between France and Hanoi were assiduously promoted in political contacts between the French and Hanoi governments through the mission headed by Jean Sainteny, one of the authors of the Franco-Vietminh agreement of March, 1946. Overestimating his skills, Sainteny apparently was convinced that with the end of the war, Franco-Vietminh cooperation had again become possible. The 1946 failure did not dismay him. He accepted his new assignment and installed himself in Hanoi on October 8. Ten days later he had the first of many meetings with Ho Chi Minh, who remained friendly but became less conciliatory as time went on. Developments soon proved that the Communists had never intended to let the French keep what they had, and certainly would not allow new French investments. The regime soon dropped its short-term practical considerations of cooperation with French business in favor of its strict and narrow economic doctrine. It was decided that socialism had to be established immediately, and totally independent of the capitalist world.

This decision was partially forced upon Hanoi by the French, who also pursued a contradictory policy on Franco-Vietminh economic cooperation. Neither French official policy nor French business made any real effort to persuade Hanoi to forgo its economic orthodoxy even temporarily. Many French firms had dismantled their factories before the French Army evacuated Haiphong. French businessmen feared, not without reason, that French firms operating in the North might be subject to American reprisals. Furthermore, they rightly suspected that ultimately the Communists would expropriate all existing and all new private investments, foreign as well as native. They were cautious all along and were never in any real danger of being trapped.

On the other hand, the Communists did not try very hard to persuade French business to invest in a Communist state. They were unreasonable in their negotiations and petty in their treatment of French technicians, whom they needed to put mines and factories back in operation. Yet they abused them. Consequently, French technicians left and French companies continued to remove from their plants whatever was worth transporting. The regime, even before it turned to Peking and Moscow for economic assistance, was rapidly moving toward outright expropriation. All French companies were nationalized before the end of 1955, and, with two notable exceptions—the coal mines and public transportation in Hanoi—without compensation. When the hopes of the French of preserving their business interests in the North died, the Sainteny mission became pointless and it, too, gradually expired.

Even before the last French technicians had left Hanoi, the regime had begun to replace them with Chinese and Russian experts whose arrival marked the beginning of Chinese and Soviet aid. The first aid agreement with Peking, concluded in December, 1954,[32] provided for the delivery of road, railroad, postal and telegraph, and water-works repair equipment. Chinese technicians supervised the rebuilding of the Hanoi-Langson Railroad. But aid on a much vaster scale and over longer periods was needed. To obtain such aid, Ho Chi Minh, accompanied by his ministers of finance, industry, agriculture, education, and health, went to Peking on June 22, 1955. On July 7, the two governments announced that Peking would extend Hanoi economic aid in the amount of 800 million yuan (about $200 million).

From Peking, Ho and his party went to Moscow, and on July 18, the Soviet Union announced that it would grant Hanoi 400 million rubles (about $100 million) in economic aid. (The amount of military aid from Peking and Moscow was, of course, never made public.) Russia had already begun to assist Hanoi before this agreement. The Soviets had supplied mining equipment, enabling Hanoi to operate the old mines and open a new one at Quang Tri. Of greater importance, however, was a three-cornered deal between the Soviet Union, Burma, and Hanoi at the beginning of 1955, by which North Vietnam received badly needed rice from Burma in return for Russian industrial equipment. Without the Burmese rice, the North undoubtedly would have suffered widespread famine in 1955.

Apart from pharmaceutical products and assistance in organizing medical services, the rice deal was the only instance where aid was of direct benefit to the suffering people. All other assistance from China, Russia, and later from the other "fraternal countries" went toward reconstruction and industrialization.

Even after the threat of famine was averted by relatively good harvests in 1955 and 1956, the diet of the people remained woefully inadequate and consumer goods virtually unavailable. The new industries, even producers of consumer goods, worked chiefly for export. Profits from the steadily growing exports went largely toward the acquisition of industrial equipment. The regime refused to import textiles, shoes, or essential household utensils and allocated a minimum of its resources to their production at home. For years the people went in rags, undernourished and without medical care. And when goods, medical services, and even some recreation and entertainment became available, they were largely limited to the privileged minority in official and Party positions. For the rest, life remained dreary, and for the politically persecuted it was worse than under the French. The only product dished out in truly generous helpings was propaganda.

The ruling elite and the lower echelons of Party and administration had good reason to be content, and they took pride in their country's remarkable industrial achievement. Some of North Vietnam's modern factories compare favorably with modern production sites anywhere in the world. Even before the Soviet Union in 1960 granted Hanoi a long-term loan for forty-three new industrial plants, North Vietnam was well on the road toward becoming the most industrialized country of Southeast Asia. Yet despite the phenomenal advances, austerity was to remain the lot of the masses for a long time to come.

Thanks to foreign aid, Hanoi also made rapid advances in the training of skilled personnel for its factories, public services, and the many new institutions through which the state directs and controls the country's economy. Thousands of students and workers have gone to China and Russia for training in plants, technical schools, and universities. Still larger numbers were trained at home by foreign experts. Hanoi remained short of skilled specialists and professionals, and hundreds of young people continued to be sent to Chinese and Russian universities. But as in many other respects, North Vietnam wished to progress without having to rely on China and Russia, and it has almost succeeded in making itself independent of this type of aid. By 1963, the regime could boast not only that the bulk of its industry was being run by native technicians, but also of having its own banking and trade experts, its own statisticians, and thousands of new young doctors, researchers, and teachers. Less than ten years after the initiation of its ambitious industrialization program, North Vietnam was producing items which are not as yet being produced in the South: machine tools, electric motors, office equipment, bicycle tires, and even small ocean craft.

12

The impressive industrial achievements of Hanoi again offer a lesson which Western critics have difficulty in absorbing, namely that the Communists are capable of achieving success under the most adverse conditions, and that they are able to overcome the grave errors and basic faults of their economic policy by sheer energy, persistence, and above all ruthlessness.

But persistence and ruthlessness failed to produce spectacular results in the vast field of small-scale, nonagricultural activity in which the Vietnamese had always excelled. In this area, too, the prime motive was the elimination of a property-owning middle class and the establishment of government control over this sector of the economy. One of the means employed was political terror. Known or suspected enemies of the regime belonging to this class were imprisoned or sent to labor camps and their possessions confiscated. Many more went out of business because the goods in which they traded were not available, and still others were ruined through excessive taxation. The aim was to abolish every vestige of a free market and to dictate the prices at which the small producer could buy and sell. But because the government was also interested in maintaining local production, outright expropriation of small enterprises was avoided. Under the slogan "peaceful socialization," the regime turned most small enterprises into joint state and private enterprises. "Capitalists" whose skills were needed were kept in their former positions and eventually ended up as salaried employees of the state. This group of businessmen— the "national bourgeoisie," "former exploiters"—ceased to exist. Statistically they have become part of the class of "manual and intellectual workers," whose number was given as 750,000 at the end of 1961.[33]

Small traders and artisans fared differently. Labeled "toilers" rather than "exploiters," they were regarded as part of the working class. It was thought that their adherence to the Communist state could be brought about through a change in their social status. "Individual workers" were to be turned into "collective workers" by the formation of handicraft "cooperatives." Such cooperatives did not result in greater production, but they altered the social position of these workers, chiefly by putting a stop to their freedom to buy, sell, and produce as they pleased. They were now under state control. Yet according to an authoritative official source, these people continued to cling to their old habits of private ownership, resisting cooperative production and maintaining "a more or less spontaneous tendency to capitalism."[34] This complaint was even truer of the small traders, who, although classified as "toilers," fared considerably worse than the handicraft workers. Although many were ruined by taxation and by state-owned retail outlets, the attempt to transform them into members of the "working class" failed. At most half joined cooperatives, and only about 5 per cent changed from trade to production.[35] The real extent of the regime's failure to integrate this segment into its socialist economy was revealed during the food crises of 1960 and 1962. Strict rationing in the cities and pressure in the villages for greater food deliveries at official prices led to widespread peasant hoarding, to the unauthorized slaughtering of livestock, and to clandestine sales of food. According to an official paper, the "free" markets in Hanoi attracted as many as 6,000 persons who gave up their old professions for trade.[36]

Even more distressing for the masters of the North than this "resurgence of capitalism" was its cause: the regime's failure to provide enough food for the population, which was increasing at the annual rate of 3.5 per cent, or about 600,000. The North had been a food-deficit area long before it became Communist, and feeding its population without imports would have been difficult under any conditions. The solution would lie in increasing the productivity of the available rice lands through improved production methods and incentives for the peasants. In 1955, North Vietnam harvested 3.6 million tons of rice. The regime hoped to more than double this amount for 1960. The population increase alone necessitated an additional 200,000 tons annually. But in 1960, instead of the projected 7.6 million tons, the harvest was a mere 4.1 million. The main reason for this spectacular failure was the regime's policy toward the more than four-fifths of the population living in the country's 15,000 villages. The story of the land reform in Communist North Vietnam is a story of unbelievable terror, disastrous mismanagement on all Party levels, and of crisis brought on by widespread popular discontent which the regime could master only through a combination of brutal force and hasty political retreat.

The first steps in the socialization of agriculture, decided upon in March, 1953, called for the redistribution of land in favor of landless agricultural workers and poor peasants, a very indirect move toward collectivization. But the Party knew that the road toward "socialized agriculture" was a long one and that a number of political problems would have to be solved before more direct steps could be taken, among them how to abolish the landlords and the basically anti-Communist class of the rich peasants, and also of how to create a mass basis for the regime by winning the gratitude and support of the mass of landless and poor peasants. But the Communists foresaw that once all land was divided into more or less equal holdings, most families would still not own enough. It was then that the peasants would have to be convinced of the necessity of collectivization.

The political motivations underlying the agrarian reform were revealed most tellingly by the manner in which the land was distributed. The rural population was divided into five categories: landlords, rich peasants, middle peasants, poor peasants, and landless agricultural laborers. To eliminate the first two groups as a social class, it was not enough to reduce them to the status of middle or poor peasants through partial expropriation. Since they were enemies of Communism and of collectivized agriculture, they had to be eliminated from village life, if need be physically. Consequently they were accused of all sorts of crimes, tried, sentenced to prison or forced labor, and some to death. Their physical elimination brought an additional advantage: those imprisoned or executed were completely expropriated and thus more land was made available for distribution to those whom the Communists wished to woo.

Nothing in the history of Communist persecution can rival the scheme of North Vietnam to rid itself of as many peasants as possible who owned more than a couple of acres of land. As a prelude to the ugly spectacle of public trials and punishment, a hate campaign against the "rich" was organized by special Party cadres. Trials were conducted by specially created People's Agricultural Reform Tribunals composed of the poor and the landless. Since more than 60 per cent of all land consisted of landholdings of around 1 acre, there was an embarrassing dearth of "rich" landlords. The necessary quota of victims to be tried by the Agricultural Tribunals could be found only through the promotion of owners of 2–4 acre parcels to the status of "landlord." And in order to obtain sentences, crimes had to be invented and charges leveled, even against supporters of the Vietminh. Of course, many landowners had cruelly exploited and mistreated the poor, but the Party was not concerned with justice. Its aim was the eradication of a social class, and to this end it mobilized hate and greed and personal vengeance. The procedure was designed to gain enough land to make distribution worthwhile and also to make the poor and the landless accomplices of the regime in the crimes committed against the "rich."

The first wave of land reform rolled over a few provinces in 1953, but fear that the action might get out of control and harm the war effort made the Vietminh decide to call a halt. But in 1955, after the war was over, land reform through "mass mobilization" was resumed. According to an official announcement of December 13, 1955, more than 100,000 persons had taken part in trials of landlords in villages near Hanoi. The campaign was conducted "with the utmost ferocity"[37] in several more "waves," lasting until the fall of 1956, when it was called off, apparently before the murderous momentum of the special cadres had exhausted itself.

Some aspects of the campaign had been causing concern among the leaders in Hanoi for some time. On August 17, Ho Chi Minh in a letter to his "compatriots in the country" admitted "errors" in the execution of the land reform and promised "corrections." On August 24, the Party paper *Nhan Dan* reported that among those wrongly classified, convicted, and executed were former Vietminh fighters and even Party members. At the end of October, the head of the campaign, Truong Chinh, was dismissed as Party secretary and replaced by Ho Chi Minh himself. The minister of agriculture was also dismissed. Party and government began to indulge in an orgy of self-criticism. The purpose of the "Campaign for the Rectification of Errors" had already been spelled out in Ho Chi Minh's letter of August 17—the re-establishment of the rights and prerogatives of those who had been victims of "erroneous judgment."[38] On November 1, the government announced the release of 12,000 persons from prisons and labor camps, and on November 8, the People's Agricultural Reform Tribunals were officially abolished.

It is generally believed that between 10,000 and 15,000 persons were killed in the course of the "erroneous" execution of the land-reform program, and another 50,000 to 100,000 deported and imprisoned. Many of those arrested were released, though not all regained their former rights and possessions; but the Rectification of Errors campaign had its limitations, for, as Ho Chi Minh grimly remarked, "One cannot wake the dead."[39]

What the agrarian reform had failed to accomplish was to satisfy the need for land of those for whose benefit it allegedly was undertaken. The regime was able to give 1.5 million landless and poor peasant families slightly more than 1 acre each. Also, one buffalo was given to groups of thirteen families each. Welcome as these gifts were, they were not enough to turn the poor peasants into enthusiastic supporters of the regime. On the contrary, the injustices and atrocities produced widespread resentment, unrest, and eventually open rebellion. The brutality of the cadres embittered not only the victims but also those lucky enough to have escaped persecution. In addition there was discontent over the high taxes and the increasing pressure for bigger and bigger food deliveries to the state at greatly depressed prices.

The regime, long deaf to the voices of dissatisfaction, began to listen to them in the summer of 1956, suddenly aware of the dangers that threatened it. But its warnings in August and its measures in October came too late. Open rebellion broke out early in November in the province of Nghe An, a region long known for its strong pro-Vietminh sentiments. Hanoi immediately acted to suppress the spontaneous insurrection, entrusting this bloody task to the 325th Division. Western observers claim that about 1,000 peasants were killed or wounded between November 10 and 20, and several thousand arrested and deported.[40] Smaller outbreaks occurred in other parts of the country. By putting an end to the land-reform campaign, the regime undoubtedly prevented other rebellions from breaking out, but not until late February, 1957, did the government feel secure enough to withdraw its regular army units from the affected areas and hand over the maintenance of order to local militias.

XVII

Toward the Second
Indochina War

1

IN 1956, THE COMMUNIST REGIME of North Vietnam was heading toward a serious political crisis. For Diem in the South, 1956 was the first year in which he was no longer threatened by rival forces. By the end of 1956, Diem had convinced both his admirers and critics of his ability to survive.

Diem, in eliminating the sects, ousting Bao Dai, and winning the withdrawal of the French Expeditionary Corps, seemed to meet South Vietnam's urgent need for an outstanding political leader. His presence revived hopes for the future of South Vietnam, hopes which for some years remained firmly linked to his name. But these hopes were stronger in the West, particularly in the United States, than in Vietnam itself. Indeed, the history of South Vietnam after 1954 cannot be divorced from the story of American acceptance of, enthusiasm for, and eventual disenchantment with Ngo Dinh Diem, whose fate ultimately was determined by the evolution of American political thinking during the nine years of his rule.

The story of American policy toward Diem illustrates the power of wishful thinking, the shortcomings of U.S. diplomacy, and U.S. ignorance of the most effective methods of fighting Communism. In principle no fault can be found with the decision to help South Vietnam survive as a non-Communist state, if that turned out to be what the people wanted. But whether or not this was the wish of the people could not be fairly determined in 1954. No free elections could have been held immediately after the Geneva conference. And more important, no real choice existed. The procolonial regime the people detested was on its way out and an alternative did not yet exist. Elections in 1954, therefore, would not have offered the people the chance to decide for themselves whether a non-Communist regime was preferable to the Communist regime of the Vietminh. To bring about such a choice was the main reason that the American people supported Washington's efforts to keep the anti-Communist, anticolonial Diem government in power and to help it build a viable state. The hope of most Americans for such an anti-Communist Vietnam was for a state that brought its people prosperity, social justice, and the gradual realization of the freedoms for which they had fought in the long struggle for independence. This, according to some Vietnamese nationalists, was the South's vocation, and only if these conditions were fulfilled could the South become viable, defensible, and worthy of survival. The South had to become what a dishonest propaganda in the West proclaimed it to be: free. No "free" Vietnam existed as yet. The American people would not have supported their government's policy of aiding South Vietnam after 1954 had they foreseen that the country, ruled by brutal and sterile dictatorships, could survive only if the United States went to war.

What makes this story so tragic is that a viable South Vietnam could have been built, the hold of the Communists on the people could have been broken, and a tragic war could have been avoided. Despite the ravages of the first Indochina War, the South economically was in better shape than the North. It had the potential for a food surplus and it had rubber plantations, but most important of all, it had plenty of land for the landless and the poor. The millions of poor, exploited peasants and tenants who looked toward a Vietminh victory could have been turned into supporters of a non-Communist regime. This could have been achieved through the recultivation and distribution of almost 1 million acres of abandoned rice land as well as a radical program of agrarian reform. In the Mekong Delta region, half the cultivated land was owned by 2.5 per cent of landlords, and 80 per cent of the land was worked by tenant farmers.[1] Diem himself had said repeatedly that he considered agrarian reform one of the most urgent tasks, and it therefore seemed inconceivable that he would reject land distribution.

In 1956, the regime seemed ready to begin the task of building a better and freer life for its people. Despite almost two years of civil disorder and political uncertainty, the threat of economic collapse had been averted. True, this had been made possible by massive U.S. assistance, but without some measure of resolve and administrative ability on the part of the regime it could not have been done so well and so quickly.

One universally acknowledged achievement of the Diem regime was its handling of the refugees from the North. By the end of 1957, at least 300,000 refugees had been settled in 300 new villages, most of which were expected to become self-sufficient; by the end of 1959, however, only about 50 had.[2] The solution of the refugee problem was of course made possible by U.S. financial assistance. Between 1954 and 1956, a substantial portion of the total U.S. aid to Vietnam went into the care and final settlement of the refugees. The success of the program moreover was greatly facilitated by two local factors: the availability of land abandoned during the war years and the presence of competent, energetic leaders, largely Catholic priests, among the refugees themselves. This local leadership compensated for the many shortcomings on both higher and lower administrative levels as well as for some of the incredible bureaucratic delays in the distribution of authorized funds from Washington. Their remarkable success in organizing self-help among the refugees was probably the outstanding feature of the entire resettlement effort.

2

The solution of the refugee problem showed what a combination of local leadership, natural wealth, and American assistance could do. The very success in this area emphasizes the poor performance of the Diem regime in tackling the economic, social, administrative, and political problems of the country.

National survival dictated economic, social, and political measures designed to win the loyalty of the people, to make them determined to defend the regime against armed uprisings. The degree of popular support enjoyed by Diem cannot be easily measured, but there is no doubt that between 1955 and 1957, he made some progress along these lines. Even some of his most implacable critics have admitted that, at least briefly, he enjoyed some popular support, which merely underscores that history offered Diem a real chance.

If the degree of support Diem enjoyed at home is uncertain, the support in the United States is not. American aid was vital for South Vietnam, and there were those in the United States who regarded aid not as a condition but rather as a substitute for popular support, as did Diem himself once he realized that he had not won over either the masses or the educated middle classes.

By 1960 it had become obvious that Diem was not using American aid to woo his people, though at one time it seemed as if under his direction anti-Communist nationalism might become a force capable of counteracting the attraction of the Vietminh. Instead, the harvest of Diem's policy was popular discontent. But how did he succeed in retaining U.S. support for years after his political deficiencies had become obvious? And why did so many well-informed, politically astute, concerned Americans continue to defend him for so many years?

In order to understand more easily the enduring faith of his American defenders, it might prove helpful to divide the nine years of Diem's rule into three periods. The first lasted roughly a year, during which Diem against all expectations succeeded in maintaining himself in office and in laying the foundations of his rule. The belief that all was well and that a miracle had happened took firm roots only during the second period, which probably lasted no more than two years. Any lingering doubt about the stability of Diem's position disappeared almost completely in the first year of this second period, and although the regime was beginning to manifest disturbing political tendencies, it was during this period that the belief in its ability to act constructively was born.

It is hard to say exactly when the third period began. In Vietnam itself, disenchantment was widespread already in 1957; in the United States, many former admirers of Diem ceased to support him after 1960. In official American circles, however, the conviction that Diem was a failure began to take root only after the so-called Buddhist crisis early in 1963.

American optimism about Diem was nourished chiefly by the very need for it. Only good news from Saigon could sustain the belief that the miracle of Vietnam was real and not a mirage. This need for good news prompted worried anti-Communist observers to overlook or at least play down the shortcomings of Diem that threatened to make his achievements worthless.

An early instance of this tendency to gloss over Diem's faults was the reluctance of most supporters to admit that his approach to agrarian reform was a political disaster. Instead of being criticized for the inadequacy of his program, Diem was praised for the careful manner in which he tackled the delicate issue of agrarian reform. His modest proposals, said those of his supporters who regarded a radical land reform as the most urgent measure in the struggle against the Vietminh, were only a beginning.

The land-reform program was inadequate in several respects. It was started too late, was carried out too slowly, did not go far enough, and its provisions for payment by the peasants who were given land created unnecessary hardships and were a serious political blunder. Nothing whatever was done during 1954. Only in 1955, after months of prodding by American advisers, including Ambassador Collins, did Diem take the first cautious steps to reduce land rents, safeguard the rights of tenants through contracts, and provide land for the resettlement of refugees from the North.[3] As to the much more important problem of land transfers from large owners to tenants, nothing at all was done until October, 1956, when, by ordinance, 700,000 hectares were made available for distribution. Still worse than the delay, however, was the manner in which the government embarked on this crucial task, thereby revealing a complete lack of understanding for the disastrous political consequences that failure to act forcefully was bound to produce.

All figures, no matter how impressive at first glance, bear out the disheartening inadequacy of the transfer program. The government boasted that 1.725 million acres of cultivated, abandoned land had been made available for transfer. But this was only 20 per cent of the total cultivated rice area. (Only rice land was subject to transfer.) Of these 20 per cent, less than two-thirds (1.062 million acres) had actually "changed hands" by 1962— six years after the institution of the program. Moreover, not all the land that had changed hands had gone to the poor peasants. Much of the land purchased from French owners was sold to the highest bidder. Diem and his American defenders proudly pointed to the 109,438 peasants—mostly tenants—who as of July, 1961, had benefited from the land transfers. But they neglected to say that more than 1 million tenants had received no land whatever.

The limited scope and lagging execution of the land-transfer program were not its only deficiencies. No less disastrous were the provisions for payment by the tenants for land that had in effect been theirs for years. In the Vietminh-controlled regions, the land of large absentee owners had been given to the tenants. Diem's transfers by and large constituted nothing but a legalization of an existing situation. The only change produced was that most of the so-called beneficiaries now had to pay for land which they had long considered their own. Payment had to be made in six yearly installments, too short a period for most; titles were provisional. The result was that those who received land were as dissatisfied with the land-reform program as was the vast majority who did not. Peasant dissatisfaction became the main theme of Communist propaganda in the South.

As to rents and security of tenancy through contracts, Diem's agrarian reform no doubt provided some relief for the more than 1 million tenants, most of whom had been completely at the mercy of the landlords. But the lack of impartial enforcement agencies greatly reduced the benefits the peasants might have derived from these reforms. Though conditions improved, the failure to provide for democratic representation of the tenants meant that the rural population continued to be victimized by landlords and government officials. The legal rent limit of 25 per cent of the crop was widely disregarded. Tenants paying a mere 30 per cent considered themselves fortunate. Even after 1960, when the battle for peasant support became the overriding political issue, abusive treatment of peasants remained widespread. Rents as high as 60 per cent of the crop were not uncommon.

Diem was unable to see that Vietnam's national revolution could be completed and the last vestiges of colonialism wiped out only through radical economic and social reforms. Since exploitation under a feudal land regime had been the dominant reality of colonialism, the peasant masses equated it with landlordism. The landlords, far from being eliminated, were in fact more than any other group able to assert their interests under Diem. Dissatisfied with the provisions for compensation for expropriated land, they first succeeded in radically curtailing the scope of the program and later in sabotaging it altogether.

But was landlord opposition alone responsible for Diem's totally inadequate agrarian reform? It would be folly to believe that Diem could not have broken landlord resistance to a really meaningful program of land reform. Why, then, did he neglect a task which even moderate "bourgeois" nineteenth-century reformers recognized as a necessary precondition for the development of democracy? The answer could not be more simple: Diem was too much of a conservative to discharge his historical mission.

The banality of this explanation makes it difficult to realize that therein lies the key to Diem's failure. Diem was radical only as a nationalist and anti-Communist. His nationalism did not include the idea of changing the social structure created by colonialism. Diem's concept of a "free" Vietnam did not encompass the social aspirations of the masses, and as it turned out it was also hostile to the political aspirations of the elite. Once the French were gone and the Communists had been kept at bay, South Vietnam, as far as Diem was concerned, was by definition "free." His nationalism had little social content and his anti-Communism none at all. Had Diem understood that mass support was indispensable in his struggle against Communism, he would probably have eradicated landlordism. But Diem the conservative rejected revolutionary social change as a means of reducing the appeal of

Communism, and this rejection gradually led him to rely more and more on antidemocratic methods and naked force.

3

In 1956, Diem's defenders in the West could hardly have foreseen that his agrarian reform, never fully realized, would turn out to be not merely a beginning, as they had hoped, but the sum total of his social reforms. This sad truth became apparent to the people of Vietnam long before Diem's foreign admirers came to suspect it. The Vietnamese people cared little about the service Diem was allegedly rendering the "free world" by staying in power. They were concerned with what his regime was doing for them. They needed no expertise to measure the immediate value of his achievements. While in Vietnam disenchantment began to turn into hostility after 1956, American support for Diem continued to grow for some years. The United States by and large remained unaware that concern for the social and political aspirations of both the masses and the elite was steadily diminishing. What continued to matter to most Americans was that Diem was fighting the battle against Communism on an exposed front, that he had saved the South, that he had proved himself as anticolonialist as Ho Chi Minh, and that he had shown the people that in order to achieve full independence they did not have to support the Vietminh. This was a truly historic achievement, and for most Americans this alone counted in their decision whether or not to support him. No matter what the shortcomings of Diem's regime, as long as it seemed effective in combating Communism, he remained a hero in the eyes of most Americans.

But some of Diem's supporters in the West were not fully convinced that the South was definitely saved, nor that he had given sufficient evidence of being the man to complete the still unfinished task. If Communism in the South were to be defeated permanently, Diem would have to prove that he was more than a determined anticolonialist. Without social and political reforms designed to gain and consolidate mass support for Diem or any other anti-Communist regime, the survival of the South was not assured. In the United States, Senator John F. Kennedy in June,

1956, concisely stated what would have to be done if Communism in South Vietnam was to be defeated: "What we must offer [the Vietnamese people] is a revolution—a political, economic, and social revolution far superior to anything the Communists can offer—far more peaceful, far more democratic, and far more locally controlled."

Yet Kennedy and even people with fewer illusions about Diem continued to support him long after disturbing news from Vietnam gave rise to the fear that the chance for the survival of the South was being dissipated. Conditions, it was argued, did not yet permit certain reforms, particularly reforms aimed at greater political freedom. Perhaps Diem was too timid and moving too slowly, and perhaps he was not yet sufficiently convinced of the need for reform, but once the time was ripe he would take whatever action was needed. Some suspected that Diem did not hold with the generally accepted meaning of terms like "democracy" and "social revolution," but most of his defenders tended to believe that conditions, not Diem himself, prevented the realization of his aims. To others the question of whether or not to continue to support Diem posed no dilemma at all. Democracy, they said, was impossible under existing conditions; reforms simply had to wait until the battle against the Communists was won. Diem needed more aid, particularly more military assistance. All else was unimportant for the time being. The United States had no choice but to support Diem even if he was dictatorial. Those who argued thus did not realize that they were accepting the discredited Communist dictum about the end justifying the means.

The history of the Diem regime, from its unexpected early triumphs to its inglorious end, had a lasting effect on American political thinking, which continued to determine the fate of Vietnam. The real lesson to be learned is not that the policy of supporting Diem beyond the initial years of his rule was a mistake. Much more important is the realization that the decision to stop supporting him signified no break with this policy. Diem was dropped not because he was a dictator but because his dictatorship had proved ineffective. There was and remains little or no awareness that the failure of the struggle against Communism was the result not of his personal shortcomings as a dictator but of the reactionary character of his regime.

4

Evidence of Diem's intention to fight Communism by building a dictatorial regime emerged only slowly and hence remained unconvincing for some years. There is no doubt that the strength and determination of the Communists justified temporary dictatorial measures if democracy was to have a chance in the South. Communist activities had to be curbed as long as they threatened the new regime, and the consolidation of this new regime through social and economic reforms could not be accomplished overnight. Force, sharply restricted and judiciously used within the context of a broad political strategy, should have been merely an adjunct of policy. A consistent anti-Communist doctrine required the advocacy and pursuit of political freedom, even if conditions demanded that freedom be denied to the Communists. The regime's pseudo-doctrine of "personalism" could never become a workable substitute for a genuine doctrine of political freedom and humanism. There could have been devoted cadres only if the youth, the intellectuals, and all anti-Communist groups had been allowed freely to participate in the political life of their country.

The Diem regime failed not only because it opposed the political aspirations of the Communists, but because it also trampled underfoot the aspirations of the entire people. Not less but more democracy, a basic condition of social justice, would have made the Diem regime politically effective against Communism.

It would of course be absurd to maintain that there was no difference between the regimes of the North and the South. Their aims were irreconcilable, their ideologies as different as day and night, and their political positions could not have been more divergent. But Diem pursued his goal, the eradication of Communism, with means copied from or identical with the Communists'. Diem's republic, says Robert Scigliano, was "for practical purposes a one-party state," which had "its political re-education camps, its Communist denunciation rallies, its ubiquitous propaganda extolling the leader and damning the enemy, its mass organizations."[4] Like the North, it also had its controlled elections, its secret police, and a constitution whose guarantees of civil liberties and political freedom were completely ignored. Here as there, opposition was not tolerated. The elected legislature was a tool of the government and the press was gradually reduced to blind praise and support of the leader.

One of the means employed by Diem in his efforts to obscure the true nature of his rule was controlled elections. Four such were held after the referendum of October, 1955, which ousted Bao Dai and made Diem president. A constituent assembly was elected on March 4, 1956, a national assembly on August 30, 1959, a presidential election was held on April 9, 1961, and a final assembly election on September 27, 1963. Like the October referendum, all the elections were poorly disguised exercises in totalitarian techniques. Both the North and the South, Scigliano has said, permitted elections only to the extent that they could control their results.[5]

Since mass approval of the regime was the real purpose of the elections, mass participation was a·vital concern. To achieve the desired voter turnout, the government fell back on intimidation by local officials and an army of civil servants. Fraud was used only as a last resort, yet it must have been rather common in view of the surprisingly big turnout in districts known to be under Communist control, such as the An Xuyen Province on the Camau Peninsula, where in 1959 more than 95 per cent of the people were reported to have voted, and in 1961 no less than 98 per cent —all of course for government candidates. In Saigon, the regime's inability to coerce an almost unanimously hostile population, and the desire to show the world a democratic façade, ruled out the more blatant measures of intimidation and fraud. Consequently, no more than 75 per cent of Saigon's registered citizens voted in the elections of 1961, as compared to 95 per cent in the rest of the country.

To make sure that only government supporters would be elected to the assembly, no others were allowed to run. Contests between candidates were generally encouraged, but the choices offered were meaningless, since every candidate, whether a member of an official government party or a so-called independent, was a firm supporter of the regime. Ngo Dinh Nhu, for instance, the second-most powerful man in the South, ran as an "independent" in both the 1956 and 1959 elections, as did the other members of his Personalist Labor Party whom he decided to put up for election. In 1959, Diem permitted two real but undistinguished opposition candidates to run in Saigon, expecting them to be defeated. When, in spite of all official precaution, they nonetheless won (one of them, Dr. Phan Quang Dan, who ran against fifteen other candidates, received 63 per cent of all votes cast), both were deprived of their seats through officially instituted court action.

The main task of the legislature elected on March 4, 1956, was the adoption of a constitution for the Republic of Vietnam. The constitution, "basically an executive-drafted document,"[6] was promulgated on October 26, 1956, the first anniversary of the proclamation of the republic, after the assembly, in a reasonably convincing show of democratic discussion, unanimously accepted it. The constitution could hardly pass muster as a pioneering document for countries starting out on the road to democracy. Robert Shaplen found that it contained only few safeguards against one-party rule and dictatorship.[7] It granted the president excessive legislative powers, the right to govern by decree when the assembly was not in session, and also empowered him to suspend any law in any part of the country even when the assembly was in session. Stating that "the President of the Republic may decree a temporary suspension of the rights of freedom of circulation and residence, of speech and the press, of assembly and association, and of the formation of labor unions and strikes, to meet the legitimate demands of public security and order and national defense,"[8] Article 98 undid, at least for the period of the assembly's first legislative term, whatever merits it may have possessed otherwise. Diem continued to rule on this basis even after the powers granted him by Article 98 had expired.

Still more important, however, than this legalization of the emerging dictatorship was that Diem acted as though the conditional safeguards of the constitution simply did not exist. "As time went on," Shaplen wrote, "Diem and Nhu came to ignore the Constitution completely and acted by decrees and by personal —and often private—orders to underlings all the way down to the village level."[9]

The elimination of all surviving remnants of village democracy followed on the heels of an administrative reorganization aimed at bringing local government on all levels under direct central control. South Vietnam was organized into forty-one provinces headed by province chiefs appointed by the president and directly responsible to him. The authority the province chiefs enjoyed extended not only over police and security activities but frequently also over the regular armed forces. In their hands was placed control of all lower governmental organs—the chiefs of the 233 districts into which the provinces were divided, their 2,560 villages, and their approximately 16,000 hamlets. In the end, the administrative system of the Republic of Vietnam was more centralized than it had been under either the emperors or the French.[10]

5

It has been remarked that for all practical purposes, South Vietnam under Diem was a one-party state. This requires modification. To begin with, Diem, like Ho Chi Minh in the North, permitted a number of parties to exist, to camouflage the fact of one-party rule. The Social Democratic Party, Socialist Party, and Restoration League—all minor groupings—served "only as fronts for the ruling group. . . . All three were taken over by the regime and their continued existence [depended] upon its benevolence and subventions."[11] Both in the North and South the parties other than the official ones were artificial creations, but with one significant difference: the artificiality of the party system in the South extended also to the official government parties—the National Revolutionary Movement, the National Revolutionary Civil Servants League, and the Personalist Labor Party.

Unlike the Communist Party in the North, the Personalist Labor Party of Ngo Dinh Nhu, Diem's brother and chief adviser, was not an organizational expression of the political aspirations of the masses or of an avant-garde. Its aims were not pursued through organization and propaganda; its chief activity was spying on enemies of the regime and uncovering and denouncing defectors; its membership was restricted almost solely to key civil servants. The Personalist Labor Party never held a convention, never took a public stand on any issue, and its governing body never met as a group. It was run by Nhu alone, and it provided him with information about whomever he wished to know something—members of the government, Army officers, administrators, and ordinary citizens. Its usefulness to its members consisted in their "access . . . to Nhu and in the material benefits which flow to them through the party's financial graft and related sources of income."[12] Fear and greed, not conviction, held the party together.

The National Revolutionary Civil Servants League was no less artificial. Its membership included practically everybody working for the government, South Vietnam's main employer next to agriculture. Nearly 500,000 persons made their living from the state, the majority in the armed services. About 125,000 persons were employed in the civil bureaucracy, a large portion of them as police and security agents.

The National Revolutionary Movement (NRM), which like the League was based on civil service, succeeded, by official intimidation and other means, in attracting members outside the government. The NRM formed the "majority faction" in the assembly. Diem was its honorary head, and members of his "official family" were its acting chairmen. Real control of the powers and resources of the NRM rested in the hands of Diem's brothers Nhu and Can. In its organizational practices the NRM followed Communist methods, but it lacked devoted and well-trained cadres, as did all official parties in the South. They were effective only in so far as they operated as adjuncts of the regime's apparatus of intimidation and suppression, and consequently they disappeared on the very day the Diem regime was toppled.

The typical local political leader was at best paternalistic and at worst a corrupt bully. But whichever he was, he considered himself vastly superior to the rest of the people. An experienced and sympathetic observer, Malcolm W. Browne, commented that of the thousands of Vietnamese officials he had known, he could not think of any who did not more or less hold the people in contempt.[13] When insurrection started in the South, the Communists, Browne pointed out, often killed government officials because they knew that this would please the local people.[14] David Halberstam reports that in areas where the people suffered under bad local government, the Viet Cong would execute offending village officials while the people watched.[15]

Not only the newspapermen but most American officials in Vietnam knew that the average Vietnamese official "looked down upon the common people . . . while at the same time milking them for kickbacks."[16] John Mecklin reports that in 1961, General Taylor exacted a long list of promises from Diem, mostly on urgently needed reforms, and that on the political level, the United States pressed the Vietnamese Government toward such reforms as punishment of dishonest village officials.[17] But why should it have been necessary to "press" for such reforms under a government headed by a man generally regarded as a determined foe of corruption?

6

If Diem had ever seriously attempted to improve the performance of his officials, he would have found himself faced by an impossible task. Opposed by the intellectuals, despised by the educated middle class, rejected by businessmen, hated by the youth and all politically ambitious nationalists, and totally devoid of mass support, the Diem government had to rely on coercion. It had to have administrators willing to side with it against practically the entire people. Its officials could not be the servants of the people but their watchdogs, a function which in the long run could not be carried out by decent, honest men. Diem initially attracted some dedicated men, but as time went on they became exceedingly rare. Sooner or later such men either resigned or were dismissed and replaced by others ready to serve the government unconditionally. That people willing to serve their country existed no one could doubt. The Vietminh enlisted them by the thousands. But once the character of Diem's regime had become apparent, it attracted only men fit to serve in a corrupt, inefficient, despised police state.

Indeed, to have asked the Diem regime to punish lazy, corrupt, or brutal officials would have meant asking it to liquidate itself. Those who sided with the people had to be eliminated. Once the regime set foot on the road of moral decline, it instituted truly vicious methods of punishing officials suspected of disloyalty. The Communists were known to kill those whose integrity and dedication were roadblocks to their work of inciting the people against the regime. Hence, incredible though this may seem, men whom the regime considered untrustworthy were sent into regions where their chances of survival were almost nil.

But even if the very nature of the regime had not prevented it from creating an administration able to serve both the people and the state, Diem's government itself had become the greatest obstacle to any attempt at reforming the officialdom. Power rested not in the hands of one man acting as leader of a totalitarian organization. It was exercised by a small clique which soon comprised only members of Diem's immediate family. The cabinet was composed almost solely of second-rate men whom Diem treated with his customary contempt for careerists.

The ruling family also kept shrinking, until it consisted only of three of Diem's brothers and Mme. Nhu. The people who even more than Diem himself determined the conduct of affairs were his younger brothers Nhu and Can, Nhu's wife, and to a lesser degree Diem's older brother Ngo Dinh Thuc, Archbishop of Hue and dean of the Catholic episcopacy of Vietnam—"an extralegal elite which, with Diem, directs the destiny of Vietnam today."[18]

Thuc, who held no official post, acted as unofficial adviser to the president, as head of the Catholic clergy, and occasionally as one of the regime's propagandists abroad. Ngo Dinh Can also held no official position, but he was in effect the governor of central Vietnam, issuing orders to all officials appointed by Saigon, usually his hand-picked choices. In addition, he built up a publicly financed private network of police and security agents, many of whom he placed in agencies of the central government. To what extent he personally benefited from his corrupt practices cannot be ascertained. He himself led a rather simple and secluded life. He seemed to use corruption as an instrument of power. Yet it was he who monopolized the cinnamon trade, controlled local shipping, and sold at enormous profit rice obtained cheaply from the government to alleviate local shortages.

More crucial for the destiny of South Vietnam and the fate of the Diem regime than Can's reckless abuse of power was the role played by Ngo Dinh Nhu, who also exercised enormous influence without holding any kind of official position. His power, which was generally thought to be greater than that of Diem himself, derived from the influence he exerted on Diem, from his role as head of the Personalist Labor Party, and from his control of the various secret and police services.

The corruptive effect of Nhu's power over government and people made itself felt in many ways. The various instruments of control over the population created by Nhu earned the Diem regime the hatred of even those on whose support it depended: the heads of the armed forces. The secret service and special intelligence and police forces took their orders from Nhu. The most important of Nhu's secret services was an organization of informers inside the administration headed by Dr. Tran Kim Tuyen, whose euphemistic title was Director of the Service for Political and Social Research of the Presidency. Nhu held Communist-style "self-criticism" sessions in the semisecret Personalist Party, and his uniformed Republican Youth imitated Fascist methods of popular control. The so-called Special Forces, and the manner in which Nhu employed them in 1963, were reminiscent of the Nazi Storm Troopers. On the other hand, the setting up of secret cells in existing organizations and in the administration, the attempt to organize all citizens into small groups whose leaders were held responsible for the loyalty of its members, the rallies denouncing Communists, the propaganda techniques, and the constant harassment of a tired population with meetings and "spontaneous" demonstrations in support of the regime and its exalted leader—all these methods were borrowed from the Communists. There was not one totalitarian stratagem that Nhu failed to employ. The only weapons he never resorted to in the fight against Communism were those of democracy.

If there was anyone in Vietnam able to outdo Nhu in arrogance, suspicion, power drive, lack of candor and humanity, it was his "catastrophic wife, Tran Le Xuan (Beautiful Spring), who was best known as Mme. Nhu."[19] Her fiery disdain, pride, and willfulness made the sobriquet "Dragon Lady" patently appropriate. Her influence on Diem was extraordinary. The help she gave the faltering Diem regime was the sort of help rendered a drowning man by a rock tied to his neck. She acted as official hostess at the Presidential Palace, but this was a role that satisfied only her vanity, not her all-consuming power drive. Like her husband, Mme. Nhu interfered directly with the running of the government and even of the Army. Everyone knew that disobeying her orders was risky and therefore usually hastened to comply.

With a great show of militant feminism, which however did nothing to strengthen the rights of women, Mme. Nhu created her own private party, the Women's Solidarity Movement, and her own private army, a paramilitary corps of young women used chiefly to embellish the parades by which the government tried to impress the people. The so-called Family Code which she pushed through the legislature at the end of 1958, and the Law for the Protection of Morality which Diem signed in May, 1962, sought not only to end divorce and polygamy, but also to impose upon the population a code of behavior that clashed with their accepted mores. "With a stroke of the pen," wrote Malcolm Browne, "Mme. Nhu outlawed divorce, dancing, beauty contests, gambling, fortune-telling, cockfighting, prostitution and a hundred other things dear to the heart of Vietnamese men. Neither her husband nor his brother, the President, dared interfere with these amazing legislative decrees."[20] Harsh penalties were provided for the use of contraceptives and for marital infidelity, "which included being seen in public with a person of another sex."[21] Dancing eventually was forbidden even in private homes, and in order to promote the war effort, Mme. Nhu in April, 1963, banned what she considered "sentimental songs."

Among the people generally and the intellectuals in particular, these efforts to control public and private morals gave rise to cynical allusions to Mme. Nhu's allegedly less than perfect moral comportment. Nhu and his wife became the two most hated people in South Vietnam. There was nothing they were not held capable of—spying on their collaborators, arbitrary arrests of suspected enemies, and large-scale graft. Proof of their corruption was of course impossible to obtain, but it was common knowledge that they extracted huge sums from Chinese and Vietnamese businessmen who sought import licenses and contracts for public works. Abuse of power, nepotism, corruption, contempt for inferiors, and cruel disregard of the needs of the people were the example set by the "Family" for the ministers, legislators, generals, province chiefs, and village commissioners whom they used as pawns. In agreeing to play their despicable roles, these tools of the Family earned the disdain of their masters as well as of the population.

As the abuses heaped on those who had incurred the Family's displeasure worsened and became common knowledge, more and more people asked why Diem, whom even many of his enemies regarded as honest and well-intentioned, tolerated these conditions. Those who believed in his integrity expected that sooner or later he would get rid of the Nhus. Why he refused to do so even after he knew that Washington wanted him to remains a puzzle. John Mecklin describes the Diem-Nhu relationships as "a psychiatric curiosity." Almost everyone who has written about it has stressed Diem's family loyalty. But even if Diem would rather have sacrificed his right arm than get rid of Nhu, family loyalty is a poor excuse for tolerating corruption. The reason Diem refused to drop the Nhus was political. Diem knew that his brother's spies, secret services, and political parties were indispensable to the regime. The eradication of the existing evils, particularly of the inefficient, graft-ridden, repressive administration, would have required more than simply a break with Nhu. It would have required a radical change in Diem's political philosophy, in the dictatorial character of a regime whose foremost exponent he was. Diem should be credited with knowing exactly what he was doing when he refused to his dying day to be separated from Nhu. Therefore Diem must be held responsible for the evils of his regime, including the corruption which he no doubt despised but embraced willingly as a means of retaining power.

7

In justifying the harsh measures against its enemies, the regime liked to point to the dangers threatening the republic unless opposition to Diem was stamped out, thereby implying that all criticism was either Communist or Communist-inspired, or at least aided the Communists. The regime denied that any significant opposition existed aside from the Vietminh, and claimed that the inmates of its concentration camps and prisons were without exception criminals and Communists.

The anti-Diem, anti-Communist nationalists in the South were deeply divided among themselves. Most were intellectuals and professionals. Not one of the known opposition spokesmen was a truly popular leader. Like Diem himself, these men were largely products of the past. Many were discredited because of past collaboration with the French; others with a predilection for intrigue and sectarianism believed that people can be manipulated instead of having to be won over. Since conditions for developing their potential for popular leadership had been denied them in the past and were denied them still, these people in fact had no chance for maturing politically. They never tried to organize a popular movement, either overtly or clandestinely. Their aim was not necessarily a democratic Vietnam, although in seeking American support they paid lip service to democracy. They were primarily vying for official positions for which they fought against Diem and among themselves. Their feebleness as a force capable of leading the country on a new road was demonstrated after the fall of Diem.

It is evident that such an opposition, even if it had managed to agree on a program and on united action, could never have become a threat to the Diem regime, and Diem obviously knew that. He could have let them talk, which was about all they did. He could even have allowed them to hold meetings and publish papers, and such concessions to democratic practices would have been fervently applauded by Diem's American supporters. But his intolerance, authoritarianism, and profound suspicion of the motives of others made it impossible for him to ignore even mild expressions of disagreement, particularly if voiced by intellectuals, whom he despised.

Diem's persecution of his non-Communist opponents became more and more vindictive as time went on. By August, 1963, "all outspoken anti-Communist, anti-Diem leaders had left the country or were imprisoned."[23]

In an unusual and ephemeral show of unity, a group of prominent anti-Communist critics of the regime gathered in April, 1960. Calling themselves the Bloc for Liberty and Progress, they met at the Hotel Caravelle on April 26 and issued a coura-geous document voicing their grievances and demands. They did not plan to overthrow the Diem regime; all they wanted was liberalization and an end of the Family domination of the civil service and armed forces. The signers of the Caravelle manifesto included former leaders of the sects, the Dai Viet, the old Na-tionalist Party, and dissident Catholic groups. Eleven of its eight-een members were former cabinet ministers; four had held other high positions. Among the signers prominent before Diem's acces-sion to power, and again after his fall, were Phan Khac Suu, Phan Huy Quat, Tran Van Do, Tran Van Huong, and Tran Van Tuyen. Though the demands of the Caravelle group were modest, the language of the manifesto was surprisingly bold. Diem, it stated, had brought the people neither a better life nor greater freedom. The constitution was merely a piece of paper; the na-tional assembly simply carried out the wishes of the government. Elections were called "antidemocratic," and all this was "copied from the dictatorial Communist regimes."[24]

As if to confirm the charge of the signers that "public opinion and the press are reduced to silence," no Vietnamese newspaper printed the manifesto. The regime liked to boast that the press was not censored. And indeed, control was less overt, more devious, and more callous: mob action against press criticism rather than resort to outright legal restraints. If a paper criticized the govern-ment too freely or dared to print anything uncomplimentary about a member of the Ngo family, hoodlums hired by one of Nhu's secret services staged a demonstration of "popular indignation," which invariably ended with the wrecking of the paper's offices and plant. By 1958, all opposition papers were suppressed.

The Caravelle group ceased to be after its one vain attempt to publicize the grievances and demands of Diem's anti-Com-munist critics. But Diem and his brothers neither forgot nor for-gave the audacity of the eighteen signers. An attempted coup by a group of paratroopers on November 11, 1960, was followed by a wave of mass arrests of anti-Communists suspected of nurturing the hope that the regime would fall. Although only one member of the Caravelle group, Phan Khac Suu, was accused of being involved in the coup, most of the others were also arrested, and some were held in jail without trial until the fall of Diem.

The West paid little attention to the manner in which Diem dealt with men who attempted to steer the regime toward a less authoritarian course. American readers remained ignorant of the manifesto of the Caravelle group and of the subsequent arrest of its members. This was in sharp contrast to the sensational reporting and endless propagandistic exploitation of a strikingly similar development in the North, the "intellectual revolt" in Hanoi in the fall and winter of 1956–57.

Like Diem's critics, the intellectual rebels in the North were not in principle opposed to the existing regime. They wanted to liberalize and humanize it. Both groups failed, and for the same reason: the reforms they demanded were incompatible with the nature of their regimes.

As far as the anti-Communists in the West were concerned, they did not recognize until too late that in the South, too, public criticism of the regime, even if voiced by proved anti-Communists, was taboo. Diem never ceased to talk about the lack of freedom in the North though he himself had most of the signers of the Caravelle manifesto jailed without trial. Diem was too weak to suppress the population and the intellectuals as effectively as Ho Chi Minh, but to the extent that he was able to apply terror he did so without restraint.

8

The inefficiency and lack of dynamism that characterized the Diem dictatorship soon slowed down action in all fields where progress was vital if South Vietnam was to survive. War damages could not be repaired and public services rebuilt efficiently by a regime that equated initiative with insubordination. Diem, apparently convinced that any decision, no matter how simple, was valid only if it was his own, would delay indefinitely rather than grant local administrators and technicians power of decision. He even decided on who should be allowed to study in foreign countries, who should be granted a passport, whose wife should be allowed to accompany her husband abroad. His desk was piled high with papers containing proposals submitted to him for decisions he had not had time to study.

The general inertia this produced on all levels of government was one of the reasons for the lack of appreciable economic progress. This failure was particularly pronounced in the industrial sector. Compared with the dynamic growth of industry in the North, the South was practically stagnant. For every factory built under Diem—fewer than two dozen altogether—the North built fifty.

In discussions about economic progress under Diem, much has been made of the introduction of industrial crops (jute, ramie, and kenaf), the increase in the production of rubber, and about the not fully corroborated fact that food production increased by about 7 per cent annually and ultimately surpassed prewar levels.[25] In view of the 50 per cent population increase since 1938, the attainment of prewar food-production levels would at best have been a mediocre achievement.

What industrial plans the regime had, and how much of its first five-year plan of 1957 was fulfilled, is not known, for the plan was kept secret. By 1962, fewer than a dozen new industrial enterprises (mostly small) had either been put into operation or brought close to completion. Mounting insecurity was the reason generally given for the fact that the first five-year plan was not fulfilled in time, and was probably also the reason for the relatively modest scope of the second plan (1962–66).

More important than guerrilla warfare, however, in slowing down industrial development was the government's attitude toward projected aims and methods used in its realization. Diem, here too the final arbiter, had little understanding of economic problems and could never quite decide whether to promote industrialization through public or private enterprise. Also, the state of political uncertainty prevented any significant mobilization of private capital for industrialization. And finally, funds for a development policy based on public enterprise were not available. No sizable industrial project could have been undertaken without U.S. help. But the United States looked with disfavor upon the use of aid money for industries run as public enterprises.

As to private enterprise, the belated and lukewarm efforts to attract foreign investors failed as conspicuously as did the feeble attempts to mobilize indigenous capital for industrial development. American capital in particular showed little inclination to support efforts to make South Vietnam prosperous, and this caution hardly encouraged local capitalists to overcome their traditional fear of possible losses or inadequate profit. Few of the landowners who had received government bonds in compensation for expropriated land changed any part of them into industrial shares. The portion of these bonds invested in industrial enterprises came to less than 1 per cent of the total bonds distributed.[26]

If the United States opposed the use of aid funds for financing public enterprise, should Diem not have fought for his views, as he did—usually successfully—whenever he and Washington failed to see eye to eye? If 78 per cent of the total U.S. aid was absorbed by the military establishment, and only 1.25 per cent went into industrial development and mining, it was because both the United States and Diem thought of security and survival primarily in military terms and neglected the social, economic, and political requirements for making the country secure.

American aid to Vietnam has been the subject of much investigation, public debate, and Congressional scrutiny. The sums involved were enormous (by mid-1960, the total had reached $1.311 billion), and the question of why still more was demanded quite understandably agitated the American people. But the debate rarely focused on the disproportion of military and economic aid: Congress always favored the first. It concentrated chiefly on waste in the program's administration, and, in a more serious vein, on the direct impact of aid on the lives of the people.

Nobody would deny that there was some waste, but most of the sensational charges were either false or grossly exaggerated. The aid program on the whole was well administered, but what was left after funds for military purposes had been allocated was entirely inadequate to meet the social and economic needs of the people. Aid for nonmilitary projects, usually referred to as "project aid," totaled no more than 22 per cent of all assistance. Of this, 40 per cent was spent on transportation, mostly on rebuilding the country's highway system. Agriculture, including the administration of the land-reform program and of agricultural credit and cooperatives, was allotted 17 per cent of nonmilitary aid. The same amount was spent for administration, most of which was devoured by the police and security services, largely for equipment. This left 7 per cent of nonmilitary aid for health and sanitation, 7 per cent for education, and 3 per cent for the much-vaunted community-development programs, social welfare, and housing. This 3 per cent amounted to approximately 0.6 per cent of the total aid, or 50 cents per person per year. It should not come as a surprise that this failed to produce a noticeable improvement in the lives of the people.

It might be said that the economy as a whole must have been stimulated by the influx of such vast sums, and there can be no doubt that whatever modest economic progress was made was due to American aid. The recruitment of hundreds of thousands into the Army and the various paramilitary forces helped to reduce unemployment. These people, although unproductive, were consumers, and thus they created employment for others, and public and private construction created employment on an even larger scale. The point here is not that this was too little but that it contributed almost nothing to economic development. The data on the type of construction carried out between 1957 and 1960 are revealing: 47,000 square meters of cinemas and dance halls, but only 6,500 square meters of hospitals; 3,500 square meters of rice mills, but 56,000 square meters of churches and pagodas.[27] Nothing was done about city slums. They were hardly ever mentioned by the people who liked to compare the drabness of Hanoi with the glitter of Saigon. "This is the sort of thing," wrote Bernard Fall, "far more than weapons and infiltrators from across the 17th parallel, that makes Communist guerrillas out of peaceable peasants."[28] And he might have added: out of city-dwellers too.

9

If the enemies of Diem had been only the divided, unorganized anti-Communist nationalists, the regime's failures and denial of basic freedoms could hardly have threatened its existence. But there also existed a well-organized, strong Communist opposition. The Vietnamese Communists after 1954 enjoyed greater popular support and were closer to victory than any other Communist movement in the world. The fate of the Diem regime therefore depended chiefly on the success or failure of the measures to reduce, and eventually put an end to, the lethal power of the country's native Communist movement.

When the military units of the Vietminh were withdrawn from the South in accordance with the Geneva agreement, the Vietminh remained in control of the countryside. In some areas it even grew stronger. After the fighting ceased and the French left, the Vietminh no longer needed to secure control by military means. The arms left behind by the troops who had gone North were buried; Vietminh power, for the time being, was to be based on organization and on the influence the movement had gained over the people. They were convinced that victory was already theirs, even if its consummation had to await the elections of July, 1956.

This was the situation Diem faced during the first two years of his reign. It would seem that a leader of even moderate political acumen should have been able to determine which strategy would be most likely to defeat the Communist threat to the South. But Diem, dogmatic and convinced that he alone was destined to save his country, was unable to devise the measures that might have turned allies of the Communists into friends of his regime—i.e., the right to organize, to voice grievances and demands freely, and eventually also to share in the government. Granted a minimum of political freedom, the people could have been persuaded to break with the Vietminh. Even more important would have been a strategy designed to deprive the Communist cadres of their true source of strength—popular support. Everybody in Vietnam, including the spokesmen of the regime, knew that such a strategy called for the realization of Diem's much-vaunted "social revolution" and "genuine democracy." This is what the people were waiting for and what Ho Chi Minh and his Communist cadres in the South feared.

The fear of the Communists turned out to be unfounded. Diem's method of fighting Communism was to destroy the cadres, if necessary physically, rather than rendering them politically impotent by depriving them of their mass base. He had failed to learn the lesson of the Indochina War—i.e., that a political movement cannot be destroyed by killing its exponents. He and Nhu subscribed to the simple notion that the only good Communist was a dead one rather than a politically helpless one without popular support. The idea that a dead Communist might prove more dangerous than a live one never occurred to them. They never realized that for every Communist killed, particularly one who had fought in the resistance, two new ones were likely to spring up.

The persecution of former resistance fighters, whether Communists or not, and the denial of their democratic freedoms constituted a breach of the Geneva agreement. But Diem maintained that South Vietnam was neither legally nor morally bound by the agreement. And Hanoi, itself no less culpable, certainly did not have the moral right to complain about Diem's noncompliance with the provisions about reprisals and democratic liberties. But quite aside from legal or moral considerations, Diem's persecution of Vietminh supporters was politically disastrous, an almost incomprehensible violation of common sense, and the major factor in the success of the future Communist-led insurrection.

The manhunt against the Vietminh began only after the regime's military and police apparatus was sufficiently developed and firmly under government control. Two major campaigns were undertaken, the first one, which swept through the provinces west of Saigon, lasting from June 8 to October 31, 1956. The second, which lasted from June 17, 1956 to December 15, 1957, covered the territory east of Saigon, which encompassed many important Vietminh bases the French had never succeeded in dislodging. Very little reliable information exists on the manner in which these and later campaigns to uproot the Vietminh were conducted. Though Communist propaganda claims of hundreds of thousands killed and imprisoned cannot be taken seriously, there can be no doubt that innumerable brutal, senseless crimes against real and suspected Communists and friendly villagers were committed.

Saigon's military and police campaigns were accompanied by civic action whose positive aspects were cited as evidence of the benefits foreign aid brought to the villagers. Roads were repaired, bridges rebuilt, and schools and infirmaries reopened, though not nearly enough to meet existing needs. However, another aspect of civic action—the psychological campaign to remove the poison of Communism from the people's minds—made gratitude for these gifts difficult. The methods used included brainwashing in "re-education camps," denunciation rallies similar to those held in the North during the land-reform campaign, nightly meetings with loudspeakers blaring for hours, and, worst of all, an attempt to establish control over the population through a system of groups, the smallest of which comprised five families. The members of these groups were supposed to watch one another, with the group leader being responsible for the conduct of the members. The "theoretician" of this program, Tran Chanh Thanh, appropriately enough was Vietminh-trained. He had left the Vietminh zone in 1951, and in 1955 had become the intellectual father of the many schemes of "rural pacification" through which Diem and his successor regimes had tried, largely without success, to regain control of the countryside. Everything was copied from the Vietminh; the campaign added up to an "experiment in defeating Communism by boisterous Communist methods."[29]

According to official figures, 20,000–30,000 former Vietminh cadres were put into concentration camps (though most official observers believe the number to be considerably higher). P. J. Honey, who had occasion to visit these camps, reported that the majority held there were neither Communists nor pro-Communists.[30] The true result of the attempt to destroy the Vietminh, according to Bernard Fall, was that in 1958–60, the countryside largely went Communist.[31]

The Communist leaders South and North persistently worked toward gaining mastery over the entire country, though not necessarily by force. They prepared for the elections provided for by the Geneva agreement, even though they had doubts about when, if ever, such elections would be held. Diem's refusal to hold general elections became official on July 16, 1955. In a statement that ranks among the most preposterous he ever made, Diem not only extolled "free elections" and "true democracy," but also promised the people of the North that the national government would bring them independence in freedom.[32] This was Diem's answer to Hanoi's request to hold preliminary discussions for the July, 1956, elections. All further requests by Hanoi, as well as the many proposals for postal, cultural, and economic exchanges between North and South, remained unanswered. Diem held to the position that his government, not having signed the Geneva agreements, was not bound by them and that moreover the North would not live up to the stipulation of free elections.

In view of the curious nature of the Geneva agreement, there has been no satisfactory answer as to who stood on firmer "legal grounds": Ho Chi Minh in demanding elections or Diem in rejecting them. But the legal aspects were and are irrelevant. What mattered was the impact of the policies of the two regimes on the people of Vietnam, and to a lesser degree on world opinion. The question is not so much a legal as a moral and political one. Diem's moral right to ignore the agreement was contingent upon his fulfillment of his obligations toward the Vietnamese people, including those who had fought with the Vietminh against the French. Among these obligations was to grant the people of the South democratic freedom.

Although the Vietnamese Communists, and Moscow and Peking as well, did nothing more than protest Diem's refusal to hold the elections, it was a mistake to believe that Hanoi would ever resign itself to permanent partition, a belief that gained currency because the Communists decided to use force only belatedly, and only after exhausting all diplomatic channels for achieving their objective through elections. However, force was an alternative for which they had been preparing themselves ever since accepting the temporary partition at Geneva.

Few people below the 17th parallel realized that life under the Hanoi regime was harsher than in the South. Saigon harped on the misery of life under Communism, but in a country where the claims of official propaganda were contradicted by everyday experience, this was not believed. The greater the skepticism toward the claims of official propaganda, the more readily the people accepted the propaganda claims of the North. But the North's inability to provide the better life they spoke of was largely why Hanoi could not resign itself to permanent partition and why the Communists were compelled to attempt to win control of the South by force. Food production could not keep pace with the rise in population, and the forced industrialization barred imports that might have relieved the appalling consumer-goods shortages.

The forcible overthrow of the Diem regime and the "liberation" of the South did not receive quasi-formal endorsement until

September, 1960, when the third congress of the Lao Dong Party convened. Le Duan, a Southerner, and secretary of the Party, directed the campaign to bring the insurrection in the South under a unified military command. He also brought directives for a political platform broad enough to attract all elements ready to overthrow the Diem regime. The aim was to create a "democratic coalition" not necessarily pledged to early reunification with the North. His efforts resulted in the formation of the National Front for the Liberation of the South (generally referred to as National Liberation Front) at a congress held on December 20, 1960, "somewhere in the South." A hundred delegates representing a dozen or more political parties and religious groups, including some of the old sects, are said to have attended. The composition and the program of the new organization testified to the proved ability of the Communists to adapt their strategy to the needs of a new situation. Emerging as a broad yet Communist-dominated political coalition, the National Liberation Front was truly the Vietminh reborn. The resemblance of the Vietminh and the Front was underlined by the manner in which the Communists spoke of their own role as that of a minority faction within a broad front of non-Communist groups. They formed an openly Marxist group with which they controlled the Front as effectively as they had controlled the Vietminh. A new party, the People's Revolutionary Party, ostensibly independent of the Communist Party in the North, was founded in the South on January 15, 1962. The Communists obviously felt that the tactics they had pursued successfully ever since 1941 were still valid, and that they could achieve their ultimate goal—a Communist regime for the whole of Vietnam—only as the guiding force of a non-Communist "popular front."

Both East and West have given greatly distorted versions of the outbreak of the fighting in South Vietnam that was to lead to the second Indochina War. The Communist version speaks of a spontaneous uprising of the vast majority of the population which the Communists could not refuse to join. But the truth is that the uprising was organized by the Communists, and while it would have made little headway without broad popular support, neither would it have had its amazing success without guidance and assistance from the North.

The Saigon-Washington version, which strays even farther from historical fact, flatly asserts that the Vietnam war was the result of external aggression. Neither Saigon nor Washington, despite strenuous effort, have been able to produce evidence that anti-Diem terror and guerrilla warfare was the result of the infiltration of men and weapons from the North. No significant infiltration occurred before 1960, and very little during the next four years. The Saigon-Washington version, which attempts to deny that the war began as a civil war in the South, omits, as Bernard Fall says, "the embarrassing fact that anti-Diem guerrillas were active long before infiltrated North Vietnamese elements joined the fray."[33] In 1961, years before any large-scale infiltration, the Communists had in fact extended their influence to about four-fifths of the countryside.[34]

While it is likely that the Communists, deprived of the chance to win the South in elections, would sooner or later have resorted to terror and guerrilla warfare, the fact remains that force was first used by Diem, not by the Communists. Diem's terror against former Vietminh fighters, known Communist cadres, and villages and regions suspected of Vietminh sympathies started long before the Communists loosed their own terror campaign. Unlike the indiscriminate government terror, the Communist terror was selective, and although frequently also directed against the innocent it was guided by clearly defined political considerations: to paralyze the Diem administration by murdering or kidnaping its officials and by disrupting communications between the countryside and Saigon.

The murder of officials began in 1957. By 1960, the movement that had begun with isolated acts of terrorism had become a full-fledged insurrection supported by the peasants in the Mekong Delta and coastal provinces northeast of Saigon and of the ethnic minority tribes in the highlands of central Vietnam. The insurrection took the form of guerrilla action against villages still under government control and usually ended with the surrender or wiping-out of local self-defense units and Civil Guards charged with ousting the guerrillas. Organized, indoctrinated, and Communist-led, the Vietcong, as these guerrillas were henceforth called, soon controlled almost the entire countryside. (The term "Vietcong" was coined by Saigon and means "Vietnamese Communists." It was intended not only to be derogatory, but to imply that everyone who fought Diem was a Communist. The term has now come into general use and does not necessarily connote agreement with the implication that all guerrillas are Communists.) The Vietcong set up their own administration, imposed their own taxes, conscripted local youth, provided education and medical care, collected food for their fighting units, dug shelters, built defense works in the regions they controlled, and trained new men for stepped-up military operations. For years they added to their fighting force (if not to their cadres) entirely through local recruiting, and they supplemented their arms supply with captured weapons rather than with weapons from the North. Beginning in 1960, they operated with increasingly larger groups, attacked and overran government outposts, and ambushed and destroyed units sent in to relieve besieged outposts. Saigon's chief problem was to maintain a minimum of security along the main lines of communication. By 1963, its military situation had become catastrophic; exactly how catastrophic became obvious to at least some American military advisers in January of that year, when a major offensive against a guerrilla force in the Mekong Delta revealed that the National Army could neither match the fighting spirit of the Vietcong nor cope with their strategy.

This episode has gone down in the history of the war as the battle of the Ap Bac. On January 2, 1963, a 2,500-man force equipped with automatic weapons and armored amphibious personnel carriers and supported by bombers and helicopters failed to defeat a group of 200 guerrillas, who, after inflicting heavy casualties on the Army and shooting down five helicopters, managed to escape almost intact.

It did not need a military expert to see that the Vietnamese Army had been trained for the wrong kind of warfare. Organized under American direction, it was technically unprepared to counter insurgency. After 1960, some of the military leaders came to realize that guerrillas had to be fought on their own terms, and suddenly everybody began to talk about the need for organizing counterinsurgency units. But the little that was done could not affect the senseless and futile manner in which the war was being conducted.

But the main reason for the failure to contain the Vietcong were political conditions that thwarted the reforms which might have made the Army effective and which prevented it from becoming a determined fighting force against the Vietcong. There is overwhelming evidence that neither men nor officers were willing to lay down their lives in this war.

The effects of Diem's demand for blind loyalty were even more disastrous in the Army than in the civil service. Almost all senior officers were political appointees of "uncertain character and intelligence."[35] But even men completely loyal to the President, as for a long time most senior officers undoubtedly were, ran the risk of incurring disfavor. Not only was it dangerous for them to stand out and become popular with their troops, it was equally unsafe to conduct the war energetically and risk losses, even if the enemy was beaten back.

Under these conditions even more dedicated troops could scarcely have performed feats of bravery. Desertions were too numerous to be ignored and morale was unbelievably low. Because of the inefficiency and corruption of their officers, the troops were poorly cared for and frequently had to steal food.

Another aspect of the war was the brutal treatment of real or suspected members of the Vietcong. The torture of prisoners and villagers suspected of harboring guerrillas and the shooting of prisoners were everyday occurrences, but neither torture nor murder could defeat the Vietcong. Nor did the regime come closer to ridding the countryside of Vietcong through the establishment of so-called agrovilles, and later of strategic hamlets. The building of agrovilles—large concentrations of villagers in fortified "peasant towns"—was soon abandoned as impractical, but not before the brutality with which the peasants were driven from their villages had created fresh hatred against the regime.

The military purpose of the strategic hamlets—the fortification of existing villages—was to prevent the Vietcong from overrunning villages in open battle and from "infiltrating" them at night. This was to be achieved by enclosing the hamlets with barbed wire, ditches, hedges, and fences of pointed bamboo stakes, and by setting up defense posts at the entrances. The people had to remain inside the enclosures after nightfall, which were guarded at night by the Civil Defense Corps. Communist propaganda referred to the strategic hamlets as "concentration camps."

Not only Diem but also his American advisers expected this program, initiated late in 1961, to help break Vietcong control of the countryside. When this expectation failed to materialize, most Americans blamed the failure on "overextension" and on the unrealistic pace of its execution. But the main reason for the failure here too was political, and like all the other failures in the struggle to defeat the Vietcong, this one also was rooted in the nature of the regime. When the Vietcong began to attack the hamlets they met with mounting success not so much because the regime lacked adequate military forces, but rather because of the low morale of its soldiers and the people's reluctance to defend these hamlets against Vietcong attacks. More often than not the attackers had allies inside the hamlets who, even if known to the people, were rarely betrayed. That is why this last attempt under Diem to regain control of the countryside began to collapse in mid-1963, and why the chief American adviser on the program, Rufus Phillips, warned Washington in September, 1963, that the strategic-hamlet program in the Mekong Delta was in a "rotten state."[36]

This late warning was apparently listened to; but earlier ones had been dismissed by the heads of the U.S. Mission in Saigon, the Pentagon, the State Department, and the White House. Such warnings came almost exclusively from American correspondents stationed in Saigon, who thereby earned not only the enmity of U.S. officials, but the fierce hostility of the Diem regime, particularly of Mme. Nhu. Some were forced to leave South Vietnam; those who remained were shadowed, attacked, and manhandled by Nhu's agents. Their telephones were tapped and they were prevented from filing uncensored reports. The U.S. Mission was anything but forceful in defending the American correspondents. Ambassador Nolting and General Harkins in particular were incensed by the correspondents' indictment of the regime. Both stanchly believed that there was no alternative to Diem and were therefore inclined to accept its claim that the Vietcong were being defeated. Washington's belief in Diem and in his final victory was apparently unshakable. Secretary McNamara called

Diem "one of the great leaders of our time," and Vice-President
Johnson in 1961 likened Diem to Winston Churchill. As to Diem's
chances for victory, skeptics were referred to General Maxwell
Taylor, who in 1962 spoke of a great national movement that
was crushing the Vietcong. And Ambassador Nolting went so
far as to predict that the Republic of Vietnam would take its place
in history as the country in which the myth of Communist in-
vincibility was forever shattered.[37]

It would, however, be a mistake to believe that the U.S. Mission
in Saigon, the State Department, the Pentagon, and President
Kennedy were not aware of or not disturbed by the decline of
the Diem regime and its obvious inability to deal effectively with
the insurrection. In 1961, President Kennedy sent three missions
to Vietnam: the first was headed by Vice-President Johnson; the
second by Professor Staley of Stanford University; the third by
General Taylor. After the report of the Taylor mission, the only
one that seriously dealt with the need for administrative, social,
and political reforms, U.S. officials began to demand that the
measures promised by Diem in return for increased U.S. aid be
carried out. Diem's reaction came in a series of articles in the
government-controlled press protesting American "imperialist" interference in Vietnamese affairs.[38] None of the many reforms
proposed by the Taylor mission was ever acted upon.

For almost two years after the Taylor mission diagnosed some
of the evils in South Vietnam, Washington and the U.S. Mission
in Saigon either allowed themselves to be deceived about the
performance of the Diem regime or excused their support of it
with the astonishing assertion that the United States could not
interfere in the country's internal affairs. This implausible argu-
ment was dropped only in 1963, the year that brought conclusive
evidence that Diem was losing the war.

10

Until spring, 1963, the actions of the Diem regime had caused
a steady but slow drift from crisis to crisis; after May, the regime
embarked on a mad race toward disaster. In the words of David

Halberstam, it was like watching a government trying to commit suicide.[39] The accumulated failures and repressions finally also drove the non-Communist portion of the population into open rebellion. The fear that even confirmed anti-Communists might join the National Liberation Front convinced the country's military leaders that the Army had to overthrow Diem if South Vietnam were to remain non-Communist.

Now began the last and most turbulent phase in the life of the Diem government. It started when the President added to the pile of popular discontent by provoking a religious clash between the majority of the population, which is Buddhist, and the government. The Buddhists had long complained that Catholics, who made up 10 per cent of the population, held a disproportionate number of high official posts. Almost all province chiefs were Catholics, as were many other high officials and army officers, many of them recent converts to Catholicism.

But open conflict between the regime and the Buddhists did not erupt until May, 1963, in a tragic event at Hue, which the Vietnamese Buddhists regard as their religious capital. Shortly before the celebration of the 2,587th anniversary of Buddha's birth, the government issued an order forbidding the display of religious flags. This senseless order was the more provocative as the Catholics of Hue only a short time before had celebrated the twenty-fifth anniversary of Ngo Dinh Thuc's elevation to the bishopric with a profuse display of flags. On May 8, the Buddhists staged a huge demonstration protesting the decree and demanding its rescission. Troops were sent to disperse the demonstrators, and when tear gas failed, they were ordered to fire into the crowd. Nine persons, including three women and two children, were killed.

The news of this brutal attack spread rapidly throughout the country. The younger Buddhist priests in a sudden release of pent-up anger spoke out forcefully. And the older conservative leaders also spoke up. Thich Tam Chau, the head of the Buddhists in Saigon, formulated a number of demands, including the punishment of those responsible for the killings at Hue and the compensation of the families of the victims. The government, instead of putting out the flames that were threatening to turn into a gigantic conflagration, rejected these demands. Diem maintained that the nine Buddhists slain at Hue were the victims of a plastic bomb planted by the Vietcong, a preposterous claim effectively rebutted by foreign eyewitnesses.[40]

Being refused satisfaction, the Buddhists prepared for battle. Buddhist religious zeal soon was coupled with barely disguised political aspirations. Thich Tri Quang, a brilliant young monk from Hue, became the leader of the movement. On May 30, hundreds of Buddhist monks staged a peaceful demonstration in Saigon, and a thousand monks and nuns began a protest fast in the pagodas of Hue. Then, on June 11, Thich Quang Duc, an elderly Buddhist monk, in a world-shaking act of personal heroism, set fire to himself in the center of Saigon. Between June and November, six more monks and one nun gave their lives thus to dramatize the plight of the Vietnamese people. The world was horrified, not only by the self-immolations, but also by Mme. Nhu's callous dismissal of the suicides as "barbecues," and by her expressed hope that there would be more. Ngo Dinh Nhu, not to be outdone by his wife, announced that "if the Buddhists want to have another barbecue, I will be glad to supply the gasoline."[41]

In the early summer of 1963, the Buddhists were still concerned primarily with obtaining redress for their grievances. Although they kept on demonstrating, fasting, praying in the streets, and exhorting their followers, they continued their attempts to negotiate with Diem, who hesitated to suppress the movement by force but at the same time refused to make meaningful concessions. When, on August 18, a Buddhist call for a demonstration brought out 15,000 people in Saigon, most American officials in Saigon thought that Diem could not fail to see the danger of a continued refusal to meet Buddhist demands.

Indeed, nowhere did the Buddhist crisis cause as great a shock as in the United States. Guilt feelings over the continued support of a regime apparently practicing religious persecution and fear that growing resistance could hardly help to win the war drastically reduced American sympathy for Diem. Washington strongly advised Diem to accept the Buddhist demands. The views of the Kennedy Administration were forcefully presented to Diem by Ambassador Nolting's deputy, William Trueheart, who, according to Mecklin, applied a degree of pressure seldom attempted with a sovereign, friendly government.[42] Washington's firmness was largely a response to the shock and indignation of the American public over the growing evidence of religious persecution. Saigon's claim that the Buddhist protests were Communist-inspired was given little credence. The danger existed that the Vietcong might exploit the situation, but not a shred of evidence has ever been produced that Communists had infiltrated the Buddhist leadership.

The manner in which Diem "settled" the Buddhist affair must have incensed even his faithful American admirer Ambassador Nolting. On the night of August 21, units of the Special Forces and armed detachments of Nhu's secret police brutally attacked the Buddhists in their pagodas, and arrested all the monks and nuns they could find. Pagoda raids were also carried out at Hue, Quang Nam, Phan Thiet, Quang Tri, and other cities. Thousands of Buddhist monks were jailed and many others were killed. At the Xa Loi Pagoda in Saigon "the orgy lasted about two hours."[43]

As a result of the attempt to settle the Buddhist affair by suppression and terror, the movement grew stronger and more political. Convinced that Diem had decided to crush them, the Buddhist leaders began to turn their thoughts toward overthrowing the regime.

Men who for years had supported Diem now began to turn against him. Foreign Minister Vu Van Mau resigned his post, denounced the raids in a speech before the Faculty of Law at Saigon University, shaved his head as a symbol of solidarity with the Buddhists, and asked for permission to go on a pilgrimage to India. (He was arrested as he tried to leave.) An even greater blow for Diem was the resignation on August 23 of the ambassador to the United States, Tran Van Chuong, Mme. Nhu's father. His wife resigned her position as observer at the United Nations. Saigon propaganda, past master in the flat denial of facts, said that Vu Van Mau had not been arrested and that Tran Van Chuong had not resigned, but that he had been dismissed. But except for a handful of U.S. officials, no one in Saigon any longer believed anything the government said.

On August 24, the students at Saigon University began a series of demonstrations. In spite of ruthless police action, during which a young girl was killed, the young people continued to pour into the streets demanding Diem's resignation. More than 4,000 students were rounded up and jailed within the next few days. But the demonstrations continued. The universities of Saigon and Hue were closed, as were all of Saigon's secondary schools.

The reaction of the ruling family to the growing evidence of popular hostility became more and more frantic. Many of the thousands in jails were brutally beaten by Nhu's thugs. Nhu drafted a directive requiring civil servants to make "sincere confessions" of their attitude toward the Buddhists. In a five-hour talk for the benefit of U.S. officials, he called supporters of the Buddhist movements fools and openly accused Diem of weakness in dealing with the Buddhist leaders. Angered by American expressions of displeasure, Nhu and his wife became more and more preposterous in their denunciation of the United States and in their attacks on Americans in Vietnam. Nhu even attempted to frighten Washington into continued unconditional support of Diem by threatening openly to enter into negotiations with Hanoi.

President Kennedy was said to have been outraged by the attacks on the pagodas. In a press conference shortly after the raids, Kennedy appealed to Diem to show respect for the rights of others, and in a television interview on September 2, he spoke of "repression," deplored the fact that the government had "gotten out of touch with the people," and even said that the chances of winning the war under such a regime were "not very good." The great sensation of this interview, however, was Kennedy's reference to "changes in policy and perhaps personnel," which could only mean a demand that Diem get rid of the Nhus.

American patience with Diem had obviously reached the breaking point. In their flight from reality, Diem and Nhu behaved as outrageously toward Americans as they did toward their own people. After the August 21 raids, the barbed wire and guards around the Xa Loi Pagoda were extended—"for security reasons" —to the building of the U.S. Mission. As soon as the raids began, the telephones of U.S. officials and newsmen were disconnected. Reporters, unable to send uncensored dispatches out of the country, had air stewardesses or GI's smuggle them out via Hong Kong, Manila, Singapore, or Bangkok. A number of foreign newsmen were threatened with arrest, and some even with assassination.

The new U.S. Ambassador, Henry Cabot Lodge (Nolting had returned to the United States on August 15), made it clear from the very outset that Washington's attitude toward the Diem regime had ceased to be one of uncritical acceptance. He insisted on the removal of John Richardson, the CIA chief and stanch supporter of Diem. Yet despite the great change in its thinking, Washington still shrank from putting really effective pressure on Diem. On September 24, a high-ranking mission headed by Secretary McNamara and General Taylor arrived in Saigon and within twenty-four hours informed newsmen that the war was "getting better rather than worse." But McNamara seems to have returned to Washington with considerably greater skepticism. A statement released by McNamara and Taylor after their return seemed to hold out some hope and express some regard for Diem, but President Kennedy's actions did not match the restraint of his words. Washington demanded that Saigon send the 2,000 members of Nhu's Special Forces in Saigon to fight the Vietcong. Kennedy lent weight to this request by ordering the cancellation of the funds used to maintain these forces.

This and similar steps may not have done immediate material harm to the regime, but they had a tremendous psychological impact. The Vietnamese were given the impression that Washington was ready to drop Diem, even though it claimed that its only objective was to make Diem change his ways. However, an atmosphere was being created in which an anti-Diem coup was becoming possible. Washington's only fear now was that South Vietnam's resistance against the advancing Vietcong might collapse before the crumbling Diem regime could be overthrown.

11

It is still too early for an accurate and complete account of the coup that toppled Diem. Yet although the story is incomplete, and in some respects inaccurate, there can be no doubt about the political significance of the coup and the motives of the men who carried it out. The Vietcong and the Buddhists had brought the Diem regime to the brink of military and political disaster, but it was Diem's own army that put an end to his rule. The colonels and generals who organized the coup were motivated not so much by revolutionary zeal or democratic convictions as by their concern

over the regime's inability to fight and defeat the Vietcong. Moreover, they were convinced that their project, though never publicly
endorsed by authorized American spokesmen, had the blessings of
the United States. This more than anything else explains why the
coup came about. Although no U.S. Government agent was actively engaged in its preparation, Washington nevertheless made a
"substantial" contribution.[44] The coup became possible only because Washington, after nine years of supporting Diem, concluded
that he had to be replaced if South Vietnam was to survive.

The persons and forces involved in the coup present a complex
and highly confusing picture. Not only were there two groups of
plotters working toward the same goal throughout the summer of
1963, but the government too, at least in the person of Ngo Dinh
Nhu, was preparing a coup, or rather a countercoup, to trap and
eliminate its enemies.

Ironically, the most ardent of the conspirators was one of the
regime's highest officials, Dr. Tran Kim Tuyen, the sinister head
of the Political and Social Research Service of the Presidency, and
for more than eight years one of Nhu's most valuable henchmen.
Dr. Tuyen, who fell out of favor in early 1963, began to organize
a group of young colonels eager to stage a coup. In September,
Dr. Tuyen was appointed consul general to Cairo, but by that time
his group was sufficiently well organized to manage without his
personal guidance. Headed by Colonel Do Mau, who was in
charge of military security, and Colonel Pham Ngoc Thao, the
military inspector of the strategic-hamlet program, the group succeeded in enlisting General Tran Thien Khiem of the Joint Chiefs
of Staff. Khiem had a major voice in troop deployment and enjoyed Diem's confidence. It was he who in the early summer of
1963 established contact between the colonels and the senior officers also working toward the overthrow of Diem. This second
group was led by the Generals Duong Van Minh, Tran Van Don,
and Le Van Kim, none of whom had command posts. The
colonels wanted to strike in July, but the generals, more cautious,
thought this premature.

General Tran Van Don was the man who kept the Americans
informed about the preparations for the coup. A high civilian
official whose identity is still unknown was the contact man between the generals and the U.S. Government. General Don in-

formed this official on October 2 that a coup was in preparation and it was this same official, according to Robert Shaplen, who told General Duong Van Minh on October 10 that Washington would not stand in the way of a military coup.[45] At least one American correspondent is fully convinced that the coup could not have taken place without the approval of President Kennedy.[46]

One of the problems facing the plotting generals was Nhu's scheme to foil the coup with his countercoup. Nhu's coup was of course intended only as a maneuver, to be quickly put down by loyal troops, the Special Forces, and the Palace Guard. They were to round up all enemies of the regime after "putting down" Nhu's phony revolt.

The generals knew that they had to strike before Nhu, whose first deceptive act was an order to the Special Forces to leave Saigon on October 20. But they could not do so before solving a second major problem. The troops of the Saigon garrison and a division near Saigon were commanded by two officers apparently determined to fight for Diem: General Huynh Van Cao, the unbelievably incompetent commander of the 4th Army Corps, whose 7th Division was stationed at Mytho, and General Ton That Dinh, a "boisterous, eccentric, whisky-drinking paratrooper"[47] in his mid-thirties whom Diem trusted implicitly and treated like a son. Dinh—cunning, vain, ambitious, but not too bright—was the only high-ranking officer with prior knowledge of the pagoda raids. Both Cao and Dinh were recent converts to Catholicism and members of Nhu's Personalist Labor Party.

There is no need to go into the intrigues that led to the removal of General Cao and his 7th Division. Suffice it to say that on the day the generals struck, the 7th Division was under the command of a conspirator and General Cao was under arrest.

In dealing with General Dinh, the plotters faced a trickier problem. Dinh was too strong to be beaten in battle, even if the loyalty of his troops to the regime was not certain. He was too cunning to be maneuvered into a position of neutrality and too ambitious to remain a bystander in a power struggle whose outcome was uncertain. Trying to win Dinh's cooperation also held its dangers, since his loyalty was certain to be extremely fragile. The generals hit upon the simple solution of playing on Dinh's vanity. They told him that he was the most important man in

Vietnam, that without him Diem could not stay in power, that it was a shame that he and other key generals were being kept out of a government they were helping to sustain, that Diem ought to appoint some generals to the cabinet, but above all that he, Dinh, in recognition of his vital role in buttressing the regime, ought to be made minister of the interior.

When Dinh voiced these demands, Diem predictably rejected them angrily. At that point the generals told Dinh that Diem would be overthrown and that if Dinh joined the coup he would become the new government's minister of the interior. The plotters even bribed a fortuneteller to help persuade Dinh that a great political future lay before him. Although Dinh remained undecided up to the very last, the conspirators' psychological gamble paid off.

When the coup finally got under way, two important members of the Ngo family were out of the country: Monsignor Ngo Dinh Thuc had been ordered to the Vatican, and Mme. Nhu had left Vietnam on September 9 on a propaganda tour that took her from Belgrade to Rome to Paris to the United States. (Official Washington ignored her visit and her parents refused to see her, but curiosity and a sense of fair play gave Mme. Nhu a hearing accorded to few nonofficial foreign visitors to the United States.)

On Friday, November 1, the day of the coup, Ambassador Lodge accompanied Admiral Felt on a farewell visit to the Palace. This was at about 10:30 A.M. Diem remarked that they should disregard any rumors of a coup they might have heard. Diem apparently thought that Nhu's countercoup was about to get under way.

Army, navy, marine, air force, and paratroop units commanded by officers supporting the coup began to move into Saigon. The generals, as was their custom every Friday, had invited all important high-ranking officers to a luncheon meeting. General Don told the gathering that a coup was under way. General Minh read a proclamation setting forth the aims of the conspirators and asked every officer ready to go along to so state. Nobody dared to protest. Four unreliable officers had already been arrested, and the pro-Diem commander of the navy had been shot by the escort sent to bring him to the meeting. Dinh, whom the plotters did not trust completely, had been told to remain at his headquarters.

Colonel Tung of the Special Forces was forced at gunpoint to order his troops to lay down their arms. Later in the afternoon he himself was shot.

The coup was carried out with great precision. The Palace was surrounded by troops under the command of Colonel Thao and attacked by tanks and mortars. General Dinh, seeing which way the wind was blowing, decided so firmly in favor of the coup that he later came to regard himself as its chief organizer. Nhu called Dinh's headquarters at 1:30 P.M. and ordered him to counterattack, but Dinh did not answer the phone; instead, he brought additional troops into Saigon in support of the coup.

When Diem and Nhu realized what was happening, they sent out a call for help, urging their chiefs of provinces and corps commanders to come to the rescue of the legitimate government. Not one responded. Diem also called on the Civil Guard and Nhu ordered his Republican Youth and his wife's paramilitary women's corps to take up arms against the rebels. Nobody stirred. The regime's political bankruptcy was total.

When the generals called on Diem to surrender, Diem invited them for "consultation," but the rebels were not ready to discuss anything but surrender. At 4 P.M., Diem called Ambassador Lodge, who advised him to give up and offered him asylum. Diem replied that he would try to restore order. He still hoped for help from General Cao's 7th Division, but some of its units had joined the coup.

According to most reports, Diem and Nhu fled from the Palace at 8 P.M. The Palace Guard was not told that the men it was fighting to protect were no longer there. The two brothers allegedly left the building through a tunnel and drove to Cholon, where they found refuge in the house of a wealthy Chinese. There they learned in the early morning hours of the next day that the rebels had taken the Palace and that most of their "loyal" troops had made common cause with the insurgents. Shortly before 7 A.M., Diem telephoned General Don that he was willing to surrender, but dissatisfied with the conditions he was offered, he refused to say where he was. However, his hiding place had apparently been betrayed to Colonel Thao, who came there in person. But Diem and Nhu managed to escape and took refuge in a nearby Catholic church. From there Diem at about 9 A.M.

managed to get to a telephone and once more offered to surrender. Speaking to General Khiem, Diem told him where he and Nhu could be found. An armored car was sent for them. With it arrived the commander of the Civil Guard, Colonel Duong Ngoc Lam, whom Diem considered loyal. Lam, who had in fact joined the coup only at a late hour, was accompanied by General Mai Huu Xuan, one of the original conspirators. Xuan, allegedly acting in full accord with General Duong Van Minh, is believed to have given the order for the murder of Diem and Nhu. Diem and Nhu were dead when the armored car arrived at Saigon. Their bodies were brought to the General's headquarters at 11 A.M. At 4 P.M., they were identified at St. Paul's Hospital by a relative, the wife of Tran Trung Dung, a former cabinet member who had long before broken with Diem.

Thus did the reign of Ngo Dinh Diem come to an end.

Only three weeks after the death of Diem, President Kennedy was assassinated. It is impossible to say whether the Vietnamese conflict would have developed in the direction it did after 1964 if either Diem or Kennedy had lived. After their deaths, the fate of Vietnam was determined by the generals who had overthrown Diem and by Kennedy's successor, Lyndon B. Johnson. It was the policies of these men that, within little more than a year's time, brought about the Americanization of the Vietnamese war.

XVIII

The Americanization
of the War

1

WHAT SOUTH VIETNAM needed more desperately at the end of 1963 than in 1954 was the revolution, social and political, which Diem had celebrated in words but blocked by deed. Unfortunately, the generals who overthrew Diem had no understanding of this need. They had done nothing beyond executing a coup, a change of government accompanied by some uninspired political reforms, such as the lifting of the most absurd and vexing restrictions on freedom imposed by the Diem regime. But they were totally devoid of constructive political ideas and took no measures to organize the country's anti-Communist nationalists; and though they were generals, they did not even have a military plan for dealing with the growing force of the Communist-led insurrection. Of the need for drastic social reforms they remained so completely unaware that the words "land reform" were never even uttered. The

475

new rulers, a military junta headed by the popular General Duong Van Minh, not only ignored the plight of the people, from whom they remained remote, but they also failed to deal with the evil of corruption, which continued to undermine the nation's well-being. Most of the venal and incompetent officials of the Diem regime remained in their positions. The new head of police, Mai Huu Xuan, had for years served as an official of the French police. It soon became known that he arrested people only to set them free for large cash payments.[1]

Instead of political reorganization and modest democratic progress, which had been the promise of the coup, the political chaos in the camp of anti-Communist nationalism continued. Six weeks after the coup, South Vietnam had no less than sixty-three political parties, few of which counted more than several dozen followers. A Council of Notables, created as a substitute for a parliament, consisted largely of old, inefficient, and discredited former collaborators of the French, without a single peasantry or labor representative. For the Vietnamese people, therefore, the coup, although greeted as a deliverance from evil, soon turned into just another disappointment.

Relieved of the burden of defending the ugly features of the Diem regime, Washington supported the new government with open enthusiasm, but unfortunately with no deeper understanding of the problems and needs that were plaguing South Vietnam. Failing to realize that military progress was impossible without a radical change in the country's political life, Ambassador Lodge kept insisting that the junta should concentrate its energies not on political reforms but on greater military effort.

After only three months, the easygoing regime set up by the leaders of the anti-Diem coup was abruptly removed. Political life under the junta had not become the active concern of the mass of the people; it continued to be the monopoly of small cliques, now composed chiefly of South Vietnam's fifty-two generals, most of whom were engaged in a power struggle. One of these generals, Nguyen Khanh, together with the chief plotter against Diem, General Tran Thien Khiem, succeeded, on January 30, 1964, in a surprise move against the junta to arrest a number of its members and to put himself at the head of a new regime. As such he continued in various military and government positions, with ever-diminishing influence, for a whole year, surviving a number of attempts to oust him through popular demonstrations, largely by students, and coup-attempts by his military colleagues. Throughout that entire year, the country's political fabric loosened and military strength continued to decline; there was growing unrest and serious military reverses. Desperate efforts by the new American ambassador, General Maxwell Taylor, to elevate Nguyen Khanh into the position of a strong man devoted to the war effort and the United States ended in failure. Khanh was almost overthrown when, in August, 1964, he proclaimed a constitution that would have given him dictatorial powers. Long before 1964 came to a close, it had become evident that Khanh too was not to be the savior of which his country was in need.

Nor did the civilian aspirants to power, with whom Khanh tried to bolster his unstable regime, give evidence of being able to repair the damage that had been done to South Vietnam's body politic and military strength during the last years of the Diem regime. The Dai Viet leader Nguyen Ton Hoan, recalled from Paris and made vice premier, failed as dismally as did the old nationalist Phan Khac Suu, whom the military under Khanh briefly allowed to become president on October 27, 1964, and Tran Van Huong, who was made premier a few days later. An attempt under Khanh to resume more drastically the program of land distribution to the landless led nowhere; the landlords in the government and high administrative posts succeeded in killing this as well as all subsequent attempts at land reform. As under Diem earlier, and Air Vice-Marshal Nguyen Cao Ky two years later, land reform remained a dead issue. The tenants were still forced to pay rents of up to 60 per cent or more of their crops to absentee landlords. Moreover, landlords who returned to villages reoccupied by the Saigon armed forces after having been under Vietcong control for years, were allowed to extract rents for past years from the tenants, thus making sure that the poor peasants regretted their liberation from Vietcong control. The masses of the villagers also suffered more and more from the increased tempo of the war and soon became totally indifferent to the frequent coups that shook the fragile Saigon power structure erected by the military, the high administrators, a small business community, and the growing number of war profiteers, a structure sustained only by the lavish U.S. expenditures for the Vietnamese war.

No less than nine changes of government took place before Nguyen Cao Ky, briefly the protector of Khanh, rose on the Saigon horizon and set himself above all other military aspirants for power. Khanh was ousted by the so-called Armed Forces Council, of which he was chairman, on February 20, 1965. Ky, a young and immature political adventurer, embarrassed the United States with his awkward admission that Adolf Hitler was his hero. But the Washington leadership, which for a whole year had been saying that the choice was between Khanh or chaos, soon decided to embrace the new man. Ky quickly acquired the skills needed to manipulate the vast powers that U.S. aid put in his hands, until, in the fall of 1967, his star began to wane, undermined by his rival, General Nguyen Van Thieu.

The ten changes of government since the fall of Diem are not worth being recorded in detail, but what they proved deserves discussion. Like the Diem regime, these governments were all unpopular, and some also fell owing to mass opposition; the generals proved that they were unable to settle their internal rivalries and lay the ground for a viable government based on popular consent, while the failure of the nonmilitary office holders demonstrated that the divisions among the civilian nationalists were also too deep and too destructive to overcome the tragic political weakness of the anti-Communist forces. This weakness partly explains why the United States opted for the more stable military dictatorship of Nguyen Cao Ky, who openly took power on June 19, 1965.

A deeper reason, however, for America's support of men like Khanh and Ky was their greater reliability as proponents of the aims pursued by the Johnson Administration in Vietnam. It is significant that Khanh tried to justify the ouster of the junta that ruled briefly after the overthrow of Diem by accusing some of its leading generals of "neutralism," a catchword invariably applied to all who sought a compromise solution of the war, who did not believe in the possibility of a military solution, or only at the risk of the country's total destruction. Accusations similar to "neutralism"—i.e., charges of being "soft on Communism"—were leveled also against the more promising, briefly tolerated government of Dr. Phan Huy Quat, in the spring of 1965. But more conclusive evidence that Washington insisted on a government determined to uphold the American policy of intensified warfare was produced in March, 1966, when Buddhist opposition to Ky could be suppressed only with active American help. Every open manifestation of the people in South Vietnam since the fall of Diem had "neutralist" tendencies, demonstrated a desire for peace, and expressed reservations regarding American policy and presence. This was particularly true of the Buddhists, whose movement was a genuinely indigenous force and enjoyed considerable mass support. The militant Buddhists regarded the conflict in Vietnam primarily as a civil war among Southerners; peace, they said, could not come through increased warfare, which might continue indefinitely; it must be based on a political solution, which could only be a compromise. As far as the military supported by Washington was concerned, the war was never anything but the result of "aggression," and therefore aggression had to be defeated before peace could come. In supporting Ky against the Buddhists and any other "neutralists" or "peace candidates," Washington confirmed that its policy, in spite of Johnson's repeated readiness to talk peace, remained committed to the elusive aim of a military victory over the Vietcong, to be achieved after the Hanoi regime had been bombed into willingness to end its support of the Southern insurrection.

But the harsh reality of a Saigon military dictatorship determined to achieve a military victory was always politically embarrassing to Washington, because it conflicted with the claim that the struggle for Vietnam was one between dictatorship and freedom and that Johnson was ready to achieve peace through negotiations. Consequently, a constituent assembly was elected in September, 1966. Elections for a president and a senate, on the basis of a constitution tailored to the needs of the ruling military clique, were held in September, 1967, quite obviously in order to camouflage the reality of the existing dictatorship, which Washington considered necessary in order to contain the upsurge of "neutralist" and "peace" sentiments among the vast majority of the people. The conditions under which the elections were held showed them to have been not an exercise in, but rather a denial of, political freedom. The constitutionally affirmed freedom of the press remained on paper. During the campaign no less than four Saigon newspapers were suppressed by the Ky government. The sale of newsprint remained a government monopoly. There was no freedom of assembly, and electioneering by the candidates was severely curtailed. The former head of state, General Duong Van Minh, was barred from running; suspected of "neutralism" and feared because of his popularity, he was forbidden to return from his exile in Bangkok. Also barred was Au Truong Thanh, formerly a minister in Ky's cabinet but later converted to the quest for peace. The Buddhist slate for the senate election was rejected under the flimsiest of pretexts, and the several thousand Buddhist activists arrested by the Ky government in the spring of 1966 were kept in prison. When the election was over, the defeated civilian candidates produced proof of shocking election frauds, and popular demonstrations by students and Buddhists supported the demand that the result be annulled. This demand was accepted by a commission of the Constituent Assembly by 16 to 2 votes, but the Assembly itself, deliberating in the presence of a strong police force headed by the chief of police, accepted the election result by a vote of 58 to 43.

In spite of all governmental precautions, the military candidates Thieu and Ky received only 35 per cent of the votes, while an avowed peace candidate gained the largest number of votes among their civilian opponents. The government boasted of an 80 per cent participation in the elections. But elections could be held only in the regions free of Vietcong control, which meant that only 56 per cent of those of voting age cast their ballots, a fact the American press failed to note. It is clear, therefore, that the "popular base" of the elected presidential government added up to less than 20 per cent of the electorate of South Vietnam. Measured by the propaganda requirements of Washington, this "step toward self-determination" was an evident fiasco. The new regime, far from representing the will of the South Vietnamese people, remained the old Thieu-Ky military regime; it could have been dropped only if the South Vietnamese forces that desired a peaceful solution of the conflict had not been rejected by the United States.

2

The fall of Diem contained a lesson which the leaders of the United States unfortunately were not able to learn: i.e., that military success against the Communist-led insurgency required bold political measures, that the problem was not how many Communists could be killed but rather how successfully the population could be immunized against Communist propaganda and attached to an anti-Communist regime. By 1964, it was already easy to predict where the alternative to such a course, namely, the reliance on military efforts, would eventually lead: since the military strength of the Saigon regime would continue to decline, a collapse could in the end be averted only if the United States intervened with its own military forces.

Whether such an intervention was advisable or not had been a subject of discussion as far back as 1961, both in regard to the question of bombing the North and of sending American combat troops into the South. As regards the question of bombing, General Maxwell Taylor wrote in his recent book: "I do not know of any element in the Vietnamese situation which caused longer debate, longer discussions."[2] Although most of President Kennedy's advisers favored the commitment of American combat troops long before the fall of Diem, Kennedy held to his view that this was a Vietnamese war, that the fighting had to be done by Vietnamese soldiers, and that America's role was merely to help —with supplies and advisers, not with combat troops.[3] But Kennedy certainly did not contemplate a withdrawal from the Vietnamese conflict. He compromised between withdrawal and full Americanization of the war by steadily increasing the teams of American military "advisers," who, it soon became known, were more and more actively engaged in combat direction, and he lavishly supplied the South Vietnamese army with modern equipment. The number of "advisers" rose from about 800 at the end of 1960 to 17,000 at the beginning of 1964, only weeks after America's Vietnam policy had become President Johnson's responsibility.

There is no way of knowing whether or not the United States, had Kennedy lived, would, at the end of 1967, have found itself committed with nearly half a million soldiers to a war which more and more qualified observers said might last another five to ten years. Even the question of whether Johnson would have taken this course had he known that escalation was an open-ended road cannot be answered with certainty. 1964 was the last year during which a solution could have been sought before the war became primarily American and before it was extended to the North. But peace through political concessions to the forces fighting the Saigon regime was never contemplated, either in Saigon or in Washington, although Washington might have considered such a course had it foreseen where the attempt to defeat the Vietcong militarily would eventually lead. Unfortunately, Washington failed to realize the extent to which the South continued to disintegrate politically and militarily, and instead of seeking a compromise chased after the mirage of a swift victory over the Vietcong.

In the early summer of 1964, however, the political and military apparatus of Saigon presided over by General Khanh gave clear signs of further disintegration. It was then that Khanh began to insist on American support for carrying the war to the North— at a time when President Johnson, beginning his election campaign, had started to attack his Republican opponent, Barry M. Goldwater, for demanding that American bombs and combat troops be employed to achieve a quick victory over the Vietnamese Communists. As early as August 12, 1964, Mr. Johnson, speaking as the critics of his policy would speak two years later, said in New York: "Some others are eager to enlarge the conflict. They call upon us to supply American boys to do the job that Asian boys should do. They ask us to take reckless action which might risk the lives of millions and engulf much of Asia and certainly threaten the peace of the entire world. Moreover, such action would offer no solution at all to the real problems of Vietnam." On August 29, he declared in Texas that he had rejected the advice "to load our planes with bombs and to drop them on certain areas" and thus broaden the war. However, very few people noticed a passage in a later Johnson rejection of bombing raids against the North, made on September 28 in Manchester, New Hampshire. There Mr. Johnson stated: "So we are not going north and drop bombs *at this stage of the game*" (italics added). Indeed, even before his election, Johnson's secret intentions were the opposite of what his vigorous peace rhetoric led the American people to believe.

Thus did the President himself open up the chasm between the words and deeds of the Administration that later became known as the "credibility gap"—a polite term for the fact that more and more people began to realize the untruthfulness of important American official statements about Vietnam. As *The New York Times* revealed on May 20, 1966, as early as the summer of 1964, "Premier Khanh was promised a bombing offensive against the North, presumably on Presidential authority, to extract pledges from Saigon of governmental stability and efficacy." To bolster the sagging morale in the South was in fact later one of the reasons given for bombing the North. At least as far as the Saigon military leadership was concerned, this aim was achieved: Premier Ky let it be known after the bombing raids on February 7, 1965, that this was "the most beautiful day of his life."

This introduced the beginning of the systematic bombing of the North. An isolated instance of a bombing attack had occurred in August, 1964, in the so-called Tongking incident, when, in reprisal for alleged attacks by North Vietnamese torpedo boats on American destroyers on August 2 and 4, Johnson ordered retaliatory air attacks on the North Vietnamese torpedo-boat bases and their oil-storage depots. The incident offered Johnson an opportunity to have his policy of escalation unconditionally endorsed by Congress in the so-called Gulf of Tongking resolution, which authorized the President "to take all necessary measures to repel any armed attack against the forces of the United States and to prevent further aggression." Johnson regarded the resolution as a blank check for any action he deemed necessary. The resolution was presented as a spontaneous reaction of the Administration and Congress to North Vietnamese aggression, but it soon became known that Mr. Johnson and some of his aides had carried a draft of it around with them for weeks. As regards North Vietnamese aggression, a rather reliable participant in the secret Senate hearings on the Tongking incident, Senator Fulbright, had this to say: "But the Gulf of Tongking incident, if I may say so, was a very vague one. We were briefed on it, but we have no way of knowing, even to this day, what actually happened. I do not know whether we provoked the attack in connection with supervising or helping a raid by the South Vietnamese or not."[4]

The lack of evidence for the claims designed to justify the first attacks on the North did nothing to remove the feeling that the public was being misled by official propaganda. But the credibility gap widened even more after bombing raids on the North became routine in February, 1965, shortly after Johnson had been elected on a platform of refusing to "go north and drop bombs." The bombing of February 7, 1965, also was presented as a U.S. reprisal —in this case for a Vietcong guerrilla attack against an American camp at Pleiku in which 7 American soldiers were killed and 109 wounded. But in this instance as well, the decision to bomb the North in retaliation for the Pleiku attack was anything but spontaneous. As a matter of fact, Johnson "had made the momentous *decision* to bomb North Vietnam nearly four months earlier," as *Newsweek* correspondent Charles Roberts wrote later. "That decision was made, it can now be revealed, in October 1964, at the height of the presidential campaign."[5] To the question why the North was being punished for an attack committed by the Vietcong, the answer was supplied by Secretary of State Dean Rusk, but only a year later, since it would have been impossible for him to produce, in February, 1965, evidence for the story he told. Rusk, testifying before the Senate Foreign Relations Committee on January 28, 1966, stated that between November, 1964, and January, 1965, the 325th Division of the North Vietnamese army came down to South Vietnam. Rusk underlined that this aggression had taken place before any bombing of the North, that therefore "escalation" had been started by the North Vietnamese. "At no stage have we ourselves wanted to escalate this war," he said at another hearing on February 18, 1966.

The truth about infiltration from the North was certainly not easy to come by; however, the Rusk statement shows that even American propaganda did not claim the infiltration of organized Northern army units before the end of 1964; yet for years it had been denied that the fighting in the South was a civil war; instead it was described as the result of "aggression from abroad." Small groups of "advisers" from the North were no doubt operating in the South before 1965, but certainly fewer than the 17,000 American advisers in the South. But Rusk's claim that a whole division was infiltrated before February, 1965, was untrue, and was soon denounced by the opposition to the war as an intentional deception of the American public. Secretary McNamara, likely to be better informed on military matters than Rusk, had in fact given the true figures and dates on April 27, 1965. The first North Vietnamese units—not a whole division, but a battalion of 400–500 men—he said, had entered the South during March, 1965. Senator Mike Mansfield, the Democratic majority leader and an expert on Vietnam, confirmed this in a speech delivered on June 16, 1966, at Yeshiva University: "When the sharp increase in the American military effort began in early 1965, it was estimated that only about 400 North Vietnamese soldiers were among the enemy forces in the South, which totaled 140,000 at that time." This was obviously another attempt to correct Rusk, who, on May 17, 1966, again had stated at a press conference: "The 325th North Vietnamese Division came from North Vietnam into South Vietnam before we started bombing North Vietnam."

The 325th Division, nonexistent in the South in February, 1965, was also Rusk's explanation for the buildup of the American ground forces, which took a new and decisive turn on March 7, 1965, when 3,500 Marines were landed at Danang, bringing the total number of U.S. troops to 27,000. By July, 1965, U.S. combat troops numbered 75,000. On July 28, President Johnson announced a further immediate increase to 125,000. Four months later, a total of 165,000 American troops had been brought into South Vietnam. By the end of 1967, the number was 475,000, but it was still regarded as insufficient by the U.S. military command, which extracted an increase of another 45,000 men from the President.

As to the bombing of the North, which steadily grew in intensity, it was said that by March, 1966, the United States was dropping two-and-a-half times the bomb load per month that it had dropped in Korea. Combat statisticians have figured out that in 1965 more than one ton of bombs, napalm, and rockets had been dropped for each Vietcong fighter in the South.

What were the real reasons that persuaded the U.S. leadership to start this gigantic military effort in Vietnam? It could not have been the appearance of 400–500 North Vietnamese soldiers in the spring of 1965 that pushed the United States into a nearly total Americanization of the war. The truth is that because of the continuing political deterioration of the Saigon regime and the ever-growing strength of the insurrection, South Vietnam, in the spring of 1965, was on the point of collapse. General Earl G. Wheeler confirmed this two years later: "By late spring of that year [1965], due to a combination of circumstances the Viet Cong/North Vietnamese army was threatening to overwhelm the armed forces of South Vietnam."[6] A commission report submitted by Senator Mansfield bluntly stated: "In short, a total collapse of the Saigon government's authority appeared imminent in the early months of 1965."[7] This, and not the appearance of one North Vietnamese battalion, triggered the massive U.S. military intervention in the South. Richard N. Goodwin, a former assistant to President Johnson and now one of his severest critics, reported that the bombing of the North was also related to the political situation in the South. He wrote that "early in 1965, the President was advised that morale in South Vietnam could be revived only if we bombed military targets in North Vietnam. This would assure Saigon of our determination to stay the course."[8]

Again, as under Diem, the deeper reasons for the near collapse of the Saigon regime were of course primarily political. The military balance could hardly have been affected by the appearance of North Vietnamese soldiers, of whom, according to U.S. military intelligence, no more than 1,200–1,400 had crossed into the South as of August, 1965. This crisis was created, on the one hand, by the increase in popular support for the Vietcong and the rise in the number of Southern guerrillas, and on the other hand by the reluctance of the Saigon armed forces to fight. One out of every six soldiers of the National Army deserted during 1965. By 1966, the desertion rate per month stood at 10,000–12,000, and the year's total loss through desertion was 110,000. As Theodore Draper put it in his recent book, one of many publications attacking U.S. policy in Vietnam: "The crisis in 1965 in South Vietnam was far more intimately related to South Vietnamese disintegration than to North Vietnamese infiltration."[9]

By early spring 1966, U.S. intervention had achieved the negative aim of preventing the collapse of the Saigon government. But it had not produced the other objectives of the U.S. buildup in the South and the bombing of the North. The guerrillas, although unable to cope with the mounting number of U.S. soldiers and its huge supply of modern equipment, nevertheless remained undefeated; at the end of 1967, they were considerably stronger than in the spring of 1965. The bombing of the North did not stop infiltration. And as to the attempt to break the morale of the North Vietnamese people and their leaders, the result was obviously quite contrary to all of Johnson's expectations. Saigon held the cities and the places where the Americans had erected their enormous installations, but the villages on the whole continued to be held by the Vietcong. According to a *New York Times* report of October 2, 1967, of the 12,537 hamlets in the South, the government fully controlled (meaning also by night) a bare 2,000. More optimistic reports put out by the Administration in November, 1967, met with general skepticism.

That the steady escalation of the air war failed to stop the growth of enemy strength is attested to by official U.S. statistics, which are unlikely to favor enemy claims. Early in 1965, estimates of Vietcong strength ranged from 116,000 to 140,000, of which only about 15 per cent had received training in the North. By August, 1966, the number of enemy soldiers had reached 280,-000, although Vietcong losses of 73,000 had been given for the preceding year. The figures of real losses, however, were inaccurate, and not only because of the tendency of the military to inflate them. All experienced observers have remarked on the difficulty of determining who was a real Vietcong. The French journalist Jean Lacouture offered the somewhat sarcastic explanation that in the eyes of American military statisticians any dead Vietnamese was a Vietcong. Assuming, however, that the figure of Vietcong losses of 73,000 for 1965 was correct, this would mean that the enemy forces, having replaced these losses and grown to 280,000 by August, 1966, must have succeeded in adding nearly 240,000 new fighters to their ranks. Since, again according to U.S. intelligence, no more than about 45,000 Northern soldiers had been in the South at the end of 1966, the increase of enemy strength must have come primarily from recruitment in the South. In spite of severe losses and the difficulties of infiltration caused by the bombing, the strength of the Northern contingent continued to grow; it was estimated at 55,000 by the end of 1967, and the number of Southern fighters was estimated at 240,000. A new way of counting enemy strength was adopted for the propaganda campaign of

November, 1967, through which the Administration tried to convince the American public that steady progress was being made in the war. But the juggling of figures, which produced the new lower estimate of a total of 240,000 enemy fighters only by leaving out previously counted Vietcong units failed to prove that enemy strength had declined.

Thus it was evident that two and a half years of steady escalation had brought the United States no nearer to its real goal, which was to force the enemy to make peace on U.S. and South Vietnamese terms. Infiltration from the North of troops and supplies continued despite the increased bombing raids. And what the nearly 500,000 American combat troops had achieved by the summer of 1967 was aptly summed up in a *New York Times* report from Saigon, dated August 7, 1967: The Americans, it said, are no longer losing battles, but they are also not winning the war.

3

Ever since the war had become fully Americanized, its costs, loss of lives, and the failure to end it had become a deep American concern. The war in Vietnam soon became the subject of violent political dissension, as well as a burden on the conscience of all Americans who do not believe that in the struggle against Communism the end justifies all means. Thanks to the vigor that characterizes press freedom in the United States, the attempts to manipulate the news coming out of Saigon and the propaganda barrage emanating from Washington did not succeed in withholding the truth about the war in Vietnam from the American public.

As this truth became known to more and more people, opposition to Mr. Johnson's conduct of the war, and, even more, opposition to the war itself, began to grow—slowly in 1965–66, but alarmingly for the Administration in the year 1967. No longer was it possible for the Administration to brush aside criticism of its policy because the serious exponents of the opposition did not reach the masses. Nor could public protests in universities and street demonstrations any longer be denounced as the work only of left-wingers, draft-dodgers, beatniks, and other "un-American" elements. Veteran Administration critics, such as Professor Hans Morgenthau and columnist Walter Lippmann in the press, and J. William Fulbright, Wayne Morse, and Ernest Gruening in the Senate, were now joined by a growing number of other experts in foreign and military policy, such as former Ambassadors George Kennan, John Kenneth Galbraith, and General James M. Gavin, who in testimony before Congress as well as in speeches and articles effectively attacked the strategic and foreign-policy concepts underlying the Administration aims in Vietnam. Harsh criticism of Johnson also came from such former White House advisers as Arthur Schlesinger Jr. and Richard N. Goodwin, both of whom wrote books expressing their serious reservations about Washington's Vietnam policy. In October, 1967, Theodore C. Sorensen, President Kennedy's closest White House aide, joined these critics, thus reviving speculation as to whether President Kennedy would have allowed the Vietnamese war to become fully Americanized.[10]

While President Johnson could long afford to disregard the numerous protests by professors, writers, artists, clergymen, doctors, lawyers, and occasional business executives, the growing opposition in Congress could not be lightly dismissed. Highly respected Democrats and Republicans joined Senators Fulbright, Morse, and Gruening in speaking out against further escalation as well as against support of the reactionary military dictatorship in Saigon. The speeches by Senators Stephen Young of Ohio, Frank Church of Idaho, Vance Hartke of Indiana, George McGovern of South Dakota, Joseph Clark of Pennsylvania, and Eugene J. McCarthy of Minnesota, to name only a few, revealed not only a growing uneasiness about the wisdom of the U.S. presence in Vietnam at all, but also a surprising familiarity with the sad military, social, and political conditions in the South. It came as quite a shock to the Administration and the Republican leadership backing Johnson's Vietnam policy when, in October, 1967, this policy was fiercely attacked by a number of prominent Republican Senators, including Clifford Case of New Jersey, John Sherman Cooper of Kentucky, Charles Percy of Illinois, Mark O. Hatfield of Oregon, and Thruston Morton of Kentucky. Some, like Cooper, demanded an end to the bombing of the North, while Morton, in a personal attack on the President, said that he had been "brainwashed" by the "military-industrial complex" into believing in the possibility of a military solution. Referring to the growing credibility gap, Hatfield accused the Administration of "doubletalk and deceit" on Vietnam. All of this coincided with the debate in the U.N. General Assembly, where not only France and the Scandinavian countries, but even such friends of the United States as Canada and anti-Communist Indonesia demanded a stop to the bombing of North Vietnam.

As to the American public, its doubts about the wisdom of the course in Vietnam had been growing slowly for some time after the summer riots in many cities, and President Johnson's request for a 10 per cent tax increase made the question whether Vietnam was worth the cost in money and American lives suddenly more acute. American casualties in dead and wounded surpassed 100,000 late in 1967; soon the 750th plane was downed over the North (some of the planes, such as the F-4 jet, cost as much as $2.5 million). While it was hard for anybody to grasp the meaning of the sum of $26 billion for one year of war, the fact, established by several critics, that it cost more than $300,000 to kill one Vietcong demonstrated rather plainly some of the more absurd aspects of the war. Flying one of the heavy bombers used over the South from its Guam base to its target costs $1,300 per hour, which adds up to $13,000 for the round trip. Senator Hartke, in an article in the *Saturday Evening Post* of April 22, 1967, told of a huge amphibious American operation in the Mekong Delta 35 miles south of Saigon which cost the U.S. taxpayers $16 million. Since a total of twenty-one enemies were killed in this operation, Hartke pointed out that it cost no less than $800,000 to kill one of these Vietcong. (The family of a civilian killed accidentally by the Americans is entitled to an indemnity of $34.00).

No wonder that, after the summer riots of 1965 once more called attention to the dreadful conditions in most large American cities, more and more people began to agree with General Gavin, who, in his testimony before the Senate Foreign Relations Committee in February, 1967, stated: "I recommend that we bring hostilities in Vietnam to an end as quickly and reasonably as we can, that we devote those vast expenditures of our national resources to dealing with our domestic problems; that we make a massive attack on the problems of education, housing, economic opportunity, lawlessness, and environmental pollution." At least half a dozen other retired generals have also spoken up against the war, some even more forcefully than Gavin, who, in resigning from the Massachusetts Democratic Advisory Council because he could not support the re-election of President Johnson again made it clear that the sacrifices demanded for the Vietnamese war increased opposition to it. "Obviously," Gavin said, "our domestic programs are grossly underfunded, especially in the poverty area, and I look at this as a consequence of the Vietnam war."[11] Senator Percy echoed the same sentiment by stating that we "spend $66 million a day trying to save the 16 million people of South Vietnam while leaving the plight of 20 million urban poor in our own country unresolved."[12]

But other aspects of the war, not merely its astronomical costs, also strengthened the opposition, largely because of their effect upon the moral conscience of America. Most disturbing for many Americans was the great number of civilian casualties caused by the manner in which this war was being conducted. Government propaganda tried to prove that civilian casualties were the result as much of Vietcong terror as of American military bombing, the widespread use of napalm and artillery against villages suspected of harboring Vietcong units, and the policy of shooting at anything that moved within a combat zone. Written and pictorial reports gave the American public a gruesome picture of the havoc that the uninhibited use of America's modern military equipment wrought upon the lives and the habitations of the Vietnamese people. There was no doubt that Vietnamese civilians met death from both sides, but the deaths caused by Vietcong terror constituted a small fraction of the total of civilian casualties, which Senator Edward M. Kennedy estimated at 150,000 per year. Vietcong terror, no matter how vicious, remained selective, unlike the thousands of tons of bombs that rained upon the hapless villagers from skies dominated entirely by the Americans. The Vietcong killed civilians chiefly with knife or rifle, rarely with plastic bombs and mortars, and only lately with rockets. These means have no doubt caused much suffering among civilians, but incomparably less than that caused by U.S. and South Vietnamese artillery, and by the bombs dropped from planes on Vietnam. *The New York Times* wrote at the end of August, 1967, that the bomb tonnage dropped on Vietnam "each week is larger than that dropped on Germany at the peak of World War II." And reminding the reader that an air raid on August 9 in the Mekong Delta caused more than 100 civilian casualties, the *Times* continued: "Civilian casualties and the alienation of peasant loyalty are not the only results when air power and artillery are employed on such a scale outside of large-unit ground engagements. The social structure of the countryside is being smashed; and the Communists may be the ultimate beneficiaries of the wreckage, however the conflict ends." It is true that American charitable intentions led to private and governmental help for the victims of this type of warfare. But whatever medical and other aid was being supplied was less than the proverbial drop in the bucket. It was more like a drop in a river, instantly carried away by the rising flood of misery which the war creates every day. Senator Edward Kennedy, intimately acquainted with conditions in South Vietnam through his visits, made this disturbing remark on the subject of civilian casualties: "We have continued to allow scandalous conditions to exist in the few hospitals equipped to deal with civilians injured in the war, and we have paid little or no attention to ways in which the number of casualties and civilian deaths could be lessened."[13]

Another growing burden on the American conscience was the dislocation of millions from their homes and villages and the fate of these victims of the war. The peasants' desire to flee the conditions that were threatening their lives in the zones of combat led to a refugee population of more than 2 million (some estimates range as high as 4 million). Most of these people were miserably housed in improvised camps, poorly fed, and virtually without means of self-help. The American policy of removing the population from villages and towns which for strategic reasons were to be destroyed greatly swelled the ranks of these unfortunate victims of the war. Edward Kennedy inspected many refugee camps and found conditions outrageous. In some he even found that thousands were "literally starving to death." Expenditures for the entire refugee program, he revealed, were less per year than what the United States expended on the war in half a day.[14]

The war led not only to ever-increasing material destruction and social disintegration, but also to the moral disintegration of large segments of the population. "Young Buddhist Says War Perils the Country's Human Values," read a headline in *The New York Times* of May 17, 1967. Another headline in the *Times* of November 13, 1966 said that corruption was taking up to 40 per cent of U.S. Vietnam aid. The monies stolen went largely into the pockets of contractors, administrators, landowners, generals, and others whom the war has made rich or richer. Those with money bribe officials to exempt their sons from military service. Amounts as high as $10,000 have been paid for permission for a young man to study abroad.[15] Other newspaper headlines told other shocking stories, such as one in the *Times* of May 19, 1967: "Pro-Saigon Troops Said to Terrorize a Province"; the subtitle added: "Irregulars Equipped by U.S. Are Accused of Brutality and Thefts in Delta." These troops, the article claimed, "regularly rape, beat, and rob the villagers they are supposed to protect." Other issues that weighed on the American conscience was the torture by the Vietnamese army of Vietcong prisoners and the spread of prostitution in the cities and near American military camps.

Opposition to the war has been nourished also by the widespread fear of what the war was doing to many Americans. The American soldier who observed these moral and political conditions could only react with cynicism to the claim that he was fighting to preserve freedom for the people of South Vietnam. In the United States, the fear kept growing that he was no less subject to the danger of having his conscience numbed and his behavior brutalized than was his Vietnamese colleague. "We burned every hut in sight," wrote a G.I. in a letter to his family, published in *War/Peace Reports* of May, 1967. "[The people] watch in terror as we burn their homes, personal possessions and food. Yes, we burn all rice and shoot all livestock." Letters in which young American soldiers expressed their horror over such procedures, although numerous, seldom found their way into the press. But the incidents they described could not be denied and demanded official explanation, which always was that a village thus treated had been used by the Vietcong whom the peasants had failed to denounce. And in the case of crop destruction with chemicals, the reason given was that the Vietcong had to be denied food supplies, even at the risk of starvation for the non-combatants, almost solely old men, women, and children. When, on September 19, 1967, the heads of the U.S. Government-sup-

506 • Vietnam at War

ported International Voluntary Services (IVS) resigned in protest against the war, after having worked two years in Vietnam, their statement indicated how deeply they were shocked by the physical destruction and moral decline. One of the heads, Don Ronk of Arcata, California, declared: "Not only do I speak against the dying and maiming of the body. . . . I also speak against the dying and maiming of those qualities separating man from beast."[16]

To the shocking disclosures of the conditions created by the war in the South was added, after 1966, a steadily growing number of accounts about the effect of American bombing raids in the North. There, civilian casualties were held to a minimum by protective measures such as evacuations from cities and the digging of shelters in town and country; but most cities and many hundreds of villages near railroads, highways, and bridges were destroyed as completely as the military and industrial establishments chosen as the objects of the raids.

The raids in the North as well as in the South came under increasing attack not only for political reasons, but also because more and more Americans found them morally objectionable—an attitude which began to be expressed ever more forcefully by writers and artists who opposed the war almost unanimously, and by a growing number of churchmen—Protestant, Jewish, and Catholic. The late Dr. Martin Luther King soon emerged as the leading spokesman of religious-political opposition against the war, denouncing it as a political crime and a moral outrage. It came as a surprise to many Americans when Bishop Fulton Sheen spoke up no less forcefully against the war. An open letter by nine Catholic college presidents addressed to their coreligionists and published by *The New York Times* of March 19, 1967, indicated the nature and depth of the concern in religious circles. "We ask you," the letter said, "to join us in condemning emphatically and unambiguously at least the following aspects of American involvement in Vietnam: (1) Indiscriminate bombing which grossly destroys any sufficient distinction between combatant and civilian; (2) The horrible destruction of human life by means of napalm and fragmentation bombs; (3) Depriving the populace of necessary food supplies through crop destruction; (4) The torture of prisoners in any form whatsoever."

The voices demanding a quick end to the war through further

drastic escalation, including the possible invasion of the North, were far from silent as the debate on Vietnam sharpened in the fall of 1967; but the majority of the growing critical voices of Johnson's conduct of the war consisted of people inclined to believe, or actually convinced, that the war was a political mistake and morally intolerable, and that the victory pursued by the military establishment was a utopian goal.

4

Toward the end of 1967, the debate about Vietnam gave signs of dividing the American people more fiercely than any national issue since the Civil War. Both the aims and the methods of achieving them were newly questioned. After almost three years of bombing the North and putting more and more American soldiers into the field, victory or any other kind of solution looked as remote as ever. The U.S. ambassador to South Vietnam, Ellsworth Bunker, and the U.S. commander, General William C. Westmoreland, were employed in a campaign to counteract the feeling that the war was a stalemate; but as authoritative a voice as Senator Mansfield dismissed this campaign with a warning against deluding ourselves.

In contrast to the anxious months of spring, 1965, it was now clear that the enemy was no longer able to achieve a military victory. But had he not already won the war politically? There was overwhelming evidence that no progress was being made in the so-called pacification program, proving that the people, even when they began to tire of Vietcong taxes and recruiting, were as far as ever from feeling any loyalty toward the Saigon regime. Cautious realists merely allowed that at the going rate, pacification of most of the South would take at least ten years. The great hope, stimulated by the U.S. Government and large sections of the press, that the elections of a president and a two-chamber parliament would at last create a popular base for the Saigon regime proved to be just another self-deception. Amid their disappointment over the ugly postelection mood in Saigon, the American people were reminded by those opposed to the war that

Premier Ky had stated on May 13, 1967, that he would act militarily against any elected president with whose policy he disagreed. Since the articulate sections of the Vietnamese people rejected the elections as undemocratic and fraudulent, the U.S. Government could hardly convince the American people that they had been democratic and free. It was the dominant belief in the United States that the new government of South Vietnam was still the old dictatorship without a popular mandate to govern. No one doubted that in a truly free contest, even one without participation of the National Liberation Front, the Thieu-Ky regime would have been wiped out.

On the military front, the outlook remained dismal. The more than one million American, "allied," and South Vietnamese troops were as far from decisive military success against the enemy as ever. There was little comfort in, and much doubt about, casualty figures which frequently showed a ratio of one or no American killed for every ten Vietcong. If these claims were true, then why, it was asked, had the Vietcong not already been wiped out completely? If their numbers did not actually increase, their supplies, particularly of new and heavier weapons, increased in spite of the stepped-up bombing attacks on routes, depots, and transport facilities in the North. Even military experts in the field and at the Pentagon began to echo what some had been saying for a long time: that at the existing tempo of the war, hostilities might continue another ten years, even if the number of American troops were raised to a million. In their frustration, many of the U.S. military leaders began to consider the bombing of the dykes in the North, the mining and bombing of the harbor of Haiphong, through which most of the supplies from the Soviet Union entered Vietnam, and some even considered an invasion of the North. If the world's greatest military power and richest nation was unable to subdue a small and backward country in Asia, these strategists maintained, the reason was simply that they were not allowed the unrestrained use of their military means. With these means, in the words of the former chief of the Air Force, Curtis LeMay, North Vietnam could be bombed back into the Stone Age. But, of course, this, in Barry Goldwater's words, meant that one would have to forget "about all that civilian stuff" (i.e., the countless innocent victims of such warfare) and dismiss the danger of a wider conflict of which more and more world leaders, including the Pope, repeatedly warned.

Even the so-called man in the street, inclined to follow his government blindly, began to worry when confronted with the choice of a tax rise to pay for the endless war, or the specter of a $30 billion budget deficit. The more sophisticated among the public asked how the U.S. military would react if in answer to an invasion of the North the "fraternal socialist countries" sent half a million well-equipped "volunteers" (in case Ho Chi Minh believed that his own still-intact and well-trained army could not deal with an American landing north of the demilitarized zone). It was these fears that increased the opposition against the war in the intellectual community of America, in Congress, in the churches, and, as opinion polls showed, even among "ordinary Americans." The opposition continued to grow more vocal and more forceful, and although the cries of the "hawks" became louder too, the mood of the country began to favor those critics who had long been engaged in the search for a peaceful settlement through negotiations.

Of the many attempts made by people concerned with the disaster for the entire world which the Vietnamese war might possibly bring about, one, initiated by U.N. Secretary U Thant, revealed clearly why an end to the conflict through negotiations had not come about before the war had become fully Americanized. In September, 1964, U Thant, with Russian help, succeeded in persuading Hanoi to agree to peace talks. Washington, apparently led by its then chief delegate to the U.N. Adlai Stevenson, for a long time considered accepting this offer. But when, with the consent of the Burmese Government, talks were scheduled to open at Rangoon on January 18, 1965, Washington let it be known that it was not interested in negotiations. The official excuse, given much later, after U Thant had publicly indicated that talks could have been held, was a lame one: Washington could not negotiate with Hanoi without the presence of the Saigon government, whose morale would be undermined by such talks. (Hanoi had obviously not insisted that the National Liberation Front be represented at the conference table.) The true reason for Washington's refusal was the awareness that the Saigon regime was close to collapse, that the enemy's position for negotiations was then too strong, and that Saigon therefore had to be strengthened through more massive U.S. military intervention before peace talks could begin. Instead of sending delegates to Rangoon in January, Johnson decided to start bombing the North in February, and to send Marines to the South in March.

U Thant's initiative and Hanoi's acceptance were not made public, but Secretary Rusk, alluding to rumors about them, admitted in March that the United States was not interested in such negotiations. A "crucial element," he said, was missing in the attitude of the enemy, namely "any indication that Hanoi is prepared to stop doing what it is doing. The absence of this crucial element affects the current discussion of something called 'negotiations.' "[17] Johnson himself simply denied that a chance for negotiations existed, and, having just done what he could to ruin any such chance by his air attacks on the North, stated on March 25 that "at present the Communist aggressors have given no sign of any willingness to move in this direction." He thus confirmed an angry remark made by U Thant at a press conference on March 15, that "in times of war, the first casualty is truth." Negotiations early in 1965 were rejected by Washington in favor of quick and drastic intervention in a war which South Vietnam was about to lose.

Another attempt to bring about negotiations was made by the French soon afterward, and revealed by Foreign Minister Couvé de Murville in May, 1965. It was rejected by Washington for the same reasons, with excuses that marked a drastic decline in the quality of U.S. propaganda, for whose dishonesty Secretary Rusk and the President himself were held responsible by the opposition. In a statement that earned him the ridicule of his critics, Rusk said that his "antennae" had not yet picked up a "key signal" from Hanoi. He did not elaborate on the "key signal," but even so it was clear that it could not have been anything but some condition on which Washington insisted before going to a conference—just about a month after President Johnson, in his widely discussed speech at Johns Hopkins University on April 7, 1965, had stated his readiness for "unconditional discussions."

Another half-dozen cautious expressions of Hanoi's willingness to negotiate were made between the spring of 1965 and the fall of 1967 to Polish, Italian, British, and private American intermediaries, but not a single one was taken up by the United States, not even if only to test the sincerity of Hanoi. After several "bombing pauses," American escalation of the air attacks on the North at the crucial moment forced Hanoi back into repeating its rigid demands for the withdrawal of all American troops before peace negotiations could begin. Responsibility for the failure to bring about peace through negotiations may rest partly with Hanoi, whose leaders very likely relied heavily on the ability of the Vietcong to prevent, with ever-increasing support from the North, an American victory—prevent it long enough to turn the American people against an Administration that refused to extricate their country from this burdensome and profitless venture. But Johnson's guilt for these failures greatly outweighs whatever responsibility Ho Chi Minh may bear. It was Johnson who prevented talks before the civil war in the South widened into a war between the United States and North Vietnam, a war begun by Washington before Hanoi had sent any units of its regular army to the South. Johnson rejected talks in the spring of 1965 because Hanoi, thanks to the strength of the Vietcong, would undoubtedly have insisted on, and very likely would have obtained, a compromise solution consisting in a sharing of power in the South between the anti- and pro-Communist forces. It was Johnson who escalated the war in order to avoid the necessity of compromising and who, all throughout 1966 and 1967, chased after the phantom of a military victory over the Vietcong by terrorizing the North into ending all support for the forces of the National Liberation Front. In the absence of any indication of what concessions the enemy might be granted through a negotiated settlement, the Vietcong and Hanoi could not be blamed for assuming that Washington's aim was still total victory, that for Washington, the settlement to be negotiated was the enemy's surrender, and that the "key signal" expected from Hanoi was never less than a one-sided renunciation of the struggle, a demand which Washington always insisted on at the very moment when more U.S. bombs were thrown on the North and more American troops and equipment shipped into the South.

Washington consistently avoided any discussion of the key question that should have been dealt with if negotiations were to be something other than a demand that the enemy agree to the conditions of surrender. The question was: What kind of South Vietnam should emerge from the conflict? The "free" Vietnam in which the United States upheld a regime acceptable to a mere fraction of the people and therefore necessarily dependent for its survival on the continued presence of an American army of occupation? No sane person, either in America or anywhere else in the world, could believe that such an outcome of the conflict would ever be accepted by the forces that fought so effectively for so many years for a different kind of South Vietnam. A peaceful solution in Vietnam therefore was impossible so long as Washington wanted to deny these forces the share in power to which they were entitled by the popular support they enjoyed. A peaceful settlement of the Vietnamese war, therefore, required that the United States accept the National Liberation Front as a partner equal to the Saigon regime in any negotiations, something which even a cautious political strategist like the late Robert Kennedy and the moderate Mike Mansfield recognized as a precondition for meaningful negotiations.[18]

Another precondition for peace talks, almost universally recognized in the fall of 1967 by any government that was not dependent on the United States, was an unconditional end of the bombing attacks on North Vietnam. Before the end of 1967, it was indeed generally assumed that Hanoi would enter into negotiations if the bombing were stopped. This was a long retreat from the "Four Points" put forward by Hanoi in April, 1965, in which the withdrawal of the American forces from Vietnam was made a condition for peace talks. Washington, however, refused to end the bombing without an "act of reciprocity," a demand which even in America more and more people, including influential senators, began to attack as unjustified and a mere excuse for the refusal to enter into negotiations. Our government would certainly have a right, these critics said, to insist on "reciprocity" if North Vietnam bombed American installations in Vietnam, or railroads in the United States. Washington even failed to state that no new American troops and supplies would enter the South if the North took similar action. Washington simply ignored the important fact that the means of military action engaged in by North Vietnam and the United States were drastically unequal. Even after the end of the bombing, the American forces in the South would still have been almost ten times as large as those infiltrated by Hanoi, and no degree of infiltration from the North could ever have matched the amount of equipment and the number of troops the United States continued to pour into Vietnam. As Sorensen put it, the demand that the North stop sending men and supplies to the South means that we expect them to "stop fighting the war altogether—while we continue to fight."[19]

If the bombing were stopped and the National Liberation Front accepted by Washington and Saigon as a partner in peace negotiations, the opponents of Johnson's policy maintained, negotiations would probably start very soon. A cease-fire might be proclaimed soon afterward. How long such negotiations would last, no one could foresee. But they could produce a settlement only under the following conditions: the parties of the National Liberation Front, in exchange for ending the armed struggle for power, would be legalized, permitted to organize freely, and to take part in elections held under a provisional coalition government. The North would withdraw its units and the Vietcong lay down their arms at the rate at which the American troops would withdraw. This withdrawal and demobilization, as well as the elections, would have to be internationally supervised, and the final agreement also be subject to international control. Whatever the outcome of free elections, the question of unifying the country, although exclusively an internal affair, should by agreement be postponed for a number of years—five or possibly more. However, close economic and cultural exchanges between North and South should be entered upon after peace is restored, and the United States and Russia should assist in the reconstruction of both the South and the North. In peaceful competition with their capable opponents, the anti-Communist forces would be given another chance to win the popular support necessary for their survival; and the United States, reversing a course bound to drive Vietnam into the arms of Communist China could thus assist Vietnamese nationalism in resuming its historical role of blocking China's advance into Southeast Asia.

As the year 1967 drew to a close, it was impossible to predict in which direction U.S. policy would move. The year 1968, when the people, in a Presidential election, would be given another opportunity to choose between advocates of peace or of continued war, held no certain promise. The options were open in both directions; the forces that threatened to provoke war with China were as active as ever. But those seeking a compromise peace seemed to be gaining in strength, giving life to the hope that the suffering of the Vietnamese people and the decline of America's prestige in the world might be brought to a halt.

Unfortunately, however, the possibility that the war would continue through 1968 and beyond could not be ruled out. Systematic misinformation of the public about the nature of this war could bring about popular support for further drastic escalation and thus increase the danger that the Vietnamese war might turn out to have been merely a prelude to World War III.

Postscript

SINCE DECEMBER, 1967, when the last chapter of this book was
written, the fear expressed in its final paragraph has unexpectedly made way for the hope that a peaceful solution of the
Vietnamese conflict may yet come about. This hope was aroused
by President Johnson's announcement, on March 31, 1968, that
the bombing of North Vietnam would be significantly restricted,
and that he would not seek re-election.

The general reaction to the President's speech was that he had
at last opened the road to peace negotiations with Hanoi. It was
assumed in the United States and abroad that the President no
longer believed in the possibility of a military victory over the
combined forces of the Vietcong and North Vietnam, and that
he had furthermore become aware of a change in American public
opinion: More and more people apparently began to prefer a

compromise solution to the prospect of several more years of inconclusive warfare.

The chief reason for this change in the mood of the American people, and subsequently in the attitude of President Johnson, was the enemy's great Tet offensive of February, 1968—a shocking development not only to Washington but also to the American and South Vietnamese commanders in the field. In November, 1967, U.S. official propaganda had begun to boast of the progress, both military and political, that had been made in the struggle against the Vietcong during that year, and prophesied more of the same for 1968. The notion of a military stalemate was ridiculed, and a steady consolidation of the Saigon regime became a daily claim. The Saigon government, it was said, "controlled" 68 per cent of the population—an increase of 13 per cent over 1966; more villages were constantly pacified and made as secure as the cities had always been. The enemy fighters were re-estimated and found to number no more than 223,000. Vietcong morale was described as·low and Vietcong desertion rates as high, in contrast to the higher morale and lower desertion rates of the Saigon army, whose fighting capacity was said to be steadily improving. This meant that the enemy, beaten in every battle, was no longer able to initiate any major military action. American military spokesmen, seeing once more "the light at the end of the tunnel," predicted that a withdrawal of some American troops was possible in the near future.

By February 3, 1968, the enemy's Tet offensive, only a few days old, had completely shattered this edifice of mindless optimism. Vietcong and North Vietnamese forces, after preparations that must have gone on for months without being discovered by the many American and South Vietnamese intelligence services, and without a single instance of betrayal by the population, were able to mount attacks on no fewer than 102 cities and military installations. This demonstrated that no part of the country was effectively controlled by the Saigon regime or was held secure by the "allied" troops against attack. In Saigon, where street fighting lasted almost two weeks, the Vietcong even succeeded in penetrating the American Embassy during the first hours of the offensive. In the old Imperial city of Hue, it took almost four weeks and a near total destruction of the city by American artillery fire and bombing raids before the stubborn and skillful enemy fighters were forced to withdraw. Hue, parts of Saigon, and several other cities suffered the same fate as Bentre in the Mekong Delta, of which an American officer said that "we had to destroy the city in order to save it." Thousands of civilians lost their lives. In a report from Saigon published by *The New Yorker* of March 23, 1968, Robert Shaplen wrote: "Nearly four thousand civilians were killed in Hue, most of them by American air and artillery attacks." Countless families all over the country were made homeless, and more than 600,000 persons were added to the more than 2 million already suffering in miserable refugee camps.

Only the lowest level of American military thinking (which apparently prevails on the highest levels of command) could have produced the conclusion that in the Tet offensive the enemy had suffered a disastrous defeat. Hanoi, it was said, seeing that its cause had become hopeless, "went for broke" and lost, although it had thrown everything it had into the battle. The popular uprising against the Saigon regime, on which the enemy leadership allegedly had counted, had not materialized; not a single city was permanently lost to the Vietcong, who, at the beginning of March, were back where they had been at the end of January. However, during February alone, 50,000 of the enemy's fighters had been killed, and even if he had suffered only two wounded for each killed, his combined losses must therefore have been 150,000, or more than two-thirds of his entire strength.

But the American people were no longer inclined to believe the statements of men who had for years attempted to prove that all was going well with the war in Vietnam. Official optimism was discredited as never before, and propaganda based on it proved at least temporarily ineffective. The conclusion millions of Americans drew from the Tet offensive was not so much that it had created an entirely new and highly critical situation; rather, it brought a sudden awareness that the situation had really always been critical—before the offensive as well as after it. The public had learned that the enemy had not been weakend by three years of massive American military intervention and became persuaded that he evidently could not be defeated at all. Almost overnight, the Tet offensive had wiped out the picture drawn by the Administration at the end of 1967, while emphatically confirming almost everything the critics of the Administration had been saying for the past three years.

As a consequence, the months of February and March brought an unprecedented outpouring of revealing reports and of scathing criticism in the press and in Congress. This made it unnecessary for the American public to seek out what was said by the propagandists of Hanoi, whose claims were even more fantastic than those of their counterparts in Saigon and Washington. According to the Hanoi English-language *Vietnam Courier* of February 12, 1968, the Vietcong had killed 40,000 American and "puppet" soldiers, dispersed or captured 200,000 members of the Saigon armed forces, destroyed 1,500 planes and helicopters, as well as 4,000 military vehicles, and captured or blown up 1 million tons of bombs and ammunition.

More important for the American public than these little-known enemy claims were Washington's official admissions and the American press revelations. The damage done to U.S. and South Vietnamese military installations and equipment, as well as the number of casualties suffered by the Allies, was indeed unparalleled. A single, belated official admission allowed a clue to the extent of this damage: No fewer than 800 planes had been damaged on the ground and 200 completely destroyed during the first hours of the offensive.

These losses could no doubt be replaced without much delay. The political setback suffered by the Saigon regime as a result of the Tet offensive was not as easily repaired. American correspondents in Vietnam reported almost unanimously that the Saigon administrative structure had been severely damaged; that the pacification program had come to a virtual halt; that most of the so-called Revolutionary Development teams had either fled the villages they were supposed to protect or were called back to assist in the defense of the threatened cities; and that, in consequence, vast rural areas had fallen back under Vietcong control. It was in these regions that the Vietcong succeeded, according to Charles Mohr in *The New York Times* of March 20, 1968, in fully replacing the losses suffered in the offensive, said to have been 40,000, a figure "disputed by some [American] intelligence officials." Robert Shaplen in his article in *The New Yorker* held that, by early March, the Vietcong had recruited at least 30,000 fresh troops.

These two highly knowledgeable correspondents also wrote about the psychological effects of the Tet offensive on many non-Communist Vietnamese in Saigon and other cities. Reactions ranged from an increase of neutralist activity to preparations for flight and desertion to the Vietcong. "For the first time," an American official told Charles Mohr, "a small number of urban youth have been 'defecting' or slipping away from the towns to join the Vietcong in recent weeks, indicating that some Vietnamese believe that the Vietcong are winning, not losing."

If the enemy had merely replaced the losses suffered, he should at best have regained his former strength of some 230,000, of which 55,000 reportedly were regular North Vietnamese units. But it seems that both the Vietcong and the North Vietnamese have done a great deal better. Charles Mohr wrote that, in early March, 1968, the number of North Vietnamese had reached 84,000; more surprising, however, was his report that total enemy strength, as estimated by the Central Intelligence Agency, stood somewhere between 515,000 and 600,000. The unassailable explanation given for these startling figures was that earlier estimates had been too low.

But whatever the true figures, which nobody seems to know, the fact remains that the enemy was able to strike at 102 sites, most of which had been considered invulnerable, and that he is now said to be at least twice as strong as before his offensive.

The reaction of the military, who are not renowned for their ability to learn from experience, was somewhat contradictory: The enemy had suffered a disaster, but in order to defeat him, another 200,000 troops were needed—a request that found no favor with the American public. The public was more inclined to listen to the critics of the Administration who used the Tet offensive as an occasion to intensify their attacks. Senator Albert Gore said on February 17 that the United States had to get out of the morass of Vietnam: "We are destroying the country we profess to be saving." In a Senate debate on March 7, Senator Fulbright demanded that Congress be consulted before any new troops were sent to Vietnam. Robert F. Kennedy said it was "immoral and intolerable" to continue what America was doing in Vietnam, and Mike Mansfield, warning against any further escalation, stated: "We are in the wrong place and we are fighting the wrong kind of war." Mansfield also said that he would not have voted for the Tongking resolution (on which the President has based his policy of continued escalation) if he had known then what he knew now.

The press too began to reflect the anger, concern, and changing mood of the country. Significant for the reappraisal of the American position in Vietnam by the press was a long article in *Newsweek* of March 18 claiming that even Washington officials privately "admitted that the U.S. has suffered a stunning defeat." What was needed now was "the courage to face the truth," which was that "all the U.S. can reasonably hope to achieve in Vietnam now is a military stalemate," and that Washington must seek a peaceful settlement, in spite of the risks this involves. "For when the risks of this course are compared with the mounting price which the U.S. will pay in domestic discord and international impotence if a settlement is not reached, chancing a Communist South Vietnam might well appear the lesser of two considerable evils." One week later, *Newsweek*, with obvious approval, quoted the conservative *Wall Street Journal*. "We think," the *Journal* said, "the American people should be getting ready to accept, if they haven't already, the prospect that the Vietnam effort may be doomed."

Another unmistakable sign of the country's changing mood was the unexpected success achieved by the "peace candidate" Senator Eugene McCarthy in the New Hampshire Democratic Presidential primary. Overnight, McCarthy became so serious a contender for the nomination that Robert Kennedy no longer hesitated to proclaim himself a candidate, for fear of losing to McCarthy the large peace vote and the enthusiastic support of the American youth which an opponent of the war was apparently able to command.

This change in the mood of the American people must have been the main reason that President Johnson decided to seek a way out for the country and for himself from the domestic and international difficulties which his Vietnam policy had created. The direction in which he was moving was first indicated when he refused to escalate the war by sending another 200,000 U.S.

soldiers to Vietnam. Instead, he decided that General Westmoreland should be relieved of his post as U.S. commander. Then came his sensational announcement that he would not seek re-election, coupled with his order restricting bombing raids on North Vietnam, evidently meant as a first step toward serious negotiations with Hanoi.

After four weeks of wrangling over a meeting site acceptable to both parties, negotiations between Washington and Hanoi opened on May 13 in Paris. How long they will last and what their outcome will be no one can predict. But they can succeed, and thereby forestall an intensification of the war with all the attendant dangers to world peace, only under one condition: if Washington is willing to accept a compromise peace providing for the right of the National Liberation Front freely to participate in the political life of South Vietnam.

June, 1968

Notes

I. INTRODUCING VIETNAM
(pp. 3–18)

1. See L. Aurousseau, "Notes sur les origines du peuple annamite," *Bulletin de l'Ecole Française d'Extrême Orient*, XXIII, 263 f.; Jeanne Cuisinier, *Les Muongs: Géographie humaine et sociologie* (Paris, 1948); Le Thanh Khoi, *Le Viet-Nam: Histoire et civilisation* (Paris, 1955).
2. See Charles Robequain, *L'Indochine* (3d ed.; Paris, 1952), p. 40; Le Thanh Khoi, *op. cit.*, p. 52.
3. Paul Mus, *Viet-Nam: Sociologie d'une guerre* (Paris, 1950), p. 236.
4. See Le Thanh Khoi, *op. cit.*, p. 20.

II. ONE THOUSAND YEARS OF CHINESE RULE
(pp. 19–36)

1. See Pierre Huard and Maurice Durand, *Connaissance du Viet-Nam* (Paris and Hanoi, 1954), pp. 7–8; Le Thanh Khoi, *Le Viet-Nam*, pp. 82–83.
2. D. G. E. Hall, *A History of South-East Asia* (New York, 1955), p. 8.
3. See Duong Quang Ham, *Leçon d'histoire d'Annam à l'usage des élèves des cours moyen et supérieur des écoles franco-annamites* (Hanoi, 1927), p. 13.

512 · *Notes*

4. René Grousset, *The Rise and Splendor of the Chinese Empire* (Berkeley, Calif., 1953), p. 60.

III. NINE HUNDRED YEARS OF INDEPENDENCE AND GROWTH
(*pp. 37–54*)

1. See Le Thanh Khoi, *Le Viet-Nam*, p. 140.
2. See D. G. E. Hall, *A History of South-East Asia*, pp. 359 ff.
3. Charles B. Maybon, *Histoire moderne du pays d'Annam (1592–1820)* (Paris, 1920).

IV. MISSIONARIES, MERCHANTS, AND CONQUERORS
(*pp. 55–74*)

1. D. G. E. Hall, *A History of South-East Asia*, p. 206.
2. *Ibid.*, p. 202.
3. See John Crawfurd, *Journal of an Embassy from the Governor-General of India to the Courts of Siam and Cochin China; Exhibiting a View of the Actual State of Those Kingdoms* (London, 1830), II, Appendix, 443, 445.
4. See "Les Européens qui ont vu le Vieux Hué: Cristoforo Borri," *Bulletin des Amis du Vieux Hué*, July–December, 1931, p. 308.
5. See Alexander de Rhodes, *Voyages et Mission* (Lille, 1884), pp. 66–67.
6. Saint-Phalle's memoirs have never been published, but large portions were used by the Abbé Richard in his *Histoire naturelle, civile et politique du Tonkin*, 2 vols. (Paris, 1778).
7. Georges Taboulet, *La geste française en Indochine*, 2 vols. (Paris, 1955 and 1956), p. 146.
8. Henri Cordier, *Histoire générale de la Chine et de ses relations avec les pays étrangers depuis les plus ancien jusqu'à la chute de la dynastie Mandchoue* (Paris, 1920), p. 226.
9. Taboulet, *op. cit.*, p. 210.
10. L. E. Louvet, *La Cochinchine religieuse*, 2 vols. (Paris, 1885), II, 41 f.

V. THE CONQUEST OF FRENCH INDOCHINA
(*pp. 75–98*)

1. John F. Cady, *The Roots of French Imperialism in Eastern Asia* (Ithaca, N.Y., 1954), pp. 33–40.
2. For the confidential instructions, see Georges Taboulet, *La geste française en Indochine*, pp. 349–52.
3. Cady, *op. cit.*, p. 29.
4. Taboulet, *op. cit.*, p. 361.
5. Cady, *op. cit.*, p. 32.
6. *Ibid.*, p. 79.
7. Adrien Launay, *Histoire générale de la Société des Missions Etrangères depuis sa fondation jusqu'à nos jours*, 3 vols. (Paris, 1894), III, 219–22.
8. Taboulet, *op. cit.*, pp. 384–86.
9. See Cady, *op. cit.*, p. 99.
10. See letter of Marquis de Courcy to the French Foreign Minister, in Taboulet, *op. cit.*, p. 387.

11. *Ibid.*, p. 349.
12. *Ibid.*, p. 406.
13. *Ibid.*, p. 404.
14. See *ibid.*, p. 407.
15. A. Thomazi, *La conquête de l'Indochine* (Paris, 1934), p. 32.
16. Cady, *op. cit.*, p. 277.
17. Charles Gosselin, *L'empire d'Annam* (Paris, 1904), p. 89.
18. Taboulet, *op. cit.*, p. 694.
19. Quoted by P. Boudet, "Francis Garnier," *Cahiers de l'Ecole Française d'Extrême-Orient*, Nos. 20–21, 1939, p. 46.
20. See letter of Admiral d'Hornoy, dated September, 1873, in Taboulet, *op. cit.*, pp. 699–70.
21. See *ibid.*, p. 738.
22. Gosselin, *op. cit.*, p. 183.

VI. THE MAKING OF FRENCH INDOCHINA
(pp. 101–16)

1. According to Admiral Rieunier, as quoted by Paulin Vial, *Les premières années de la Cochinchine*, (Paris, 1874), and by Jean Chesneaux, *Contribution à l'histoire de la nation vietnamienne* (Paris, 1955), p. 115.
2. Paul Doumer, *L'Indo-Chine française: Souvenirs* (Paris, 1903), p. 85.
3. *Ibid.*, p. 314
4. *Ibid.*, p. 315
5. *Ibid.*, pp. 335, 363.
6. Virginia Thompson, *French Indo-China* (London, 1937; New York, 1967), p. 206.
7. André Masson, *Histoire de l'Indochine* (Paris, 1950), p. 99.

VII. THE METHODS AND AIMS OF FRENCH RULE
(pp. 117–47)

1. From a speech delivered at the competition of scholars at Nam Dinh, in André Masson, *Histoire de l'Indochine*, p. 99.
2. Virginia Thompson, *French Indo-China*, p. 84.
3. *Ibid.*, p. 82.
4. Jean Ajalbert, *L'Indochine en péril* (Paris, 1906), p. 64.
5. Ajalbert, *Les destinées de l'Indochine* (Paris, 1909 [?]), p. 297.
6. For some recent works on the subject, see Bernard B. Fall, *The Two Viet-Nams: A Political and Military Analysis* (2d rev. ed.; New York, 1967); Paul Isoart, *Le phénomène national vietnamien: De l'indépendance unitaire à l'indépendance fractionée* (Paris, 1961); Donald Lancaster, *The Emancipation of French Indochina* (London and New York, 1961).
7. Senator Issac, President of the National Colonial Congress, 1889–90; as quoted by Raymond F. Betts, *Assimilation and Association in French Colonial Theory: 1890–1914* (New York, 1961), p. 31.
8. See Stephen H. Roberts, *History of French Colonial Policy: 1870–1925*, 2 vols. (London, 1929), p. 103.

514 • *Notes*

9. Betts, *op. cit.*, p. 23, and p. 180, n. 28.
10. See the many speeches of Jules Ferry and his collected writings in *Discours et opinions de Jules Ferry*, 5 vols. (Paris, 1895–98). Pierre-Paul Leroy-Beaulieu's principal work was *De la colonisation chez les peuples modernes* (Paris, 1874).
11. Leroy-Beaulieu, *op. cit.* (2d ed.; Paris, 1882), p. viii.
12. Jules Blois, "Les anglais dans l'Indie," *Revue bleue*, XIX, April 11, 1903, 477; cited by Betts, *op. cit.*, p. 44.
13. Jules Harmand, *Domination et colonisation* (Paris, 1910), p. 12.
14. In *Essai sur la colonisation* (Paris, 1907), a pamphlet written by Régismanset under the pseudonym of Charles Siger.
15. See Betts, *op. cit.*, p. 147.
16. See Auguste Billiard, *Politique et organisations coloniales* (Paris, 1899).
17. Henri Brunschwig, *La colonisation française* (Paris, 1949), pp. 276–77.
18. Albert de Pouvourville, *Les défenses de l'Indochine et la politique d'association* (Paris, 1905), pp. 112–13.
19. Henri Lorin, "La sécurité de l'Indochine," *Dépêche Coloniale*, March 28, 1905.
20. "La défense de l'Indochine, rapport Deloncle," *Dépêche Coloniale*, May 10, 1905.
21. Speech of Etienne Clementel at the annual banquet of the Syndicat de la presse coloniale française, cited in the *Dépêche Coloniale*, March 28, 1905.
22. *Journal Officiel*, April, 1909, as cited by B. Camilli, *La représentation des indigènes en Indochine* (Paris, 1914), p. 1.
23. For an early profile of Sarraut, see Claude Farrère, *Les civilisés* (Paris, 1921).
24. Joost van Vollenhoven (January, 1914–March, 1915); Ernest Nestor Roùme (March, 1915–May, 1916); Eugène Jean Charles (May, 1916–January, 1917).
25. Thompson, *op. cit.*, p. 88.
26. For instance, Thomas E. Ennis writes that the "thirty-nine-year-old governor-general refused to be led by the military group in Indochina, who attempted to bring him to a harsh assimilative program as an antidote to the disorders. In opposition to their demands he declared that he looked forward to the day when the Indochinese would be admitted into the French family as brothers" (*French Policy and Developments in Indochina* [Chicago, 1936], p. 102).
27. In *French Colonization on Trial*, the second volume of Ho Chi Minh's *Selected Works* (Hanoi, 1960 and 1961), Ho levels this charge against Sarraut.
28. Ennis, *op. cit.*, p. 103.
29. Roberts, *op. cit.*, p. 660.
30. Philippe Devillers, *Histoire du Viet-Nam de 1940 à 1952* (Paris, 1952), p. 43.
31. *Le Temps*, March 12, 1926.
32. Pasquier wrote a widely read popular history of Vietnam entitled *L'Annam d'autrefois* (Paris, 1930), a rather superficial and condescending account of Vietnamese civilization.

Notes · 515

VIII. THE MOVEMENTS OF NATIONAL RESISTANCE
(pp. 148–60)

1. Charles Gosselin, *L'empire d'Annam*, p. 271.
2. Baille, *Souvenir d'Annam* (Paris, 1891), p. 72.
3. See Jean Chesneaux, *Contribution à l'histoire de la nation vietnamienne*, p. 141, and Paul Isoart, *Le phénomène national vietnamien*, p. 153.
4. Nguyen Van Thai and Nguyen Van Mung, *A Short History of Vietnam* (Saigon, 1958), p. 305.
5. According to Chesneaux (*op. cit.*, p. 139), Piquet brought on his dismissal by filing a continuous stream of optimistic reports to Paris.
6. Sun Yat-sen's main doctrines are to be found in his *Three Principles of the People*, trans. F. W. Price (Shanghai, 1927), and *Outlines of National Reconstruction*, trans. E. B. S. Lee and S. S. Chow (Nanking, 1929).
7. This account is based on an article by Dao Trinh Nhat, in *Cai Tao (Reform)* (Hanoi), October 30, 1948, entitled "Mot Viec Bi Mat Chua Ai No Ra" (A Secret That Has Never Been Disclosed"). For a version far less flattering to Ho Chi Minh, see P. J. Honey (ed.), *North Vietnam Today: Profile of a Communist Satellite* (New York, 1962), p. 4.

IX. THE ROOTS OF NATIONALISM AND COMMUNISM
(pp. 161–83)

1. The main work on the subject is Charles Robequain, *The Economic Development of French Indo-China* (London, 1944).
2. For details on industrial development, see Paul Isoart, *Le phénomène national vietnamien*, pp. 264–68.
3. W. MacMahon Ball, *Nationalism and Communism in East Asia* (Melbourne, 1952), p. 70.
4. *Ibid.*
5. Pham Quynh, *Les paysans tonkinois à travers les parlers populairs* (Hanoi, 1930), p. 60.
6. Isoart, *op. cit.*, p. 180.
7. Virginia Thompson, *French Indo-China*, p. 132.
8. See Isoart, *op. cit.*, p. 294.
9. Le Thanh Khoi, *Le Viet-Nam*, p. 412.
10. See Paul Bernard, *Nouveau aspects du problème économique indochinois* (Paris, 1934), and Grégoire Kherian, "La querelle de l'industrialisation," *Revue Indochinoise Juridique et l'Economique*, IV, 1938, on the French refusal to establish local industries in Vietnam. Isoart (*op. cit.*, pp. 184–91) also deals with this subject, as do many American and British postwar writers on Southeast Asia.
11. See Isoart, *op. cit.*, p. 180. On the exploitation and profits of mines, see also Jean Chesneaux, *Contribution à l'histoire de la nation vietnamienne*, pp. 171, 173.
12. Donald Lancaster, *The Emancipation of French Indochina*, p. 62.
13. *Ibid.*, pp. 62–63.

516 · *Notes*

14. This information is based largely on I. Milton Sacks, "Marxism in Viet Nam," in Frank N. Trager (ed.), *Marxism in Southeast Asia: A Study of Four Countries* (Stanford, Calif., 1959), pp. 113 and 117, nn. 26, 27, 28.
15. Isoart, *op. cit.*, p. 241.
16. *Ibid.*, p. 287.
17. For an account of the process of party unification, see *ibid.*, pp. 287–88.
18. *Ibid.*, p. 291.

X. THE FRENCH LOSE INDOCHINA
(pp. 184–210)

1. For a discussion of the problem of British and American help, see *Memoirs of Cordell Hull* (New York, 1948); Winston Churchill, *The Second World War* (Boston, 1949); Georges Catroux, *Deux actes du drame indochinois* (Paris, 1959); Jean Decoux, *A la barre de l'Indochine: Histoire de mon gouvernement général—1940–1945* (Paris, 1952); Paul Isoart, *Le phénomène national vietnamien*; Philippe Devillers, *Histoire du Vietnam*; Ellen J. Hammer, *The Struggle for Indochina* (Stanford, Calif., 1954).
2. See Hammer, *op. cit.*, p. 19.
3. For a more detailed account of these events, see Decoux, *op. cit.*, pp. 117–22; also André Gaudel, *L'Indochine française en face du Japon* (Paris, 1947), p. 92.
4. Bernard B. Fall, *The Two Viet-Nams*, p. 45.
5. For a detailed account of Japanese activities in Vietnam during this period, see Devillers, *op. cit.*, pp. 88–95
6. A. M. Savani, *Visage et images du Sud Viet-Nam* (Saigon, 1955), p. 87.
7. I. Milton Sacks, "Marxism in Viet Nam," in Frank N. Trager (ed.), *Marxism in Southeast Asia*, p. 322, n. 127.
8. Fall, *op. cit.*, p. 63.
9. Nguyen Kien Giang, *Les grandes dates du parti de la classe ouvrière du Viet Nam* (Hanoi, 1960), p. 48.
10. This version of Diem's relations with the Japanese is based on information given me in a private talk with a Vietnamese who at that time was close to Diem (and a close relative as well).
11. Le Thanh Khoi, *Le Viet-Nam*, p. 462.
12. There are two schools of thought on the chronology of these events. Jean Chesneaux (*Contribution à l'histoire de la nation vietnamienne*, p. 233) says that Ho Chi Minh created the Liberation Committee on August 7, and that on that same date the guerrillas took the name "Liberation Army." Devillers (*op. cit.*, p. 135) gives the same date, adding that Ho Chi Minh gave the order for the general insurrection on August 10. Le Thanh Khoi (*op. cit.*, p. 465) also mentions August 7 as the decisive date. Sacks (*op. cit.*, p. 151), Fall (*op. cit.*, p. 63), and Isoart (*op. cit.*, p. 328) give August 13. The official Communist version agrees with my dates. Cf. the following North Vietnamese documents: *Viet Nam's Fight Against Fascism (1940–1945)*, and *Breaking Our Chains: Documents on the Vietnamese Revolution of August, 1945* (Hanoi, 1960).
13. See Hammer, *op. cit.*, p. 104.

XI. THE FRENCH RETURN TO VIETNAM
(*pp. 211–43*)

1. Charles de Gaulle, *War Memoirs of Charles de Gaulle* (New York, 1960), III, 163.
2. Jean Sainteny, *Histoire d'une paix manquée* (Paris, 1953), p. 33.
3. Harold R. Isaacs, *No Peace for Asia* (New York, 1947), pp. 235 ff.
4. Sainteny, *op. cit.*, p. 51.
5. Jean-Michel Hertrich, *Doc Lap! L'indépendance ou le mort* (Paris, 1946), p. 49.
6. Sir Anthony Eden, *Full Circle* (Boston, 1960), p. 88.
7. Andrien Dansette, *Leclerc* (Paris, 1952), p. 187.
8. Sainteny, *op. cit.*, p. 91, n. 1.
9. Paul Isoart, *Le phénomène national vietnamien*, p. 346, n. 86, quoting *Missi* (the official organ of the Catholic missions), No. 184, November, 1954, pp. 296–98.
10. Ellen J. Hammer, *The Struggle for Indochina*, p. 146.
11. I. Milton Sacks, "Marxism in Viet Nam," in Frank N. Trager (ed.), *Marxism in Southeast Asia*, p. 157.
12. For the full English text of the Sino-French agreement of February 28, 1946, see Harold R. Isaacs, *New Cycle in Asia* (New York, 1947), pp. 166–68.
13. Hammer, *op. cit.*, p. 163.
14. *Ibid.*, p. 155.
15. Philippe Devillers, *Histoire du Vietnam*, pp. 228 ff.

XII. THE ROAD TO WAR
(*pp. 244–71*)

1. Donald Lancaster, *The Emancipation of French Indochina*, p. 139.
2. See Ellen J. Hammer, *The Struggle for Indochina*, pp. 122–23.
3. *Le Monde*, January 13–14, 1946.
4. Philippe Devillers, *Histoire du Viet-Nam*, p. 244.
5. See Paul Isoart, *Le phénomène national vietnamien*, p. 357; also Devillers, *op. cit.*, pp. 256–66.
6. See Hammer, *op. cit.*, pp. 167–68.
7. *Ibid.*, pp. 166–67.
8. Lancaster, *op. cit.*, p. 162.
9. For the full text of the *modus vivendi* of September 14, 1946, see *Notes documentaires et études*, No. 548; also Jean Sainteny, *Histoire d'une paix manquée*, pp. 248–52; and Allan B. Cole (ed.), *Conflict in Indochina and International Repercussions: A Documentary History, 1945–1955* (Ithaca, N.Y., 1956), p. 46.
10. Hammer, *op. cit.*, p. 184, n. 10.
11. See *ibid.*, p. 150, and Bernard B. Fall, *The Two Viet-Nams*, p. 240.
12. See Lancaster, *op. cit.*, p. 149, and Fall, *op. cit.*, p. 208.
13. See I. Milton Sacks, "Marxism in Viet Nam," in Frank N. Trager (ed.), *Marxism in Southeast Asia*, pp. 161 and 327, n. 181.
14. Le Thanh Khoi, *Le Viet-Nam*, p. 467.

15. Truong Chinh, *The August Revolution* (Hanoi, 1958), p. 37.
16. For further details on this incident, see Pierre Naville, "La guerre du Viet-Nam," *La Revue Internationale*, 1949, p. 113; Devillers, *op. cit.*, p. 338, n. 7; Le Thanh Khoi, *Le Viet-Nam*, p. 471, n. 117; Henri Larroue, "Comment a debuté la guerre du Viet-Nam," *Cahiers Internationaux*, No. 40, November, 1952, pp. 77, 78; Dr. Boutbient (ed.), *Rapport de la commission d'enquête parliamentaire*; and *Les origines du conflit franco-vietnamien*, issued by the Vietnamese delegation in Paris, 1948.
17. Hammer, *op. cit.*, p. 183, n. 6.
18. *Ibid.*, p. 183.
19. Devillers, *op. cit.*, pp. 339–40.
20. See *ibid.*, p. 351.
21. *Le Monde*, August 29, 1946.
22. Cole (ed.), *op. cit.*, pp. 17–18.

XIII. THE "BAO DAI SOLUTION"
(pp. 277–314)

1. Philippe Devillers, *Histoire du Viet-Nam*, p. 459.
2. See Ellen J. Hammer, *The Struggle for Indochina*, p. 191.
3. *Ibid.*, p. 199.
4. *Ibid.*, p. 189.
5. Andrien Dansette, *Leclerc*, p. 216.
6. Jean Lacouture and Philippe Devillers, *La fin d'une guerre: Indochine 1954* (Paris, 1960), p. 20.
7. Philippe Devillers, "Vietnamese Nationalism and French Policies," in William L. Holland (ed.), *Asian Nationalism and the West* (New York, 1953), pp. 210–11.
8. Paul Mus, *Viet-Nam*, pp. 315–16.
9. Devillers, *Histoire du Viet-Nam*, p. 394, n. 1.
10. French Information Service, *Notes documentaires et etudes*, No. 752, July 5, 1947.
11. For excerpts from Bollaert's Ha Dong speech, see Allan B. Cole (ed.), *Conflict in Indochina and International Repercussions*, pp. 62–66.
12. Jean Chesneaux, *Contribution à l'histoire de la nation vietnamienne*, p. 261.
13. Pierre Dabezies, *Forces politiques au Viet-Nam* (mimeographed; 1957 [?]), p. 171.
14. Lacouture and Devillers, *op. cit.*, p. 19.
15. *Le Monde*, May 15, 1948, and Paul Isoart, *Le phénomène national vietnamien*, p. 379, n. 166.
16. For a list of its members, see Devillers, *Histoire du Viet-Nam*, p. 430, n. 1.
17. Devillers, "Vietnamese Nationalism and French Policies," *op. cit.*, p. 236.
18. Hammer, *op. cit.*, p. 241.
19. *Ibid.*
20. *Ibid.*, p. 245.
21. See Donald Lancaster, *The Emancipation of French Indochina*, p. 250.
22. Dabezies, *op. cit.*, p. 187.

XIV. POLITICAL FAILURE AND MILITARY DECLINE
(*pp.* 315–53)

1. See Edgar O'Ballance, *The Indo-China War, 1945–1954: A Study in Guerrilla Warfare* (London, 1964), p. 112.
2. *Ibid.,* p. 82.
3. For a more detailed account of this struggle, see Bernard B. Fall, *Street Without Joy: Insurgency in Indochina, 1946–1963* (4th rev. ed.; Harrisburg, Pa., 1964); Lucien Bodard, *La guerre d'Indochine: L'enlisement* (Paris, 1963); J. P. Dannaud, *Guerre morte* (Paris, 1954).
4. Cf. Jean Chesneaux, *Contribution à l'histoire de la nation vietnamienne,* p. 305.
5. O'Ballance, *op. cit.,* p. 116.
6. Fall, *op. cit.,* p. 30.
7. A French translation, entitled *La resistance vaincra* appeared in Hanoi in 1962; an English translation is to be found in Truong Chinh, *Primer for Revolt: The Communist Takeover in Viet-Nam* (New York, 1963), with an introduction and notes by Bernard B. Fall. Fall has called this book "the fullest expression of Vietminh doctrine."
8. For a more detailed account of these three battles, see O'Ballance, *op. cit.,* pp. 120–39.
9. Donald Lancaster, *The Emancipation of French Indochina,* pp. 221–23.
10. *Ibid.,* p. 242.
11. *Ibid.,* p. 243.
12. *Ibid.*
13. Jean Lacouture and Philippe Devillers, *La fin d'une guerre,* p. 36.
14. Quoted by Phan Quang Dan, *The War in Indochina: A Comparative Study of the Vietminh and the French Union Forces* (mimeographed; 1954), p. 26.
15. O'Ballance, *op. cit.,* p. 175.
16. Lacouture and Devillers, *op. cit.,* p. 23.
17. Le Thanh Khoi, *Le Viet-Nam,* p. 490.
18. For this comparatively little-known aspect of the war, see Fall, *op. cit.,* particularly the section "The Commando Groups," pp. 262–74.
19. Paul Isoart, *Le phénomène national vietnamien,* p. 394.
20. Bodard, *op. cit.,* p. 172.
21. Lancaster, *op. cit.,* p. 270.
22. Pierre Dabezies, *Forces politiques au Viet-Nam,* p. 190.
23. For the English text of Tam's land-reform program, see Allan B. Cole (ed.), *Conflict in Indo-China and International Repercussions,* pp. 166–68.
24. Dabezies, *op. cit.,* p. 190.
25. *Ibid.,* p. 196.
26. For the complete text of the resolution of October 17, see Cole (ed.), *op. cit.,* pp. 168–70, and also for Bao Dai's message of thanks to the delegates, in which he gracefully bowed to demands he could not reject.
27. For details on Operation Lorraine, see O'Ballance, *op. cit.,* pp. 179–84, and Fall, *op. cit.,* pp. 58–103.
28. Joseph Laniel, *Le drame indochinois: De Dien-Bien-Phu au pari de Genève* (Paris, 1957), p. 17.

XV. THE END OF FRENCH INDOCHINA
(pp. 354–83)

1. Paul Isoart, Le phénomène national vietnamien, p. 383.
2. Ibid., p. 384.
3. For a most impressive account of the terrible fate of Mobile Group 100, see Bernard B. Fall, Street Without Joy: Insurgency in Indochina, 1946–1963 (4th rev. ed.; Harrisburg, Pa., 1964), pp. 182–246.
4. Department of State Bulletin, XXII, No. 554 (February 13, 1950), 244.
5. Dean Acheson, in a speech before the Commonwealth Club, San Francisco, March, 1950.
6. Donald Lancaster, The Emancipation of French Indochina, p. 293.
7. The New York Times, April 20, 1954.
8. Ibid.
9. Ibid., April 30, 1954.
10. Dwight D. Eisenhower, The White House Years: Mandate for Change (New York, 1963), p. 351.
11. The New York Times, April 10, 1954.
12. See Jean Lacouture and Philippe Devillers, La fin d'une guerre, pp. 217–18.
13. Ibid., pp. 244–45.
14. For the full text of General Bedell Smith's statement, see Allan B. Cole (ed.), Conflict in Indo-China and International Repercussions, pp. 175–76.
15. Bernard B. Fall, "The Cease-Fire in Indochina: An Appraisal," Far Eastern Survey, September, 1954.
16. Quoted by Ton That Thien, "The Geneva Agreements and Peace Prospects in Vietnam," India Quarterly, October–December, 1956, p. 378.
17. Le Monde, August 4, 1954.
18. For the full text of Secretary Dulles' statement, see Department of State Bulletin, XXXI, No. 788 (August 2, 1954), 163–64.
19. As reported by Emmet John Hughes, The Ordeal of Power (New York, 1964), p. 182.
20. Lacouture and Devillers, op. cit., p. 286.

XVI. INDEPENDENCE WITHOUT UNITY OR FREEDOM
(pp. 384–429)

1. Bernard B. Fall, The Two Viet-Nams, p. 245.
2. Bulletin du Haut Commissariat du Viet-Nam en France, No. 87, December, 1954, p. 2.
3. U.S. Senate Commission on Foreign Relations, Report by Senator Mike Mansfield on a Study Mission to Vietnam, Cambodia, Laos (Washington, D.C., 1954).
4. Donald Lancaster, The Emancipation of French Indochina, p. 383.
5. The New York Times, March 11, 1955.
6. Fall, op. cit., p. 245.
7. The New York Times, April 7, 1955.

8. *Ibid.*, April 8, 1955.
9. *The New Republic*, April 19, 1955.
10. Diem's Speech to the Free World, May 8, 1955 (Vietnamese Embassy, Washington, D.C., Press and Information Service, May 13, 1955).
11. *Le Monde*, April 30, 1955.
12. As reported in *The Times* (London), April 30, 1955.
13. See William Henderson, "South Vietnam Finds Itself," *Foreign Affairs*, XXXV (January, 1957), 289.
14. See *The Christian Science Monitor*, April 30, 1955.
15. For the composition of the Revolutionary Committee, see Francis J. Corley, "Vietnam Since Geneva," *Thought*, XXXIII, No. 131 (Winter, 1958–59), p. 546.
16. See Denis Warner, *The Last Confucian* (New York, 1963), p. 84.
17. Lancaster, *op. cit.*, p. 392.
18. Max Clos, in *Le Monde*, May 3, 1955.
19. Corley, *op. cit.*, p. 545.
20. Ellen J. Hammer, *The Struggle for Indochina Continues* (Stanford, Calif., 1955), p. 38, n. 31.
21. For various accounts of The's death, see Nguyen Kien, *Le Sud Viet-Nam depuis Dien-Bien-Phu* (Paris, 1963), p. 65; Georges Chaffard, *Indochine: Dix ans d'indépendance* (Paris, 1964), p. 89; Lancaster, *op. cit.*, p. 394; Robert Shaplen, *The Lost Revolution* (New York, 1965), pp. 125, 126.
22. *The New York Times*, May 30, 1955.
23. Lancaster, *op. cit.*, pp. 397–98.
24. B. S. N. Murti, *Vietnam Divided: The Unfinished Struggle* (New York, 1964), p. 142, n. 21.
25. Lancaster, *op. cit.*, p. 399.
26. Warner, *op. cit.*, p. 86.
27. *Le Monde*, October 14, 1955.
28. Chaffard, *op. cit.*, p. 101.
29. See Frédéric-Dupont, *Mission de la France en Asie* (Paris, 1956), p. 232.
30. See Bui Van Luong, in Richard W. Lindholm (ed.), *Viet-Nam, the First Five Years: An International Symposium* (East Lansing, Mich., 1959), p. 49; Corley, *op. cit.*, pp. 523–31; Fall, *op. cit.*, p. 154.
31. For text of letter, see Chaffard, *op. cit.*, pp. 115–16.
32. See *The New York Times*, December 29, 1954.
33. See Roy Jumper and Marjorie Weiner Normand, in George McTurnan Kahin (ed.), *Government and Politics of Southeast Asia* (2d ed.; Ithaca, N.Y., 1964), p. 466.
34. General Secretary Le Duan, in his "Political Report of the Central Committee of the Viet Nam Workers' Party," in *Third International Congress*, 1960.
35. Jumper and Normand, *op. cit.*, p. 469, n. 31.
36. P. J. Honey, "The Democratic Republic of Vietnam in 1962," *China News Analysis*, March 15, 1963, p. 2.
37. Fall, *op. cit.*, p. 155.
38. *Ibid.*, p. 156.
39. *Ibid.*, p. 157.
40. See *ibid.*, pp. 156–57.

XVII. TOWARD THE SECOND INDOCHINA WAR
(*pp. 430–74*)

1. Wesley R. Fishel, *Vietnam, Is Victory Possible?*, Foreign Policy Association Headline Series, No. 163, February, 1964, p. 32.
2. *Migration Facts and Figures*, No. 20, September–October, 1959.
3. For American efforts regarding land reform, see John D. Montgomery, *The Politics of Foreign Aid* (New York, 1962), pp. 121–27.
4. Robert Scigliano, *South Vietnam: Nation Under Stress* (Boston, 1963), pp. 88, 91.
5. See *ibid.*, pp. 99–100.
6. *Ibid.*, p. 26.
7. Robert Shaplen, *The Lost Revolution*, p. 134.
8. Bernard B. Fall, *The Two Viet-Nams: A Political and Military Analysis* (New York, 1963), p. 431.
9. Shaplen, *op. cit.*, p. 134.
10. See Scigliano, *op. cit.*, p. 33.
11. *Ibid.*, pp. 79, 85 ff.
12. *Ibid.*, p. 76.
13. Malcolm W. Browne, *The New Face of War* (Indianapolis, Ind., and New York, 1965), p. 196.
14. *Ibid.*
15. David Halberstam, *The Making of a Quagmire* (New York, 1965), p. 115.
16. John Mecklin, *Mission in Torment: An Intimate Account of the U.S. Role in Vietnam* (Garden City, N.Y., 1965), p. 86.
17. *Ibid.*, pp. 20, 25.
18. Scigliano, *op. cit.*, p. 60.
19. Mecklin, *op. cit.*, p. 471.
20. Browne, *op. cit.*, p. 170.
21. Scigliano, *op. cit.*, p. 44.
22. Mecklin, *op. cit.*, p. 43.
23. Halberstam, *op. cit.*, p. 195.
24. For the text of the Caravelle Manifesto, see Fall, *The Two Viet-Nams* (2d rev. ed.; New York, 1967), Appendix II, pp. 435–41.
25. See *A Threat to Peace: North Viet-Nam's Effort to Conquer South Viet-Nam* (Washington, D.C., 1961), p. 6.
26. See Lloyd D. Musolf, "Public Enterprise and Development Perspectives in South Vietnam," *Asian Survey*, III, No. 8 (August, 1963), 370–71.
27. *Annual Statistical Bulletin*, USOM, No. 4, 1961, p. 105.
28. Fall, *op. cit.*, p. 315.
29. Scigliano, *op. cit.*, p. 168.
30. P. J. Honey, "The Problem of Democracy in Vietnam," in *The World Today*, February 16, 1960, p. 73.
31. Fall, *op. cit.* (2d rev. ed.), p. 272.
32. Embassy of Vietnam, Washington, D.C., *Press and Information Service*, I, No. 18 (July 22, 1955).
33. Fall, *op. cit.* (2d rev. ed.), p. 345.
34. Scigliano, "A Country at War," *Asian Survey*, III, No. 1 (January, 1963), 1.

35. Mecklin, *op. cit.*, p. 104.
36. Halberstam, *op. cit.*, p. 172.
37. See Mecklin, *op. cit.*, p. 117.
38. See Scigliano, *South Vietnam*, p. 212.
39. Halberstam, *op. cit.*, p. 199.
40. See Erich Wulff, "The Buddhist Revolt," *The New Republic*, August 31, 1963; Halberstam, *op. cit.*, pp. 195, 196; Mecklin, *op. cit.*, pp. 153, 154.
41. Mecklin, *op. cit.*, p. 178.
42. *Ibid.*, p. 169.
43. Halberstam, *op. cit.*, p. 231.
44. Scigliano, "Epilogue: The Coup d'Etat," in *South Vietnam*, p. 222.
45. See Shaplen, *op. cit.*, pp. 203–4.
46. *Ibid.*, p. 212.
47. Mccklin, *op. cit.*, p. 183.

XVIII. THE AMERICANIZATION OF THE WAR
(pp. 475–502)

1. Robert Shaplen, *The Lost Revolution*, p. 221.
2. Maxwell D. Taylor, *Responsibility and Response* (New York, 1967), pp. 25–26.
3. See the reports on these discussions by Arthur M. Schlesinger, Jr., in *A Thousand Days* (Boston, 1965); and Theodore C. Sorensen, in *Kennedy* (New York, 1965).
4. "Why Our Foreign Policy Is Failing," an interview with Senator Fulbright by Eric Sevareid, in *Look*, May 3, 1966, pp. 25–26.
5. Charles Roberts, *LBJ's Inner Circle* (New York, 1965), pp. 20–21.
6. Quoted by Theodore Draper, *Abuse of Power* (New York, 1967), p. 84.
7. *Ibid.*, p. 82.
8. Richard N. Goodwin, *Triumph or Tragedy: Reflections on Vietnam* (New York, 1966), p. 31.
9. Draper, *op. cit.*, p. 85.
10. See Sorensen's article "The War in Vietnam—How Can We End it," *Saturday Review*, October 21, 1967.
11. See the article "Big Brass Lambs," *Esquire*, December, 1967, which quotes the following six retired generals and one admiral as being opposed to the Vietnam war: Rear Admiral Arnold E. True, Brigadier General Samuel B. Griffith II, Brigadier General William Wallace Ford, General David M. Shoup, Brigadier General Hugh B. Hester, and General Matthew B. Ridgway.
12. Quoted by Marriner S. Eccles, chairman of the Utah Construction and Mining Co., and former chairman of the Federal Reserve Board, in an article in *War/Peace Report* of October, 1967, entitled "Vietnam—The Effect on the Nation."
13. See Edward M. Kennedy's article "The 'Other War' in Vietnam," *The New Leader*, November 20, 1967.
14. *Ibid.* For a description of the removal of a whole village and the manner of its resettlement, see Jonathan Schell, *The Village of Ben Suc* (New York, 1967). The misery of the refugee population has also been vividly

described in a long report by Tom Buckley in *The New York Times* of October 28, 1967.

15. For some amazing details about corruption in South Vietnam, see David Halberstram's report in *Harper's*, December, 1967.
16. *The New York Times*, September 20, 1967.
17. Department of State *Bulletin*, March 15, 1965, p. 636.
18. For a comprehensive exposition of Robert Kennedy's views on the war, see his article "What Can We Do To End the Agony of Vietnam," in *Look*, November 28, 1967.
19. Sorensen, in *Saturday Review*, October 21, 1967.

Selected Bibliography

The following bibliography contains a selection from the more comprehensive listings in *The Smaller Dragon* and *Viêtnam: A Dragon Embattled,* and almost as many additional titles, most of which have been published since 1966. Because of the enormous outpouring of books on Vietnam during the past five years, the existing bibliographies on the subject are not up to date, including the latest one to appear, *Bibliographie critique sur les relations entre le Viet-Nam et l'Occident,* by Nguyen Thé-Anh (Paris: G. P. Masonneuve & Larose, 1967). Obviously, a new English-language bibliography on Vietnam is badly needed. Just during the last three years, more than 300 new titles dealing with Vietnam have come to my attention.

Most books listed below are briefly annotated, except those whose titles seemed sufficiently descriptive and those published by the Foreign Languages Publishing House in Hanoi. All that need be said about the latter is that their meager factual information is generally buried amid propaganda.

Aid to Vietnam. New York: American Friends of Vietnam, 1959. A record of a conference held on April 17, 1959, on the effect of U.S. aid to Vietnam.

AJALBERT, JEAN. *Les nuages sur l'Indochine*. Paris: Louis-Michaud, 1912. A continuation of the author's earlier books of criticism of French colonial rule of Indochina.

AMERICAN FRIENDS SERVICE COMMITTEE. *Peace in Vietnam: A New Approach in Southeast Asia*. Rev. ed. New York: Hill and Wang, 1967. A brief historical summary and proposal for a settlement.

ANH VAN and JACQUELINE ROUSSEL. *Movements nationaux et lutte des classes au Viet-Nam*. Marxisme et Colonie, Publications de la IVᵉ Internationale. Paris: Imprimerie Réaumur, 1947. A Trotskyite account of colonial history and a sharp condemnation of Vietminh policy in 1945 and 1946.

BAIN, CHESTER A. *Vietnam: The Roots of Conflict*. Englewood Cliffs, N.J.: Prentice-Hall, 1967. A brief, reliable survey of Vietnamese history from the beginning up to the present U.S. military intervention.

BALL, W. MACMAHON. *Nationalism and Communism in East Asia*. Melbourne, Australia: Melbourne University Press, 1952. Important facts on land ownership and on peasant exploitation by landlords.

BATOR, VICTOR. *Viet-Nam: A Diplomatic Tragedy*. Dobbs Ferry, N.Y.: Oceana Publications, 1965. A critique of U.S. policy toward Vietnam offering little-known details, and a keen analysis of the strategy of John Foster Dulles before and during the Geneva conference in 1954.

BERNARD, FERNAND. *L'Indo-Chine, erreurs et dangers: Un programme*. Paris: Bibliothèque-Charpentier, 1901. The book is primarily a polemic against the policies of Governor General Paul Doumer.

BERNARD, PAUL. *Le problème économique indochinois*. Paris: Nouvelles Editions Latines, 1934. Criticism of the antidevelopmental nature of French economic policy in Indochina.

BETTS, RAYMOND F. *Assimilation and Association in French Colonial Theory: 1890–1914*. New York: Columbia University Press, 1961. A scholarly discussion of French colonial policy, dealing largely with Indochina and based on a study of all important works on the subject. With an extensive bibliography.

BODARD, LUCIEN. *The Quicksand War*. Boston: Little, Brown and Company, 1967. A vivid firsthand picture of guerrilla warfare and of corruption in Saigon, with a few contemptuous vignettes of U.S. officials before the departure of the French.

Breaking Our Chains: Documents on the Vietnamese Revolution of August, 1945. Hanoi: Foreign Languages Publishing House, 1960. Important documents issued by the Indochinese Communist Party.

BROWN, ROBERT MCAFEE, ABRAHAM HESCHEL, and MICHAEL HOVAK. *Vietnam: Crisis of Conscience*. New York: Association Press, 1967. A statement of opposition to the Vietnam war on religious and moral grounds.

BROWNE, MALCOLM W. *The New Face of War*. Rev. ed. Indianapolis, Ind., and New York: The Bobbs-Merrill Company, 1968. A vivid description of the failure of Diem's army to cope with the fighting techniques of the Vietcong, and of the decline of the Diem regime. The most important book on the nature of the war before the arrival of American combat troops.

BURCHETT, WILFRED G. *The Furtive War: The United States in Vietnam and Laos*. New York: International Publishers, 1963. The Communist view, ably presented by an Australian journalist.

―――. *Vietnam: Inside Story of the Guerrilla War*. New York: International Publishers, 1965. A follow-up on Burchett's *Furtive War*, based on firsthand observation in the Vietcong areas.

BUTTINGER, JOSEPH. "The Ethnic Minorities in the Republic of Vietnam," in Wesley R. Fishel (ed.), *Problems of Freedom* (see below), pp. 99–103.

CADY, JOHN F. *The Roots of French Imperialism in Eastern Asia*. Ithaca, N.Y.: Cornell University Press, 1954. A basic study of French policy in Asia up to and through the conquest of Indochina.

―――. *Southeast Asia: Its Historical Development*. New York: McGraw-Hill Book Company, 1964. A scholarly, up-to-date study.

CAMERON, JAMES. *Here Is Your Enemy*. New York: Holt, Rinehart & Winston, 1966. A report by the well-known British journalist of a visit to North Vietnam during the winter of 1965–66.

CATROUX, GEORGES. *Deux actes du drame indochinois*. Paris: Librairie Plon, 1959. A defense by former Governor General Catroux of his policy in Indochina in 1939–40 and a discussion of the battle of Dien Bien Phu.

CHAFFARD, GEORGES. *Indochine: Dix ans d'indépendance*. Paris: Calmann-Lévy, 1964. The views of an experienced French reporter who spent much of the ten years under discussion in Vietnam, both in the South and in the North. Particularly valuable for its detailed account of Diem's struggle with the sects.

CHAPPOULIÉ, HENRI. *Aux origines d'une église: Rome et les missions d'Indochine au XVIIe siècle*. 2 vols. Paris: Bloud and Gay, 1943–1947. A standard work on the subject.

CHESNEAUX, JEAN. *The Vietnamese Nation*. Sydney, Australia: Current Books, 1966. A translation from the French (*Contribution à l'histoire de la nation vietnamienne*, Paris, 1955). The author is a Marxist.

COEDES, GEORGES. *The Indianized States of Southeast Asia*. Honolulu: East-West Center Press, 1965. India's influence in Southeast Asia prior to 1500, described by the leading French scholar in the field.

CULTRU, P. *Histoire de la Cochinchine française des origines à 1883*. Paris: Challamel, 1910. One of the earliest and best accounts of the colonial regime and the political and administrative institutions created by the French in Cochinchina.

DAREFF, HAL. *The Story of Vietnam: A Background Book for Young People.* New York: Parents' Magazine Press, 1966. An excellent introduction to Vietnamese history.

Democratic Republic of Vietnam, 1945–1960: Impressions of Foreigners. Hanoi: Foreign Languages Publishing House, 1966.

DESPUECH, JACQUES. *Le trafic des piastres.* Paris: Editions des Deux Rives, 1953. The author reveals some of the more unsavory scandals in the piaster transactions.

DEVILLERS, PHILIPPE. *Histoire du Viet-Nam de 1940 à 1952.* Paris: Editions du Seuil, 1952. The best account, by an author with first-hand experience, of French policy in Vietnam during and after World War II. Indispensable for an understanding of the causes of Communist strength and the failure of the French in fighting the Vietminh.

———. "Vietnamese Nationalism and French Policies," in William L. Holland (ed.), *Asian Nationalism and the West.* New York: The Macmillan Company, 1953. A well-known French author's criticism of French policy in Vietnam.

DOUMER, PAUL. *L'Indo-Chine française: Souvenirs.* Paris: Vuibert et Nony, 1905. Doumer's self-congratulatory report on his achievements as Governor General of Indochina.

DRAPER, THEODORE. *Abuse of Power.* New York: The Viking Press, 1967. The case against the Administration's Vietnam policy. Well documented.

DUMAREST, ANDRÉ. *La formation des classes sociales en pays annamite.* Lyons: Imprimerie Ferréol, 1935. A probing study of the social structure of colonial Vietnam.

EDEN, SIR ANTHONY. *Full Circle: Memoirs of Sir Anthony Eden.* Boston: Houghton Mifflin Company, 1960. Important for the discussion of the Geneva conference.

———. *Toward Peace in Indochina.* Boston: Houghton Mifflin Company, 1966. A call for reconvening Geneva conference, by one of its chairmen in 1954.

ELY, PAUL. *L'Indochine dans la tourmente.* Paris: Librairie Plon, 1964. The memoirs of the last French Commander in Chief and High Commissioner of Indochina. Important on the role of the French in Vietnam during 1954–55.

EMERSON, RUPERT, et al. *Government and Nationalism in Southeast Asia.* New York: Institute of Pacific Relations, 1952. See in particular Rupert Emerson's Introduction and Part III, Virginia

Thompson's "Nationalism and Nationalist Movements in Southeast Asia."

ENNIS, THOMAS E. *French Policy and Developments in Indochina.* Chicago: University of Chicago Press, 1936. A scholarly study of French rule in Indochina with deep insight into the effect on the educated circles of Vietnam and the nature of Vietnamese Communism.

Escalation War and Songs about Peace. Hanoi: Foreign Languages Publishing House, 1965.

FALK, RICHARD A. (ed.) *The Vietnam War and International Law.* Princeton, N.J.: Princeton University Press, 1968. A collection of articles, speeches, and documents.

FALL, BERNARD B. *Hell in a Very Small Place: The Siege of Dien Bien Phu.* Philadelphia & New York: J. B. Lippincott Company, 1967. The story of the decisive battle of the Indochina war, dramatically told.

———. *Last Reflections on a War.* Garden City, N.Y.: Doubleday & Company, 1967. A collection of Fall's most recent articles and his last interview. The well-known author was killed in Vietnam in February, 1967.

———. *Street Without Joy: Insurgency in Indochina, 1946–1963.* 4th rev. ed. Harrisburg, Pa.: Stackpole, 1964. A first-rate contribution to the military history of the Indochina War and its aftermath. The only book in English describing in convincing detail the agonies and frustrations of the French in the struggle against the ubiquitous Vietminh guerrillas.

———. *The Two Viet-Nams: A Political and Military Analysis.* 2d rev. ed. New York: Frederick A. Praeger, 1967. An account and analysis of both South and North Vietnam almost up to the fall of Diem. The book abounds in statistics. It contains a comparison of institutions and achievements of both regimes and an up-to-date biography of Ho Chi Minh. Highly critical of the Diem regime and of U.S. policy in Vietnam.

———. *The Viet-Minh Regime.* Ithaca, N.Y.: Cornell University Southeast Asia Program and the Institute of Pacific Relations, 1956. (The book appeared later in French as *Le Viet Minh: La République Démocratique du Viet-Nam, 1945–1960.* Paris: Armand Colin, 1960.) The most comprehensive study of the evolution, military organization, and government of North Vietnam.

———. *Viet-Nam Witness, 1953–66.* New York: Frederick A. Praeger, 1966.

FISHEL, WESLEY R. (ed.). *Problems of Freedom: South Vietnam Since Independence.* Chicago: Free Press of Glencoe, 1961. Contains papers presented at a conference in New York, in October,

1959, organized by the American Friends of Vietnam. The contributors are Joseph Buttinger, John C. Donnel, John T. Dorsey, Jr., Wesley R. Fishel, William Henderson, James B. Hendry, Wolf Ladejinsky, Craig S. Lichtenwalner, Robert R. Nathan, Edgar N. Pike, Tran Ngoc Lien, and Vu Van Thai. With an introduction by Senator Mike Mansfield.

FOURNIAU, CHARLES. *Le Vietnam face à la guerre.* Paris: Editions Sociales, 1966. A Communist version of the events in Vietnam since the end of World War II, particularly since the U.S. military intervention.

FULBRIGHT, J. WILLIAM. *The Arrogance of Power.* New York: Random House, 1967. A critique of U.S. foreign policy by the chairman of the Senate Committee on Foreign Relations.

GALBRAITH, JOHN KENNETH. *How to Get Out of Vietnam: A Workable Solution to the Worst Problem of Our Time.* New York: New American Library, 1967. A "broadside," originally published in *The New York Times Magazine.*

GAVIN, JAMES M. (in collaboration with Arthur T. Hadley). *Crisis Now.* New York: Random House, 1968. The General's view on the folly of the Vietnam war and its effect on the U.S.

GETTLEMAN, MARVIN E. *Vietnam: History, Documents, and Opinions on a Major World Crisis.* New York: Fawcett World Library, 1965. A collection with an introduction and comments by Mr. Gettleman, of documents, excerpts from books, articles, public statements, and government declarations ranging in time from precolonial Vietnam to the present discussion on U.S. policy on Vietnam.

GIGON, FERNAND. *Les Américains face au Vietcong.* Paris: Flammarion, 1965. A neutral view of the American involvement presented by a Swiss journalist.

GITTINGER, J. PRICE. "Communist Land Policy in North Viet Nam," *Far Eastern Survey,* XXVII (August, 1959), 113–26. Still the best report on the Communist efforts in the North to create a new pattern of land ownership in preparation for their policy of collectivization of agriculture.

GOODWIN, RICHARD N. *Triumph or Tragedy: Reflections on Vietnam.* New York: Random House, 1966. These reflections, although informed and sophisticated, lead to rather contradictory conclusions. Goodwin defends the Administration policy of vigorous warfare, yet accepts the opposition demand for a political settlement through negotiations with the Vietcong.

GOSSELIN, CHARLES. *L'empire d'Annam.* Paris: Perrin, 1904. A surprisingly good history of precolonial Vietnam and of the period of conquest by a French officer turned amateur-historian who took part in the conquest and pacification of Indochina.

GOUROU, PIERRE. *The Peasants of the Tonkin Delta.* 2 vols. New Haven, Conn.: Human Relations Area File Press, 1955. Originally published in French under the title *Les paysans du delta tonkinois: Etude de géographie humaine.* Paris: Editions d'Art et d'Histoire, 1936. The most exhaustive demographic study on the life of the North Vietnamese peasants by a great French scholar.

GRUENING, ERNEST, and HERBERT W. BEASER. *Vietnam Folly.* Washington, D.C.: The National Press, 1968. The Senator from Alaska, a longtime opponent of U.S. military intervention, summarizes his case.

HALBERSTAM, DAVID. *The Making of a Quagmire.* New York: Random House, 1965. South Vietnam in 1962–63 as seen by the then *New York Times* correspondent. A devastating critique of the Diem regime, with a detailed description of the events that led to the overthrow of Diem by the Army.

HALL, D. G. E. *A History of South-East Asia.* 2d ed. New York: St Martin's Press, 1964. The standard work on the region.

HAMMER, ELLEN J. *The Struggle for Indochina, 1940–1955.* Stanford, Calif.: Stanford University Press, 1966. A pioneering English-language work on the subject, particularly strong and well-documented on French policy toward the Vietminh and the pro-Bao parties between 1945 and 1953.

——. *Vietnam Yesterday and Today.* New York: Holt, Rinehart and Winston, 1966. A brief general introduction.

HARVEY, FRANK. *Air War—Vietnam.* New York: Bantam Books, 1967. Factual and partly shocking information about the bombing of Vietnam.

HICKEY, GERALD C. *Village in Vietnam.* New Haven, Conn., and London: Yale University Press, 1964. A broad study, based on the author's earlier work for the Michigan State University Vietnam Advisory Group. The standard text in English on life in a South Vietnamese village.

HIGGINS, MARGUERITE. *Our Vietnam Nightmare.* New York: Harper and Row, 1965. A defense of Diem, and critique of U.S. policy, by the late correspondent for the New York *Herald Tribune.*

HILSMAN, ROGER. *To Move a Nation: The Politics of Foreign Policy in the Administration of John F. Kennedy.* Garden City, N.Y.: Doubleday & Company, 1967. A long section is devoted to Vietnam. The author, who served as Assistant Secretary of State for Far Eastern Affairs in the Kennedy Administration, writes candidly of his experiences.

Ho Chi Minh. *Selected Works*. 3 vols. Hanoi: Foreign Languages Publishing House, 1960 and 1961.

Ho Chi Minh on Revolution: Selected Writings, 1920–66. Ed. Bernard B. Fall. New York: Frederick A. Praeger, 1967. Fall compiled a selection of Ho's writings spanning his entire career, and added an introduction and notes.

Honey, P. J. (ed.). *North Vietnam Today: Profile of a Communist Satellite*. New York: Frederick A. Praeger, 1962. Contains nine articles previously published in *The China Quarterly*. Introduction and an essay discussing the North Vietnamese leadership by P. J. Honey. Other contributors are Bernard B. Fall, Philippe Devillers, William Kaye, and Hoang Van Chi.

Huard, Pierre, and Maurice Durand. *Connaissance du Viet-nam*. Paris and Hanoi: Imprimerie National, Ecole Française d'Extrème Orient, 1954. The most comprehensive study of Vietnamese civilization, with brief chapters on prehistory and history.

In the Name of America. Published by the Clergy and Laymen Concerned About Vietnam. With contributions by Seymour Melman and Richard Falk. Annendale, Virginia: The Turnpike Press, Inc. 1968. A collection of documents showing how the conduct of the war contravenes the laws of war binding on the United States Government and on its citizens.

Isaacs, Harold R. *No Peace for Asia*. Cambridge, Mass.: The MIT Press, 1967. The chapter on Indochina is probably the first comprehensive report on the events of Vietnam in 1945–46 by an American eyewitness. Isaacs then was the Asian correspondent of *Newsweek*. His report, originally published in 1947, still makes exciting reading.

Isoart, Paul. *Le phénomène national vietnamien: De l'indépendance unitaire à l'indépendance fractionée*. Paris: Librairie Général de Droit et de Jurisprudence, 1961. The last of the great French scholarly works on the history of Vietnam. Isoart's work is up to date, richly documented, and despite the author's lapses of apologies for colonialism, he is objective in his evaluation of French rule in Vietnam. Excessively critical of American policy after 1954.

Janse, Olov R. T. *Archaeological Research in Indo-China: The District of Chiu-chên During the Han Dynasty*. 3 vols. Cambridge, Mass.: Harvard University Press, 1947, 1949, 1951. The main work on the subject in English.

Joiner, Charles A. "South Vietnam's Buddhist Crisis: Organization for Charity, Dissidence, and Unity," *Asian Survey*, IV, No. 7 (July, 1964). A detailed report on the Buddhist crisis of 1963 before the fall of Diem.

JUMPER, ROY. "The Communist Challenge to South Vietnam," *Far Eastern Survey*, XXV (November, 1956), 161–68. An early warning of the threat the Communist appeal to the peasants in the South posed to the Diem regime

———. "Mandarin Bureaucracy and Politics in South Vietnam," *Pacific Affairs*, XXX (March, 1957), 44–58. An analysis of the role played by the Vietnamese mandarins under the colonial regime and of the problems of mandarin mentality for postcolonial Vietnam.

KAHIN, GEORGE MCTURNAN, and JOHN W. LEWIS. *The United States in Vietnam*. New York: The Dial Press, 1967. An analysis of the history of America's involvement in Vietnam, aimed at destroying some of the assumptions that underlie U.S. propaganda and policy.

KARNOW, STANLEY. "The Edge of Chaos," *The Saturday Evening Post*, September 28, 1963. The Buddhist crises, the failure of the Diem regime to win popular support, the "Family" dictatorship, and its lack of success in fighting Communism. A fierce attack on the destructive role of Mme. Nhu.

KNOEBL, KUNO. *Victor Charlie: The Face of War in Vietnam*. New York: Frederick A. Praeger, 1967. With an introduction by Bernard B. Fall. Observations by an Austrian journalist who entered NLF-controlled territory by way of Cambodia.

KOLPACOFF, VICTOR. *The Prisoners of Quai Dong*. New York: New American Library, 1967. A novel about the interrogation and torture of a Vietcong soldier.

LACOUTURE, JEAN. *Ho Chi Minh*. New York: Random House, 1968. An up-to-date biography by the well-known French author on Vietnam.

———. *Vietnam: Between Two Truces*. New York: Random House, 1966. With an introduction by Joseph Kraft. Largely a collection of articles on both South and North Vietnam. Important for its information on the founding and composition of the National Liberation Front. Highly critical of the Diem regime and its conduct of the war.

——— and Philippe Devillers. *La fin d'une guerre: Indochine 1954*. Paris: Editions du Seuil, 1960. (An English-language edition is announced for publication by Praeger in 1969). The authors, probably the two best-informed Frenchmen on Vietnam, trace the political and military events of the Indochina War up to the defeat of the French at Dien Bien Phu. The book also contains the best account of the Geneva conference.

LANCASTER, DONALD. *The Emancipation of French Indochina*. London and New York: Oxford University Press, 1961. A well-documented survey of French Indochina from the conquest to the establishment of the two Vietnams by a British diplomat who spent the critical early 1950's in Vietnam.

LAUNAY, ADRIEN. *Histoire générale de la Société des Missions Etrangères depuis sa fondation jusqu'à nos jours.* 3 vols. Paris: 1894 (and 1920). A standard work on the Catholic missions in Vietnam.

LE DUAN. *On the Socialist Revolution in Vietnam.* 2 vols. Hanoi: Foreign Languages Publishing House, 1965. By the Secretary-General of the Lao Dong (Communist) Party of North Vietnam.

LE HONG LING, and VUONG THANH DIEN. *Ap Bac: Major Victories of the South Vietnamese Patriotic Forces in 1963 and 1964.* Hanoi: Foreign Languages Publishing House, 1965.

LE THANH KHOI. *Le Viet-Nam: Histoire et civilisation.* Paris: Editions de Minuit, 1955. A scholarly work on the history of Vietnam from its origin to 1953 by a pro-Vietminh author.

LEDERER, WILLIAM J. *Our Own Worst Enemy.* New York: W. W. Norton & Company, 1968. The well-known author submits shocking evidence of corruption in South Vietnam.

LINDHOLM, RICHARD W. (ed.). *Viet-Nam, the First Five Years: An International Symposium.* East Lansing, Mich.: Michigan State University Press, 1959.

LURO, ELIACIN. *Le pays d'Annam* (2d ed.). Paris: Leroux, 1897. A basic study of Vietnamese political and social institutions by one of the outstanding early French officials in Vietnam. Based on the author's lectures at the Collège des Stagiaires (training institute for French administrators) at Saigon.

LYND, STAUGHTON, and TOM HAYDEN. *The Other Side.* New York: New American Library, 1967. An account of a visit to North Vietnam by two members of the so-called New Left.

McCARTHY, EUGENE. *The Limits of Power.* New York: Holt, Rinehart and Winston, 1967. A critique of U.S. policy. (One chapter deals with Vietnam.)

McCARTHY, MARY. *Vietnam.* New York: Harcourt, Brace and World, 1967. Impressions of a novelist and critic opposed to U.S. intervention in Vietnam.

MARSHALL, S. L. A. *Battles in the Monsoon: Campaigning in the Central Highlands, South Vietnam, Summer 1966.* New York: William Morrow, 1967. An account of military action in Vietnam.

MASSON, ANDRÉ. *Histoire du Vietnam.* Paris: Presses Universitaires de France, 1960. A short and informative book, though rather uncritical of the colonial regime.

MAYBON, CHARLES B. *Histoire moderne du pays d'Annam (1592–1820): Etude sur les premiers rapports des européens et des annamites et sur l'établissement de la dynastie.* Paris, 1920. Preface by Henri Cordier.

MECKLIN, JOHN. *Mission in Torment: An Intimate Account of the U.S. Role in Vietnam.* Garden City, N.Y.: Doubleday & Company, 1965. An account, by a former American official in Vietnam, of the failure of the Diem regime and the conflict between American correspondents and the U.S. Mission in Saigon.

MONET, PAUL. *Les jauniers: Histoire vrai.* Paris: Gallimard, 1931. On the recruiting and mistreatment of plantation labor.

MONROE, MALCOLM. *The Means Is the End in Vietnam.* White Plains, N.Y.: Murlagan Press, 1968. A conservative lawyer, businessman, and churchman condemns the Vietnamese war as "illegal and immoral."

MONTGOMERY, JOHN D. *The Politics of Foreign Aid: American Experience in Southeast Asia.* New York: Frederick A. Praeger, 1962. The only comprehensive report, analysis, and criticism of American aid to Southeast Asia, with heavy emphasis on Vietnam.

MORGENTHAU, HANS J. *Vietnam and the United States.* Washington, D.C.: Public Affairs Press, 1965. Articles by a noted critic of U.S. policy.

MULLIGAN, HUGH A. *No Place to Die: The Agony of Vietnam.* New York: William Morrow, 1967. The author is an Associated Press correspondent.

MURTI, B. S. N. *Vietnam Divided: The Unfinished Struggle.* New York: Asia Publishing House, 1964. The views of an Indian member of the International Control Commission. Critical of both the North and South Vietnamese regimes.

MUS, PAUL. *Viet-Nam: Sociologie d'une guerre.* Paris: Editions du Seuil, 1950. A profound study of Vietnamese life and of nationalism and Communism in Vietnam.

MUSOLF, LLOYD D. "Public Enterprise and Development Perspectives in South Vietnam," *Asian Survey,* III, No. 8 (August, 1963), 357–72. A study of the problem of industrialization of South Vietnam and the conflict of public and private enterprise. In the author's opinion, the regime failed in both respects.

NAVARRE, HENRI. *Agonie de l'Indochine.* Paris: Librairie Plon, 1956. The views of the Commander in Chief of the French Union forces in Indochina during the last year of the Indochina War.

NAVILLE, PIERRE. *La guerre du Viet-Nam.* Paris: Editions de la Revue Internationale, 1949. A collection of articles written during 1947 and 1948 on political, economic, and military subjects by a leftist opponent of French policy in Indochina.

NGHIEM DANG. *Viet Nam: Politics and Public Administration.* Honolulu: East-West Center Press, 1966. A scholarly study by a Vietnamese author.

NGO VAN CHIEU. *Journal d'un combattant Viet-Minh.* Paris: Editions du Seuil, 1955. Probably the best of all descriptions of combat operations from the Communist side.

NGUYEN AI QUOC (HO CHI MINH). *Le procès de la colonisation française*. Paris, 1926. The famous brochure by Ho Chi Minh on French colonial exploitation and police terror. The writing is mediocre, the charges exaggerated and poorly documented.

NGUYEN KIEN. *Le Sud Viet-Nam depuis Dien-Bien-Phu*. Paris: François Maspéro, 1963. A Communist account of South Vietnam under Diem.

NGUYEN KIEN GIANG. *Les grandes dates du parti de la classe ouvrière du Viet Nam*. Hanoi: Éditions en Langues Etrangères, 1960. Important dates in the history of the Communist movement in Vietnam from 1919 to 1954.

NGUYEN THAI. *Is South Viet-Nam Viable?* Manila: Carmelo and Bauerman, 1962. A devastating critique of the Diem regime by a close collaborator of Diem who for several years headed the government's press service.

NGUYEN VAN VINH. *The Vietnamese People on the Road to Victory*. Hanoi: Foreign Languages Publishing House, 1966.

NHAT HANH THICH. *Vietnam: Lotus in a Sea of Fire*. New York: Hill and Wang, 1967. The conflict in Vietnam as seen by a Buddhist monk.

NIGHSWONGER, WILLIAM A. *Rural Pacification in Vietnam*. New York: Frederick A. Praeger, 1966. A complete survey, with emphasis on administration and organization, by an American who served as an AID provincial representative in Vietnam.

O'BALLANCE, EDGAR. *The Indo-China War, 1945–1954: A Study in Guerrilla Warfare*. London: Faber & Faber, 1964. The only study of the subject in English. An excellent outline and analysis.

PARKS, DAVID. *G.I. Diary*. New York, Evanston, and London: Harper & Row, 1968. A young Negro soldier's moving record of service in Vietnam, who "never felt he was fighting for any particular cause."

PHAM VAN DONG. *Let Us Hold Aloft the Banner of Independence and Peace*. Hanoi: Foreign Languages Publishing House, 1965. .

—— and THE COMMITTEE FOR THE STUDY OF THE HISTORY OF THE VIETNAMESE WORKERS' PARTY. *President Ho Chi Minh*. Hanoi: Foreign Languages Publishing House (n.d.). Two articles offering a quasi-official and highly propagandistic biography of Ho Chi Minh with many quotations from Ho Chi Minh's writings.

PHAN THY QUYEN. *Nguyen Van Troi: The Way He Lived*. National Liberation Front, South Vietnam, 1965. Told by his widow. The subject of this biography was executed for plotting to kill Secretary of Defense Robert McNamara in Saigon.

PIKE, DOUGLAS. *Viet Cong.* Cambridge, Mass.: M. I. T. Press, 1966. The standard work on the subject, strongly anti-Vietcong.

RASKIN, MARCUS G., and BERNARD B. FALL (eds.). *The Viet-Nam Reader*, Rev. ed. New York: Random House, 1968. Articles and documents on American foreign policy and the Vietnam crisis.

REPUBLIC OF VIETNAM. *La politique agressive des Viet-Minh communistes et la guerre subversive communiste au Sud Viet-Nam.* Saigon, 1962. Documented account of guerrilla activities inside South Vietnam during 1961–62. A follow-up was published in 1964 under the title *Communist Aggression Against the Republic of Viet-Nam.*

RHODES, ALEXANDER DE. *Rhodes of Vietnam: The Travels and Missions of Father Alexander de Rhodes in China and Other Kingdoms of the Orient.* Westminster, Md.: Newman Press, 1966. The English translation of a book by the famous Jesuit missionary, published first in Paris in 1653.

ROBEQUAIN, CHARLES. *The Economic Development of French Indo-China.* London: Oxford University Press, 1944. The basic book on the French colonial economy. First published in French in 1939. The English edition has a supplement by John K. Andrus and Katrine R. C. Greene, "Recent Developments in Indo-China, 1939–1943."

ROBINSON, F. M., and E. KEMP (eds.). *The Truth About Vietnam: Report on the U.S. Senate Hearings.* Analyses by Senator Wayne Morse. Foreword by Senator J. W. Fulbright. San Diego, Calif.: Greenleaf Classics, 1966.

ROUBAUD, LOUIS. *Viet-Nam: La tragédie indochinoise.* Paris: Valois, 1931. A French journalist reports on the rebellion in 1930 and the subsequent persecution of nationalists in a book generally harshly critical of the colonial administration.

ROVERE, RICHARD. *Waist Deep in The Big Muddy: Personal Reflections on 1968.* Boston: Little, Brown and Company, 1968. Searching commentaries on what the Vietnam War is doing to America, by the national affairs correspondent of *The New Yorker.*

ROY, JULES. *The Battle of Dienbienphu.* New York: Harper & Row, 1965. With an introduction by Neil Sheehan. A dramatic and comprehensive account of the fateful battle by a French officer and author of several works on the Indochina War.

SAINTENY, JEAN. *Histoire d'une paix manquée.* Paris: Amiot Dumont, 1953. The memoirs of the leading spokesman of the Free French in Kunming (China) during World War II, and the first French official to return to North Vietnam from China after the Japanese collapse. Important because of the leading role of Sainteny in the negotiations between the French and Ho Chi Minh. Strongly anti-American.

SALISBURY, HARRISON E. *Behind the Lines—Hanoi.* New York, Evanston, and London: Harper and Row, 1967. The first story by an American on the effect, material, moral and political, of the bombing of North Vietnam.

SCHELL, JONATHAN. *The Military Half: An Account of Destruction in Quang Ngai and Quang Tin.* New York: Alfred A. Knopf, 1968. What American planes and artillery are doing to the country and people of Vietnam.

————. *The Village of Ben Suc.* New York: Alfred A. Knopf, 1967. An eye-witness account of the tactics used in the relocation of populations in the Iron Triangle, South Vietnam.

SCHLESINGER, ARTHUR M., JR. *The Bitter Heritage: Vietnam and American Democracy, 1941–1966.* Boston: Houghton Mifflin Company, 1966. A balanced criticism of American policy in Vietnam, and a plea for a negotiated settlement of the war.

————. *A Thousand Days.* Boston: Houghton Mifflin Company, 1965. An account of the Kennedy Administration, containing information on U.S. policy on Vietnam.

SCHOENBRUN, DAVID. *Vietnam: How We Got In, How To Get Out.* New York: Atheneum Publishers, 1968. A debater's handbook, strongly opposed to U.S. policy in Vietnam.

SCHURMANN, FRANZ, PETER DALE SCOTT, and REGINALD ZELSIK. *The Politics of Escalation in Vietnam.* Greenwich, Conn.: Fawcett Publications, 1966. A study of U.S. responses to pressures for a political settlement of the Vietnam war, covering the period from November, 1963, to July, 1966; by three members of the faculty of the University of California at Berkeley. Critical of U.S. policy.

SCIGLIANO, ROBERT. *South Vietnam: Nation Under Stress.* Boston: Houghton Mifflin Company, 1963. The best political analysis in English of South Vietnam under Diem. Scigliano acquired his first-hand knowledge during his years of service in South Vietnam as an administrative adviser to the government.

————, and GUY H. FOX. *Technical Assistance in Vietnam: The Michigan State University Experience.* New York: Frederick A. Praeger, 1965. A critical assessment of Michigan State University's role in advising the government of South Vietnam.

SHAPLEN, ROBERT. *The Lost Revolution: The U.S. in Vietnam, 1946–1966.* Rev. ed. New York: Harper & Row, 1966. The comments of a long-time observer on recent Vietnamese history. Important especially for the chapter on the crisis that ended the Diem regime.

SHEEHAN, SUSAN. *Ten Vietnamese.* New York: Alfred A. Knopf, 1967. Reports of interviews in South Vietnam describing life in times of war.

SORENSEN, THEODORE C. *Kennedy.* New York: Harper & Row, 1965. Background information on the policies of the Kennedy Administration, by the Special Counsel to the late President.

TABOULET, GEORGES. *La geste française en Indochine.* 2 vols. Paris: Adrien Maisonneuve, 1955 and 1956. Documents, many never published before, and comments on French policy prior and through the period of conquest. A most important source book on Vietnamese history from the seventeenth to the twentieth centuries.

TANHAM, GEORGE K. *Communist Revolutionary Warfare: From the Vietminh to the Viet Cong.* Rev. ed. New York: Frederick A. Praeger, 1967. An analytic report on the organization, tactics, and political indoctrination of the Vietminh and Viet Cong armies, and a discussion of the reasons for their success in fighting first the French and then the Americans.

———, with W. ROBERT WARNE, EARL J. YOUNG, and WILLIAM NIGHSWONGER. *War Without Guns: American Civilians in Rural Vietnam.* New York: Frederick A. Praeger, 1966. Mr. Tanham reports on the program he administered as Director of Provincial Operations for AID; three provincial representatives contribute chapters on their experiences.

TAYLOR, MAXWELL D. *Responsibility and Response.* New York: Harper & Row, 1967. A brief account of U.S. policy in Southeast Asia, by the General and former Ambassador to South Vietnam. A defense of American policy in Vietnam.

TAYLOR, MILTON C. "South Vietnam: Lavish Aid, Limited Progress," *Pacific Affairs,* XXXIV, No. 3 (1961), 242–56. Very critical of the entire aid program and the Diem government's economic policy.

The Vietnam Hearings. Introduction by J. William Fulbright. New York: Random House, 1966.

THOMPSON, VIRGINIA. *French Indo-China.* London: Allen & Unwin, 1937; New York: Octagon Books, 1967. The standard work in English on the French colonial regime in Indochina. A well-balanced account of its achievement and shortcomings.

TRAGER, FRANK N. *Why Vietnam?* New York: Frederick A. Praeger, 1966. A routine defense of Administration policy with a brief historical introduction.

——— (ed.). *Marxism in Southeast Asia: A Study of Four Countries.* Stanford, Calif.: Stanford University Press, 1959. Contains I. Milton Sacks's study "Marxism in Viet Nam," indispensable for an understanding of Vietnamese Communism. The editor summarizes and discusses the findings of his contributors in a separate essay.

TRAN VAN DINH. *No Passenger on the River.* New York: Vantage Press, 1965. A novel by a former Vietnamese diplomat about the Diem regime.

TRUMBULL, ROBERT. *The Scrutable East: A Correspondent's Report on Southeast Asia.* New York: David McKay, 1964. The views of a long-time Far Eastern correspondent of *The New York Times.* Chapters 13 through 16 deal with Vietnam.

TRUONG CHINH. *Ho Chi Minh.* Hanoi: Foreign Languages Publishing House, 1966. The author is a leading theoretician of the Lao Dong Party in North Vietnam.

———. *Primer for Revolt: The Communist Takeover in Viet-Nam.* New York: Frederick A. Praeger, 1963. A facsimile edition of two books by Truong Chinh—*The August Revolution* (Hanoi, 1958) and *The Resistance Will Win* (Hanoi, 1960). The latter describes the political and military strategy of the Vietminh against the French, which is based on Mao Tse-tung's writings on guerrilla warfare.

U.S. DEPARTMENT OF STATE. *Aggression from the North: The Record of North Viet-Nam's Campaign to Conquer South Viet-Nam.* ("Department of State Publication 1839") Washington, D.C.: Government Printing Office, 1965. The second of two major statements in justification of official military policy in Vietnam. The first ("Department of State Publication 7308") was released in December, 1961.

———, BUREAU OF PUBLIC AFFAIRS, OFFICE OF PUBLIC SERVICE. *A Threat to Peace: North Vietnam's Effort to Conquer South Vietnam.* Washington, D.C.: Government Printing Office, 1961. Detailed report, with a documentary appendix, of Communist subversive activities in South Vietnam since 1954.

Vietnam: Issues for Decision. ("Headline Series No. 188.") New York, Foreign Policy Association, 1968. A sober and impartial exposition of the Vietnam problem as it presented itself in April, 1968.

VO NGUYEN GIAP. *"Big Victory, Great Task."* New York: Frederick A. Praeger, 1968. With an Introduction by David Schoenbrun. In a series of articles first published in Hanoi in 1967, North Vietnam's Minister of Defense assesses the course of the war.

———. *Dien Bien Phu.* Hanoi: Foreign Languages Publishing House, 1954. The battle of Dien Bien Phu as seen by the commander in chief of the Vietminh Army.

———. *Once Again We Will Win.* Hanoi: Foreign Languages Publishing House, 1966.

———. *People's War, People's Army: The Viet Cong Insurrection Manual for Underdeveloped Countries.* New York: Frederick A. Praeger, 1962. A facsimile edition of Giap's rather undistinguished collection of articles on the subject of guerrilla warfare published under the same title in Hanoi in 1961. With an introduction by Roger Hilsman and a biographical study of Giap by Bernard B. Fall.

WARNER, DENIS. *The Last Confucian.* New York: The Macmillan Company, 1963. A well-known Australian journalist presents his assessment of South Vietnam after years on the spot. Extremely critical of the Diem regime.

We Will Win: Statements by the Central Committee of the South Vietnam National Front for Liberation. Hanoi: Foreign Languages Publishing House, 1965.

WEINSTEIN, FRANKLIN B. *Vietnam's Unheld Elections: The Failure to Carry Out the 1965 Reunification Elections and the Effect on Hanoi's Present Outlook.* Ithaca, N.Y.: Cornell University Press, 1966. A carefully documented study, important for an understanding of Hanoi's present attitude toward a settlement.

WEINTAL, EDWARD, and CHARLES BARNETT. *Facing the Brink: An Intimate Study of Crisis Diplomacy.* New York: Charles Scribner's Sons, 1967. Policy-making under Eisenhower, Kennedy, and Johnson, by two Washington correspondents. See especially Chapter 5, "Sonic Booms Over Hanoi."

WHITE, RALPH K. "Misperceptions and the Vietnamese War," *The Journal of Social Issues,* XXII, No. 3 (July, 1966). Deals with the propaganda slogans and false ideas that dominate much of the discussion of Vietnam.

WOODRUFF, LLOYD W. *Local Administration in Vietnam.* Saigon: Michigan State University, Vietnam Advisory Group, 1961. One of the many valuable reports on the many aspects of Vietnam's administration put out by the Advisory Group. (For other studies by this and other authors on administrative problems of South Vietnam, see Robert Scigliano, *South Vietnam,* Bibliography, pp. 218–219.)

ZINN, HOWARD. *Vietnam—The Logic of Withdrawal.* Boston: Beacon Press, 1967. The case for American withdrawal, irrespective of the political consequences to South Vietnam.

Index

543

"Greater East Asia Co-Prosperity Sphere," 190, 206
Greene, Graham, quoted, 406
Griffith, General Samuel B., II, 523
Grousset, René, 512
Gruening, Ernest, 489
Guam, 490
Guerrilla warfare, 45, 87, 103, 127, 325–26, 335; Diem and, 413; French suppression of, 128, 151, 191, 227; against Japanese, 204; in Second Indochina War, 460–61, 484; Vietminh, 202, 203, 208–9, 260, 294, 317–20, 325
Guizot, François, 76–78, 80
Gurkha troops, 221, 226

Ha Dong, 293, 416
Ha Giang, province of, 267
Haidung, province of, 152
Hainan Island, 185
Haiphong, 13, 254, 306, 309, 319, 420–21; customs dispute at, 262–63; massacre at, 266; military action at, 263–66, 316; railroad in, 114
Halberstam, David, 443–44, 464–65
Hall, D. G. E., 511, 512
Ham Ngi, Emperor, 148–50
Hammer, Ellen J., 516, 517, 518, 521
Han dynasty, 22, 26, 27, 32, 33
Han River, 26
Han Wu Ti, Emperor, 26, 27, 44
Hangchow, 159
Hankow, 93, 239
Hanoi, 18, 41; French occupation of, 94, 97, 98; French reoccupation of, 268–69, 284, 306, 309, 316; military action at, 44, 45, 54, 71, 94; missionaries in, 62; railroads in, 114, 422; resistance movements in, 26–27, 143; University of, 120–21, 128, 139, 233; Vietminh control of, 217, 228–31, 416
Hanoi Government, 382–83, 417–29; composition of, 232, 237–38, 257–58; diplomatic recognition of, 239, 245, 294–95, 337–38; "intellectual revolt" against, 451; South Vietnam and, 457–58; threat by Nhu to negotiate with, 468; U.S. and, 497–99;

see also Democratic Republic of Vietnam; Ho Chi Minh, government of
Hanoi-Langson Railroad, 422
Harbors, 115
Harkins, General Paul D., 463
Harmand, Jules, 135
Hartke, Vance, 489, 490
Hatfield, Mark O., 489–90
Hatien, province of, 69, 72
Ha Tinh, province of, 149, 179
Heath, Donald, 378, 403
Hester, Brigadier General Hugh B., 523
Hieu, 150
Hitler, Adolf, 182, 183, 185, 201, 478
Ho Chi Minh, 183, 199–203 *passim*, 415–17, 499, 516; alleged duplicity of, 245–46; character of, 200, 242–43, 515; on duration of war, 316; early career of, 159–60, 176; French and, 282, 285–93, 296, 315, 355; on Geneva conference, 362–63; government of, 208–10, 228, 232, 234–38, 241–42, 263, 288, 294–96, 298, 337, 422, 428, 451, 497; negotiations by, 214, 238, 239–42, 245–46, 249, 253, 264, 268, 289–92; quoted, 243, 267, 294; U.S. and, 231, 359–62
Ho Dac Lieu, 292
Ho Huu Tuong, 181–82, 400
Ho Thong Minh, 404
Hoa Binh, 325
Hoa Hao, 194–97, 217, 220, 259, 260, 296, 298, 299, 313, 331, 344; Diem and, 392, 393–94, 397, 399, 400, 401, 412–13; Nhu and, 346
Hoang Hoa Tham; *see* De Tham
Hoang Minh Giam, 257, 269, 295
Honey, P.J., 457, 515
Hong Bang dynasty, 19, 20
Hong Kong, 76, 77, 185, 468; Vietnamese exiles in, 157, 288, 291–92, 297, 300
Hongay, 256, 420
Houa Pham, province of, 350
Huc, Father, 81, 83
Hue, 9, 17, 32, 159, 294, 318, 352; Buddhist crisis at, 465–67; imperial

Plain of Reeds (Plaine des Joncs), 183, 318
Plaine des Jarres, 351
Pleiku: attack on base at, 484; province of, 252, 254, 356
Pleven, René, 205
Plutocracy, Vietnamese, 139
Poivre, Pierre, 68–69
Poland, 378
Police forces, South Vietnamese, 393, 398, 446, 454, 476, 480
Political indoctrination, 319, 332–33, 335–36
Political parties (France), 279–81
Political parties (Vietnam), 173–79, 182, 196–98, 297–99, 476; pro-Chinese, 235, 237, 241, 249, 256–57, 261; South Vietnamese, 442–43; *see also* Communist Party (Vietnam); Socialists, Vietnamese; Trotskyist parties; Vietminh
Political-religious sects; *see* Binh Xuyen; Cao Dai; Hoa Hao
Polygamy, 65, 447
Pondicherry, 59, 70, 71, 72
Popular Front (France), 145, 147, 182
Portugal, 51, 55–63 *passim*
Potsdam conference, 215, 216, 221, 223
Poulo Condore, island of, 68, 87, 122–23, 180
Pourissement, tactic of, 320, 323
Press: British, 226–27; colonial, 127, 129, 267, 450; Diem and correspondents of U.S., 463, 468, 471; French, 268, 290, 352, 402; U.S., 295, 480, 488, 506, 508
Press, Vietnamese, 145, 173, 220, 223, 450, 480, 506; Diem and, 405–6, 450; suppression of, 480; of Vietminh, 240
Prices, 166, 170, 190
Prisoners, political, 119, 122, 128, 146, 147, 180, 220, 224, 225; Hanoi Government and, 128; Saigon Government and, 449, 450, 451, 457, 467–68
Prisoners of war, 353

Profiteering, 108, 166, 167, 169, 416, 445, 478
Propaganda: anti-Communist, 361, 431, 451, 458; anti-French, 193; colonial, 127, 151; Communist, 201, 332, 355, 389, 456, 463, 506; Japanese, 193; U.S. official, 484, 488, 491, 498, 504, 505; Vietnamese nationalist, 128; Western, 431
Protectorates, French, 74, 135; of Cochinchina, 90; of Tongking and Annam, 97–98, 104–5, 106
Provisional Executive Committee for the South, 217, 220–21, 222–23, 224, 228
Public opinion: colonial, 279; French, 132, 180, 185–86, 267, 279, 285, 294; U.S., 466–67, 490, 503–4
Public utilities, 233
Public works, 30, 113–15, 119, 131, 447
"Puppet governments," 305–7, 311–14, 342–47
Puritanism, Vietnamese, 47, 447

Quang Binh, province of, 149
Quang Nam, 9, 150, 467
Quang Ngai, province of, 179
Quang Tri, 319, 352, 422, 467
Queuille, Henri, 307
Qui Nhon, 318, 356
Quoc Ngu, 62

Racism, 193
Radford, Admiral Arthur W., 365–66, 368
Radical parties (France), 137, 280, 285–86, 287, 290, 355
Railroads: construction of, 111, 114, 118; disruption of, 388; rebuilding of, 418, 422
Ramadier, Paul, 282, 285, 287, 289, 293
Rassemblement Populaire Française, 279, 303
Rationing, 425
Rebel chiefs, 149–55 *passim*
Rebellions, Vietnamese, 31, 34, 42, 88–89, 158, 179–80; encouraged by Japanese, 191; of peasants, 54, 122,